2005 | 2006

SUNDAY SCHOOL
COMMENTARY

Based on the International Lesson Series

Eighty-fifth Edition

Writers
Dr. David A. Hodge, Sr.
Dr. William Burwell, Jr.
Dr. E. Christopher Jackson
Dr. Walstone E. Francis

Editor
Rev. Ottie L. West

Sunday School Publishing Board
National Baptist Convention, USA, Inc.
Dr. E. L. Thomas, *Executive Director*

CONTENTS

Three-year Cycle v
List of Printed Texts vi
Preface vii
Acknowledgements viii
Know Your Writers ix

Fall Quarter, 2005—*You Will Be My Witnesses*

General Introduction 1
September: UNIT I—*In Jerusalem*
  4 The Coming of the Spirit (Acts 2:1-8, 38-42) 3
  11 Life Among the Followers (Acts 2:43-47; 4:32-35) 12
  18 Peter and John Heal a Lame Man (Acts 3:1-16) 21
  25 The Time for Boldness (Acts 4:1-4, 23-31) 31

October: UNIT II—*In All Judea and Samaria*
  2 Stephen (Acts 6:8-15; 7:53-60) 40
  9 The Samaritans and Philip (Acts 8:4-17) 50
  16 The Ethiopian Official (Acts 8:26-38) 60
  23 Cornelius and the Gentiles (Acts 10:1-20) 70
  30 Peter in Prison (Acts 12:1-16) 80

November: UNIT III—*To the Ends of the Earth*
  6 Paul Becomes a Follower (Acts 9:3-18) 88
  13 Lydia: A Committed Woman (Acts 16:6-15) 97
  20 Priscilla and Aquila: Team Ministry (Acts 18:1-4, 18-21, 24-28) 105
  27 Paul's Farewell (Acts 20:17-28, 36-38) 113

Winter Quarter, 2005-2006—*God's Commitment—Our Response*

General Introduction 121
December: UNIT I—*God's Redeeming Love*
  4 Justice for All (Isaiah 42:1-8) 123
  11 Strength for the Weary (Isaiah 49:5-6; 50:4-9) 131
  18 Hope for Those Who Suffer (Isaiah 53:1-3; Luke 1:47-55) 139
  25 Good News for the World (Isaiah 61:1-2; Luke 2:8-20) 147

January: UNIT II—*God's Gifts of Leadership*
  1 God Gives Strength (1 Timothy 1:12-20) 155
  8 Pray for Everyone (1 Timothy 2:1-8) 162
  15 God Calls Church Leaders (1 Timothy 3:2-15) 170
  22 Guidance for Teaching (1 Timothy 4:1-16) 178
  29 God Desires Justice and Mercy (1 Timothy 5:1-8, 17-24) 187

February: UNIT III—*Faithful Followers, Faithful Leaders*
  5 Be True to Your Christian Heritage (2 Timothy 1:3-14) 195
  12 Develop Christian Character (2 Timothy 2:14-26) 204

19 Follow a Good Mentor (2 Timothy 3:10—4:8) 212
26 Live the Truth, Teach the Truth (Titus 2:1-15) 221

Spring Quarter, 2006—*Living in and as God's Creation*

General Introduction 229

March: UNIT I—*The Glory of God's Creation*

5 God Made Us Special (Psalm 8:1-9) 231
12 God Created Wonderful Things (Psalm 104:1-13) 238
19 God Created and Knows Us (Psalm 139:1-3, 7-14, 23-24) 247
26 A Hymn of Praise to the Creator (Psalm 145:1-13) 255

April: UNIT II—*Living with Creation's Uncertainty*

2 When Tragedy Occurs (Job 1:14-15, 18-19, 22; 3:1-3, 11) 263
9 When All Seems Hopeless (Job 14:1-2, 11-17; 32:6, 8; 34:12; 37:14, 22) 271
16 God Responds with Life (Job 38:1, 4, 16-17; 42:1-2, 5; Mark 16:1-7, 9-14, 20) 279
23 Finding Life's Meaning (Ecclesiastes 1:1-9; John 20:19-23) 288
30 In God's Time (Ecclesiastes 3:1-8, 14-15) 297

May: UNIT III—*Lessons in Living*

7 A Treasure Worth Seeking (Proverbs 2:1-5; 3:1-6, 13-18) 305
14 Wisdom's Invitation (Proverbs 8:1-5, 22-31) 313
21 The Path of Integrity (Proverbs 11:1-14) 321
28 Living Out Wisdom (Proverbs 31:8-14, 25-30) 329

Summer Quarter, 2006—*Called to Be a Christian Community*

General Introduction 337

June: UNIT I—*Servants of God*

4 Servants of Unity (1 Corinthians 1:10-17) 339
11 Servants of Wisdom (1 Corinthians 2:1, 6-16) 347
18 Servants Together (1 Corinthians 3:1-15) 357
25 Servants in Ministry (1 Corinthians 4:1-13) 368

July: UNIT II—*Called to Obedience*

2 Called to Relationships (1 Corinthians 7:2-15) 377
9 Called to Help the Weak (1 Corinthians 8:1-13) 387
16 Called to Win the Race (1 Corinthians 9:24—10:13) 396
23 Called to the Common Good (1 Corinthians 12:1-13) 406
30 Called to Love (1 Corinthians 13:1-13) 416

August: UNIT III—*The Spirit of Giving*

6 Giving Forgiveness (2 Corinthians 2:5-11; 7:2-15) 425
13 Giving Generously (2 Corinthians 8:1-15) 436
20 Giving Is a Witness (2 Corinthians 9:3-15) 445
27 The Giving of Sufficient Grace (2 Corinthians 12:1-10) 454
Glossary of Terms 463
Bibliography of Resources 468

CYCLE OF 2004-2007

Arrangement of Quarters According to the
Church School Year, September Through August

	Fall	Winter	Spring	Summer
2004-2005	The God of Continuing Creation (Bible Survey) Theme: Creation	Called to Be God's People (Bible Survey) Theme: Call	God's Project: Effective Christians (Romans and Galatians) Theme: Covenant	Jesus' Life, Teachings and Ministry (Matthew, Mark, Luke) Theme: Christ
2005-2006	"You Will Be My Witnesses" (Acts) Theme: Community	God's Commitment—Our Response (Isaiah; 1 and 2 Timothy) Theme: Commitment	Living in and as God's Creation (Psalms, Job, Ecclesiastes, Proverbs) Theme: Creation	Called to Be a Christian Community (1 and 2 Corinthians) Theme: Call
2006-2007	God's Living Covenant (Old Testament Survey) Theme: Covenant	Jesus Christ: A Portrait of God (John, Philippians, Colossians, Hebrews, 1 John) Theme: Christ	Our Community Now and in God's Future (1 John, Revelation) Theme: Community	Committed to Doing Right (Various Prophets, 2 Kings, 2 Chronicles) Theme: Commitment

LIST OF PRINTED TEXTS—2005-2006

The Printed Scriptural Texts used in the 2005-2006 *Townsend Press Sunday School Commentary* are arranged here in the order in which they appear in the Bible. Opposite each reference is the page number on which Scriptures appear in this edition of the *Commentary*.

Reference	Page	Reference	Page
Job 1:14-15, 18-19, 22	263	Acts 7:53-60	41
Job 3:1-3, 11	263	Acts 8:4-17	50
Job 14:1-2, 11-17	271	Acts 8:26-38	60
Job 32:6, 8	272	Acts 9:3-18	88
Job 34:12	272	Acts 10:1-20	70
Job 37:14, 22	272	Acts 12:1-16	80
Job 38:1, 4, 16-17	279	Acts 16:6-15	97
Job 42:1-2, 5	279	Acts 18:1-4, 18-21, 24-28	105
Psalm 8:1-9	231	Acts 20:17-28, 36-38	113
Psalm 104:1-13	238	1 Corinthians 1:10-17	339
Psalm 139:1-3, 7-14, 23-24	247	1 Corinthians 2:1, 6-16	347
Psalm 145:1-13	255	1 Corinthians 3:1-15	357
Proverbs 2:1-5	305	1 Corinthians 4:1-13	368
Proverbs 3:1-6, 13-18	305	1 Corinthians 7:2-15	377
Proverbs 8:1-5, 22-31	313	1 Corinthians 8:1-13	387
Proverbs 11:1-14	321	1 Corinthians 9:24-27	396
Proverbs 31:8-14, 25-30	329	1 Corinthians 10:1-13	396
Ecclesiastes 1:1-9	288	1 Corinthians 12:1-13	406
Ecclesiastes 3:1-8, 14-15	297	1 Corinthians 13:1-13	416
Isaiah 42:1-8	123	2 Corinthians 2:5-11	425
Isaiah 49:5-6	131	2 Corinthians 7:2-15	425
Isaiah 50:4-9	131	2 Corinthians 8:1-15	436
Isaiah 53:1-3	139	2 Corinthians 9:3-15	445
Isaiah 61:1-2	147	2 Corinthians 12:1-10	454
Mark 16:1-7, 9-14, 20	280	1 Timothy 1:12-20	155
Luke 1:47-55	139	1 Timothy 2:1-8	162
Luke 2:8-20	147	1 Timothy 3:2-15	170
John 20:19-23	289	1 Timothy 4:1-16	178
Acts 2:1-8	3	1 Timothy 5:1-8, 17-24	187
Acts 2:38-42	4	2 Timothy 1:3-14	195
Acts 2:43-47	12	2 Timothy 2:14-26	204
Acts 3:1-16	21	2 Timothy 3:10-17	212
Acts 4:1-4, 23-31	31	2 Timothy 4:1-8	213
Acts 4:32-35	12	Titus 2:1-15	221
Acts 6:8-15	40		

PREFACE

The *Townsend Press Commentary* on the International Bible Lessons for Christian Teaching is a production of the Sunday School Publishing Board, National Baptist Convention, USA, Incorporated. These lessons were developed consistent with the curriculum guidelines of the Committee on Uniform Series, Education and Leadership Ministries Commission, National Council of the Churches of Christ in the United States of America. Selected Christian scholars and theologians—who themselves embrace the precepts, doctrines and positions on biblical interpretation that we have come to believe—are contributors to this publication. By participating in Scripture selection and the development of the matrices for the Guidelines for Lesson Development with the Committee on Uniform Series, this presentation reflects the historic faith that we share within a rich heritage of worship and witness.

The format of the *Townsend Press Commentary* consists of: Unit Title, General Subject with age-level topics, Printed Text from the *King James* and the *New Revised Standard Versions* of the Bible, Objectives of the Lesson, Points to Be Emphasized, Topical Outline of the Lesson, Biblical Background of the Lesson (under discussion), Sidebar, Exposition and Application of the Scripture, Special Features (that correlate the lesson with our own experiences as a people)—including Concluding Reflections (designed to focus on the salient points of the lesson)—and the Home Daily Bible Readings. Each lesson concludes with a prayer. The color sidebar featured in each lesson highlights background information, insights and concepts that are relevant to the lesson, but may not be addressed specifically in the exposition.

The 2005-2006 *Commentary* features two additions to supplement the teaching/learning process of users: a Glossary of Terms and a Bibliography of Resources featuring many of the resources used by the writers in developing the lesson material.

The *Townsend Press Commentary* is designed as an instructional aid for persons involved in the ministry of Christian education. While the autonomy of the individual soul before God is affirmed, we believe that biblical truths find their highest expression within the community of believers whose corporate experiences serve as monitors to preserve the integrity of the Christian faith. As such, the Word of God must not only be understood, but also embodied in the concrete realities of daily life.

The presentation of the lessons anticipates the fact that some concepts and Scripture references do not lend themselves to meaningful comprehension by children. Hence, when this occurs, alternative passages of Scripture are used along with appropriate content emphases that are designed to assist children in their spiritual growth.

We stand firm in our commitment to Christian growth, to the end that lives will become transformed through personal and group interaction with the Word of God. The challenge goes forth: "Do your best to present yourself to God as one approved by him, a worker who has no need to be ashamed, rightly explaining the word of truth" *(2 Timothy 2:15, NRSV)*.

ACKNOWLEDGEMENTS

The *Townsend Press Commentary* is the centerpiece of a family of church school literature designed especially to aid teachers in their presentation of the lessons as well as to broaden the knowledge base of students from the biblical perspective. Our mission is to provide religious educational experiences and spiritual resources for our constituency throughout this nation as well as many foreign countries. To achieve this end, a coterie of persons in concert with each other provides the needed expertise in the various areas of the production process. Although under the employ of the Sunday School Publishing Board, personnel too numerous to list approach their respective tasks with the dedication and devotion of those who serve God by serving His people. This *Commentary* is presented with gratitude to God for all those who desire a more comprehensive treatment of the selected Scriptures than is provided in the church school quarterlies, and is intended to be a complementary resource thereto.

Our gratitude is hereby expressed to Dr. David A. Hodge, Sr. (Fall); Dr. William Burwell, (Winter); Dr. E. Christopher Jackson (Spring); and Dr. Walstone E. Francis (Summer); for their devotion in the development of the respective lessons. These writers bring diversity and a broad spectrum of ministerial and educational experience to bear on the exposition and application of the Scripture.

The Sunday School Publishing Board consists of employees with expertise in their assigned area whose self-understanding is that of "workers together with God" and partners with those who labor in the vineyard of teaching the Word of God in order to make disciples and nurture others toward a mature faith.

Special appreciation is appropriately accorded to Dr. E. L. Thomas, Executive Director of the Sunday School Publishing Board, for his insightful leadership and motivation. His vision and determination in seeking to meet the needs of our constituency by providing top-quality curriculum materials is not only reflected in this publication, but pervades the vast array of resources for the enrichment and enhancement of the people of God. It is to his credit that the employees have embraced the mission of the Sunday School Publishing Board with a self-perspective that accrues to personal commitment to the cause of Christ as they interface with one another and with the greater community of faith.

Our work would be in vain were it not for the many readers for whom this publication has been prepared. Their faithfulness has been enduring for over a century, and we are more than blessed to be their servants in the work of the Lord. It is our prayer that God's grace will complement our efforts so that lives will become transformed within the context of classroom interaction that is undergirded by the Spirit of God. Through it all, may God grant each of us the power to live for Him who died for us, even Jesus Christ, our Lord and Savior.

Ottie L. West
Senior Editor

Know Your Writers

Dr. David A. Hodge, Sr. ▼
Fall Quarter

Dr. David Augustin Hodge, Sr. was born in St. Thomas, Virgin Islands and raised in Perth Amboy, New Jersey. Upon graduating from Charlotte Amalie High School in St. Thomas, he attended American Baptist College in Nashville, Tennessee, before enrolling in Oral Roberts University where he earned a Master of Arts degree in Education Administration. Shortly thereafter, Dr. Hodge enrolled at Candler School of Theology, Emory University in Atlanta, Georgia where he earned his Master of Theological Studies degree. Prior to completing his degree at Emory, he was invited to pursue the Doctor of Ministry degree at Columbia Theological Seminary where he graduated with a doctorate in Gospel and Culture. He is a Ph.D. candidate at the University of Miami where he is working on his graduate degree in philosophy, primarily focusing in philosophical theology and ethics.

Dr. Hodge has received numerous awards including *Who's Who Among Students in American Colleges and Universities, National Dean's List, All-American Collegiate Scholar,* and *Who's Who Among Teachers in American Colleges and Universities.*

Dr. Hodge is Assistant Professor of Religion and Philosophy at Florida Memorial College, Miami.

He is married to his best friend, Theresa Paula Hodge. They live in Pembroke Pines with their three children, David II, Avia and Jonathan.

Dr. William Burwell ▼
Winter Quarter

The Reverend Dr. William Burwell comes to us with a rich background of education and experience. He holds several graduate and post-graduate degrees, including the Master of Divinity from Talbot Theological Seminary and the Doctor of Philosophy from the University of Southern California.

Dr. Burwell is a teacher of preachers and a regular lecturer at the National Baptist Convention USA's National Conference of Christian Educators. Through this conference, Dr. Burwell has utilized his insight and inspiration to guide those in attendance to effectively confront problems and explore possibilities in their local congregations. Because he is a renowned preacher, revivalist, lecturer, consultant and worship coordinator, Dr. Burwell has been a featured guest at ministers' conferences across the nation and in Germany, including the Oakcliff Baptist Ministers' Conference of Dallas, Texas; the Illinois Baptist Congress; and the Baptist Ministers' Conference of Oklahoma City, Oklahoma.

In addition to serving as Director of Christian Education at the Bethany Baptist Church in West Los Angeles, CA from 1979 to 1981, Dr. Burwell organized the First Berean Christian Church of Los Angeles in 1983. In just eight years, that congregation grew from 12 members to over 350 congregants. Since 1991, Dr. Burwell has been a full-time teacher and evangelist and CEO of Burwell Ministries.

Dr. E. Chris Jackson ▼
Spring Quarter

Dr. E. Christopher Jackson is a native of Chattanooga, Tennessee. He is an ordained minister who received his Bachelor of Arts degree in English Literature from the University of Tennessee-Knoxville. He completed his Master of Divinity degree at Southern Baptist Theological Seminary in Louisville, Kentucky and his Doctor of Ministry degree at United Theological Seminary in Dayton, Ohio.

His ministry experience includes serving in campus ministry at the University of Tennessee and the University of Louisville. His full-time professional campus ministry positions include nine years at Lincoln University in Missouri and ten years at Tennessee State University and Fisk University in Nashville. In 1999, he and his wife co-founded Creative Ministry Consultants, which provides seminars, counseling and ministry consulting on a national basis. Locally, he serves as Staff Pastor and Minister of Nurture at the Temple Church where the Rev. Darrell Drumwright is Senior Pastor.

Dr. Jackson is an accomplished writer and the author of two books internationally published by Zondervan Publishing House: *Straight Talk on Tough Topics*, and *The Black Christian Single's Guide to Dating and Sexuality*. His most recent publication is an inspirational desk-mate resource entitled, *Have You Fed Your Dream Today?* He has written the international daily instructional guide for the Baptist World Youth Conference and has also written extensively for the Sunday School Publishing Board and for LifeWay Christian Resources magazines. He has been referenced in *Essence* and *Ebony*. Nationally, he is a frequent facilitator for universities, singles' groups, marriage conferences and various churches.

He is married to Dr. Coreen D. Jackson, a licensed minister who holds a Ph.D. from Howard University. Their sons are Joshua, Juleon and Jemiah. International travels include West Africa, Bahamas, Jamaica, Spain and Venezuela. One of his primary objectives in life is to help other people to discover their life purpose. His personal mission statement is "To honor God, pursue purpose, and empower people through practical and creative ministries of teaching, writing, conferencing, and producing the arts."

Dr. Walstone E. Francis ▼
Summer Quarter

Dr. Walstone E. Francis is a native of Nassau, Bahamas, where he received his elementary and high school education. He was awarded the Bachelor of Theology and Bachelor of Arts degrees from American Baptist College of the American Baptist Theological Seminary, Nashville, Tennessee. He is the recipient of an honorary Doctor of Divinity degree from Selma University, Selma, Alabama. He became a United States citizen in July 1994.

Prior to becoming pastor of the Shiloh Baptist Church of Waukegan, Illinois in 1992, Dr. Francis served as pastor of Mt. View Baptist Church in Smyrna, Tennessee, and the Alpha Baptist Church in Franklin, Kentucky. In addition to the pastoral ministry, Dr. Francis is an instructor in the Sister Theresa B. Stackhouse Leadership School, Baptist General State Congress of Christian Education, and the Congress of Christian Education of NBC, USA, Inc. Other affiliations include: Volunteer Chaplain of the Victory Memorial Hospital and the Lake County Jail, Waukegan, Illinois; Fourth Vice President and Chairman of Foreign Missions, Baptist General State Convention of Illinois; and organizer and moderator of the Lake Shore Baptist District in Waukegan and vicinity.

Dr. Francis is married to Angelia Rene Otey Williams, and they are the proud parents of one son, Ronald.

You Will Be My Witnesses

GENERAL INTRODUCTION

During this quarter, our attention will be directed to the book of Acts that chronicles the early years of the Christian community. The three units of this study focus on how the early church developed in Jerusalem, its spread into Judea and Samaria, and the process by which the Gospel was extended "to the ends of the earth."

Unit I, *In Jerusalem*, has four lessons that focus on the beginning of the church in Jerusalem. The first lesson deals with the coming of the Holy Spirit at Pentecost. Herein, we see the power of the Gospel to be communicated across cultural boundaries, preceded by repentance, baptism, and adherence to the faith. While the gift of the Holy Spirit was a public, dramatic experience, there are those today whose experience with the Holy Spirit is more quiet and private. The second lesson looks at how the early faith community broke bread together, worshiped, and shared their possessions. This portrayal of the early church contrasts the Gospel's call to an inclusive community and the commitment of present-day culture to individualism. The third lesson examines how the apostles continued to preach, teach and heal despite official opposition. While God does not always heal in such a dramatic way as pointed out in this lesson, the question may be posed as to what makes the Christian ministry of healing distinct from other forms of healing. The fourth lesson explores how the new leaders continued to witness boldly, even when their lives were placed at risk. Although we live in a society that values free speech that may invite opposition, distinction must be made between fanaticism on the one hand, and the faithful upholding of the truth implicit in the message of the Bible on the other.

Unit II, *In All Judea and Samaria*, consists of five lessons that center on how the Gospel traveled to outlying communities and to people who had previously been considered as outsiders. Lesson five looks at how Stephen was instrumental in the spreading of the Gospel. While some churches have difficulty finding leadership that has integrity, courage and spiritual power, it will be to our advantage to explore the relationship between the quality of church leadership and the level of political and social comforts the church enjoys today in society. Lesson six explores how Philip and others extended the Gospel beyond Judea into Samaria. There is a direct relationship between the extension of the Gospel to Samaria and the persecution of the Christians in Jerusalem.

This lesson affords us the opportunity to discuss how church growth or persecution and official opposition spur on missionary activity. The seventh lesson discusses Philip's encounter with the Ethiopian official. Of special interest is the fact that some Christian traditions insist that biblical interpretation be done by scholars and authoritative specialists. Believing in the accountability of each individual soul before God, how does this impact personal Bible study and meditation upon Scripture? Lesson eight moves into Cornelius' story and the spread of the Gospel to the Gentile population. The lesson draws attention to the reality that sometimes outsiders are shown to be open to God's voice while insiders are bogged down in prejudice and reluctance. In such cases, what does this say about the way in which God's Spirit works? The final lesson in this unit presents the evangelism that resulted from Peter's miraculous escape from prison. Keep in mind that prayer for those who are persecuted is powerful, resulting in inner peace and a conviction that one's cause is right. This stance of faith enables Christians to be calm in the presence of opposition or other difficult circumstances.

Unit III, *To the Ends of the Earth,* has four lessons that continue the further spread of the Gospel. The tenth lesson explores the conversion of Paul who had come to believe that his understanding of God's will was right and assumed that his activities were pleasing to God, until God intervened directly in his life and commissioned him for a greater task. Lesson eleven introduces Lydia, a committed believer. While the complexities of contemporary society may place a strain upon accepting hospitality offered by others, the fact cannot be denied that God-fearing people are often eager to learn from others about the faith. Lesson twelve looks at the team ministry of Priscilla and Aquila. Herein, the emphasis is placed upon team ministry in recognition of the belief that sometimes God calls persons to particular ministries because they will more easily reach others who may be engaged in the same work. God's promise to build the church is actualized when Christians work to support and teach each other. The final lesson concludes with Paul's prayerful farewell to the church in Ephesus. While prayer can help Christians to deal better with difficult or sad times in their lives, strength and comfort come from knowing that their actions are predicated upon their personal understanding of the will of God within the context of community.

In each of these lessons, we see the Gospel of Christ moving further into the world through the work of dedicated believers who not only embraced the challenge of the Great Commission, but also dared to share their faith with others under circumstances that proved their commitment. Our task is to emulate them who imitated the Christ.

Lesson 1

The Coming of the Spirit

ADULT TOPIC: Encountering the Spirit
YOUTH TOPIC: Power for My Life
CHILDREN'S TOPIC: God's People Get the Power

UNIT I
In Jerusalem

CHILDREN'S UNIT
The Church in Jerusalem

DEVOTIONAL READING: Psalm 16
BACKGROUND SCRIPTURE: Acts 2:1-42
PRINT PASSAGE: Acts 2:1-8, 38-42

Acts 2:1-8, 38-42—KJV

AND WHEN the day of Pentecost was fully come, they were all with one accord in one place.

2 And suddenly there came a sound from heaven as of a rushing mighty wind, and it filled all the house where they were sitting.

3 And there appeared unto them cloven tongues like as of fire, and it sat upon each of them.

4 And they were all filled with the Holy Ghost, and began to speak with other tongues, as the Spirit gave them utterance.

5 And there were dwelling at Jerusalem Jews, devout men, out of every nation under heaven.

6 Now when this was noised abroad, the multitude came together, and were confounded, because that every man heard them speak in his own language.

7 And they were all amazed and marvelled, saying one to another, Behold, are not all these which speak Galilaeans?

8 And how hear we every man in our own tongue, wherein we were born?

KEY VERSE

Peter said unto them, Repent, and be baptized every one of you in the name of Jesus Christ for the remission of sins, and ye shall receive the gift of the Holy Ghost.—Acts 2:38

OBJECTIVES

After completion of this lesson, students should understand:

1. The Pentecost account and its fulfillment in the coming of the Holy Spirit.

2. That the Gospel expanded into the world through the transforming power of the Holy Spirit.

3. That the Holy Spirit works in the lives of individual persons and churches.

..…

38 Then Peter said unto them, Repent, and be baptized every one of you in the name of Jesus Christ for the remission of sins, and ye shall receive the gift of the Holy Ghost.

39 For the promise is unto you, and to your children, and to all that are afar off, even as many as the Lord our God shall call.

40 And with many other words did he testify and exhort, saying, Save yourselves from this untoward generation.

41 Then they that gladly received his word were baptized: and the same day there were added unto them about three thousand souls.

42 And they continued stedfastly in the apostles' doctrine and fellowship, and in breaking of bread, and in prayers.

Acts 2:1-8, 38-42—NRSV

WHEN THE day of Pentecost had come, they were all together in one place.

2 And suddenly from heaven there came a sound like the rush of a violent wind, and it filled the entire house where they were sitting.

3 Divided tongues, as of fire, appeared among them, and a tongue rested on each of them.

4 All of them were filled with the Holy Spirit and began to speak in other languages, as the Spirit gave them ability.

5 Now there were devout Jews from every nation under heaven living in Jerusalem.

6 And at this sound the crowd gathered and was bewildered, because each one heard them speaking in the native language of each.

7 Amazed and astonished, they asked, "Are not all these who are speaking Galileans?

8 And how is it that we hear, each of us, in our own native language?"

..…

38 Peter said to them, "Repent, and be baptized every one of you in the name of Jesus Christ so that your sins may be forgiven; and you will receive the gift of the Holy Spirit.

39 For the promise is for you, for your children, and for all who are far away, everyone whom the Lord our God calls to him."

40 And he testified with many other arguments and exhorted them, saying, "Save yourselves from this corrupt generation."

41 So those who welcomed his message were baptized, and that day about three thousand persons were added.

42 They devoted themselves to the apostles' teaching and fellowship, to the breaking of bread and the prayers.

POINTS TO BE EMPHASIZED
ADULTS
Key Verse: Acts 2:38
Print: Acts 2:1-8, 38-42
—The Feast of Pentecost (Feast of Weeks) was held at the end of the wheat harvest on the sixth of the third month

(June) to commemorate the giving of the Law of Moses.

—The Holy Spirit is associated with the elements of wind and fire.

—Through the power and influence of the Holy Spirit, a covenant community takes shape among those who experienced and witnessed the event.

—Pentecost is a reversal of the Old Testament story of Babel. While Babel represented judgment, Pentecost represents the new redeemed community in all its diversity.

YOUTH

Key Verse: Acts 2:4
Print: Acts 2:1-8, 38-42

—The apostles had gathered for Pentecost, a Jewish holiday that is fifty days after Passover.

—A sound like the rush of a violent wind filled the entire house.

—Repentance, baptism, forgiveness and the gift of the Holy Spirit are related.

CHILDREN

Key Verse: Acts 2:1, 4a
Print: Acts 2:1-8, 38-39, 41-42

—The Holy Spirit was sent in fulfillment of a promise made by Jesus.

—God gave the Holy Spirit as a special gift to believers.

—Tongues, as a fire, on each believer showed the Holy Spirit's presence.

—The Holy Spirit strengthened the believers to share the Good News.

■ TOPICAL OUTLINE OF THE LESSON

I. INTRODUCTION
  A. The Ministry of the Holy Spirit
  B. Biblical Background

II. EXPOSITION AND APPLICATION OF THE SCRIPTURE
  A. The Coming of the Holy Spirit *(Acts 2:1-8)*
  B. The Work of the Holy Spirit *(Acts 2:38-42)*

III. SPECIAL FEATURES
  A. Preserving Our Heritage
  B. Concluding Reflections

I. INTRODUCTION
A. The Ministry of the Holy Spirit

The Holy Spirit is the third person in the Godhead (1 John 5:7, KJV)—the other two being the Father and the Son. The Bible teaches monotheism; this means that there is only one God (Deuteronomy 6:4-8). Is the reality of the Godhead to be considered a contradiction in the Word of God? Far from it. The Father, the Son and the Holy Spirit are three distinct personalities, but they are unified in one whom we call God. This unification is known as the Trinity.

One can justifiably suggest that each of the three not only has a particular function, but that each one "reigns" during a particular dispensation. First, the Father, generally referred to as *God*, functions as the primary person. God's primary action is to disseminate God's judgment and love throughout the world community that God created. The role of the second person of the Trinity, which is the preexistent manifestation of the *Son* (Jesus Christ), is the incarnated expression of the love of God: "For God [the Father] so loved the world, that he gave his only begotten Son, that whosoever believeth in him should not perish, but have everlasting life" (John 3:16). Simply stated, the role of the Son is to offer grace to (and confer it upon) fallen (and sinful) humanity. The role of the Spirit is to keep us in communion with the Father (see 2 Corinthians 13:14).

Secondly, the three are one, and as such, they do not manifest a competitive existence. Rather, they work together in harmony. At a given time, the presence and authority of one may be more accentuated than one of the others, but this is only in regard to the particular dispensation. For example, in the Old Testament, there was a greater presence of the Father. In the New Testament, particularly in the four Gospels, the ministry focus was on Jesus Christ, who was God incarnate (i.e., God *in the flesh*; John 1:14). And now, in the Acts of the Apostles, the work of the Holy Spirit is accentuated as the early Christians continued the work started by Jesus. Being fully human, Jesus was limited by time and space; He could not be everywhere at the same time. On the other hand, Jesus, as fully God, was not limited to time and space. He, in the person of the Holy Spirit, was in each disciple at the same time, empowering him or her to do the work of ministry.

In the Acts of the Apostles, the early Christians began the mammoth task of evangelizing the world. When they were given the Great Commission (Matthew 28:18-20), they were also told to expect a Helper known as the Holy Spirit (John 14:15-18; 15:26-27; 16:15). To their probable question of "How can we do this without you Jesus?" came the wonderful gift of the Holy Spirit—Jesus Himself in a more expansive, non-spatial form.

B. Biblical Background

The Acts of the Apostles is the first documented church history book. It is a rich book that outlines many salient factors pertaining to the ministry of the Holy Spirit, the activities of the first disciples, the commencement of the church, and evangelization of the world. Beyond these developmental activities and institutions are the less palatable moments of beatings, imprisonment and martyrdom. It is easy to see the movement of the Holy Spirit in the developmental stages of the early church, but how are we to understand the Holy Spirit's work and ministry in the wake of oppression, suffering and death? The real-world dimensions of Acts help us on these matters. First, the Acts of the Apostles was written by Luke, the physician, as a sequel to his Gospel work (Acts 1:1-3; Luke 1:1-4). Both books were written to an intended audience with the Grecian name, Theophilus. This name, which is a combination of two Greek words (*Theos*—"God," and *philus*—"love"), means "Lover of God." Thus, Theophilus may have been a Roman official of note (Acts 24:3; 26:25) or a community of people who loved God—we may never know. What we do know is that Luke wrote these books because of his deep commitment to documenting the ministry of Jesus (the gospel of Luke) and the ministry of the Holy Spirit (Acts of the Apostles).

Second, we must understand that the book of Acts is a record of transitions, the most notable being the practical working out of the New Covenant (i.e., the New Testament). The first covenant (the Old Testament) was given to Abraham and solidified by his descendents, the most notable being Moses—to whom God gave the Law (Exodus 19-24). The death of Jesus Christ—the shedding of His blood—was the beginning of the New Covenant (Luke 22:20). Consequently, the ministry of the Holy Spirit is not independent of the ministry of Jesus—it is a continuation of it. Luke's identification of Jesus' primary job description shows an aspect of the Holy Spirit's function: "The Spirit of the Lord is upon me, because he hath anointed me to preach the gospel to the poor; he hath sent me to heal the brokenhearted, to preach deliverance to the captives, and recovering of sight to the blind, to set at liberty them that are bruised, To preach the acceptable year of the Lord" (Luke 4:18-19).

II. Exposition and Application of the Scripture
A. The Coming of the Holy Spirit *(Acts 2:1-8)*

The "coming" of the Holy Spirit is somewhat misleading. To say that the Holy Spirit came on the Day of Pentecost is not to suggest that this was the first time that the Holy Spirit's presence was manifested in the created world; for the Spirit was indeed present at the beginning (Genesis 1:2). What we are seeing here is the beginning of a new dispensation— a continuation of an ongoing saga in which God reconciles humanity back to Himself. This new dispensation began on the Day of Pentecost.

We have no reason to doubt that the disciples were still in the Upper Room (Acts 1:13), where about 120 of them

Pentecost is the fiftieth day after Passover—the popular Feast of Weeks of the early harvest. The "sound of the rush of a violent wind" recalls the loud sound of God's presence at Sinai (Exodus 19:16-19). Fire indicates divine presence. Devout Jews were observant of the law. In the Greek, they "hear in their own dialect." All of these groups represent Jewish communities, including Gentiles, who had become Jews (proselytes) spread throughout the world—now gathered in Jerusalem. This is a miracle of both speech and hearing, since they now heard in their own languages (in Greek "tongues"). The subject matter of inspired witness is God's deeds of power. "Is filled with new wine" is a judgment intended to discredit the disciples' prophetic speech. Jesus has been attested from Scripture as God's Lord and Messiah, which is to charge all who were involved in His crucifixion. To be "cut to the heart" is a profoundly physical response of contrition. John's warning to "repent and be baptized" was to avert the wrath to come; but, now that Christ has come, forgiveness and the gift of the Holy Spirit are promised.

gathered (1:15) to consider their next move and await the Holy Spirit (1:8). What follows next must be understood very clearly.

First, the Holy Spirit came. Notice that the Spirit came, not as the result of prayer, fasting, or any human activity. The Spirit came because God's sovereign will necessitated His arrival. There are some who seem to believe that the indwelling of the Holy Spirit is subject to human authority, but this is not what the Word of God says. The disciples did not conjure up the Spirit of God; they only waited.

Secondly, the Holy Spirit came on the Day of Pentecost. This too is a very important notation. The word *Pentecost* means "fiftieth." Fifty days after the Passover (thus fifty days after the Resurrection) was the Day of Pentecost. In the Old Testament, it was known as the Feast of Weeks (Exodus 34:22-23) or the Feast of Harvest (Exodus 23:16). These feasts were always held on the first day of the week, which of course is Sunday, and fifty days after the Passover (Leviticus 23:15). It was also the day that the people of Israel brought their *firstfruit* offering. Since Jesus was the symbolic Passover Lamb (1 Corinthians 5:7), and "the firstfruits of those who are asleep" (1 Corinthians 15:20), it is only fitting that the Holy Spirit would come fifty days later. Those who accepted Him on that day were the firstfruit of Christianity.

Thirdly, with the coming of the Holy Spirit, the believers are introduced to another phenomenon. Twice (in verses 3 and 8), the word "tongues" is mentioned. When tongues are mentioned the first time, they refer to the shape of the descending fire. The word refers to the same symbolism that occurred when the Holy Spirit descended as a dove and rested on Jesus after His baptism (Luke 3:22). This was a collective blessing in which each person received the promised Comforter.

The second time the word "tongues" is used, it is not visual, but auditory. And in contrast to the tongues of 1 Corinthians 12-14, it is linguistic rather than ecstatic. In Acts, the tongues are linguistic, meaning that everyone heard and understood in their own language (2:8). In 1 Corinthians, the tongues are unintelligible to the others (14:22-25). Given the ubiquitous nature of the Great Commission ("Go and make disciples of all nations"), it is clear that the first disciples logically understood that there would be a communication problem: "How can we communicate with other nations if we do not speak their language?" In a great sense, the disciples' ability to speak in tongues at Pentecost was an undoing of the confusion associated with the builders of the Tower of Babel (see Genesis 11). The first lesson that the Holy Spirit taught them was that language would not be a barrier to the spreading of the Gospel. It was not at all similar to the tongues in Paul's epistle.

B. The Work of the Holy Spirit
(Acts 2:38-42)

Peter's words in verse 38 are in direct

response to the audience's reaction to his preaching. After mentioning, at the end of his message, their culpability for the Messiah's execution, the hearers were "stabbed" in their heart. They were overtaken with remorse and guilt when they discovered that their long-awaited Messiah had indeed come; however, their failure to recognize who He was, and their willingness to turn Him over to the Roman officials, directly resulted in His crucifixion. Confronted with this information and the new knowledge that the Messiah had arisen from the dead (verse 32), they were terrified that they were now on the wrong side of His impending wrath. Their collective inquiry was well-founded: "Brothers, what shall we do?"

This question is similar to the question asked by Paul (Acts 22:10) and the Philippian jailer (16:30): "What must I do to be saved?" Peter immediately seized this opportunity to lead them into a saving knowledge of Jesus Christ. Now, much ado has been made over this pericope from two different directions: "be baptized, everyone of you, in the name of Jesus"; and "baptized for the forgiveness of your sins." In other words, should we be baptized in the name of the Father, Son and Holy Spirit as Jesus commands, or should we be baptized in the name of Jesus Christ? Secondly, since baptism precedes salvation in this text, it begs the question: Does baptism save?

In response to the former question regarding the name in whom we baptize, we must separate our practice today from what was done at the genesis of the Christian movement. Today, Baptists immerse believers in the name of the Father, Son and Holy Spirit, as is proper. As it relates to this specific event, however, it must be kept in mind that the great number that had gathered to hear Peter's message had no knowledge of the Holy Spirit, and only partial knowledge of the Father. Therefore, to ask them to be baptized in the name of the full Trinity would be to use language that was irrelevant to them. Secondly, these same people previously were antagonistic to Jesus—but not necessarily to God the Father, and certainly not to the Holy Spirit (of whom they had never heard). So, baptism in the name of Jesus was a necessary public pronouncement to indicate that they had aligned with Jesus of Nazareth.

Concerning the latter question, "Can baptism save?", the sequence of events here should not lead one to interpret that baptism brings about salvation. Notice the true word order: "Repent and be baptized." Repentance leads to forgiveness. Encompassed in the meaning of repentance is that God will forgive. The two go together. Once a person repents (and is forgiven), baptism is the next step. If we were to infer that baptism precedes forgiveness, we misrepresent what repentance genuinely means, and postulate a salvation of works rather than grace—a direct violation of the will of God. Paul reminds us, "For by grace you have been saved through faith, and this is not your own doing; it is the gift of God—not the result of works, so that no one may boast" (Ephesians 2:8-9, NRSV). We find further confirmation at the end of this passage: "They that gladly received his word baptized" (verse 41). The only persons who were baptized "gladly received" the Gospel. It was not the case that some were baptized then accepted the message. Belief in Jesus Christ is a prerequisite to baptism, not the reverse.

III. SPECIAL FEATURES
A. Preserving Our Heritage

During slavery, it was illegal for the enslaved to be taught how to read or write. Ironically, more than any other text, they desired to learn how to read the Bible; but for the overwhelming majority of them, this dream was too far deferred. One former slave commented, "Mama 'nem always felt dey'd be free. I don't know why dey belieb dis. The Spirit musta 'veiled it unto dem." Even when the saved slaves didn't have access to the Bible, they had access to the revelation of God in the form of the Holy Spirit leading and guiding them to Truth.

Historically, the Holy Spirit has also been a significant part of our Black Baptist understanding in the form of "shouting." For decades, shouting has been viewed as evidence of a believer having the indwelling of the Spirit of God. However, we know that the indwelling of the Holy Spirit cannot be limited to a two-minute experience that happens during worship. There is a much more that should underline the meaning when we say that someone "got the Holy Ghost."

The "shout" has been a genuine expression of the Spirit's indwelling; it has also been abused and politicized in the worship setting. Nevertheless, the expressive forms of worship associated with the Spirit's presence have a much-needed and distinct role in worship. Professor/author Henry Mitchell has observed the following regarding contemporary believers' recognition of their need for guidance from the Holy Spirit: "Charismatic Christian groups are growing rapidly, while "major brand" denominations shrink. One very important reason for this could be a widespread hunger for the presence and guidance of the Holy Spirit in a very personal, folk-oriented way. Traditional denominations, once prone to be suspicious of the supposedly over-subjective tendencies of charismatics and their kin, must be increasingly open to the spontaneity and expressiveness which charismatics associate with the presence of the Holy Spirit."

B. Concluding Reflections

When the Holy Spirit takes residence in the hearts of believers, that indwelling is an ongoing part of our faith experience, and one that is to be evidenced in every aspect of a believer's life, not just during worship. Indeed, when Christ promised the gift of a Comforter, "getting the Holy Ghost" would serve as the empowerment given to believers, not an outward test to determine one's faith.

As Jesus departed this earth, He gave His followers a tall order; but He also promised them power to aid them in their work toward fulfilling that order. True to His promise, as always, every believer is empowered with gifts through the Holy Spirit (Romans 12:6-8) to prepare God's people for the work they must do (see also 1 Corinthians 12:1-11). The mission instituted by God the Father and fulfilled in God the Son remains energized and mobilized through God the Spirit.

There is a story told about a lady who went to her jeweler to have her watch fixed. The jeweler disappeared into the back room and soon returned with her watch, running perfectly. Surprised, she asked the jeweler how he was able to repair the watch so quickly. He explained to her that the watch only needed a new battery. "Battery?" she questioned. "No one said anything about it needing a battery when I bought it. I've been winding it up every morning!"

Many Christians are like the woman winding her battery-operated watch. They act as though they do not realize the power of the Holy Spirit is available to help them by taking matters into their own hands. When the circumstances of life are moving to our liking and in our favor, it becomes easy to forget the importance of relying on the Spirit. The Holy Spirit not only gifts us and directs us in Kingdom work, He is our Comforter. Moreover, He is our "insurance policy," or guarantee that Christ will return for His people.

HOME DAILY BIBLE 📖 READINGS

for the week of September 4, 2005
The Coming of the Spirit

Aug. 29, Monday
—Joel 2:23-29
—God's Spirit Will Be Poured Out
Aug. 30, Tuesday
—Psalm 16:5-11
—God Is Always with Us
Aug. 31, Wednesday
—Acts 2:1-13
—The Holy Spirit Comes
Sept. 1, Thursday
—Acts 2:14-21
—Peter Speaks to the Crowd
Sept. 2, Friday
—Acts 2:22-28
—Peter Speaks About the Crucified Jesus
Sept. 3, Saturday
—Acts 2:29-36
—Peter Speaks About the Risen Christ
Sept. 4, Sunday
—Acts 2:1-8; 37-42
—Three Thousand Are Baptized

PRAYER

Eternal God our Father, our estranged condition resulted in our being separated from You. Thank You for reconciling us with Yourself through Your Son Jesus Christ. May we use the gifts we have been given to take bold action for the Kingdom. Amen.

Lesson 2

UNIT I
In Jerusalem

CHILDREN'S UNIT
The Church in Jerusalem

Life Among the Followers

ADULT TOPIC: Sharing Community
YOUTH TOPIC: We Belong Together
CHILDREN'S TOPIC: God's People Share

KEY VERSE

All that believed were together, and had all things common.—Acts 2:44

DEVOTIONAL READING: Romans 8:9-17
BACKGROUND SCRIPTURE: Acts 2:43-47; 4:32-35
PRINT PASSAGE: Acts 2:43-47; 4:32-35

OBJECTIVES

After completion of this lesson, students should understand:

1. The early Christian community's way of caring and sharing together.

2. How the Word, love and worship of God served as the foundation for true community in the early church.

3. How to live as loving, caring and sharing members of a faithful Christian community.

Acts 2:43-47; 4:32-35—KJV

43 And fear came upon every soul: and many wonders and signs were done by the apostles.

44 And all that believed were together, and had all things common;

45 And sold their possessions and goods, and parted them to all men, as every man had need.

46 And they, continuing daily with one accord in the temple, and breaking bread from house to house, did eat their meat with gladness and singleness of heart,

47 Praising God, and having favour with all the people. And the Lord added to the church daily such as should be saved.

. . . . .

32 And the multitude of them that believed were of one heart and of one soul: neither said any of them that ought of the things which he possessed was his own; but they had all things common.

33 And with great power gave the apostles witness of the resurrection of the Lord Jesus: and great grace was upon them all.

34 Neither was there any among them that lacked: for as many as were possessors of lands or houses sold them, and brought the prices of the things that were sold,

35 And laid them down at the apostles' feet: and distribution was made unto every man according as he had need.

Acts 2:43-47; 4:32-35—NRSV

43 Awe came upon everyone, because many wonders and signs were being done by the apostles.

44 All who believed were together and had all things in common;

45 they would sell their possessions and goods and distribute the proceeds to all, as any had need.

46 Day by day, as they spent much time together in the temple, they broke bread at home and ate their food with glad and generous hearts,

47 praising God and having the goodwill of all the people. And day by day the Lord added to their number those who were being saved.

. . . . .

32 Now the whole group of those who believed were of one heart and soul, and no one claimed private ownership of any possessions, but everything they owned was held in common.

33 With great power the apostles gave their testimony to the resurrection of the Lord Jesus, and great grace was upon them all.

34 There was not a needy person among them, for as many as owned lands or houses sold them and brought the proceeds of what was sold.

35 They laid it at the apostles' feet, and it was distributed to each as any had need.

POINTS TO BE EMPHASIZED
ADULTS
Key Verse: Acts 2:44
Print: Acts 2:43-47; 4:32-35
—The transforming power of the Holy Spirit possessed the early believers and enabled them to form a genuine community of sharing.
—The powerful movement of the Holy Spirit inspired and guided the worship, action and service of the early believers.
—Powerful signs accompanied the witness of the early church, proclamation of the resurrection of Jesus, and an increase in numbers. "Wonders" and "signs" are familiar Old Testament words used to describe miracles.

YOUTH
Key Verse: Acts 2:46-47
Print: Acts 2:43-47; 4:32-35
—So great was the concern for one another that all things were held in common with some members selling their property and turning over their money to the community.

—The life of the community was characterized by gathering together for prayer in the temple, breaking bread together at home, eating together with joy, and praising God.
—The apostles witnessed to their faith in the resurrected Lord.
—The early church was a vibrant, growing church in which members were committed to God and to one another.

CHILDREN
Key Verse: Acts 2:44
Print: Acts 2:44-47; 4:32-35
—As a result of the coming of the Holy Spirit, the apostles performed many supernatural acts that held the people in awe.
—The Holy Spirit empowers Christians to be able to express compassion, care and concern among themselves.
—Christians' witness to others results in an increase in new converts.
—The Christian community is called upon to respond to the diverse needs of others.

TOPICAL OUTLINE OF THE LESSON

I. INTRODUCTION
   A. The Ministry of Giving and Sharing
   B. Biblical Background

II. EXPOSITION AND APPLICATION
   OF THE SCRIPTURE
   A. They Devoted Themselves to Purposeful Things *(Acts 2:43)*

   B. They Were Unified in Their Mission *(Acts 2:44-47)*
   C. They Shared and Gave to Others *(Acts 4:32-35)*

III. SPECIAL FEATURES
   A. Preserving Our Heritage
   B. Concluding Reflections

I. INTRODUCTION
A. The Ministry of Giving and Sharing

Our present political climate seems adversarial to giving and sharing. During the Reagan Administration, there was an oft-used phrase known as *rugged individualism*. This phrase meant precisely what it suggests—a rigorous preoccupation with individuality, even at the expense of the community. This philosophy, however, fails to correspond with the teachings of the early church. Christianity did not begin with a desire to protect one's own interests, neither did it advance legislation that would enable the ascension of one group or race over another. On the contrary, Christianity had a nobler venture: *Now the whole group of those who believed were of one heart and soul, and no one claimed private ownership of any possessions, but everything they owned was held in common.* This was the beginning of the Christian faith community. In many respects, particularly in regard to our embrace of Western culture's preoccupation with individualism, we have neglected our *giving and sharing* roots; indeed, we have abandoned a critical function of Jesus' mission.

How can we return to this mission, and re-invent ourselves to be like our Christian progenitors? The answer is found in the introduction to our text. The early Christians did not have an imprudent approach to their faith. Quite the opposite—they quickly invested in the ministry of Jesus' students (disciples), known as the apostles (i.e., the remaining eleven of the twelve men whom Jesus chose to be His learners; Judas, the twelfth apostle, had committed suicide after his betrayal of Jesus; cf., Acts 1:18-20; 3:16-19).

The early Christians were known as "People of The Way" (Acts 9:2). These people "devoted themselves to the apostles' teaching and fellowship, to the breaking of bread and the prayers" (Acts 2:42, NRSV). Notice that the text did not say that they shared their possessions and gave to those in need before it first gave recognition to their commitment to the ministry of Jesus. To be sure, these virtuous aspects of their lives—teaching, fellowship, breaking of bread, and prayer—were the impetus that gave rise to their giving and sharing. As such, they are worthy of investigation.

Although only four impetuses are listed above as the prevailing features of the early disciples, there is one that is more foundational than functional: salvation. Those who were devoted were first saved. We are told (verse 41) that three thousand souls accepted the Gospel and were baptized that same day. This was the beginning of the first church. In the midst of a hostile environment, due in part to Jewish hostility to those who imitated the crucified Jesus, three thousand people still committed themselves to participate. Though they would do many things thereafter—including devoting themselves to teaching, fellowship, breaking of bread and prayer—nothing they would ever do compared to their acceptance of Christ as their Lord and Savior.

The word of the Lord to Hosea is instructional: "My people are destroyed for lack of knowledge" (Hosea 4:6). The early Christians' willingness to be taught also showed their unwillingness to be destroyed due to a lack of knowledge. Over and over, we are introduced to passages of Scripture where teaching is elevated: *And the things that thou hast heard of me among many witnesses, the same commit thou to faithful men, who shall be able to teach others also* (2 Timothy 2:2). Once someone hears the Gospel through the preached Word and accepts Christ as Lord and Savior, that person need not hear the Gospel appeal again. Their next step is delving into the taught Word—teaching. Whereas preaching is the proclamation of the Gospel of Jesus Christ unto salvation, teaching is explanation of the Word of God toward edification. These early Christians were able to give and share because they were taught what it means to be a disciple of Christ. Truly, He was the ultimate Giver and Sharer (John 3:16).

B. Biblical Background

The new converts were in a strange dilemma. For a number of reasons, they faced hostility and conflict from every possible direction. First, Jesus did not come to establish a new religion; He came that sinners may be saved. "He came to what was his own, and his own people did not accept him. But to all who received him, who believed in his name, he gave power to become children of God" (John 1:11-12, NRSV). Although Christianity is not Judaism (neither is it a sect of Judaism), it emerged from a Jewish teacher (Jesus) and His band of disciples. Therefore, at the onset, the initial converts were in a quandary as to what they should and should not do. They were accustomed to going to the temple for prayer and other religious ceremonies on the Sabbath—and this was where the other Jews would congregate. So, instead of abolishing this practice outright, they continued going to the temple (Acts 3:1), and this act caused tension.

Secondly, not only did they face antagonism from their own people (8:1), they were also subject to Roman oppression. Generally, the Romans were not concerned about religious rituals and dogma, so long as the religionists paid their taxes. At the beginning of the period, Nero was the emperor of Rome. Initially, he was a good emperor, reducing taxes, eliminating bloodshed in the coliseum, and putting an end to capital punishment. But, as is often the case, "Power corrupts and absolute power corrupts absolutely." Nero's insecurities and paranoia led to his assassination of his mother and many others. In order to ingratiate himself with the people of Rome, in a sordid attempt to build a city after his own likeness, it is believed that he was the one who set Rome ablaze in a fire that lasted nine days. He then shifted blame from himself to the Christians—after all, were they not known for their conversations about eternal fire? Many Christians were put to death under Nero's psychopathic regime, not the least of whom was the apostle Paul.

The Jewish Christians were in quite a conundrum. They were unsafe at home and they were mutilated and murdered abroad because of their belief in the resurrected Messiah.

At the beginning of the Christian movement, the temple remained the natural gathering place for prayer. As the major Jewish institution that Romans allowed, the temple had its own officials and security force. The disciples' prayer to the Sovereign Lord invoked God's royal dominion over everything. "All who believed" means those who conscientiously affirmed the doctrine concerning the incarnation, crucifixion, resurrection and ascension of Jesus Christ. Holding all things in common was a voluntary practice. Luke's picture of common ownership expresses a vision of the practices of the community of the Resurrection. On the distribution "as any had need" anticipates the dispute that arises in Acts 6. Barnabas is identified as a Levite (note that the Levites had no allotment in land; see Deuteronomy 14:27) whose gift, laid at the disciples' feet, acknowledged their authority without coercion. "Laid it at the apostles' feet" may reflect an old legal convention by which property was transferred by placing it at or under the feet of the recipient.

II. EXPOSITION AND APPLICATION OF THE SCRIPTURE

A. They Devoted Themselves to Purposeful Things (Acts 2:43)

They devoted themselves to the apostles' teaching and fellowship, to the breaking of bread and the prayers (verse 42, NRSV). This verse is difficult to place because it is instructive, both at the end of the narrative that precedes it and at the commencement of the one that follows. Given its mobility with either narrative, attention is given to it in the introduction.

This verse is predicated upon the salvation of the first converts. Once they were saved and baptized, their next move was functional. They availed themselves of the apostles' teachings (i.e., the teachings rendered by Jesus), fellowship (i.e., the partnership among themselves, Jesus Christ and other believers; cf., Hebrews 10:24-25), the breaking of bread (i.e., a combination of the Lord's Supper and their regular fellowship meal) and prayer. Their dedication to these particular functions of the church enabled and strengthened the development of the new movement.

Awe came upon everyone, because many wonders and signs were being done by the apostles (verse 43). The word "awe" in this passage is translated from the Greek *phobos*, which means "fear." For example, we attach "phobia" to other prefixes to specify particular fears (as in claustrophobia—fear of enclosed spaces). "Fear" in this passage refers to the holy fear associated with being in the presence of God. Notice that the number of people who were awestruck was absolute: it was not the case that someone was in the presence of God (or could be in the presence of God) without being awestruck.

It follows, then, that as the apostles conducted many signs and wonders, the believers were able to identify the presence of the Lord in these works. Indeed, this was the purpose of such works. Signs and wonders were not meant to serve as isolated "magical" acts for entertainment or to excite spectators. On the contrary, the purpose of signs and wonders was to point to the message and the truth of Jesus Christ in the same way that Jesus Himself pointed to His Father (John 14:9-11).

B. They Were Unified in Their Mission (Acts 2:44-47)

And all that believed were together, and had all things common; And sold their possessions and goods, and parted them to all men, as every man had need (verses 44-45). This verse, if interpreted incorrectly, might suggest that the disciples lived in a commune—but this was not the case. The emphasis in this passage is on the unity of the believers and their *common* mission. There is a direct relationship between the "fellowship" of verse 42 and what is being acted out here. The fact that they *had all things common* demonstrates their willingness to be unified in an ongoing fellowship where they brought their goods to be given so that "there will be no poor among [them]" (Deuteronomy 15:4). These early believers would sell what they had and place all of their resources in a pool to be redistributed later. Such a commitment to unity is an affront to the individualistic movement that is often consistent with what it means to live in the capitalistic West. There is often the tendency to forget about the needy and outcast, but this was not the mission celebrated by the early church. Right away, they exemplified their commitment to being Christlike.

Every day they continued to meet together in the temple courts (NIV). Notice how often they went to the temple. In Athens, the people congregated around the city square; in today's world, the church is a major gathering place. But in ancient Judaism, the place to meet and greet was in the temple courts. We should not read into this that they were trying to recapture their Jewish heritage. They understood that if they were going to convert others, they would have to go where the people were. In this case, it was the temple.

They broke bread at home and ate their food with glad and generous hearts, praising God and having the goodwill of all the people. The new converts did their witnessing at the temple, but they did their fellowshiping, which included the Lord's Supper, in their homes. Many times, we limit the Communion meal to the first Sunday of the month; but the Word of God places us under no such restriction. We can do it as often as we please. The early disciples did it as a way of maintaining fellowship and focus. This is where the glad and sincere hearts come into view: the more we focus on the Master, the greater the possibility of our joy. Remember, the Lord's Supper is a meal that symbolizes Jesus Christ. The bread represents His body, which was broken for our sins; the wine represents His blood that was shed for us. When we partake of the bread and wine, we are embracing the life, ministry and concerns of Jesus Christ. When we break bread in fellowship around the Communion table, we can rejoice in the fact that our blinded eyes have been opened, according to His promise (Luke 24:30-31).

And day by day the Lord added to their number those who were being saved (Acts 2:47). What happened next in the life of the early church should be regarded as a significant lesson for our modern experience. Because of their faithfulness to the apostles' teaching, fellowship, the breaking of bread, and prayer, God exacted an ongoing revival in their midst—indeed, the conjunction "and" avails this interpretation. But it is also important (and even critical) to note that the daily additions to the church were motivated by God's own will: *"The Lord added."* In other words, they could have done the very same things and the Lord could have opted not to add to their numbers. It is always the case that God's will be done—it is never the case that *our* will be done.

C. They Shared and Gave to Others
(Acts 4:32-35)

This pericope is almost identical to the passage already outlined and commented on in the previous section—the only difference is that it is offered in reverse order. The atmosphere of fellowship and revival was enough to encourage new converts to share their belongings with others. Their voluntary attitude toward sharing was based on a clear understanding that "The earth is the LORD's, and the fulness thereof; the world, and they that dwell therein" (Psalm 24:1).

Like Jesus, of whom the Word of God testified, "increased in wisdom and in years, and in divine and human favor" (Luke 2:52), we see here that the early Christians had the same characterization. In the world, they were favored because of their benevolent attitude. In the body of Christ, they were favored with God's ongoing grace.

III. SPECIAL FEATURES
A. Preserving Our Heritage

Communitas is a Latin term that is extremely important and relevant for the philosophical and cultural perspective of the descendants of Africa in America. It means the "singularity of organizational focus." We are all familiar with the African proverb, "It takes a village to raise a child." At the times of great stress or in an effort to rally people of color around a viable *mantra* (a commonly repeated word or phrase), we often invoke this great saying because we sense a deep connection to its roots. African villages were made up of tribes, and African tribes were made up of households. These households had families—mother, father and children. Village leaders realized centuries ago that if they failed to protect their children, their families would be lost. If they failed to protect their families, their tribes would be lost. And if they failed to protect their tribes, their villages would be lost. Thus, they had to maintain a strong sense of unity.

The early Christian *communitas* began this way as well. It follows, therefore, that as Africans and as Christians, we should always be community-minded and look out for each other. Indeed, this is a basic part of our ethnic and religious heritage.

B. Concluding Reflections

Christians today face some perplexing challenges, in some cases to the extent that there is little "unity in the community." The Christian community is divided on a number of issues, many of which have little to do with the faith. Though debates on matters of doctrine and ritualism would later arise, the early Christians focused their attention on more basic matters. As the faith community grew more diverse and complex, other issues arose and demanded their attention. However, this early period is a beautiful picture of an unpolluted, sincere desire for worship and fellowship among believers.

Perhaps the tragedy of September 11, 2001 gives us some understanding of the early Christians' unity. When the World Trade Centers of New York were demolished and the Pentagon in Washington D.C. was damaged by terrorists, Christians of every denomination banded together to do all that they could to help those in need. Indeed, they shared a common concern that superseded their various tenets of doctrine or polity.

Perhaps the impending threat of persecution caused the early faith community to band together and focus on matters deemed more central to their faith rather than dividing themselves on issues that were less central to their existence.

The sad truth is, nothing binds human beings more closely than shared tragedy. The neighbors who barely know each other bond while boarding up the broken windows of their homes after a tornado. While it would be wonderful if human beings could live in this kind of intimate sharing on a continual basis, our culture is becoming increasingly suspicious of "others," whether next door or across the continent. Our suspicion of others often crosses racial, ethnic, cultural, economic, educational and religious boundaries. Yet, the early believers had among them people of various races, cultures and religious backgrounds.

Through Christ we can live in the reality of Galatians 3:28: "There is no longer Jew or Greek, there is no longer slave or free, there is no longer male and female; for all of you are one in Christ Jesus" (NRSV). Our Gen X and Gen Y population has adopted a phrase, "Don't hate!

Celebrate." While Christians can ill afford to embrace every wind of change, the rhyme emphasizes the need for us to celebrate differences instead of looking upon them with suspicion and disdain.

HOME DAILY BIBLE READINGS

for the week of September 11, 2005
Life Among the Followers

Sept. 5, Monday
—Deuteronomy 15:4-8
—Share with Those in Need
Sept. 6, Tuesday
—Isaiah 55:1-7
—Come to an Abundant Life
Sept. 7, Wednesday
—Luke 12:13-21
—The Parable of the Rich Fool
Sept. 8, Thursday
—Luke 12:22-34
—Do Not Worry About Possessions
Sept. 9, Friday
—Acts 2:43-47
—The Believers Grow in Faith
 Together
Sept. 10, Saturday
—Acts 4:32-37
—The Believers Share Their
 Possessions
Sept. 11, Sunday
—Acts 5:12-16
—Many Sick People Are Cured

PRAYER

O Lord our God, may we never shrink in assembling ourselves together for strength, aided by Your Holy Spirit. Amen.

Lesson 3

Peter and John Heal a Lame Man

ADULT TOPIC: The Gift of Healing
YOUTH TOPIC: Healing the Whole Person
CHILDREN'S TOPIC: God's People Heal

DEVOTIONAL READING: Luke 7:18-23
BACKGROUND SCRIPTURE: Acts 3:1-26
PRINT PASSAGE: Acts 3:1-16

UNIT I
In Jerusalem

CHILDREN'S UNIT
The Church in Jerusalem

KEY VERSE

Peter said, Silver and gold have I none; but such as I have give I thee: In the name of Jesus Christ of Nazareth rise up and walk. —Acts 3:6

Acts 3:1-16—KJV

NOW PETER and John went up together into the temple at the hour of prayer, being the ninth hour.

2 And a certain man lame from his mother's womb was carried, whom they laid daily at the gate of the temple which is called Beautiful, to ask alms of them that entered into the temple;

3 Who seeing Peter and John about to go into the temple asked an alms.

4 And Peter, fastening his eyes upon him with John, said, Look on us.

5 And he gave heed unto them, expecting to receive something of them.

6 Then Peter said, Silver and gold have I none; but such as I have give I thee: In the name of Jesus Christ of Nazareth rise up and walk.

7 And he took him by the right hand, and lifted him up: and immediately his feet and ancle bones received strength.

8 And he leaping up stood, and walked, and entered with

OBJECTIVES

After completion of this lesson, students should understand:

1. The significance of Peter and John's healing of a crippled beggar.

2. The apostles' ability to heal was a sign of their participation in Jesus' healing ministry—made possible through the power of the Holy Spirit.

3. Christians should become involved in the church's holistic healing of those who are wounded, whether physically, emotionally, or spiritually.

them into the temple, walking, and leaping, and praising God.

9 And all the people saw him walking and praising God:

10 And they knew that it was he which sat for alms at the Beautiful gate of the temple: and they were filled with wonder and amazement at that which had happened unto him.

11 And as the lame man which was healed held Peter and John, all the people ran together unto them in the porch that is called Solomon's, greatly wondering.

12 And when Peter saw it, he answered unto the people, Ye men of Israel, why marvel ye at this? or why look ye so earnestly on us, as though by our own power or holiness we had made this man to walk?

13 The God of Abraham, and of Isaac, and of Jacob, the God of our fathers, hath glorified his Son Jesus; whom ye delivered up, and denied him in the presence of Pilate, when he was determined to let him go.

14 But ye denied the Holy One and the Just, and desired a murderer to be granted unto you;

15 And killed the Prince of life, whom God hath raised from the dead; whereof we are witnesses.

16 And his name through faith in his name hath made this man strong, whom ye see and know: yea, the faith which is by him hath given him this perfect soundness in the presence of you all.

Acts 3:1-16—NRSV

ONE DAY Peter and John were going up to the temple at the hour of prayer, at three o'clock in the afternoon.

2 And a man lame from birth was being carried in. People would lay him daily at the gate of the temple called the Beautiful Gate so that he could ask for alms from those entering the temple.

3 When he saw Peter and John about to go into the temple, he asked them for alms.

4 Peter looked intently at him, as did John, and said, "Look at us."

5 And he fixed his attention on them, expecting to receive something from them.

6 But Peter said, "I have no silver or gold, but what I have I give you; in the name of Jesus Christ of Nazareth, stand up and walk."

7 And he took him by the right hand and raised him up; and immediately his feet and ankles were made strong.

8 Jumping up, he stood and began to walk, and he entered the temple with them, walking and leaping and praising God.

9 All the people saw him walking and praising God,

10 and they recognized him as the one who used to sit and ask for alms at the Beautiful Gate of the temple; and they were filled with wonder and amazement at what had happened to him.

11 While he clung to Peter and John, all the people ran together to them in the portico called Solomon's Portico, utterly astonished.

12 When Peter saw it, he addressed the people, "You Israelites, why do you wonder at this, or why do you stare at us, as

though by our own power or piety we had made him walk?

13 The God of Abraham, the God of Isaac, and the God of Jacob, the God of our ancestors has glorified his servant Jesus, whom you handed over and rejected in the presence of Pilate, though he had decided to release him.

14 But you rejected the Holy and Righteous One and asked to have a murderer given to you,

15 and you killed the Author of life, whom God raised from the dead. To this we are witnesses.

16 And by faith in his name, his name itself has made this man strong, whom you see and know; and the faith that is through Jesus has given him this perfect health in the presence of all of you."

POINTS TO BE EMPHASIZED
ADULTS
Key Verse: Acts 3:6
Print: Acts 3:1-16
—Both the healing and the apostles' explanation to the crowd are centered on Jesus Christ as the source of healing.
—The narrative of the healing shows the power of the Gospel for the poor and those without silver and gold.
—Beggars choose strategic places to ask for help, because when people are on their way to worship or pray, they tend to be more generous.
—The disciples sought to continue the healing ministry of Jesus by allowing the Spirit to work miracles through them.

YOUTH
Key Verse: Acts 3:6
Print: Acts 3:1-16
—Although lame persons were considered to be "blemished," or unclean (Leviticus 21:16-23), Peter continued Jesus' compassion for those who were in need of healing and wholeness.
—The disabled man was "carried" to the temple to beg.
—The healing of the disabled man changed his life as well as the lives of those who witnessed this miracle.
—The amazing acts of God can be used as teaching moments.

CHILDREN
Key Verse: Acts 3:7
Print: Acts 3:1-10
—God wants us to put our faith into action.
—God chooses people to help others in times of difficulty.
—God often uses other people to give us blessings that we do not expect.
—Believers praise and thank God for interceding in their lives.

TOPICAL OUTLINE OF THE LESSON

I. INTRODUCTION
   A. The Gift of Healing in the New Testament
   B. Biblical Background

II. EXPOSITION AND APPLICATION OF THE SCRIPTURE
   A. The Need of the Sick
      (Acts 3:1-3)

B. The Act of Healing *(Acts 3:4-8)*
C. The Explanation of Jesus' Role in Healing *(Acts 3:9-16)*

III. SPECIAL FEATURES
   A. Preserving Our Heritage
   B. Concluding Reflections

I. INTRODUCTION
A. The Gift of Healing in the New Testament

The matter of healing and the gift of healing tend to elicit a myriad of emotions from two poles. Those who believe in miraculous healing, and those who do not, have very clear lines of demarcation concerning whether or not this gift was prevalent in the New Testament, and whether or not it is extant in our postmodern world. Despite this polarization, the Word of God does not provide us with a concise dictum on the gift of healing; however, we can glean some guidance from the advice of the apostle James: "Are any among you sick? They should call for the elders of the church and have them pray over them, anointing them with oil in the name of the Lord. The prayer of faith will save the sick, and the Lord will raise them up; and anyone who has committed sins will be forgiven. Therefore confess your sins to one another, and pray for one another, so that you may be healed. The prayer of the righteous is powerful and effective" (James 5:14-16, NRSV).

While James offers encouragement for healing, Scripture further teaches that prayer alone is not enough. All prayer is answered only insofar as the prayer is consistent with the will of God: "And this is the boldness we have in him, that if we ask anything according to his will, he hears us. And if we know that he hears us in whatever we ask, we know that we have obtained the requests made of him" (1 John 5:14-15, NRSV).

Whether or not healing is acknowledged as a gift, we must concede that people will get sick and many will die as a result of their illness. For "just as it is appointed for mortals to die once, and after that the judgment" (Hebrews 9:27, NRSV). Because of sin's entrée into the world, humankind was cursed to die (cf., Genesis 2:15-17; Romans 5:12). Therefore, everyone cannot be healed; dying is a part of what it means to be human. If this is the case, how then are we to understand the healing activities that took place in the New Testament, particularly in the book of Acts?

First, it is essential that we define and understand the New Testament term, "gifts of healings" (1 Corinthians 12:28). Scriptural evidence suggests that healing was a temporary gift to call people's attention to the preached Word and to authenticate the works of Jesus and the apostles. Whenever Jesus or the apostles entered a new region, they would commit an act of healing in order to be authenticated. Once the curiosity of the unsaved was grasped, the Word could go forth with new fervor. Secondly, the Bible does not show any evidence that the gift of healing was widespread or arbitrarily used. The only people using this gift in a public forum were Christ (Matthew 8:16-17), the apostles (Matthew 10:1), the seventy (Luke 10:1) and Philip, a close acquaintance of the apostles (Acts 8:5-7). Each person or group who utilized this gift always did so as a precursor to the Gospel message. It was never the case that healing was the central event—it always pointed to the Gospel.

Thirdly, it is important to note that when an act of healing would have stood by itself, rather than point to the Gospel message (i.e., when someone with the gift was not attempting to heal a saved friend or relative), it was not used. For example, there are several places where Paul and others did not heal themselves or a sick brother or sister in the faith (Philippians 2:27; 1 Timothy 5:23; 2 Timothy 4:20). It is important to note that with Epaphroditus (see Philippians 2), God intervened on behalf of Paul's petition. Paul did not arbitrarily heal whomever he wanted. Finally, as indicated above, healing was always done in the name of Jesus (except by Jesus Himself), for the purpose of pointing to the Gospel. Saved people were never saved as a result of the gift of healing; they were healed as a result of prayer.

B. Biblical Background

The previous chapter climaxes with a stunning invocation from the hearers of Peter's message (Acts 2:37): "Now when they heard this, they were pricked in their heart, and said unto Peter and to the rest of the apostles, Men and brethren, what shall we do?" Peter's message brought home the point that their rebellious attitudes and antagonism to the Messiah created the atmosphere that resulted in His crucifixion. Peter said about their participation, "Jesus of Nazareth, a man attested to you by God with deeds of power, wonders, and signs... you crucified and killed by the hands of those outside the law" (Acts 2:22, 23, NRSV). Consequently, the atmosphere, primarily for those who "were cut to the heart," was starting to become polarized. As the disciples continued the ministry of Jesus, those who were antagonistic to Jesus would begin to reveal their annoyance over the perpetuation of His work.

As more and more converts repented and made professions of faith in Jesus as the Messiah, made public through baptism, the more people began to take the ministry of Jesus and His followers seriously. Until now, the apostles had not done anything of physical consequence; their work was limited to preaching the Word. What took place with the lame man whom Peter and John healed was the beginning of a new dispensation in their ministry. They would not only preach and teach as Jesus preached and taught, they would also heal as Jesus did (Mark 16:17-18), according to His promise.

Their encounter with the lame man would prove to be a powerful evangelistic opportunity. Separation from their faith, their heritage and their loved ones often characterized the life many persons afflicted with a disease or other physical condition. Jewish tradition held that people who had any type of physical infirmity, whether congenital or contracted later in life, were unclean. Thus, those so afflicted could not be cleansed sufficiently to enter the temple. Furthermore, practicing Jews feared that any contact with persons deemed unclean would render them unclean also and thereby subject them to the rituals and sacrifices of cleansing as well. Consequently, the lame man secured his daily sustenance by begging outside the temple—as he could not go inside.

As one with an infirmity, the lame man had no hope of living as an upright member of the community. Furthermore, the entry of an unclean person into the temple area was no small issue. So, the paralytic had no hope of seeing the interior of the temple. Later, after Jesus' ascension, the apostle Paul would be thrown into prison after creating a riot when some of his enemies rumored that he had taken an unclean person into the temple.

This is a marvelous passage of Scripture, especially for those of us who have seen or experienced a greater portion of life's inequities. The man Peter and John encounter on their way to worship suffered from a congenital condition that rendered him unable to walk. In their culture, most people earned their living from the ground, be they farmers of agriculture or livestock. Therefore, this man's paralysis precluded his participation in the workforce. Although Jewish religion had made provisions for this kind of situation—by allowing begging and the reciprocation of alms—it is likely that this man, and others in his predicament, would have preferred physical mobility.

II. Exposition and Application of the Scripture
A. The Need of the Sick *(Acts 3:1-3)*

In this pericope, Peter and John enter a new world, quite different from the one to which they had grown accustomed. They had been present while Jesus healed, cast out demons, performed a myriad of miracles, and raised the dead. Now, consistent with Jesus' prophetic words, "They shall lay hands on the sick, and they shall recover" (Mark 16:18). They did not go looking for someone to heal or inviting others to come and participate in a "healing and deliverance" service. In the normal course of their day, Peter and John happened upon an opportunity that had mega-implications: a sick man needed healing.

One day Peter and John were going up to the temple at the time of prayer—at three in the afternoon (NIV). It is imperative to remember that Peter and John were Jews. Much ado has been said and inferred about the early disciples' temple participation, especially on the Sabbath. The early disciples were not called Christians immediately; this did not come until later (Acts 11:27). They were known as the "people of The Way." In understanding the apostles' constant appearances at the temple or various synagogues, we must keep in mind the context of their faith. It also must be kept in mind that Jesus did not come to commence a new religion, or, for that matter, to abolish Judaism. He came, in part, to renovate, reform and refocus Judaism. Therefore, as devout messianic Jews, Peter and John were in the proper place. Three times each day, they would go up to the temple for prayer (Psalm 55:17; Daniel 6:10).

At the same time, *a man lame from birth was being carried in. People would lay him daily at the gate of the temple called the Beautiful Gate so that he could ask for alms from those entering the temple.* This man's full-time occupation was begging—and what a wise beggar he was. First, he knew *when* to beg. The time of Peter and John's arrival was about three in the afternoon. He likely was postured at the temple gate at the times when people came to worship, thus increasing the odds that his appeals would be successful. Second, the paralytic knew *where* to beg. There were three fundamental requirements of Judaism: The Torah (the Law), worship, and giving of alms (charity: giving aid to the poor, sick, and less fortunate). Being positioned at the temple three times a day as devout Jews (wanting to fulfill their almsgiving before worship passed by) was not a bad place to be! But more significantly was the designation, *gate... called Beautiful.* Our best estimate places this gate at the eastern side between the Gentile court and the women's court. He begged at the most beautiful gate, where there was certain to be high traffic and a willingness to give.

Among those who came to the temple on this particular day were Peter and John. It was not unusual to see these two disciples together, for they were close associates before Jesus invited them to minister with Him (cf., Matthew 17:1; Mark 5:37; 9:2; 13:3; 14:33; Luke 8:51; 9:28). In the book of Acts, they continued to work together as ministers of the Gospel (cf., 4:13, 19; 8:14). When the beggar saw these two men, he unwittingly made a request that would change his life forever. The text notes that this man was born crippled. Therefore, he would have had no reason to imagine a life that included physical mobility. He had learned to survive as a crippled beggar. In an agrarian society, he did not have many choices beyond this. Thus, he asked Peter and John, and other passersby, for money.

B. The Act of Healing (Acts 3:4-8)

It may be interesting to note the confidence and resolve to which Peter and John approached this situation: *"Look on us,"* Peter commanded. This man epitomized one of the two Greek words for poor: *penichros* (someone who barely has his or her daily sustenance met) and *ptochos* (a beggar; someone who is so poor that he has nothing; cf., Matthew 5:2). Their physical disposition is one that is bent. The latter description is the closest depiction of this man. He was so destitute that he had not the self-esteem or self-image that would allow him to make eye contact with his benefactors: he bowed his head to the ground and extended his hand for alms. Peter, noting this humbling characteristic, commanded an immediate response.

Quite possibly, this man had never heard it on this wise. Most of his previous benefactors gave only to fulfill their religious convictions. They had no interest in becoming familiar with the man or his circumstances. By contrast, the disciples of Jesus demonstrated their love for this man by going deeper than surface kindness—they wanted to see his eyes.

But Peter said, "I have no silver and gold, but I give you what I have; in the name of Jesus Christ of Nazareth, walk." Peter's words were likely a tremendous disappointment to the beggar. Shortly, however, the paralyic would discover that what these two ordinary-looking men possessed was much more significant—in the name of Jesus Christ, they knew that they could heal the man.

Their act of healing demonstrated that there is something that Christ has to offer that is far more valuable than silver and gold (cf., Proverbs 3:14; Job 28:12). To be sure, this raises a critical question of the believer: You may not have money, but what do you possess that you can offer? All believers can offer the gifts that we receive as heirs to the Kingdom.

Another important thrust in Peter's words was his invocation of the name of Jesus Christ. He did not heal on his own, but *in the name of Jesus Christ of Nazareth*. The man had no real reason to believe in (or to even know for that matter) *the name of Jesus Christ*. Peter's words were an indication that an authentic healing of this man could not have been done apart from the Messiah's sovereign will. What happened next is an indication of how the bona fide gift of healing works: it was instantaneous. We can expect that when saints pray for the healing of another saint, the person will recover (James 5:14). But when the gift of healing was engaged, there was no recovery period—it was instantaneous (cf., Matthew 8:13; Mark

5:29; Luke 5:13; 17:14; John 5:9). With the assistance of Peter's outstretched hand, the man immediately *leaping up stood, and walked, and entered with them into the temple, walking, and leaping, and praising God.* Notice the exuberance of someone who had been touched by the grace of God! We may have been depraved or destitute like this poor beggar, but once we have been impacted by grace, our testimony cannot be silenced.

C. The Explanation of Jesus' Role in Healing *(Acts 3:9-16)*

Whereas the people were confused about this man who, until recently, had been a temple fixture, he himself was not confused. He clung to Peter and John as though they were his dear friends that had stopped by to visit him. They gathered under the porch that Solomon had initially erected, where Herod had ambitiously built upon in order to retain for himself some of the mystique and grandeur therein. Peter immediately posed two questions for the crowd: *Men of Israel, why does this surprise you? Why do you stare at us as if by our own power or godliness we had made this man walk?* Peter believed that the answer to both questions should have been obvious.

In Peter's estimation, they should have known that what they were seeing was from Jesus Christ. His disciples were now doing the kinds of works that He had done—but they were doing these works in His name, not according to their own piety or power.

Peter seized this teachable moment and began preaching. His message had one basic thrust: proclaim the name and power of Jesus. Over and over again, he pointed out the crowd's culpability in the death of Jesus: "You handed him over to be killed, and you disowned him"; "You disowned the Holy and Righteous One and asked that a murderer be released"; "You killed the author of life." And, over and over again, he used a different title to express who Jesus really was: Servant, Jesus, Holy and Righteous One, Prince of Life, and Christ. With great candor and sincerity, Peter outlined who Jesus was, what they did when they killed Him, and that it was in His name that this man, whom they all knew and recognized, was healed.

III. SPECIAL FEATURES
A. Preserving Our Heritage

Historically, our people have known what it means to serve a God who can "make a way out of no way." African Americans are more economically prosperous than ever; but for most of our history, Black people could assert, like Peter and John, "Silver and gold have I none...." What we did have, however, often served as a powerful testimony, just as Peter and John did in healing the lame man. Despite having meager economic resources and even less political or social clout, the faith of many Black Christians has wrought miraculous results. The logbook of testimonies in the Black church is replete with stories of eviction notices deferred, groceries that mysteriously appeared, or the sick rising from their bed of affliction without the benefit of professional medical care. These events were (and are) interpreted as the providential hand of God mercifully moving in the lives of His children. Moreover, having received God's goodness, those who experienced deliverance were glad to tell it. Like the lame man, their deliverance was joyful occurance that moved the believer to testify, "I just couldn't keep it to myself."

B. Concluding Reflections

Christians do not live with the same religious dictums regarding those with infirmities as the Hebrews, but many of us have our own prejudices regarding people who are wounded in some way. The paralytic in this passage was consigned to a life of begging because the religious people of his day could not make room for him in their understanding of the family of God. Peter and John were willing to challenge barriers imposed by religious doctrine to minister to someone in need (as Jesus had done so many times) as they shared His message of hope. But more than anything else, their concern was to call attention to the Savior through their ministry.

Persons with physical infirmities generally are not regarded with such disdain today; however, the community of faith must stand ready to use its various gifts to offer comfort to the afflicted. The gifts and resources available to us as people of faith are not reserved for our own purposes, nor are they to be confined to church walls.

HOME DAILY BIBLE READINGS

for the week of September 18, 2005
Peter and John Heal a Lame Man

Sept. 12, Monday
—Luke 7:18-23
—Jesus Tells of His Healing Power
Sept. 13, Tuesday
—Luke 9:1-6
—The Twelve Receive Power to Heal
Sept. 14, Wednesday
—Luke 4:31-37
—Jesus Rebukes a Demon
Sept. 15, Thursday
—Acts 3:1-5
—A Beggar Asks for Alms
Sept. 16, Friday
—Acts 3:6-10
—A Man Is Healed
Sept. 17, Saturday
—Acts 3:11-16
—Peter Speaks to the People
Sept. 18, Sunday
—Acts 3:17-26
—Peter Tells the People to Repent

PRAYER

Eternal God, when we are confronted with human need, grant us the grace to give not only the sustenance on which a person can survive, but also that for which he or she can live. May your love constrain us so that we minister not in our strength, but in the power of Your Holy Spirit. In Jesus' name, we pray. Amen.

Lesson 4

The Time for Boldness

ADULT TOPIC: Power to Be Bold
YOUTH TOPIC: Courage to Speak Out
CHILDREN'S TOPIC: God's People Speak Boldly

UNIT I
In Jerusalem

CHILDREN'S UNIT
The Church in Jerusalem

DEVOTIONAL READING: Ephesians 6:10-20
BACKGROUND SCRIPTURE: Acts 4:1-31
PRINT PASSAGE: Acts 4:1-4, 23-31

KEY VERSE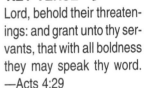

Lord, behold their threatenings: and grant unto thy servants, that with all boldness
they may speak thy word.
—Acts 4:29

Acts 4:1-4, 23-31—KJV

AND AS they spake unto the people, the priests, and the captain of the temple, and the Sadducees, came upon them,

2 Being grieved that they taught the people, and preached
through Jesus the resurrection from the dead.

3 And they laid hands on them, and put them in hold unto
the next day: for it was now eventide.

4 Howbeit many of them which heard the word believed;
and the number of the men was about five thousand.

.....

23 And being let go, they went to their own company, and
reported all that the chief priests and elders had said unto them.

24 And when they heard that, they lifted up their voice to
God with one accord, and said, Lord, thou art God, which hast
made heaven, and earth, and the sea, and all that in them is:

25 Who by the mouth of thy servant David hast said, Why
did the heathen rage, and the people imagine vain things?

26 The kings of the earth stood up, and the rulers were
gathered together against the Lord, and against his Christ.

27 For of a truth against thy holy child Jesus, whom thou

OBJECTIVES

**After completion of this
lesson, students should
understand:**

1. How Peter and John
   boldly proclaimed the
   Gospel in the face of
   persecution.

2. The background infor-
   mation on the persecu-
   tion that Peter and John
   faced.

3. How to help participants
   identify and commit to
   ways they can witness
   boldly themselves.

hast anointed, both Herod, and Pontius Pilate, with the Gentiles, and the people of Israel, were gathered together,

28 For to do whatsoever thy hand and thy counsel determined before to be done.

29 And now, Lord, behold their threatenings: and grant unto thy servants, that with all boldness they may speak thy word,

30 By stretching forth thine hand to heal; and that signs and wonders may be done by the name of thy holy child Jesus.

31 And when they had prayed, the place was shaken where they were assembled together; and they were all filled with the Holy Ghost, and they spake the word of God with boldness.

Acts 4:1-4, 23-31—NRSV

WHILE PETER and John were speaking to the people, the priests, the captain of the temple, and the Sadducees came to them,

2 much annoyed because they were teaching the people and proclaiming that in Jesus there is the resurrection of the dead.

3 So they arrested them and put them in custody until the next day, for it was already evening.

4 But many of those who heard the word believed; and they numbered about five thousand.

.....

23 After they were released, they went to their friends and reported what the chief priests and the elders had said to them.

24 When they heard it, they raised their voices together to God and said, "Sovereign Lord, who made the heaven and the earth, the sea, and everything in them,

25 it is you who said by the Holy Spirit through our ancestor David, your servant:

'Why did the Gentiles rage, and the peoples imagine vain things?

26 The kings of the earth took their stand, and the rulers have gathered together against the Lord and against his Messiah.'

27 For in this city, in fact, both Herod and Pontius Pilate, with the Gentiles and the peoples of Israel, gathered together against your holy servant Jesus, whom you anointed,

28 to do whatever your hand and your plan had predestined to take place.

29 And now, Lord, look at their threats, and grant to your servants to speak your word with all boldness,

30 while you stretch out your hand to heal, and signs and wonders are performed through the name of your holy servant Jesus."

31 When they had prayed, the place in which they were gathered together was shaken; and they were all filled with the Holy Spirit and spoke the word of God with boldness.

POINTS TO BE EMPHASIZED
ADULTS
Key Verse: Acts 4:29
Print: Acts 4:1-4, 23-31
—The proclamation of Jesus' resurrection

challenged the authority of the Sadducee sect, which denied the reality of life beyond the grave.

—The large following that the apostles had gathered represented a political threat to the Jewish establishment.

—As is common in Acts, there is a strong association of the Holy Spirit with boldness, prayer, and powerful acts of God.

—The prayer of thanksgiving (Acts 4:23-30) is a song that is similar in style to several in the Old Testament (see Psalm 30).

YOUTH

Key Verse: Acts 4:31
Print: Acts 4:1-4, 23-31

—The Sadducees did not believe in the Resurrection and reacted vehemently against Peter and John for proclaiming the resurrection of Jesus.

—Although the council of religious leaders ordered Peter and John not to teach in Jesus' name, they insisted that they would continue to proclaim Jesus' message in obedience to God.

—The Holy Spirit enabled Peter and John to preach with boldness.

CHILDREN

Key Verse: Acts 4:31b
Print: Acts 4:1-5, 18-21, 23, 31

—Some people are annoyed by anyone who talks about the Lord.

—Persons who do not have a relationship with Jesus Christ can develop such a relationship because of our faithful witness.

—Christians praise God in both good and bad times.

—The Holy Spirit makes bold witnesses.

TOPICAL OUTLINE OF THE LESSON

I. INTRODUCTION
  A. Evolving into Boldness
  B. Biblical Background

II. EXPOSITION AND APPLICATION OF THE SCRIPTURE
  A. The Disciples Were Arrested for Teaching and Preaching *(Acts 4:1-4)*
  B. The Disciples Prayed Boldly *(Acts 4:23-30)*
  C. The Disciples' Prayer Was Answered *(Acts 4:31)*

III. SPECIAL FEATURES
  A. Preserving Our Heritage
  B. Concluding Reflections

I. INTRODUCTION
A. Evolving into Boldness

The Peter who is featured prominently in Acts 4 for speaking so boldly about Christ seems to have nothing in common with the man who ran away weeping after denying that he knew Jesus (see Luke 22). The radical transformation of Peter serves to encourage and affirm the sovereign knowledge of our Lord. He does not give up on us, even when it seems to us that we have little to offer Him. Obviously, He saw something in Peter that was not apparent, especially as he stood in the courtyard, vehemently denying his relationship with Jesus.

By the Day of Pentecost, a different Peter has begun to emerge. Neither Luke nor the other gospel writers provides a detailed account of the apostles' transformation from the fearful band who went into seclusion while their Teacher was being crucified, to men who spoke boldly for Christ, adding thousands to the number of believers. Empowered by the Holy Spirit, Peter and John were no longer afraid of the Jewish religious authorities—particularly the 71 men who comprised the Sanhedrin.

B. Biblical Background

During Jesus' three years of earthly ministry, several antagonists, mainly the scribes, Pharisees, Sadducees and priests, confronted Him. Given Jesus' enemies' disdain for Him, it is no surprise that they were equally ferocious toward His disciples, particularly those who did similar works as the faith was beginning to amass a following. In order to understand their contempt for Jesus' disciples, it is important to look at the enemies of Jesus, particularly the priests, the captain of the temple and the Sadducees.

Regarding the three immediate rivals of the apostles—the priests, the captain of the temple and the Sadducees—the setting was ripe for a showdown. Immediately after their authentic healing of a man who was born lame—legitimated by the many who knew the man's history—Peter and John began to speak to the people. There were many temple priests, but they were divided into groups and served based upon the drawing of lots. Thus, each man greatly anticipated the day when he would be able to minister in the temple before the multitude of people who came to present their evening sacrifice. Peter and John represented a distraction from the priests' pivotal moment. They were an interruption that had to be annihilated; thus, we have the captain of the temple.

The captains of the temple were descendants of Levi (the tribe of Israel from which the priests were selected), but sanctioned under the Roman government to act as temple police. As such, the only Jewish leader with a higher authority was the high priest to whom the captains reported. So, they carried out whatever the high priest charged; thus, we have the Sadducees.

For quite a while, the Sadducees were the high priests in Israel. They were wealthy landowners with strong political connections. Unlike the Zealots who were oppositional to the political might and oppression of the Roman Empire, the Sadducees had a strong conflict of interest. Their tenure as high priests, combined with their aristocratic disposition, fostered their acquiescence to Rome. They knew that it was to their benefit to conform to Rome if they were going to stay in power. Their opposition to the apostles, however, had a different rationale than the priests or captains. The Sadducees did not believe in the resurrection of the dead, which was the central doctrine of the apostles' message, which included their personal testimony of Jesus Christ's resurrection. This teaching, fortified by the lame man being healed in Jesus' name, and coupled with the fact that Peter and John had the ear of the people, was enough of a distraction to cause insurgency. Just as they had moved against Jesus (John 11:47-50), they were now moving against His disciples.

II. Exposition and Application of the Scripture

A. The Disciples Were Arrested for Teaching and Preaching
(Acts 4:1-4)

Evidently, Peter and John's healing of the lame man had caused quite a stir, and people wanted to know more about the source of their power. It is likely that many of them remembered that only a few years prior, Peter and John had been partners in a fishing business. Then, for reasons beyond most people's ability to comprehend, they shut down their business, which was probably a lucrative enterprise in a community that upheld serious cuisine restrictions (cf., Leviticus 11), and began traversing the land with an itinerant teacher. These same former fishermen, having no credentials, no training, and no sanction by the elite Sadducees, were now *speaking to the people... [and] teaching the people and proclaiming that in Jesus there is the resurrection of the dead.*

This speaking, teaching and preaching were far more than mere distractions to the Jewish religious hierarchy; remember that thousands had already believed and had been converted. Beyond this,

many more had seen their healing work with the lame man (chapter 3), and were becoming more and more convinced of their authority. Therefore, in the minds of their antagonists, this new teaching threatened the financial income, way of life, religious authority and the Jewish faith as a whole. As far as the Jewish leaders were concerned, the disciples could legitimate the resurrection of Jesus, then the Sadducees' objection to teaching life after death would be proven false. If this major theological point was discredited, their doctrinal authority would be undermined.

Their response to this potential (and grave) disruption of their teaching was similar to what they did to Jesus—arrest them, then get rid of them. They immediately had the apostles arrested, but it was too late: *many of those who heard the word believed; and they numbered about five thousand.* The ministry of Jesus was now officially established in His disciples and was on the move. Aristotle once said, "The role of a teacher is infinite." Jesus initially taught twelve, but those twelve (imbued with His Spirit) had reached thousands of others; and now the number of persons who had come to Christ is inestimable.

B. The Disciples Prayed Boldly
(Acts 4:23-30)

Here we find the disciples at a place that should not be unusual for a mature Christian: they are at the crossroads of their lives. Prior to now, the opposition was of a simple sort: they only had to

As the major Jewish institution, that the Romans allowed, the temple had its own officials and security force. The Sadducees, who did not believe in the Resurrection, regarded proclamation of the resurrection of Jesus as a threat to the temple. The five thousand believers indicate a substantial response. The question of power or name is a challenge of the legitimacy of the authority of the temple's council. Luke emphasizes that the rulers of the people and elders were now confronted with the authority of the Holy Spirit. The public trial of the apostles was again an occasion for testimony to all Israel, and another indictment for their crucifixion of the Messiah. Psalm 118:22 is again used as a charge against the authorities. In Luke's narrative, to be saved means physical, social and spiritual well-being. The apostles were known for their boldness in speech, no matter what the consequences. The officials were frustrated in their effort to silence the apostle because of the people. This unusual healing was a sign of hope because it pointed to God's fulfillment of His promise of restoration.

contend with inquisitive speculators regarding the message they spoke. Now, however, they faced a totally different, elite group of antagonists. The members of the Sanhedrin Council (i.e., the ruling court) came together in an impromptu meeting in order to discuss what to do with the followers of Jesus, who were doing works that were similar to that of their leader.

Peter and John did not back down and were not intimidated by this high council of Jewish leaders. Sounding very much like Martin Luther, the Protestant reformer, they refused to recant their earlier words. When asked to take back his written objections to the Catholic Church (October 31, 1517), Luther said, "Here I stand; I can do no other. God help me. Amen." Regardless of what happened, Peter and John would not stop invoking the name of Jesus Christ. The apostles had been greatly impacted by their three-year experience with Jesus, and Peter had already denied Him three times, just as Jesus had prophesied. Given their testimony and Peter's personal experience of denial, they boldly said, *Whether it be right in the sight of God to hearken unto you more than unto God, judge ye. For we cannot but speak the things which we have seen and heard* (19-20).

Not wanting to further agitate the crowd that had witnessed the miracle that was wrought in the lame man, and unwilling to change from their dogmatic preoccupation with their association with Jesus, the Council reprimanded Peter and John then released them. The two apostles went back to their company and reported all that had occurred. The disciples, who were gathered in that one space, did the only thing familiar to them: they prayed. Many times, we opt to use human reasoning to liberate us from unfamiliar territory. We call friends or we may be given to nefarious counsel from horoscopes, tarot cards, or palm readings. But none of these is consistent with the will of God. Faced with difficult and unfamiliar circumstances, and having no idea how to proceed, they decided to pray.

The opening of their prayer expressed their sincere commitment to follow the will of God: *"Sovereign Lord,"* they said. The Greek word for *"Lord"* in this passage is unusual in the New Testament. It renders the English *despot*, which means "an authoritative figure or owner or ruler." The *"Sovereign"* prefix helps us to understand the weight of the term. In other words, the Lord was their total and complete leader. To Him and Him alone would they look in their moments of despair.

Once they finished their acknowledgements in their prayer, they did three things. First, they acknowledged God as Creator of the earth and everything in it, *"who didst make the heaven and the earth and the sea and everything in them."* Secondly, they outlined who God was in relationship to the prophets of old. Quoting Psalm 2:1-2, they acknowledged that the same Jesus who was crucified was the same Messiah who was to come. Remember, the word "Messiah" is the Hebrew rendering and "Christ" is the Greek word—which mean "the Anointed One." Indeed, *"The kings of the earth set themselves in array, and the rulers were gathered together, against the Lord and against his Anointed."* Moreover, the praying disciples went on to identify these kings and rulers. Herod and Pilate, along with *the Gentiles and the people of Israel*, were all culpable for the Messiah's death.

Once the foundation of their prayer was laid, the disciples began their supplications. *"And now, Lord, look upon their threats, and grant to thy servants to speak thy word with all boldness."* Although they had already spoken *with great boldness* as they stood before the Sanhedrin, the Bible does tell us that we should "pray without ceasing" (1 Thessalonians 5:17). Even though they had already exhibited the capacity to speak boldly, they needed and wanted to keep it. Despite their arrest experience they knew that boldness to speak about Christ was a necessary ingredient in taking the Gospel to every nation.

The closing of their prayer was spectacular. Shortly before they met to pray, the same Council that ordered them to cease speaking in the name of Jesus cautioned them. One might think that their prayer would have included a request to be relieved of their assignment, but this was not the case. Their prayer was for fortification and determination to do even more: *By stretching forth thine hand to heal; and that signs and wonders may be done by the name of thy holy child Jesus.* They were undeterred. Instead of recoiling to pressure, they maximized their efforts by prayerfully springing into boldness. Their response was similar to Daniel's before the king. When he knew that the writ had been signed that prohibited him from praying to any deity save the king, "He went into his house; and his windows being open in his chamber toward Jerusalem, he kneeled upon his knees three times a day, and prayed, and gave thanks before his God, as he did aforetime" (Daniel 6:10).

C. The Disciples' Prayer Was Answered *(Acts 4:31)*

God answered the disciples' prayer in a manner reminiscent of the Day of Pentecost. *And when they had prayed, the place in which they were gathered together was shaken; and they were all filled with the Holy Spirit and spoke the word of God with boldness* (NRSV). In many ways, this clarifies the language Baptists may hear about the necessity of being filled with the Holy Spirit more than once, with the evidence of speaking in tongues. Notice here that three things occurred *after* prayer: first, the place was shaken; second, they were filled with the Holy Spirit; and third, they spoke the Word of God boldly.

Many times, we overlook the importance of prayer, or we pray as an afterthought; but in this text, the disciples immediately recognized their limitations and began praying (cf., Nehemiah 1:1-5; 2:1-5). As it was on the Day of Pentecost, the presence of God was expressed with a physical force, as the place began to shake. Unlike Pentecost, however, the initial experience of speaking in a foreign language was gone. This filling of the Holy Spirit was not another filling or a new filling in the sense that there was not a prior filling, but rather it was a continuous reenergizing of the power of God.

Interestingly, their prayer was to continue doing the very thing that led to their incarceration. Their fervent prayer led to a renewal of the Spirit with the power to speak boldly.

III. SPECIAL FEATURES
A. Preserving Our Heritage

Black history and the early church share an important commonality in that, as a result of persecution, they resorted to prayer for a solution to their predicament. Nothing fosters an atmosphere for prayer in the human spirit like the resolve that derives from persecution. Also, the many Black people who have fought against persecution have exhibited boldness in that struggle. Abolitionist Sojourner Truth spoke boldly in her famous speech delivered in 1851 at the Women's Convention in Akron, Ohio. Some in the audience were not pleased that a poor, Black woman had the audacity to address them. Some historians speculate that Truth was booed and hissed by some, yet she had the courage to speak with boldness.

Though few Blacks spoke as boldly as Sojourner Truth and Frederick Douglass, many in the slave community found other ways to boldy continue in the faith. For example, the genre of spirituals that grew out of that oppressive experience served a dual purpose as code language for secret communication. Spirituals like "Steal Away," and "Swing Low, Sweet Chariot" encouraged slaves to seek liberation through prayer and action, but many of them served as alerts that there would be a secret worship service, perhaps "Down by the Riverside." The enslaved community had bold determination to worship God and praise Him despite their oppressive conditions.

B. Concluding Reflections

All human beings face times when it is necessary to speak up for what is right. For some people, the ability to do this comes naturally. Others cultivate the ability to speak boldly as they mature, both in age and in Christ. Still, speaking boldly for Christ is a difficult thing for many Christians to do. Since Christianity is a way of life for so many Americans, speaking about Jesus today normally does not evoke vehement opposition. Being bold for Christ today often means the willingness to share our faith or speak out for Christ at the risk of being ridiculed or rejected. Yet, many Christians find themselves unable or unwilling to risk even moderate forms of rejection or ridicule in order to share the Gospel. Our Lord needs people who are willing to push past their fears and tell others about Him.

We are not persecuted or killed for our faith like the early disciples were. The Greek word for "witness," *Mautauria,* is the root of the English word *martyr.* A witness during the early days of the faith was quite literally someone who died for what he or she believed. This is why prayer was an essential part of their faith activity.

Bill Hybels has written a marvelous book, *Too Busy Not to Pray,* in which he outlines the need to carve out specific prayer times. Because Christ still seeks disciples who are willing to boldly go about the ministry of evangelism and witnessing, it is essential that we pray—and pray without ceasing.

HOME DAILY BIBLE READINGS

for the week of September 25, 2005
The Time for Boldness

Sept. 19, Monday
—Ephesians 6:10-20
—Be Strong in the Lord
Sept. 20, Tuesday
—1 Thessalonians 2:1-8
—Paul Preaches the Gospel
Courageously
Sept. 21, Wednesday
—Acts 4:1-7
—Peter and John Are Arrested
Sept. 22, Thursday
—Acts 4:8-12
—Peter Speaks About Jesus Christ
Sept. 23, Friday
—Acts 4:13-17
—Peter and John Are Warned
Sept. 24, Saturday
—Acts 4:18-22
—Peter and John Refuse to Stop
Sept. 25, Sunday
—Acts 4:23-31
—The Believers Pray for Boldness

PRAYER

O Thou who art our God, in a pluralistic religious society, may we as Your servants be not afraid to claim and proclaim the name of Jesus Christ, and to affirm Him boldly as the Model and Example for those who would find life in Thee. Grant us grace that will accrue to the magnification of Your name on earth. In Jesus' name, we pray. Amen.

October 2, 2005

Lesson 5

UNIT II
In All Judea and Samaria

Stephen

CHILDREN'S UNIT
The Church Grows

ADULT TOPIC: Faithful Servant
YOUTH TOPIC: Me, a Leader?
CHILDREN'S TOPIC: God's Special Helpers

KEY VERSE
Stephen, full of faith and power, did great wonders and miracles among the people. —Acts 6:8

DEVOTIONAL READING: Isaiah 6:1-8
BACKGROUND SCRIPTURE: Acts 6:8—7:60
PRINT PASSAGE: Acts 6:8-15; 7:53-60

OBJECTIVES
After completion of this lesson, students should understand:

1. Church leadership should possess integrity, courage and spiritual power to minister to the people of God.
2. Religious leadership can be the worst enemies of strong church leaders.
3. There is persecution of Christians today, although in more subtle ways than it was in the early church.
4. Persecution should make us better witnesses for Christ.

Acts 6:8-15; 7:53-60—KJV

8 And Stephen, full of faith and power, did great wonders and miracles among the people.

9 Then there arose certain of the synagogue, which is called the synagogue of the Libertines, and Cyrenians, and Alexandrians, and of them of Cilicia and of Asia, disputing with Stephen.

10 And they were not able to resist the wisdom and the spirit by which he spake.

11 Then they suborned men, which said, We have heard him speak blasphemous words against Moses, and against God.

12 And they stirred up the people, and the elders, and the scribes, and came upon him, and caught him, and brought him to the council,

13 And set up false witnesses, which said, This man ceaseth not to speak blasphemous words against this holy place, and the law:

14 For we have heard him say, that this Jesus of Nazareth shall destroy this place, and shall change the customs which Moses delivered us.

15 And all that sat in the council, looking stedfastly on him, saw his face as it had been the face of an angel.

53 Who have received the law by the disposition of angels, and have not kept it.

54 When they heard these things, they were cut to the heart, and they gnashed on him with their teeth.

55 But he, being full of the Holy Ghost, looked up stedfastly into heaven, and saw the glory of God, and Jesus standing on the right hand of God,

56 And said, Behold, I see the heavens opened, and the Son of man standing on the right hand of God.

57 Then they cried out with a loud voice, and stopped their ears, and ran upon him with one accord,

58 And cast him out of the city, and stoned him: and the witnesses laid down their clothes at a young man's feet, whose name was Saul.

59 And they stoned Stephen, calling upon God, and saying, Lord Jesus, receive my spirit.

60 And he kneeled down, and cried with a loud voice, Lord, lay not this sin to their charge. And when he had said this, he fell asleep.

Acts 6:8-15; 7:53-60—NRSV

8 Stephen, full of grace and power, did great wonders and signs among the people.

9 Then some of those who belonged to the synagogue of the Freedmen (as it was called), Cyrenians, Alexandrians, and others of those from Cilicia and Asia, stood up and argued with Stephen.

10 But they could not withstand the wisdom and the Spirit with which he spoke.

11 Then they secretly instigated some men to say, "We have heard him speak blasphemous words against Moses and God."

12 They stirred up the people as well as the elders and the scribes; then they suddenly confronted him, seized him, and brought him before the council.

13 They set up false witnesses who said, "This man never stops saying things against this holy place and the law;

14 for we have heard him say that this Jesus of Nazareth will destroy this place and will change the customs that Moses handed on to us."

15 And all who sat in the council looked intently at him, and they saw that his face was like the face of an angel.

.....

53 "You are the ones that received the law as ordained by angels, and yet you have not kept it."

54 When they heard these things, they became enraged and ground their teeth at Stephen.

55 But filled with the Holy Spirit, he gazed into heaven and saw the glory of God and Jesus standing at the right hand of God.

56 "Look," he said, "I see the heavens opened and the Son of Man standing at the right hand of God!"

57 But they covered their ears, and with a loud shout all rushed together against him.

58 Then they dragged him out of the city and began to stone him; and the witnesses laid their coats at the feet of a young man named Saul.

59 While they were stoning Stephen, he prayed, "Lord Jesus, receive my spirit."

60 Then he knelt down and cried out in a loud voice, "Lord, do not hold this sin against them." When he had said this, he died.

POINTS TO BE EMPHASIZED
ADULTS
Key Verse: Acts 6:8
Print: Acts 6:8-15; 7:53-60
—Even though Stephen was originally appointed to "wait on tables" (6:2), the church recognized his gifts as a speaker and miracle worker.
—Stephen defended the Gospel through a speech that narrated the story of God's work through Israelite history.
—Stephen became the church's first martyr.
—Supernatural signs and visions, consistent with his ministry, accompanied Stephen's trial and execution.

YOUTH
Key Verse: Acts 6:8
Print: Acts 6:8-15; 7:53-60
—Stephen was a Greek-speaking Jewish Christian who was among those selected to assure fair distribution of food among Hellenist widows.
—Stephen's witness to his faith in the resurrection of Christ aroused the anger of others within the synagogue.
—Stephen accused the members of the Sanhedrin of killing the prophets and the Messiah.
—Stephen's bold witness resulted in his being stoned to death, while he prayed for the forgiveness of his killers.

CHILDREN
Key Verse: Acts 6:3
Print: Acts 6:1-12, 15
—The church has experienced tremendous growth despite internal conflicts, disputes and turmoil.
—The church has developed rituals for recognizing persons whom God has chosen for ministry.
—Some Christians have been mistreated for expressing their faith.
—Christian leaders spread the Gospel message without regard for their personal safety.

TOPICAL OUTLINE OF THE LESSON
I. INTRODUCTION
  A. The Charge of Being a Witness for Christ
  B. Biblical Background

II. EXPOSITION AND APPLICATION OF THE SCRIPTURE
  A. True Disciples Speak with Wisdom and Power *(Acts 6:8-10)*
  B. True Disciples Are Often in Opposition to the World *(Acts 6:11-15)*

C. True Disciples Emulate Jesus—
Even unto Death *(Acts 7:53-60)*

III. SPECIAL FEATURES
A. Preserving Our Heritage
B. Concluding Reflections

I. INTRODUCTION

A. The Charge of Being a Witness for Christ

The word "witness" has a paradoxical nature. The only time that this word is mentioned in this passage (verse 58), it means one thing—but once attached to the life of Stephen (or any disciple who is willing to give his or her life for Christ), it means something quite different. For this reason, we are compelled to take a closer, more analytical look at what is at work with this word in order to comprehend our roles as disciples of Christ.

In the normal sense (that is, in the way we commonly use the word *witness*), a witness is someone who has a firsthand account of something; but if a person in Old Testament times was corrupt and offered false witness, there would be dire consequences. Because offering false witness could cost a life, it was prohibited by the Ten Commandments. But as austere as this definition of *witness* appears to be, it is not as stringent as the New Testament meaning, particularly as typified by Stephen, and later by many others from the second century onward.

The word *witness* is derived from the Greek word *martyria*, which means "someone who is willing to die for an important cause." For the disciples of Jesus, being a witness was not just looking on at what was happening with objectivity and indifference; they believed it included living a life that emulated the life of Jesus—even if they died in the process (Acts 22:20; Hebrews 12:1; Revelation 2:13).

Herein lies the paradox: the world's understanding of "witness" is to look on (verse 58); the Christian conception of "witness" is to be a martyr—to die for one's beliefs (verse 60), which is what Stephen embodied in his life and ministry.

B. Biblical Background

There came a time in the life of the early church when the work outgrew the practicality of the disciples doing it all by themselves. The disciples wisely reasoned that it was a more urgent task for them to deal with "prayer, and to the ministry of the word" (Acts 6:4). The men chosen to assist the church were not identified as deacons, but traditionally they are considered the first deacons. The word "deacons" comes from the Greek *diakonos*, which means a "servant" or "minister."

Stephen's selection was itself unique, even in regard to the others chosen. His was one of two names that had commentary attached to it: namely, *a man full of faith and of the Holy Ghost*. The other was *Nicolas, a proselyte of Antioch*. This brief description was also given to alert the reader that Stephen had a special ministry function; for later Stephen is cited as a man *full of faith and power, did great wonders and miracles among the people* (6:8).

Stephen's uniqueness at the time seems inconsequential, but nothing can be more untrue. In fact, there are several consequences that came through Stephen. Furthermore, his ministry, life and death were very similar to Jesus'. Both Jesus and Stephen were brought to court on trumped-up charges. Both were unwilling to give a personal defense for their actions. Both were accused of speaking against the temple and the Jewish laws and customs. Both willingly gave their lives in obedience to the great plan of the heavenly Father. Perhaps this is why Stephen, like the Master, received such a great reception into the Kingdom by the heavenly hosts.

Among his many gifts, Stephen was also a preacher and a miracle worker, doing a work similar to that of the apostles. He was perhaps the first recorded Christian theologian who showed the inclusivity of the Gospel. Stephen is what we would call an *apologist* for the faith. The word *apology* in this context does not mean to be contrite or to beg forgiveness; here, it means "to defend" one's belief. Stephen's speech/sermon before the Sanhedrin was actually given as a defense of the universality of the Christian faith. In the minds of the Jews, their history and religion were limited to themselves, but in terms of the new dispensation (that is, the commencement of the Christian era), the history of Judaism is essential to the history of Jesus and Christianity.

Above all his many gifts and abilities, Stephen is best known in Christendom for being the first martyr of the faith.

When we read the footnote that shows Saul's presence during the persecution of Stephen, we can almost anticipate (from its ambiguity) that Saul would have a more functional and intentional role in the narrative. Although at this point in the text the two men are at opposite poles of the faith, the fact remains that Stephen's and Paul's lives are inextricably bound to the expansion of Christianity.

II. EXPOSITION AND APPLICATION OF THE SCRIPTURE

A. True Disciples Speak with Wisdom and Power
(Acts 6:8-10)

Luke, in his description of Stephen, was careful to acknowledge that he was *"full of grace and power,* [and] *did great wonders and miracles among the people."* Stephen was a disciple of Jesus Christ, a role he took very seriously. The word *full* in this passage means "to be filled up." We are told that Stephen was filled with faith, grace and power. To be filled by faith indicates that he trusted Christ immeasurably for his well-being. In this way, he seems consistent with one of Paul's testimonies: "If we live, we live to the Lord, and if we die, we die to the Lord; so then, whether we live or whether we die, we are the Lord's (Romans 14:8, NRSV).

Stephen was not only filled with faith (that is, the ability to trust in God regardless of the situation), he also was filled with grace. To have grace means to have received favor from someone (God, in this case) such that one has an inward joy, delight, or charm. But the gift of grace did not come mysteriously upon Stephen as he stood before the Sanhedrin. The grace that so typified his character was a result of his relationship with the Lord. He was so filled with grace that his face looked "as it had been the face of an angel" (6:15, NRSV).

Being filled with faith, Stephen was able to trust God; but being filled with grace, he was able to approach any situation with a sense of calm or delight. Indeed, Stephen had power! We have here the manifestation of a promise. Jesus said, "But ye shall receive power, after that the Holy Ghost is come upon you: and ye shall be witnesses [martyrs] unto me both in Jerusalem, and in all Judaea, and in Samaria, and unto the uttermost part of the earth" (Acts 1:8). The word *power* here means "ability to do." Stephen demonstrated his power by showing his ability to do *great signs and miracles among the people.*

Equipped with faith, grace and power, *They were not able to resist the wisdom and the Spirit by which he spake.* This is the mark of a true disciple—one who has the gifts and who understands how to utilize these gifts for the building up of the Kingdom. What we see in Stephen is part of the ongoing directive that Jesus gave to His disciples: "Behold, I send you forth as sheep in the midst of wolves: be ye therefore wise as serpents, and harmless as doves" (Matthew 10:16). To be wise is to be clever and skillful in how one responds to various situations.

B. True Disciples Are Often in Opposition to the World
(Acts 6:11-15)

Stephen found himself in a public debate, which was not an unusual occurrence in and around Jerusalem. Five hundred years earlier, Socrates the philosopher and many others had wandered from place to place publicly debating esoteric issues. In a similar fashion, the Diaspora Jews from

As a deacon, nothing is said about Stephen serving the needs of the widows, but his great wonders and signs manifest the work of God through him as through the apostles. The charge against Stephen is similar to that brought against Paul (21:18). The security of Israel was believed to rest on the sanctity of the Law and the Temple. Stephen's transformation with his face like the face of an angel was a warning of contending with God. Stephen's interrogation recalls Jesus' trial before the high priest and Pilate. The extended retelling of the stories from Genesis displays careful interpretation of the Greek version known as the Septuagint (LXX), where the contrast between present promise and future possession originates. As the stories are retold, they emphasize God's initiative and activity. Among all the stories of the patriots, Stephen's focus on Joseph highlights a divided Israel with God taking special care of Joseph, for God was with him. Stephen citing Israel's history "in witness against you" is a call to repentance. Stephen invokes the passage from Deuteronomy (18:15) that was used to identify Jesus as "the prophet like Moses."

Asia and Africa (those who were dispersed and made into slaves when they were captured by Pompey in 63 BC) were, for whatever reason, resident in Jerusalem. They apparently were more zealous than indigenous Jews and began a public debate with Stephen. Upon losing their debate against Stephen they immediately sought a way to redeem themselves: *Then they suborned men, which said, We have heard him speak blasphemous words against Moses, and against God.* The NRSV reports, "Then they *secretly instigated* men." Because they were unable to handle Stephen's wisdom, they resorted to a tried and true method employed earlier against Jesus: "Now the chief priests, and elders, and all the council, sought false witness against Jesus, to put him to death" (Matthew 26:59) on charges of blasphemy.

Blasphemy was an offense punishable by death (Leviticus 24:16). In order to do away with Stephen, they sought and found persons who were willing to lie under oath. By tossing about an accusation of blasphemy as a charge, the spectators were *stirred up*—they were moved to action. They took hold of Stephen and, as the NRSV suggests, "seized him," which is a violent act. Like Jesus, Stephen did speak some of the words that they accused him of saying, but their deception was in the subtle (and deadly) misrepresentation of the actual words and intent.

The charge was clear in the minds of these religious fanatics: *This man ceaseth not to speak blasphemous words against* *this holy place, and the law.* The holy place (the temple where they believed God resided) and the Law of Moses were both sacred. They could not have devised a more sacred venue than the temple, or a more sacred writing than the Law.

They immediately connected Stephen to Jesus of Nazareth. This showed their disdain for Stephen in no less than two ways. First, they were careful to remind the onlookers that Jesus was from Nazareth, the place from which nothing good could emerge (cf., John 1:46). Secondly, they misconstrued Jesus' words to "destroy this temple" (John 2:19). At the time, Jesus was referring to His antagonists as those who would destroy the temple; and, more importantly, the temple to which He was referring was Himself (cf., John 2:21).

Next, they determined that Stephen's alignment with Jesus was anathema to the temple and irreverent to Moses. For the Jews, the Law of Moses represented something similar to Christian salvation. Even though the Jews themselves struggled with the Law, it was nevertheless near and dear to their hearts. The Ten Commandments of Moses had been expanded to include upwards of six thousand ceremonial laws or ordinances. Jesus Himself said, "Think not that I am come to destroy the law, or the prophets: I am not come to destroy, but to fulfil. For verily I say unto you, Till heaven and earth pass, one jot or one tittle shall in no wise pass from the law, till all be fulfilled" (Matthew 5:17-18). But what was this fulfillment of which he spoke?

The Law had a specific purpose as a temporary and symbolic Messiah. The *New Living Translation* puts it this way: "Let me put it another way. The law was our guardian and teacher to lead us until Christ came. So now, through faith in Christ, we are made right with God. But now that faith in Christ has come, we no longer need the law as our guardian" (Galatians 3:24- 25). Stephen understood this particular function of the Law—it was to point to its fulfillment in Christ. Mosaic Law can never be done away with, in that it finds fulfillment in Christ, the expected Hope. But this was not the spirit in which it was represented to the council. Jesus was seen as the one who intended to eradicate the Law and all the customs of Judaism.

As they were speaking, the image of Stephen was transformed before their eyes; they *saw that his face was like the face of an angel.*

C. True Disciples Emulate Jesus— Even unto Death *(Acts 7:53-60)*

At the end of Stephen's rousing oration, he showed no fear as he advised the council of their historic refusal to accept anyone who spoke of Jesus—*who have received the law by the disposition of angels, and have not kept it*—until they ultimately murdered the Incarnated One Himself. Prophets spoke of the One who was to come, but it was to no avail. Rather than accept their words, they eliminated them. Now that the Christ had actually come, Stephen said bluntly, "you have now betrayed and murdered" Him (Acts 7:52).

These words were a direct indictment against their hypocrisy. *When they heard these things, they were cut to the heart, and they gnashed on him with their teeth.* In all likelihood, the council probably agreed with much of what Stephen was saying in his opening testimony. Then their supposed agreement turned to agitation as they understood the direction Stephen's monologue would take: he was comparing them to their ancestors who killed prophets for what they were prophesying, but their context was much worse. They actually *betrayed and murdered* Him. The phrase *cut to the heart* literally means "divided in two." Stephen's words were so piercing that they were beside themselves in frustration and anger.

The phrase *gnashed at him with their teeth* literally means "to hate someone with the intent of destroying him or her." In the Old Testament, it referred to righteous persons who became sinners because they thought they were doing the will of God but were sorely wrong and misguided in their efforts. They had not only killed the Messiah, but now they were hardening their hearts to the Messiah's messenger. On at least two other occasions, they heard the Gospel message (cf., 4:8ff, 5:27ff); they were told exactly who Jesus was—but they chose to operate with impunity.

While Stephen's antagonists were *hardening* their hearts against him and the words he spoke, Stephen was *opening* his heart to the work of the Holy Spirit. *But he, being full of the Holy Ghost, looked up stedfastly into heaven, and saw the glory of God, and Jesus standing on the right hand of God.* We should not be surprised by Stephen's response to the council's destructive hatred. Luke's introduction of Stephen indicates that he was "a man full of faith and the Holy Spirit." The message for modern Christians is compelling: we should open our hearts to the indwelling of the Holy Spirit in our daily work so that we are not unduly disconnected from God and peace when adversity comes. While his adversaries were seeing hatred and destruction, Stephen was seeing victory and triumph as Jesus stood gloriously at the right hand of God.

The word *glory* literally means "something that has weight or importance." David helps us to understand what this truly means when he called God "the King of Glory" (Psalm 24). There is none who has more weight or importance than God! Stephen saw God's glory and Jesus standing at God's right side, and he immediately revealed what he saw: *And said, Behold, I see the heavens opened, and the Son of man standing on the right hand of God.* But this was the last thing they wanted to hear. Like disobedient children, *They cried out with a loud voice and stopped their ears and rushed together upon him.* The idea that the person whom they had crucified only recently was at the "right hand" of the King of Glory (a reference with which they were familiar) was more than they could handle. In collusion, they seized Stephen to murder him.

It is amazing how these pious citizens were so quickly reduced to mob violence in the name of religion. What is more amazing is that even though they lost their composure, they did not lose their memory concerning such matters: "Take the blasphemer outside the camp; and let all who were within hearing lay their hands on his head, and let the whole congregation stone him" (Leviticus 24:14, NRSV). They did not stone him until he was first removed from the city: *And cast him out of the city, and stoned him.*

Standing in the wings was the person whose letters would later occupy the greater portion of the New Testament. Saul was observing this wicked mob violence from the sidelines. Later, his direct role in the persecution of Christians would increase; however, his function at this point was limited to that of an observer.

We already have detailed similarities between the events surrounding Jesus' crucifixion and Stephen's martyrdom. Stephen did and said many things that are reminiscent of Jesus. For example, we can compare, "Then Jesus, crying with a loud voice, said, 'Father, into your hands I commend my spirit.' Having said this, he breathed his last" (Luke 23:46, NRSV). In Stephen's case, *Lord Jesus, receive my spirit. And he kneeled down, and cried with a loud voice, Lord, lay not this sin to their charge. And when he had said this, he fell asleep.* Both Jesus and Stephen committed their spirits to a member of the Deity, and both forgave their assailants. And, of course, having done this, they both breathed their last breath and fell asleep.

III. SPECIAL FEATURES
A. Preserving Our Heritage

There have been many martyrs in the African American struggle for justice and liberation. During slavery, there were many unsung heroes—those whose contribution to the struggle may never be known. From the holding chambers on the shores of the West African coast, to the Middle Passage, to the auction block, Africans were routinely killed. There have been martyrs among the ranks of Baptists, witnesses who were killed for the cause in which they believed. Like Stephen, they believed they were correct to assert their rights to human dignity.

B. Concluding Reflections

There's a saying, "Everybody wants to go to heaven but nobody wants to die." All Christians enjoy the benefits of our faith, yet we are often reluctant to embrace its sufferings. Although it is unlikely in our modern culture, being a Christian means having the willingness to die for Him, too. Every believer should live with the reality that death may come to us because of our witness for Christ. This should be the extent of our conviction.

Come what may, we should strive to maintain our course for the kingdom of God.

HOME DAILY BIBLE READINGS
for the week of October 2, 2005
Stephen

Sept. 26, Monday
—Acts 6:8-15
—Stephen Is Arrested
Sept. 27, Tuesday
—Acts 7:1-8
—Stephen Speaks to the Council
Sept. 28, Wednesday
—Acts 7:9-16
—Stephen Tells the Joseph Story
Sept. 29, Thursday
—Acts 7:17-29
—Stephen Tells Moses' Early Story
Sept. 30, Friday
—Acts 7:30-43
—Stephen Tells of Moses, the
Liberator
Oct. 1, Saturday
—Acts 7:44-53
—Stephen Challenges His Hearers
Oct. 2, Sunday
—Acts 7:54-60

—Stephen Is Stoned to Death

PRAYER
Eternal God, grant that our lives may mirror Your love so that others will see Christ in us. May we embrace opposition as the opportunity to witness to Your holy name. We pray in the name of Jesus Christ, and for His sake. Amen.

Lesson 6

The Samaritans and Philip

KEY VERSE 💡

When the apostles which were at Jerusalem heard that Samaria had received the word of God, they sent unto them Peter and John.—Acts 8:14

ADULT TOPIC: Christians Without Borders
YOUTH TOPIC: Old Enemies—New Friends
CHILDREN'S TOPIC: God's People Tell Good News

DEVOTIONAL READING: Acts 19:1-10
BACKGROUND SCRIPTURE: Acts 8:4-25
PRINT PASSAGE: Acts 8:4-17

OBJECTIVES

After completion of this lesson, students should understand that:

1. Philip spread the Good News of God's love beyond Judea, bringing healing and joy to new believers.

2. Participants gain a concept of the geographical and cultural barriers that Philip fought in going to Samaria.

3. Participants commit to overcoming barriers that keep us from accepting others.

Acts 8:4-17—KJV

4 Therefore they that were scattered abroad went every where preaching the word.

5 Then Philip went down to the city of Samaria, and preached Christ unto them.

6 And the people with one accord gave heed unto those things which Philip spake, hearing and seeing the miracles which he did.

7 For unclean spirits, crying with loud voice, came out of many that were possessed with them: and many taken with palsies, and that were lame, were healed.

8 And there was great joy in that city.

9 But there was a certain man, called Simon, which beforetime in the same city used sorcery, and bewitched the people of Samaria, giving out that himself was some great one:

10 To whom they all gave heed, from the least to the greatest, saying, This man is the great power of God.

11 And to him they had regard, because that of long time he had bewitched them with sorceries.

12 But when they believed Philip preaching the things concerning the kingdom of God, and the name of Jesus Christ, they were baptized, both men and women.

13 Then Simon himself believed also: and when he was baptized, he continued with Philip, and wondered, beholding the miracles and signs which were done.

14 Now when the apostles which were at Jerusalem heard that Samaria had received the word of God, they sent unto them Peter and John:

15 Who, when they were come down, prayed for them, that they might receive the Holy Ghost:

16 (For as yet he was fallen upon none of them: only they were baptized in the name of the Lord Jesus.)

17 Then laid they their hands on them, and they received the Holy Ghost.

Acts 8:4-17—NRSV

4 Now those who were scattered went from place to place, proclaiming the word.

5 Philip went down to the city of Samaria and proclaimed the Messiah to them.

6 The crowds with one accord listened eagerly to what was said by Philip, hearing and seeing the signs that he did,

7 for unclean spirits, crying with loud shrieks, came out of many who were possessed; and many others who were paralyzed or lame were cured.

8 So there was great joy in that city.

9 Now a certain man named Simon had previously practiced magic in the city and amazed the people of Samaria, saying that he was someone great.

10 All of them, from the least to the greatest, listened to him eagerly, saying, "This man is the power of God that is called Great."

11 And they listened eagerly to him because for a long time he had amazed them with his magic.

12 But when they believed Philip, who was proclaiming the good news about the kingdom of God and the name of Jesus Christ, they were baptized, both men and women.

13 Even Simon himself believed. After being baptized, he stayed constantly with Philip and was amazed when he saw the signs and great miracles that took place.

14 Now when the apostles at Jerusalem heard that Samaria had accepted the word of God, they sent Peter and John to them.

15 The two went down and prayed for them that they might receive the Holy Spirit:

16 (for as yet the Spirit had not come upon any of them; they had only been baptized in the name of the Lord Jesus).

17 Then Peter and John laid their hands on them, and they received the Holy Spirit.

POINTS TO BE EMPHASIZED

ADULTS
Key Verse: Acts 8:14
Print: Acts 8:4-17
—Philip's preaching to the Samaritans is one result of the scattering of the Jerusalem church because of persecution.
—Samaria was a region composed of people whom Jerusalem Jews considered outcasts because of their mixed ancestry and their form of religious practice.
—The birth of the church in Samaria begins the movement of the church's witness outward from Jerusalem.
—Simon is one of several magicians and false teachers mentioned in Acts, indicating the spiritual thirst of people in the world of the first century.
—The intervention of Peter and John so that the Samaritans would receive the Holy Spirit indicates the solidarity of the "mother church" with new offshoots.

YOUTH
Key Verse: Acts 8:5
Print: Acts 8:4-17
—Following the death of Stephen, a severe persecution was launched against the church in Jerusalem, causing many followers to scatter from Jerusalem to proclaim the Gospel in other places.
—Philip went to Samaria and proclaimed the Messiah to people who were considered unclean half-breeds.
—Samaritans eagerly responded to Philip

as unclean spirits were cast out and people were healed.
—By carrying the Gospel into Samaria and baptizing men and women there, Philip was extending the community of faith, geographically and culturally.

CHILDREN
Key Verse: Acts 8:5
Print: Acts 8:4-6, 8-17
—The persecution of Christians led to their being scattered, but they still preached the Gospel.
—Many people believed in Jesus Christ because of the preaching of the displaced Christians.
—The power of God is still manifested through the efforts of faithful Christians.
—Samaritans were rejected by the Jews, but accepted by the early Christians.

TOPICAL OUTLINE OF THE LESSON

I. INTRODUCTION
   A. The Two Worlds: Darkness and Light
   B. Biblical Background

II. EXPOSITION AND APPLICATION OF THE SCRIPTURE
   A. When People Accept Jesus, There Will Be Joy *(Acts 8:4-8)*
   B. What It Means to Accept Jesus *(Acts 8:9-13)*
   C. People Who Accept Jesus Receive the Holy Spirit *(Acts 8:14-17)*

III. Special Features
    A. Preserving Our Heritage
    B. Concluding Reflections

I. Introduction

A. The Two Worlds: Darkness and Light

In this passage, we have the collision of two worlds: the world of darkness and the world of light. Stated another way, we can look at this as the collision of evil and good. After all is said and done, these are the two main designations in the world—the only options from which humankind can choose. In this passage, Simon is representing the world of darkness with his magical trickery. Representing the world of light is Philip, with his miracles and message about Jesus Christ. Sometimes, the line of demarcation between good and evil is more subtle than we may think; it is not as obvious as black and white. We probably have to deal with more grey areas in our lives than the more clearly defined black-and-white issues.

In this narrative, we find that Simon was in a similar position. He was a sorcerer (a magician) who tricked the people into believing that illusions were real. A few years ago, our television airwaves were inundated with advertisements for "psychic hotlines" to call and receive advice from a clairvoyant or fortune-teller. Such behavior can fall into one of only two categories: darkness or light; good or evil. It cannot be both! Simon so believed his own hype that he went from place to place *saying that he was someone great* (Acts 8:9, NRSV). He was not great—he was but another charlatan who used deception to lure people to walk with him in darkness.

As Christians, we are supposed to follow but one person: "For to this you have been called, because Christ also suffered for you, leaving you an example, so that you should follow in his steps" (1 Peter 2:21, NRSV). And what is this step that we should follow? "This then is the message which we have heard of him, and declare unto you, that God is light, and in him is no darkness at all. If we say that we have fellowship with him, and walk in darkness, we lie, and do not the truth: But if we walk in the light, as he is in the light, we have fellowship one with another, and the blood of Jesus Christ his Son cleanseth us from all sin" (1 John 1:5-7). We must decide whether we want to live in the world of darkness (i.e., to be lukewarm; cf., Revelation 3:15-16; Joshua 24:15), or whether we want to live as children of God, committed to the will of God (1 John 3:1-3).

B. Biblical Background

The book of Acts tells powerful stories of believers breaking down human barriers that would embrace some people in the kingdom of God and reject others. After His resurrection, Jesus' Great Commission to His disciples was, "Go therefore and make disciples of all nations, baptizing them in the name of the Father and of the Son and of the Holy Spirit" (Matthew 28:19, NRSV). Later, in the book of Acts, He gave the parameters within which this mandate would take place: "But you will receive power when the Holy Spirit has come upon you; and you will be my witnesses in Jerusalem, in all Judea and Samaria, and to the ends of the earth" (Acts 1:8, NRSV). The Jews had at times refused to share the message of God with other nations. Jonah's calamity at sea is but one example of Jewish resistance to sharing their God with others. Instead of going to Ninevah as the Lord had directed him, Jonah tried to run from his call by running to Tarshish. The Ninevites' wickedness was well-known. Still, Jonah had no interest in evangelizing them to show them a way out of their wickedness (Jonah 1).

The New Covenant was a correction of this exclusive attitude. Luke takes special care in sharing the fact that "From one ancestor he made all nations to inhabit the whole earth, and he allotted the times of their existence and the boundaries of the places where they would live" (Acts 17:26, NRSV).

Consequently, the disciples were charged to start in Jerusalem, then leave the comfort of their geographical location and expand the ministry of Jesus to the rest of the world (Acts 1:8). But by the time we arrive at Acts 8, the disciples were still residing in Jerusalem. Philip moved to change this by bringing the Gospel to the Samaritans, which was precisely what Jesus had outlined. What is also important is their motivation to move beyond Jerusalem. They did not move until persecution forced them to move. This is important even for our own lives. Many times, God allows situations to come our way to persuade us to do God's will. Think back to some of the persecutions or challenges you have had in your life. Did this persecution or challenge bring you into a more intimate understanding of who Jesus really is and what His will is for your life? Paul reminds us, "For he has graciously granted you the privilege not only of believing in Christ, but of suffering for him as well" (Philippians 1:29, NRSV).

II. Exposition and Application of the Scripture

A. When People Accept Jesus, There Will Be Joy (Acts 8:4-8)

Therefore they that were scattered abroad went every where preaching the word. We have before us the Christian Diaspora. The word *diaspora* means "dispersion." Following Stephen's execution, and on the wake of Saul's merciless persecution of the Christian church, the disciples finally began to move beyond the borders of Jerusalem as Jesus had commanded. This is the irony of our faith; the disciples did not leave their comfort zone until severe persecution prompted them to evangelize elsewhere. And is not this the case for us as well? Do we not remain comfortable, even irresponsible in our prayer lives, until we are prompted from our bed of ease by some affliction?

Luke leaves nothing uncovered on these matters, for he is the one who quotes Jesus regarding Satan's intent: "Simon, Simon, listen! Satan has demanded to sift all of you like wheat, but I have prayed for you that your own faith may not fail; and you, when once you have turned back, strengthen your brothers." (Luke 22:31-32, NRSV). In the first part of this verse, "Satan has demanded," the "you" is singular and personal. Satan asked for Peter by name for the purpose of "sifting," which means "to shake violently."

Jesus followed His words to Peter with a more general claim: "But I have prayed for you." The "you" in this section is plural. He warned Peter that Satan had a personal attack prepared for him; but Jesus realized that this personal attack was to be levied against all believers, so He has prayed for us all. Jesus was well aware that He would be sending His followers into hostile territory, but He had undergirded us with prayer to take on the challenge.

Then Philip went down to the city of Samaria, and preached Christ unto them. Here, for the first time, we are witnessing the bold move to leave Judea and enter the non-Jewish world. Philip, who was one of the original seven chosen to serve as *diakonos*, was the first to go into Samaria for the purpose of preaching the Gospel. Remember, the Jews and the Samaritans were estranged cousins. A well-known adage at the time of Jesus was that the Jews had "no dealings with the Samaritans" (John 4:9; compare Luke 9:52-53). The enmity between them heightened when the Jews refused to allow the Samaritans—on their return from Babylonian captivity—to participate in the building of the temple because they had intermarried with other races. The Samaritans subsequently built their own temple and their own theology. The Jews so despised their amalgamated relatives and their religion that they refused to even enter Samaria. They would take a longer route to avoid putting their footsteps on Samarian soil. In this regard, Philip's determination to preach the Gospel in

Samaria marked the beginning of a reversal of long-held prejudices.

And the people with one accord gave heed unto those things which Philip spake, hearing and seeing the miracles which he did. Philip began his ministry assisting the apostles by taking care of the practical needs of the people (Acts 6:1-6). In chapter 8, however, we begin to see an expanded role taking place. Philip was now an evangelist who had the ability to perform genuine miracles and to heal others: *For unclean spirits, crying with loud voice, came out of many that were possessed with them: and many taken with palsies, and that were lame, were healed.*

Given our modern climate's penchant for extremes, it is important to note that the acts of healing that Philip did, like Jesus and the others who had the gift, were not done in absence of preaching. Healing and other miracles were done to garner people's attention in order for them to hear the Word of God. As we will see in the next section, it is a mistake to be more preoccupied with healing (or any other gift) than with the preached Word. Healings and miracles cannot save a person's soul; belief in Jesus Christ as a response to the Gospel message can.

Once the Gospel is preached and people accept it, there is a corresponding joy that ensues. This does not mean that all problems are solved and all pains are gone; on the contrary—it means that a saved person has access to "the peace of God, which surpasses all understanding" (Philippians 4:7, NRSV). Once this takes place, the community's testimony will be, *And there was great joy in that city.*

B. What It Means to Accept Jesus
(Acts 8:9-13)

But there was a certain man, called Simon, which beforetime in the same city used sorcery, and bewitched the people of Samaria, giving out that himself was some great one. What we know of Samaria in recent times—notwithstanding the historical estrangement between them and the Jews—is that while Jesus was here He evangelized that province (John 4). But sometime after His departure, Simon Magus (i.e., Simon the conjurer) did mystifying works among them. His illusions did not have the intent to teach them about God or worship; rather, the intention was to have the people believe that he was a great man. And this they did.

To whom they all gave heed, from the least to the greatest, saying, This man is the great power of God. Simon was highly regarded for his powers; there is no indication that there were any others on his level; he even captured the attention of Luke. All of the people who knew of him were mesmerized by the mystical acts Simon was performing, so much so that they elevated him to divine status. Unable to equate his greatness with any human being, and believing that no human being could perform the many feats he was doing, the people of Samaria conceded that *This man is the great power of God.* Simon Magus had the people under his total control: *And to him they had regard, because that of long time he had bewitched them with sorceries.*

What happens next is a verification of the overwhelming power of God. These people had already conceded that Simon was on another level, such that he had the power of God at his disposal. Enter now the authentic man of God—Philip. Once they saw Philip's miracles and heard the words he spoke, their perception was elevated to a level beyond what they felt about Simon. *But when they believed Philip preaching the things concerning the kingdom of God, and the name of Jesus Christ, they were baptized, both men and women.* They did not hesitate. We each have within us the capacity to recognize the truth of God; but, at the same time, each of us possesses the option to reject the truth of God. En masse, the same people who saw and believed the magical works of Simon were the same persons who converted to Jesus Christ. Without question, they accepted the kingdom of God as the only dimension that had a true rule over their lives. Then, as a final blow to the magical episodes of Simon, the people showed their public adoration for Jesus by being baptized.

God will never be outdone by anyone. If it appears that God is silent on an issue, it is not the case that God cannot handle it; rather, God has chosen not to handle it yet. For however long, Simon had free reign in Samaria. People of all ages believed that he had some kind of divine mandate, such that he could have been the Son of God. But when the true authority arrived on the scene, *Then Simon himself believed also: and when he was baptized, he continued with Philip, and wondered, beholding the miracles and signs which were done.* Simon's conversion is but another confirmation of the Gospel's power to convict sinners. While later passages would indicate that Simon had not given up all of his former ways, in that regard his is no different from many believers in that we grow in discipleship as we grow in grace and understanding of the faith. Apparently somewhat fixated on the power that came from being a believer, Simon followed Philip everywhere, fascinated by what the Holy Spirit had empowered Philip to do.

C. People Who Accept Jesus Receive the Holy Spirit *(Acts 8:14-17)*

Now when the apostles which were at Jerusalem heard that Samaria had received the word of God, they sent unto them Peter and John. This must have been an inspiring moment. The apostles were aware of both the historical animosity and the reconciliation effort that Jesus Himself initiated with the woman at the well (John 4). Now they had received the news that Philip's preaching had made inroads and was tearing down the invisible (but very real) barriers.

What is also noteworthy is the apostles who came to his aid and why. First, they came to his aid because even though Philip was a servant of the Lord who possessed extraordinary gifts—namely, the gifts of evangelism, miracles and healings—he was not an apostle. God is a God of order. Paul reminds us that "all things should be done decently and in order" (1 Corinthians 14:40, NRSV). God has a particular order for how leadership is to take place, and rarely do we find God deviating from this. Psalm 33 serves as further demonstration of this fact. Notice the direction that the oil, which is symbolic of the anointing, flows. It flows from top to bottom, not from bottom to top. Philip was an evangelist, not an apostle. The apostles were anointed to do certain things—in this instance, passing on the Holy Spirit to new converts.

The two went down and prayed for them that they might receive the Holy Spirit (for as yet the Spirit had not come upon any of them; they had only been baptized in the name of the Lord Jesus). Then Peter and John laid their hands on them, and they received the Holy Spirit. We must always remember that the book of Acts deals with the continuation of the ministry of Jesus to the ministry of the Holy Spirit as manifested in the apostles and other believers. Furthermore, we must keep in mind that the only persons who knew there was a Holy Spirit who was to come were those disciples who were with Jesus in John 14:15-18 and the disciples who were in the Upper Room. There were no telecommunication devices to alert people who were not in the vicinity that the Holy Spirit was coming. Consequently, when Paul went to Ephesus, he was faced with the prospect of meeting believers who had not known about the coming Helper. While there, he found some disciples and asked them, "'Did you receive the Holy Spirit when you became believers?' They replied, 'No, we have not even heard that there is a Holy Spirit'" (Acts 19:2, NRSV). "When Paul had laid his hands on them, the Holy Spirit came upon them, and they spoke in tongues and prophesied" (19:6, NRSV).

The method of getting the news across that the Holy Spirit had come in the apostolic age was face-to-face, by the laying on of hands. But now we have the Word of God to instruct us concerning the work of the Spirit. Now, when we believe, the Holy Spirit comes upon us and seals us immediately for the day of redemption (Ephesians 4:30; cf., Philippians 1:6). This narrative is similar to Paul's experience in Ephesus. In both cases, apostles arrived on the scene after salvation had already taken place in order to teach and deliver to them the Holy Spirit's anointing.

III. SPECIAL FEATURES
A. Preserving Our Heritage

Our core beliefs as African Americans are predicated upon the fact that God is good, regardless of how trying the circumstances of life may be. This foundation of our faith has empowered us to be gracious and loving, even toward those who oppose us. One such example can be found in the story of young Ruby Bridges. At six years old in the spring of 1960, young Ruby entered the doors of William Franz Elementary School surrounded by federal marshalls. But the agents could not protect her from the barrage of verbal harassment from the White community. Her mother reminded her that she had no need to be afraid because she could always pray. "Remember, if you get afraid, say your prayers. You can pray to God anytime, anywhere. He will always hear you." So each day, as she walked into the school, Ruby prayed for those who hurled insults at her—because she was different.

B. Concluding Reflections

Many Christians are reluctant to share the Gospel with others, but especially to those who are radically different from them. Having no idea how he would be received, Philip ventured beyond his comfort zone to share the Good News.

The powerful message of hope is still available to move lives today. There are a myriad of human beings who identify and define themselves as "Christian." Among the ranks of the faithful are persons from a variety of backgrounds and experiences. And though people experience the wonders of the Gospel differently because of our various diversities, we all recognize that the same Gospel binds us together. Therefore, it is imperative that we focus on the tie that binds and not the issues that divide. The salvation of humanity is a far more significant and pressing matter than our personal biases.

HOME DAILY BIBLE READINGS
for the week of October 9, 2005
The Samaritans and Philip

Oct. 3, Monday
 —Matthew 19:1-12
 —Jesus Teaches in Judea
Oct. 4, Tuesday
 —Matthew 20:29-34
 —Healing in Jericho
Oct. 5, Wednesday
 —Luke 19:1-10
 —A Visit in Jericho
Oct. 6, Thursday
 —John 4:1-10
 —Jesus Meets a Samaritan Woman
Oct. 7, Friday
 —John 4:11-5
 —Water Gushing Up to Eternal Life
Oct. 8, Saturday
 —Acts 8:4-13
 —Philip Preaches in Samaria
Oct. 9, Sunday
 —Acts 8:14-25
 —Peter and John Preach in Samaria

PRAYER
Eternal God, grant that as we accept the Christ as our personal Savior and Lord that we will lay aside all selfish motives and submit ourselves to Him and Your will for our lives. Grant us grace to live for Him and His kingdom. Amen.

Lesson 7

UNIT II
In All Judea and Samaria

The Ethiopian Official

CHILDREN'S UNIT
The Church Grows

ADULT TOPIC: Interpreting the Word
YOUTH TOPIC: Commitment to Study
CHILDREN'S TOPIC: God's People Tell About Jesus

KEY VERSE
Then Philip opened his mouth, and began at the same scripture, and preached unto him Jesus.
—Acts 8:35

DEVOTIONAL READING: Acts 11:19-26
BACKGROUND SCRIPTURE: Acts 8:26-40
PRINT PASSAGE: Acts 8:26-38

OBJECTIVES
After completion of this lesson, students should understand:

1. The story of how the Holy Spirit sent Philip to teach an African official the Good News about Jesus.

2. The various interpretations of how the Holy Spirit helps Christians understand and apply Scripture.

3. The need to commit to regular reading of the Scripture and listening for God's Spirit to help them see how the Scripture speaks to their lives.

Acts 8:26-38—KJV

26 And the angel of the Lord spake unto Philip, saying, Arise, and go toward the south unto the way that goeth down from Jerusalem unto Gaza, which is desert.

27 And he arose and went: and, behold, a man of Ethiopia, an eunuch of great authority under Candace queen of the Ethiopians, who had the charge of all her treasure, and had come to Jerusalem for to worship,

28 Was returning, and sitting in his chariot read Esaias the prophet.

29 Then the Spirit said unto Philip, Go near, and join thyself to this chariot.

30 And Philip ran thither to him, and heard him read the prophet Esaias, and said, Understandest thou what thou readest?

31 And he said, How can I, except some man should guide me? And he desired Philip that he would come up and sit with him.

32 The place of the scripture which he read was this, He was led as a sheep to the slaughter; and like a lamb dumb before his shearer, so opened he not his mouth:

33 In his humiliation his judgment was taken away: and who shall declare his generation? for his life is taken from the earth.

34 And the eunuch answered Philip, and said, I pray thee, of whom speaketh the prophet this? of himself, or of some other man?

35 Then Philip opened his mouth, and began at the same scripture, and preached unto him Jesus.

36 And as they went on their way, they came unto a certain water: and the eunuch said, See, here is water; what doth hinder me to be baptized?

37 And Philip said, If thou believest with all thine heart, thou mayest. And he answered and said, I believe that Jesus Christ is the Son of God.

38 And he commanded the chariot to stand still: and they went down both into the water, both Philip and the eunuch; and he baptized him.

Acts 8:26-38 —NRSV

26 Then an angel of the Lord said to Philip, "Get up and go toward the south to the road that goes down from Jerusalem to Gaza." (This is a wilderness road.)

27 So he got up and went. Now there was an Ethiopian eunuch, a court official of the Candace, queen of the Ethiopians, in charge of her entire treasury. He had come to Jerusalem to worship

28 and was returning home; seated in his chariot, he was reading the prophet Isaiah.

29 Then the Spirit said to Philip, "Go over to this chariot and join it."

30 So Philip ran up to it and heard him reading the prophet Isaiah. He asked, "Do you understand what you are reading?"

31 He replied, "How can I, unless someone guides me?" And he invited Philip to get in and sit beside him.

32 Now the passage of the scripture that he was reading was this: "Like a sheep he was led to the slaughter, and like a lamb silent before its shearer, so he does not open his mouth.

33 In his humiliation justice was denied him. Who can describe his generation? For his life is taken away from the earth."

34 The eunuch asked Philip, "About whom, may I ask you, does the prophet say this, about himself or about someone else?"

35 Then Philip began to speak, and starting with this scripture, he proclaimed to him the good news about Jesus.

36 As they were going along the road, they came to some water; and the eunuch said, "Look, here is water! What is to prevent me from being baptized?"

37, 38 He commanded the chariot to stop, and both of them, Philip and the eunuch, went down into the water, and Philip baptized him.

POINTS TO BE EMPHASIZED
ADULTS
Key Verse: Acts 8:35
Print: Acts 8:26-38
—The Ethiopian eunuch was a Gentile worshiper of Israel's God, and came from a faraway country.

—Eunuchs in Old Testament law were limited in the extent to which they could participate in communal worship.

—The Scripture passage from which the eunuch was reading was from the "servant songs" in Isaiah, which the early church understood to apply to Jesus the Messiah.

—Even though the eunuch was baptized alone, the rite signified his joining the community of faith.

YOUTH

Key Verse: Acts 8:30-31
Print: Acts 8:26-38

—The Ethiopian official was a Gentile worshiper who had visited Jerusalem.

—While rulers often placed eunuchs in positions of trust, Jewish law considered them to be "blemished."

—The Ethiopian eunuch made a decision to be baptized after hearing the explanation of the Scripture from Philip.

—It is important both to seek and to offer help in interpreting and understanding the Scripture.

CHILDREN

Key Verse: Acts 8:35
Print: Acts 8:26-38

—God performs great works through disciples who recognize and act on God's message to them.

—Christians share their faith with all who ask.

—People can recognize the power of God at work in the lives of others.

—Preaching God's Word is a powerful instrument when used to lead others to Christ.

TOPICAL OUTLINE
OF THE LESSON

I. Introduction
  A. Interpreting the Word of God
  B. Biblical Background

II. Exposition and Application
  #### of the Scripture
  A. Disciples Must Be Open to God's Lead *(Acts 8:26-29)*
  B. Disciples Must Be Willing to Ask Questions About God's Word *(Acts 8:30-35)*
  C. Disciples Must Respond Appropriately to God's Word *(Acts 8:36-38)*

III. Special Features
  A. Preserving Our Heritage
  B. Concluding Reflections

I. Introduction
A. Interpreting the Word of God

The text for today's discussion deals with the importance of correct biblical interpretation. The term used to refer to this discipline is *hermeneutics*. Before preachers and teachers (in particular) and all Christians (in general) come to a conclusion on the correct understanding of a particular text, there should be several steps that are adhered to and a sober state of mind that one must adopt. First, when we come to a text, we must understand that the *text* has *texture*. To be sure, all texts possess a certain feel, a certain character that is indispensable and indigenous to the text. Hermeneutics says that we must be *diligent* about trying to discover this "feel." No text stands by itself—it is in a triangular relationship that includes: (1) the text; (2) the reader; and (3) the author. Specifically, the text itself has a particular character, but so do the reader and the author. Both the reader and the author have an inherent bias that is predicated upon their race, religion, culture, class, gender, and a myriad of other subjective (internal) categories. When each one approaches the text, whether to read it or to write it, there are always historical biases to consider. This is why prayer is essential to biblical interpretation of the Bible. We must ask God to subvert our biases so that the Holy Spirit can reveal to us what God desires to share. In short, we must ask God—irrespective of our race, religion, culture, class, gender, or any other subjective (internal) categories—to keep us open to God's will for our individual and collective lives.

Secondly, for hermeneutics to be effective, open and honest, we must develop a sense of distance (a/k/a *distanciation*) from the text in order to remain objective. Too many people interpret the Bible in light of their personal experiences, rather than interpreting their lives in light of biblical revelation. The task of hermeneutics is not to make the Bible relevant for our lives; more accurately, it serves to make our lives more relevant to the Bible. "For the word of God is quick, and powerful, and sharper than any twoedged sword, piercing even to the dividing asunder of soul and spirit, and of the joints and marrow, and is a discerner of the thoughts and intents of the heart" (Hebrews 4:12).

The Bible is a living document! It is not just a book; it has the breath of God on it (cf., Genesis 2:7), which gives it life. As such, it should not be treated as any ordinary book. When we attempt to interpret it, we must understand that we cannot—unless the Holy Spirit gives us guidance; for the Spirit of God inspired the text in the first place (see 2 Timothy 3:16-17).

B. Biblical Background

This section of the text records the continuing ministry of Philip. When Philip was introduced in Acts 6:5, his name did not carry the same kind of fanfare as Stephen's, the one who became the first martyr of the Christian church. But what was lacking in his introduction to the New Testament was made up for in his work to build up the Kingdom. Philip, upon the death of Stephen, immediately went to work as an evangelist. At a time when young Saul was leading the vicious and vehement persecution of the church, Philip was still willing to go where the Spirit led him in order to share the Word of God.

It is evident from the narrative that Philip was the first disciple who was daring enough to leave the Jerusalem comfort zone for the express purpose of following the mandate that was given by Jesus, "But you will receive power when the Holy Spirit has come upon you; and you will be my witnesses in Jerusalem, in all Judea and Samaria, and to the ends of the earth." (Acts 1:8, NRSV). Previously, we witnessed the persecution of individuals or disciples of Christ, but now we transition to the persecution of the church itself. Thus, Philip went into Samaria and began preaching there.

Among the first converts to Philip's preaching ministry was a shadowy figure named Simon who thought himself to be much, but Peter and John quickly dispensed of him by outlining who he was and where he was headed if he did not repent. Notice that Philip did not deal with any of these pastoral or apostolic matters. He was an evangelist. The word *evangelist* is derived from the Greek word "evangel," which is itself a derivative of the Greek *"euanggelion"* or the English "gospel." Consequently, an evangelist is someone who proclaims the Good News of Jesus Christ. The Gospel is what was proclaimed (preached), but the fuller or more specific message is known as the *kerygma* (i.e., the life, death, resurrection and exaltation of Jesus Christ).

Since Philip was not an apostle, or prophet, or pastor-teacher, he stayed within his calling. No one person can do everything. God has given each of us gifts to make the church more functional. Each of us has been directed to "walk worthy of the vocation wherewith ye are called" (Ephesians 4:1), in order to maximize the total effectiveness of the church. Philip stayed within his calling and God directed him along those specific lines. So when God needed someone to interpret Scripture for an Ethiopian official, thereby leading him to a fuller understanding of Jesus Christ, God sent Philip—a brother who already had proven himself as an evangelist.

II. EXPOSITION AND APPLICATION OF THE SCRIPTURE
A. Disciples Must Be Open to God's Lead *(Acts 8:26-29)*

And the angel of the Lord spake unto Philip, saying, Arise, and go toward the south unto the way that goeth down from

Jerusalem unto Gaza, which is desert. On the heels of a successful evangelical journey into Samaria, Philip remained open to the leading of the Lord. Angels are, by definition, messenger beings—this is their primary function—through whom God furnished Philip with the directions for his newest assignment. If he thought that going to Samaria was a difficult prospect, particularly because of the historical estrangement between the Jews and the Samaritans, then this next assignment was going to require a different level of faith and patience. Gaza was located to the south of Jerusalem and represented the final populated community before entering the desert on what had to be a slow and laborious trek toward Egypt.

Philip's response was what we would expect from someone of his stature, someone who had a proven track record regarding difficult tasks: *And he arose and went.* What an awesome force he was for the kingdom of God! Imagine the whole economy of this text: he was sent to the desert with no assistance, no supplies, and no transportation, yet he did not complain. His compliant response was simply to go where the Lord instructed. But is not this typical of the early Christians? When Jesus approached the two sets of brothers (Peter and Andrew; James and John), He challenged them, "Follow me, and I will make you fish for people." Matthew declared that "Immediately they left their nets and followed him" (see Matthew 4:18-22).

The object of Philip's evangelism was probably a stranger spectacle than any he had encountered previously. Luke describes him as *a man of Ethiopia, an eunuch of great authority under Candace queen of the Ethiopians, who had the charge of all her treasure, and had come to Jerusalem for to worship, was returning, and sitting in his chariot read Esaias the prophet.* There are several important components within Luke's description of him, and each part points to another reason why his presence was so peculiar; why it is conceivable that he was the kind of person who likely would have dismissed any need for our Christ. First, he was an Ethiopian; he was a foreigner from North Africa. Africans have always had a very rich and diverse religious heritage. Their conception of God was very large. For them, God was a way of life; sacred and secular ideas had no line of distinction. If an African was in the fields, his God was with him. If she was walking along the way, her God was present. God and ancestral spirits were always there to guide that African.

Given this strong religious culture, it must have been intriguing to see this Ethiopian worshiping at the gates of the Jerusalem temple, which leads to the second point: he was a eunuch. There were two kinds of eunuchs. The first was a man who was born that way. The second was a slave who was emasculated as a boy in order to work as a keeper of the harem and/or a keeper of the treasury. A male who was incapable of sexual function was deemed less of a liability, and thus more trustworthy. It remains unanswered whether a person of such tremendous importance, and of such high rank, would travel so far just to worship—especially since there was a prohibition against eunuchs entering the temple (cf., Deuteronomy 23:1).

Nonetheless, as this high official was returning from worship, he was probably reclining in his slow-paced, ox-driven chariot, reading from the book of Isaiah. This is yet another anomaly for the region: someone was actually reading. Even though North Africa was quite advanced and admired by even the Greeks and Romans, only a few of the elite class were literate people—most were unable to read. Though reading is normative in our postmodern, cosmopolitan world, such was not the case in the ancient world. The ordinary vehicle for maintaining a story was by way of oral tradition (i.e., the passing down of stories from one generation to another). In those days, a person who could read was quite educated and, more than likely, a scribe. Evidently, this official was valuable to Candace, his queen.

Once again, we see Philip's receptivity to going beyond his comfort zone to share the Gospel: *Then the Spirit said unto Philip, Go near, and join thyself to this chariot.* Very often, God calls His people to move outside what is familiar and safe to do something for Him. However, a person who is closed to the move of the Holy Spirit will discover that the Spirit will come calling less and less frequently. Our Lord seeks willing laborers for the growth of His kingdom.

B. Disciples Must Be Willing to Ask Questions About God's Word
(Acts 8:30-35)

Philip was on foot, but he wasted no time in trying to catch up to the official. *And Philip ran thither to him, and heard him read the prophet Esaias, and said, Understandest thou what thou readest?* Reading ancient Hebrew may have been a cumbersome ordeal for this minister of finance. And given the fact that reading was such a lonesome art that much of it was done aloud, the Ethiopian was reading aloud, trying his best to make sense out of a difficult text. How was he to understand something as opaque as the *kerygma* (the proclaimed word) without a Christian interpreter: *He was led as a sheep to the slaughter; and like a lamb dumb before his shearer, so opened he not his mouth: In his humiliation his judgment was taken away: and who shall declare his generation? for his life is taken from the earth.*

We can add another plus to the repertoire of this Ethiopian: he was a humble man who recognized what he did not know. Someone has rightly said, "He who knows not, but does not know that he knows not, is a fool—shun him. But he who knows not and knows that he knows not, is wise—follow him." This eunuch was wise in that he immediately responded,

How can I, except some man should guide me? And he desired Philip that he would come up and sit with him. Not only did he acknowledge his limited understanding, but also he invited Philip into the chariot for a more in-depth conversation on the matter.

The first thing the Ethiopian did was to go against one of our modern conventions espousing that we should not question God. He asked, *of whom speaketh the prophet this? of himself, or of some other man?* The Ethiopian was reading prophecy from the book of Isaiah. By its very nature, prophecy is often difficult to comprehend. The Ethiopian is to be admired for his willingness to ask questions in order to gain understanding and knowledge. Although he was a man of great authority, the Ethiopian was willing to admit that he did not understand what he was reading. His desire for greater understanding is a model for all disciples to follow. Believers are encouraged to "Ask, and it shall be given you; seek, and ye shall find; knock, and it shall be opened unto you: For every one that asketh receiveth; and he that seeketh findeth; and to him that knocketh it shall be opened" (Matthew 7:7-8).The Holy Spirit sent Philip to facilitate the Ethiopian's understanding.

The crux of his question was to identify this man who was going to be humiliated. Was the text talking about Isaiah himself or was it talking about someone else altogether? The high official had no idea—but Philip did. *Then Philip opened his mouth, and began at the same scripture, and preached unto him Jesus.* This is not the first time we see this in the text. In Luke 24:45, we find that Jesus opened the Scriptures to the two disciples on the road to Emmaus and taught them who He was. Remember that at this time there was no New Testament—there would be no New Testament for another 290 years. The only Scripture available to them was the Old Testament, the Hebrew Bible. In accepting the dictum that the "Old Testament is the New Testament concealed; the New Testament is the Old Testament revealed," there is a substantial amount of concealed information that points toward Jesus. These were the texts that Philip unraveled for the Ethiopian.

In his unraveling the Scripture, *Philip preached unto him Jesus.* Preaching is the practice of sharing the Gospel, the Good News of Jesus Christ. It is part of the Great Commission that begins with the preaching of the Gospel and ends with the baptism of the converted. For the Ethiopian, once he heard the message and believed, baptism was the next logical step.

C. Disciples Must Respond Appropriately to God's Word
(Acts 8:36-38)

And as they went on their way, they came unto a certain water: and the eunuch said, See, here is water; what doth hinder me to be baptized? The monotony of the long, exhaustive trip had finally been broken. The Word of God had been preached and now a response was needed. Having heard the message of Jesus, the eunuch's questions had been answered. He was so excited that he could wait no longer—he wanted to be baptized. Baptism is a public expression of an inner commitment, similar to a wedding, a funeral and communion. They all are public confessions done out of obedience and are more necessary for the audience than they are for the person who is going through it.

A person with as much power and position as this Ethiopian official probably had one or more servants with him. How humbling an experience it must have been for him to be baptized, totally immersed in water, upon his confession of faith. *And Philip said, If thou believest with all thine heart, thou mayest. And he answered and said, I believe that Jesus Christ is the Son of God. And he commanded the chariot to stand still: and they went down both into the water, both Philip and the eunuch; and he baptized him.* There is an appropriate response to the Gospel, and an inappropriate one. The Ethiopian eunuch gave an appropriate response. He was deeply concerned and profoundly interested in the reference to Jesus Christ in the Old Testament and what all of this meant to his life. Consequently, he did the only thing necessary for salvation. Paul gave us the method for salvation when he said, "That if thou shalt confess with thy mouth the Lord Jesus, and shalt believe in thine heart that God hath raised him from the dead, thou shalt be saved. For with the heart man believeth unto righteousness; and with the mouth confession is made unto salvation. For the scripture saith, Whosoever believeth on him shall not be ashamed" (Romans 10:9-11). The Ethiopian official followed this to the letter and immediately sought baptism.

III. SPECIAL FEATURES
A. Preserving Our Heritage

The last seventy years have witnessed the birth of two religious traditions that focus on the divinely ordained supremacy of Black people. The first is the Nation of Islam. Their claim is that long before White missionaries Christianized portions of Africa, and long before the slave trade, Africa was already an Islamic nation. But the facts do not support this diatribe. Four hundred years before Muhammad, the founder of Islam, Philip had already evangelized the Ethiopian eunuch, who then returned to his native land. Are we to suppose then that this great Ethiopian official had no influence to evangelize others once he arrived back home?

The second religion is the Rastafarian religion that was birthed in Jamaica. For many reasons, this religion is still a religio-cultural movement in search of a theology. Their fundamental claim is that Haile Selassie I, the Emperor of Ethiopia during World War II, whose real name was Ras Tafari, was actually the Christ. Their claim, which is even less sophisticated than that of the Nation of Islam, lacks any kind of documentation or recognizable testimony.

The Ethiopian official's encounter with Philip invalidates any claims that Christianity belongs to a particular race of people. From the early days of the church, Africans were a part of the faith community.

B. Concluding Reflections

Philip demonstrated the willingness to leave the comfort of the familiar in order to be obedient to the Lord. Likewise, the Ethiopian demonstrated his own willingness to step away from the comfort zone of his high rank in order to discover more about the things of God.

Sometimes, and probably more often than not, God may call upon us to go to a place outside of our comfort zone in order to tell someone else about Jesus Christ and His love for humankind. Like Philip, and like Abraham before him, we must be willing to go without hesitation. An educated pastor of a large, prestigious suburban church may be called to an inner city church that has little regard for theology, doctrine, or tradition. A person who has earned average grades in school may be charged to go to Bible college to develop further in ministry. In the end, it is not our comfort that matters, but rather, our obedience to God's call.

◼ HOME DAILY BIBLE READINGS

for the week of October 16, 2005
The Ethiopian Official

Oct. 10, Monday
—Matthew 5:38-42
—Jesus Teaches About Responding to Others
Oct. 11, Tuesday
—Matthew 12:36-42
—Jesus Teaches About Signs
Oct. 12, Wednesday
—John 3:1-15
—Jesus Teaches Nicodemus About Rebirth
Oct. 13, Thursday
—Matthew 15:1-9
—Jesus Rebukes the Pharisees and Scribes
Oct. 14, Friday
—Matthew 22:41-46
—Jesus Asks the Pharisees a Question
Oct. 15, Saturday
—Acts 8:26-31
—Philip Meets the Ethiopian Official
Oct. 16, Sunday
—Acts 8:32-40
—Philip Proclaims the Good News

PRAYER

Eternal God, You are the Creator and Father of all humankind.Because You loved us first, enable us by Your Spirit to love and care for others that they too may come to accept the saving grace of our Lord and Savior Jesus Christ. Amen.

Lesson 8

UNIT II
In All Judea and Samaria

CHILDREN'S UNIT
The Church Grows

Cornelius and the Gentiles

ADULT TOPIC: Breaking the Gospel Barriers
YOUTH TOPIC: God's Favorite: Everyone
CHILDREN'S TOPIC: God's People Baptize

KEY VERSE

While Peter thought on the vision, the Spirit said unto him, Behold, three men seek thee. Arise therefore, and get thee down, and go with them, doubting nothing: for I have sent them. —Acts 10:19-20

DEVOTIONAL READING: Acts 13:44-49
BACKGROUND SCRIPTURE: Acts 10:1-48
PRINT PASSAGE: Acts 10:1-20

OBJECTIVES

After completion of this lesson, students should understand:

1. The significance of Peter's vision and the visit to Cornelius.

2. The prejudices between Jews and Gentiles that Peter and Cornelius had to overcome.

3. How to acknowledge their prejudices and commit to trying to overcome them in God's name.

Acts 10:1-20—KJV

THERE WAS a certain man in Caesarea called Cornelius, a centurion of the band called the Italian band,

2 A devout man, and one that feared God with all his house, which gave much alms to the people, and prayed to God always.

3 He saw in a vision evidently about the ninth hour of the day an angel of God coming in to him, and saying unto him, Cornelius.

4 And when he looked on him, he was afraid, and said, What is it, Lord? And he said unto him, Thy prayers and thine alms are come up for a memorial before God.

5 And now send men to Joppa, and call for one Simon, whose surname is Peter:

6 He lodgeth with one Simon a tanner, whose house is by the sea side: he shall tell thee what thou oughtest to do.

7 And when the angel which spake unto Cornelius was departed, he called two of his household servants, and a devout soldier of them that waited on him continually;

8 And when he had declared all these things unto them, he sent them to Joppa.

9 On the morrow, as they went on their journey, and drew nigh unto the city, Peter went up upon the housetop to pray about the sixth hour:

10 And he became very hungry, and would have eaten: but while they made ready, he fell into a trance,

11 And saw heaven opened, and a certain vessel descending unto him, as it had been a great sheet knit at the four corners, and let down to the earth:

12 Wherein were all manner of fourfooted beasts of the earth, and wild beasts, and creeping things, and fowls of the air.

13 And there came a voice to him, Rise, Peter; kill, and eat.

14 But Peter said, Not so, Lord; for I have never eaten any thing that is common or unclean.

15 And the voice spake unto him again the second time, What God hath cleansed, that call not thou common.

16 This was done thrice: and the vessel was received up again into heaven.

17 Now while Peter doubted in himself what this vision which he had seen should mean, behold, the men which were sent from Cornelius had made enquiry for Simon's house, and stood before the gate,

18 And called, and asked whether Simon, which was surnamed Peter, were lodged there.

19 While Peter thought on the vision, the Spirit said unto him, Behold, three men seek thee.

20 Arise therefore, and get thee down, and go with them, doubting nothing: for I have sent them.

Acts 10:1-20—NRSV

IN CAESAREA there was a man named Cornelius, a centurion of the Italian Cohort, as it was called.

2 He was a devout man who feared God with all his household; he gave alms generously to the people and prayed constantly to God.

3 One afternoon at about three o'clock he had a vision in which he clearly saw an angel of God coming in and saying to him, "Cornelius."

4 He stared at him in terror and said, "What is it, Lord?" He answered, "Your prayers and your alms have ascended as a memorial before God.

5 Now send men to Joppa for a certain Simon who is called Peter;

6 he is lodging with Simon, a tanner, whose house is by the seaside."

7 When the angel who spoke to him had left, he called two of his slaves and a devout soldier from the ranks of those who served him,

8 and after telling them everything, he sent them to Joppa.

9 About noon the next day, as they were on their journey and approaching the city, Peter went up on the roof to pray.

10 He became hungry and wanted something to eat; and while it was being prepared, he fell into a trance.

11 He saw the heaven opened and something like a large sheet coming down,

being lowered to the ground by its four corners.

12 In it were all kinds of four-footed creatures and reptiles and birds of the air.

13 Then he heard a voice saying, "Get up, Peter; kill and eat."

14 But Peter said, "By no means, Lord; for I have never eaten anything that is profane or unclean."

15 The voice said to him again, a second time, "What God has made clean, you must not call profane."

16 This happened three times, and the thing was suddenly taken up to heaven.

17 Now while Peter was greatly puzzled about what to make of the vision that he had seen, suddenly the men sent by Cornelius appeared. They were asking for Simon's house and were standing by the gate.

18 They called out to ask whether Simon, who was called Peter, was staying there.

19 While Peter was still thinking about the vision, the Spirit said to him, "Look, three men are searching for you.

20 Now get up, go down, and go with them without hesitation; for I have sent them."

POINTS TO BE EMPHASIZED
ADULTS
Key Verse: Acts 10:19-20
Print: Acts 10:1-20
—Based on Old Testament law and tradition, some first-century Jews had strict rules against associating with Gentiles because they were considered unclean.

—Cornelius was a Gentile who respected God and lived an upright life.

—The voice in Peter's vision instructed him to eat ritually unclean animals, which was specifically forbidden by Old Testament law and carried severe consequences.

—Peter's concern for ritual purity is in the context of his lodging at the house of a tanner who, because of his work with unclean animal carcasses, would have been marginalized in some segments of Jewish society.

YOUTH
Key Verse: Acts 10:34-35
Print: Acts 10:1-20
—All creation is good; therefore, humans are not to discriminate against or favor others.

—God's Spirit intervenes to bring diverse people together so that the Good News of Jesus Christ may be shared.

—Peter learned that no one is inherently "unclean" or unacceptable to God.

—People who are open to God's Spirit receive guidance.

CHILDREN
Key Verse: Acts 10:48
Print: Acts 10:1-3, 5-8, 21-24, 34-36, 44-48
—God answers the prayers of faithful and devout followers.

—God's answers to prayer are specific, though at times we do not acknowledge the answers.

—God brings people into our lives for specific purposes.

—God loves and calls all people.

TOPICAL OUTLINE OF THE LESSON

I. INTRODUCTION
  A. What Does the Lord Require?
  B. Biblical Background

II. EXPOSITION AND APPLICATION OF THE SCRIPTURE
  A. Cornelius, a Pious Gentile, Has a Vision *(Acts 10:1-8)*
  B. Peter, a Prejudiced Jew, Has a Vision *(Acts 10:9-15)*
  C. The Jew Visits the Gentile *(Acts 10:16-20)*

III. SPECIAL FEATURES
  A. Preserving Our Heritage
  B. Concluding Reflections

I. INTRODUCTION
A. What Does the Lord Require?

This lesson explores what happens when we come face-to-face with our own prejudices. Peter grew up believing that Jews were clean and pure before God, and that non-Jews (i.e., Gentiles) were unclean and impure. The idea of spending time with a non-Jew was an abomination in his mind. He simply could not break through the cultural façade, until he had a vision that contradicted his tradition.

Many of us live with a truncated knowledge of the will of God. We act out our prejudices against others as though we have an ascendancy that others do not possess. Some go as far as claiming a strong devotion to God, but a not-so-strong devotion to others. Such thinking is arrogant, misleading and antithetical to the teachings of Jesus. We must never forget that the second greatest commandment that Jesus gave us was, "Thou shalt love thy neighbor as thyself" (cf., Mark 12:30-31; see also Matthew 5:44; John 15:12-13; Romans 12:10; 1 Peter 1:21). Our neighbors are not only the people who live in our neighborhood, but as Jesus demonstrated in the Parable of the Good Samaritan, our neighbor is anyone who needs us (Luke 10:30-35). Loving our neighbors, particularly those we do not know, is always the right thing to do.

The theological discipline that deals with understanding what is right and what is wrong is called Christian ethics. Theologian Paul Lehman has offered that "The goal of Christian ethics is Christian maturity." In a nutshell, Christian ethics is about understanding the will of God and committing ourselves to doing God's will regardless of the implications for our personal lives. So how are we to understand the will of God? Where is the starting point for this understanding?

The starting point for understanding God's will can begin with the Ten Commandments (the Decalogue). God gave Moses the Ten Commandments to give to the children of Israel (Exodus 20). The first four of these commandments are vertical in nature; they deal with our responsibility toward God. The last six are horizontal in nature; they deal with our relationship to humankind (i.e., our neighbors). In terms of the commandments that deal with our relationship to God, we find reference for this in the Shema (Deuteronomy 6:4-9), Israel's classical demonstration of monotheism: "Hear, O Israel: the Lord our God, the Lord is one; you shall love the Lord your God with all your heart, and with all your soul, and with all your mind, and with all your strength" (Mark 12:29-30, NRSV). This verse is repeated in the New Testament, adding to it a second part that demonstrates the importance of the horizontal relationship: "love your neighbor as yourself" (Mark 12:31, NRSV). This is what the Lord requires of us—that we love God and love our neighbors, regardless of who they are or where they are. The story of Cornelius and Peter helps us recognize that, biblically defined, Cornelius was Peter's neighbor even though Peter was in Joppa and Cornelius was in Caesarea.

B. Biblical Background

A post-modern description of Peter is that he was an ethnocentric individual (i.e., he had a preoccupation with his own ethnicity). Although he received the Great Commission from the Lord, his historic marginalization of other peoples because of their pedigree remained a barrier to the accomplishment of the will of God. What is most apparent in this passage is the progress that came as a result of three major events in the life of the early church.

In the first event, Jesus gave His disciples the Great Commission, which was to "Go ye into all the world, and preach the gospel to every creature" (Mark 16:15). If the early disciples had any questions or if they needed a confirmation, this was clarified in Acts 1:8: "But ye shall receive power, after that the Holy Ghost is come upon you: and ye shall be witnesses unto me both in Jerusalem, and in all Judaea, and in Samaria, and unto the uttermost part of the earth." The mandate was specific, measurable, achievable (with the Holy Spirit), realistic and time-sensitive.

Secondly, the events on the Day of Pentecost made it clear that there would be no barrier to spreading the Gospel. Beyond their age-old prejudices, they likely identified another possible barrier early on—How could they reach every human being if they didn't know their various languages? This was all put to rest when Peter preached on that day and everyone heard the Gospel in their own language, even though Peter was speaking in his native tongue. It is God's will that all nations come to know the Son of God, and God would not allow language to be a barrier to the Gospel explosion.

Thirdly, the persecution event teaches us that the disciples were content to remain in their comfort zone, even though they were supposed to go beyond the borders of Jerusalem and Judea. We are told that: "Therefore they that were scattered abroad went every where preaching the word" (Acts 8:4). Philip (the disciple who became an evangelist) was the first to demonstrate a commitment to this charge. We ought not short-circuit the importance of Samaria being the first non-Jewish nation that the disciples, namely Philip, evangelized. This was the same non-Jewish nation to which Jesus extended His ministry (cf., John 4).

Consequently, these events collectively prepare us for the Peter/Cornelius narrative. Peter's preoccupation with his own tradition, even though he was given a clear and specific charge to go beyond his comfort zone, precluded his willingness to go and seek out Cornelius, the Roman centurion.

II. EXPOSITION AND APPLICATION OF THE SCRIPTURE
A. Cornelius, a Pious Gentile, Has a Vision (Acts 10:1-8)

The story of Cornelius has some commonalities with the story of the Ethiopian eunuch of chapter seven. In both instances, they were foreigners. Those who were historically excluded from the Old Covenant took it upon themselves to learn more about God. And in both instances, the two foreigners were missing pertinent information that only a disciple of Jesus Christ could supply. Both men were persons of influence—the Ethiopian was a minister of finance, and Cornelius was a Roman centurion who had servants and soldiers serving him continuously.

Caesarea, located on the Mediterranean Sea almost thirty miles from Joppa, served as the Roman capital of Judea for almost a century. Named after the emperor Caesar, it was also the place where the Roman governor resided. Its political importance necessitated the presence of a garrison for its ongoing protection. We are told that Cornelius was the commander of an Italian regiment or cohort. A Roman legion consisted of six thousand men. A cohort or regiment consisted of six hundred men. These men were divided into groups of one hundred men, each lead by a centurion. In Caesarea, it was the responsibility of a regiment to protect

Fearing God, giving alms and praying marked Cornelius as righteous according to the Law, although he was a Gentile. Three o'clock was the ninth hour of the day—the hour of prayer. Peter and Cornelius had a double vision of a heavenly messenger appearing in two places. The centurion called the angel "Lord," addressing the messenger's authority. Peter's vision dealt with the profane or unclean, as Israel was commanded to make a distinction among the four-footed creatures with respect to eating. "What God has made clean" now included creatures that previously had been identified as unclean. The word "profane" means vulgar and could not be used to refer to all the nations chosen of God or set apart by their observance of the law as holy to God. Peter got his first signal of the presence of the creatures directly from the Spirit. He was to go without hesitation or objection. The boundaries of what was lawful in relationship between Jews and Gentiles were drawn carefully in various Jewish traditions, but few were so strict as to prevent association or visits.

the governor's residence. In all probability, this was the role of Cornelius.

Luke does not end his description here. He goes on to say that Cornelius was *a devout man, and one that feared God with all his house, which gave much alms to the people, and prayed to God always.* It is one thing to be great or powerful; it is quite another matter to be elevated in this manner and still be devout and God-fearing. George Orwell's political novel/satire, *Animal Farm*, carried the theme, "Power corrupts and absolute power corrupts absolutely." Often when people gain access to power, they are deceived by it. A person so deceived finds it difficult to be pious or spiritually inclined. This was another peculiarity of Cornelius. He was a sincere, God-fearing man, even though he was a man of power and prestige.

A further distinctive characteristic of Cornelius was his philanthropic and prayerful attitude. We do not read in the text where he was converted to Judaism by conceding to the ritualistic act of circumcision, but we do find that he was committed to the more functional aspects of the faith, such as prayer and giving alms to the needy. Furthermore, it was about the time of prayer—*the ninth hour of the day* (3:00 p.m.), which was the most important prayer time (cf., Acts 3:1)—that he had a vision of an angel of God coming to him.

Cornelius' immediate response to the angel of the Lord was similar to others in the Bible who had the same experience (cf., Judges 6:22; 13:20; 1 Chronicles 21:16; Daniel 10:4-9; Matthew 28:2-5; Luke 1:11-13, 30; 2:9-10). Notwithstanding the fact that Cornelius was a trained man of war, a soldier of high rank, he was still struck with fear in the presence of the Most High saying, *What is it, Lord?* But the Lord quickly calmed his fears by sharing the reason for approaching him: because of his devotion to the Lord, particularly in the areas of prayer and almsgiving, God was moved to take the relationship even further. *Send men to Joppa, and call for one Simon, whose surname is Peter.*

Is this not characteristic of God? Apparently, the apostles had struggled with leaving their familiar Judean surroundings as they had failed to undertake the Great Commission expeditiously. However, as they moved out, fleeing the threat of persecution, God placed Cornelius and Peter on a collision course similar to that of Philip and the Samaritans, or Philip and the Ethiopian eunuch. Upon hearing the Word of God, Cornelius dispatched two servants and one soldier to Joppa to retrieve Peter. It is interesting that Peter initially came to Joppa when he was summoned to participate in the funeral of Dorcas, a woman devoted to "good works and acts of charity" (Acts 9:36, NRSV). Reminiscent of Jesus putting out the crowd before He raised Jairus' daughter from the dead (Mark 5:40), Peter put everyone out and proceeded to pray for Dorcas' restoration to life.

Dorcas was Tabitha's Greek name, but

the implication is that, since Joppa was in the Judean territory (south of Caesarea, but northwest of Jerusalem), she was a Christian convert from Judaism. This revelation opens the door to a rather interesting metaphor: Peter had no objection to raising her from a *physically* dead state to a living state. On the contrary, as we will soon discover, he had perennial objections about leading Cornelius from a *spiritually* dead state to a born-again state.

Beyond the most obvious metaphors outlined above, there is another that might be of interest: the word *Joppa* means "beautiful." In the place named *Beautiful* resided a man who was going to impart a whole new meaning to Cornelius' life.

B. Peter, a Prejudiced Jew, Has a Vision *(Acts 10:9-15)*

While Cornelius' men were *en route*, God was working on Peter. They were not simply traveling to an arbitrary situation; God was preparing the vineyard for their arrival. *As they were on their journey and approaching the city, Peter went up on the roof to pray* (verse 9). It is an intriguing notion that both the pious Gentile and the prejudiced Jew had the same point of interest. Both of them believed in God and were committed to prayer. One can be faithful in prayer and still possess malignant traits. His grace is sufficient to cover all of our imperfections. The fact that we have an undesirable trait, be it bigotry or any other, is never justification to surrender to the will of Satan, however. Peter

was a bigot, but he still maintained his commitment to prayer.

As he prayed, Peter became hungry. No doubt his host, Simon the tanner (or one of his servants) began to prepare a meal for Peter. In the meanwhile, with the menacing hunger upon him, Peter fell into a trance. What happened next was truly an enigma for Peter. *Heaven opened, and a certain vessel descending unto him, as it had been a great sheet knit at the four corners, and let down to the earth: Wherein were all manner of four-footed beasts of the earth, and wild beasts, and creeping things, and fowls of the air.* The reference to the sheet knit at the four corners could be an allegorical reference to the prevailing assumption of that day— namely, that the earth was four-cornered. Thus, the sheet containing both clean and unclean animals was symbolic of the whole world and the need for a non-discriminatory missionary effort. Though the conclusion is consistent with the rest of the narrative, allegory ("this" means "that") is not the best interpretive strategy.

In the vision, God told Peter to *kill and eat,* but Peter protested saying, *I have never eaten anything that is profane or unclean* (verse 14). Indeed, Peter was ritualistically and biblically justified in his argument as Mosaic Law did dictate that certain animals were unclean (cf., Leviticus 11:2-47; Deuteronomy 14:3-21). Thus, there has to be a deeper implication for this vision. One can argue that Leviticus 20:24-26 is further justification for Peter's alignment of unclean animals with people, but at the same time, one must understand that Jesus is the fulfillment of the Law (cf., Galatians 3:23- 29). His arrival broke down the division between Jews and Gentiles (cf., Ephesians 2:14-15; Colossians 2:14-16). Jesus' Great Commission was further indication of His ministry of reconciliation (Matthew 28:18-19; Mark 16:15-18; Acts 1:8). His instruction to go to all nations should have relieved Peter and the other apostles of their discriminatory traditions.

C. The Jew Visits the Gentile
(Acts 10:16-20)

As Peter pondered the deeper implications of this vision, Cornelius' men arrived on the scene, inquiring where to find Simon's house. Once again, the Spirit of the Lord came to Peter to instruct him: *Get up, go down, and go with them without hesitation; for I have sent them.* He needed to ponder the vision no further. God was making it very clear to him. He was not just in a hunger trance; God was orchestrating events so that the overall plan—namely, the evangelization of the whole world—could go forward.

In the eighth chapter, we saw how persecution was the primary motivation for the Gospel's departure from Jerusalem. Here, God used a vision to motivate the apostles to leave their comfort zone. Given his knowledge and understanding of the Law, Peter apparently was willing to argue for the separation of God's people for God's purpose, as indicated by his resistence in the vision to touch anything he considered "unclean." However, the incarnation and the resurrection of Jesus had done away with all such notions of clean and unclean. Jesus' arrival on earth broke down the wall of division between races. Now, there was no Jews or Gentiles—we are all one in Christ.

III. SPECIAL FEATURES
A. Preserving Our Heritage

The implication of this narrative for America is clear. Peter, prior to his vision, was a bigot, not unlike the bigotry used to justify the slavocracy of the seventeenth through the nineteenth centuries. Atheists did not initiate the slave trade. It was started by believers in Jesus Christ, white Christians who thought it was their duty to save African "savages" by bringing them to a slave world. Notwithstanding the Northern abolitionists, rarely did the Southern slaveholders see incongruity between their *practice* and their *preaching*. So pervasive were their intentions and actions that they even named their ships after biblical characters, the most intriguing being the slave ship *Jesus*.

Moreover, in their hearts, Blacks—both slave and free—resisted Paul's letters because the master was inclined to use the texts that seemed to enable slavery: "Servants, be obedient to them that are your masters…as unto Christ." Upon emancipation, and given the Southern states' preoccupation with Jim Crow laws, free men and women avoided any biblical reference that seemed to condone the greatest offense they had ever known.

Peter's vision in modern times has a dual interpretation: Just as it was incorrect and offensive for Whites to marginalize Blacks—seeing them as three-fifths human and unclean—it is just as pejorative for Blacks to marginalize Whites or any other race due to our historical estrangement. No one has the authority to call any of God's creation unclean and profane.

B. Concluding Reflections

It is important for each of us to constantly examine our own prejudices. Many of us continue to use racially offensive language and gender exclusionary words. We seem to forget that God said, "What God has made clean, you must not call profane." Discrimination and bigotry are sin, for they reduce the value of the human personality to the level of things.

The church faces a great challenge today as a number of moral issues are being addressed in the political arena, such as human rights issues. While we know that we cannot discriminate against anyone, at the same time, we know that we cannot support any agenda that is anti-biblical. The church must deal seriously with this and all such ethical considerations. We are mandated to proclaim the Word. The Word of God contains the moral code by which we must conduct our lives.

◼ HOME DAILY BIBLE 📖 READINGS

for the week of October 23, 2005
Cornelius and the Gentiles

Oct. 17, Monday
   —Acts 10:1-8
   —Cornelius Has a Vision
Oct. 18, Tuesday
   —Acts 10:9-16
   —Peter Has a Vision
Oct. 19, Wednesday
   —Acts 10:17-22
   —Cornelius' Men Call on Peter
Oct. 20, Thursday
   —Acts 10:23-33
   —Peter Visits Cornelius
Oct. 21, Friday
   —Acts 10:34-43
   —Peter Shares the Good News
Oct. 22, Saturday
   —Acts 10:44-48
   —Gentiles Receive the Holy Spirit
Oct. 23, Sunday
   —Acts 11:1-15
   —Peter Explains How Gentiles Also Believed

PRAYER

Eternal God, You created us as persons with the freedom of will. Grant us the grace to refuse to abuse Your love for us, but to exercise our God-given freedom in ways that are consistent with Your will for our lives. Because You loved us with an everlasting love, grant us the grace to love others and to witness to them with Your sacrificial work on our behalf. Amen.

Lesson 9

UNIT II
In All Judea and Samaria

CHILDREN'S UNIT
The Church Grows

Peter in Prison

ADULT TOPIC: Never Alone
YOUTH TOPIC: An Unbelievable Rescue
CHILDREN'S TOPIC: God's People Are Rescued

DEVOTIONAL READING: Psalm 46
BACKGROUND SCRIPTURE: Acts 12:1-17
PRINT PASSAGE: Acts 12:1-16

KEY VERSE

Behold, the angel of the Lord came upon him, and a light shined in the prison: and he smote Peter on the side, and raised him up, saying, Arise up quickly. And his chains fell off from his hands. —Acts 12:7

OBJECTIVES

After completion of this lesson, students should understand:

1. How Peter, imprisoned for his faithfulness, was freed and protected in surprising ways by God.
2. The circumstances that led to Peter's imprisonment.
3. How to compare and contrast God's rescue of Peter with the ways in which God helps us today.

Acts 12:1-16—KJV

NOW ABOUT that time Herod the king stretched forth his hands to vex certain of the church.

2 And he killed James the brother of John with the sword.

3 And because he saw it pleased the Jews, he proceeded further to take Peter also. (Then were the days of unleavened bread.)

4 And when he had apprehended him, he put him in prison, and delivered him to four quaternions of soldiers to keep him; intending after Easter to bring him forth to the people.

5 Peter therefore was kept in prison: but prayer was made without ceasing of the church unto God for him.

6 And when Herod would have brought him forth, the same night Peter was sleeping between two soldiers, bound with two chains: and the keepers before the door kept the prison.

7 And, behold, the angel of the Lord came upon him, and a light shined in the prison: and he smote Peter on the side, and raised him up, saying, Arise up quickly. And his chains fell off from his hands.

8 And the angel said unto him, Gird thyself, and bind on

thy sandals. And so he did. And he saith unto him, Cast thy garment about thee, and follow me.

9 And he went out, and followed him; and wist not that it was true which was done by the angel; but thought he saw a vision.

10 When they were past the first and the second ward, they came unto the iron gate that leadeth unto the city; which opened to them of his own accord: and they went out, and passed on through one street; and forthwith the angel departed from him.

11 And when Peter was come to himself, he said, Now I know of a surety, that the Lord hath sent his angel, and hath delivered me out of the hand of Herod, and from all the expectation of the people of the Jews.

12 And when he had considered the thing, he came to the house of Mary the mother of John, whose surname was Mark; where many were gathered together praying.

13 And as Peter knocked at the door of the gate, a damsel came to hearken, named Rhoda.

14 And when she knew Peter's voice, she opened not the gate for gladness, but ran in, and told how Peter stood before the gate.

15 And they said unto her, Thou art mad. But she constantly affirmed that it was even so. Then said they, It is his angel.

16 But Peter continued knocking: and when they had opened the door, and saw him, they were astonished.

Acts 12:1-16—NRSV

ABOUT THAT time King Herod laid violent hands upon some who belonged to the church.

2 He had James, the brother of John, killed with the sword.

3 After he saw that it pleased the Jews, he proceeded to arrest Peter also. (This was during the festival of Unleavened Bread.)

4 When he had seized him, he put him in prison and handed him over to four squads of soldiers to guard him, intending to bring him out to the people after the Passover.

5 While Peter was kept in prison, the church prayed fervently to God for him.

6 The very night before Herod was going to bring him out, Peter, bound with two chains, was sleeping between two soldiers, while guards in front of the door were keeping watch over the prison.

7 Suddenly an angel of the Lord appeared and a light shone in the cell. He tapped Peter on the side and woke him, saying, "Get up quickly." And the chains fell off his wrists.

8 The angel said to him, "Fasten your belt and put on your sandals." He did so. Then he said to him, "Wrap your cloak around you and follow me."

9 Peter went out and followed him; he did not realize that what was happening with the angel's help was real; he thought he was seeing a vision.

10 After they had passed the first and the second guard, they came before the iron gate leading into the city. It opened

for them of its own accord, and they went outside and walked along a lane, when suddenly the angel left him.

11 Then Peter came to himself and said, "Now I am sure that the Lord has sent his angel and rescued me from the hands of Herod and from all that the Jewish people were expecting."

12 As soon as he realized this, he went to the house of Mary, the mother of John whose other name was Mark, where many had gathered and were praying.

13 When he knocked at the outer gate, a maid named Rhoda came to answer.

14 On recognizing Peter's voice, she was so overjoyed that, instead of opening the gate, she ran in and announced that Peter was standing at the gate.

15 They said to her, "You are out of your mind!" But she insisted that it was so. They said, "It is his angel."

16 Meanwhile Peter continued knocking; and when they opened the gate, they saw him and were amazed.

POINTS TO BE EMPHASIZED
ADULTS
Key Verse: Acts 12:7
Print: Acts 12:1-16
—King Herod (grandson of Herod the Great, king at the birth of Jesus) was a political opportunist among the Jews, and a puppet of the Romans.
—Peter was imprisoned by King Herod, but remained calm as he slept between the soldiers.

—The gathered church at prayer underscores the importance of interceding on behalf of fellow members.
—The believers were incredulous when Peter came to them, which illustrates human tendency to be amazed when our prayers are actually answered.

YOUTH
Key Verse: Acts 12:7
Print: Acts 12:1-16
—Peter was imprisoned for his belief in Jesus Christ.
—God acts to help people who find themselves in difficult circumstances.
—Intercessory prayer has power to bring about good.
—We should pray with the expectation that our prayers will be answered.

CHILDREN
Key Verse: Acts 12:17
Print: Acts 12:1-16
—Evil, corrupt governments are still persecuting the Christian church.
—Prayer transforms difficult situations into stepping stones for increased faith.
—Prayer can unlock any type of prison doors—psychological, economic, social, or physical.

TOPICAL OUTLINE OF THE LESSON
I. INTRODUCTION
   A. Destined for Persecution
   B. Biblical Background

II. Exposition and Application
   of the Scripture
   A. Disciples Sometimes Need
      Deliverance *(Acts 12:1-5)*
   B. God Delivers as a Result of
      Our Prayers *(Acts 12:6-11)*
   C. Disciples Must Expect God's
      Deliverance When They Pray
      (Acts 12:12-16)

III. Special Features
   A. Preserving Our Heritage
   B. Concluding Reflections

I. Introduction

A. Destined for Persecution

As Christians, there are certain expectations that we should have concerning our faith. A primary expectation is that we should expect some suffering to come our way. There are some types of suffering that are going to come in the process of living, but some suffering will come because we are Christians. The apostle Paul affirmed this when he said, "For he has graciously granted you the privilege not only of believing in Christ, but of suffering for him as well—since you are having the same struggle that you saw I had and now hear that I still have" (Philippians 1:29-30, NRSV). Notice the way Paul says this: it is a *privilege* to suffer. And not only this, but that suffering will take place.

This lesson gives us greater insight into the kind of suffering and persecution suffered during the days of the early Christians, most notably James and Peter. Before his ascent to eternal glory, Jesus had warned His disciples of impending persecution. However, in Peter's case, there was an even more profound and prophetic expectation. Some twenty years before, Jesus had already prophesied to Peter saying, "Simon, Simon, listen! Satan has demanded to sift you like wheat" (Luke 22:31). Apparently, Satan had singled out Simon Peter as one to attack, one who would endure pressures and persecution. We must remain perfectly clear that the Adversary and his agents will attempt to wreak havoc in our lives. This is his role as the "prince of the power of the air" (Ephesians 2:2). In short, he was demanding his right to violently shake Peter.

What is promising for both Peter and for all believers is Jesus' response to Satan's demand: "but I have prayed for you that your own faith may not fail." Although the Greek rendering expresses the sentiment more clearly, Satan had designs on sifting Peter ("Satan desires to sift "you," which is singular), but Jesus has "prayed for you" (here, a plural "you," meaning all of His disciples). It is important for the children of God to understand that although Satan will try to prevent us from doing God's will, our Lord will do His part as He has promised. Peter was delivered from prison.

B. Biblical Background

The focal passage has taken place during a wave of persecution against the early Christians, initiated by King Herod

Agrippa I. The Herod family dynasty had long served as chief antagonist against the cause of Christ. It was King Herod the Great who ordered the massacre of the baby boys in Bethlehem in an attempt to do away with the baby Jesus. It was his son, King Herod the Tetrarch, who ordered the beheading of John the Baptist. In Acts 12, the third generation, Herod Agrippa I, used the season of Passover to launch a new wave of persecution against the church in Jerusalem.

As the days of the Passover celebration were coming to an end, Jewish pride and nationalism were beating in every heart. Herod was partially Jewish, causing the Jewish people to grudgingly accept him; some related to him fairly well. No matter how they may have felt about him, Herod was strong on building alliances with his Jewish subjects. Bible historians indicate that Herod did all that he could to be popular with the Jews—even observing certain Jewish customs. To help relieve Judiasm of the menacing followers of "the Way," he took an action that was certain to enhance his popularity among Jewish nationalists and religious authorities like the Pharisees and Sadducees. First, Herod apprehended the apostle James and had him executed hastily. Possibly to gain further political mileage among his Jewish subjects, Herod arrested Peter, putting him in a maximum-security prison, but delaying his execution until the Feast of Passover had ended.

II. Exposition and Application of the Scripture
A. Disciples Sometimes Need Deliverance (Acts 12:1-5)

Consistent with the whole notion of what it means to be a Christian in ancient Palestine, chapter 12 opens with the only New Testament record of an apostle's death. King Herod, in this text, was the grandson of the wicked Herod the Great who was so malignant that he had his wife, Marianne, along with his five sons and mother-in-law, executed in order that they not receive higher praise than him. Later, he ordered the genocide of all Jewish male children in his rabid attempt to kill the Christ child (Matthew 2:16). His grandson was no better. He murdered his father Aristobulus; then, because of

The persecution of Stephen accounts for the expanding mission so far still limited to the Jews. The Jews whom the execution pleased are probably "the Judeans" who regarded the followers of Jesus as a threat to the temple and its leadership. The fervent prayers of the church hope for God to act. These prayers produced that miraculous interference without which Peter could not have escaped, being bound to the left hand of one soldier, and by the right to another. The angel of the Lord accomplishes Peter's release from prison. Peter has been confounded by visions before (10:10, 17; 12:11), but the gate opening of its own accord is miraculous, being influenced by the unseen power of the angel. The angel departed, having brought Peter to a place where he no longer needed his assistance. Peter's verdict is a lucid declaration of the meaning of his rescue. It was only when the angel left him that he was fully convinced that all was real. "It is an angel." It was common opinion among the Jews that each person has a guardian angel; the Jews also believed that angels often assumed the likeness of particular persons.

his strained relationship with Rome, waited until the Passover to ingratiate himself with the Jews by attacking the church. In so doing, he had *James, the brother of John, killed with the sword.*

The fact that James was killed *with the sword* indicates that the Jewish elite, whom the king was trying to impress, believed that the apostles were teaching about false gods, or, more specifically, a god who was not Yahweh. (YHWH in the Hebrew is the preferred name for God in the Old Testament. The name was considered so holy that Jews refrained from uttering it or even spelling it completely.) Consequently, the penalty for such an infraction was death by the sword (cf., Deuteronomy 13:12-15).

After James was dead, Herod's (Agrippa I) four squads seized Peter. King Herod may have heard about Peter's previous escape (cf., 5:19), so in order to secure Peter until he could *bring him out* for trial and execution (similar to what they did with Jesus and Stephen), they placed him under maximum security. Four squads (sixteen men) would guard Peter so that there would be no chance of escape. The first two squads would watch him for an agreed-upon period, then the other two would be rotated in.

While Peter was kept in prison, the church prayed fervently to God for him. The early church understood what many of us have come to understand today: namely, there will be times when the only answer for our troubles is prayer (Jeremiah 23:23; Psalms 4:3; 55:17; 1 John 5:14-15; James 5:16; Colossians 4:2; 1 Thessalonians 5:17). So the church came together to pray.

B. God Delivers as a Result of Our Prayers *(Acts 12:6-11)*

When we are going through a distasteful situation, we have the tendency to wonder whether God is against us or whether we will not make it out of the situation. Peter's demeanor during this entire episode is a wonderful testimony for any believer in the time of trial. With the death of his co-laborer fresh in his memory, surrounded by guards and with the threat of imminent death, Peter went to sleep. Because he had seen the handiwork of God when he was in a similar situation (cf., 4:23-31), Peter had no need to fear. Our previous experiences with God's movement in our lives should enable us to trust Him for *future* challenges. Peter later testified, "Cast all your anxiety on him, because he cares for you" (1 Peter 5:7, NRSV).

While the church prayed for Peter's deliverance, God dispatched an angel to deliver him. Peter was so soundly asleep in his cell, comfortably situated between two guards, that the angel had to shake him! Immediately, *the chains fell off his wrists.* The angel's instructions are helpful as we try to imagine the scene. While the church was praying as Peter was facing imminent death, he slept calmly.

Peter's recent vision in Acts 10 that

prompted his openness to see Cornelius was now apparent in his present state of mind: *he did not realize that what was happening with the angel's help was real; he thought he was seeing a vision.* But this was not the only miracle for the morning. As he followed the angel, miraculous events continued to occur. There is a lesson to be learned here: as long as we remain without prayer and without God, we will see no miracles. But if we follow God's will and directions, miracles (and deliverance) will occur all around us. The church prayed, the angel of deliverance came, and Peter walked past the first and second team of guards without being hindered. As they approached the main gate, *it opened for them of its own accord.*

His mission completed, the angel disappeared and Peter was left to reflect on his recent deliverance. There are cynics and unbelievers who would doubt that this deliverance ever took place, but we have the testimony of Peter stating the fact of his release: *And when Peter was come to himself, he said, Now I know of a surety, that the Lord hath sent his angel, and hath delivered me out of the hand of Herod, and from all the expectation of the people of the Jews.*

C. Disciples Must Expect God's Deliverance When They Pray
(Acts 12:12-16)

During the early days of the church, they did not have edifices and complexes like we have today; they met at the homes of various saints. Peter knew where the other disciples could be found; they would be at the house of one of the saints. John Mark was Barnabas' cousin (Colossians 4:10) and is credited for writing the gospel that bears his name. (Though the gospel of Mark is second in the New Testament, it was the first one written. Matthew and Luke used Mark's gospel as a template for their own.) Hence, Peter appeared at Mary's house and knocked on the door. What follows remains an intriguing matter for most Christians.

A maid by the name of Rhoda went to the outer gate to find out who was knocking. She became excited upon realizing that Peter himself was at the gate: *And when she knew Peter's voice, she opened not the gate for gladness, but ran in, and told how Peter stood before the gate. And they said unto her, Thou art mad. But she constantly affirmed that it was even so. Then said they, It is his angel.* Here is the intriguing matter: they were praying—and probably praying for his deliverance—but when Peter miraculously appeared, they were unprepared. They were so amazed that, initially, they thought it was an angel rather than Peter himself delivered.

Indeed, *Peter continued knocking: and when they had opened the door, and saw him, they were astonished.* God had responded so rapidly to their requests. They, like us, should take note of David's testimony, "The eyes of the LORD are upon the righteous, and his ears are open unto their cry" (Psalm 34:15).

III. SPECIAL FEATURES
A. Preserving Our Heritage

The history of African Americans is fraught with stories of how the faithful prayed for deliverance from various forms of persecution. The story is told of how, as a young woman, Harriet Tubman prayed that if God wouldn't change her master's stubborn heart, he would be struck down dead. Soon afterward, her master mysteriously died; however, she was devastated that he never came to know Christ. Like many others, Tubman sought relief from her persecution; however, if she had been treated more humanely as a slave, she might never have been moved to become a conductor in the Underground Railroad. These are the "Jameses" in our history—men and women who died because of persecution; but there are others who experienced deliverance that only the faithful can know.

B. Concluding Reflections

Why did God deliver Peter, yet fail to intervene on behalf of James? Sometimes God allows God's human will to prevail—this is what we see in the James event. At other times, God's divine will prevails—as in Peter's case. Regardless of which one occurs, we must be willing to accept both. Indeed, we may think that James got the worst end of the deal, but is this what the Bible teaches elsewhere? Placed in its proper context, the truth of the matter is that, as Paul puts it, "To live is Christ, and to die is gain" (see Philippians 1:21).

HOME DAILY BIBLE READINGS

for the week of October 30, 2005
Peter in Prison

Oct. 24, Monday
—Acts 9:32-42
—Peter Heals One and Revives Another

Oct. 25, Tuesday
—Luke 4:1-13
—Jesus Is Tempted

Oct. 26, Wednesday
—Matthew 26:36-46
—Jesus Prays in Gethsemane

Oct. 27, Thursday
—Mark 15:33-37
—Jesus Dies on the Cross

Oct. 28, Friday
—Acts 12:1-5
—James Is Killed and Peter Imprisoned

Oct. 29, Saturday
—Acts 12:6-11
—An Angel Frees Peter from Prison

Oct. 30, Sunday
—Acts 12:12-17
—Peter Tells the Others What Happened

PRAYER

Our Father and our God, grant us the grace to cast all of our cares upon You, rather than depend upon our own ingenuity to negotiate the trials of life. May we lift up our voices in prayer for Your help when we face that which we consider to be the impossibilities of life. Amen.

Lesson 10

UNIT III
To the Ends of the Earth

CHILDREN'S UNIT
Witnessing to All the World

Paul Becomes a Follower

ADULT TOPIC: Encountering Truth
YOUTH TOPIC: From Persecutor to Believer
CHILDREN'S TOPIC: Paul's Life Changes

KEY VERSE
Immediately there fell from his eyes as it had been scales: and he received sight forthwith, and arose, and was baptized.—Acts 9:18

DEVOTIONAL READING: Acts 9:23-31
BACKGROUND SCRIPTURE: Acts 9:1-31
PRINT PASSAGE: Acts 9:3-18

OBJECTIVES
After completion of this lesson, students should understand:

1. How Saul was transformed from a persecutor to a believer when he saw a vision of Jesus Christ.
2. The radical nature of Paul's transformation.
3. The actions and attitudes that show they, too, have encountered and been transformed by Jesus Christ.

Acts 9:3-18—KJV

3 And as he journeyed, he came near Damascus: and suddenly there shined round about him a light from heaven:

4 And he fell to the earth, and heard a voice saying unto him, Saul, Saul, why persecutest thou me?

5 And he said, Who art thou, Lord? And the Lord said, I am Jesus whom thou persecutest: it is hard for thee to kick against the pricks.

6 And he trembling and astonished said, Lord, what wilt thou have me to do? And the Lord said unto him, Arise, and go into the city, and it shall be told thee what thou must do.

7 And the men which journeyed with him stood speechless, hearing a voice, but seeing no man.

8 And Saul arose from the earth; and when his eyes were opened, he saw no man: but they led him by the hand, and brought him into Damascus.

9 And he was three days without sight, and neither did eat nor drink.

10 And there was a certain disciple at Damascus, named

Ananias; and to him said the Lord in a vision, Ananias. And he said, Behold, I am here, Lord.

11 And the Lord said unto him, Arise, and go into the street which is called Straight, and enquire in the house of Judas for one called Saul, of Tarsus: for, behold, he prayeth,

12 And hath seen in a vision a man named Ananias coming in, and putting his hand on him, that he might receive his sight.

13 Then Ananias answered, Lord, I have heard by many of this man, how much evil he hath done to thy saints at Jerusalem:

14 And here he hath authority from the chief priests to bind all that call on thy name.

15 But the Lord said unto him, Go thy way: for he is a chosen vessel unto me, to bear my name before the Gentiles, and kings, and the children of Israel:

16 For I will show him how great things he must suffer for my name's sake.

17 And Ananias went his way, and entered into the house; and putting his hands on him said, Brother Saul, the Lord, even Jesus, that appeared unto thee in the way as thou camest, hath sent me, that thou mightest receive thy sight, and be filled with the Holy Ghost.

18 And immediately there fell from his eyes as it had been scales: and he received sight forthwith, and arose, and was baptized.

Acts 9:3-18—NRSV

3 Now as he was going along and approaching Damascus, suddenly a light from heaven flashed around him.

4 He fell to the ground and heard a voice saying to him, "Saul, Saul, why do you persecute me?"

5 He asked, "Who are you, Lord?" The reply came, "I am Jesus, whom you are persecuting.

6 But get up and enter the city, and you will be told what you are to do."

7 The men who were traveling with him stood speechless because they heard the voice but saw no one.

8 Saul got up from the ground, and though his eyes were open, he could see nothing; so they led him by the hand and brought him into Damascus.

9 For three days he was without sight, and neither ate nor drank.

10 Now there was a disciple in Damascus named Ananias. The Lord said to him in a vision, "Ananias." He answered, "Here I am, Lord."

11 The Lord said to him, "Get up and go to the street called Straight, and at the house of Judas look for a man of Tarsus named Saul. At this moment he is praying,

12 and he has seen in a vision a man named Ananias come in and lay his hands on him so that he might regain his sight."

13 But Ananias answered, "Lord, I have heard from many about this man, how much evil he has done to your saints in Jerusalem;

14 and here he has authority from the chief priests to bind all who invoke your name."

15 But the Lord said to him, "Go, for he is an instrument whom I have chosen to bring my name before Gentiles and kings and before the people of Israel;

16 I myself will show him how much he must suffer for the sake of my name."

17 So Ananias went and entered the house. He laid his hands on Saul and said, "Brother Saul, the Lord Jesus, who appeared to you on your way here, has sent me so that you may regain your sight and be filled with the Holy Spirit."

18 And immediately something like scales fell from his eyes, and his sight was restored. Then he got up and was baptized.

POINTS TO BE EMPHASIZED
ADULTS
Key Verse: Acts 9:18
Print: Acts 9:3-18
—Saul accepted the message from Jesus and the Holy Spirit transformed his life.
—Saul was convinced before his conversion that he was doing the right thing by persecuting followers of the Way.
—Ananias was instrumental in God's plan for changing Saul.
—The story of Paul's conversion is recounted again later in Acts, and in Paul's epistles.

YOUTH
Key Verse: Acts 9:5-6
Print: Acts 9:3-18
—Saul, who persecuted Christians, was transformed into Paul, who ceaselessly preached the Good News of Jesus Christ.
—Saul, whose name was changed to Paul, was chosen by God to preach the Gospel.
—God worked through the lives of others (beginning with Ananias) to guide Paul in ways that led to his ministry.
—Saul's transformation begins with the Damascus road experience.

CHILDREN
Key Verse: Acts 9:15
Print: Acts 9:3-12, 17-20
—Jesus changed the direction of Paul's life.
—Although blind, Paul received new "insight," and so can believers today.
—Paul was as committed to preaching the Gospel after his transformation as he was to persecuting the followers of the Way before his transformation.

TOPICAL OUTLINE OF THE LESSON
I. INTRODUCTION
  A. Counting the Cost
  B. Biblical Background

II. EXPOSITION AND APPLICATION OF THE SCRIPTURE
  A. God Meets Us Where We Are (*Acts 9:3-6*)
  B. God Sends Us to a Diverse Population (*Acts 9:7-16*)
  C. God Wants Us to Publicly Acknowledge Him (*Acts 9:17-18*)

III. SPECIAL FEATURES
    A. Preserving Our Heritage
    B. Concluding Reflections

I. INTRODUCTION
A. Counting the Cost

Two major transformations take place in this passage of study: the man known as Saul, a persecutor of Christians, is transformed into a lover of Christians and a missionary to the Gentile world. At the same time, Ananias, a devout Christian, must put his fears aside in order to visit with a notorious persecutor. For both men, this is a life-changing event; but this is what it means to be a Christian. Salvation is free, but discipleship is costly. True discipleship exacts a price.

Secondly, we must be willing to be transformed. In his letter to the Romans, the apostle Paul says, "I beseech you therefore, brethren, by the mercies of God, that ye present your bodies a living sacrifice, holy, acceptable unto God, which is your reasonable service. And be not conformed to this world: but be ye transformed by the renewing of your mind, that ye may prove what is that good, and acceptable, and perfect, will of God" (Romans 12:1-2). Each and every day, we must undergo a metamorphosis—we must transform our thinking.

It is our nature to respond defensively to matters. If we are wronged, we often respond in the flesh, most often through some kind of verbal conflict, but at times through physical confrontation as well. Even though we know the right thing to do, this is not what we do (cf., Romans 7:14-24). Our study for today examines these two features of our faith—counting the cost and transformation. Both men came to a better understanding of what this really means.

Shortly after his conversion experience, Saul was referred to exclusively as Paul, although it is not believed that his name was changed because of his conversion. From this point in the lesson study, however, Saul will be referred to as Paul.

B. Biblical Background

The man that Christendom recognizes as the apostle Paul was originally named Saul, after the first king of Israel. Even though he was born a Jew, Paul was no ordinary Jew. He was both a scholar and a leader. Paul studied in Jerusalem under the famed religious scholar, Gamaliel (Acts 22:3) and later became one of the Pharisees (23:6). And because his father was a Roman citizen, he inherited the same distinction with its various privileges.

As a Pharisee, Paul was among the religious elites who were motivated to annihilate Christians because their love and loyalty to Jesus Christ was a threat to Judaism. When Stephen was murdered, Paul stood on the sidelines, giving consent to the persecution (7:58; 8:1). This same young man was so vehemently against the disciples that he went to the high priest to garner support to further persecute the people of "the Way."

There are at least two ways that we can look at Paul's vehement opposition to

Christians. First, as a loyalist to the Jewish tradition and Law, one can say that Paul was defending the honor of the Most High God, particularly with regard to the first commandment: "You shall have no other gods before me" (Exodus 20:3, NRSV). It seems plausible to suggest that Paul believed he was only following the commandments. The fact that the disciples believed Jesus was the eternal God who came in the flesh (John 1:1-3, 14) only served to further vilify them in the eyes of the loyalist Jews.

Secondly, as a Pharisee, Paul was very familiar with the Law and the prophets. Isaiah prophesied saying, "Therefore the Lord himself shall give you a sign; Behold, a virgin shall conceive, and bear a son, and shall call his name Immanuel" (Isaiah 7:14). He, along with all of the other Jews, should have been expecting the Messiah. The Savior would not be a normal prophet; He was to be God incarnate: "For unto us a child is born, unto us a son is given: and the government shall be upon his shoulder: and his name shall be called Wonderful, Counseller, The Mighty God, The Everlasting Father, The Prince of Peace. Of the increase of his government and peace there shall be no end" (Isaiah 9:6-7).

As an expert in the Law, Paul was without excuse for persecuting the children of God. A preponderance evident that the Scriptures had been fulfilled was right before him.

II. EXPOSITION AND APPLICATION OF THE SCRIPTURE
A. God Meets Us Where We Are
(Acts 9:3-6)

Paul was seeking Christians wherever they could be found. Because they were spread all over—as a result of the persecution in Jerusalem (Acts 8:4)—it made his task a little more laborious. Thus, Paul obtained permission from the high priest in Jerusalem to go to Damascus, a distance of 160 miles, seeking people of the Way to harass. In verse 2, we note that they were called people of *the Way*, which was a derivation of Jesus' personal description, "I am the Way, the Truth, and the Life" (John 14:6). Pastor-teacher John MacArthur suggests,

"This was an appropriate title because Christianity is the way of God (18:26), the way into the Holy Place (Hebrews 10:19-20), and the way of truth (John 14:6; 2 Peter 2:2)."

Luke does not tell us what Paul was thinking as he traveled, but it is reasonable to assert that his thoughts were focused on the task that lay ahead. As a Pharisee (i.e., a religious loyalist), it is conceivable that he may have been praying for God's help to annihilate the Christians, the menace of Judaism. Somewhere along his 160-mile trek, Paul's thoughts were suddenly interrupted by a light that *shone around him from heaven*. John has already given us clarity concerning this light, for he said about Jesus, "In him was life, and the life was the light of all people. The light shines in the darkness, and the darkness did not overcome it." (John 1:4-5). The light of Jesus' glory shone from heaven and blinded Paul (cf., Acts 22:6; 26:13).

This text provides additional support for God's election (cf. Romans 9:11). Though there were several others on the road with paul, he alone was singled out. God's sovereignty says, "What then are we to say? Is there injustice on God's part? By no means! For he says to Moses, "I will have mercy on whom I have mercy, and I will have compassion on whom I have compassion." So it depends not on human will or exertion, but on God who shows mercy" (Romans 9:14-16, NRSV).

What happens next is truly magnificent: *And he fell to the earth, and heard a voice saying unto him, Saul, Saul, why persecutest thou me? And he said, Who art thou, Lord? And the Lord said, I am Jesus whom thou persecutest: it is hard for thee to kick against the pricks.* To Jesus' question, Paul gives a very potent response: *Who are You, Lord?* Notice that although Paul was inquiring about his interrogator, he was also identifying Him by name when he said, "Lord." Instinctively, Paul recognized and acknowledged that he was an unwitting participant in a miraculous experience.

Paul may have thought that he was only persecuting Christians, but this is never the case with Jesus, who takes such attacks as personal affronts (cf., Matthew 25:31-36). Anyone who attacks Christians is attacking Christ Himself. Paul was vicariously persecuting Christ as he persecuted His disciples.

Notwithstanding Paul's vocation, which placed him at odds with the cause of Christ, the Lord still wanted to use him. Christ recognized something in Paul that no human being would ever have seen. In response to Christ's call, Paul submitted himself to Jesus and Jesus immediately gave him instructions: the *Lord said unto him, Arise, and go into the city, and it shall be told thee what thou must do.*

B. God Sends Us to a Diverse Population *(Acts 9:7-16)*

The Bible uses the phrase "eyes were opened" no less than three times; each time, the ramifications were extremely impressive. First, in Genesis 3:7

(NRSV), the text says, "Then the eyes of both were opened." Referring to Adam and Eve's departure from the will of God, they both were able to see evil. Their innocence was lost; guilt and shame would forever have dominion over them and their subsequent generations.

Secondly, Luke 24:31 (NRSV) reads, "Then their eyes were opened, and they recognized him; and he vanished from their sight." This instance is the reverse of Adam and Eve's. Whereas they were able to see evil once their eyes were opened, the disciples on the road to Emmaus were now able to see righteousness.

Finally, in the case of Paul, when he possessed physical sight, he was spiritually blind; upon gaining spiritual sight, he was rendered physically blind, although this was only a temporary condition. For three days, Paul fasted without benefit of sight. As he fasted in darkness, he awaited instructions from God. In the meantime, the narrative is similar to Philip and the Ethiopian eunuch (Acts 8:26-39), and Peter and Cornelius (Acts 10:1-43). In this case, it is *a certain disciple at Damascus, named Ananias; and to him said the Lord in a vision, Ananias. And he said, Behold, I am here, Lord*. While Peter was praying, the delegation came from Cornelius; while Paul was praying, God was arranging a visit from Ananias to Paul. But there was a minor problem: while Ananias was quick to respond to God's call (verse 10), he was hesitant when he discovered what God's will included. *Then Ananias answered, Lord, I have heard by many of this man,* *how much evil he hath done to thy saints at Jerusalem: And here he hath authority from the chief priests to bind all that call on thy name.* For good reason, Ananias was less than excited about this charge. His going to see the infamous Jew was a radical statement of his commitment to obedience to the Lord.

Without question, Paul had a notorious reputation when it came to Christians— he hated them. But as important a factor as this may have been for the early Christians, this was not a factor for God. His concern is that His will be obeyed. If there are any repercussions, God will fight those battles. God may send us to people whom we may not care to associate with, but our reluctance may lead us to violate God's command. The mission is greater than us! For the hesitant Ananias, the mission that God had for Paul was greater than Ananias' insecurities. God wanted Paul to be a missionary to *Gentiles, kings, and the children of Israel*. In his lifetime, Paul fulfilled his charge. But there is more.

Paul wrote thirteen New Testament books (fourteen if Hebrews is included). His letters went to churches from Palestine to Rome. As an evangelist, he was far excelled beyond any other. To this day, his writings are still converting *Gentiles, kings, and the children of Israel* for the kingdom of God. He began as a man with a putrid reputation, but God made him into someone worthy of honor. Many of us began like Paul, misguided and confused; but God transformed us into persons passionately determined to obey His will.

C. God Wants Us to Publicly Acknowledge Him *(Acts 9:17-18)*

Three spectacular things happened at the close of this narrative. First, Ananias, who was initially afraid of Paul because of his reputation, called him "Brother." This was quite a turnabout for someone to move from enemy to brother. Once we are born again, we enter into the family of God. We are no longer strangers or enemies—we are now brothers and sisters. The highest accolade that one Christian can give another is not to call him or her by a title (although there is nothing wrong with showing respect by using titles), but rather to acknowledge him or her as a brother or sister.

Secondly, Ananias laid his hands on Paul so that he could receive the Holy Spirit. This was another dramatic turnabout. Three days before, he was an enemy of the Christian faith, but then he received the Holy Spirit.

Finally, Paul left Jerusalem on his way to Damascus, Syria in order to persecute Christians. He was so notorious that Ananias and others knew about his reputation. Yet, the chief persecutor of Christians made a public profession of faith in Jesus Christ (baptism). In three days, his life was totally turned around. God can do the same today for the most heinous, immoral individual on earth.

III. SPECIAL FEATURES
A. Preserving Our Heritage

Wouldn't it have been amazing if Birmingham Public Safety Commissioner Eugene "Bull" Connor had responded positively to Martin Luther King, Jr.'s show of love? Conner, along with the Ku Klux Klan and the White Citizen's Council in the city, among others, had a similar disposition to Paul's prior to his conversion. Because they considered Black people to be inferior to Whites, they became enraged at the possibility of equality. Furthermore, they rejected (in the name of Christ) the possibility of any good and decent relationship between the races.

Today, we still have people of a similar mentality. But this lesson is poignantly clear: if God can transform—from our misguided ways—a man like Paul, defender of the faith, God can do the same for the worst enemies of the faith.

B. Concluding Reflections

Some of us had foul reputations before we were saved. We did things that probably still would make us feel ashamed if we dwell upon them. It is tremendously important that we do not allow anyone to take us back to the place from which God has delivered us. Once Paul encountered Christ, no person, place, or circumstance could turn him away from his passionate pursuit.

Paul's transformation was so radical that theologians have dubbed similar experiences a "Pauline conversion." While Paul's Damascus Road experience is a rather extreme conversion account, Christendom has many souls that can testify to Christ having caused a radical transformation in their lives. A raging alcoholic is transformed, never desiring the taste of liquor again. A habitual criminal gives up his life of crime and becomes a model of obedience and discipleship.

The power of Christ to change lives is evident among many of the men and women who have enrolled in our nation's Bible colleges and seminaries. Many of them had no intention of pursuing a vocation in Christian ministy. Some were successful engineers, computer programmers, and stockbrokers, yet, they gave up lucrative careers to pursue a greater calling.

Whether our conversion experience is dramatic and intense like Paul's, or a more subdued, inner revolution, when we are called out by Christ for transformation, our lives are never the same. When God saves us, everything that we have done wrong is in the past. "As far as the east is from the west, so far hath he removed our transgressions from us" (Psalm 103:12). We become new creatures in Christ.

HOME DAILY BIBLE 📖 READINGS

for the week of November 6, 2005
Paul Becomes a Follower

Oct. 31, Monday
    —Luke 5:4-11

—Jesus Calls Disciples and Changes Lives
Nov. 1, Tuesday
    —Acts 11:1-10
    —Peter Responds to Criticism from Believers
Nov. 2, Wednesday
    —Acts 11:11-18
    —The Believers in Jerusalem Praise God
Nov. 3, Thursday
    —Acts 9:1-9
    —Saul Sees a Vision of Jesus
Nov. 4, Friday
    —Acts 9:10-16
    —Ananias Receives Instructions in a Vision
Nov. 5, Saturday
    —Acts 9:17-22
    —Saul Begins to Proclaim Jesus
Nov. 6, Sunday
    —Acts 9:23-31
    —Saul and the Disciples Proclaim Jesus

PRAYER

Eternal God, keep us humble and receptive to Your mandates so that we can stay on the path, which You have laid out for us as Your children. Amen.

Lesson 11

Lydia:
A Committed Woman

ADULT TOPIC: Offering of Oneself
YOUTH TOPIC: A Gracious Convert
CHILDREN'S TOPIC: Lydia Welcomes New Friends

DEVOTIONAL READING: Acts 16:25-34
BACKGROUND SCRIPTURE: Acts 16
PRINT PASSAGE: Acts 16:6-15

Acts 16:6-15—KJV

6 Now when they had gone throughout Phrygia and the region of Galatia, and were forbidden of the Holy Ghost to preach the word in Asia,

7 After they were come to Mysia, they assayed to go into Bithynia: but the Spirit suffered them not.

8 And they passing by Mysia came down to Troas.

9 And a vision appeared to Paul in the night; There stood a man of Macedonia, and prayed him, saying, Come over into Macedonia, and help us.

10 And after he had seen the vision, immediately we endeavoured to go into Macedonia, assuredly gathering that the Lord had called us for to preach the gospel unto them.

11 Therefore loosing from Troas, we came with a straight course to Samothracia, and the next day to Neapolis;

12 And from thence to Philippi, which is the chief city of that part of Macedonia, and a colony: and we were in that city abiding certain days.

13 And on the sabbath we went out of the city by a river

UNIT III
To the Ends of the Earth

CHILDREN'S UNIT
Witnessing to All the World

KEY VERSE

When she was baptized, and her household, she besought us, saying, If ye have judged me to be faithful to the Lord, come into my house, and abide there. And she constrained us. —Acts 16:15

OBJECTIVES

After completion of this lesson, students should understand:

1. The role of Lydia and the implications of her conversion.

2. The importance of hospitality in the ancient world.

3. How they can offer hospitality and service to others in the same spirit that Lydia demonstrated.

side, where prayer was wont to be made; and we sat down, and spake unto the women which resorted thither.

14 And a certain woman named Lydia, a seller of purple, of the city of Thyatira, which worshipped God, heard us: whose heart the Lord opened, that she attended unto the things which were spoken of Paul.

15 And when she was baptized, and her household, she besought us, saying, If ye have judged me to be faithful to the Lord, come into my house, and abide there. And she constrained us.

Acts 16:6-15—NRSV

6 They went through the region of Phrygia and Galatia, having been forbidden by the Holy Spirit to speak the word in Asia.

7 When they had come opposite Mysia, they attempted to go into Bithynia, but the Spirit of Jesus did not allow them;

8 so, passing by Mysia, they went down to Troas.

9 During the night Paul had a vision: there stood a man of Macedonia pleading with him and saying, "Come over to Macedonia and help us."

10 When he had seen the vision, we immediately tried to cross over to Macedonia, being convinced that God had called us to proclaim the good news to them.

11 We set sail from Troas and took a straight course to Samothrace, the following day to Neapolis,

12 and from there to Philippi, which is a leading city of the district of Macedonia and a Roman colony. We remained in this city for some days.

13 On the sabbath day we went outside the gate by the river, where we supposed there was a place of prayer; and we sat down and spoke to the women who had gathered there.

14 A certain woman named Lydia, a worshiper of God, was listening to us; she was from the city of Thyatira and a dealer in purple cloth. The Lord opened her heart to listen eagerly to what was said by Paul.

15 When she and her household were baptized, she urged us, saying, "If you have judged me to be faithful to the Lord, come and stay at my home." And she prevailed upon us.

POINTS TO BE EMPHASIZED
ADULTS
Key Verse: Acts 16:15
Print: Acts 16:6-15
—Lydia and the other women gathered for Sabbath prayers beside the river, indicating that there was no synagogue in Philippi.
—As a dealer in purple, Lydia may have been a prominent businessperson.
—Lydia accepted the words of Paul as true and was baptized with her household, becoming the first-named Christian convert in Europe.
—After demonstrating a faithful response to the Lord, Lydia offered her home to Paul and the other travelers.

YOUTH

Key Verse: Acts 16:15

Print: Acts 16:6-15

—Paul went to Europe instead of staying in Asia Minor because God's Spirit guided him there by means of a vision.

—Paul valued women when culture, religion and society did not.

—Lydia was an unusual person because she was an independent woman in a time when almost all women were dependent upon men.

—Lydia's most apparent gift is her hospitality and generosity.

CHILDREN

Key Verse: Acts 16:15

Print: Acts 16:9-15

—The Holy Spirit sends messengers to people in unusual places.

—Salvation is available to all people who are willing to accept it.

—The belief in Jesus by one person in the household can influence other members to receive salvation.

—Hearing the Gospel with an open heart can lead to belief in Jesus.

TOPICAL OUTLINE OF THE LESSON

I. **INTRODUCTION**
   A. Hospitality in the Biblical World
   B. Biblical Background

II. **EXPOSITION AND APPLICATION OF THE SCRIPTURE**
   A. God Directs His Saints
      (Acts 16:6-10)

   B. A Woman of Faith Meets the Disciples *(Acts 16:11-15)*

III. **SPECIAL FEATURES**
   A. Preserving Our Heritage
   B. Concluding Reflections

I. INTRODUCTION

A. Hospitality in the Biblical World

This lesson introduces us to a way of life that was normative for the ancient world, but highly unlikely in our modern civilization. Our text deals, in part, with the concept of hospitality. We are a hotel generation. We will not travel too far on any highway before we will see a host of signs offering overnight accommodations, with several different levels of luxury. We are so accustomed to pulling off the highway and turning into one of these commuter paradises that we think nothing of it. This was not the case in the ancient world.

By the time that events in Acts occurred, there were few public inns, and these could often be dangerous. Most travelers relied on the beneficence of village people who were willing to open their doors for a stranger. A person or family traveling on foot or on a donkey all day would enter a village and post at the city square until someone was kind enough to invite them in. This practice was such an important way of life that God would punish those who failed to be hospitable (Deuteronomy 23:3-4); indeed, this was a way for persons to show their faithfulness to God. Furthermore, by assisting a stranger, by inviting him into one's household, one might even entertain the Lord as a guest (Genesis 18:1-8) or his angels (Judges 6:17-23; 13:15-21; cf., Hebrews 13:2).

A benchmark story for this kind of hospitality is what occurred when strangers came to town in Genesis 18. Abraham went out of his way to feed them and make them feel at home. Later, the same is true when the angel of the Lord visited Manoah to inform him that he was going to be the father of a special young man named Samson. Manoah instinctively asked the angel to stay while he cooked a young goat (Judges 13:15). The same was true with the Shunammite woman who saw the prophet Elisha going back and forth each day. She invited him in to have a meal, which initiated a tradition between them (2 Kings 4:8).

In the New Testament, the tradition of hospitality continued. Jesus was especially conscientious about this. "Then turning toward the woman, he [Jesus] said to Simon, 'Do you see this woman? I entered your house; you gave me no water for my feet, but she has bathed my feet with her tears and dried them with her hair. You gave me no kiss, but from the time I came in she has not stopped kissing my feet. You did not anoint my head with oil, but she has anointed my feet with ointment.'" (Luke 7:44-46, NRSV). Thus, the hospitality tradition continued.

In the early church, because there were no established worship centers, the disciples had to rely upon the tradition of hospitality in order to be successful in their current endeavor. In the chapter we are studying, Lydia showed hospitality to the apostles as a demonstration of her faith. As a result of her hospitality, Paul and his troupe of missionaries had a stable base from which to operate and plant a new church, which was the church at Philippi.

B. Biblical Background

As we have already seen in previous lessons, after Philip evangelized the Samaritans, the apostles saw where they would have to subordinate their personal will to the will of God. But they were not entirely sold on the idea of going to the Gentile population. If going to their archrivals, the Samaritans, was a major mental stretch, then going to the Gentiles would require a complete worldview change. Peter's perception of the Gentiles' uncleanness is evident in Acts 10.

Paul and Barnabas were the first to enter the Gentile world for the purpose of evangelism. In the sixteenth chapter, Paul teamed with Silas and continued the commission by going to the ends of the earth. Macedonia is now a part of modern-day Europe. By going to Macedonia, Paul was truly out of his Judean comfort zone, but he had an inexhaustible zeal to go further. But given the radical transformation that had already occurred in Paul's life, going to Macedonia probably required no great faith effort on his part. One may rightly ask, "What was Paul's motivation for being so inexhaustible in his missionary effort?" Paul realized that his role as a persecutor of Christians had made him a persecutor of Christ (Acts 9:5). Since he was forgiven of much, Paul felt a desire to do more than the average believer. Jesus once told Peter, "Wherefore I say unto thee, Her sins, which are many, are forgiven; for she loved much: but to whom little is forgiven, the same loveth little" (Luke 7:47).

The Macedonian ministry saw the end of one team and the beginning of a new one. On a previous trip, John Mark had departed from Paul and the others in Pamphylia and did not go on to complete the work (15:38). Paul felt that his failure made him an unsuitable choice for this work. Such a work was only hampered by novices or immature help; he needed seasoned workers. "And the contention was so sharp between them, that they departed asunder one from the other: and so Barnabas took Mark, and sailed unto Cyprus; And Paul chose Silas, and departed" (Acts 15:39-40). Their separation was not an amicable one, but they later reconciled (1 Corinthians 9:6). It was a good thing that Paul chose Silas as his companion. As a prophet and a Jew, he was able to proclaim the Word as well as enter the synagogues. He was also a Roman citizen; so, like Paul, he had the covering of the Roman government on matters.

II. Exposition and Application of the Scripture
A. God Directs His Saints *(Acts 16:6-10)*

At first glance, it may seem that there are only cursory events in these passages, but even here we can see the handiwork of God in the process. First, they were *forbidden by the Holy Spirit to speak the word in Asia.* Apparently, Paul had deemed it logical for the group to head to Asia and spread the Good News in new territory. Luke does not tell us why the Holy Spirit forbade them to go into Asia. What we do know is that each of the major cities of Asia (Ephesus, Smyrna, Philadelphia, Laodicea, Colosse, Sardis, Pergamos and Thyatira) was eventually evangelized, established churches, and (with the exception of Colosse) was identified

Paul's mission moved to Europe. Mark's earlier departure was interpreted as a desertion. Silas and Judas were chosen earlier by the Jerusalem authorities to represent the agreement that validated the mission of Paul and Barnabas, and Syria and Cilicia were crucial areas for the message. Derbe and Lystra were the sites of the mission. Timothy's circumcision was intended to make him acceptable as a Jew without compromising the decisions reached by the apostles and elders about the Gentiles. The Holy Spirit and the Spirit of Jesus are alternative terms for the same divine agency that redirected the mission by preventing their plans. A vision was a means of divine communication to cross a boundary now beyond Asia Minor to Macedonia. The place of prayer was clearly a gathering for Jewish worship, whether or not it was a proper synagogue, and Lydia was already a worshiper of God, whether Jewish or Gentile. To say that the Lord opened her heart to listen is to suggest a miracle of faith. The merchant Lydia had sufficient means to support the mission, urging her hospitality as a sign of acceptance.

in Revelation 2–3 as the churches for which Jesus had a word.

Secondly, *After they were come to Mysia, they assayed to go into Bithynia: but the Spirit suffered them not.* For a second time, the missionaries' plans were thwarted. The first time their plans were redirected by the Holy Spirit (verse 6). The second time, their plans were again redirected by the *Spirit.* Upon leaving Mysia, they traveled southwest to Troas, a harbor city located about ten miles south of the city of Troy. Troas was an important seaport in the Roman Empire, trafficking many merchants traveling between Asia Minor and Macedonia.

As the church moved away from its Jerusalem comfort zone, the members found themselves in foreign, strange territory. More than ever, they needed divine guidance, and this guidance came to them in the form of visions (as we have already referenced). In Paul's vision, a man pleaded for Paul to come to Macedonia to help them. There was no church there and the Gospel had to be preached. So Paul heeded the vision and continued on to Macedonia, *assuredly gathering that the Lord had called us for to preach the gospel unto them.*

Luke gives us no insight into how Paul knew that the man in his dream was from Macedonia. Regardless of how the man's nationality was made known to Paul, after two attempts, Paul had received a clear directive. They were to go to Macedonia. There was an urgent need in Macedonia to hear the Gospel. Paul's vision, commonly known as the Macedonian Call, has been interpreted by some scholars as the start of the Gospel movement in Europe. This may not be true, however, as Paul's letter to the Romans indicates that Christianity had been in Rome since the early days of the movement.

Paul's experience in discerning his next ministry field holds an important truth for us today. There are times when we clearly believe we know the best action to take based on our human knowledge and understanding. However, God's knowledge is much greater. The time was right to evangelize in Macedonia, not Asia or Bithynia.

B. A Woman of Faith Meets the Disciples *(Acts 16:11-15)*

On the sabbath, Paul and company went by the riverside and spoke to a group of women who had gathered there. Why was Paul talking to a group of women? It is believed there was no synagogue in the city because there were not enough Jewish males residing there who met the necessary qualifications. In order for there to be a synagogue in a city, there was a minimum requirement of ten Jewish male heads of household.

Paul's usual evangelistic strategy was to go to the local synagogue and begin to teach or debate the truth—that of Jesus of Nazareth being the Promised Messiah. Paul and the other apostles employed this strategy for two reasons. First, Paul and the other believers were not trying to start a new religion; their intention was to expand Judaism to accept the arrival of the Messiah as prophesied by the Old Testament prophets. Furthermore, Paul, as a trained Pharisee, was a rabbi. All synagogues did not have rabbis, so his presence in any city that had a Jewish population was a rare treat.

Secondly, Paul was commissioned to take the Gospel to the Gentile world. There was always a chance that by going to the synagogue, he would find Gentile converts worshiping with the Diaspora Jews (cf., 8:27; 10:2). What the missionaries did instead was access a body of water located in the open air, and have a prayer meeting *by a river side*. It became a custom for exiled Jews to go to a river and weep because they were away from their homeland. In the absence of a synagogue, Paul must have felt certain that he could find local Jews who followed this custom of praying by the riverside on the Sabbath.

Contrary to the prevailing assumption that Paul was a male chauvinist, Paul and his company broke tradition when they *sat down and spoke to the women who had gathered there*. Among the women was Lydia, *a seller of purple, of the city of Thyatira, which worshipped God*. Lydia was not just an entrepreneur, she was an unusual woman of means during a time when few women had their own money, let alone a business that catered to the elite of society. Only royalty and wealthy aristocrats could afford such the luxurious purple cloth that Lydia sold. Although she was a woman of means, Lydia was not arrogant concerning the things of God. Thus, she *was listening* to them. Luke correspondingly says that the Lord opened her heart and *she attended unto the things which were spoken of Paul*.

Like the Ethiopian eunuch, when Lydia received the Word of God, she desired to be baptized that same time. Their proximity to water worked on their behalf; she and her household (cf., 11:14) were all baptized. It is not clear who comprised Lydia's household, but her commitment to the faith was firm in that she determined that her entire household would be followers of the Way.

The narrative ends as Lydia persuaded the missionaries to stay at her home. Hers was not a casual or insincere invitation. The fact that she had enough space to house this many travelers verifies that she was well-to-do. Lydia's hospitality to the men of God was as though she was doing it to Christ Himself, whereas Saul's persecution of the Christians was an evil, contentious act, as though he was doing it to Christ Himself. Her hospitality evidenced her faith in and commitment to Christ.

III. Special Features
A. Preserving Our Heritage

The African American community is familiar with hospitality being demonstrated as evidence of a deep and abiding faith. The Underground Railroad operated on a hospitality principle. Escaped slaves would travel from home to home as they moved under the cover of night. They would stay with one family during the daylight hours, and then travel by night as they tried to locate the next station on the secret "Railroad."

After slavery, segregation laws did not afford Blacks the opportunity to stay in southern hotels and motels, eat in restaurants, or use public restroom facilities. For their basic needs, Blacks, especially in the South, had to rely upon the hospitality of other Blacks.

B. Concluding Reflections

The story of Paul's encounter with Lydia is an important story of faith and obedience—the obedience of Paul as well as that of Lydia. These two people could not have been more different, yet both were willing to use what they had to build up the body of believers.

Every person has something to offer the kingdom of God. For some, it is their passion for sharing the Gospel and making disciples, like Paul did. Others may have the economic means or spirit of hospitality, like Lydia did. Both were needed to establish the church at Philippi, which continued to be a blessing to others.

Is there fertile ground awaiting your gifts and resources? More importantly, are you willing to give them freely for the sake of the Gospel?

■ HOME DAILY BIBLE 📖 READINGS

for the week of November 13, 2005
Lydia: A Committed Woman

Nov. 7, Monday
    —Hebrews 13:1-6
    —Show Hospitality to Strangers
Nov. 8, Tuesday
    —Luke 10:38-42
    —Mary and Martha Welcome Jesus
Nov. 9, Wednesday
    —1 Peter 4:7-11
    —Serve One Another Using Your
        Gifts
Nov. 10, Thursday
    —Acts 16:11-15
    —Lydia Becomes a Faithful Follower
Nov. 11, Friday
    —Acts 16:16-24
    —Paul and Silas Are Imprisoned
Nov. 12, Saturday
    —Acts 16:25-34
    —Converted, the Jailer Shows
        Hospitality
Nov. 13, Sunday
    —Acts 16:35-40
    —Paul and Silas Are Freed

PRAYER

Our Father, in a world wherein there are conflicting perceptions of how to accomplish Your will, give us the grace to transcend gender, class and race to embrace each other. Grant us the spirit of cooperation, knowing that we do not engage in the task alone, but as workers together with God, to accomplish Your will. Amen.

Lesson 12

Priscilla and Aquila: Team Ministry

UNIT III
To the Ends of the Earth

CHILDREN'S UNIT
Witnessing to All the World

ADULT TOPIC: Working Together in Ministry
YOUTH TOPIC: Team Players
CHILDREN'S TOPIC: T. E. A. M.
(Together Everyone Accomplishes More)

DEVOTIONAL READING: Luke 10:1-11
BACKGROUND SCRIPTURE: Acts 18:1—19:10
PRINT PASSAGE: Acts 18:1-4, 18-21, 24-28

KEY VERSE
Because he was of the same craft, he abode with them, and wrought: for by their occupation they were tentmakers.—Acts 18:3

Acts 18:1-4, 18-21, 24-28—KJV

AFTER THESE things Paul departed from Athens, and came to Corinth;

2 And found a certain Jew named Aquila, born in Pontus, lately come from Italy, with his wife Priscilla; (because that Claudius had commanded all Jews to depart from Rome:) and came unto them.

3 And because he was of the same craft, he abode with them, and wrought: for by their occupation they were tentmakers.

4 And he reasoned in the synagogue every sabbath, and persuaded the Jews and the Greeks.

.....

18 And Paul after this tarried there yet a good while, and then took his leave of the brethren, and sailed thence into Syria, and with him Priscilla and Aquila; having shorn his head in Cenchrea: for he had a vow.

19 And he came to Ephesus, and left them there: but he

OBJECTIVES
After completion of this lesson, students should understand that:
1. People of various trades, gifts and skills are led to minister to others.
2. Team ministry has its advantages.
3. Team ministry provides an effective support system.

himself entered into the synagogue, and reasoned with the Jews.

20 When they desired him to tarry longer time with them, he consented not;

21 But bade them farewell, saying, I must by all means keep this feast that cometh in Jerusalem: but I will return again unto you, if God will. And he sailed from Ephesus.

.....

24 And a certain Jew named Apollos, born at Alexandria, an eloquent man, and mighty in the scriptures, came to Ephesus.

25 This man was instructed in the way of the Lord; and being fervent in the spirit, he spake and taught diligently the things of the Lord, knowing only the baptism of John.

26 And he began to speak boldly in the synagogue: whom when Aquila and Priscilla had heard, they took him unto them, and expounded unto him the way of God more perfectly.

27 And when he was disposed to pass into Achaia, the brethren wrote, exhorting the disciples to receive him: who, when he was come, helped them much which had believed through grace:

28 For he mightily convinced the Jews, and that publickly, showing by the scriptures that Jesus was Christ.

Acts 18:1-4, 18-21, 24-28—NRSV

AFTER THIS Paul left Athens and went to Corinth.

2 There he found a Jew named Aquila, a native of Pontus, who had recently come from Italy with his wife Priscilla, because Claudius had ordered all Jews to leave Rome. Paul went to see them,

3 and, because he was of the same trade, he stayed with them, and they worked together—by trade they were tentmakers.

4 Every sabbath he would argue in the synagogue and would try to convince Jews and Greeks.

.....

18 After staying there for a considerable time, Paul said farewell to the believers and sailed for Syria, accompanied by Priscilla and Aquila. At Cenchreae he had his hair cut, for he was under a vow.

19 When they reached Ephesus, he left them there, but first he himself went into the synagogue and had a discussion with the Jews.

20 When they asked him to stay longer, he declined;

21 but on taking leave of them, he said, "I will return to you, if God wills." Then he set sail from Ephesus.

.....

24 Now there came to Ephesus a Jew named Apollos, a native of Alexandria. He was an eloquent man, well-versed in the scriptures.

25 He had been instructed in the Way of the Lord; and he spoke with burning enthusiasm and taught accurately the things concerning Jesus, though he knew only the baptism of John.

26 He began to speak boldly in the synagogue; but when Priscilla and Aquila

heard him, they took him aside and explained the Way of God to him more accurately.

27 And when he wished to cross over to Achaia, the believers encouraged him and wrote to the disciples to welcome him. On his arrival he greatly helped those who through grace had become believers,

28 for he powerfully refuted the Jews in public, showing by the scriptures that the Messiah is Jesus.

POINTS TO BE EMPHASIZED
ADULTS
Key Verse: Acts 18:3
Print: Acts 18:1-4, 18-21, 24-28
—Paul chose to work with people who had the same employment as he did.
—Priscilla and Aquila confronted Apollos in order to train him in the appropriate interpretation of the Scripture, who was then strengthened and enabled to strengthen others.
—Priscilla and Aquila accompanied Paul to Ephesus.
—God used the Jewish Diaspora to facilitate the spread of the Gospel.

YOUTH
Key Verse: Acts 18:26
Print: Acts 18:1-4, 18-21, 24-28
—In Corinth, Paul met Priscilla and Aquila—who had left Rome when Claudius ordered Jews to leave Rome.
—Priscilla and Aquila were team players both in their ministry and in the ministry they shared with Paul.

—Priscilla and Aquila were tentmakers, which was the same trade that Paul practiced.
—The team skills of Priscilla and Aquila were demonstrated by the way in which they called Apollos aside to help him become more accurate in his message.

CHILDREN
Key Verse: Acts 18:3
Print: Acts 18:1-3, 18a, 19-21, 24-26
—Working with Priscila and Aquila made Paul's challenging task easier.
—Knowing a trade provides a livelihood.
—Paul did not rely on others for financial support.
—Those who know the Word of God are obligated to share it with others.

TOPICAL OUTLINE OF THE LESSON

I. INTRODUCTION
  A. The Meaning of Preaching and Teaching in the New Testament
  B. Biblical Background

II. EXPOSITION AND APPLICATION OF THE SCRIPTURE
  A. Paul Preaches and Teaches in Corinth *(Acts 18:1-4)*
  B. Paul Preaches and Teaches in Ephesus *(Acts 18:18-21)*
  C. Apollos Is Instructed in Ephesus *(Act 18:24-28)*

III. SPECIAL FEATURES
  A. Preserving Our Heritage
  B. Concluding Reflections

I. INTRODUCTION

A. The Meaning of Preaching and Teaching in the New Testament

Modern times have given us a framework for preaching and teaching that is not altogether accurate. At times, we possess rather sophomoric ideas of what preaching and teaching are. This confusion leads to a misguided notion and eventually creates theological defilement in terms of gifts and office. As we follow Paul's movement, we see that he was engaged in both preaching and teaching. Though they sound alike phonetically, they are not the same. They both have very singular goals and audiences.

An essential goal of preaching is to *proclaim* the name of Jesus Christ such that others will accept Him as their Lord and Savior. In this sense, everyone who is born again is a preacher of the Gospel. Jesus' directions were not exclusive of any convert; rather, His charge was inclusive of all believers. Jesus said, "Go ye into all the world, and preach the gospel to every creature" (Mark 16:15). The fact that our vernacular expresses the notion of being "called to preach" is somewhat misleading. In fact, we are all *sent* to preach. Preaching in and of itself is not an office or a gift—rather, it is a command given for the purpose of evangelizing and making disciples.

Teaching, on the other hand, has a goal and audience as well. The goal of Christian teaching is edification and education about how to live in the kingdom of God.

The Kingdom is not for unbelievers—it is not for the lost. The kingdom of God is for those who have heard preaching—that is, Jesus Christ is the Son of God and He died as a sacrifice for our sins—and believed. Such persons are no longer lost—they are believers; they are saved. Paul tells us, "The gifts he gave were that some would be apostles, some prophets, some evangelists, some pastors and teachers" (Ephesians 4:11, NRSV). Notice that the gift of pastor is paired with the gift of teaching. The pastor is a shepherd who equips the sheep for life. Preaching and teaching are the skills (gifts) granted to pastors and teachers to bring the kingdom of God to fruition.

B. Biblical Background

From his conversion until his arrival in Corinth, Paul was moving at a rapid pace, preaching and teaching everywhere. At one point, he was stoned almost to death (Acts 14:19) and later beaten with many stripes and imprisoned (16:23). As if this were not enough, he was later placed in the stockade (verse 24). This was followed by a lengthy discourse in Athens.

Paul's next undertaking was quite engaging. By the time of Paul's entrance into Corinth, the city was both a political and commercial city. This cosmopolitan city was like a modern-day Las Vegas, New York City or Los Angeles, accompanied by the moral decay that often accompanies more populated areas. The temple of Aphrodite, the goddess of love, was located in Corinth. In the evening, one thousand temple prostitutes converged on the city to work their trade. So infamous was this town that the name "Corinth" became synonymous with whoredom and debauchery. It was a bustling metropolis because traffic flowing from northern to southern Greece had to pass through this trade center. Corinth was the opposite of Athens, the intellectual city. So, as Paul left Athens going to Corinth, he was entering fertile ground for a highly motivated evangelist.

II. EXPOSITION AND APPLICATION OF THE SCRIPTURE
A. Paul Preaches and Teaches in Corinth (Acts 18:1-4)

Amid the debauchery that is usually associated with Corinth, Paul unexpectedly found new friends in a husband-and-wife team—Aquila and Priscilla. Back in Rome, Emperor Claudius, motivated by anti-Semitic sentiments, issued a decree that all Jews must leave Rome. Among the Jews who fled potential hostility in Rome were Aquila and Priscilla. Apparently, the couple had a tent-making business in Italy and were perhaps converted to Christianity while there. But even though they were Christians, Rome was unconcerned about the particulars of their faith; they were still Jews in the eyes of the Empire.

Paul, like the husband-and-wife team, was a tentmaker. Jewish sons followed in their fathers' footsteps. Just as Joseph was a carpenter and Jesus followed in the same vein, it is likely that Paul's father was also a tentmaker. Rabbis were not excluded from learning a trade. They, too, had to support their families. By earning a living independently, they were free to teach, without concern for obtaining income. So, Paul joined the team and the threesome began plying their trade.

Unlike the small town of Philippi that had no synagogue, Corinth, even with its moral depravity, was much different. Paul maintained his Sabbath day practice of going to the synagogue to teach. Once there, Paul *reasoned* (*argued*, NRSV) with the Jews and Greeks there regarding the faith. Perhaps the reason why Luke indicates that Paul reasoned rather than

Aquila and Priscilla appear as partners in the ministry with Paul. Claudius' edict expelling the Jews from Rome is dated around 49 BC. Like rabbis and philosophers who worked with their hands, they practiced their trade of tentmaking to avoid becoming a burden to their hearers. To *shake the dust from their clothes* is a prophetic act of judgment consistent with holding people responsible for their own lives. "Do not be afraid, I am with you" is the assurance of divine presence. The charge against Paul was not general sedition, but violation of the law of Israel, and Gallio refused to become involved in an intra-Jewish debate. Paul apparently cut his hair at the beginning of taking a special vow, in contrast to shaving his head as the completion of the vow in the temple. Paul's visit to Jerusalem indicates his respect for the church at Jerusalem. The baptism of John represents repentance and was preparation for the baptism of the Holy Spirit. Baptism in the name of Jesus is accompanied by the laying on of hands and confirmed by the Holy Spirit. Priscilla and Aquila were teachers of "The Way" and had a great impact upon Apollos' mission to Achaia.

taught was because they all may have been influenced by the Greek method of Socratic dialogues that emphasized a give-and-take, question-and-answer conversation. These intellectuals were not interested in lectures or simple answers to opaque questions or concepts. They were most interested in dialogue.

Both the Jews and the Greeks (who were converts to Judaism) were familiar with the singular God of Israel, but they were unfamiliar with Jesus Christ and His ministry. Paul reasoned with the Jews and the Greeks until they were convinced of the Gospel.

B. Paul Preaches and Teaches in Ephesus *(Acts 18:18-21)*

There are a couple of citations in this passage that lack clarity. First, the fact that Paul was allowed to *tarry there yet a good while* is an indication that he was not under any kind of persecution. It appears that he could have continued his practice of tent-making on weekdays and reasoning in the synagogue on the Sabbath. Certainly, Corinth could have used his witness. But, without explanation to the reader, Luke says that Paul terminated his ministry in Corinth and sailed to Syria. He left the brothers behind and sailed to his next port-of-call, accompanied by his friends and business partners, Priscilla and Aquila.

A second feature of verse 18 that remains unclear is the cryptic reference to *having shorn his head in Cenchrea: for*

he had a vow. Nothing more on the matter of Paul's vow precedes this verse and nothing follows it. Some have speculated that this was perhaps a temporary Nazarite vow (cf., Numbers 6:1-21). A vow was a sacred observance within Mosaic Law (Deuteronomy 23-21-22). The Nazarite vow was a solemn promise that a man made to God to abstain from intoxicants, to let his hair grow and to avoid entering any house containing a dead body or attending any funeral.

According to theologian Albert Barnes, in Paul's day it was common for Jews to make such vows to God as an expression of gratitude or devotedness to His service, or when they had been delivered from sickness, danger, or calamity. Vows of this nature were also made by the Gentiles on occasions of deliverance. Barnes reasoned that it is possible Paul made such a vow in consequence of his deliverance from the numerous perils to which he was exposed. What is most intriguing is that Paul, a devoted Christian evangelist and teacher, would maintain a connection to these antiquated Jewish customs. Indeed, he was a follower of Christ, but he remained loyal to the traditions of his religion, even though he knew that there was no salvific meaning behind such observances.

Paul journeyed to Ephesus with Priscilla and Aquila. While in Ephesus, he made a cursory visit to the synagogue and reasoned with the Jews, but when they requested his presence for a longer time, he opted out, saying, *I must by all means keep this feast that cometh in Jerusalem: but I will return again unto you, if God will. And he sailed from Ephesus.* He does not indicate which feast he was trying to keep, but most probably it was the Passover Feast. Being a devout Jew, he maintained his loyalty to the holy days. Paul had to move quickly to catch the boat. His friends, Priscilla and Aquila, the loyal team, remained in Ephesus.

C. Apollos Is Instructed in Ephesus
(Acts 18:24-28)

Luke introduces Apollos on a high plane: *born at Alexandria, an eloquent man, and mighty in the scriptures, came to Ephesus.* The Greek word for "eloquent" is used only here in the entire New Testament. It can either mean "a man of words" or "a learned man." Both fixations seem probable for Apollos, particularly given Luke's gracious introduction. Apollos was not only an excellent speaker, but he was well-trained. He did not grow up in Jerusalem, but there was a sizable population of Jews in Alexandria, such that he could receive superior training.

The Greek word for "mighty" is *dunatos* and is related to *dunamis*. *Dunamis* renders the English words "power" and "dynamite." Paul said, "I am not ashamed of the gospel of Christ: for it is the power of God unto salvation" (Romans 1:16). Every time Apollos stood up to speak, his words were like dynamite. He was a believer who was taught in the way of the Lord, which is an Old Testament expression (Genesis 18:19; Judges 2:22). But even with his limitations, *and being fervent in the spirit, he spake and taught diligently the things of the Lord, knowing only the baptism of John.* Apollos did the best he could with what he had. He accurately taught what the prophets said about Jesus, even though he did not have complete information.

Aquila and Priscilla, being themselves trained and having shared with Paul regularly, very tactfully *took him unto them, and expounded unto him the way of God more perfectly.* They were tentmakers; he was an eloquent scholar. He had the ability to debate—the fact that he was introduced as he was indicates that he had no equal in Ephesus. He could convince many to believe the things that were near and dear to his heart. Still, he allowed himself to be taught by this couple. He was a "great" preacher with a humble spirit. They wisely took him aside privately, and he wisely submitted to their teaching about the Gospel.

III. SPECIAL FEATURES
A. Preserving Our Heritage

African American Christianity is like no other. Like any other racial or cultural group, we have our problems, but we also have a very rich and powerful history. Germane to our history is the richness of Black preaching. The profound eloquence of such great pulpiteers is unparalleled. We need not go far to find an "Apollos" among our people, scholarly and eloquent persons who preach and teach the Gospel as if their lives depended on it. Every time the trained Black preacher mounts the pulpit, there is convergence of scholarship and eloquence that result in persons accepting Christ as their Lord and Savior.

B. Concluding Reflections

During a Special Olympics game held in Seattle, nine contestants, all physically or mentally disabled, assembled at the starting line for the 100-yard dash. At the gun, they all started out, possessing little athletic skill but a great desire to run the race to the finish and win, except for the little boy who stumbled on the asphalt, tumbled over a couple of times and began to cry. When the other eight competitors heard the boy crying they slowed down to look back. Every one of them all turned around and went back to see about the fallen boy. In a beautiful expression of humanity, all nine children then linked arms and walked across the finish line together.

Too often, competition overshadows team effort. This group of "special" children understood what Paul, Aquila and Priscilla recognized through faith. A great deal more is accomplished by working as a team than when we are more concerned about achieving for our own benefit. Christians should recognize that lives are at stake; therefore, we must depend on each other to accomplish the Great Commission given to every believer.

HOME DAILY BIBLE READINGS

for the week of November 20, 2005
Priscilla and Aquila: Team Ministry

Nov. 14, Monday
  —Luke 10:1-11
  —Jesus Sends Disciples Out in Pairs
Nov. 15, Tuesday
  —Luke 19:28-34
  —Go and Find a Colt
Nov. 16, Wednesday
  —Acts 18:1-8
  —Paul Preaches in Corinth
Nov. 17, Thursday
  —Acts 18:9-17
  —Paul's Preaching Stirs Up
    Controversy
Nov. 18, Friday
  —Acts 18:18-23
  —Paul, Priscilla and Aquila Travel
    Together
Nov. 19, Saturday
  —Acts 18:24-28
  —Priscilla and Aquila Help Apollos
Nov. 20, Sunday
  —Romans 16:3-16
  —Paul Thanks Priscilla and Aquila

PRAYER

O God, when we encounter those who are weak in the faith, grant us the grace to reach out in love as we seek to bring them to a fuller knowledge of Thy truth. In Jesus' name, we pray. Amen.

Paul's Farewell

ADULT TOPIC: Saying Good-bye
YOUTH TOPIC: Sad Good-byes
CHILDREN'S TOPIC: It's So Hard to Say Good-bye

Witnessing to All the World

DEVOTIONAL READING: Acts 20:31-35
BACKGROUND SCRIPTURE: Acts 20:17-38
PRINT PASSAGE: Acts 20:17-28, 36-38

Acts 20:17-28, 36-38—KJV

17 And from Miletus he sent to Ephesus, and called the elders of the church.

18 And when they were come to him, he said unto them, Ye know, from the first day that I came into Asia, after what manner I have been with you at all seasons,

19 Serving the Lord with all humility of mind, and with many tears, and temptations, which befell me by the lying in wait of the Jews:

20 And how I kept back nothing that was profitable unto you, but have shown you, and have taught you publickly, and from house to house,

21 Testifying both to the Jews, and also to the Greeks, repentance toward God, and faith toward our Lord Jesus Christ.

22 And now, behold, I go bound in the spirit unto Jerusalem, not knowing the things that shall befall me there:

23 Save that the Holy Ghost witnesseth in every city, saying that bonds and afflictions abide me.

24 But none of these things move me, neither count I my life dear unto myself, so that I might finish my course with joy, and the ministry, which I have received of the Lord Jesus,

KEY VERSE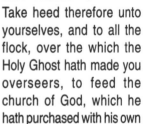

Take heed therefore unto yourselves, and to all the flock, over the which the Holy Ghost hath made you overseers, to feed the church of God, which he hath purchased with his own blood.—Acts 20:28

OBJECTIVES
After completion of this lesson, students should understand:

1. How terribly sad Paul's friends were when they said good-bye to him for the last time.

2. How to identify some of the "sad good-byes" that people experience today.

3. How to express gratitude for sources of support that can help them cope during difficult times.

to testify the gospel of the grace of God.

25 And now, behold, I know that ye all, among whom I have gone preaching the kingdom of God, shall see my face no more.

26 Wherefore I take you to record this day, that I am pure from the blood of all men.

27 For I have not shunned to declare unto you all the counsel of God.

28 Take heed therefore unto yourselves, and to all the flock, over the which the Holy Ghost hath made you overseers, to feed the church of God, which he hath purchased with his own blood.

…..

36 And when he had thus spoken, he kneeled down, and prayed with them all.

37 And they all wept sore, and fell on Paul's neck, and kissed him,

38 Sorrowing most of all for the words which he spake, that they should see his face no more. And they accompanied him unto the ship.

Acts 20:17-28, 36-38—NRSV

17 From Miletus he sent a message to Ephesus, asking the elders of the church to meet him.

18 When they came to him, he said to them: "You yourselves know how I lived among you the entire time from the first day that I set foot in Asia,

19 serving the Lord with all humility and with tears, enduring the trials that came to me through the plots of the Jews.

20 I did not shrink from doing anything helpful, proclaiming the message to you and teaching you publicly and from house to house,

21 as I testified to both Jews and Greeks about repentance toward God and faith toward our Lord Jesus.

22 And now, as a captive to the Spirit, I am on my way to Jerusalem, not knowing what will happen to me there,

23 except that the Holy Spirit testifies to me in every city that imprisonment and persecutions are waiting for me.

24 But I do not count my life of any value to myself, if only I may finish my course and the ministry that I received from the Lord Jesus, to testify to the good news of God's grace.

25 And now I know that none of you, among whom I have gone about proclaiming the kingdom, will ever see my face again.

26 Therefore I declare to you this day that I am not responsible for the blood of any of you,

27 for I did not shrink from declaring to you the whole purpose of God.

28 Keep watch over yourselves and over all the flock, of which the Holy Spirit has made you overseers, to shepherd the church of God that he obtained with the blood of his own Son."

…..

36 When he had finished speaking, he knelt down with them all and prayed.

37 There was much weeping among them all; they embraced Paul and kissed him,

38 grieving especially because of what he had said, that they would not see him again. Then they brought him to the ship.

POINTS TO BE EMPHASIZED
ADULTS
Key Verse: Acts 20:28
Print: Acts 20:17-28, 36-38

—Paul's visit to Miletus marks the end of his third missionary journey and precedes his imprisonment in Jerusalem and his transfer as a prisoner to Rome.

—Ephesus was a city filled with many religious influences, mainly pagan.

—Paul encouraged the Ephesian elders by sharing about his own call, and explaining why he had to travel to Jerusalem despite expectations of persecution.

—The Ephesian elders also encouraged Paul for the continuation of his ministry, through their presence, their tears and their love.

YOUTH
Key Verse: Acts 20:37-38
Print: Acts 20:17-28, 36-38

—Upon Paul's request, the leaders of the church in Ephesus came to meet Paul in the port of Miletus to bid him farewell.

—As a "captive to the Spirit," Paul vowed to go to Jerusalem, certain only that persecution and imprisonment lay ahead of him, because the Spirit had so informed him.

—Paul informed the Ephesian Christians that, having taught and prepared them as best he could, he must now hand over to them the responsibility for the church that had been entrusted into their hands by the Holy Spirit.

CHILDREN
Key Verse: Acts 20:37-38
Print: Acts 20:18-24, 35-38

—Giving to others is a measure of our love.

—The life of a Christian includes both working for personal and physical needs and working for the spiritual needs of others.

—Christian mission efforts can remove barriers between people from different backgrounds.

—God's universal love is extended to the rich as well as the poor.

TOPICAL OUTLINE OF THE LESSON

I. INTRODUCTION
   A. Why Bad Things Happen to Good People
   B. Biblical Background

II. EXPOSITION AND APPLICATION OF THE SCRIPTURE
   A. Facing Tribulation with Joy *(Acts 20:17-28)*
   B. Final Good-byes *(Acts 20:36-38)*

III. SPECIAL FEATURES
   A. Preserving Our Heritage
   B. Concluding Reflections

I. INTRODUCTION

A. Why Bad Things Happen to Good People

Christ is the ultimate example of what suffering is all about. In a previous lesson, we talked about the inherent humiliation of the Creator being subject to the creation—even unto death. Christ was in eternity participating in creation as the Word of God (John 1:1-3). Then He abdicated His throne and came down to suffer in our place. Thus, He has set an example of what suffering is all about.

The more difficult part to comprehend is that just as it was granted or gifted us to believe, it is also gifted us to suffer. Suffering for, with and in Christ is part of the entire package. We cannot have one without the other! Suffering is a means God sometimes uses in order to pull us closer to Jesus Christ. Remember Paul's words? "I want to know him intimately, and the power of his resurrection and the fellowship of sharing in his suffering" (Philippians 3:10). Yes, there is a camaraderie that develops as we suffer with Christ. Not only do we feel like we are not alone, but there is a sense in which we feel like we are a part of a greater network. It is in this regard that we can comfortably say, "No weapon formed against us can prosper." It is in this context that we can say, "We are more than conquerors."

Life brings its share of ups and downs, yet, as believers, we can affirm that we are more than conquerors despite the challenges we face. We must live our faith, recognizing that bad things happen—to good people, to bad people, to any people. Regardless of the situation or how bad it seems, God can churn good out of that situation. Even if it takes our lives doing so, ultimately, our eternal life in Christ gives us an opportunity to rejoice. But as we live in faith, "We know that all things work together for good for those who love God, who are called according to his purpose" (Romans 8:28, NRSV).

B. Biblical Background

Paul's newest journey was a scary one indeed. In a speech that reminds us of the last public words of Martin Luther King, Jr. on April 3, 1968, Paul said, "the Holy Spirit testifies in every city, saying that chains and tribulations await me." When a disciple of Jesus is faced with these kinds of pressures, what options does he have? This is worthy of investigation.

In Psalm 139, David does not allow too much room for negotiation. Even if we try running from God, God is still with us! God knows us and expects a relationship with us—in spite of ourselves. Paul could have tried running away from the cup that bore his name; but, like Jesus, he chose to drink of the cup with honor.

It was difficult for Paul to return to Jerusalem and face possible persecution, but it was also difficult for him to leave a group of people with whom he had cultivated great mutual love and affection. Paul had resided in Ephesus longer than any other city he visited, staying there for more than two years. His departure for Jerusalem also signaled the close of his third missionary journey. As difficult as it must have been to leave, Paul would carry with him memories of some of his greatest missionary accomplishments. The city had served as his base of operations while he spread the Gospel throughout parts of Asia. While in Ephesus, Paul planted at least three other churches—at Colossae, Laodicea and Hierapolis.

II. EXPOSITION AND APPLICATION OF THE SCRIPTURE
A. Facing Tribulation with Joy
(Acts 20:17-28)

A dark and imminent cloud had come over Paul's life and ministry. Like Jesus, who set His face toward Jerusalem, knowing full well that He was going to be killed once He arrived, Paul did likewise. And as Jesus called His disciples together for a final chat, Paul sent a message to the elders at Meletus to request their presence at his final farewell. *And when they were come to him, he said unto them, Ye know, from the first day that I came into Asia, after what manner I have been with you at all seasons.* For three years they saw his faithfulness. He was stoned, beaten, imprisoned and maligned, but he never gave up. He had some lonely moments and he met some new friends, but at all times *and in all seasons* he remained true to his calling. Indeed, the same zeal with which he practiced Judaism, and the same zeal with which he persecuted Christians, was the same zeal with which he approached the evangelical task.

Now Paul was about to move into a new and unfamiliar area—that of being on the opposite side of powerful Jews. He was no longer a Jewish power broker. He was an enemy of the Jewish religious elite: *Serving the Lord with all humility of mind, and with many tears, and temptations, which befell me by the lying in wait of the Jews.* Like Jesus, who cried when He thought about the unbelievers in Jerusalem, people saw Him and His work and still chose to disbelieve their own eyes. Paul, too, was saddened over the unbelief of those who

Pentecost was the time for an annual Jewish pilgrimage to Jerusalem. The elders of the church were appointed locally with divine authority comparable to the apostles, and Paul's account of his ministry and farewell commendation was addressed to them. The apostle's trials were spiritual tests as well as human conflicts. Humility and tears are signs of a ministry like that of Jesus. "I did not shrink" is another way of claiming apostolic boldness. The content of repentance toward God (or conversion) is, specifically, faith toward our Lord Jesus. To be captive to "the Spirit who testifies to me in every" city is to be bound by God's determined purpose in suffering rather than power. Paul's directed journey comes to a climax in the temple in Jerusalem. The journey or mission is compared to an athletic course to finish. "The ministry ...I received from the Lord Jesus" stands in contrast to Paul's earlier self-appointed mission. The elders of the congregation were entrusted with the office of overseers, and the church of God is both local and a larger spiritual reality. Paul's warning against wolves was an alert against false teachers who distort the truth.

chose not to listen to the Word of God. Paul says in Romans, "I have great sorrow and unceasing anguish in my heart. For I could wish that I myself were accursed and cut off from Christ for the sake of my own people, my kindred according to the flesh" (9:2-3, NRSV). Beyond this, Paul also had a weak spot for Christians who struggled in their faith. These were his internal sufferings. For the sake of others, he shed many tears.

At the same time, Paul had to contend with external temptations or trials that came as a result of plotting Jews (cf., 2 Corinthians 11:24, 26). They saw his shift from Judaism to Christianity as the ultimate betrayal. He was one of them; he was taught by them. Then, while on a journey to kill their Christian enemies, he became the very person that he and his Jewish fellows despised most. But even worse than becoming a disciple of Jesus of Nazareth, Paul began to assist in the conversion of others. Even more troubling to the Jews, he also taught them: *And how I kept back nothing that was profitable unto you, but have showed you, and have taught you publickly, and from house to house, Testifying both to the Jews, and also to the Greeks, repentance toward God, and faith toward our Lord Jesus Christ.* This is Paul as a teacher. He was a man of many gifts, not the least of them was his teaching ability. The gift of teaching was among the highest gifts that Paul admonishes believers to desire (1 Corinthians 12:31). However, the apostle James cautions that those who teach will be judged by a higher standard (see James 3:1).

As Paul outlined all that he had done and was doing, he humbly mentioned the end result of doing the things that he had done. The words of Martin Luther King, Jr. are reminiscent of Paul, who said, *I go bound in the spirit unto Jerusalem, not knowing the things that shall befall me there.* He had an idea of what was going to happen when he returned in his old community. The same people that he once counted as colleagues, teachers and friends were laying in wait until his arrival: *Save that the Holy Ghost witnesseth in every city, saying that bonds and afflictions abide me.* The Holy Spirit had already cautioned him. The NRSV says, "imprisonment and persecutions."

Next, Paul taught the church the correct response to tribulations. Our natural response is either revenge or to get angry that something was being done to us. After Paul outlined the many things that he had done for the sake of the ministry, and after he expressed his belief that there was a group plotting against him, Paul then says, *none of these things move me, neither count I my life dear unto myself, so that I might finish my course with joy.* Regardless of the malady—and there were many—*none of these things moved* him! This is quite a testimony. He was stoned, beaten, and tossed in prison, yet he remained unmoved.

If you are living in the will of God, count it a joy to be going through suffering.

There is a peculiar little verse in James 1:2-3 (NRSV): "My brothers and sisters, whenever you face trials of any kind, consider it nothing but joy, because you know that the testing of your faith produces endurance." James says that regardless of your situation, consider it joy. Trials are those episodes that break your pattern of peace or comfort. You are going along well, at peace with the world and comfortable with yourself. All of a sudden, oftentimes when you least expect it, something happens to break your peace. You are going along well with your husband and children, then out of nowhere your husband stops coming home. Out of nowhere your children turn to gangs and drugs to be cuddled, rather than to you. Or even worse, you turn yourself to some vice to comfort and cuddle you. In the book of Ruth, Naomi was doing well, and then tragedy came and broke her peace and comfort. She turned to bitterness. Paul took the opposite approach—he turned to joy.

B. Final Good-byes *(Acts 20:36-38)*

This is a sad and potent end. What began with Ananias being afraid to approach Paul ends with the disciples not wanting to see him go. And when he had thus spoken, he kneeled down and prayed with them all. *And they all wept sore, and fell on Paul's neck, and kissed him.* The walk to the ship must have been done in slow motion. Everyone had their own thoughts about the richness that this man of God had brought to their lives. He was a true jewel. There are many parallels between this story and the death of Jesus, the most telling being the profound sadness that we have when we experience personal loss. Even when we know that we are going to a better place, our humanity often dictates something quite contradictory. In such case, faith should transcend our personal predicament.

Sorrowing most of all for the words which he spake, that they should see his face no more. And they accompanied him unto the ship.

III. SPECIAL FEATURES
A. Preserving Our Heritage

Joy in tribulation is a tall and difficult order for anyone, but it is even more difficult to achieve when one's total existence is wrought with despair on a regular basis. In Alex Haley's *Roots: The Saga of an American Family,* probably one of the best examples of this can be found. Kunta Kinte's daughter, Kizzy, was sold away when it was discovered that she wrote the pass to aid her boyfriend's escape. The result of her "wrong" was to sell her off to another plantation farther south. She never saw her parents alive again.

Like so many enslaved Blacks, the overwhelming grief and loss that Kunta and his wife and family experienced is possibly the most painful that a human being can endure. The pain associated with the loss of a child is crippling.

The African American community is no stranger to grief and loss. In recent times, families have experienced fragmentation resulting from the structure of our welfare system—which enables and supports female-headed households, or from gang and drug violence—which have sent many sons and fathers to jail or to the grave. Our task is to work to eradicate these conditions that produce unnecessary painful good-byes.

A gospel song popular in many Black churches a few decades ago was, "There's a Bright Side Somewhere." The song encouraged the neverending search of the faithful to look to all of life's circumstances through the eyes of hope. Through all of our difficult times as a people, the Black Christian community has always searched for the bright side of life.

B. Concluding Reflections

Good-byes are often difficult and heart-wrenching. The few special and loving relationships we are blessed to have in a lifetime are painful to lose. Usually, we lose such relationships to death, divorce, departure, or disagreement.

When we know for certain that a good-bye is final, such as death, it brings on a special kind of grief. Knowing this, we should be especially careful to honor our relationships. We should treat our church leaders with honor and respect because they invest themselves in us for the sake of our own spiritual edification.

HOME DAILY BIBLE READINGS

for the week of November 27, 2005
Paul's Farewell

Nov. 21, Monday
—Ruth 1:6-14
—Naomi and Ruth Part with Orpah
Nov. 22, Tuesday
—1 Samuel 20:32-42
—David and Jonathan Part
Nov. 23, Wednesday
—Acts 20:1-6
—Paul Stops in Greece and Macedonia
Nov. 24, Thursday
—Acts 20:7-12
—Paul's Farewell Visit to Troas
Nov. 25, Friday
—Acts 20:17-24
—Paul Speaks to the Ephesian Elders
Nov. 26, Saturday
—Acts 20:25-31
—Paul Warns Elders to Be Alert
Nov. 27, Sunday
—Acts 20:32-38
—Paul and the Elders Say Good-bye

PRAYER

Eternal God, as we face the crises of living in a world of changing relationships, may we embrace the faith that the transient will be replaced by the eternal and that we will be united in a world not made with hands, but eternal in heaven. Amen.

God's Commitment—Our Response

GENERAL INTRODUCTION

This quarter consists of three units that are structured to explore the redeeming acts of God and some appropriate responses that move Christians toward spiritual wholeness.

Unit I, *God's Redeeming Love,* has four lessons. The first two are based on passages from Isaiah, while the last two focus on passages from both Isaiah and Luke. These lessons explore how God brings justice to the world, strengthens a weary people, offers hope to those who suffer, and brings the Good News to all people of the earth. The final lesson, which is set on Christmas Day, explores how Christians experience God's redeeming love in the birth of Jesus Christ. This unit affords opportunities to discuss the role of the church in seeking justice for all persons, including those whose vision of justice is not consistent with the ministry of Jesus. Christians can exchange experiences on how strength is gained through dedicating quiet time with God that is enhanced by mutual support from the faith community. Opportunity is provided for interaction with the fact that the image of the Suffering Servant implies our suffering in solidarity with the poor and hungry that will accrue to their greater welfare. The point is that God identifies Himself with those who are despised by society, but exalted by God. We must open ourselves to the belief that sharing the Good News of Jesus Christ enables all who embrace it to achieve a better quality of life. We must not forget that retelling the story of the coming of Christ into the world invigorates our faith as we identify with that which God has accomplished through His love.

Unit II, *God's Gifts of Leadership,* consists of five lessons based on First Timothy, a letter that shows how the apostle Paul worked with this young pastor. Paul puts forth instruction for a number of goals and tasks: relying on God for strength, praying, answering one's call, teaching, and working for justice and mercy. Each lesson shows how the development of the gift for leadership is part of our faithful response to the love of God. The unit encourages our understanding of the strength that comes from God in the process of carrying out His will. This is cause to thank God for those successes that we accomplish in His name. In a society that is self-absorbed, we should not forget to pray for others as members of the community of faith, as well as those who are invested with authority to manage the affairs of society. Prayer affects the person who prays as well as those for whom we pray. The leadership prerequisites of those who are appointed or elected to take responsible positions within the church of Jesus Christ are detailed for discussion—such persons deserve our respect and admiration. We must understand when leadership grows ineffective or makes appropriate evaluation that is not consistent with biblical principles. In our day, vibrant teaching must exist in the creative tension between novelty and traditionalism. No one is excluded from the necessity to act for both justice and mercy within and beyond the community of faith. As much as lies within our power, believers should treat one another with the respect that is accorded to them as members of the human family.

Unit III, *Faithful Followers, Faithful Leaders,* has four lessons based on passages from Second Timothy and from Titus. They are designed to encourage all members of the faith community to be true to our Christian heritage, to develop Christian character, to follow a Christian mentor, and to live and teach the truth. All of these goals are part of our faithful response to God's redeeming acts of love. The unit provides the opportunity for believers to assist others in the development of latent gifts that need to be stirred into action. Consistent with the insights of Paul, faith is often instilled by family elders or other older adults that have the effect of bringing others into the community of faith. While there is a difference between one's posture of faith that may be inconsistent with the beliefs of others, Christian leaders should not participate in senseless controversies that will not result in faith confirmation, but should exercise control over the words that they speak. One's action can invalidate the words that are implored to support one's point of view. In this case, the Word of God is the essential guideline—with emphasis placed upon exemplary Christian behavior. The point is that Christian discipleship means living a life that others can emulate, as personal examples provide instruction for faithful discipleship. As actions validate commitment to the faith, leaders merit the obligation for others to listen to the doctrine that they proclaim in the name of Christ.

Lesson 1

Justice for All

ADULT TOPIC: Serving Others
YOUTH TOPIC: God's Servant Messiah
CHILDREN'S TOPIC: An Angel Visits Zechariah

UNIT I
God's Redeeming Love

CHILDREN'S UNIT
The Gift of Jesus

DEVOTIONAL READING: Isaiah 41:8-13
BACKGROUND SCRIPTURE: Isaiah 41—42
PRINT PASSAGE: Isaiah 42:1-8

Isaiah 42:1-8—KJV

BEHOLD MY servant, whom I uphold; mine elect, in whom my soul delighteth; I have put my spirit upon him: he shall bring forth judgment to the Gentiles.

2 He shall not cry, nor lift up, nor cause his voice to be heard in the street.

3 A bruised reed shall he not break, and the smoking flax shall he not quench: he shall bring forth judgment unto truth.

4 He shall not fail nor be discouraged, till he have set judgment in the earth: and the isles shall wait for his law.

5 Thus saith God the LORD, he that created the heavens, and stretched them out; he that spread forth the earth, and that which cometh out of it; he that giveth breath unto the people upon it, and spirit to them that walk therein:

6 I the LORD have called thee in righteousness, and will hold thine hand, and will keep thee, and give thee for a covenant of the people, for a light of the Gentiles;

7 To open the blind eyes, to bring out the prisoners from the prison, and them that sit in darkness out of the prison house.

8 I am the LORD: that is my name: and my glory will I not give to another, neither my praise to graven images.

KEY VERSE

I the LORD have called thee in righteousness, and will hold thine hand, and will keep thee, and give thee for a covenant of the people, for a light of the Gentiles. —Isaiah 42:6

OBJECTIVES

Upon the completion of this lesson, students should know that:

1. God keeps His Word.
2. God deals justly with all people.
3. God calls for His people to be just in their dealings with others irrespective of age, race, or class.
4. The Messiah is God's instrument to bring salvation and justice to all mankind.

Isaiah 42:1-8—NRSV

HERE IS my servant, whom I uphold, my chosen, in whom my soul delights; I have put my spirit upon him; he will bring forth justice to the nations.

2 He will not cry or lift up his voice, or make it heard in the street;

3 a bruised reed he will not break, and a dimly burning wick he will not quench; he will faithfully bring forth justice.

4 He will not grow faint or be crushed until he has established justice in the earth; and the coastlands wait for his teaching.

5 Thus says God, the LORD, who created the heavens and stretched them out, who spread out the earth and what comes from it, who gives breath to the people upon it and spirit to those who walk in it:

6 I am the LORD, I have called you in righteousness, I have taken you by the hand and kept you; I have given you as a covenant to the people, a light to the nations,

7 to open the eyes that are blind, to bring out the prisoners from the dungeon, from the prison those who sit in darkness.

8 I am the LORD, that is my name; my glory I give to no other, nor my praise to idols.

POINTS TO BE EMPHASIZED
ADULTS

Key Verse: Isaiah 42:6

Print: Isaiah 42:1-8

—The early church saw Jesus in Isaiah's image of the suffering servant.

—Justice is established by the service of the strong for the sake of the weak, not by force.

—God's justice includes all people.

YOUTH

Key Verse: Isaiah 42:1

Print: Isaiah 42:1-8

—God values each person and calls all people to serve.

—God speaks through Isaiah to a defeated people in exile.

—God promised to send a servant messiah to bring justice for the oppressed.

—God renewed the covenant with the people to bring light and freedom to the nations.

CHILDREN

Key Verse: Luke 1:13b

Print: Isaiah 40:3; Luke 1:13-24

—Zechariah and Elizabeth's prayer was answered, and it fulfilled God's purpose for them.

—Disobedience and not believing in God's purpose for us sometimes prevents us from living up to our potential.

—God gives us opportunities to prove our faithfulness and obedience.

—Angels are used as God's messengers.

TOPICAL OUTLINE OF THE LESSON

I. INTRODUCTION

    A. Chosen for a Purpose

    B. Biblical Background

II. EXPOSITION AND APPLICATION
OF THE SCRIPTURE
  A. The Servant's Mission
     (Isaiah 42:1)
  B. The Servant's Method
     (Isaiah 42:2-3)
  C. The Servant's Commitment
     (Isaiah 42:4)
  D. The Servant's Master
     (Isaiah 42:5-8)

III. SPECIAL FEATURES
  A. Preserving Our Heritage
  B. Concluding Reflections

I. INTRODUCTION
A. Chosen for a Purpose

God chose Israel to be His people and His instrument for bringing salvation to humanity. As such, they are often referred to in the Bible as "My Servant." However, instead of behaving as true servants of God, they deserted and forsook Him. Israel's failure, however, did not thwart God's plan to bring justice to all humankind. God sent His Son as Messiah, whom He also referred to as "My Servant," who would accomplish for Him what Israel had failed to do.

It should be noted that God has acquitted Himself from any possible charges of being unjust for choosing Israel, rather than the Gentiles, as His instrument. In spite of Israel's unfaithfulness, God sent His Son as Savior—not only of Israel, but of the entire world. In this lesson, we hear the prophet Isaiah extolling the virtues of the Servant who is to bring about God's salvation.

B. Biblical Background

The theme of the book of Isaiah is expressed in the meaning of the name Isaiah—"the Lord saves" or "the Lord is Savior." The book of Isaiah may be divided into two main sections. The first section, chapters 1-39, speaks of God's judgment that would come upon Judah because of her failure to follow the Mosaic Covenant. God's punishment would prove that He fulfills His Word. Despite their punishment, the prophet emphasized that blessings would eventually come because of Israel's covenantal relationship with the Lord. The second section of the book (Deutero-Isaiah), chapters 40-66, focuses upon the blessings coming to God's people.

The prophecies of deliverance found in the first section were local and temporary in nature. These belonged to the distant future, and were worldwide in their interest. Their deliverance under Cyrus, which Isaiah here foretells by prophetic suggestion, carried them on to the greater deliverance under the Messiah, the Savior of the Jews and Gentiles, and the restorer of Israel and Head of the worldwide kingdom, both literal and spiritual.

Assyria was the hostile power in the first section, which refers to Isaiah's own time. Babylon served as the hostile power in the second, which refers to a subsequent period. At this point in the text, Judah is seen under captivity in Babylon, and the city of Jerusalem is in ruins.

God chose the prophets and used them to communicate divine messages of warning, judgment and deliverance. When

God's people failed to heed the warnings and the exhortations to repent and return to Him, God executed judgment. Nevertheless, even in judgment God gave them hope. He reminded them of His covenantal promises with Abraham and sent them messages of deliverance. The deliverance He promised was twofold. First, they would receive actual and historical deliverance from their earthly enemies. This deliverance would, however, prove to be only temporary, as they would resort back into their practice of forsaking Him for other gods, prompting judgment once again. Total and final deliverance would come in the person of the Messiah, referred to as "My Servant."

The book of Isaiah, as is often pointed out, is like a miniature Bible. The first thirty-nine chapters (like the thirty-nine books of the Old Testament) are filled with judgment upon an immoral and idolatrous people. God's people, Judah, had sinned; the surrounding nations had sinned; the whole earth had sinned. Judgment had to come, for God could not allow such blatant sin to go unpunished forever. The final twenty-seven chapters (like the twenty-seven books of the New Testament) declare a message of hope. The Messiah would come as a Savior to bear a cross and to wear a crown for the redemption of all humanity.

Isaiah 42:1-8 is the first of Isaiah's "Servant Songs" referring to the Messiah. Inasmuch as Isaiah refers to Israel as the "Servant of the Lord" (41:8; 42:19; 43:10; 44:1-2, 21; 45:4; 48:20) and the Messiah by the same title (cf., 49:3, 5-7; 50:10; 52:13; 53:11), the Servant to which Isaiah was referring in each passage must be determined by the context and the characteristic assigned to the servant. In some cases, the Servant is Israel; at other times, it is the Messiah.

In studying the lesson, it must be borne in mind that God's Servant, Israel, was supposed to help bring the world to the knowledge of God, but she failed. So the Messiah, the Lord's Servant, who would epitomize the nation of Israel, would take on the challenge and—motivated by love for humanity and obedience to the Father—fulfill God's will.

II. EXPOSITION AND APPLICATION OF THE SCRIPTURE

A. The Servant's Mission
(Isaiah 42:1)

The first verse tells us that the mission of the Servant would be to *bring forth justice,* not only to Israel, but also to *the nations (Gentiles).* Previously, the revelation of God's justice was given to the Jews only. The *justice* to be ushered in by the *Servant* would not be limited to the Jews only, but would be extended to all *the nations* also. And so it must be with those of us who claim to be believers; we, too, are charged with the duty of extending and ensuring *justice* to all, without regard to race, gender, rank, or nationality.

The verse begins with God exhorting the saints of old, and us, the saints of the present, to *Behold.* The definition of behold extends beyond a mandate to simply "see"; rather, it implies an emphatic command to investigate with serious consideration. In so doing, we are to take note of the relationship that the Servant had with the Father. Although He was God incarnate (cf., John 1:1), He humbled Himself by taking on the form of a servant. As a Servant, He modeled obedience to the will of the Father as He practiced it. Therefore, our confession of Him as Lord should lead us to follow His example. Irrespective of our life situation, we, too, should become servants seeking to obey God and advance His kingdom. Such an attitude of servanthood moves God to place honor upon God's people by calling them *My servant.*

God's reference to the Servant as *mine elect* affirms that He was chosen by God. He did not enter into this work by His own initiation; He was chosen and appointed by God for the task. And so it must be for all who desire to be called servants of God. We, too, must wait for God's calling and leading before attempting to do a work for God. When we wait for God's call, rather than proceeding on our own, then we have the assurance that God will *uphold (tamak,* support) us and strengthen us for the task. God's soul will take *delight (ratsa,* take pleasure) in our going and coming. As God's chosen servants, we can be confident in the knowledge that God's Spirit is in us. In the Old Testament, His Spirit is was placed *upon* His servants; but those of us under the New Covenant have the more blessed assurance that, in this dispensation, He has placed His Spirit *in* us (cf., 1 Corinthians 6:19).

B. The Servant's Method
(Isaiah 42:2-3)

He shall not cry, nor lift up, nor cause his voice to be heard in the street. This is a description of the manner in which the Servant will carry out His mission. Quietness, humility, meekness and anonymity characterized Jesus' ministry. On several occasions, He admonished those whom He healed not to tell anyone by whom they had received healing (Matthew 8:4; 9:30). His methods differed from the self-proclaimed "faith-healers" and televangelists of our day who bring attention to themselves with great fanfare, and make frequent appeals for financial support. The Servant did not come to town in a parade preceded by noisy retinues.

A bruised reed shall he not break, and the smoking flax shall he not quench: he shall bring forth judgment unto truth. This is a reference to how the Servant will respond to the feeble and fragile, as well as how He will respond to those who are violent in their opposition. He is tender with those who are easily broken and patient with those who are hostile and violent. The Servant patiently "endured the contradiction of sinners against himself" (Hebrews 12:3). How instructive it is for us today, we who are so eager to contradict, confront and condemn those who do not share our beliefs.

He shall bring forth judgment unto truth, is perhaps a reference to the *judicial* aspect of the Servant at His second coming. His mild-mannered method at His first coming was manifested to reveal *truth,* but in His second appearance, it will be to reveal *judgment.* The word *judgment* may be translated as *justice.* The idea is that the triumph of truth is God's *judgment* or justice. As God's servants today, we also must administer both justice and truth to all—for where there is no judgment, truth loses its effect and becomes merely good advice.

C. The Servant's Commitment
(Isaiah 42:4)

He shall not fail nor be discouraged. The word *fail* means "to faint and become like the flax, almost extinguished." The word *discouraged* means "to be broken," that is, loss of zeal. In other words, "He will not be too slow on the one hand, nor run too hastily on the other," *till he have set judgment in the earth: and the isles shall wait for his law.* God's Law was given to the entire world, not simply to the Jews. His Law, if faithfully established and adhered to, will ensure justice for all humanity, even those in the remotest parts of the earth.

Matthew 12:18-21 quotes Isaiah 42:1-4 with some minor variations, relating it to Jesus and His ministry in Israel. As God's Servant, Jesus did what Israel could never do: He perfectly carried out the will of the Father so that people everywhere may believe in the Holy One of Israel.

Unlike many today that become discouraged in the face of ambivalence and opposition and easily give up or quit the race, the Servant would stay the course with absolute determination, enduring the shame and being obedient to the Father, even to His death on the cross.

D. The Servant's Master
(Isaiah 42:5-8)

Thus says God the Lord. The Servant's Master is here identified as no less than the Lord God Himself...*he that created the heavens, and stretched them out; he that spread forth the earth, and that which cometh out of it.* Reference, here, is made to the creation of the heavens and the earth and God as the Creator (Genesis 1) *that giveth breath unto the people upon it, and spirit to them that walk therein.* God offers, as a part of His credentials, the creation of humanity. In so doing, we are reminded that God's creation of humankind included the pivotal moment when God "breathed into his nostrils the breath of life" (Genesis 2:7).

It should be understood that what God breathed into Adam was "spirit." This made humans spiritual beings with a capacity for serving and fellowshiping with God. It is a reaffirmation of God creating humankind in God's own image (Genesis 1:27). It should be remembered that God is Spirit and that humans are created in God's likeness, as spiritual beings.

I the LORD have called thee in righteousness, and will hold thine hand. To be called in *righteousness* means to be held responsible for doing God's righteous will. The Servant was promised that God would empower the Servant to carry out God's will by holding Him by the hand. One who is called to be a servant of God must remember that, ultimately, the calling is to execute the righteous will of God. We can only expect to be empowered by God and held by God's mighty hand when we are faithful to God's righteous cause. Further, God promises the Servant that He *will keep thee, and give thee for a covenant of the people, for a light of the Gentiles.* The Servant would fulfill God's covenant promises to Israel, and would also be a light to the Gentiles. God's commitment *to open the blind eyes* meant that spiritually unredeemed Israel and the Gentiles were blind to God's Word. They were not able to see it clearly; therefore, they were incapable of understanding and responding to it with obedience. God's reason for giving them spiritual sight would be *to bring out the prisoners from the prison, and them that sit in darkness out of the prison house.* This is a reference first to the Jewish captivity, a promise that God would free them from exile, which God accomplished through King Cyrus. However, the promise speaks more prominently to the spiritual release (cf., Isaiah 61:1; John 8:32), sight (cf., John 9:39-41) and light (cf., John 8:12) that would be given to those who trust God. This spiritual salvation to both Jews and Gentiles would result in the glorious messianic Kingdom.

III. SPECIAL FEATURES
A. Preserving Our Heritage

Ever since the revolution of the 1960s era, there have been many accusations and indictments in the African American community against the Bible, the church and even God and His sent Messiah. These charges generally promoted the idea that Christianity is a "White man's religion" that had no salvation to offer people of color. For that reason, it was to be rejected by all African Americans who wanted to be true to their heritage. These indictments were given credence because of racist Whites who erringly twisted the Scriptures to support their self-serving agenda—everything from slavery to segregation to poverty.

It is of utmost importance, however, that those of us charged with the responsibility of teaching in the National Baptist arena be diligent in pointing out the errors of such biblical interpretations. We should use this lesson and others to demonstrate that in the church of the Lord Jesus Christ, *"There is neither Jew nor Gentile, neither bond nor free, neither male nor female, but we are all one in Christ Jesus"* (Galatians 3:28).

We must take care to point out that there is one true God, and He is a God of equality and justice for all peoples, regardless of nationality, gender, race, or color.

B. Concluding Reflections

The current strife in the Middle East between Jews and Arabs is often interpreted in a way that calls for blind loyalty to the Jews and Israel, as they are God's chosen people. Such interpretations insist that we adopt an attitude of "Israel, right or wrong!" They seem to forget or ignore the fact that the justice of God is such that His very character demands justice for all. Therefore, He will not ignore or bless injustices done by any—even if it is done in His name. In keeping with His moral character of justice, we, the members of His household of faith, must likewise demand that justice be done to both Arabs and Jews alike.

HOME DAILY BIBLE READINGS

for the week of December 4, 2005
Justice for All

Nov. 28, Monday
—Isaiah 41:1-7
—An Eastern Victor Is Roused
Nov. 29, Tuesday
—Isaiah 41:8-13
—God Will Strengthen Israel
Nov. 30, Wednesday
—Isaiah 41:14-20
—God Will Care for the People
Dec. 1, Thursday
—Isaiah 41:21-29
—God Is Greater than Babylon's Deities
Dec. 2, Friday
—Isaiah 42:1-9
—My Servant Will Bring Forth Justice
Dec. 3, Saturday
—Isaiah 42:10-17
—Sing Praise to God
Dec. 4, Sunday
—Isaiah 42:18-25
—Blind and Deaf to God's Instruction

PRAYER

Gracious, merciful God our Father, we praise You for being a God who metes out mercy and justice to all peoples. Thank You for Your Son who made it possible for us to stand before You as saints rather than as the sinners we surely are. Amen.

Lesson 2

Strength for the Weary

ADULT TOPIC: Strength from God
YOUTH TOPIC: Power Aid
CHILDREN'S TOPIC: An Angel Visits Mary

UNIT I
God's Redeeming Love

CHILDREN'S UNIT
The Gift of Jesus

DEVOTIONAL READING: Isaiah 49:7-13
BACKGROUND SCRIPTURE: Isaiah 49—50
PRINT PASSAGE: Isaiah 49:5-6; 50:4-9

Isaiah 49:5-6; 50:4-9—KJV

5 And now, saith the LORD that formed me from the womb to be his servant, to bring Jacob again to him, Though Israel be not gathered, yet shall I be glorious in the eyes of the LORD, and my God shall be my strength.

6 And he said, It is a light thing that thou shouldest be my servant to raise up the tribes of Jacob, and to restore the preserved of Israel: I will also give thee for a light to the Gentiles, that thou mayest be my salvation unto the end of the earth.

.....

4 The Lord GOD hath given me the tongue of the learned, that I should know how to speak a word in season to him that is weary: he wakeneth morning by morning, he wakeneth mine ear to hear as the learned.

5 The Lord GOD hath opened mine ear, and I was not rebellious, neither turned away back.

6 I gave my back to the smiters, and my cheeks to them that plucked off the hair: I hid not my face from shame and spitting.

KEY VERSE

For the Lord GOD will help me; therefore shall I not be confounded: therefore have I set my face like a flint, and I know that I shall not be ashamed.
—Isaiah 50:7

OBJECTIVES

After completing this lesson, students should affirm that:

1. God's love and strength are both made manifest in God's Son.
2. God's people may also be called upon to demonstrate His love by enduring sufferings and persecutions on behalf of others.
3. Those who suffer are assured of the power of God's love to sustain and strengthen them in their struggles.

7 For the Lord God will help me; therefore shall I not be confounded: therefore have I set my face like a flint, and I know that I shall not be ashamed.

8 He is near that justifieth me; who will contend with me? let us stand together: who is mine adversary? let him come near to me.

9 Behold, the Lord God will help me; who is he that shall condemn me? lo, they all shall wax old as a garment; the moth shall eat them up.

Isaiah 49:5-6; 50:4-9—NRSV

5 And now the Lord says, who formed me in the womb to be his servant, to bring Jacob back to him, and that Israel might be gathered to him, for I am honored in the sight of the Lord, and my God has become my strength—

6 he says, "It is too light a thing that you should be my servant to raise up the tribes of Jacob and to restore the survivors of Israel; I will give you as a light to the nations, that my salvation may reach to the end of the earth."

.....

4 The Lord God has given me the tongue of a teacher, that I may know how to sustain the weary with a word. Morning by morning he wakens—wakens my ear to listen as those who are taught.

5 The Lord God has opened my ear, and I was not rebellious, I did not turn backward.

6 I gave my back to those who struck me, and my cheeks to those who pulled out the beard; I did not hide my face from insult and spitting.

7 The Lord God helps me; therefore I have not been disgraced; therefore I have set my face like flint, and I know that I shall not be put to shame;

8 he who vindicates me is near. Who will contend with me? Let us stand up together. Who are my adversaries? Let them confront me.

9 It is the Lord God who helps me; who will declare me guilty? All of them will wear out like a garment; the moth will eat them up.

POINTS TO BE EMPHASIZED
ADULTS
Key Verse: Isaiah 50:7
Print: Isaiah 49:5-6; 50:4-9
—The Servant recognized that God had created Him for a purpose.
—The Servant listened for the Word of God, and He responded with obedience and trust.
—In difficult times, the Servant discovered that God provided strength and encouragement.

YOUTH
Key Verse: Isaiah 49:5
Print: Isaiah 49:5-6; 50:4-9
—God's desire is that everyone be saved.
—God formed the Servant Messiah to restore the nation of Israel and to bring salvation to the Gentile nations.
—God empowered the Servant Messiah to teach and sustain the weary.

—God has made the Servant obedient and enabled Him to be faithful in the midst of difficult times.

CHILDREN
Key Verse: Luke 1:30
Print: Isaiah 49:8; Luke 1:26-33
—Jesus was born in fulfillment of God's promise to send a Redeemer to save us from eternal damnation.
—God always keeps His promises.
—God always finds a way to use those who are faithful, despite their youth.
—God may select individual persons for service before their birth.

TOPICAL OUTLINE OF THE LESSON

I. INTRODUCTION
   A. The Servant Identified
   B. Biblical Background

II. EXPOSITION AND APPLICATION OF THE SCRIPTURE
   A. Messiah Sent First to Restore Israel *(Isaiah 49:5)*
   B. Messiah Sent as a Light to Gentiles *(Isaiah 49:6)*
   C. The Servant Is Equipped by God *(Isaiah 50:4)*
   D. The Servant Submits His Mind to God *(Isaiah 50:5)*
   E. The Servant Submits His Will to God *(Isaiah 50:6)*
   F. The Servant Receives His Strength from God *(Isaiah 50:7)*
   G. The Servant Is Justified by God *(Isaiah 50:8-9)*

III. SPECIAL FEATURES
   A. Preserving Our Heritage
   B. Concluding Reflections

I. INTRODUCTION
A. The Servant Identified

This lesson is about Jesus, the true Servant of God, and how God would strengthen Him for the assignment. Herein, we are to glean that God calls all of us to become servants with the assurance that He will supply us with the strength needed. The fact that, here, Jesus is referred to as "Servant" may seem out of place among all the splendiferous titles which Isaiah gave Him: "The Holy One" "The Redeemer," "The Sovereign Lord" and "The Everlasting God." The contrast between these images of the Sovereign Lord, acting in power, and His image of the Servant, suffering for others, was indeed puzzling to the Old Testament saints. But now, in Jesus, we at last understand the unity of God's plan. Jesus suffered, but will return in glory. And, in Isaiah's vision of a Suffering Servant, we see our Lord more clearly—and we better understand our calling to be servants also.

B. Biblical Background

Isaiah 40–66 is often called the "New Testament section" of the book. It has twenty-seven chapters in it, similar to the twenty-seven books of the New Testament, and its emphasis is Christ and salvation. It begins with the ministry of John the Baptist (40:3-4 with Matthew 3:1-3) and its emphasis is Christ and salvation. At the very heart of this section is chapter

53, the strongest Old Testament prophecy of Christ's death on the cross. While Isaiah 1–39 emphasizes God's judgment on His people, Isaiah 40–66 sounds a note of comfort and redemption. It was written to encourage the Jewish remnant that they would be delivered from the Babylonians after their seventy years of captivity. Yet, Isaiah wrote this amazing prophecy over 150 years before the remnants would ever need it for their encouragement.

As you read these chapters, several major ideas will stand out. The first is the constant emphasis, "Fear not" (see 41:10, 13-14; 43:1, 5; 44:2, 8). Of what were the Jews afraid? They feared the great Gentile nations that were moving in conquest across the land. Israel had been taken by Assyria; Judah had been captured by Babylon, and by this time a new empire—the Persians—was emerging on the scene. Worse, all these nations worshiped idols. "If these nations are so victorious," some of the Jews argued, "then their gods must be the true gods, and Jehovah cannot be trusted." This leads to the second major idea: the greatness of God and the falseness of the heathen idols. Read carefully 40:18-20; 41:6-7, 29; 42:8, 17; 43:10-12; 44:9-20 (a scathing exposure of the stupidity of idol worship); 45:16, 20; 46:1-2, 5-7. Please note the repeated statement that God is true and there is no other god to be compared with Him (40:18, 25; 43:10-11; 44:6, 8; 45:5-6, 14). In each of these chapters, Isaiah exposes the folly of idols and exalts the greatness of Jehovah.

As you read these chapters, keep in mind that they had immediate fulfillment in Cyrus and the return of the remnant from Babylon, and ultimate fulfillment in Jesus Christ and the redemption we all have in Him. The remnant's deliverance from Babylon is a picture of the redemption that Christ purchased for us on the Cross. King Cyrus, though a heathen ruler, is in this sense a picture of Christ, our Redeemer (45:1-4). Isaiah 42:1-9 presents Christ as God's obedient Servant, bringing glory to the Jews and salvation to the Gentiles. (Compare these verses with Matthew 12:18-20.)

II. EXPOSITION AND APPLICATION OF THE SCRIPTURE

A. Messiah Sent First to Restore Israel *(Isaiah 49:5)*

Jesus, the great Author and Finisher of our faith, knew very well that God had *formed him from the womb to be his servant,* and had begun early to prepare Him for it. This indicates that those whom God designs to employ as His servants are fashioned and prepared to be so, long before they themselves or others are aware of it. It is for this reason that those of us who are called ought not to speak of "when we were called"; but, rather, more appropriately, we should speak of when we "responded to the call." God forms the human spirit within Him. Christ was to be *his servant, to bring Jacob again to him,* that had treacherously departed from Him. The seed of Jacob, therefore, according to the flesh, would first be dealt with, along with the means established to bring them back. Christ and the word of salvation was therefore sent first to them. Christ would come in person to them only, *to the lost sheep of the house of Israel* (Matthew 10:6). But what if Jacob would not be brought back to God and Israel would not be gathered? It is shown here that even if that were the case, *Christ will be glorious in the eyes of the Lord.* Though few of the Jewish nation were converted by Christ's preaching and miracles, and many of them loaded Him with ignominy and disgrace, God put honor upon Him and made Him glorious—at His baptism, and in His transfiguration—spoke to Him from heaven, sent angels to minister to Him, and made even His shameful death glorious by the many prodigies that attended it, much more His resurrection.

B. Messiah Sent as a Light to Gentiles *(Isaiah 49:6)*

The Lord God addressed the Servant and said, *It is a light thing that thou shouldst be my servant, to raise up the tribes of Jacob* to the dignity and dominion they would expect by the Messiah, and to *restore the preserved of Israel,* and make them a flourishing nation and state. Considering what a handful of people the Israelites were, it would be but a small matter, in comparison, for the Messiah to be the Savior of them only; and therefore *I will give thee for a light to the Gentiles* (many great and mighty nations by the Gospel of Christ shall be brought to the knowledge and worship of the true God), *that thou mayest be my salvation,* the Author of that salvation which I have designed for lost humankind— *To the end of the earth,* to nations at the greatest distance. Hence, Simeon learned to call Christ *a light to lighten the Gentiles* (Luke 2:32), and Paul's exposition of this text is what we ought to abide by, as it serves as a key to the context (Acts 13:47). *Therefore,* says he, we turn to the Gentiles, to preach the Gospel to them, *because so has the Lord commanded us, saying, I have set thee to be a light to the Gentiles.*

Israel's servant mission will reach beyond the survivors of the former Israel, and will bring light (salvation) to the nations. The task of restoring the tribes of Jacob consists of establishing the land, apportioning the desolate heritage, and releasing the prisoners. Exiles will be able to return. Syene (perhaps southern Egypt) is an example of the distant locations to which the people had fled. The apparent impossibility of the promised restoration of the ruined city is now possible, due to the compassion and love that God has for it. What might sometimes rarely be possible in human terms—that a human tyrant may set his captives free—is possible with God. The questions posed at the beginning of chapter 50 highlight the need for choice between a positive, believing response and an unbelieving rejection; the contrast is between the submissive and obedient servant, and the mocking and insolent rebels. The prophet contrasts those who seek light (salvation) in order to walk by it, and those who use torches (firebrands) to kindle destruction for a similar use of the picture of light becoming fire.

C. The Servant Is Equipped by God
(Isaiah 50:4)

The Servant begins here to speak of how God has equipped Him for the task: *The Lord God has given Me.* Whom God sends, He also equips. *The tongue of the learned.* God Himself has taught the Servant His true message that will be readily recognized by the so-called "learned." When Jesus had finished giving the Beatitudes, *He taught them as one having authority* (Matthew 7:29). *That I should know how to speak a word in season to him who is weary.* God gave Moses the tongue of the learned to speak against the terror and conviction of Pharaoh (Exodus 4:11-12). He gave to Christ the tongue of the learned, to speak a word in season for the comfort of those that are weary and heavily laden under the burden of sin (Matthew 11:28). Grace was poured into His lips, and they are said to drop sweet-smelling myrrh. Indeed, one of the best attributes of a minister is to know how to comfort troubled consciences, and to speak pertinently, properly and plainly to the various cases of poor souls. An ability to do this is God's gift, and it is one of the best gifts, which we who do ministry should covet earnestly.

D. The Servant Submits His Mind to God *(Isaiah 50:5)*

The Lord God has opened my ear, and I was not rebellious. The Servant acknowledged the faithfulness of God in awaking Him freshly, but also, His willingness to receive instruction. Our case calls for continual, fresh supplies of divine grace to free us from the dullness we contract daily. The morning, when our spirits are most lively, is a proper time for communion with God. The Servant rejoiced that the Lord God had not only wakened His ear to hear, but opened His ear to receive that instruction, and comply with it. *Nor did I turn away* implies that the Servant submitted His mind to God, as a willing humble student, even though the instruction He received for His ministry involved a great deal of difficulty and discouragement. Even though He was called to divest Himself of His majesty and submit Himself to that which was very mean, yet He did not complain.

It is instructional for us to open our ears continually and attentively to the instructions of God for the task to which He has called us. We must take pains to be sure that what we have heard is truly from God, and then go to great lengths to make sure that we clearly understand what we have been instructed to do.

E. The Servant Submits His Will to God *(Isaiah 50:6)*

This verse speaks prophetically of the humiliation and suffering the Servant endured on the night before His crucifixion: *I gave my back to those who struck me—* He submitted to the pain and indignity of being whipped (cf., Matthew 27:30); *and my cheeks to those who plucked out the beard—* which was a greater degree both of pain and of ignominy. *I hid not my face from shame and spitting.* To be spat upon was an expression not only of contempt, but also of abhorrence and indignation. The Servant did not turn His face nor seek to avoid it. All this Christ underwent for us, and voluntarily, to convince us of His willingness to save us. Although we are not called to suffer physically (that is, we are not called to be physically beaten as He was), nevertheless, we are called to suffer, and such suffering may involve indignities.

F. The Servant Receives His Strength from God *(Isaiah 50:7)*

The Servant is able to endure the suffering, pain and shame because He was certain *the Lord God will help me.* He was confident that the Lord would give Him the strength, both physically and emotionally, to persevere. Those whom God employs He will assist and will take care to ensure that they confidently receive the help that they or their work requires. Not only will He assist Him in His work, but He will fully accept Him. *Therefore I will not be disgraced.* The Servant knew that He would be falsely accused and put to shame, but He would remain steadfast. *Therefore I have set my face like flint.* The words "like a flint" are used with reference to the hoofs of horses (cf., Isaiah 5:28). This expression is used here and in Ezekiel 3:9 to indicate that the Messiah would be firm and resolute amid all contempt and scorn which He would meet. He had made up His mind to endure it and would not shrink from any kind or degree of suffering necessary to accomplish the great work in which He was engaged.

G. The Servant Is Justified by God *(Isaiah 50:8-9)*

He is near who justifies me. The Servant was confident of being in the will of God, and therefore in the right, as against all the slanderers and foes. The word *justify* (Hebrew, *sadaq*) is a forensic term meaning "acquit," "declare righteous"—the opposite of "condemn." In Scripture, God is "the Judge of all the earth" (Genesis 18:25), and His dealings with human beings are constantly described in forensic terms. *Who will contend with me? Let us stand together.* The Servant saw Himself standing before God the Judge as a defendant and summoned His opponents to stand alongside of Him as plaintiffs. *Who is my adversary?* "Who is it," the Servant asked, "who would pretend to enter an action against Me?" *Let him come near to me.* The Servant challenged His adversaries to prove any crime against Him. *Surely the Lord God will help me.* The Servant again echoed His confidence in God as a righteous Judge to vindicate Him.

III. SPECIAL FEATURES
A. Preserving Our Heritage

As Christians, and particularly, as African Americans, we witness crimes in our communities that seem to go unpunished, racism in the larger community that seems to go unchecked, and suppression of the good and exaltation of the bad. This leaves us sometimes wondering if there is any justice anywhere in the world, as good things seem to happen to bad people, while good people continuously suffer wrong. It is difficult to understand why the drug dealers are acquitted in the courts, while the drug addicts are locked up. It is tough to witness the drive-by murders of the innocent and the carefree attitude of the guilty. Yet, this lesson assures us that justice will one day prevail—not in the earthly courts, but at the judgment seat of our Lord. He Himself, and we as His people, will one day see justice prevail for all humanity.

B. Concluding Reflections

Note that four times in this lesson the Servant uses the name "Lord God." *Jehovah Adonai* can be translated "Sovereign Lord," and you will find this title nowhere else in the "Servant Songs." Accordingly, it connotes that God is the Owner of each member of the human family, and that He consequently claims the unrestricted obedience of all. So the emphasis here is on the Servant's submission to the Lord God in every area of His life and service.

His *mind* was submitted to the Lord God so that He could learn His Word and His will. The Servant's *will* was also yielded to the Lord God. An "opened ear" is one that hears and obeys the voice of the master.

HOME DAILY BIBLE 📖 READINGS

for the week of December 11, 2005
Strength for the Weary

Dec. 5, Monday
    —Isaiah 40:1-5
    —Comfort, O Comfort My People
Dec. 6, Tuesday
    —Isaiah 40:27-31
    —God Strengthens the Powerless
Dec. 7, Wednesday
    —Isaiah 49:1-7
    —My God Has Become My Strength
Dec. 8, Thursday
    —Isaiah 49:8-13
    —The Lord Has Comforted His
        People
Dec. 9, Friday
    —Isaiah 49:14-18
    —I Will Not Forget You
Dec. 10, Saturday
    —Isaiah 49:22-26
    —I Am the Lord, Your Savior
Dec. 11, Sunday
    —Isaiah 50:4-11
    —The Lord God Helps Me

PRAYER

Loving God, our Father, we praise You for Your eternal love for us and all humankind as demonstrated in the gift of Your Son. We ask that You would continue wrapping Your mighty arms of protection around us and granting us the grace to continue as servants in Your eternal kingdom. In Jesus' name, we pray. Amen.

Lesson 3

Hope for Those Who Suffer

ADULT TOPIC: Hope for Those Who Suffer
YOUTH TOPIC: God Keeps Promises
CHILDREN'S TOPIC: Mary Sings Praise to God

DEVOTIONAL READING: Romans 12:9-16
BACKGROUND SCRIPTURE: Isaiah 53; Luke 1
PRINT PASSAGE: Isaiah 53:1-3; Luke 1:47-55

Isaiah 53:1-3; Luke 1:47-55—KJV

WHO HATH believed our report? and to whom is the arm of the LORD revealed?

2 For he shall grow up before him as a tender plant, and as a root out of a dry ground: he hath no form nor comeliness; and when we shall see him, there is no beauty that we should desire him.

3 He is despised and rejected of men; a man of sorrows, and acquainted with grief: and we hid as it were our faces from him; he was despised, and we esteemed him not.

.....

47 And my spirit hath rejoiced in God my Saviour.

48 For he hath regarded the low estate of his handmaiden: for, behold, from henceforth all generations shall call me blessed.

49 For he that is mighty hath done to me great things; and holy is his name.

50 And his mercy is on them that fear him from generation to generation.

KEY VERSE
His mercy is on them that fear him from generation to generation. —Luke 1:50

OBJECTIVES
Upon completion of this lesson, students should understand that:
1. Suffering may be part of God's plan for the believer.
2. God's comfort is available in the midst of suffering.
3. Servanthood often involves the choice to suffer for a greater good.
4. Comfort from the knowledge gained through suffering identifies us with Christ, whose suffering preceded His exaltation.

51 He hath shown strength with his arm; he hath scattered the proud in the imagination of their hearts.

52 He hath put down the mighty from their seats, and exalted them of low degree.

53 He hath filled the hungry with good things; and the rich he hath sent empty away.

54 He hath helped his servant Israel, in remembrance of his mercy;

55 As he spake to our fathers, to Abraham, and to his seed for ever.

Isaiah 53:1-3; Luke 1:47-55—NRSV

WHO HAS believed what we have heard? And to whom has the arm of the LORD been revealed?

2 For he grew up before him like a young plant, and like a root out of dry ground; he had no form or majesty that we should look at him, nothing in his appearance that we should desire him.

3 He was despised and rejected by others; a man of suffering and acquainted with infirmity; and as one from whom others hide their faces he was despised, and we held him of no account.

. . . . .

47 "and my spirit rejoices in God my Savior,

48 for he has looked with favor on the lowliness of his servant. Surely, from now on all generations will call me blessed;

49 for the Mighty One has done great things for me, and holy is his name.

50 His mercy is for those who fear him from generation to generation.

51 He has shown strength with his arm; he has scattered the proud in the thoughts of their hearts.

52 He has brought down the powerful from their thrones, and lifted up the lowly;

53 he has filled the hungry with good things, and sent the rich away empty.

54 He has helped his servant Israel, in remembrance of his mercy,

55 according to the promise he made to our ancestors, to Abraham and to his descendants forever."

POINTS TO BE EMPHASIZED

ADULTS
Key Verse: Luke 1:50
Print: Isaiah 53:1-3; Luke 1:47-55
—God's redemptive purpose is revealed through the image of the Suffering Servant.
—The Suffering Servant reveals a God in solidarity with the poor and hungry.
—Servanthood often involves the choice to suffer for a greater good.
—That which people despise, God exalts.

YOUTH
Key Verse: Luke 1:52
Print: Isaiah 53:1-3; Luke 1:47-55
—God keeps His promises.
—God spoke words of hope through Isaiah to the suffering Israelites in exile.
—The suffering Messiah would not be a glamorous heroic person but one who suffered.
—Mary rejoiced that God had kept His promise to send a servant Messiah to liberate people.

CHILDREN

Key Verse: Luke 1:46

Print: Isaiah 52:7; Luke 1:46-55

—Those who find the Savior will discover the purpose for their lives.

—Humility can be demonstrated through praise songs.

—Some praise songs focus on God's actions in helping those in need.

—Jesus came to help those who are suffering.

TOPICAL OUTLINE OF THE LESSON

I. INTRODUCTION
   A. Redemptive Suffering
   B. Biblical Background

II. EXPOSITION AND APPLICATION
    OF THE SCRIPTURE
   A. The Message of Hope Is Rejected
      (Isaiah 53:1)
   B. Hope for Those of Humble
      Beginnings *(Isaiah 53:2)*
   C. Hope for the Despised and
      Rejected *(Isaiah 53:3)*
   D. Hope Expressed in Praise
      (Luke 1:47-49)
   E. Hope for Future Generations
      (Luke 1:50)
   F. Hope for the Helpless *(Luke 1:51)*
   G. Hope for the Humble *(Luke 1:52)*
   H. Hope for the Hungry *(Luke 1:53)*
   I. Hope for the Covenanted
      (Luke 1:54-55)

III. SPECIAL FEATURES
   A. Preserving Our Heritage
   B. Concluding Reflections

I. INTRODUCTION

A. Redemptive Suffering

This chapter is the very heart of Isaiah 40-66, as it takes us to the Cross. We are given a graphic literary portrait of the Suffering Servant, which tells us of the glorious work He would undertake in order that the sin matter would be settled forever to the perfect satisfaction of the Holy One.

The Suffering Servant prophecy begins with 52:13-15. Verse 13 tells of Christ's exaltation, while the rest of the section deals with His humiliation. It is this strange dichotomy that perplexed the Old Testament prophets (see 1 Peter 1:10-11). They did not realize that there would be a long period between the Messiah's coming as the Suffering Servant unto death and His return as the exalted Sovereign to reign.

Our lesson focuses on the life and ministry of Christ, who came into the world to give hope to all who suffer under the weight of sin. The Old Testament passage from the book of Isaiah speaks prophetically of His humble beginning (verse 2), His common physical appearance (verse 2), and His earthly sojourn (verse 3). The Gospel passage from Luke is a prayer or song uttered by the Virgin Mary during her visit with Elizabeth, the mother of John the Baptist, whereupon she received confirmation that she had been chosen to be the mother of the Messiah. These poetic words of Mary have been widely adopted and are used as a liturgical hymn by the Roman Catholic Church as well as

Protestant groups, though not so much among Baptists. Its widespread usage has given rise to its entitlement, *The Magnificat*, from the Latin word "magnify." Loosely translated, it means "The Magnificent."

God's choice of barren Elizabeth and the Virgin Mary is an apt illustration of the hope that God provides for all humanity. It is especially encouraging for those of lowly estate to recognize that God often chooses the despised and downtrodden of the world as His instruments of hope to all who suffer.

B. Biblical Background

Isaiah is often called "the evangelical prophet" because of his prophecies of Christ and His great salvation. In studying Isaiah's great predictions, it should be remembered that he was expressing the general hope of Israel, which also appears in other prophecies. Isaiah's prophecies do not stand alone, however. The stream of messianic prophecy, which began with Genesis 3:15, expanded markedly with God's promises to David (2 Samuel 7).

The work of the Suffering Servant (Isaiah 53) would open the door not only for pardon from sin, but also to the glorious vistas of peace throughout the earth.

Upon learning that the Lord would use her as the vessel to birth the Hope of Israel (Luke 1:26-38), Mary went to visit the home of Zechariah and Elizabeth. Luke states that this was a city in Judah in the hill country. Tradition identifies the town as "Ain Karim," a village five miles west of Jerusalem. If so, Mary traveled some eighty miles from Nazareth to visit her relative. It was there that she received the prophetic confirmation from Elizabeth that she was *the mother of my Lord.*

II. EXPOSITION AND APPLICATION OF THE SCRIPTURE

A. The Message of Hope Is Rejected *(Isaiah 53:1)*

The Servant as viewed by humanity would be rejected and despised. *Who hath believed our report* is literally, "the thing heard" (i.e., by the prophet from God). Hence, the prophetic message, *our report*—the message of Isaiah and his fellow prophets—is rejected. The speaker is believed to portray the repenting Jews in the latter ages of the world who would come to believe in Jesus as Messiah. *To whom is the arm of the Lord revealed?* is a phrase always used to designate special interventions in human affairs whereby God delivers His people and punishes His foes. It is especially used in reference to the miracles of the Exodus.

B. Hope for Those of Humble Beginnings *(Isaiah 53:2)*

For He shall grow up before Him as a tender plant is more literally understood as a suckling (used of a baby at her mother's breast, as well as of a shoot from a tree stump). The Messiah did not appear suddenly as an adult, as in the case of Melchizedek, the high priest of old (Genesis 14:18). It is indeed a miracle that

God Himself would condescend to the lowly estate of a baby to accomplish the work of human redemption. This allows Him to claim full identification with humankind. Had He not come into the world as an infant, it might be claimed that He was not fully human.

He hath no form nor comeliness is not meant to suggest that Jesus was physically unattractive; it emphasizes that it was not His physical appearance that attracted people to Him. The Servant was an ordinary man in His physical appearance. Those who desire to serve the Lord ought not be chosen because of their physical appearance. Conversely, it means that the lack of physical attractiveness need not be a hindrance to serving Him.

C. Hope for the Despised and Rejected
(Isaiah 53:3)

He is despised and rejected of men, more exactly, he was rejected by the elite, persons of distinction. In other words, those persons of prestige and honor, the learned and the religious leaders despised and rejected Him as Messiah. It is the same for many today as it was during His earthly sojourn; many persons of wealth and prestige reject Him as the Messiah.

A man of sorrows, and acquainted with grief. That is, His distinguishing characteristic was *sorrows*, and He was one familiar with *grief.* Indeed, part of His sorrow resulted from His intense identification with humankind in general and Israel in particular (Matthew 10:36). He sympathized with those who labored under the burden of sin. His ministry did not include the pursuit of personal comfort or luxury. He did not own a place of residence (Luke 9:58).

He was despised, and we esteemed him not speaks first of His rejection by Israel. It speaks further of those who do not want to be associated with Him and consider the name "Christian" to be a reproach or something to be denied. People still resist giving honor to Him; despite their rejections, He remains the Holy One of Israel at whose feet all will bow.

The Servant would suffer as a result of His commitment to God's assigned task. The Servant's mission would be divisive in its challenge; not all hearers would respond to His demands, and many had already shown themselves to be rebellious. It is those who identified with this servant's task whose fate is described. There is a positive and reassuring outlook that sees beyond the immediate pain to the rich reward of such endurance. There is a sensitivity to the way in which the righteous often suffer at the hands of wrongdoers that leads to the perception of meaning in suffering. Isaiah prophesied that a virgin (Hebrew—*young woman*) would bear a son. To be a "favored one" is to be blessed by God and chosen for a special role. "Jesus" is a form of the common Hebrew name *Joshua* (he saves). Mary's question, "How can this be?," is echoed as trust and wonder in her acceptance. God's Holy Spirit overshadows Mary (like Israel) to protect her from harm and shield her from God's holiness; so Mary is protected in a divine conception that Elizabeth's pregnancy confirms. "Nothing will be impossible with God" reflects God's Word to Sarah's laughter about her pregnancy.

D. Hope Expressed in Praise
(Luke 1:47-49)

Having been given the message that the time had come for the Hope of Israel to appear, Mary began her song of praise with *My soul doth magnify the Lord, And my spirit hath rejoiced in God my Saviour.* Mary viewed herself as part of the godly remnant that had served Yahweh and lived in the hope of seeing the Messiah. She knew that His appearing was near and she would be a part of that fulfillment. Therefore her *soul*, her entire being, "magnified," His coming. Mary was able to magnify God because she knew Him. Hope in the Lord is inextricably bound with knowledge of Him and His promises.

For he hath regarded the low estate of his handmaiden. Mary's praise to God was an acknowledgement of her lowly state and her need to trust the Lord for her eternal salvation. The term *handmaiden* is also translated as *bondslave,* and means "one of servile condition, or lowliness." Not only had God saved her, but He had also chosen her to be the mother of the Messiah (Luke 1:48). He had *regarded* her; God looked upon her with favor.

For, behold, from henceforth all generations shall call me blessed. The verse highlights the importance the ancients placed on one's honor and name enduring after one's death. As God's humble *handmaiden*, Mary magnified Him for placing honor upon her such that future generations would look upon her as blessed.

For he that is mighty hath done to me great things; and holy is his name is another use of parallelism—namely, that almighty God had chosen this virgin girl from a common family in Nazareth to be the recipient of this greatest of blessings. The *great things* refer not only to His choice of her, but also to the means by which she gave birth.

E. Hope for Future Generations
(Luke 1:50)

And his mercy is on them that fear him from generation to generation. This is an allusion to Psalm 103:17, which in context emphasizes God's unending faithfulness to those who fear Him. This faithfulness, *from generation to generation,* is an indication of the perpetuity of His mercy. We who are recipients of His mercy can rest assured that our progeny can depend upon Him for mercy. But the duty of every generation is to ensure that they are taught reverential fear of Him.

F. Hope for the Helpless *(Luke 1:51)*

He hath shown strength with his arm. The *arm* is often used in Scripture as a metaphor for strength and power, and always in the New Testament to represent the power of God. *He hath scattered the proud in the imagination of their hearts.* It is always God's way to cross the expectations of the proud, and to proceed quite apart from what they have envisioned. God, therefore, has a particular interest in disappointing the expectations of the proud who imagine that they have no need of Him. On the other hand, God takes great joy in exalting, strengthening and enriching the helpless (Luke 22:43; Acts 9:22). This means that those among us who are seemingly helpless in the face of those who appear strong before God may derive strength from the knowledge that "Though the Lord be high, yet hath he respect unto the lowly: but the proud he knoweth afar off" (Psalm 138:6).

G. Hope for the Humble *(Luke 1:52)*

He hath put down the mighty from their seats, and exalted them of low degree. We have yet another use of synonymous parallelism. In verse 52 we see the images of kings, queens, rulers and others who sat upon *thrones*, a metaphor for kingly power and a negative reference for haughtiness. Mary praised God for His historical record of defeating kings and rulers and giving victory to those who are *lowly,* but also who possess greater faith in the one God. Humility is a great force when offered to God in hope.

H. Hope for the Hungry *(Luke 1:53)*

He hath filled the hungry with good things; and the rich he hath sent empty away. Notice that parallelism may be synonymous (repeating the same thing) or antithetical (comparing two things that are the antithesis or the opposite). This verse illustrates the antithetical in that one line in the stanza shows God's attitude toward the low and the hungry: *He has filled the hungry with good things.*

I. Hope for the Covenanted *(Luke 1:54-55)*

He has helped his servant Israel, in remembrance of his mercy, according to the promise he made to our ancestors, to Abraham and to his descendants forever (NRSV). It was always expected that the Messiah would be the strength and glory of His people, Israel. God's covenant with Abraham was unconditional, having nothing to do with Israel's faithfulness, but, rather, upon the faithfulness of God. Throughout the Old Testament, we witness Jehovah helping *(antilambano),* literally "taking by the hand," *his servant Israel.* Notice here that the *servant* is Israel, whereas in our former lesson, the *servant* referred to the Messiah. Israel was under the burden of a broken covenant of innocence and was helped by the blessings of a renewed covenant of grace.

And to his seed forever: refers to Abraham's spiritual seed (Galatians 3:7). The carnal seed (Israel) was cut off by their rejection of the Messiah and will not be helped again until the return of Jesus at His second coming. But the spiritual seed, those who are His by faith, shall receive the blessings of the Messiah. In this final verse, Mary magnifies God for His bountiful blessing, "That the blessing of Abraham might come on the Gentiles through Jesus Christ; that we might receive the promise of the Spirit through faith" (Galatians 3:14).

III. SPECIAL FEATURES
A. Preserving Our Heritage

The image of Christ as the Suffering Servant reveals a God in solidarity with the poor, despised and rejected people of the world—images that are all too familiar to African Americans. Therefore, perhaps more than any other people, we can identify with the Suffering Servant, and embrace Him as our Liberator.

When we look at the history of our people in this country, we can clearly see the hand of God moving and acting on our behalf. We can identify with the assertions of James Cone, noted author of *Black Theology,* that "Christianity is essentially a religion of liberation." We can see that the Messiah unreservedly identified with the oppressed—expressing His "job description" to "heal the brokenhearted, to preach deliverance to the captives" (Luke 4:18).

B. Concluding Reflections

Suffering and death help us to gain some understanding why we, as His followers, are subject to suffering. The biblical context of this lesson teaches us about "vicarious suffering"—that is, the suffering one endures for the sake of another. We suffer because we are under the *penalty* and the *power* of sin, and we live in a world filled with the *presence* of sin.

Jesus Christ came into the world to defeat sin and, through His victory, to demonstrate that it is through service and sacrifice that we can gain victory over the deepest suffering.

HOME DAILY BIBLE READINGS
for the week of December 18, 2005
Hope for Those Who Suffer

Dec. 12, Monday
   —Isaiah 52:13—53:3
   —Despised, Rejected, a Man of
     Suffering
Dec. 13, Tuesday
   —Isaiah 53:4-12
   —He Bore the Sins of Many
Dec. 14, Wednesday
   —Luke 1:5-17
   —John the Baptist's Birth Foretold
Dec. 15, Thursday
   —Luke 1:26-38
   —The Birth of Jesus Foretold
Dec. 16, Friday
   —Luke 1:39-45
   —Mary Visits Elizabeth
Dec. 17, Saturday
   —Luke 1:46-55
   —Mary's Song of Praise
Dec. 18, Sunday
   —Romans 5:1-11
   —Hope Comes Through Suffering

PRAYER
Merciful, gracious God our Father, we humbly bow in Your presence to say thank You. Thank You for loving us so that You looked beyond our faults and saw our great need. Amen.

Lesson 4

Good News for the World

UNIT I
God's Redeeming Love

CHILDREN'S UNIT
The Gift of Jesus

ADULT TOPIC: Be Joyful
YOUTH TOPIC: The Messiah Is Born
CHILDREN'S TOPIC: Jesus Is Born!

KEY VERSE

For unto you is born this day in the city of David a Saviour, which is Christ the Lord. —Luke 2:11

DEVOTIONAL READING: Isaiah 52:7-12
BACKGROUND SCRIPTURE: Isaiah 61:1-3; Luke 2:8-20
PRINT PASSAGE: Isaiah 61:1-2; Luke 2:8-20

OBJECTIVES

Upon completing this lesson, students should understand that:

1. The birth of Jesus was "good news" for all mankind.
2. Christmas has significance for all persons.
3. The birth of Jesus gives hope to everyone.
4. They should share the Good News of Christmas with others.

Isaiah 61:1-2; Luke 2:8-20—KJV

THE SPIRIT of the Lord GOD is upon me; because the LORD hath anointed me to preach good tidings unto the meek; he hath sent me to bind up the brokenhearted, to proclaim liberty to the captives, and the opening of the prison to them that are bound;

2 To proclaim the acceptable year of the LORD, and the day of vengeance of our God; to comfort all that mourn.

…..

8 And there were in the same country shepherds abiding in the field, keeping watch over their flock by night.

9 And, lo, the angel of the Lord came upon them, and the glory of the Lord shone round about them: and they were sore afraid.

10 And the angel said unto them, Fear not: for, behold, I bring you good tidings of great joy, which shall be to all people.

11 For unto you is born this day in the city of David a Saviour, which is Christ the Lord.

12 And this shall be a sign unto you; Ye shall find the babe wrapped in swaddling clothes, lying in a manger.

13 And suddenly there was with the angel a multitude of the heavenly host praising God, and saying,

14 Glory to God in the highest, and on earth peace, good will toward men.

15 And it came to pass, as the angels were gone away from them into heaven, the shepherds said one to another, Let us now go even unto Bethlehem, and see this thing which is come to pass, which the Lord hath made known unto us.

16 And they came with haste, and found Mary, and Joseph, and the babe lying in a manger.

17 And when they had seen it, they made known abroad the saying which was told them concerning this child.

18 And all they that heard it wondered at those things which were told them by the shepherds.

19 But Mary kept all these things, and pondered them in her heart.

20 And the shepherds returned, glorifying and praising God for all the things that they had heard and seen, as it was told unto them.

Isaiah 61:1-2; Luke 2:8-20—NRSV

THE SPIRIT of the Lord GOD is upon me, because the LORD has anointed me; he has sent me to bring good news to the oppressed, to bind up the brokenhearted, to proclaim liberty to the captives, and release to the prisoners;

2 to proclaim the year of the LORD's favor, and the day of vengeance of our God; to comfort all who mourn;

.....

8 In that region there were shepherds living in the fields, keeping watch over their flock by night.

9 Then an angel of the Lord stood before them, and the glory of the Lord shone around them, and they were terrified.

10 But the angel said to them, "Do not be afraid; for see—I am bringing you good news of great joy for all the people:

11 to you is born this day in the city of David a Savior, who is the Messiah, the Lord.

12 This will be a sign for you: you will find a child wrapped in bands of cloth and lying in a manger."

13 And suddenly there was with the angel a multitude of the heavenly host, praising God and saying,

14 "Glory to God in the highest heaven, and on earth peace among those whom he favors!"

15 When the angels had left them and gone into heaven, the shepherds said to one another, "Let us go now to Bethlehem and see this thing that has taken place, which the Lord has made known to us."

16 So they went with haste and found Mary and Joseph, and the child lying in the manger.

17 When they saw this, they made known what had been told them about this child;

18 and all who heard it were amazed at what the shepherds told them.

19 But Mary treasured all these words and pondered them in her heart.

20 The shepherds returned, glorifying and praising God for all they had heard and seen, as it had been told them.

POINTS TO BE EMPHASIZED
ADULTS
Key Verse: Luke 2:11
Print: Isaiah 61:1-2; Luke 2:8-20
—The Spirit of the Lord came upon the servant to liberate, heal and comfort people.
—The Gospels portray Isaiah's prophecy as being fulfilled in Jesus' birth.
—The Good News of Jesus' birth came first to the shepherds.

YOUTH
Key Verse: Luke 2:11
Print: Isaiah 61:1-2; Luke 2:8-20
—The birth of the Messiah was foretold through Isaiah's prophecy.
—God sent the Messiah for a specific purpose.
—The angel announced to the shepherds the Good News of the birth of the Messiah in Bethlehem.
—The shepherds responded to the Good News by going to Bethlehem, where they found Mary, Joseph and the baby.

CHILDREN
Key Verse: Luke 2:11
Print: Isaiah 61:1-2; Luke 2:8-20
—The shepherds were overwhelmed by the sudden appearance of the angel.
—Great joy comes when God is working among us.

—Great joy and answers to difficult circumstances come to those who carefully listen to God.
—True believers always remember to praise and thank God for bountiful blessings.

TOPICAL OUTLINE OF THE LESSON

I. INTRODUCTION
  A. The Ministry Identified
  B. Biblical Background

II. EXPOSITION AND APPLICATION OF THE SCRIPTURE
  A. The Good News Prophesied *(Isaiah 61:1)*
  B. The Good News Explained *(Isaiah 61:2)*
  C. The Angelic Announcement *(Luke 2:8-10)*
  D. The Joyful Announcement *(Luke 2:11)*
  E. A Joyful Sign *(Luke 2:12-14)*
  F. A Joyful Visit *(Luke 2:15-20)*

III. SPECIAL FEATURES
  A. Preserving Our Heritage
  B. Concluding Reflections

I. INTRODUCTION
A. The Ministry Identified

In this lesson, we study portions of Isaiah 61, the passage to which Jesus directed His hearers' attention when He went into the synagogue at Nazareth. After His baptism in the Jordan and His temptation in the wilderness, He came up through Judea into Galilee, and entered the city where He had been raised—Nazareth.

The Luke passage focuses on the news concerning Jesus' birth as announced to the shepherds in the field watching their flock.

B. Biblical Background

There are many aspects of the writings of Isaiah which are perhaps beyond our present comprehension. Like the other prophets, Isaiah wrote at the command of the Lord, and then searched his own Scriptures to try and discern what he was called to prophesy. The portions that deal with the birth and suffering that took place at His first advent have become amazingly clear in the light of the Gospels. Those that have to do with the glories that shall follow at His second advent, while linked with all prophecy as to that glorious advent, will never be fully understood until the day of fulfillment arrives. As we study this book, we may seem to look through a glass darkly, but we may be assured of real blessing as we weigh carefully before God that which He commissioned Isaiah to proclaim.

II. EXPOSITION AND APPLICATION OF THE SCRIPTURE

A. The Good News Prophesied
(Isaiah 61:1)

The Spirit of the Lord GOD is upon me: The prophets had the Spirit of God moving them at various times, both instructing and empowering them regarding their message. As the mouthpiece of God, the prophet was called into such close identification with his God that often he speaks in the first person, using the pronouns "I" and "me." All three Persons of the Trinity are presented in this verse, but the subsequent use of this passage by Jesus in reference to Himself tells us that in this passage the *me* refers to the Messiah. *Because the LORD has anointed me.* The kings of Israel, dating back to the time of Saul and David, were anointed with oil, symbolizing the presence and power of the Holy Spirit upon them. As King of kings, the Lord Jesus is anointed by the Spirit; in His case, it is not oil but, rather, the Spirit's anointing that is seen in the form of a dove and confirmed by the voice of God the Father: "This is my beloved Son, in whom I am well pleased" (Matthew 3:17).

B. The Good News Explained
(Isaiah 61:2)

The ministry of the Messiah was to serve first as a preacher; He was *to preach good tidings*. The phrase initially meant "to publish good news," but later came to be associated with the English word "gospel," which means "good message." When used of Christ's ministry and message in the New Testament, it came to refer to the good tidings of the kingdom of God and of salvation through Him: *to the poor,* and in some translations, *to the meek.* The idea is that He was sent to proclaim Good News to the penitent, and humble, and poor in spirit. These individuals are commonly best disposed to receive the Gospel (James 2:5), while the rich and haughty are apt to reject and despise it. It was this attitude of receptivity to which Jesus referred in the Beatitudes when He said, *"Blessed are the poor in spirit...and the meek"* (Matthew 5:3, 5). The Gospel is good news only to those who see themselves in need of such.

C. The Angelic Announcement *(Luke 2:8-10)*

And there were in the same country shepherds abiding in the field, keeping watch over their flock by night. In His day, shepherds were at the lowest rung of the social ladder. Their work not only kept them away from the temple and the synagogue, but it made them ceremonially unclean. The mere fact that God in His grace chose lowly shepherds to give the first announcement of the Savior's birth, rather than the religious leaders or scribes and priests, illustrates that God delights in showing favor to those whom the world considers the least important (Luke 1:51-53; 1 Corinthians 1:26-29).

And, lo, the angel of the Lord came upon them. First, one angel appeared and gave the glad announcement; and then a chorus of angels joined him and gave an anthem of praise. *And the glory of the Lord shone round about them: and they were sore afraid.* Angelic appearances, the revelation of God's glory and consequent fear among the humans present were common in the Old Testament when God was acting in human history in special ways (Exodus 16:10; 20:18; 2 Chronicles 7:1). The Greek word, translated *afraid,* literally means "They feared a great fear" and stresses the intensity of their fright.

D. The Joyful Announcement *(Luke 2:11)*

And the angel said unto them, Fear not: The angel's words, *Fear not,* were the usual greeting to persons for whom such an appearance would be terrifying (cf., 1:13, 30). *For, behold, I bring you good tidings of great joy, which shall be*

The year of the Lord's favor—everything God had promised regarding the rebuilding and restoration of Jerusalem—would shortly be fulfilled. The expectation of God's direct action to overthrow the present world order becomes a marked feature of the hope of Israel. The hand of God had been recognized in the rise of Cyrus, king of Persia, to direct the destiny of Judah; now Israel awaited a more direct, divine intervention. Assurance that this transformation would take place was derived from the very nature of God Himself. Luke projects Jesus' birth against the background of the whole Roman order, while Matthew draws attention to King Herod's reign in Judea. The Romans used registration as a means to establish control of taxes, lands and military conscription. Bethlehem was also King David's birthplace, and his tending sheep was legendary. The phrase, "Jesus is Lord," is thoroughly Jewish and scriptural, as the titles "Messiah" and "Anointed One" are for Israel's King. Without asking for confirmation, the shepherds were given the sign of the child in the manger, and were exemplary in telling what they had heard and seen.

to all people. This phrase, *tidings of great joy,* is expressed in English by the word "gospel" and gives rise to the thought of the Gospel as "Good News" *of great joy which shall be to all the people.* Throughout Luke, "joy" (Greek: *chara*) is often associated with salvation. This Gospel announcement, though sent specifically to the Jews, was to bring good news and great joy to all people of the earth. This is a very strong indication that from the first announcement, the Savior's mission was designed to provide salvation for all humanity. This means that the angelic announcement was intended to bring joy to all who would accept it. The true joy of Christmas, then, is the gift of Christ.

For unto you is born this day in the city of David a Savior. The place of the Messiah's birth had been foretold by the prophets—that He was to be of the household of David (2 Samuel 7:1-17; Isaiah 9:6). Luke broadens the concept to make Jesus a Savior by the use of the term *Christ the Lord.* The word *Christ* means "anointed." The Messiah of Israel was the promised Deliverer and "Lord" of all.

E. A Joyful Sign *(Luke 2:12-14)*

Ye shall find the babe wrapped in swaddling clothes, lying in a manger. Mothers in that day wrapped their infants in long bands of cloth to give the limbs strength and protection. The word translated *manger* here is translated *stall* in Luke 13:15 and can either mean a feeding trough or an enclosure for animals—the point being that the birth occurred in a place where animals were kept. It is indeed surprising that the Son of God would be born in such a lowly place. Perhaps this was done to indicate to succeeding generations that one's place of birth need not become a hindrance to one's usefulness and potential for greatness in the kingdom of God.

And suddenly there was with the angel a multitude of the heavenly host. The angelic messenger, believed by many to be Gabriel, was suddenly joined by an untold number of other angels who joined him in *praising God.* The angels had praised God at Creation (Job 38:7), and now they praised Him at the beginning of a new creation.

Glory to God in the highest: The whole purpose of God's plan of salvation is "glory to God" (Ephesians 1:6, 12, 14). God's glory had dwelt in the tabernacle (Exodus 40:34) and in the temple (2 Chronicles 7:1-3), but had departed because of Israel's sin (1 Samuel 4:21; Ezekiel 8:4). Now, God's glory was returning to earth in the person of His Son (John 1:14). *And on earth, peace, good will toward men!* The *New Revised Standard Version* follows a different manuscript and gives a better sense of what is meant by the translation, *and on earth peace among those whom he favors!* The distinction places the emphasis on God rather than people. God's peace is not given to human beings who possess goodwill, but, rather, to those who are the recipients of God's goodwill or favor.

F. A Joyful Visit (Luke 2:15-20)

And it came to pass, as the angels were gone away from them into heaven, the shepherds said one to another, Let us now go even unto Bethlehem, and see this thing which is come to pass, which the Lord hath made known unto us. Their collective agreement to journey to the site suggests that they did not doubt the reality of the angel's proclamation. *Which the Lord hath made known to us* is an indication that they received the announcement as one coming from God.

They lost no time, but *came with haste* to the place, which probably means that the angel gave them more specific directions than is recorded ("Go to the stable of such an inn"). *And they came with haste, and found Mary, and Joseph, and the babe lying in a manger.* The verb *found* means "found after a search," which suggests that they had to go to several stables to locate the one where the baby lay. Bethlehem was not a large town.

And when they had seen it, they made known abroad the saying which was told them concerning this child. These shepherds are good examples for us to imitate today. They received the message God sent them and by faith responded with immediate obedience. After finding the baby, they reported the Good News to others. It is not enough that we experience the joy of Jesus ourselves; it is both our solemn obligation and great privilege to share this joy with others.

But Mary kept all these things, and pondered them in her heart. This is probably an indication that the shepherds shared with Mary the things they had heard from the angels. This becomes further confirmation of what she had heard from the angel Gabriel, in addition to the testimony of Elizabeth (Luke 1:39-56).

And the shepherds returned, glorifying and praising God for all the things that they had heard and seen, as it was told unto them. The shepherds returned to their work in the fields, and in so doing, they praised God for what *they had heard* from the angel, and for what they had seen—the babe *in the manger*—for it was the babe in the manger who would later become the Christ of the Cross, ushering in good news and joy to all who would believe.

III. SPECIAL FEATURES
A. Preserving Our Heritage

Madison Avenue and the mass media spend millions of dollars each year on the commercialization of Christmas. They have done so by focusing on a fictionalized old gentleman called "Santa Claus" and his reindeer, who purportedly fly through the air on the night before Christmas, descending into chimneys distributing toys and gifts to households across the country. His fictionalized activity of gift giving creates in the psyche of the American consumer an insatiable obligation to engage in lavish gift giving to family, friends and coworkers, but especially to children. This gift-giving ritual is accompanied by the obligatory decorating of houses and trees with colored lights and various paraphernalia.

In such an atmosphere, it is helpful for those of us charged with the privilege and responsibility of teaching God's Word to emphasize the joy of Christ and what we receive through Him rather than the joy of receiving gifts.

B. Concluding Reflections

Neither the term *Christmas* (a derivative of Christ + mass) nor the actual celebration of the anniversary of the birth of Christ is recorded in the Bible. By the end of the fourth century, the eastern churches had adopted special services commemorating the birth of Christ, the adoration of the Magi, and Christ's baptism by John. Apparently, these services were held at first on January 6, but later were divided between December 25 and January 6.

Today, in most western churches, the observance of Christmas emphasizes the immediate events surrounding the birth of Christ.

The biblical emphasis connected with the birth of Jesus Christ is evidenced by: adoration and worship (Luke 2:8-12); giving gifts to God (Matthew 2:1-11); and the expression of peace and goodwill (Luke 2:13-14).

▌HOME DAILY BIBLE READINGS 📖

for the week of December 25, 2005
(Christmas)
Good News for the World

Dec. 19, Monday
—Isaiah 51:1-6
—God's Justice and Deliverance Never End

Dec. 20, Tuesday
—Isaiah 52:7-12
—God's Messenger Brings Good News

Dec. 21, Wednesday
—Isaiah 60:17-22
—God Will Be Your Glory

Dec. 22, Thursday
—Isaiah 61:1-7
—Good News for the Oppressed

Dec. 23, Friday
—Isaiah 61:8—62:3
—God Gives Salvation and Righteousness

Dec. 24, Saturday
—Luke 2:1-7
—Mary Has a Baby

Dec. 25, Sunday
—Luke 2:8-21
—The Angels Bring Good News

PRAYER

Dear God, our heavenly Father, thank You for the gift of Your Son. Help us to recognize the great opportunity afforded us at this time of the year to share Your gift with those with whom we shall converse with this week. In Jesus' name, we pray. Amen.

Lesson 5

God Gives Strength

ADULT TOPIC: Finding Strength to Serve
YOUTH TOPIC: Powered Up for Service
CHILDREN'S TOPIC: Good Leaders Thank God

UNIT II
God's Gifts of Leadership

CHILDREN'S UNIT
God Gives Good Leaders

DEVOTIONAL READING: Romans 16:17-27
BACKGROUND SCRIPTURE: 1 Timothy 1
PRINT PASSAGE: 1 Timothy 1:12-20

1 Timothy 1:12-20—KJV

12 And I thank Christ Jesus our Lord, who hath enabled me, for that he counted me faithful, putting me into the ministry;

13 Who was before a blasphemer, and a persecutor, and injurious: but I obtained mercy, because I did it ignorantly in unbelief.

14 And the grace of our Lord was exceeding abundant with faith and love which is in Christ Jesus.

15 This is a faithful saying, and worthy of all acceptation, that Christ Jesus came into the world to save sinners; of whom I am chief.

16 Howbeit for this cause I obtained mercy, that in me first Jesus Christ might show forth all longsuffering, for a pattern to them which should hereafter believe on him to life everlasting.

17 Now unto the King eternal, immortal, invisible, the only wise God, be honour and glory for ever and ever. Amen.

18 This charge I commit unto thee, son Timothy, according to the prophecies which went before on thee, that thou by them mightest war a good warfare;

KEY VERSE

I thank Christ Jesus our Lord, who hath enabled me, for that he counted me faithful, putting me into the ministry. —1 Timothy 1:12

OBJECTIVES

Upon the completion of this lesson, students should understand that:

1. Every believer is called to serve.
2. God has equipped every believer for service.
3. The only ability needed for service is availability.
4. God's strength is sufficient to empower every believer to be successful in ministry.

19 Holding faith, and a good conscience; which some having put away concerning faith have made shipwreck:

20 Of whom is Hymenaeus and Alexander; whom I have delivered unto Satan, that they may learn not to blaspheme.

1 Timothy 1:12-20—NRSV

12 I am grateful to Christ Jesus our Lord, who has strengthened me, because he judged me faithful and appointed me to his service,

13 even though I was formerly a blasphemer, a persecutor, and a man of violence. But I received mercy because I had acted ignorantly in unbelief,

14 and the grace of our Lord overflowed for me with the faith and love that are in Christ Jesus.

15 The saying is sure and worthy of full acceptance, that Christ Jesus came into the world to save sinners—of whom I am the foremost.

16 But for that very reason I received mercy, so that in me, as the foremost, Jesus Christ might display the utmost patience, making me an example to those who would come to believe in him for eternal life.

17 To the King of the ages, immortal, invisible, the only God, be honor and glory forever and ever. Amen.

18 I am giving you these instructions, Timothy, my child, in accordance with the prophecies made earlier about you, so that

by following them you may fight the good fight,

19 having faith and a good conscience. By rejecting conscience, certain persons have suffered shipwreck in the faith;

20 among them are Hymenaeus and Alexander, whom I have turned over to Satan, so that they may learn not to blaspheme.

POINTS TO BE EMPHASIZED
ADULTS
Key Verse: 1 Timothy 1:12
Print: 1 Timothy 1:12-20
—Paul thanked Christ Jesus for being his strength for his ministry.
—Paul made clear to Timothy that without the power and strength that had come to him through Christ Jesus, he, Paul, was unworthy of the ministry that he had received.
—Paul wrote his first letter to Timothy, his spiritual son, who was a pastor in Ephesus.

YOUTH
Key Verse: 1 Timothy 1:12
Print: 1 Timothy 1:12-20
—Paul wrote his first letter to Timothy—who was a pastor in Ephesus—as a father would advise a son.
—Paul gave thanks to God for saving him and strengthening him for ministry.
—God empowered and equipped Paul because he was faithful.
—Paul encouraged Timothy to persevere despite hardships.

CHILDREN

Key Verse: 1 Timothy 1:12

Print: Acts 16:1-5; 1 Timothy 1:12, 14, 17

—Parents who live by Christian traditions and moral values often reap the benefit of seeing their children committed to serving God.

—Christian faith can be strengthened through the teachings of committed persons.

—God's kingdom will be enlarged if persons called to ministry follow God's instructions.

TOPICAL OUTLINE OF THE LESSON

I. INTRODUCTION
  A. Timothy and His Ministry
  B. Biblical Background

II. EXPOSITION AND APPLICATION OF THE SCRIPTURE
  A. Paul Called by Christ into Ministry *(1 Timothy 1:12-13)*
  B. Grace More Abundant than Sin *(1 Timothy 1:14-16)*
  C. A Closing Doxology *(1 Timothy 1:17)*
  D. Fight the Good Fight *(1 Timothy 1:18-19)*
  E. Apostates Who Departed from the Faith *(1 Timothy 1:20)*

III. SPECIAL FEATURES
  A. Preserving Our Heritage
  B. Concluding Reflections

I. INTRODUCTION

A. Timothy and His Ministry

Timothy was a young man who responded to Christ's call to help build His church. He was one of the apostle Paul's special assistants. Along with Titus, Timothy tackled some of the tough assignments in the churches that Paul had founded. Timothy was brought up in a religious home (2 Timothy 1:5) and had been assisted with faith in Christ by Paul himself who called him, "my own [genuine] son in the faith" (1 Timothy 1:2).

But in spite of his calling, his close association with Paul, and his spiritual gifts, Timothy was easily discouraged. The last time Paul had been with Timothy, he had encouraged him to stay on at Ephesus and finish his work (1 Timothy 1:3). Apparently, Timothy had experienced some physical problems (1 Timothy 5:23) as well as periods of discouragement; and one gets the impression that some of the church members were not giving their pastor the proper respect as God's servant (1 Timothy 4:12; 2 Timothy 2:6-8).

B. Biblical Background

First Timothy, along with 2 Timothy and Titus, belongs to the group of Paul's writings known as the Pastoral Epistles. They are so named because they were addressed to two of Paul's dear sons in the faith, Timothy and Titus, who had pastoral duties. Timothy was in charge of the church at Ephesus, and Titus of those on the island of Crete. Along with Philemon, they are the only letters Paul addressed to an individual.

Paul's reason for writing 1 Timothy was so that Timothy "may know how one ought to conduct himself in the household of God, which is the church of the living God, the pillar and support of the truth" (1 Timothy 3:15). Public worship, the selection and qualification of church leaders, the pastor's personal life and public ministry, how to confront sin in the church, the role of women, the care of widows, and how to handle money are among the matters discussed. Besides the wealth of practical information they contain, the Pastoral Epistles also teach important doctrinal truths about the Scriptures, salvation and the Savior.

II. EXPOSITION AND APPLICATION OF THE SCRIPTURE
A. Paul Called by Christ into Ministry *(1 Timothy 1:12-13)*

And I thank Christ Jesus our Lord who has enabled me, because He counted me faithful, putting me into the ministry. The apostle returns thanks to Jesus Christ for putting him into the ministry. He wants us to know that he did not volunteer for the work, but Christ in His sovereign grace appointed him to the work of ministry. The first practical thing that we are to learn is that it is Christ's work to appoint persons in ministry (Acts 26:16-17).

In order to magnify more the grace of Christ in putting him into the ministry, the apostle gives an account of his conversion. *Although I was formerly a blasphemer, a persecutor, and an insolent man.* Saul breathed out threats and slaughter against the disciples of the Lord (Acts 9:1). He made havoc of the church (Acts 8:3). He was a *blasphemer,* "blasphemos"—one who speaks evil, slanderous words and curses against the name of God, *a persecutor,* "dioktes"— one who commits acts of injury *to the saints of God,* and an *insolent man,* "hybristes"—one who is uplifted with pride. Frequently, those who are designed for great and eminent services are left to themselves before their conversion, to fall into great wickedness, that the mercy of God may be the more glorified in their remission, and the grace of God in their regeneration. The greatness of sin is no barrier to our acceptance with God, or to our being employed for Him, if the sinner was truly repentant.

But I obtained mercy. Paul's wretchedness was met with God's compassion. Mercy differs from grace in that grace removes guilt, while mercy takes away the misery caused by sin. Paul received the undeserved relief of misery that accompanies saving grace. God granted him mercy *because I did it ignorantly in unbelief.* He was no hardened apostate rejecting the full light of God's revelation. He did it out of *ignorance (agnoeo),* a lack of understanding. He did not understand the ramifications of his actions. The Old Testament made a distinction between sins committed in ignorance as opposed to those committed in full knowledge; the sacrifice was less for the former (Numbers 15:22-29).

B. Grace More Abundant than Sin
(1 Timothy 1:14-16)

The apostle takes notice of the abundant grace of Jesus Christ. *And the grace of our Lord was exceeding abundant.* Abundant sin gives way to the more than abundant grace. The salvation of great sinners is owing to the grace of Christ, His exceedingly abundant grace. The surpassing measure of God's grace is greater than humanity's sin (Romans 5:20). With exceedingly abundant grace comes the *faith and love which are in Christ Jesus.* Faith and love are often linked with salvation in the New Testament (cf., Ephesians 1:5; 3:17; Colossians 1:4), since they are part

of the salvation package. The grace of God outpaced Paul's grievous sins that were committed in unbelief; God poured out faith. Where there had been violent aggression against God and His people, now God poured out the love of Christ.

Christ's purpose for coming into this fallen world was *to save sinners.* "To save" is to deliver from death and darkness, from sin, from hell, and from judgment. *Sinners* was a word that Jews used to refer to Gentiles (cf., Galatians 2:15), but our Lord used it to refer to all of fallen humanity (cf., Matthew 9:13). It refers to humankind's constant violation of God's law; humans are sinners by nature. Therefore, all persons stand in need of God's salvation. He came into the world, *not to call the righteous but sinners to repentance* (Matthew 9:13). In the close of the verse, Paul applied it to himself: *Of whom I am chief.* Paul was a sinner of the first rank, so he acknowledged himself to have been, for he breathed out threats and slaughter against the disciples of the Lord (cf., Acts 9:1-2). It is an expression of his great humility; he that elsewhere calls himself the *least of all saints* (Ephesians 3:8), here calls himself the chief of sinners.

C. A Closing Doxology *(1 Timothy 1:17)*

Having begun the passage with a thanksgiving, Paul closed it with a doxology. *Now unto the King eternal* literally means "of the ages." It refers to the two ages in Jewish thought—the present age and the age to come. God had no beginning and will have no end. He exists outside of time, though He acts in it. He is *immortal,* imperishable and incorruptible. He will never know death or decay or lose strength. Because He is *invisible,* He can only be known by His self-revelation. That He is *the only (wise,* some manuscripts omit this word*) God* is a fundamental truth of Scripture and emphasizes His uniqueness in a typical Jewish monotheistic fashion. He alone is worthy of *honor and glory for ever and ever.* The doxology ends with the emphatic *Amen,* meaning, "let it be so."

D. Fight the Good Fight
(1 Timothy 1:18-19)

This charge I commit to you. Paul here again uses military language to enforce his statement, for the word *charge* means "an urgent command handed down from a superior officer." *Son Timothy.* This phrase shows the apostle's intimate affection for his spiritual son. *According to the prophecies previously made concerning you.* Paul reminded Timothy that his choice of him for the ministry was at the behest of the Holy Spirit and was confirmed by prophetic utterances of other godly men (see Acts 13:1-3 for an example of this procedure). Timothy was to hold fast to and not depart from the *faith.* As a good soldier, he had to remember that his first responsibility was to remain loyal and unwavering to the objective body of revealed truth.

E. Apostates Who Departed from the Faith *(1 Timothy 1:20)*
...of whom are Hymenaeus and Alexander. Paul cited two examples of those who have departed and suffered shipwreck. Alexander is probably the Alexander of 2 Timothy 4:14, who opposed the apostolic teaching. Hymenaeus is mentioned in 2 Timothy 2:17, as one whom ungodliness has eaten away as a canker or spread like gangrene. *Whom I delivered to Satan that they may learn not to blaspheme.* To deliver to Satan indicates that they had not before been fully in his power. Those who are to be delivered to Satan must have previously been in some way under the umbrella of the church's protection, but, now, are being turned over to Satan.

Church leaders who refuse to be disciplined by the church and who persist in pursuing ungodliness and teaching false doctrine are *blaspheming* the very name of God and must be dealt with. Our Lord taught in Matthew 18 that those who continue in sin are to be put out of the church. Such people who are excommunicated are delivered to Satan.

III. SPECIAL FEATURES
A. Preserving Our Heritage

The apostle Paul's life experience recorded in Scripture should prove comforting and encouraging to us as we recognize that in spite of his past, it did not determine his future. It matters little from whence we came; it matters most where we are going. As ministers of the Gospel of Jesus Christ, we should not seek to portray ourselves as self-righteous individuals in whom there is found no guile. Rather, it is both liberating to us and to those to whom we minister when we openly and earnestly acknowledge not only where we are at present, but also, from whence we have come. In so doing, we encourage others in their journey toward holiness. "There is no secret what God can do, what He has done for others, He will do for you!"

B. Concluding Reflections

Grace may be defined as "God's loving forgiveness," by which He grants exemption from judgment, and the promise of temporal and eternal blessing to guilty and condemned sinners freely—without any worthiness on their part, and based on nothing they have done or failed to do. Paul emphasized that he had been a recipient of that grace by expressing four aspects of God's grace in his life.

First, for "electing grace"—Paul was ever conscious of God's choice of him, both for salvation and apostleship. Second, for "enabling grace"—through God's grace, Paul was strengthened. God not only graciously elected him to salvation, but also graciously gave him the strength he did not have or deserve, but needed to live out that salvation. Third, for "entrusting grace"—God considered him faithful, or trustworthy, and it was that grace that made him so. Fourth, for the "employing grace" that put him into service—for this grace, he used the Greek word *diakonia* (service), which refers to lowly, humble service.

HOME DAILY BIBLE READINGS

for the week of January 1, 2006
God Gives Strength

Dec. 26, Monday
  —Psalm 119:25-32
  —Strengthen Me, O God
Dec. 27, Tuesday
  —Romans 16:17-27
  —God Is Able to Strengthen You
Dec. 28, Wednesday
  —1 Thessalonians 3:1-5
  —We Sent Timothy to Strengthen You
Dec. 29, Thursday
  —1 Thessalonians 3:6-13
  —May God Strengthen Your Hearts
Dec. 30, Friday
  —Acts 16:1-5
  —Paul, Silas and Timothy Strengthen Churches
Dec. 31, Saturday
  —1 Timothy 1:1-11
  —Paul Writes to Timothy
Jan. 1, Sunday
  —1 Timothy 1:12-20
  —Strengthened by Christ

PRAYER

Our heavenly Father, we readily confess that we do not measure up to Your standard, but we also readily present our bodies to You as living sacrifices, praying that You would so account us as being trustworthy servants and place us in Your ministry. In the name of Jesus Christ, we pray. Amen.

Lesson 6

Pray for Everyone

CHILDREN'S UNIT
God Gives Good Leaders

ADULT TOPIC: Everyone Needs Prayer
YOUTH TOPIC: Who Needs Prayer?
CHILDREN'S TOPIC: Good Leaders Pray for Everyone

KEY VERSE
I exhort therefore, that, first of all, supplications, prayers, intercessions, and giving of thanks, be made for all men. —1 Timothy 2:1

DEVOTIONAL READING: 1 Thessalonians 5:16-22
BACKGROUND SCRIPTURE: 1 Timothy 2
PRINT PASSAGE: 1 Timothy 2:1-8

1 Timothy 2:1-8—KJV

I EXHORT therefore, that, first of all, supplications, prayers, intercessions, and giving of thanks, be made for all men;

2 For kings, and for all that are in authority; that we may lead a quiet and peaceable life in all godliness and honesty.

3 For this is good and acceptable in the sight of God our Saviour;

4 Who will have all men to be saved, and to come unto the knowledge of the truth.

5 For there is one God, and one mediator between God and men, the man Christ Jesus;

6 Who gave himself a ransom for all, to be testified in due time.

7 Whereunto I am ordained a preacher, and an apostle, (I speak the truth in Christ, and lie not;) a teacher of the Gentiles in faith and verity.

8 I will therefore that men pray every where, lifting up holy hands, without wrath and doubting.

1 Timothy 2:1-8—NRSV

FIRST OF all, then, I urge that supplications, prayers, intercessions, and thanksgivings be made for everyone,

OBJECTIVES
Upon completion of this lesson, students should affirm to:
1. Emphasize the role of prayer in the life of the believer.
2. Teach the various kinds of prayers found in Scripture.
3. Emphasize the commandment to pray for one another.
4. Teach others how to pray.

2 for kings and all who are in high positions, so that we may lead a quiet and peaceable life in all godliness and dignity.

3 This is right and is acceptable in the sight of God our Savior,

4 who desires everyone to be saved and to come to the knowledge of the truth.

5 For there is one God; there is also one mediator between God and humankind, Christ Jesus, himself human,

6 who gave himself a ransom for all—this was attested at the right time.

7 For this I was appointed a herald and an apostle (I am telling the truth, I am not lying), a teacher of the Gentiles in faith and truth.

8 I desire, then, that in every place the men should pray, lifting up holy hands without anger or argument.

POINTS TO BE EMPHASIZED
ADULTS
Key Verse: 1 Timothy 2:1
Print: 1 Timothy 2:1-8
—Prayer promotes godliness.
—Paul counseled Timothy to pray for everyone—even those who might be enemies.
—Through Christ, we approach God in prayer.

YOUTH
Key Verse: 1 Timothy 2:1
Print: 1 Timothy 2:1-10
—God calls us to respect and pray for all people.
—God desires for people to live at peace with one another.

—Christians are to pray for those who are in authority, even though the authorities may be persecuting the church.
—Christians are to witness to others by example.

CHILDREN
Key Verse: 1 Timothy 2:1
Print: Acts 25:13-14, 22-23; 26:1, 12-14a, 15-16, 19, 22-23, 27-29; 1 Timothy 2:1
—Paul, a prayerful Christian leader, had been falsely accused and was on trial.
—Christians use every opportunity to tell others about Christ and His redeeming power.
—Christians often sacrifice personal safety and well-being in order to tell others about Christ.
—Christian leaders often teach young Christians to pray by example.

TOPICAL OUTLINE OF THE LESSON

I. **INTRODUCTION**
   A. Setting Priorities
   B. Biblical Background

II. **EXPOSITION AND APPLICATION OF THE SCRIPTURE**
   A. Pray for All People *(1 Timothy 2:1)*
   B. Pray for Those in Political Offices *(1 Timothy 2:2-4)*
   C. There Is One God and Mediator *(1 Timothy 2:5-7)*
   D. Believers Ought to Pray *(1 Timothy 2:8)*

III. **SPECIAL FEATURES**
   A. Preserving Our Heritage
   B. Concluding Reflections

I. Introduction
A. Setting Priorities

From his concerns about false teachers, Paul turns to matters relating to the conduct of the church broadly (cf., 3:14-15). Paul began with what he considered most important: prayer. What too often comes last in a church's priorities should actually come first.

It must be remembered that the church is an organism, as well as an organization. As such, we should see the interrelationship of the one to the other, recognizing that if an organization is *disorganized,* it will surely die. The Spirit of God keeps the organization alive and guards it against becoming disorganized. Therefore, the Spirit must be granted the freedom to operate. In so doing, it is important to remember that the "freedom of the Spirit" does not mean that the church is to be guided by the carnal ideas of some Christian who is not walking in the Spirit. Such imagined "freedom" eventually becomes anarchy, and the Spirit grieves as a church gradually moves away from the standards of God's Word.

B. Biblical Background

The importance of prayer in the lives of God's people in the Old Testament means that it must hold a position of high priority in the local church. The local church does not pray because it is the expected thing to do; it prays because prayer is vital to the life of the local church. The Holy Spirit works in the church through prayer and the Word of God (1 Thessalonians 2:13; Ephesians 3:20-21). The church that prays will have power and will make a lasting impact for Christ. Paul exhorts us to pray—it is important!

We are commanded to pray for all people, for prayer helps to maintain the peace of society. As Christians pray for leaders in government, God overrules and protects His church from the wicked. In addition, it is by praying for the salvation of the lost that we please God and glorify Christ. Christ died for all people, and God would have all people to be saved (see 2 Peter 3:9). Therefore, the Spirit directs the believer to pray for lost people.

II. Exposition and Application of the Scripture
A. Pray for All People *(1 Timothy 2:1)*

First of all. Paul lists prayer as one of the primary duties of the church. Timothy, as pastor, was to take care and ensure that this be done. The first three terms Paul uses are virtually synonymous, with some subtle shades of meaning that enrich our concept of prayer. *Supplications*—from *deesis,* also translated as *entreaties, requests,* whose root meaning is "to be deprived," or "to be without something"—is prayer that arises out of needs. Herein, Timothy was to instruct the church to pray for the needs of the church, but particularly for the need of salvation for lost souls. *Prayers,* from *proseuche,* is a general word for prayer and is used in Scripture only in reference to God. Thus, this form of prayer is that of worship and adoration. *Petitions,* from *enteuxis,* is also translated as *intercessions.* It comes from a root word meaning, "to fall in with someone," or get involved with them. The verb form from which it is derived speaks of both Christ and the Spirit's intercession for us (Romans 8:26; Hebrews 7:25). They identify with our needs and become involved in our struggles. It denotes, therefore, a word of advocacy, as well as one of empathy, sympathy, compassion and involvement. Here, believers are exhorted to pray for the needs of others. *And giving of thanks.* This type of prayer calls for us to pray with a spirit of gratitude to God for blessings already received.

The Christian church must be praying people. In so doing, our prayers are not to be restricted to ourselves or those with whom we are related; we must also pray *for all men,* for humanity in general, for particular persons who need or desire our prayers. This is a clear indication of how Christianity differs from cults or other sects, which teach a kind of exclusivism—praying only for those who belong to their group.

B. Pray for Those in Political Offices *(1 Timothy 2:2-4)*

For kings, and all those that are in authority; that is, inferior magistrates. Though the kings at this time were heathens, enemies to Christianity, and persecutors of Christians, yet they were instructed to pray for them, because it is for the public good that there should be civil government, and proper persons entrusted with the administration of it. We, likewise, must recognize the need for us to pray for those in political offices in our communities and in our country. Even though they may be unbelievers whose practices are ungodly, we must nevertheless pray for them. Our prayers for them will accrue to our benefit that *we may lead a quiet and peaceable life in all godliness and honesty.* Let us mind our duty; then we may expect to be taken under the protection both of God and the government. Indeed, our duty as Christians is summed up in these two words: *godliness*—that is, the

The qualities of right worship resemble those of a well-conducted household. The household character of church leaders can determine their ability to hold office within the church. Paul's list includes instructions about overseers (bishops), deacons and deaconesses. The aim of worship—reverence offered a divine being or supernatural power—is the salvation of all. The heaped-up language—supplications, prayers, intercessions and thanksgiving—indicates the centrality of prayer in Christian worship. There is fullness and emphasis, not distinction. The Christian must actively seek the salvation of all persons, not excluding kings and all who are in high positions. "Godliness," or religion, and "honesty," or seriousness, are the Greek counterparts to the Hebraic concept of holiness and righteousness. "Knowledge of the truth" is acceptance of a revelation of the received faith which is truth, arrived at through repentance. "Mediator" is applied to Christ, ascribing this function only to Him, excluding Jewish and Gnostic mediators, whether Moses or the law, high priests or angels.

right worshiping of God; and *honesty—* that is, a good conduct toward all people. These two must go together; we are not truly honest if we are not godly, and do not render to God His due; and we are not truly godly if we are not honest, rendering to everyone their just due. Now the reason he gives for this is *because this is good in the sight of God our Savior;* that is, the Gospel of Christ requires this. Praying in various ways for not only ourselves, but for all people is pleasing in the sight of God.

Who desires all men to be saved. One reason why our prayers should include concern for all humanity is that it shows God's love to humanity in general, bearing witness that there is but one God, and that one God bears a good will to all humankind, desiring all people to be saved. It does not mean that everyone will be saved, for only those whom God has elected will be saved. Yet, we are required to pray for everyone because we do not know whom He has elected. Our duty is to pray; God's sovereign privilege is to save whom He desires; therefore, we are to pray His heart's desire that all be saved, *and to come to the knowledge of the truth.* It is the duty of every person to get the knowledge of the truth, because that is the way to be saved. Indeed, Christ is the Way and the Truth, and so He is the Life.

C. There Is One God and Mediator
(1 Timothy 2:5-7)

For there is one God. The word "One" has no bearing on the Christian doctrine of the Trinity; it is simply intended to emphasize the uniqueness of the relationship of God to man. The oneness of God has a bearing on the practical question of human salvation. It is possible for all people to be saved, because over them there are not many gods that can exercise conflicting will power toward them, but one only… *and one Mediator between God and man.* The word "mediator" is *mesites,* "one who intervenes between two, either in order to make or restore peace and friendship, or to form a compact or ratify a covenant." Our Lord is a mediator in that by His death, He intervenes between God and humanity, making possible the restoration of harmony between the two parties. *The Man Christ Jesus.* The absence of the article before *anthropos, man* suggests the translation, *"Christ Jesus, Himself man."* As the perfect God-man, He brings God and humanity together. All who come to God must come through Him. Therefore, our prayers for humanity ought to begin with praying for them to accept Christ as Savior.

Who gave Himself. This speaks of the fact that our Lord's death was a spontaneous and voluntary sacrifice on His part. This statement necessarily implies not only the pre-existence of our Lord, but also His cooperation in the eternal counsels and purpose of the Father in regards to the salvation of humanity. *A ransom for all.* This word, *ransom,* simply means "instead of" and was a common word used of the payment for a slave or a prisoner's release.

The death of Christ was a ransom—a counter-price paid instead of death that all people deserved. *To be testified in due time.* The "due time" refers to the time of the church age—that unique, particular season for the proclamation of the Gospel based upon the historic work of Christ on the Cross. The Gospel was preached throughout the Old Testament times, but this was on the basis of a prophetic work of salvation which was yet to be worked out on the Cross.

And an apostle. The word "apostle" has the basic meaning of "one sent," and refers to someone sent with a commission and credentials to act on behalf of another. It was used of someone who was an ambassador or representative of someone else. Paul was appointed to serve as an ambassador for the Lord Jesus Christ. *I am speaking the truth and not lying.* As Paul was constantly struggling against those who doubted his position, he was apt to feel defensive by sensing the need to emphasize his standing. *Teacher of the Gentiles.* Besides his general call to the apostleship, he was commissioned particularly to preach to the Gentiles—that is, those who are not Jews by birth. *In faith and truth* refers to the sphere in which the apostle discharges his apostolic function. Truth, in the thinking of the Greeks, is that which is not covered or hidden—that which is open for inspection. Thus, the apostle preaches and teaches with a sincere faith in the Gospel, and with a truthful representation of what has been revealed.

Those who are saved must come to the knowledge of the truth, for this is God's appointed way to save sinners. Without knowledge, the heart cannot be good; if we do not know the truth, we cannot be ruled by it. Paul was ordained a minister to declare this to the Gentiles: Christ is the one Mediator between God and humankind, who gave Himself a ransom for all. This is the substance of which all ministers are to preach to the end of the world. Ministers must preach the truth—what they apprehend to be so—they must believe it themselves, and, like the apostle, they must do so in faith and sincerity.

D. Believers Ought to Pray
(1 Timothy 2:8)

I desire therefore that the men pray everywhere. The word "therefore" is resumptive, picking up again the general topic of prayer from which Paul digressed in verses 3-7. Notice the use of the definite article "the" in front of men and the use of the Greek word *aner* for "men" specifies males as opposed to females. This verse thrusted responsibility upon the men to be leaders in prayer—both publicly and privately. Their readiness in prayer would distinguish them as followers of Christ. In the subsequent verses, Paul admonished the women to carry themselves in such a way that they would be distinguished from unbelieving women. The word "everywhere" more appropriately should be *"in every place,"* a phrase used by Paul three times (cf., 1 Corinthians 1:2;

2 Corinthians 2:14; 1 Thessalonians 1:8), and in every case he uses it in reference to the official assembly of the church—that means wherever Christian congregations assemble, not in every place indiscriminately. *Lifting up holy hands.* The word "holy" here is not *hagios,* referring to being set apart for God, but *hosios,* which means "unpolluted" or "unstained by evil." Thus, it refers to hands that are pure from the pollution of sin. The idea is that those who would pray for others effectively must, first of all, cleanse their hands of sin through confession and repentance. The emphasis here is not upon a particular position or posture. Hands symbolized the activities of life, and the lifting of holy hands meant a holy life… *without wrath,* or malice, or anger at any person. We must pray in faith *without doubting* (James 1:6).

III. SPECIAL FEATURES
A. Preserving Our Heritage

Prayer has always been a prominent feature of our heritage. Our forebears, who labored under the yoke of the slave master's whip, relied upon prayer as a means of persevering. They believed that through prayer, even the hard-heartedness of the cruel slave master could be softened. They saw prayer as a means of communicating with a God who could and would intervene on their behalf. Prayer was a dominant feature of the infant Black church that was formed after our separation from the dominant White majority. Indeed, it was a vital part of the training that prepared demonstrators to face the snarling dogs of racism during the Civil Rights protest movement. If we as a people are to survive and prosper in this world of chaos and confusion, we will do so by continuing to nurture the practice of prayer.

B. Concluding Reflections

Prayer is conversing with God—the intercourse of the soul with God, not in contemplation or meditation, but in direct address to Him. Prayer may be oral or mental, occasional or constant, informal or formal. It is a: "beseeching the Lord" (Exodus 32:11); "pouring out the soul before the Lord" (1 Samuel 1:15); "praying and crying to heaven" (2 Chronicles 32:20); "seeking unto God and making supplication" (Job 8:5); "drawing near to God" (Psalm 73:28); and "bowing the knees" (Ephesians 3:14).

Prayer presupposes a belief in the personality of God, His ability and willingness to hold intercourse with us, and His personal control of all things and of all His creatures and all their actions.

Acceptable prayer must be sincere (Hebrews 10:22), offered with reverence and godly fear, with a humble sense of our own insignificance as creatures and of our own unworthiness as sinners, with earnest importunity, and with unhesitating submission to the divine will. Prayer must also be offered in the faith that God is, and is the hearer and answerer of prayer, and that He will fulfill His Word—"Ask, and ye shall receive" (Matthew 7:7-8;

21:22; Mark 11:24; John 14:13-14); and in the name of Christ (John 15:16; 16:23-24; Ephesians 2:18; 5:20; Colossians 3:17).

If the teacher-preacher is to deliver God's message with power, prayer must permeate that person's life and furnish an environment for the fruit of the Spirit (Galatians 5:22-23). Such a spiritual example causes others to take the message seriously. As followers of God, our spiritual credibility forcefully attracts others to follow us, because as trailblazers, we can be seen practicing single-minded devotion to God. In so doing, we humbly render all glory to God and submit to His Word. True godly prayer demonstrates honesty and discipline of the tongue, time, mind and body, along with fervent resourcefulness. As the teacher calls others to obedience, God uses his trailblazing leadership to mark the way. All desirable spiritual qualities, particularly godliness and dependence on God, are basic ingredients in the experience of a praying teacher-preacher.

A noble child of God, a person of prayer, is passionate in pursuing God and His values (Psalm 42:1-2). True leaders live for God and model lives shaped by the godliness they recommend for others.

HOME DAILY BIBLE READINGS

for the week of January 8, 2006
Pray for Everyone

Jan. 2, Monday
—Philippians 1:3-11
—Paul Prays for the Philippians

Jan. 3, Tuesday
—1 Thessalonians 5:16-22
—Pray Without Ceasing

Jan. 4, Wednesday
—1 Peter 3:8-12a
—God Hears Our Prayers

Jan. 5, Thursday
—Luke 18:1-8
—A Parable About Praying

Jan. 6, Friday
—Matthew 5:43-48
—Pray for Your Enemies

Jan. 7, Saturday
—1 Timothy 2:1-7
—Pray for Everyone

Jan. 8, Sunday
—James 5:13-18
—Prayer Is Powerful and Effective

PRAYER

Dear God, our merciful Father, we thank You for the privilege of prayer. Thank You for being a God who hears and answers the prayers of Your people. We readily confess that we are not worthy of such a privilege, but because of Your Word we may approach Your throne and find grace and mercy, we beseech You on behalf of our leaders. Amen.

Lesson 7

God Calls Church Leaders

CHILDREN'S UNIT
God Gives Good Leaders

ADULT TOPIC: Leading God's People
YOUTH TOPIC: Leading by Example
CHILDREN'S TOPIC: Good Leaders Serve Others

KEY VERSE
Holding the mystery of the
faith in a pure conscience.
—1 Timothy 3:9

DEVOTIONAL READING: Mark 9:33-37
BACKGROUND SCRIPTURE: 1 Timothy 3
PRINT PASSAGE: 1 Timothy 3:2-15

OBJECTIVES
At the conclusion of this
lesson, students should
affirm that:
1. God has set high stan-
   dards for those who
   serve as leaders in the
   church.
2. Scripture identifies the
   spiritual qualities that
   God desires for those
   who serve as leaders in
   the church.
3. It is important that leaders adhere to godly
   standards in their de-
   portment.

1 Timothy 3:2-15—KJV

2 A bishop then must be blameless, the husband of one
wife, vigilant, sober, of good behaviour, given to hospitality,
apt to teach;

3 Not given to wine, no striker, not greedy of filthy lucre;
but patient, not a brawler, not covetous;

4 One that ruleth well his own house, having his children
in subjection with all gravity;

5 (For if a man know not how to rule his own house, how
shall he take care of the church of God?)

6 Not a novice, lest being lifted up with pride he fall into
the condemnation of the devil.

7 Moreover he must have a good report of them which
are without; lest he fall into reproach and the snare of the devil.

8 Likewise must the deacons be grave, not doubletongued,
not given to much wine, not greedy of filthy lucre;

9 Holding the mystery of the faith in a pure conscience.

10 And let these also first be proved; then let them use the
office of a deacon, being found blameless.

11 Even so must their wives be grave, not slanderers, sober, faithful in all things.

12 Let the deacons be the husbands of one wife, ruling their children and their own houses well.

13 For they that have used the office of a deacon well purchase to themselves a good degree, and great boldness in the faith which is in Christ Jesus.

14 These things write I unto thee, hoping to come unto thee shortly:

15 But if I tarry long, that thou mayest know how thou oughtest to behave thyself in the house of God, which is the church of the living God, the pillar and ground of the truth.

1 Timothy 3:2-15—NRSV

2 Now a bishop must be above reproach, married only once, temperate, sensible, respectable, hospitable, an apt teacher,

3 not a drunkard, not violent but gentle, not quarrelsome, and not a lover of money.

4 He must manage his own household well, keeping his children submissive and respectful in every way—

5 for if someone does not know how to manage his own household, how can he take care of God's church?

6 He must not be a recent convert, or he may be puffed up with conceit and fall into the condemnation of the devil.

7 Moreover, he must be well thought of by outsiders, so that he may not fall into disgrace and the snare of the devil.

8 Deacons likewise must be serious, not double-tongued, not indulging in much wine, not greedy for money;

9 they must hold fast to the mystery of the faith with a clear conscience.

10 And let them first be tested; then, if they prove themselves blameless, let them serve as deacons.

11 Women likewise must be serious, not slanderers, but temperate, faithful in all things.

12 Let deacons be married only once, and let them manage their children and their households well;

13 for those who serve well as deacons gain a good standing for themselves and great boldness in the faith that is in Christ Jesus.

14 I hope to come to you soon, but I am writing these instructions to you so that,

15 if I am delayed, you may know how one ought to behave in the household of God, which is the church of the living God, the pillar and bulwark of the truth.

POINTS TO BE EMPHASIZED
ADULTS
Key Verse: 1 Timothy 3:9
Print: 1 Timothy 3:2-15
—Serving God in the church is a noble calling.
—Church leaders should have impeccable reputations in the community.
—Church leaders are to be temperate in all areas of life.

YOUTH
Key Verse: 1 Timothy 3:14-15
Print: 1 Timothy 3:1-15

—Paul lifts up a standard for leaders to adhere to.

—Paul identifies some moral high ground for Christian leaders.

—God calls all of us, especially leaders, to live above reproach.

CHILDREN
Key Verse: Mark 9:35
Print: Mark 9:30-37; 1 Timothy 3:14-15

—God is not pleased when church leaders argue about their personal success and position.

—Jesus taught that greatness in God's kingdom is achieved through humility and service.

—Church leaders must possess the humble, meek and mild disposition of a child as they interact with others.

—Jesus used a little child to demonstrate that church leaders who are humble and self-denying resemble Christ and are favored by God.

TOPICAL OUTLINE OF THE LESSON

I. INTRODUCTION
   A. The Posture of Leadership
   B. Biblical Background

II. EXPOSITION AND APPLICATION OF THE SCRIPTURE
   A. Qualifications to Be an Overseer
   (1 Timothy 3:2)
   B. The Overseer's Prohibitions
   (1 Timothy 3:3)
   C. Godly and Family-oriented
   (1 Timothy 3:4-5)

   D. Not a New Convert
   (1 Timothy 3:6-7)
   E. Qualifications for Deacons
   (1 Timothy 3:8-10)
   F. Deacons' Wives with Concluding Injunctions *(1 Timothy 3:11-15)*

III. SPECIAL FEATURES
   A. Preserving Our Heritage
   B. Concluding Reflections

I. INTRODUCTION
A. The Posture of Leadership

Paul moves from discussing the congregation (2:1-15) to dealing with the pastors. The ministry, effectiveness and testimony of any church are largely a reflection of its leaders. The principle of Hosea 4:9 is still true: *"And it will be, like people, like priest."* People do not usually rise above the level of their leaders. So important is it that those who lead the church be highly qualified spiritually that the detailed list of their specific qualifications are entered twice in Paul's letters—here, and in Titus 1. Church leadership is at the core of New Testament teaching, since the Lord came into this world to establish the church (Matthew 16:18).

Though the church is an organism, a living and growing body united to Christ, the church is also an organization. In fact, every organism has to be organized or it will die. The human body is a living organism, but it is also a highly organized machine. If the local church is to do its task effectively, it must have leadership, and this implies organization. Having given instructions on how the church should conduct itself, Paul turned to the crucial matter of leadership qualifications.

B. Biblical Background

The church at Ephesus had been blessed with leadership of the highest caliber. It was founded by Paul who ministered there for three years (Acts 20:31). During that time, he trained a core of godly leaders (Acts 20:17ff) to lead the church after he left. As he foresaw, however, false leaders arose after his departure from Ephesus (Acts 20:29-30). After his release from his first Roman imprisonment, Paul returned to Ephesus and dealt with two prominent ones (1:20). Leaving Timothy to deal with the rest of them, he set out for Macedonia (1:3). Not long afterward, he wrote this letter to Timothy, directing him with a strategy to correct and build up the Ephesian church. At the heart of the task was the crucial need to reestablish a godly leadership. Choosing the right elders was to be done by measuring candidates against a divinely inspired checklist of qualifications.

All the qualifications Paul lists are spiritual virtues, character traits that mark godly teachers and leaders. He says nothing about the duties of the leaders, but is concerned only with their spirituality, morality and virtue as the necessary foundation of duty. All who serve as overseers or elders in the church must measure up to these standards.

II. EXPOSITION AND APPLICATION OF THE SCRIPTURE

A. Qualifications to Be an Overseer
(1 Timothy 3:2)

The word "bishop" is a rendering of *episkopos,* "to look over, to oversee, to superintend, to exercise oversight or care over." The word originally came from secular life, referring to the foreman of a construction gang, or the supervisor of building construction. The word was adopted by the Christian church; a person with such a title was designated as overseer of any Christian church. The responsibilities of this new office have to do with the oversight and direction of the spiritual life of the local church. It, therefore, refers to those who serve as pastors or leaders of local congregations. In our day, especially with the advent of megachurches, the word "bishop" has been encumbered with much ecclesiastical trapping and implies a certain advanced level of authority. In the New Testament, however, the term was used to refer to all those who served in the role as pastor or elder. *Must be blameless.* The word "blameless" is made up of two words, whose compound meaning is "to lay hold upon." The Greek letter Alpha that renders it in the negative prefixes it. Thus, *blameless* means literally "one who cannot be laid hold upon."

Husband of one wife—literally, a "one-woman man." This ambiguous but important phrase is subject to several interpretations. The question is: How stringent a standard was Paul erecting for overseers? Virtually all commentators agree that this phrase prohibits both polygamy and promiscuity, which are unthinkable for spiritual leaders in the church. Paul is not referring to one's marital status, as the absence of the definite article in the original indicates. Rather, the issue is a church leader's moral, sexual behavior. Many men married only once are not "one-woman men," as many with one wife are unfaithful to that one wife. While remaining married to one spouse is commendable, it is no indication or guarantee of moral purity.

A "one-woman man" is a man devoted in heart and mind to the woman who is his wife. He loves, desires and thinks only of her. He maintains sexual purity in his thought, life and conduct. Paul's words do not disqualify a single person, for Paul himself was single (1 Corinthians 7:8). Nor does it disqualify one who has been previously married, for even our Lord permitted remarriage when a divorce was caused by adultery (Matthew 5:31-32; 19:9). The emphasis properly placed again is not upon marital status, but upon moral character.

B. The Overseer's Prohibitions *(1 Timothy 3:3)*

Not given to much wine is from a compound word that means "not one who sits long at his wine." Paul's meaning is that the overseer, in partaking wine, which in the first century was a common beverage not having the associations with which it is identified today, must not drink it so freely that he becomes intoxicated and hence quarrelsome. *Not violent or no striker* is from the phrase meaning one who is "a bruiser, one who is ready with a blow, a pugnacious, contentious, quarrelsome person. The leader in the church must not be a person who resorts to physical violence as a means of settling a dispute. Leaders must confront difficulties cool and calmly without becoming angry and losing their tempers. *Not greedy of filthy lucre.* He must not (be) a lover of money (cf., 6:5; Titus 1:11). Leaders neither relish fighting with others nor pursue ministry for personal

Paul exhorts good behavior as that behavior consistent with belief. The exhortations contrast right behavior with that of the deviating teachers, who practice self-control in ways that do not show the goodness of creation in the lives of believers as they seek to influence others. According to Paul, a bishop must be blameless: a person against whom no evil can be proven. He must be the husband of one wife—no polygamists. He must be vigilant, watchful: one who drinks is apt to sleep, so he who abstains is more likely to keep awake and attend to his work and charge. He must be sober: a man of sound mind, having a good understanding and complete government of all his passions. He must be of good behavior: a clownish, rude, or boorish man should never have rule of the church of Christ. Given to hospitality: one who is ready to receive into his home and relieve the necessities of strangers. Apt to teach: not only wise himself, but ready to communicate his wisdom to others. Not given to wine: one who is inordinately attached to wine, impervious, abusive, insolent, whether through wine or otherwise. Not a brawler, contentious or litigious, but quiet and peaceable.

gain (cf., 1 Peter 5:2). The leader must not be greedy, stingy, or financially ambitious. *He must be patient* refers to the quality of being able to wait for the Lord's people, to listen to them and take criticism without reacting; and, as well, having the ability to endure others' shortcomings.

C. Godly and Family-oriented
(1 Timothy 3:4-5)

He must be one who rules his own house well, having his children in submission with all reverence. As was indicated above, this does not mean that the overseer must be married or have children. However, if he is, he must oversee his own household well. The minister's children and family members must demonstrate respect and obedience. For Christians, the church is an extension of the home, and one is a reflection of the other. The minister's home life must provide a model for others. *For if a man know not how to rule his own household, how shall he rule the house of God.* There is a direct correlation between the leader's ability to oversee his own household and his ability to oversee the household of God. Has he been able, for example, to lead those of his own household to accept the lordship of Jesus in their lives? How well has he resolved conflict, built unity, and maintained love between the members of his own household? These are indices of a leader's ability, or lack thereof, to oversee the household of God.

D. Not a New Convert
(1 Timothy 3:6-7)

Not a novice is from *neophutos,* a word used to refer to newly planted palm trees, and used here of a new convert. The leader must not be a neophyte. *Lest being lifted up with pride.* Lest his rapid advancement to leadership fill him with pride and conceit, *and he fall into the condemnation of the devil.* The condemnation of the devil refers to the fact that Satan is under the condemnatory sentence of God because of his original sin of rebellion against God, a sin that was motivated by pride. A new convert that is placed into a position of leadership is being set up for falling into the sin of pride. We must guard against appointing new converts to positions of leadership in the church based upon some secular experience or standing in the community prior to their conversion experience.

An overseer must also have a good reputation with outsiders (cf., Colossians 4:5; 1 Thessalonians 4:12). Paul's thought here seems to be that church leaders, as representatives of the congregation, are constantly susceptible to the snares of the devil (cf., 2 Timothy 2:26). Satan likes nothing better than to disgrace God's work and God's people by trapping church leaders in sin before a watching world. It is important, therefore, that overseers achieve and maintain a good reputation before unbelievers.

E. Qualifications for Deacons
(1 Timothy 3:8-10)

Like overseers, deacons (cf., Philippians 1:1) must also be persons of quality, even though their function in the congregation is significantly different. The word translated "deacon" (*diakonos*) literally means "humble servant." The role of the deacons is to carry out, under the elders' oversight, some of the more menial tasks of the church so that the elders can give their attention to more important things (see Acts 6:1-6 for the prototype of what later became the "office" of deacon in the church). The qualifications for the office of deacon are almost as stringent as for elder because of their public profile in the church, and because the servant nature of their work requires strong qualities of maturity and piety. Deacons must therefore be worthy of respect—that is, be serious and carry themselves with dignity, not clowns. They must be sincere, literally, "not double-tongued," in the sense of being honest and unhypocritical. Like the overseers, deacons must not be heavy wine drinkers or greedy chasers after dishonest gain.

Most importantly, deacons must possess spiritual depth (cf., Acts 6:3). Specifically, they should understand and hold fast the deep truths of the faith. By the phrase "with a clear conscience," Paul (cf., "good conscience" in 1 Timothy 1:5) meant that there must be nothing in the conduct of these men that was glaringly inconsistent with their professed beliefs.

In other words, they must not profess one thing, but practice another.

F. Deacons' Wives with Concluding Injunctions *(1 Timothy 3:11-15)*

Similarly, the *gynaikas* ("women" or wives) are to be worthy of respect; that is, dignified (the same word, *semnas,* is used of deacons in verse 8), not slanderers (*diabolous,* from diaball "to slander;" from this verb comes the noun "devil," the chief slanderer) of others, but temperate (*nephalious,* "well-balanced"; cf. verse 2; Titus 2:2) and trustworthy (lit. "faithful") in everything. Who are these *gynaikas* Paul addressed? They were almost certainly not the women of the congregation generally. They were most likely either the wives of the deacons or a group of female deacons (cf., Phoebe, Romans 16:1). A case can be made for either of these two options, with a slim advantage falling to the first. But being dogmatic about either view is unwarranted by the exegetical data.

Like the elders, deacons must be faithful (cf., verse 2) and capable managers of their own families. Paul's reasoning behind this latter qualification is spelled out in verses 4-5.

III. SPECIAL FEATURES
A. Preserving Our Heritage

There has been nothing more damaging to the cause of Christ in the African American church than that of ungodly leaders. Far too many of our leaders have themselves been guilty of the sins which they preach against and condemn in others. Far too many have proclaimed Christ's transforming power, yet remain unchanged themselves. The National Baptist Convention can never become what God has ordained it to be if we, who proclaim God's governing power, negate it by becoming rebels ourselves. We who speak against evil ought not to be evildoers. We, who preach and teach God's threatening judgments to others, ought not to behave as if we do not fear them ourselves.

B. Concluding Reflections

From a different perspective, John R. Mott, a world leader in student circles in the early part of this century, gave the following list concerning leaders: Does he do things well? Has he learned the meaning of priorities? How does he use his leisure? Has he intensity? Has he learned to take advantage of momentum? Has he the power of growth? What is his attitude toward discouragements? How does he face impossible situations? What are his weakest points?

Those points, and many others like them, contain qualities every church leader should possess. But serving as leaders of God's people demands far more because the issue is not just leadership, but moral and spiritual example.

HOME DAILY BIBLE READINGS

for the week of January 15, 2006
God Calls Church Leaders

Jan. 9, Monday
—Deuteronomy 1:9-18
—Moses Appoints Israel's Tribal Leaders
Jan. 10, Tuesday
—Galatians 2:1-10
—Paul Is Welcomed as a Leader
Jan. 11, Wednesday
—1 Thessalonians 5:6-15
—Respect Those Who Labor Among You
Jan. 12, Thursday
—Titus 1:5-9
—Qualities of a Leader
Jan. 13, Friday
—Mark 9:33-37
—The Greatest Is Servant of All
Jan. 14, Saturday
—1 Timothy 3:1-7
—Qualifications of Overseers
Jan. 15, Sunday
—1 Timothy 3:8-15
—Qualifications of Helpers

PRAYER

God, our heavenly Father, we praise Your name and thank You for the privilege of prayer. Help us to fulfill Your design for the ministries into which You have called us. In Jesus' name, we pray. Amen.

Lesson 8

Guidance for Teaching

CHILDREN'S UNIT
God Gives Good Leaders

ADULT TOPIC: Set an Example
YOUTH TOPIC: Teaching by Example
CHILDREN'S TOPIC: Good Leaders Teach God's Word

KEY VERSE
Take heed unto thyself, and unto the doctrine; continue in them: for in doing this thou shalt both save thyself, and them that hear thee.
—1 Timothy 4:16

DEVOTIONAL READING: 1 Corinthians 3:6-11
BACKGROUND SCRIPTURE: 1 Timothy 4:1-16
PRINT PASSAGE: 1 Timothy 4:1-16

OBJECTIVES
Upon the completion of this lesson, students will be able to:
1. Explain why teaching is a spiritual gift.
2. Demonstrate the importance of teaching in the church.
3. Present the Christian virtues needed for teaching in the church arena.
4. Demonstrate the importance of role modeling for the Christian teacher.

1 Timothy 4:1-16—KJV

NOW THE Spirit speaketh expressly, that in the latter times some shall depart from the faith, giving heed to seducing spirits, and doctrines of devils;

2 Speaking lies in hypocrisy; having their conscience seared with a hot iron;

3 Forbidding to marry, and commanding to abstain from meats, which God hath created to be received with thanksgiving of them which believe and know the truth.

4 For every creature of God is good, and nothing to be refused, if it be received with thanksgiving:

5 For it is sanctified by the word of God and prayer.

6 If thou put the brethren in remembrance of these things, thou shalt be a good minister of Jesus Christ, nourished up in the words of faith and of good doctrine, whereunto thou hast attained.

7 But refuse profane and old wives' fables, and exercise thyself rather unto godliness.

8 For bodily exercise profiteth little: but godliness is profitable unto all things, having promise of the life that now is, and of that which is to come.

9 This is a faithful saying and worthy of all acceptation.

10 For therefore we both labour and suffer reproach, because we trust in the living God, who is the Saviour of all men, specially of those that believe.

11 These things command and teach.

12 Let no man despise thy youth; but be thou an example of the believers, in word, in conversation, in charity, in spirit, in faith, in purity.

13 Till I come, give attendance to reading, to exhortation, to doctrine.

14 Neglect not the gift that is in thee, which was given thee by prophecy, with the laying on of the hands of the presbytery.

15 Meditate upon these things; give thyself wholly to them; that thy profiting may appear to all.

16 Take heed unto thyself, and unto the doctrine; continue in them: for in doing this thou shalt both save thyself, and them that hear thee.

1 Timothy 4:1-16—NRSV

NOW THE Spirit expressly says that in later times some will renounce the faith by paying attention to deceitful spirits and teachings of demons,

2 through the hypocrisy of liars whose consciences are seared with a hot iron.

3 They forbid marriage and demand abstinence from foods, which God created to be received with thanksgiving by those who believe and know the truth.

4 For everything created by God is good, and nothing is to be rejected, provided it is received with thanksgiving;

5 for it is sanctified by God's word and by prayer.

6 If you put these instructions before the brothers and sisters, you will be a good servant of Christ Jesus, nourished on the words of the faith and of the sound teaching that you have followed.

7 Have nothing to do with profane myths and old wives' tales. Train yourself in godliness,

8 for, while physical training is of some value, godliness is valuable in every way, holding promise for both the present life and the life to come.

9 The saying is sure and worthy of full acceptance.

10 For to this end we toil and struggle, because we have our hope set on the living God, who is the Savior of all people, especially of those who believe.

11 These are the things you must insist on and teach.

12 Let no one despise your youth, but set the believers an example in speech and conduct, in love, in faith, in purity.

13 Until I arrive, give attention to the public reading of scripture, to exhorting, to teaching.

14 Do not neglect the gift that is in you, which was given to you through prophecy with the laying on of hands by the council of elders.

15 Put these things into practice, devote yourself to them, so that all may see your progress.

16 Pay close attention to yourself and to your teaching; continue in these things, for in doing this you will save both yourself and your hearers.

POINTS TO BE EMPHASIZED
ADULTS
Key Verse: 1 Timothy 4:16
Print: 1 Timothy 4:1-16
—Effective teaching is a gift from God.
—Teaching includes setting an example in speech, conduct, love, faith and purity.
—Teaching requires reflection and spiritual discernment.

YOUTH
Key Verse: 1 Timothy 4:12
Print: 1 Timothy 4:1-16
—Paul admonishes Timothy to teach godliness and the Good News.
—Paul advised Timothy to follow his instructions, which are based on sound teaching.
—There is a difference between true and false teaching.

CHILDREN
Key Verse: 1 Timothy 4:13
Print: Acts 11:19-26; 1 Timothy 4:7-16
—The believing Jews, who were persecuted in Jerusalem and scattered to faraway cities, proclaimed the Gospel of Jesus Christ wherever they went.
—Believers must use their God-given gifts to help the church grow spiritually and numerically.
—Timothy was confirmed by prophecy

and ordained by the elders of the church.
—Timothy served as a role model for pastors because of his purity in speech and conduct.

TOPICAL OUTLINE OF THE LESSON

I. **INTRODUCTION**
  A. Prepare for Apostasy
  B. Biblical Background

II. **EXPOSITION AND APPLICATION OF THE SCRIPTURE**
  A. Apostasy Prophesied *(1 Timothy 4:1)*
  B. Hypocrites *(1 Timothy 4:2)*
  C. False Laws of Asceticism *(1 Timothy 4:3-5)*
  D. Be an Example *(1 Timothy 4:6)*
  E. Reject Ungodliness *(1 Timothy 4:7-8)*
  F. Be an Example in Labor and Trust *(1 Timothy 4:9-11)*
  G. Youth Does Not Exempt from Example *(1 Timothy 4:12)*
  H. Public Reading of the Word *(1 Timothy 4:13-14)*
  I. An Example of Spiritual Growth *(1 Timothy 4:15-16)*

III. **SPECIAL FEATURES**
  A. Preserving Our Heritage
  B. Concluding Reflections

I. INTRODUCTION
A. Prepare for Apostasy

In this chapter, the apostle Paul warns his son Timothy of the coming apostasy and departure from the faith that would be seen in the church and how he as a minister was to deal with it. He begins by instructing him that as the repository and guardian of the truth, the church must be aware of the strategies of the enemies of truth. Timothy must recognize that spiritual error is seldom due to innocent mistakes. It is more often due to the conscious strategies of God's enemies. The false teachings, the apostle instructs, are instigated by demons. As such, their strategy is not to directly confront their victims with error; instead, they work through hypocritical liars (4:2)—that is, Satan's standard operating procedure is to select likely representatives, sear their consciences and render them beyond feeling. With seared minds, they are ready instruments in Satan's hands to do his bidding.

The work of these false teachers will result in causing many to fall away from the faith; and, additionally, Paul instructs him that the situation would degenerate as Christ's return approaches.

B. Biblical Background

The presence of apostate teachers at Ephesus is indicated from 1:3-7, 18-20. In chapters 2—3, Paul dealt with some of the ramifications of their false teaching and corruption of the church. He countered their deceptions with the divine design for men and women in the church, and the spiritual qualifications for true church leaders. Chapter 3 closed with a creedal statement affirming what apostates most directly deny and what is the central truth of the Christian faith: the person and work

of Jesus Christ. In chapter 4, Paul returns to his discussion of the false teachers themselves. While not always popular in our day of toleration and "love," there is a biblical mandate to deal directly and firmly with false teaching. Any tolerance of error regarding God's revelation is a direct form of dishonor to Him.

II. EXPOSITION AND APPLICATION OF THE SCRIPTURE

A. Apostasy Prophesied (1 Timothy 4:1)

We have here a prophecy of the apostasy of the latter times, which Paul spoke of as that to be expected and taken for granted among Christians. *The Spirit speaks expressly that in the latter times some shall depart from the faith* (2 Thessalonians 2:1). This prediction is part of the Holy Spirit's ongoing revelation in Scripture on the subject of apostasy. In the Old Testament, the Spirit warned of the consequences of apostasy (Deuteronomy 28:15ff; Ezekiel 20:38) and gave numerous examples of apostates (Exodus 32:1; 1 Samuel 15:11). He also warned about this coming apostasy in the New Testament, particularly at the time of the end, just before the Lord's return (Matthew 24:4-12; 2 Thessalonians 2:3-12). But apostasy, though escalated in the end time, is not limited to that era.

Giving heed to seducing spirits. The word "seducing" is from *planos,* "wandering, roving, misleading, leading into error." The word "spirits" refers to evil spirits who manifest themselves in humans. There is but one devil, himself a

"In latter times" refers to any times subsequent to those in which the church then lived. "Seducing spirits" are emissaries of every kind, which are employed to darken the hearts and destroy the souls of men. "Doctrine of Devils" is doctrine by Satan by which he secures his own interest and provides for his own worship. "Speaking lies in hypocrisy": persons pretending not only to have divine inspiration, but also to extraordinary degrees of holiness, self-denial and mortification. "Having their conscience seared with a hot iron": it was customary in ancient times to mark those with a hot iron who had been guilty of great crimes. "Forbidding to marry": priests pretending that a single life was much more favorable to devotion, and to the perfection of the Christian life. "To abstain from meat": prohibitions from eating certain meats; some always, others at certain times. This was contrary to the original design of God who declared every creature as good. "Put the brethren is remembrance": show the church that there is danger of apostasy and to put them on their guard against it. "Old wives' fables": profane fables that disgrace the intellect.

fallen angel. But, there are also many other fallen angels who make up Satan's demonic kingdom. The apostle says that the source of false doctrine is these demons, manifesting themselves in men who pretended to be guided by the Spirit of God (1 John 4:1).

B. Hypocrites *(1 Timothy 4:2)*

Speaking lies in hypocrisy; having their conscience seared with a hot iron refers to the human agents of the seducing spirits. Demons are spirits—free agents without physical bodies: and these are the deceiving spirits. They are the agents and emissaries of Satan, who promote these delusions by lies, forgeries and pretended miracles. It is done by their hypocrisy, professing honor to Christ, and yet at the same time, fighting against all His anointed offices, and corrupting or profaning all His ordinances. The metaphor, "branded in their conscience" is from the practice of branding slaves or criminals, the latter on the brow. These deceivers are not acting under delusion, but deliberately, and against conscience. They wear the form of godliness, and contradict their profession by their crooked conduct. The point is that one's conduct ought to be consistent with one's doctrine.

C. False Laws of Asceticism *(1 Timothy 4:3-5)*

Forbidding to marry and commanding to abstain from meats. One might have suspected that the demonic teaching would focus upon one of the more standard doctrines like the deity of Christ or the doctrine of salvation. Rather, the subtlety of the Evil One focuses upon some things from ordinary life, like marriage and food. We should be aware that anything contrary to Scripture could become the entry point of demonic teaching, and be alert to teachings that seem to be harmless. As is typical of satanic deception, both of these teachings contain an element of truth. There is nothing wrong with singleness, and such a state may aid spiritual service (cf., 1 Corinthians 7:25-35). Nor is fasting wrong; it is a spiritual discipline that is an accompaniment to prayer (cf.,

Matthew 6:16-17; 9:14-15). The deception comes in seeing those as essential elements of salvation.

For every creature of God is good, and nothing to be refused, if it be received with thanksgiving. Having mentioned their hypocritical fasting, the apostle takes occasion to lay down the doctrine of Christian liberty, which we enjoy under the Gospel. Whereas under the law there was a distinction between clean and unclean meats (such sorts of flesh they might eat, and such they might not eat), all this is now taken away; and we are to call nothing common or unclean (Acts 10:15). The dietary regulations were temporary, intended to teach Israel the importance of discernment and to isolate the nation from the pagan societies around them. We must not refuse the gifts of God's bounty or be scrupulous in making differences where God has made none; but receive them, and be thankful, acknowledging the power of God as maker of them, and the bounty of God who gives them—*for it is sanctified by the word of God and prayer.* To be sanctified is to be set apart for holy use. The means by which that is accomplished are the Word of God which had declared all foods to be clean (cf., Acts 10:9-15; Romans 14:1-12). We ought therefore to ask His blessing by prayer, and so to sanctify the creatures we receive by prayer.

D. Be an Example *(1 Timothy 4:6)*

The word "brethren" is the translation of the word for "brother," and literally means "from the same womb." Thus, Christians are all related in the sense that they have the same heavenly Father. *In remembrance* is from a mild verb meaning "to point out" or "remind." *Of those things* refers back to the unbiblical, demonic doctrines. *You will be a good minister of Jesus Christ.* The word "minister" today generally refers to a licensed clergy, but in Paul's day it referred simply to one who was a "servant" and has special emphasis upon the servant as seen in his activity of serving. Therefore, it could refer to anyone who was serving in any capacity in the church, whether as teacher, deacon, trustee, or musician.

E. Reject Ungodliness
(1 Timothy 4:7-8)

Refuse profane and old wives' sayings. Timothy is exhorted to refuse, decline, reject those things that are not of a divine character. This included not only the various philosophies of the Greeks, but also many of the Jewish traditions, with which some people fill their heads. *But exercise thyself rather unto godliness.* Timothy is exhorted to exercise with a view toward excelling in godliness. Those who would be godly must exercise themselves unto godliness; it requires the same kind of diligence and determination that is required of one who excels in athletic competition. *For bodily exercise profits little,* or for a little time. The apostle refers to the ascetic practices which he mentioned above that took the form of physical exercise. Abstinence from meats and marriage, and the like, though they pass for acts of mortification and self-denial, are of little value.

F. Be an Example in Labor and Trust
(1 Timothy 4:9-11)

This is a faithful saying and worthy of all acceptation. As noted earlier in our study of chapter 3, this refers to a statement that is self-evident. It is something so patently true that everyone acknowledges it. *For therefore we labour and suffer reproach.* Godly people must labor and expect reproach; they must do well, and yet expect at the same time to suffer ill. Toil and trouble are to be expected by us in this world, especially as saints. Nevertheless, those who labor and suffer reproach in the service of God and the work of building His kingdom may be assured that they will not suffer loss. Our guarantee is bound up in the fact that *we trust in the living God.* The God who has undertaken to be our Paymaster is the living God, who does Himself live forever and is the fountain of life to all who serve Him. *The Saviour of all men.* He is the Savior of all in the sense that our Lord is "the savior of the world" (John 4:42). He is the actual Savior of those who believe, and the potential Savior of the unbeliever as He has provided salvation at the Cross, and stands ready to save that sinner when the latter puts faith in the Lord Jesus Christ. Also, He has a general goodwill to the eternal salvation of all, not willing that any should perish, but that all should come to repentance. He desires not the death of sinners; He is the Savior of all—that none are left in the same desperate condition of fallen angels.

G. Youth Does Not Exempt from Example *(1 Timothy 4:12)*

Let no man despise thy youth; that is, give no man an occasion to despise thy youth. It is estimated that Timothy was probably from 38-40 years old at the time of this writing. This meant that many of the Ephesian elders were probably older than he was. Therefore, Paul warned him that because he had no record to establish his credibility, he would have to earn the respect of his people. The word "despise" speaks of that contempt felt in the mind, which displays itself in injurious action.

Be thou an example of the believers. The word "be" is not the ordinary verb of being in the Greek, but *ginomai,* "to become." Paul is saying, *"keep on becoming."* The word "example" refers to a "pattern." Timothy was to continue his growth and development as a young man as a pattern for other believers. Those who teach by their doctrine must teach by their lives, else they pull down with one hand what they build up with the other. They must be examples both *in word and conversation; in behavior, manner of life.* Their discourse must be edifying; their conversation must be guarded, and this will be a good example.

H. Public Reading of the Word
(1 Timothy 4:13-14)

Till I come, give attendance to reading, to exhortation, to doctrine. Timothy was to "give attendance to": literally, *"keep on putting your mind on"* the public reading of the Scriptures. The Scriptures should be read whenever the corporate body meets, whether it is for Bible study, meetings, or corporate worship. Timothy must *read and exhort*—that is, read and expound, read and press what he reads upon them. He must expound it both by way of exhortation and by way of doctrine; he must teach them both what to do and what to believe.

I. An Example of Spiritual Growth
(1 Timothy 4:15-16)

Meditate upon these things carries the idea of thinking through beforehand, planning, strategizing. It is a process often made analogous to the "chewing of the cud" done by cows. The process of meditation involves a similar activity. After the believer has studied the Word, he is to "chew on it" again, and allow the Holy Spirit to clarify it and help make application of it to the present condition. Having this work committed to him, Timothy must *give himself wholly to them.* A servant of God must have a single-minded, consuming devotion to that calling, *so that your progress may be evident to all.* None of us are yet all that we should be; we are all a work in progress, or under construction. A spiritual leader must not try to hide flaws from the people, but, rather, allow them to demonstrate personal progress in spiritual knowledge, wisdom and maturity.

Take heed to thyself and to the doctrine. Paul wraps up his charge to Timothy by commanding him to pay close attention to both himself and to his teaching. This summarizes all that he had tried to tell him in the preceding verses. First, "Pay close attention to your character to ensure that it is godly." Secondly, "Pay close attention to your teaching to ensure that it is biblical." Strive with all your being to "walk your talk." *Continue in them* carries the idea of staying by the side of a person or thing, or to stick to it. Timothy was to stay with the doctrine that he had received. There will be temptations to abandon that which is sound doctrine to take on that which is popular. The servant of God must stick to the Word of God.

III. Special Features
A. Preserving Our Heritage

We in the National Baptist arena are witnessing—perhaps more than at any time in our history—the proliferation of false and aberrant doctrines. The advent of television is making it easier than ever before to spread false doctrines among the saints. Moreover, the numerical success of these televangelists is making it more appealing to our churches. Many of our pastors are being influenced, so much so that doctrine is being sacrificed on the altar of dollars. The increasing promises of prosperity for all—health and wealth being propagated as a divine right—is causing many of our preachers to abandon sound doctrine in search of economic success.

It is imperative that we awaken from our slumber and recognize that our salvation is nearer than when we first believed. We must work while it is still day, for the night is fast approaching when no one can work. The heritage of our faith is at stake, and we dare not ignore the challenge to contend for the faith that was once delivered to the saints!

B. Concluding Reflections

Throughout the annals of time, God has always looked for those who were willing to place their lives before others as a pattern to be followed. Abraham, Moses and Joseph are a few of the patriarchs whose lives provide patterns. Paul, Peter and John were men of the New Testament whose lives provide patterns of faithful discipleship that we can use as models today. None of them were perfect; they all had flaws, as do we. But we can see them as men who struggled with their human frailties and, by the grace of God, conquered them and went on to do great things for God.

The apostle Paul commanded Timothy to "train yourself to be godly" (4:7). If we are to excel and become examples that others may follow, we must divest ourselves of everything that would present us as ungodly patterns, unfit to model.

▌HOME DAILY BIBLE 📖 READINGS

for the week of January 22, 2006
Guidance for Teaching

Jan. 16, Monday
   —Deuteronomy 4:1-8
   —Moses Teaches Israel to Obey
Jan. 17, Tuesday
   —Psalm 78:1-8
   —Give Ear to My Teaching
Jan. 18, Wednesday
   —Ephesians 4:25—5:2
   —Rules for the New Life
Jan. 19, Thursday
   —Romans 12:3-8
   —The Teacher's Gift Is Teaching
Jan. 20, Friday
   —1 Timothy 4:1-5
   —A Warning Against False Teaching
Jan. 21, Saturday
   —1 Timothy 4:6-10
   —Train Yourself in Godliness
Jan. 22, Sunday
   —1 Timothy 4:11-16
   —Put All These Things into Practice

PRAYER

Our heavenly Father, we praise You for being a Shepherd who leads, guides and protects His sheep from all harm or danger. Guide us as we pilgrim through this land. Thank You for Your Word, which serves as a lamp unto our feet and a light to our pathway. Keep our leaders from error, and help us to help those who have fallen along the way. We pray in the name of Your Son, Jesus the Christ. Amen.

Lesson 9

God Desires Justice and Mercy

ADULT TOPIC: Practicing Justice and Mercy
YOUTH TOPIC: God's Family
CHILDREN'S TOPIC: Good Leaders Respect Others

KEY VERSE

Rebuke not an elder, but entreat him as a father; and the younger men as brethren; The elder women as mothers; the younger as sisters, with all purity.
—1 Timothy 5:1-2

DEVOTIONAL READING: Matthew 23:23-28
BACKGROUND SCRIPTURE: 1 Timothy 5
PRINT PASSAGE: 1 Timothy 5:1-8, 17-24

OBJECTIVES
Upon completion of this lesson, students should:

1. Affirm the biblical principle of mutual respect for one another in the body of Christ.

2. Know the importance of leaders, and resolve to treat members of the body of Christ with dignity.

3. Insist upon the purity in relationships that enhances the ministry of the local church.

1 Timothy 5:1-8, 17-24—KJV

REBUKE NOT an elder, but entreat him as a father; and the younger men as brethren;

2 The elder women as mothers; the younger as sisters, with all purity.

3 Honour widows that are widows indeed.

4 But if any widow have children or nephews, let them learn first to show piety at home, and to requite their parents: for that is good and acceptable before God.

5 Now she that is a widow indeed, and desolate, trusteth in God, and continueth in supplications and prayers night and day.

6 But she that liveth in pleasure is dead while she liveth.

7 And these things give in charge, that they may be blameless.

8 But if any provide not for his own, and specially for those of his own house, he hath denied the faith, and is worse than an infidel.

.....

17 Let the elders that rule well be counted worthy of double honour, especially they who labour in the word and doctrine.

18 For the scripture saith, Thou shalt not muzzle the ox that treadeth out the corn. And, The labourer is worthy of his reward.

19 Against an elder receive not an accusation, but before two or three witnesses.

20 Them that sin rebuke before all, that others also may fear.

21 I charge thee before God, and the Lord Jesus Christ, and the elect angels, that thou observe these things without preferring one before another, doing nothing by partiality.

22 Lay hands suddenly on no man, neither be partaker of other men's sins: keep thyself pure.

23 Drink no longer water, but use a little wine for thy stomach's sake and thine often infirmities.

24 Some men's sins are open beforehand, going before to judgment; and some men they follow after.

1 Timothy 5:1-8, 17-24—NRSV

DO NOT speak harshly to an older man, but speak to him as to a father, to younger men as brothers,

2 to older women as mothers, to younger women as sisters—with absolute purity.

3 Honor widows who are really widows.

4 If a widow has children or grandchildren, they should first learn their religious duty to their own family and make some repayment to their parents; for this is pleasing in God's sight.

5 The real widow, left alone, has set her hope on God and continues in supplications and prayers night and day;

6 but the widow who lives for pleasure is dead even while she lives.

7 Give these commands as well, so that they may be above reproach.

8 And whoever does not provide for relatives, and especially for family members, has denied the faith and is worse than an unbeliever.

.....

17 Let the elders who rule well be considered worthy of double honor, especially those who labor in preaching and teaching;

18 for the scripture says, "You shall not muzzle an ox while it is treading out the grain," and, "The laborer deserves to be paid."

19 Never accept any accusation against an elder except on the evidence of two or three witnesses.

20 As for those who persist in sin, rebuke them in the presence of all, so that the rest also may stand in fear.

21 In the presence of God and of Christ Jesus and of the elect angels, I warn you to keep these instructions without prejudice, doing nothing on the basis of partiality.

22 Do not ordain anyone hastily, and do not participate in the sins of others; keep yourself pure.

23 No longer drink only water, but take a little wine for the sake of your stomach and your frequent ailments.

24 The sins of some people are conspicuous and precede them to judgment, while the sins of others follow them there.

POINTS TO BE EMPHASIZED
ADULTS
Key Verse: 1 Timothy 5:1-2
Print: 1 Timothy 5:1-8, 17-24
—Communities are called upon to provide systems of care for their members.
—The community of faith must devise ways and means of just resolution of problems and issues.
—Preferential treatment of some over others can cause conflict in the community.
—Christians are to deport themselves in ways that demonstrate justice and mercy.

YOUTH
Key Verse: 1 Timothy 5:8
Print: 1 Timothy 5:1-8, 17-24
—God is concerned about how we treat persons in need.
—We are accountable to God relative to how we treat one another.
—Paul advised Timothy on how to treat older and younger church members.
—Those who do not provide for family members are worse than unbelievers.

CHILDREN
Key Verse: Luke 19:10
Print: Luke 19:1-10, 1 Timothy 5:25
—Jesus did not call the qualified, but qualified the ones He called.

—Jesus ministered to the lost and calls His disciples today to do likewise.
—Jesus expanded His kingdom of love by restoring the esteem and confidence of sinners.
—Christians should live godly lives because good and bad deeds will eventually be revealed.

TOPICAL OUTLINE OF THE LESSON

I. **INTRODUCTION**
   A. Relationships Matter
   B. Biblical Background

II. **EXPOSITION AND APPLICATION OF THE SCRIPTURE**
   A. Justice and Respect for Elders and Younger Men *(1 Timothy 5:1)*
   B. Justice and Respect for Old and Young Women *(1 Timothy 5:2)*
   C. Justice and Mercy for Widows *(1 Timothy 5:3-4)*
   D. Identifying True Widows *(1 Timothy 5:5-7)*
   E. Justice Requires Provisions for One's Own *(1 Timothy 5:8)*
   F. Justice Due Elders *(1 Timothy 5:17-20)*
   G. Timothy's Charge *(1 Timothy 5:21-24)*

III. **SPECIAL FEATURES**
   A. Preserving Our Heritage
   B. Concluding Reflections

I. INTRODUCTION
A. Relationships Matter

The apostle deals with the joint themes of *justice* and *mercy* by imparting how

Timothy was to relate to the various groups of individuals within the body of Christ. At the outset, it must be understood that justice is an attribute of God as a reflection of His holiness, and mercy is an expression of His love. The servant of God is to reflect both in personal dealings with the people of God. *Justice* may be thought of as "righteousness," and when used of human beings, it refers to right rule, right conduct, or to each getting just due, whether good or bad. *Mercy* refers to the quality of pity, compassion, gentleness and forbearance. The biblical record suggests an intimate relationship between these two attributes.

B. Biblical Background

There is one metaphor of the church that fits the context of this passage—that is the metaphor of the church as a family (cf., Ephesians 2:19; 3:15; Galatians 6:10). The word "family" speaks of intimacy, care, openness and love.

Within the framework of believers' love for each other is a very necessary and often overlooked element: confrontation of sin. In the church, as in the family, disobedience must be dealt with. That is a mark of a loving family. True love cares that others enjoy the blessing of God and prosper spiritually. Because of that, it does not hesitate to confront sin. In this brief passage, Paul covers the important issue of how this is to be done in the Lord's family.

II. EXPOSITION AND APPLICATION OF THE SCRIPTURE

A. Justice and Respect for Elders and Younger Men *(1 Timothy 5:1)*

Rebuke not an elder. Though the word "elder" may be used to refer to one of ecclesiastical rank and authority, the usage here refers to one of age, not of an appointed office. Bishops or overseers are appointed from among the elders (cf., Titus 1:5; Acts 14:23). The word "rebuke" refers to harsh or violent verbal correction. The thought is that respect for age must temper the way one deals with an older man's misdemeanors. *But entreat him as a father.* As a young man, Timothy was to confront sinning, older men with the same deference and respect he would show his own father. Respect for one's father is commanded in Scripture, and Proverbs 30:17 warns about, in graphic terms, the consequences of not showing that respect: "The eye that mocks a father, and scorns to obey a mother, the ravens of the valley will pick it out, and the young eagles will eat it." Disobedience to one's father in the Old Testament could even result in death: "He who curses his father or mother shall surely be put to death" (Exodus 21:17).

And the younger men as brothers. Viewing them as brothers assumes no air of superiority; the term implies the absence of hierarchy.

B. Justice and Mercy for Old and Young Women
(1 Timothy 5:2)

The elder women as mothers. Older women are to be treated gently, as mothers. The Bible commands respect for mothers. Exodus 20:12 says, "Honor your father and your mother, that your days may be prolonged in the land which the Lord your God gives you." Older women were to receive the same respect and honor that Timothy would give to his own mother Eunice.

The younger as sisters, with all purity. Scripture is clear that the purity of younger women is to be protected. Incest was strictly forbidden by the Old Testament law (cf., Leviticus 18:9-18; 20:17-19). By commanding Timothy to treat younger women as sisters, Paul stressed that he must be indifferent to them in terms of lust.

C. Justice and Mercy for Widows *(1 Timothy 5:3-4)*

Honour widows that are widows indeed. The English word "widow" describes a woman whose husband is dead. The Greek word for *widow* includes that meaning, but is not limited to it. It is an adjective used as a noun, and means "bereft," "robbed," "having suffered loss," or "left alone." The word does not speak of how the woman was left alone; it merely describes the situation. It is broad enough to encompass those who lost their husbands through death, desertion, divorce, or imprisonment. The responsibility of the church extends to all qualifying women who have lost their husbands. The term "widows indeed" is an indication that the church was not obligated to support all widows.

D. Identifying True Widows *(1 Timothy 5:5-7)*

Now she that is a widow indeed, and desolate. The word "now" points to the contrast between the widow of verse 4 who has relatives to take care of her, and the widow of verse 5 who does not. The word "desolate" is from *mono* and means "alone." The first criterion to be used in determining true widowhood was whether or not she has been left alone with no family. *Trusteth in God, and continueth in supplications*

Rebuke means "a harsh or violent reproof," such as anyone in authority might attempt to employ, while *exhort* is a kindly, many-sided Christian word including ideas of exhortation, admonition and comfort. A widow was not just a married woman bereft of her husband; she was a married woman bereft of all kinsfolk whose relationship obliged them to support her. The "real widow" was one who had no one but God as the sole center and ground of her hope; the support of the church allowed her to truly live while she lived and not be "dead to God." Consider this against the background of too many women with official enrollment to receive assistance from the church who had grown wanton against Christ, gadding about from house to house, gossips and busybodies. Persistent pressure had to be put on families to support their widows so that the church would not be burdened beyond necessity, and have the financial resources to assist those who were "real widows." Hospitality was a virtue required of all church officials—indeed—all Christians. Christianity was a traveling religion, and adequate care must be given to members of the Christian family on journey.

and prayers night and day. The second criterion for determining widowhood is that a widow be a believer. She must have demonstrated her trust in God. The tense of the verb indicates a continual state or condition, and refers to one who has been continually in the fellowship, demonstrating these qualities. The church may and should show compassion toward all widows; however, the commandment given here was for those who belong to the fellowship. Here, it was not a matter of choice, but the church was directed to provide care for true widows in the church.

E. Justice Requires Provision for One's Own *(1 Timothy 5:8)*

Verse 8 states negatively what has already been said in verse 4: *But if anyone provide not for his own.* This phrase is purposely vague. It refers to anyone within the circle of family relationships—*and especially for those of his own house.* A believing man who is the head of a house has a mandated responsibility to provide for those in his household. This is a narrower phrase than the first and focuses upon those in his immediate family. *He hath denied the faith and is worse than an infidel.* Faith demands works and fruits. By refusing the natural duties which Christian faith implies, one practically denies his possession of faith. One who is an "infidel," an unbeliever, will perform these natural duties; therefore, the believer who fails in this area is worse than an unbeliever.

F. Justice Due Elders *(1 Timothy 5:17-20)*

Let the elders that rule well. Elders is a general term referring to those who were also called "overseers." The titles *elder, pastor* and *overseer* all describe the same person and is made clear by the use of all three words to describe the same men in Acts 20:17, 28. The term "pastor" emphasizes their shepherding or feeding function, "overseer" their authority and leading function, and "elder" their spiritual maturity. *Be counted worthy of double honour.* The word "honor" refers generally to "respect" or "regard" (cf., 6:1), but it can also be translated as "price" and refers to money given to someone to honor him (cf., Matthew 27:6, 9). The verb *axioo* reflects an estimate received by the thinking process. It is to evaluate some elders and consider them worthy of double honor. The idea is that the double honor is not a gift, but something they deserve. Paul further describes such men as *those who labour in the word and doctrine.* A servant's reward from God is proportional to the excellence of his ministry and the effort put into it.

Against an elder receive not an accusation, but before two or three witnesses. There are always people eager to falsely accuse a minister of God. They may do so because they resent calling, reject the minister's teaching, resist biblical authority, resent virtue, or are jealous of the Lord's blessing on his life. Therefore, it is of utmost importance that the church follow biblical guidelines for dealing with such an accusation. Here is the scriptural method of proceeding against an elder, when accused of any crime. There must be an accusation; it must not be a flying uncertain report, but an accusation containing a certain charge formally drawn up. Further, this accusation is not to be received unless supported by two or three credible witnesses. The elders were never to be at the mercy of frivolous, evil accusers.

Those that sin. This refers to the elders in the context, and the grammatical construction demands that it be interpreted *those who continue in sin.* Elders were to be protected against false accusations but were not to receive immunity from true ones. Elders who continued in sin bear the consequences.

G. Timothy's Charge
(1 Timothy 5:21-24)

I charge thee, or as in Greek, "I *adjure* thee"; so it ought to be translated (2 Timothy 4:1): "in the presence of God *and the Lord Jesus Christ* who will testify against you, if you disregard my injunction." He vividly set before Timothy *the last judgment,* in which God shall be revealed, and Christ seen face-to-face with His angels. *Elect angels* is an epithet of reverence. As witnesses to Paul's adjuration, angels take part by action and sympathy in the affairs of the earth (Luke 15:10; 1 Corinthians 4:9). *Observe these things without preferring one before another, doing nothing by partiality.*

Lay hands suddenly on no man. This refers to the ordination ceremony to the office of the ministry. To lay hands upon someone in this context was to affirm suitability for and acceptance into public ministry. It expressed solidarity, union and identification with them. This ought not to be done rashly and inconsiderately, and before due evidence is made of the necessary gifts and graces, abilities and qualifications for it. *Neither be partakers of other men's sins* implies that those who are too easy in granting the privileges of the church encourage others in the sins which are thus connived at, and make themselves thereby guilty. Those who are rash will make themselves partakers in the sins of others.

III. SPECIAL FEATURES
A. Preserving Our Heritage

We who minister must be mindful of the damage and danger that we have suffered as a result of the increasing failure of our young people to have respect for the elderly.

Early in the history of our people (or we who belong to previous generations), we were taught to respect our elders by responding to adult women with a "Yes, Ma'am" or "No, Ma'am," and to adult men with a "Yes, Sir" or "No, Sir." Much to our detriment, we have allowed the permissiveness of the dominant culture to infiltrate and destroy our common courtesy that was reserved for all adults, irrespective of their rank or socioeconomic status.

It is vitally important that we get back to the "good old days and the good old ways" that were practiced by our forebears and passed along to us. In so doing, we must redefine the essential three "Rs" as of old—"Respect, Restraint and Responsibility." This must be taught first and foremost in the family, then practiced in the church and community.

B. Concluding Reflections

Danger that we are warned against in this lesson is that of "laying hands on too quickly." Many of the problems that we face with those in the pulpit and those in the diaconate can be traced back to our failure to take the time to examine them and to allow enough time for us to observe their spirituality. We are too prone to license and ordain ministers to the pulpit based upon their musical or other abilities. This results in clergy who have learned to substitute "showmanship" for "scholar-ship"—believing that as long as they can make folk shout, it matters not what the content of the message is. We cannot continue to appoint deacons after they have served some period as "walking deacons" or "deacons-in-training." The apostle points out in this lesson that deacons *already* have demonstrated spiritual acumen. There is a direct correlation to the spirituality of those in the pews to the spirituality of those in leadership positions and in the pulpit.

HOME DAILY BIBLE READINGS
for the week of January 29, 2006
God Desires Justice and Mercy

Jan. 23, Monday
　—Psalm 33:1-5
　—God Loves Righteousness and
　　Justice
Jan. 24, Tuesday
　—Proverbs 28:4-13
　—Show Justice, Integrity,
　　Righteousness and Mercy
Jan. 25, Wednesday
　—Matthew 23:23-28
　—Jesus Demands Justice and Mercy
Jan. 26, Thursday
　—James 2:8-13
　—Mercy Triumphs over Judgment
Jan. 27, Friday
　—1 Timothy 5:1-8
　—Show Mercy to All Believers
Jan. 28, Saturday
　—1 Timothy 5:9-16
　—Show Justice to the Widows
Jan. 29, Sunday
　—1 Timothy 5:17-25
　—Show Justice to the Elders

PRAYER

Our Father, who is in heaven, thank You for the wonderful gift of Your Son, Jesus Christ, who died that we might live. Give us the courage to speak the truth in love. Help us to honor one another in humility and hope looking forward to that great day. Amen.

Be True to Your Christian Heritage

ADULT TOPIC: A Heritage of Faith
YOUTH TOPIC: Guard the Good Treasure
CHILDREN'S TOPIC: We Learn from Family

DEVOTIONAL READING: 2 Thessalonians 2:13-17
BACKGROUND SCRIPTURE: 2 Timothy 1
PRINT PASSAGE: 2 Timothy 1:3-14

2 Timothy 1:3-14—KJV

3 I thank God, whom I serve from my forefathers with pure conscience, that without ceasing I have remembrance of thee in my prayers night and day;

4 Greatly desiring to see thee, being mindful of thy tears, that I may be filled with joy;

5 When I call to remembrance the unfeigned faith that is in thee, which dwelt first in thy grandmother Lois, and thy mother Eunice; and I am persuaded that in thee also.

6 Wherefore I put thee in remembrance that thou stir up the gift of God, which is in thee by the putting on of my hands.

7 For God hath not given us the spirit of fear; but of power, and of love, and of a sound mind.

8 Be not thou therefore ashamed of the testimony of our Lord, nor of me his prisoner: but be thou partaker of the afflictions of the gospel according to the power of God;

9 Who hath saved us, and called us with an holy calling, not according to our works, but according to his own purpose and grace, which was given us in Christ Jesus before the world began,

KEY VERSE

When I call to remembrance the unfeigned faith that is in thee, which dwelt first in thy grandmother Lois, and thy mother Eunice; and I am persuaded that in thee also.
—2 Timothy 1:5

OBJECTIVES
Upon the completion of this lesson, students should:
1. Know the value and importance of a Christian heritage.
2. Recognize and appreciate their own heritage.
3. Remember their elderly parents and relatives in their daily prayers.
4. Recognize that they are responsible for building a Christian legacy for their youth to follow.

10 But is now made manifest by the appearing of our Saviour Jesus Christ, who hath abolished death, and hath brought life and immortality to light through the gospel:

11 Whereunto I am appointed a preacher, and an apostle, and a teacher of the Gentiles.

12 For the which cause I also suffer these things: nevertheless I am not ashamed: for I know whom I have believed, and am persuaded that he is able to keep that which I have committed unto him against that day.

13 Hold fast the form of sound words, which thou hast heard of me, in faith and love which is in Christ Jesus.

14 That good thing which was committed unto thee keep by the Holy Ghost which dwelleth in us.

2 Timothy 1:3-14—NRSV

3 I am grateful to God—whom I worship with a clear conscience, as my ancestors did—when I remember you constantly in my prayers night and day.

4 Recalling your tears, I long to see you so that I may be filled with joy.

5 I am reminded of your sincere faith, a faith that lived first in your grandmother Lois and your mother Eunice and now, I am sure, lives in you.

6 For this reason I remind you to rekindle the gift of God that is within you through the laying on of my hands;

7 for God did not give us a spirit of cowardice, but rather a spirit of power and of love and of self-discipline.

8 Do not be ashamed, then, of the testimony about our Lord or of me his prisoner, but join with me in suffering for the gospel, relying on the power of God,

9 who saved us and called us with a holy calling, not according to our works but according to his own purpose and grace. This grace was given to us in Christ Jesus before the ages began,

10 but it has now been revealed through the appearing of our Savior Christ Jesus, who abolished death and brought life and immortality to light through the gospel.

11 For this gospel I was appointed a herald and an apostle and a teacher,

12 and for this reason I suffer as I do. But I am not ashamed, for I know the one in whom I have put my trust, and I am sure that he is able to guard until that day what I have entrusted to him.

13 Hold to the standard of sound teaching that you have heard from me, in the faith and love that are in Christ Jesus.

14 Guard the good treasure entrusted to you, with the help of the Holy Spirit living in us.

POINTS TO BE EMPHASIZED
ADULTS
Key Verse: 2 Timothy 1:5
Print: 2 Timothy 1:3-14

—Paul's purpose in writing was to strengthen Timothy's faith for the task of ministry in Ephesus.

—Paul expressed great confidence in Timothy, whose spiritual heritage was rooted in Christianity.

—Paul relies on the family image when invoking memory of Lois and Eunice.

—Paul reminds Timothy that he suffers and invites him to accept suffering as he proclaimed the Gospel boldly.

YOUTH

Key Verse: 2 Timothy 1:5
Print: 2 Timothy 1:3-14

—God calls one generation to mentor the next generation.

—Paul reminded Timothy to rekindle the spirit of power, love and self-discipline that he received through his ordination.

—Paul told Timothy not to be ashamed of the Gospel, but to suffer for the sake of Jesus Christ.

—Paul was chosen as an apostle and teacher of the Gospel, and Timothy was to hold to this sound teaching and guard this good treasure.

CHILDREN

Key Verse: 2 Timothy 1:5
Print: 2 Timothy 1:2-7; 3:14-17

—Christian parents and grandparents are a child's first spiritual teachers.

—Faith is something that we cannot keep to ourselves, but must share with others.

—God deserves our praise and thanksgiving for blessing us with families.

—Families can pass on Christian traditions.

—Children take on the attitudes and behaviors of their parents, or other significant caregivers.

TOPICAL OUTLINE OF THE LESSON

I. INTRODUCTION
 A. The Value of Heritage
 B. Biblical Background

II. EXPOSITION AND APPLICATION OF THE SCRIPTURE
 A. Paul and Timothy's Godly Heritage *(2 Timothy 1:3-5)*
 B. Stir Up the Gift *(2 Timothy 1:6-7)*
 C. Be Not Ashamed *(2 Timothy 1:8-10)*
 D. Divine Appointment *(2 Timothy 1:11-12)*
 E. Hold on to the Doctrine *(2 Timothy 1:13-14)*

III. SPECIAL FEATURES
 A. Preserving Our Heritage
 B. Concluding Reflections

I. INTRODUCTION
A. The Value of Heritage

We should be reminded that Timothy was being thrust into a position of responsible Christian leadership far beyond his natural capacity. To begin with, he was relatively young. The references to his age (1 Timothy 4:12) seem to suggest that he was probably in his mid-thirties. Next, he was prone to illness. In his first letter to him, the apostle Paul referred to his "frequent ailments," though without specifying what they were. He went on to recommend a tonic. Thirdly, Timothy was timid by temperament. He seems to have been naturally shy. Possibly, he shrank from difficult tasks, so that Paul in writing to the Corinthians had to pave the way for his mission (1 Corinthians 16:10-11). Several times in this second letter the apostle exhorted Timothy to take his share of suffering and to not be afraid or ashamed, since God has not given us a spirit of cowardice (see 2 Timothy 1:7-8). These admonitions evidently were necessary.

This, then, was Timothy—young in years, frail in physique, retiring in disposition—who nevertheless was called to exacting responsibilities in the church of God. Greatness was being thrust upon him, and like Moses and Jeremiah, and a host of others before and after him, Timothy was exceedingly reluctant to accept it. Undoubtedly, his godly heritage would prove of unsurpassing value as he set out on his mission for the Kingdom.

B. Biblical Background

Timothy was no longer the leader in Ephesus; Tychicus had been sent to take his place (4:12). Apparently, Timothy was doing work as a traveling minister and evangelist in the area around Ephesus. Paul expected Timothy to come to Rome because he knew that Timothy would be in Troas (4:13) and Ephesus (1:16-18). These cities were on the road to Rome.

The letter is intensely personal. Paul was alone in Rome, awaiting trial and certain death. He longed to see his son Timothy and to encourage him to take his place

in the ministry of the Gospel. Paul saw apostasy and defeat all around him. Dr. Sidlow Baxter, in *Explore the Book,* points out that the "some" of 1 Timothy has become "all" in 2 Timothy. "Some have turned aside" (1:6); "some have made shipwreck" (1:19); "some have turned aside after Satan" (5:15); "some have been led astray" (6:10); "some have erred" (6:21)—this is the theme of his first letter. But in 2 Timothy we read: "all have turned away from me" (1:15); "all forsook me!" (4:16). The churches were turning from the faith, and Paul urged young Timothy to be true to his calling and fulfill his ministry. Woven into the exhortations of this letter are the personal sentiments and concerns of the great apostle. This letter is not a "swan song" of defeat; it is an anthem of victory!

II. Exposition and Application of the Scripture

A. Paul and Timothy's Godly Heritage
(2 Timothy 1:3-5)

Paul refers here to his own godly heritage, being conscious that he was the result of generations of God-fearing people. Paul had known God from his earliest years because he was "an Hebrew of the Hebrews" (Philippians 3:5). His ancestors had given him the orthodox Jewish faith. But when he met Jesus Christ, Paul realized that his Jewish faith was but preparation for the fulfillment Christ gave him in Christianity. The apostle viewed his own faith in Christ, not as a break from his forefathers, but in continuity with their faith. His inborn, natural instincts were all toward the service of God (Acts 22:3; 24:14). Paul, while sitting in his Roman jail cell, undoubtedly spent much time in prayer. He wanted his son Timothy to know that he was included in his prayers both day and night. What an encouragement this must have been to Timothy to know that the great apostle was praying for him. Paul, who knew Timothy's weaknesses and problems, was able to pray with a real burden on his heart. His praying was not routine; it was done with compassion and concern. This is a solemn reminder for us to pray for our children, both those of natural birth, as well as those whom we have had the privilege of leading to Christ. *Greatly desiring to see you, being mindful of your tears, that I may be filled with joy.* Paul desired greatly to see Timothy before being put to death at the hands of the Romans. In the East, tears were an appropriate expression of sadness for troubles or long partings. He remembered the tears Timothy had shed at their last parting (Acts 20:37). The tears were tears of love and loyalty to Paul and the Lord, and so were cause for joy.

When I call to remembrance the genuine faith that is in you, which dwelt first in your grandmother Lois and your mother Eunice. So many, it seems, had opposed or deserted Paul (cf., 1:15; 2:17; 3:1-9) that Timothy's genuine faith stood out in bold relief. Paul attributed Timothy's faith to the influence of his mother Eunice and his grandmother Lois. Apparently Lois was the first in the family who was won to Christ; then his mother, Eunice, was converted. Timothy's father was a Greek (Acts 16:1), so Eunice had not practiced the orthodox Jewish faith. However, Timothy's mother and grandmother had seen to it that he was taught the Scriptures (2 Timothy 3:15); this was great preparation for the hearing of the Gospel.

B. Stir Up the Gift *(2 Timothy 1:6-7)*

It is the Holy Spirit who enables us to serve God, and through Him, we can overcome fear and weakness. The word *fear* in 2 Timothy 1:7 means "timidity, cowardice." *But of*

Paul appeals to suffer for the Gospel, and links himself and his ancestors to Timothy and his mother and grandmother. Timothy's chief function in the church is to transmit—intact and unchanged—what he has heard from Paul to other faithful men who, in turn, will be able to teach others. *Sincere* literally means "without hypocrisy." A fundamental principle against cowardice precedes a direct exhortation against being ashamed of the Gospel. "Rekindle" implies continuous burning. Self-discipline is not private rigor, but God-given endurance. "Ashamed" is a key theme: believers must rely on the power of God to counter the suffering associated with the Gospel. "Appearing" refers to Jesus' future coming, but here it means His incarnation. Onesiphorus is an example of one not ashamed of the Gospel. In contrast, Phygelus and Hermogenes have turned away. "Treasure" means deposit. "If we endure": in spite of the assurance which baptismal death and resurrection bring, the Christian's blessed future is contingent upon his or her perseverance; baptism is the beginning—not the end. Only if the Christian endures will he or she share in that glorious Kingdom where the saints "shall reign forever and ever."

power. The Holy Spirit gives us power for witness and for service (Acts 1:8). It is futile for us to try to serve God without the power of the Holy Spirit. Talent, training and experience cannot replace the power of the Spirit.

Timothy did not need any new spiritual ingredients in his life; all he had to do was *stir up* (*anazopureo*: to kindle up, inflame one's mind, strength, zeal) what he already had. Paul had written in his first letter, "Neglect not the gift that is in thee" (1 Timothy 4:14). Now he added, "Stir up—stir into flame—the gift of God." The Holy Spirit does not leave us when we fail (John 14:16); but, He cannot fill us, empower us and use us if we neglect our spiritual lives. It is possible to grieve the Spirit (Ephesians 4:30) and to quench the Spirit (1 Thessalonians 5:19).

C. Be Not Ashamed *(2 Timothy 1:8-10)*

"Not ashamed" is a key idea in this chapter: Paul was not ashamed (2 Timothy 1:12); he admonished Timothy not to be ashamed. Timothy's natural timidity might make it easy for him to avoid circumstances that demand witness and involve suffering. So Paul felt it necessary to stir him up and guard him against the possibility of un-Christian dereliction of duty in a bold confession of Christ. *Shame* is the companion of *fear;* if fear is overcome, false shame flees. Paul himself (2 Timothy 1:12) and Onesiphorus (2 Timothy 1:16) were examples of fearless profession removing false shame. The

exhortation is for Timothy to be a fellow-partaker, to share with Paul and Christ's sufferings. *According to the power of God.* This phrase is connected with the verb "be thou partaker." It is the power given by God which would enable Timothy to endure suffering for the cause of Christ and the sake of the Gospel. In other words, think not that you have to bear these afflictions in your own power; it is by the power of God that you will be able to bear them.

Who hath saved us and called us. Christ has "saved us" in His eternal purpose of grace, given to us before the world began. The call of God here is that effectual call into salvation—the sinner is called and willingly accepts the salvation God offers. *With a holy calling.* The call is not only a call to salvation, but also a call to a life of holiness (Hebrews 3:1). "Holy" implies the *separation* of believers from the rest of the world unto God.

The same power that saves us also strengthens us for the battle. Paul emphasized that our calling is by grace; we do not deserve to be saved. If God permits us to suffer, after giving us such a wonderful salvation, what right have we to complain or quit? "God has a purpose in mind," Paul advised. "Let Him work out that purpose."

D. Divine Appointment
(2 Timothy 1:11-12)

Whereunto I am appointed a preacher. Jesus Christ had met Paul on the Damascus road (Acts 9) and had personally called him into the ministry. Paul was a *herald* ("preacher") of the Gospel. In ancient times, a "herald" was the official messenger of the king or emperor, and his message was treated with great respect. The fact that professed believers in Asia were rejecting Paul did not change his calling or his message. Paul was not only a herald; he was also *an apostle, "one sent with a commission."* Not every Christian was an apostle of Jesus Christ, for a person had to meet certain qualifications and be chosen by the Lord personally, or through His Spirit (see Acts 1:15-26; 1 Corinthians 9:1; 2 Corinthians 12:12). An apostle represented Jesus Christ. To reject an apostle was to reject the Lord. *A teacher of the Gentiles.* This meant that he shepherded local churches. It was this word, *Gentiles,* that put him into prison in Rome the first time (Acts 22:21ff). The Gentile believers in Asia should have shown their appreciation of Paul by rallying to his support, for, after all, it was Paul who brought them the Good News of salvation. But instead, they were ashamed of him and tried not to get involved.

For the cause which refers back to verse 11. The connection is *I also suffer these things* because I am a preacher of the Gospel, *nevertheless I am not ashamed:* "I am not disappointed of my hope." The idea is that Paul, in spite of his sufferings incurred in his service for the Lord, has not been put to shame, has not been defeated, and has not had his hopes disappointed. *For I know whom I have believed.* The word for "know" here is *oida,* and means "absolute and beyond all doubt." *And am persuaded* denotes a settled and fixed state. It is like hammering a nail through a board and clinching it on the other side—it is here to stay! *That he is able to keep.* The reference is to God's preeminent power and ability to keep *that which I have committed unto him.* This refers first to the apostle committing the salvation of his soul to the keeping of God; and secondly, to the ministry and the responsibility to preach it, that God has committed to Paul. The apostle expresses his supreme confidence in God's ability to keep guard and watch over both his soul and his ministry. *Until that day:* to the time when Paul's works will be judged at the judgment seat of Christ, the purpose of the judgment being the determination of the reward that the apostle earned.

E. Hold on to the Doctrine
(2 Timothy 1:13-14)

Hold fast the form of sound words, which thou hast heard of me in faith and love which is in Christ Jesus. Loyalty begins with loyalty to God's Word. God had given the deposit of spiritual truth to Paul (1 Timothy 1:11), and he had given it to Timothy (1 Timothy 6:20). It was now Timothy's solemn responsibility to *"hold fast"* (2 Timothy 1:13) and *"guard"* (2 Timothy 1:14, NIV) the precious deposit of Christian truth, and to pass it along to others (2 Timothy 2:2).

The word *form* (2 Timothy 1:13)

means "a pattern, an architect's sketch." There was a definite outline of doctrine in the early church, a standard by which teaching was tested. If Timothy changed this outline or abandoned it, then he would have nothing by which to test other teachers and preachers. We need to hold fast to what Paul taught for the same reason.

However, note that Timothy's orthodoxy was to be tempered with *"faith and love."* "Speaking the truth in love" (Ephesians 4:15) is the divine pattern. How easy it is to become pugnacious in our desire to defend the faith, or a witch-hunter who creates problems.

That good thing which was committed unto thee keep by the Holy Ghost which dwelleth in us. Timothy is to guard, watch and defend the truth, once and for all, delivered to the saints in view of the defection from the truth that was even then in its inception in the early church. It was the Holy Spirit who committed the truth to Timothy, and He would help him guard it. Apart from the ministry of the Spirit, we are in the dark when it comes to understanding the Word of God. It is He who must teach us (John 16:13) and enable us to guard the truth and share it with others.

III. SPECIAL FEATURES
A. Preserving Our Heritage

Not unlike Timothy, most of us in the African American church can trace our knowledge of God to our childhoods. Most of us were reared in families in which church attendance on Sundays was not an option. More than a few of us can relate to Timothy's experience in which his spirituality could be traced back to the matriarchs of his family—his mother and grandmother—rather than to his father.

Instead of this female-headed household becoming a handicap, it ended up working to Timothy's advantage. He apparently was not very involved in the sports and physical activities of his day, and may not have fit the masculine prototype of his cohorts. His absence from these activities, we may presume, left him ample time to become involved in the activities of the synagogue. After all, Paul makes reference to his having received the Scriptures at an early age.

Timothy had no godly, male role model in his home, but his grandmother and mother so nurtured him in the Word that when the apostle came to town looking for help, Timothy was readily recommended by everyone in the neighborhood. Let us imitate the actions of Eunice and Lois in rearing our children. Let us not use the absence or presence of a godly father as an excuse for failing to rear godly children. Let us stop thinking about the children and youth as the church of tomorrow; for if we accept, design programs for, and nurture them as the church of today— they will be the leaders of the church tomorrow!

B. Concluding Reflections

Despite our prayers, we worry that the values we are trying to instill within our children will be countered somehow. What strikes fear in our hearts is that our young people will fall prey to the wrong crowd, succumb to the cultural pressures, and make wrong choices that will bring them pain and suffering. Our children today face unprecedented pressure. They are exposed to sexual temptation, school violence, alcohol, illegal drugs, and a variety of influences that threaten to undo all that we try to teach them. And while we need to fear what our kids could be tempted to *do*, we need to be more concerned with what our kids are led to *believe*. At the foundation of a person's life, we find his beliefs. These beliefs shape his values, and his values drive his actions.

The alarming thing for us to recognize today as Christian parents is that the majority of our young people don't hold to a biblical belief system. Our children, even those from solid, Christian homes and churches, have distorted beliefs about God and the Bible, beliefs that are having a devastating, rippling effect into every aspect of their lives.

It is both doctrine and a way of life that Paul yearned to pass on to the next generation through the system of teaching and communication that the Pastorals describe. Christians must take seriously our Christian heritage.

HOME DAILY BIBLE READINGS

for the week of February 5, 2006
Be True to Your Christian Heritage

Jan. 30, Monday
   —Psalm 111
   —God Gives the Heritage
Jan. 31, Tuesday
   —Jeremiah 17:1-8
   —We Can Lose Our Heritage
Feb. 1, Wednesday
   —2 Thessalonians 2:13-17
   —Stand Firm, Hold Fast
Feb. 2, Thursday
   —Acts 16:1-5
   —Timothy's Mother Was a Believer
Feb. 3, Friday
   —2 Timothy 1:1-5
   —Lois and Eunice Passed on Faith
Feb. 4, Saturday
   —2 Timothy 1:6-10
   —Be Not Ashamed of Your Heritage
Feb. 5, Sunday
   —2 Timothy 1:11-18
   —Guard the Good Treasure Given You

PRAYER

Most heavenly God, our Father, we thank You for the gift of Your Holy Spirit by whom we can cry out to You with the intimate phrase, "Abba Father." We confess that we are not worthy to even be called by Your name, no less to be called Your children. We ask now that You would create in us clean hearts and renew in us a steadfast spirit whereby we may be empowered to glorify You in all we think and do. In Jesus' name, we pray. Amen.

Lesson 11

UNIT III
Faithful Followers,
Faithful Leaders

CHILDREN'S UNIT
We Give Thanks to God

Develop Christian Character

ADULT TOPIC: Pursue Righteousness
YOUTH TOPIC: Becoming a Special Utensil
CHILDREN'S TOPIC: We Learn from Teachers

KEY VERSE
Flee also youthful lusts: but follow righteousness, faith, charity, peace, with them that call on the Lord out of a pure heart.
—2 Timothy 2:22

DEVOTIONAL READING: 1 Peter 2:1-10
BACKGROUND SCRIPTURE: 2 Timothy 2
PRINT PASSAGE: 2 Timothy 2:14-26

OBJECTIVES
After completion of this lesson, students will realize that:

1. Bible study plays an important role in developing Christian character and in achieving spiritual maturity.
2. Getting caught up in useless arguments can do damage to one's character.
3. One may be a member of the church, and yet dishonor God by his or her behavior.
4. A person can become useful as a vessel of honor in God's church.

2 Timothy 2:14-26—KJV

14 Of these things put them in remembrance, charging them before the Lord that they strive not about words to no profit, but to the subverting of the hearers.

15 Study to show thyself approved unto God, a workman that needeth not to be ashamed, rightly dividing the word of truth.

16 But shun profane and vain babblings: for they will increase unto more ungodliness.

17 And their word will eat as doth a canker: of whom is Hymenaeus and Philetus;

18 Who concerning the truth have erred, saying that the resurrection is past already; and overthrow the faith of some.

19 Nevertheless the foundation of God standeth sure, having this seal, The Lord knoweth them that are his. And, Let every one that nameth the name of Christ depart from iniquity.

20 But in a great house there are not only vessels of gold and of silver, but also of wood and of earth; and some to honour, and some to dishonour.

21 If a man therefore purge himself from these, he shall be a vessel unto honour, sanctified, and meet for the master's use, and prepared unto every good work.

22 Flee also youthful lusts: but follow righteousness, faith, charity, peace, with them that call on the Lord out of a pure heart.

23 But foolish and unlearned questions avoid, knowing that they do gender strifes.

24 And the servant of the Lord must not strive; but be gentle unto all men, apt to teach, patient,

25 In meekness instructing those that oppose themselves; if God peradventure will give them repentance to the acknowledging of the truth;

26 And that they may recover themselves out of the snare of the devil, who are taken captive by him at his will.

2 Timothy 2:14-26—NRSV

14 Remind them of this, and warn them before God that they are to avoid wrangling over words, which does no good but only ruins those who are listening.

15 Do your best to present yourself to God as one approved by him, a worker who has no need to be ashamed, rightly explaining the word of truth.

16 Avoid profane chatter, for it will lead people into more and more impiety,

17 and their talk will spread like gangrene. Among them are Hymenaeus and Philetus,

18 who have swerved from the truth by claiming that the resurrection has already taken place. They are upsetting the faith of some.

19 But God's firm foundation stands, bearing this inscription: "The Lord knows those who are his," and, "Let everyone who calls on the name of the Lord turn away from wickedness."

20 In a large house there are utensils not only of gold and silver but also of wood and clay, some for special use, some for ordinary.

21 All who cleanse themselves of the things I have mentioned will become special utensils, dedicated and useful to the owner of the house, ready for every good work.

22 Shun youthful passions and pursue righteousness, faith, love, and peace, along with those who call on the Lord from a pure heart.

23 Have nothing to do with stupid and senseless controversies; you know that they breed quarrels.

24 And the Lord's servant must not be quarrelsome but kindly to everyone, an apt teacher, patient,

25 correcting opponents with gentleness. God may perhaps grant that they will repent and come to know the truth,

26 and that they may escape from the snare of the devil, having been held captive by him to do his will.

POINTS TO BE EMPHASIZED

ADULTS

Key Verse: 2 Timothy 2:22
Print: 2 Timothy 2:14-26

—Timothy is advised to exhort the believers to avoid pointless and harmful arguments.

—The faithful will not quarrel, but will set a good example for others.

—The false teachings of Hymenaeus and Philetus undermined the basic belief in the Resurrection, but appealed to the Sadducees, who denied the Resurrection.

—Arguments create disunity among those who argue and frighten the uninformed who hear the argument.

—Christians play various roles within the body of Christ.

YOUTH

Key Verse: 2 Timothy 2:15
Print: 2 Timothy 2:14-26

—Paul advised Timothy not to quibble over words with others, but to seek divine approval as a skilled preacher correctly explaining God's Word.

—Paul used the image of dinnerware to encourage Christians to improve their ability to serve God.

—Paul told Timothy to pursue Christian virtues and avoid stupid and senseless controversies.

—Paul told Timothy to be an apt and patient teacher, gently correcting opponents so they might repent.

—Christians should be sensitive to youth who may have disciplinary problems.

CHILDREN

Key Verse: 2 Timothy 2:2
Print: Acts 16:9-10; 17:1-4, 10-12; 2 Timothy 2:1-2

—Christian disciples should take every opportunity to tell and teach the Good News.

—Christians are urged to be strong in the faith.

—Christian teachers must not become discouraged by obstacles, but put their trust in God.

—Christians are encouraged to give God thanks for their teachers.

—The Good News should be shared with others.

TOPICAL OUTLINE OF THE LESSON

I. INTRODUCTION
   A. Character Counts
   B. Biblical Background

II. EXPOSITION AND APPLICATION OF THE SCRIPTURE
   A. Avoid Useless Quarreling
      (2 Timothy 2:14)
   B. Be Diligent in Study
      (2 Timothy 2:15)
   C. Avoid Useless Chatter
      (2 Timothy 2:16-18)
   D. The Christian's Character Seal
      (2 Timothy 2:19)
   E. Vessels of Honor
      (2 Timothy 2:20-21)
   F. Reject Youthful Desires
      (2 Timothy 2:22-23)

G. Be Patient with Everyone
   (2 Timothy 2:24-26)
III. SPECIAL FEATURES
   A. Preserving Our Heritage
   B. Concluding Reflections

I. INTRODUCTION
A. Character Counts

The theme of this lesson is the development and maintenance of Christian character. The exhortations and directions that the apostle Paul gives Timothy in this regard should prove useful for all of those engaged in the preaching-teaching-pastoral ministry. Let's begin our study by taking a closer look at the character of Timothy—to whom this letter is addressed.

Paul had a strong affection for Timothy as a friend he had evidently led to Christ (1 Corinthians 4:17), but he had also grown to trust Timothy as his "fellow worker" (Romans 16:21). Herein, we see the virtue of *trustworthiness*. It is not surprising, therefore, that when the first imprisonment was over, Paul left Timothy in Ephesus as the accepted leader of the church. This does not mean, however, that Timothy was without his own shortcomings.

As we study and teach this lesson on the development of Christian character, let us be reminded that God can and does use persons whose human frailties may seemingly disqualify them, if they are open to serve.

■ B. Biblical Background

The apostle Paul's own career of Gospel work was virtually over. For thirty years or so, he had faithfully preached the Good News, planted churches, defended the truth and consolidated the work. Truly he had *fought the good fight...finished the race...kept the faith* (2 Timothy 4:7). Now nothing awaited him but the victor's wreath at the winning post. A prisoner now, he would be a martyr soon.

But, what would happen to the Gospel when he was dead and gone? The emperor, Nero, bent on suppressing all secret societies and misunderstanding the nature of the Christian church, seemed determined to destroy it. Heretics seemed to be on the increase. Who then would do battle for the truth when Paul had laid down his life? This was the question which dominated and vexed his mind as he lay in chains, and to which in this letter he addressed himself.

II. EXPOSITION AND APPLICATION OF THE SCRIPTURE
A. Avoid Useless Quarreling
   (2 Timothy 2:14)

Remind them of these things, charging them before the Lord. "These things" refers to the issues of life and death set out in verses 11-13. Timothy was to keep reminding others of these things. The verb is a present imperative, which means that this was to be Timothy's regular practice.

The bulk of preaching and teaching to a knowledgeable audience frequently consists of reminding them of what they already know. In the case of the Christians at Ephesus, they were to be solemnly *charged* in the presence of God (cf., 1 Timothy 5:21) *not to strive about words to no profit.* That is, they were to stop quarreling and wrangling about empty and trifling matters, a tendency in the early church (cf., Acts 18:15).

B. Be Diligent in Study *(2 Timothy 2:15)*

Study to show thyself approved unto God. The Greek word translated *study* means "to make haste, to exert one's self, endeavor, give diligence." *Approved* means "to put to the test for the purpose of approving, and finding that the person or thing meets the specifications laid down, to put one's approval on that person or thing." A worker approved is a worker who has been put to the test, and meeting the specifications has won the approval of the one who has administered the test. Timothy was exhorted to "Do your utmost, your absolute best to present yourself to God, approved." God's approval is stamped upon the believer whose labor is characterized by diligence and zeal.

C. Avoid Useless Chatter
(2 Timothy 2:16-18)

Shun profane and idle babblings, for they will increase to more ungodliness. Shun means "to turn oneself away from," and *profane* refers to that which is "unholy," while *idle* is that which is "empty." Timothy is exhorted to avoid discussions about secular topics which have no value toward building Christian character. Such discussions only advance ungodliness, *and their message will spread like cancer.* Other translations use the word *gangrene* in place of cancer. This kind of talk, "godless chatter," is contrasted with "the Word of truth" (2 Timothy 2:15) and "the truth" (verse 18). The medical image is striking. Participating with those who engage in such profane speculations will only, literally, "give

In his admonition for endurance, Paul used three proverbial images: the soldier, the athlete and the farmer. "Be strong" recalls that God has granted believers a spirit of power (dynameos), and those believers should rely on the power of God. "Entrust" recalls deposit (treasure) and anticipates the contrast between true and false teaching. The proverbial images of the soldier, athlete and farmer are images of hard work under specific rules: the soldier seeks to please the enlisting officer; the athlete runs to receive the crown according to the rules; the farmer who labors can expect the first share of the crop. The laborer deserves to be paid. "Wrangling over words and profane chatter" are opposed to the word of truth; they are like gangrene, a spreading death of tissue caused by obstruction of blood flow. Utensils will be judged not by their materials (gold, silver, wood, clay) but by the cleanliness that makes them useful. "Rightly handling the word of truth" means to guard it, to preach it, to follow it, and to suffer for it. The Greek word for *handle* originally meant "to cut straight," a metaphor inspired by the farmer who drives (cuts) a straight furrow, or a tailor who cuts a fabric according to the pattern.

their words a feeding place like gangrene." They must be amputated instead. Two who deserved such treatment were Philetus, about whom nothing is known, and Hymenaeus, whom Paul had already "delivered over to Satan" for chastisement (1 Timothy 1:20). These two had *strayed concerning the truth* (cf., 1 Timothy 1:6; 6:21) regarding the crucial doctrine of the Resurrection…saying that is already past.

D. The Christian's Character Seal
(2 Timothy 2:19)

The defection of Philetus and Hymenaeus, and their followers, must not shake Timothy's confidence. *Nevertheless the solid foundation of God stands* (i.e., the church; cf., 1 Corinthians 3:10-15; Ephesians 2:19-22; 1 Timothy 3:15)—that is to say, the integrity of God's Word is unaffected by some who defect. The church and its doctrine are of God and will stand firm, independent of attempts to misuse and misrepresent it. *Having this seal, "The Lord knows those who are His," and "Let everyone who names the name of Christ depart from iniquity."* The foundation stone as one seal has two inscriptions, two mutually complementary parts or aspects to indicate the structure's authenticity and integrity (cf., Romans 4:11; 1 Corinthians 9:2). The first guarantees the *security*, the second the *purity* of the church. The two inscriptions emphasize, respectively, both God's sovereign control over the church and every Christian's responsibility to turn away from evil.

E. Vessels of Honor *(2 Timothy 2:20-21)*

Paul furthered his point about non-contamination by introducing a new but similar metaphor. The image changes from a building to a household (cf., 1 Timothy 3:5, 15). In a large and varied household are all sorts of containers. Some are made of gold and silver and others of wood and clay. More importantly, some are for noble purposes and some for ignoble. Clearly, the reference so far is to the faithful and the unfaithful within the church. But Paul then shifted the metaphor slightly to show how one can be an instrument for noble purposes, by cleansing oneself from the ignoble vessels. The metaphor is somewhat mixed (one would usually think of cleansing from corruption, not cleansing from the corrupted vessels), but the apostle's point is clear: Timothy was to have nothing to do with the false teachers.

F. Reject Youthful Desires
(2 Timothy 2:22-23)

Timothy was still a young man (cf., 1 Timothy 4:12), and even though he was probably mature beyond his years, he still may have displayed some of the characteristics and passions of the young: impatience, intolerance, love of argument, self-assertion and partiality. Timothy was to flee the evil desires of youth (probably Paul did not have sexual passions in mind here, at least not primarily), and pursue the opposite virtues: righteousness, faith, love (cf., 1 Timothy 6:11 for the same trio) and peace, along with those who call on the Lord out of a pure heart. While Timothy was to oppose false teachers, he was to be at peace with those who were honest before God. The clear implication is that the false teachers were dishonest before God (cf., 1 Timothy 1:5; 4:2; 6:3-5). Timothy had refused to get caught up in foolish and stupid arguments (debates) which only produce quarrels.

G. Be Patient with Everyone
(2 Timothy 2:24-26)

False teaching will always be divisive, but the Lord's servant should not be a fighter but a promoter of unity, by being kind (gentle) to everyone (cf., 1 Thessalonians 2:7), able or ready to teach (cf., 1 Timothy 3:2) those who are willing to learn, and forbearing in the face of differences. Servants must treat opponents with gentle instruction characterized by "meekness," in the hope that God will grant them repentance (a change of heart and conduct) leading them to a knowledge (full knowledge) of the truth. The goal is always remedial, never punitive, when dealing with brethren (cf., 2 Thessalonians 3:6, 15). The purpose must always be to edify Christ's body, not tear it down (cf., 1 Corinthians 14:26). Thus, when believers fall into false teaching, they must be treated with gentleness and Christian love in the hope that they will come to their senses and escape from the trap of the devil (cf., Galatians 5:1; 1 Timothy 3:7; 6:9), who has taken them captive to do his will. False teaching—and all its negative consequences—in the church is always the handiwork of Satan; but God, in His grace, often salvages the situation through the Christlike ministry of His servants.

III. Special Features
A. Preserving Our Heritage

This business of building Christian character will not prove easy in today's environment, particularly when it comes to responding to those within the church who have gone astray. The attacks upon doctrinal purity by ministers within the church make it difficult to maintain unity and fellowship. It is quite easy to get caught up in arguments that are of no lasting value. Christian integrity is needed in discerning those things which are essential to the faith and need to be defended from those things which are nonessentials that contribute to disunity. True Christian character calls for us to defend the faith on the one hand, but to grant liberty to those who may disagree with us on the other hand.

B. Concluding Reflections

Paul describes the local church as a house with a solid foundation and containing vessels of different kinds. The Jews often put Bible verses on their houses (see Deuteronomy 11:20), and it was not uncommon for Gentiles to write mottoes on their houses also. God's house has two affirmations on it: one that is toward God and one that is toward humanity. God knows His own, and His own ought to be known to others by their godly lives. Each Christian is a vessel in the great house, but some vessels are defiled and cannot be used. Timothy is warned to purge (cleanse) himself from the dishonorable vessels, lest they defile him. This is the biblical doctrine of separation (2 Corinthians 6:14–7:1). Believers should be set-apart vessels unto honor, suitable (meet) for Christ's use. Fleeing youthful lusts and following that which is spiritual would help Timothy be a prepared vessel that Christ could use for His glory.

Each of us, as God's worker, will be either approved or ashamed. The word *approved* means "one who has been tested and found acceptable." The word was used for testing and approving metals. Each trial that we go through forces us to study the Word to find God's will. As we rightly use the Word, we succeed in overcoming our trials, and we are approved by God. We cannot be approved unless we are tested.

HOME DAILY BIBLE 📖 READINGS

for the week of February 12, 2006
Develop Christian Character

Feb. 6, Monday
—Romans 4:13-25
—God's Promise Is Realized Through Faith

Feb. 7, Tuesday
—1 Peter 2:1-10
—So You May Grow into Salvation

Feb. 8, Wednesday
—Colossians 1:3-10
—Grow in the Knowledge of God

Feb. 9, Thursday
—2 Timothy 2:1-7
—A Good Soldier of Christ Jesus

Feb. 10, Friday
—2 Timothy 2:8-13
—Remember Christ Jesus

Feb. 11, Saturday
—2 Timothy 2:14-19
—Be a Worker Approved by God

Feb. 12, Sunday
—2 Timothy 2:20-26
—Pursue Righteousness, Faith, Love and Peace

PRAYER

Most high God, our heavenly Father, we praise and honor You as the one and true God, Maker of the heavens and the earth. We thank You for Your written Word and we thank You for the Word that was made flesh and dwelt among us, even, Your Son, the Lord Jesus Christ. We thank You for the example He provided for us as He lived in the flesh yet remained faithful to You by the power of Your Holy Spirit. Help us, likewise, to be empowered to walk in Your Spirit and to shun the promptings of our flesh. Give us the grace to live before others that they might see our good works and glorify You. In Jesus' name, we pray. Amen.

Lesson 12

Follow a Good Mentor

CHILDREN'S UNIT
We Give Thanks to God

ADULT TOPIC: The Marks of a Helpful Mentor
YOUTH TOPIC: Follow a Good Example
CHILDREN'S TOPIC: We Learn from the Bible

KEY VERSE

But continue thou in the things which thou hast learned and hast been assured of, knowing of whom thou hast learned them.
—2 Timothy 3:14

DEVOTIONAL READING: Psalm 119:9-16
BACKGROUND SCRIPTURE: 2 Timothy 3—4
PRINT PASSAGE: 2 Timothy 3:10—4:8

OBJECTIVES
Upon completion of this lesson, students should:
1. Know what is meant by the term "mentor."
2. Identify the qualities of a godly mentor.
3. Illustrate how each person can serve as a mentor to someone.
4. Encourage each other to find someone in their family, church or community to whom they can serve as a mentor.

2 Timothy 3:10—4:8—KJV

10 But thou hast fully known my doctrine, manner of life, purpose, faith, longsuffering, charity, patience,

11 Persecutions, afflictions, which came unto me at Antioch, at Iconium, at Lystra; what persecutions I endured: but out of them all the Lord delivered me.

12 Yea, and all that will live godly in Christ Jesus shall suffer persecution.

13 But evil men and seducers shall wax worse and worse, deceiving, and being deceived.

14 But continue thou in the things which thou hast learned and hast been assured of, knowing of whom thou hast learned them;

15 And that from a child thou hast known the holy scriptures, which are able to make thee wise unto salvation through faith which is in Christ Jesus.

16 All scripture is given by inspiration of God, and is profitable for doctrine, for reproof, for correction, for instruction in righteousness:

17 That the man of God may be perfect, thoroughly furnished unto all good works.

.....

I CHARGE thee therefore before God, and the Lord Jesus Christ, who shall judge the quick and the dead at his appearing and his kingdom;

2 Preach the word; be instant in season, out of season; reprove, rebuke, exhort with all longsuffering and doctrine.

3 For the time will come when they will not endure sound doctrine; but after their own lusts shall they heap to themselves teachers, having itching ears;

4 And they shall turn away their ears from the truth, and shall be turned unto fables.

5 But watch thou in all things, endure afflictions, do the work of an evangelist, make full proof of thy ministry.

6 For I am now ready to be offered, and the time of my departure is at hand.

7 I have fought a good fight, I have finished my course, I have kept the faith:

8 Henceforth there is laid up for me a crown of righteousness, which the Lord, the righteous judge, shall give me at that day: and not to me only, but unto all them also that love his appearing.

2 Timothy 3:10—4:8—NRSV

10 Now you have observed my teaching, my conduct, my aim in life, my faith, my patience, my love, my steadfastness,

11 my persecutions and suffering the things that happened to me in Antioch, Iconium, and Lystra. What persecutions I endured! Yet the Lord rescued me from all of them.

12 Indeed, all who want to live a godly life in Christ Jesus will be persecuted.

13 But wicked people and impostors will go from bad to worse, deceiving others and being deceived.

14 But as for you, continue in what you have learned and firmly believed, knowing from whom you learned it,

15 and how from childhood you have known the sacred writings that are able to instruct you for salvation through faith in Christ Jesus.

16 All scripture is inspired by God and is useful for teaching, for reproof, for correction, and for training in righteousness,

17 so that everyone who belongs to God may be proficient, equipped for every good work.

.....

IN THE presence of God and of Christ Jesus, who is to judge the living and the dead, and in view of his appearing and his kingdom, I solemnly urge you:

2 proclaim the message; be persistent whether the time is favorable or unfavorable; convince, rebuke, and encourage, with the utmost patience in teaching.

3 For the time is coming when people will not put up with sound doctrine, but having itching ears, they will accumulate for themselves teachers to suit their own desires,

4 and will turn away from listening to the truth and wander away to myths.

5 As for you, always be sober, endure suffering, do the work of an evangelist, carry out your ministry fully.

6 As for me, I am already being poured out as a libation, and the time of my departure has come.

7 I have fought the good fight, I have finished the race, I have kept the faith.

8 From now on there is reserved for me the crown of righteousness, which the Lord, the righteous judge, will give me on that day, and not only to me but also to all who have longed for his appearing.

POINTS TO BE EMPHASIZED
ADULTS
Key Verse: 2 Timothy 3:14
Print: 2 Timothy 3:10—4:8

—Timothy learned from people and writings he could trust.

—The Scriptures inform and offer a foundation for Christian ministry.

—God's Word must be fearlessly proclaimed.

YOUTH
Key Verse: 2 Timothy 3:14
Print: 2 Timothy 3:10—4:8

—Paul reminded Timothy that he had worked closely under him and had observed his character, his ministry and persecutions firsthand.

—Paul advised Timothy to continue in the faith that he had learned from him and to study the Scriptures.

—Paul urged Timothy to proclaim the Gospel, even when people were not receptive.

—Youth can learn from the study of Scripture.

CHILDREN
Key Verse: Psalm 119:11
Print: 2 Timothy 3:16-17; Psalm 119:1, 9-11, 33-34, 73, 97, 105, 127, 172-174

—Timothy realized the importance of the Scriptures through his family members; Paul later reinforced such.

—All Christian believers should be continuously taught, reproved, corrected and trained in righteousness through God's Word.

—God's law and commands are treasures to be learned, followed, loved and lived.

—Christians are to sing and delight in God's commands and promises.

—We should sing and delight in God's commands and promises

TOPICAL OUTLINE OF THE LESSON

I. INTRODUCTION
   A. The Mentor
   B. Biblical Background

II. EXPOSITION AND APPLICATION OF THE SCRIPTURE
   A. Faithfulness in the Face of Opposition (*2 Timothy 3:10-12*)
   B. Persecution and Deception Will Increase (*2 Timothy 3:13*)
   C. Faithfulness to God's Word (*2 Timothy 3:14—4:5*)
   D. The Faithfulness of Paul (*2 Timothy 4:6-8*)

III. SPECIAL FEATURES
   A. Preserving Our Heritage
   B. Concluding Reflections

I. INTRODUCTION
A. The Mentor

This lesson focuses upon the apostle Paul as a mentor. A mentor, in common usage today, refers to one who tutors, guides, or coaches another. Though the word itself is not found in the Bible, the concept is certainly there. Paul urged Timothy to consider him as an "example" to follow (1 Timothy 1:16). The Greek word from which we derive "example" is one used to signify an ethical or spiritual *model* or *pattern* to be followed (cf., Philippians 3:17; 1 Thessalonians 1:7). It is also used to refer to patterns to be avoided—that is, warning examples or exhibitions of God's judgment and wrath (1 Corinthians 10:6, 11; Hebrews 4:11). Therefore, the mentor is an individual who serves as a pattern or model for others to imitate and follow. The thrust of today's lesson is upon those qualities that a good model or mentor must possess.

B. Biblical Background

"The last days" is a period of time that actually began with the life and ministry of Christ on earth (Hebrews 1:1-2). However, the New Testament indicates that "the last days" refers particularly to the state of the church before the second coming of Christ. These shall be "perilous" times—that is, "difficult, hard to deal with." This is the same word used in Matthew 8:28 to describe the Gadarene demoniac. Because people will believe the "doctrines of demons" (1 Timothy 4:1ff), this world will become a "demonic graveyard" just as in Gadara. We are in those days now!

Paul compared the apostate teachers to the Egyptian magicians Jannes and Jambres, who opposed Moses by imitating what he did (Exodus 7:11ff). Satan is an imitator, and his imitation gospel and church will spread in the last days. But just as Moses overcame these imitators by the power of God coming in great judgment, so Christ will ultimately overcome these latter-day deceivers. "From such turn away!" warns Paul (verse 5). Timothy was not to get involved with Christ-denying deceivers, at any cost.

II. EXPOSITION AND APPLICATION OF THE SCRIPTURE
A. Faithfulness in the Face of Opposition *(2 Timothy 3:10-12)*

Timothy had not been a companion with Paul at the time of his persecutions at *Antioch, Iconium and Lystra* (Acts 13:50). Yet, from his mother Eunice, his grandmother Lois, and the other townspeople, Timothy was well-acquainted with the apostle's adversaries. Paul testified that *out of them all, the Lord delivered me.* Herein, Paul gives glory to God as being his Deliverer, who was ever faithful to him throughout all his persecutions. He offered this as evidence and admonition to Timothy, and to us likewise, as just cause to follow Christ. We can be assured that whatever comes our way by means of adversities and persecutions, we can rely upon God to deliver us either *from* them or *out* of them all.

B. Persecution and Deception Will Increase
(2 Timothy 3:13)

There are warnings characteristic of persons associated with the end time. "Lovers of their own selves": selfish, and studious after their own interest, regardless of the welfare of all humankind. "Covetous": lovers of money, because of the influence that riches can procure. "Boasters": vainglorious, self-assuming, valuing themselves beyond all others. "Proud": airy, light, trifling persons—those who love to make a show. "Blasphemers": those who speak unpiously of God and sacred things, and injuriously of others. "Disobedient to parents": headstrong children, whom their parents cannot persuade. "Unthankful": persons without grace, who think they have a right to the service of all persons, yet feel no obligation and consequently no gratitude. "Unholy": without piety, having no heart reverence for God. "Without natural affection": lacking that affection which parents bear to their young, and which the young bear to their parents. "Trucebreakers": those who are bound by no promise, held by no engagement, obliged by no oath—persons who readily promise anything because they never intend to perform.

Contrary to the "health, wealth and prosperity" teachings of many current-day ministers, Paul wanted Timothy, and all Christians, to realize that persecution awaits *everyone who wants to live a godly life in Christ* (cf., John 15:18-21)—hence Paul's reminder of his own experience. Consistency in the life of Christ must necessarily be opposed by the world. Yet, with the last days again in mind, Paul wrote that Timothy could actually expect the situation to get worse and the pressure to intensify.

C. Faithfulness to God's Word *(2 Timothy 3:14–4:5)*

But as for you continue in the things which you have learned, knowing from whom you have learned them and from childhood you have known the Holy Scriptures. The exhortation is to continue in the things Timothy had learned and become convinced of (cf., 1 Corinthians 15:1-2). These things had come from two sources, which Paul set side by side as of equal importance: his own testimony, and the Holy Scriptures, which at that time consisted of the Old Testament. Timothy's complete confidence in both sources would be enough to prevent any slippage in his commitment to the truth. Again, these verses may imply that Timothy's salvation occurred prior to his acquaintance with Paul (cf., 1 Timothy 1:2; 2 Timothy 1:2, 5; Acts 16:1).

Which are able to make you wise for salvation through faith which is in Christ Jesus. Paul noted that the Scriptures are able to make one wise with regard to salvation, a lesson Timothy had learned long before. But now Paul wanted to reemphasize to Timothy the crucial role of God's inspired revelation in his present ministry. Thus, Paul reminded Timothy that *all Scripture is given by inspiration of God* (*theopneustos,* "God-breathed"); that is, God's Word was given through men superintended by the Holy Spirit so that their writings are without error. This fact was virtually taken for granted by the Jews. Then Paul asserted the "usefulness" of the Word for each aspect of Timothy's ministry, whatever it might be—teaching (instructing believers in God's truths), rebuking those in sin (cf., 1 Timothy 5:20; 2 Timothy 4:2), correcting those in error (cf., 2 Timothy 2:25; 4:2), and training (*paideian,* lit., "child-training") in righteousness (guiding new believers in God's ways). For all of these and more, the written Word of God is profitable. With it, the *man of God* (one who must provide spiritual leadership to others) is *artios*: "complete, capable, proficient in the sense of being able to meet all demands." To drive home his point still more emphatically, Paul added equipped (*exertismenos,* "furnished") for every good work (cf., 2:21). Paul placed heavy burdens of ministry on his young disciple in this letter, but he did not do so irresponsibly. He was confident of Timothy's commitment to and dependence on the Scriptures, and he was even more confident of God's ability to supply all of Timothy's needs through the Word.

Paul said *"I charge thee therefore,"* which was his final charge to the young pastor, Timothy, the one upon whose shoulders he now placed responsibility for the care of all the churches and the leadership in maintaining the faith. This exhortation was given in light of the spiritual declension and departure from true doctrine which had already set in, and which in the last days would come to a head. The Greek word translated "charge"

was used in pagan Greek culture to call the gods and men to witness. As has been previously mentioned, Timothy seemed to have been deficient in the area of dogged perseverance, so the apostle used this strong word (charge) in his urging. Indeed, this *charge* represents the central thrust of every minister's task. Because the Word is inspired and profitable for all aspects of the ministry, proclaiming that Word was to be Timothy's business. *Preach!* His preaching should be characterized by that dignity which comes from the consciousness of the fact that he is an official herald of the King of kings. It should be accompanied by that note of authority which will command the respect, careful attention and proper reaction of the listeners. The pulpit is no place for "clowning around," if you will. Take careful note that the preacher is to proclaim the "Word," not book reviews, not politics, not a philosophy of positive thinking, etc. The preacher as a herald cannot choose the message. The message to be proclaimed is given by the Sovereign One. To proclaim anything contrary is to betray the trust entrusted by the King.

The exhortation to proclaim the Word is given in view of the coming defection from the faith. *For the time will come—* and no doubt was already partially present, in the apostle's opinion—*when they will not endure sound doctrine* (lit., "healthy"; cf., 1 Timothy 1:10; 6:3; 2 Timothy 1:13; Titus 1:9, 13; 2:8). The word *endure* carries the idea of standing firm against a person or thing. Thus, it refers to those who will not stand up against false doctrine. *According to their own desires.* The word *desires* is the Greek "lusts" or "cravings"; those who set themselves against Paul's doctrine are dominated by their own private, personal cravings. Chief among those is the desire for personal gratification. This gives us insight as to why the current-day doctrines of "health and wealth" are so popular...*because they have itching ears.* The word *itch*, in its active verb form, means "to scratch, to tickle." It describes that person who desires to hear for mere gratification.

Timothy was exhorted to do four things: first, he was to *watch in all things*—that is, he was to be calm and collected in spirit, dispassionate, alert; second, he must *endure afflictions*—he was to be willing to suffer evils, hardships and troubles. Too many of us today are afraid to boldly proclaim the Gospel for fear of the displeasure of some board or some group within the convention which might threaten our ecclesiastical advancement or the cutting off of our financial income; third, he was to *do the work of an evangelist*—this means that the pastor's work is always to be evangelistic in character, always bringing the Good News, ever in search of lost souls. The local pastor differs from the evangelist (cf., Ephesians 4:11); however, a pastor should be evangelistic in his message and his methods. We, today, must guard against the practice, observed among many, of loosely using the term "evangelist" to apply to women whom they do not want to license to preach, but simply want to appease. *Fulfill your ministry.* Make full proof of your ministry, or fully perform every aspect of your ministry.

D. The Faithfulness of Paul
(2 Timothy 4:6-8)

Looking back over his life, the apostle summed it up in three sentences, using the figures of a Greek wrestler, a Greek runner, and a Roman soldier. He said, using the first figure, *I have fought* the good fight. This is not an egotistical statement as the modern translation might seem to indicate. Rather, it refers to an external goodness used in Greek athletics of a contest in the Greek stadium where the games were held. It is goodness that is not moral, but aesthetic, a beauty of action that would characterize either the Greek wrestler's efforts or the Christian's warfare against evil. It speaks of an action completed in past time with present results. Paul fought his fight with sin to the finish, and was resting in a complete victory. *I have finished my course.* This refers to a racecourse, the center path of the present-day college athletic field. Like a Greek runner, he had crossed the finish line and was now resting at the goal. His life's work was over. *I have kept the faith* (cf., 1 Timothy 6:20). "The faith" here is the deposit of truth which God had entrusted to Paul, and *kept* means "to keep by safeguarding." His work of safeguarding that truth was now at an end. He had defended it against the attacks of the Gnostics, the Judaizers, and the philosophers of Athens. He had laid it down at the feet of his Captain. He, like a soldier who has grown old in the service of his country, was awaiting his discharge. But his use of illustrations from Greek athletics is not finished. He compared himself to the Greek athlete, who, having finished his race, was looking up at the judge's stand, and awaiting his laurel wreath of victory. He says, *"Henceforth, there is laid up for me a crown of righteousness."* The *henceforth* is from a word that literally means "what remains."

Crown is from the Greek word *stephanos,* referring to the victor's crown, a garland of oak leaves or ivy, given to the winner in the Greek games. The victor's crown of righteousness is the crown which belongs to or is the due reward of righteousness. *Which the Lord, the righteous judge.* The righteous Judge is the Lord Jesus Christ, the umpire who makes no mistakes and is always fair. *Shall give me at that day* is a reference to the second coming of the Lord. *And not to me only, but to all those who love his appearing.* To those who have considered His appearing precious and therefore have loved it, and as a result at the present time are still holding that attitude in their hearts— to these individuals, the Lord will give the victor's garland of righteousness. Such a reward is reserved for those who remain faithful even in the face of persecution and ultimate death.

III. SPECIAL FEATURES
A. Preserving Our Heritage

It has been correctly observed that "it takes a village to raise a child." This concept, though popularized by others, is taken from the concept of our ancestors in Africa. It is based upon the concept of the "extended family" rather than the "nuclear family."

The "nuclear family" model of Western societies views the family as consisting of a mother, father and children, all residing in the same household. In this view, the child's rearing is solely the responsibility of the biological parents. However, the African model of "extended family" views the family as consisting of not only the mother and father within the house in which they live, but also, the grandparents, uncles, aunts and cousins who live nearby. Therefore, the upbringing of the children becomes the joint responsibility of all those in the neighborhood/village.

Imagine the radical difference that would result if such an attitude in our society would develop. The most vulnerable in our society would come under the protection of the entire "village."

Here is where the church must assume the role of the *village* and take on the responsibility of helping rear the children. Every church can provide mentoring for these youngsters by establishing "Big-Brother" or "Spiritual Parents" types of ministries. In such ministries, the children can see Christian role models and receive instruction with the Scriptures being the standard of conduct. There should be no single female-headed households void of proper male role models that the church fails to assume responsibility for the upbringing of the children. This is especially critical for young males, for it has been said that "a woman can raise a boy, but it takes a man to raise a man!"

B. Concluding Reflections

The apostle Paul sets before Timothy his own example, of which Timothy had been an eyewitness, having long observed Paul. Therefore, Paul was assured that Timothy stood firm in his beliefs—he knew his doctrine by observing his duty; he knew his beliefs by observing his behavior. For, indeed, our walk tells more about us than our talk.

In a recent interview with the African American basketball star, Charles Barkley, he was asked if he considered himself to be a good role model. He responded, "I am nobody's role model—kids should seek out their parents for role models!" The faultiness of this argument is this: We are all role models whether we choose to be one or not. Charles Barkley is a role model; the only question remaining is, "What kind of role model is he?" Is he a good role model or a bad one? Is he a godly role model or an ungodly role model? The same may be said of each of us—we are all role models—but what kind of role models are we?

Lesson 13

Live the Truth, Teach the Truth

ADULT TOPIC: Teach Sound Doctrine by Example
YOUTH TOPIC: Teaching by Example
CHILDREN'S TOPIC: We Learn from Others' Examples

DEVOTIONAL READING: Ephesians 4:11-16
BACKGROUND SCRIPTURE: Titus 2:1-15
PRINT PASSAGE: Titus 2:1-15

Titus 2:1-15—KJV

BUT SPEAK thou the things which become sound doctrine:

2 That the aged men be sober, grave, temperate, sound in faith, in charity, in patience.

3 The aged women likewise, that they be in behaviour as becometh holiness, not false accusers, not given to much wine, teachers of good things;

4 That they may teach the young women to be sober, to love their husbands, to love their children,

5 To be discreet, chaste, keepers at home, good, obedient to their own husbands, that the word of God be not blasphemed.

6 Young men likewise exhort to be sober minded.

7 In all things showing thyself a pattern of good works: in doctrine showing uncorruptness, gravity, sincerity,

8 Sound speech, that cannot be condemned; that he that is of the contrary part may be ashamed, having no evil thing to say of you.

9 Exhort servants to be obedient unto their own masters, and to please them well in all things; not answering again;

UNIT III
Faithful Followers, Faithful Leaders

CHILDREN'S UNIT
We Give Thanks to God

KEY VERSE

In all things showing thyself a pattern of good works: in doctrine showing uncorruptness, gravity, sincerity.
—Titus 2:7

OBJECTIVES
Upon the completion of this lesson, students should understand:

1. The importance of holiness in the sight of God.

2. The importance of a godly lifestyle before others.

3. The reward implicit in pursuing godliness with the assurance of victory through the Holy Spirit.

10 Not purloining, but showing all good fidelity; that they may adorn the doctrine of God our Saviour in all things.

11 For the grace of God that bringeth salvation hath appeared to all men,

12 Teaching us that, denying ungodliness and worldly lusts, we should live soberly, righteously, and godly, in this present world;

13 Looking for that blessed hope, and the glorious appearing of the great God and our Saviour Jesus Christ;

14 Who gave himself for us, that he might redeem us from all iniquity, and purify unto himself a peculiar people, zealous of good works.

15 These things speak, and exhort, and rebuke with all authority. Let no man despise thee.

Titus 2:1-15—NRSV

BUT AS for you, teach what is consistent with sound doctrine.

2 Tell the older men to be temperate, serious, prudent, and sound in faith, in love, and in endurance.

3 Likewise, tell the older women to be reverent in behavior, not to be slanderers or slaves to drink; they are to teach what is good,

4 so that they may encourage the young women to love their husbands, to love their children,

5 to be self-controlled, chaste, good managers of the household, kind, being submissive to their husbands, so that the word of God may not be discredited.

6 Likewise, urge the younger men to be self-controlled.

7 Show yourself in all respects a model of good works, and in your teaching show integrity, gravity,

8 and sound speech that cannot be censured; then any opponent will be put to shame, having nothing evil to say of us.

9 Tell slaves to be submissive to their masters and to give satisfaction in every respect; they are not to talk back,

10 not to pilfer, but to show complete and perfect fidelity, so that in everything they may be an ornament to the doctrine of God our Savior.

11 For the grace of God has appeared, bringing salvation to all,

12 training us to renounce impiety and worldly passions, and in the present age to live lives that are self-controlled, upright, and godly,

13 while we wait for the blessed hope and the manifestation of the glory of our great God and Savior, Jesus Christ.

14 He it is who gave himself for us that he might redeem us from all iniquity and purify for himself a people of his own who are zealous for good deeds.

15 Declare these things; exhort and reprove with all authority. Let no one look down on you.

POINTS TO BE EMPHASIZED
ADULTS
Key Verse: Titus 2:7
Print: Titus 2:1-15

—Sound doctrine is taught by righteous example.

—If we model good works, we will minimize criticism of the Christian faith.

—As a minister, Titus was to fulfill his duty to all the groups in the church.

—Regardless of one's social status, all have the opportunity to choose a righteous life.

YOUTH
Key Verse: Titus 2:12
Print: Titus 2:1-15

—God is interested in how we demonstrate personal, spiritual growth through our daily living.

—God calls us to display attitudes and actions that are appropriate for Christian living.

—Paul admonishes Titus to teach sound doctrine.

CHILDREN
Key Verse: 1 Thessalonians 1:6-7
Print: 1 Thessalonians 1:1-7; 3:6-9

—Even in the midst of personal trauma and other difficult situations, Christian believers can be examples to others.

—When we invest time, effort and a caring spirit in teaching other believers, we will be rewarded.

—Christian teachers must continuously praise children's progress in faith formation.

—Children imitate their Christian teachers.

TOPICAL OUTLINE OF THE LESSON

I. INTRODUCTION
  A. Walking the Talk
  B. Biblical Background

II. EXPOSITION AND APPLICATION OF THE SCRIPTURE
  A. The Example of Sound Doctrine *(Titus 2:1)*
  B. The Example Required of Older Men *(Titus 2:2)*
  C. The Example Required of Older Women *(Titus 2:3)*
  D. The Example Required of Younger Women *(Titus 2:4-5)*
  E. The Example Required of Younger Men *(Titus 2:6-8)*
  F. The Example Required of Bondservants *(Titus 2:9-10)*
  G. Needed Grace Given to All *(Titus 2:11-15)*

III. SPECIAL FEATURES
  A. Preserving Our Heritage
  B. Concluding Reflections

I. INTRODUCTION
A. Walking the Talk

The letter to Titus is similar to Paul's two letters to Timothy and was written for much the same purpose—to encourage and strengthen a young pastor whom he had mentored, in whom he had great confidence, and for whom he had great love as a spiritual leader. He was passing the baton, as it were, to those young pastors who were ministering in difficult situations—

Timothy in the church at Ephesus and Titus in the numerous churches on the island of Crete. The great apostle had carefully trained both men; both were highly gifted by the Holy Spirit, and both had proven their unflagging devotion to Paul and to the Lord's work. Both men also faced formidable opposition, from within and from without the church.

This letter was designed to instruct Titus to teach the other elders on Crete who ministered under his leadership, and to instruct members of the various congregations. It also backed up Titus' leadership with Paul's authority. Chapter 1 focuses upon the qualifications of the church leadership, specifically, their theology and their personal character and conduct. Chapter 2, from which our lesson is taken, focuses upon the character and conduct of church members among themselves.

B. Biblical Background

Titus was a Gentile convert (Galatians 2:3) who had served and traveled with Paul (Galatians 2:1-3). Titus had also functioned as a faithful emissary to the troubled church in Corinth (2 Corinthians 7:6-7; 8:6, 16).

In approximately AD 63-64, sometime after they left Timothy behind in Ephesus, Paul and Titus traveled on to Crete. After a brief visit, Paul then left Titus behind to help provide leadership for the Cretan churches (Titus 1:5). Subsequently, the apostle wrote this epistle and had it delivered to Titus. The exact time and place of writing is unknown.

Paul hoped to join Titus again in Nicopolis for the winter (3:12), but there is no way of knowing whether that meeting ever took place. Titus was last mentioned by Paul (2 Timothy 4:10) as having gone to Dalmatia (Yugoslavia). Tradition has it that Titus later returned to Crete and there served for the rest of his life.

II. EXPOSITION AND APPLICATION OF THE SCRIPTURE

A. The Example of Sound Doctrine (Titus 2:1)

"But as for you." Paul began these instructions to Titus by intensively establishing a strong contrast with the false teachers he had just discussed. Speak the things which are proper for sound doctrine. Titus was to teach the congregation what is in accord with sound doctrine, or more literally, "healthy teaching." The notion of healthy teaching is common in the Pastorals (cf., 1 Timothy 1:10; 6:3; 2 Timothy 1:13; 4:3; Titus 1:9, 13; 2:2), as well as the idea that certain behavior befits sound doctrine and other behavior does not (cf., 1 Timothy 1:10; 6:3). The victims of false teachers (cf., Titus 1:16) were out of harmony with sound doctrine; but now Paul would describe the right sorts of behavior.

B. The Example Required of Older Men (Titus 2:2)

Paul addressed several groups, the first being the older men, a group he considered himself to be a part of while he was in his sixties (Philemon 9). Titus was to teach them to manifest the characteristics of maturity. Older men are to be: *sober* (*nephalious;* cf., 1 Timothy 3:2), abstaining from wine, either entirely or at least from its immoderate use; *temperate*—curbing one's desires and impulses, self-controlled; *sound in faith*—referring here to the faith, the body of Christian doctrine. They are to be *worthy of respect,* "serious-minded," "dignified," a person who is neither frivolous nor superficial. Next, older men ought to be characterized additionally by *soundness in love and perseverance.* They should demonstrate the Christian virtue of love toward God, toward His people, and toward those who do not yet know Him. They have learned the virtue of loving those who do not deserve it and even those who reject and persecute them. They lovingly forgive, and lovingly serve. They are to be patient and persevering; that is, they are to exhibit the ability to endure hardship, to accept disappointment and failure, and to be satisfied despite thwarted personal desires and plans.

C. The Example Required of Older Women *(Titus 2:3)*

Titus was *likewise* to teach the older *women to behave reverently,* referring widely to conduct in all respects and on all occasions. Though he does not specify at what age a woman must be considered to fall into this category, we may assume from his reference to the age of widows in his first letter to Timothy that it was about the age of sixty. They were not to be slanderers (cf., 1 Timothy 3:11). They should refuse to listen to, much less propagate, slanderous or demeaning words about others. They were to be *teachers of good things*—those things that are noble, excellent and lofty. He was to encourage these older women to develop a ministry of teaching younger women these virtues. Younger women with children were to keep their primary focus at home (see Titus 2:4-5), but the older women would do well to reach outside their homes and share what they had learned with those who would profit from it most.

Paul writes to Titus with instruction to prepare for the attack of false teachers. *Servant* literally means "slave of God." The letter explains appropriate behavior and its motivation and gives a general reminder of Titus' authority. *Prudent* is related to words that are translated "self-controlled." Notice the contrast between elders and false teachers: false teachers are motivated by sordid gain; the elders must not be greedy for gain, but able to control their own families. Titus was a Christian teacher of Greek origin, who was converted by Paul. He was one of those sent upon a mission to Jerusalem from the church of Antioch (Acts 5:2). God's grace indicates God's favor. "Teaching us that in denying" places Christ as teacher and Christians as His disciples. "Worldly lust": desires, affections and appetites characterized by persons who live without God. "Should live soberly": having every temper and desire under control by reason that is under the direction of the Holy Spirit. "Righteously" infers rendering to every person his or her due, injuring no one in body, mind, reputation, or property—doing unto all that which we would have them do unto us.

D. The Example Required of Younger Women *(Titus 2:4-5)*

Paul specified here what he meant by his general reference to "what is good" in verse 3. Older women could help the younger women in at least seven areas, a list that no doubt represents the apostle's understanding of a young wife and mother's proper priorities. This list emphasizes, in the original, first what young wives and mothers are to be, and then only secondarily what they are to do. Wives are to rank themselves as being in submission to their husbands' headship. It refers to function rather than essence. In essence, husbands and wives are equal, but in function, wives are to submit to their husbands—*that the Word of God may not be dishonored.* The thought here is that when all groups, within the church, collectively and individually—older men and women, young men and women, husbands and wives—all perform their duties in a biblical way, they honor God and His Word. Of course, the opposite is true. The failure to live harmoniously in accordance with God's design dishonors Him and His Word. Unbelievers judge the genuineness and value of our faith more by our living than by our theology. In doing so, they judge the truth and power of the Word of God by the way in which we live.

E. The Example Required of Younger Men *(Titus 2:6-8)*

Likewise, exhort the young men to be sober minded. Titus was to similarly encourage the young men to exercise self-control, a virtue in which far too many young men are deficient. Paul used some form of the word here translated "self-control" with each of the four groups of people (verses 2, 4, 5, 6). Various forms of the word are prominent in the Pastorals, indicating the importance of moderation, sensibleness and self-restraint. Titus qualified as a young man, too, and so received some direct advice from the apostle. He must strive to "show himself" an example (*typos,* "pattern") to all (but especially to the other young men) in every good work (cf., 1 Timothy 4:15-16). In his public ministry of teaching, Titus was charged to show integrity, seriousness, and soundness of speech that cannot be condemned. Paul was always concerned lest those who oppose be provided ammunition for their attacks.

F. The Example Required of Bondservants *(Titus 2:9-10)*

Exhort bondservants. Notice that Paul does not address the condition of slavery. He offered no judgment about its basic fairness or morality. He simply acknowledged its existence and dealt with the attitude that Christians who were bondservants or slaves should reflect. Therefore, slaves, too, who made up a significant portion of first-century congregations, were responsible to honor God with their lives. Paul listed five qualities which were to characterize Christians bonded to serve others. Titus was to teach them: (1) to be subject to their masters in everything; (2) to try to please them; (3) not to talk back to them; (4) not to steal from them; and (5) to show that they can be fully trusted. From the world's perspective, a slave should not owe any of these things to his master; but from a Christian perspective, the situation looks different. A Christian slave was in fact serving, not his earthly master, but the Lord Christ who would vindicate him in the end (Colossians 3:23-24). In the meantime, he was to avoid giving offense, and concentrate on following Christ's example in every way (cf., 1 Peter 2:18-25). In this way, his life would prove to be an adornment to the teaching about God our Savior. Thus, Paul reemphasized what had been the theme of this entire section (Titus 2:1-10): a believer's behavior is to be in accord with or befitting sound doctrine.

G. Needed Grace Given to All
(Titus 2:11-15)

Paul had been exploring the affirmation that godly living is demanded by God's truth. Now, he changed his focus to explore that central aspect of God's truth which demands godly living: grace. The word "for" (*gar*) suggests that here is the theological foundation for what the apostle had just written. *For the grace of God that brings salvation has appeared to all men.* When fully understood, it is the Gospel of the grace of God which teaches Christians how to live. This grace has brought salvation to all people. It *appeared* to all men through the life, death and resurrection of Jesus Christ. God, in His grace, sent His Son to redeem those in the bondage of sin. This salvation is for every person who receives it. There is a universal need and God has provided a universal remedy for all who believe. In each case, the reference to God as Savior (cf., 1 Timothy 2:3; 4:10; Titus 2:10) prompted Paul to affirm the universal availability of salvation through Christ. The message of God's grace, when its full implications are seen, leads Christians, negatively, to say "No" to ungodliness and worldly passions (cf., Hebrews 11:24-26), and, positively, to live self-controlled, upright, and godly lives in this present age.

The Gospel of grace affects one's present behavior, on the one hand, by focusing on God's unmerited favor in the past (see the Jesus parable in Matthew 18:23-35 for the dynamics of how this should work). But the Gospel also promotes godly living by focusing on the future. Christians look forward to the blessed hope—the glorious appearing of our great God and Savior, Jesus Christ (cf., 2 Timothy 4:8). Titus was told to step out aggressively in his public ministry, encouraging those who were doing well, rebuking those who needed to be corrected, being intimidated by no one.

III. SPECIAL FEATURES
A. Preserving Our Heritage

It is important that each church recognize the importance of age-graded ministries. Too often, because of limited space and small numbers, we are prone to lump all age groups together for study. This tendency must be resisted at all costs, for it is not only stagnating, but also counterproductive. We must recognize that individuals at different ages have had different life experiences. As such, their perspectives about life are different and their needs are likewise different. If our teaching ministries fail to meet people where they are, then we fail to teach—as people can only be met where they are and not where we want them to be.

B. Concluding Reflections

Paul's teaching to his two disciples, Timothy and Titus, reflects the importance not only of teaching precepts, but the essentiality of it being accompanied by *fellowship*. People who share common beliefs, interests and expectations seek each other's companionship. When such companionship is based on a faith-life centered in Jesus Christ, the concept changes from companionship to fellowship. And, it is in fellowship where true learning takes place. As Paul said to Titus in this lesson, "You know fully well my beliefs, because you have observed my behavior!"

HOME DAILY BIBLE READINGS

for the week of February 26, 2006
Live the Truth, Teach the Truth

Feb. 20, Monday
　　—Ephesians 4:11-16
　　—Speak the Truth in Love
Feb. 21, Tuesday
　　—2 Peter 1:3-12
　　—Be Established in the Truth
Feb. 22, Wednesday
　　—1 John 1:5-10
　　—Walk in the Light of Truth
Feb. 23, Thursday
　　—3 John 2–8
　　—Support All Believers in the Truth
Feb. 24, Friday
　　—Titus 2:1-5
　　—Teaching Older Men and Women
Feb. 25, Saturday
　　—Titus 2:6-10
　　—Teaching Younger Men and Slaves
Feb. 26, Sunday
　　—Titus 2:11-15
　　—Teach What God Expects of
　　　Believers

PRAYER

Gracious God, our heavenly Father, how we thank You for the indwelling presence of Your Holy Spirit who continually guides us into paths of righteousness. We confess that we are still given over to the lust of the flesh and the pride of life which cause us to behave in ways that are not consistent with whom we have been called to be. We ask You to forgive us for our sins and to cleanse us from all unrighteousness. Amen.

Living in and as God's Creation

GENERAL INTRODUCTION

This quarter's study affords us the opportunity to examine portions of the Wisdom Literature found in Psalms, Job, Ecclesiastes and Proverbs. The selected texts emphasize our lives as created beings within God's larger world.

Unit I, *The Glory of God's Creation,* has four lessons based on selected psalms. Lesson 1 lifts up the special qualities of human beings as part of God's creation. Lesson 2 points out the other wonders of God's creation. Lesson 3 emphasizes the omniscient and intimate character of the God who made us and knows us. Lesson 4 presets a hymn of praise to God.

This unit provides opportunity to enter into dialogue concerning dominion over creation as a faith responsibility that obligates humans to protect it. This is interrelated with the fact that God's creativity must be recognized on a daily basis. In spite of the various rituals that we employ to insulate ourselves from the presence of God, God has intimate knowledge of humans and enters their presumed space at will. While some adults find more reasons to praise God than others, praise is a natural response to God's goodness and mercy.

Unit II, *Living with Creation's Uncertainty,* has five lessons based on passages from Job and Ecclesiastes. Lessons 5 and 6 retell the story of Job. Lesson 7, which falls on Easter Sunday, combines passages from Job and the gospel of Mark to reaffirm that the Resurrection gives a sure source of hope and victory in the face of the tragedies of life. Lesson 8 continues the post-Resurrection theme by combining passages from John and Ecclesiastes that focus on the meaning of life. The final lesson explores our lives as beings who are obliged to live within that "time frame" set by God.

One facet of this unit is that it provides student-teacher interaction with the fact that we sometimes fail to find peace and meaning in life because we seek it through worldly knowledge rather than through God. This points up the need for faith to be passed on from one generation to another in order to strengthen present-day believers. As this is seen in perspective, the spiritual understanding of God's purpose for life helps us to have a balanced view of the various experiences that we encounter as humans who exist within the context of God's timing. This mandates a relationship with God that helps us cope with experiences that we would rather avoid. As true wisdom comes from God, those who are spiritually wise are called to teach those who are new in the faith.

As we study this unit, we shall discover that faith may falter during times of tragedy and difficulties, and it is understandable why one may question the meaning of life under such circumstances. But, all questions about life and living must be addressed to a power that is higher than the contingencies of the human condition. This unit will provide the opportunity to explore the value of friends in their attempt to comfort under trying conditions; the question is: Do they project their personal feelings into our individual situation and assume that they possess the appropriate answers to our dilemma? Humans may raise questions that they expect God to answer, but as Job demonstrates, we should never question God's motives—since He is totally committed to our welfare as expressed in the Resurrection faith. Whereas the writer of Ecclesiastes struggled to find meaning in a repetitive life pattern, he comes to the conclusion that accountability to God is the final destiny of humans. We can gain much from this interaction.

Unit III, *Lessons in Living,* has four sessions based upon selections from Proverbs. Lesson 10 presents wisdom as a priceless treasure. Lessons 11 and 12 explore wisdom's invitation to us to make wise choices and to follow the path of integrity. The final lesson focuses on frugal and capable behavior that the person who possesses wisdom exercises.

The lessons in this unit present opportunities for the students and the teacher to outline how Christians can rejoice that God has created and promised an enduring source for help in the choices with which they are confronted from day to day. One can easily discern the interrelationship between humans and the other aspects of God's creation, as the one is instructive to the other.

Lesson 1

God Made Us Special

ADULT TOPIC: God Made Us Special
YOUTH TOPIC: We Are Special
CHILDREN'S TOPIC: I Am Special

UNIT I
The Glory of God's Creation

CHILDREN'S UNIT
Our Creator God

DEVOTIONAL READING: Genesis 1:26-31
BACKGROUND SCRIPTURE: Psalm 8:1-9
PRINT PASSAGE: Psalm 8:1-9

KEY VERSE

What is man, that thou art mindful of him? and the son of man, that thou visitest him? For thou hast made him a little lower than the angels, and hast crowned him with glory and honour.
—Psalm 8:4-5

Psalm 8:1-9—KJV

O LORD our Lord, how excellent is thy name in all the earth! who hast set thy glory above the heavens.

2 Out of the mouth of babes and sucklings hast thou ordained strength because of thine enemies, that thou mightest still the enemy and the avenger.

3 When I consider thy heavens, the work of thy fingers, the moon and the stars, which thou hast ordained;

4 What is man, that thou art mindful of him? and the son of man, that thou visitest him?

5 For thou hast made him a little lower than the angels, and hast crowned him with glory and honour.

6 Thou madest him to have dominion over the works of thy hands; thou hast put all things under his feet:

7 All sheep and oxen, yea, and the beasts of the field;

8 The fowl of the air, and the fish of the sea, and whatsoever passeth through the paths of the seas.

9 O LORD our Lord, how excellent is thy name in all the earth!

OBJECTIVES

Upon the completion of this lesson, students should understand that:

1. There is a bond between the Creator and humans that gives them special status.

2. Humans' dominion over creation involves a faith responsibility to protect it.

3. Nature reflects the majesty of God's creation.

Psalm 8:1-9—NRSV

O LORD, our Sovereign, how majestic is your name in all the earth! You have set your glory above the heavens.

2 Out of the mouths of babes and infants you have founded a bulwark because of your foes, to silence the enemy and the avenger.

3 When I look at your heavens, the work of your fingers, the moon and the stars that you have established;

4 what are human beings that you are mindful of them, mortals that you care for them?

5 Yet you have made them a little lower than God, and crowned them with glory and honor.

6 You have given them dominion over the works of your hands; you have put all things under their feet,

7 all sheep and oxen, and also the beasts of the field,

8 the birds of the air, and the fish of the sea, whatever passes along the paths of the seas.

9 O LORD, our Sovereign, how majestic is your name in all the earth!

POINTS TO BE EMPHASIZED
ADULTS

Key Verse: Psalm 8:4-5
Print: Psalm 8:1-9
—God is in charge of the created order.
—Humans hold a special place in the created order.
—God gave humans dominion over all aspects of creation.

—God, as Creator, is worthy of our worship.

YOUTH

Key Verse: Psalm 8:5
Print: Psalm 8:1-9
—God cares about each one of us.
—The greatness of God is seen throughout the world.
—Psalm 8 affirms the value of God's creation.
—Humans hold a special place in God's creation.

CHILDREN

Key Verse: Psalm 8:9
Print: Psalm 8
—God gave humans dominion over nature.
—Scripture established a hierarchy of beings consisting of God, angels, humans and animals.
—Nature is the handiwork of God.
—God gives humans honor and glory.
—Our primary obligation is to praise and honor God.

TOPICAL OUTLINE
OF THE LESSON

I. INTRODUCTION
   A. Like God, Like Child
   B. Biblical Background

II. EXPOSITION AND APPLICATION
   OF THE SCRIPTURE
   A. The Excellence of God
     (Psalm 8:1-3)

B. The Potential of Humanity
(Psalm 8:4-9)

III. SPECIAL FEATURES
  A. Preserving Our Heritage
  B. Concluding Reflections

I. INTRODUCTION

A. Like God, Like Child

When you look at your life and you look at God's character, do you see a resemblance? Such a question requires a bit of wisdom that is exactly what is offered by the book of Psalms. This largest of the biblical books, also known as the Psalter, falls into the general category of Old Testament literature known as Wisdom Literature. This group of writing also includes Job, Proverbs, Ecclesiastes and the Song of Songs. Wisdom Literature is characterized by its content more so than by its specific writing style. In the Hebrew Bible, the word "wisdom" is a very general term that describes a variety of skills that are both physical as well as mental. Psalms is a collection of songs, laments, praises and words of practical advice. It explores the emotional and spiritual gamut of the human experience: "The Psalms have been inspired by the heights and depths of human experience. They express great faith, great doubt, and timeless prayer. In origin, it is clear that the Psalms played a crucial part in the ritual and sacrificial life of the people" (Complete Bible Handbook).

Psalm 8 asserts the sovereignty, glory, excellence and dominion of God over heaven, earth, and all that is in the earth.

God is exalted far above humanity and above all the heavenly bodies. Although the majesty of God is presented as matchless, still God is not so far removed from the world that there is no connection between the Creator and the created beings. In fact, it is strictly because of this special connection that humanity is blessed with such great potential. The eternal flame of God's glory is reflected and manifested in the spark of greatness located inside all of God's offspring. It would be impossible for One so great to produce anyone or anything lacking in all aspects of power and godly character traits. When humanity fails to realize and recognize from whence they have come, they also fail to understand how far they can go. When we begin to recognize the Source of our origin, we, then, can begin to walk in the light of our true destiny.

B. Biblical Background

The classic connection between the Creator and the created is beautifully and powerfully illustrated in this psalm. This psalm of David is a perfect example of the incredible sense of splendor and majesty embodied in the series of poetic songs called Psalms. The book of Psalms holds a unique place in biblical literature in that much of it is written from the perspective of humanity addressing God rather than God addressing humanity or humanity addressing humanity. (The Interpreter's Bible Commentary, Psalms/Proverbs, p. 3). These psalms are direct and unpretentious statements of truth. They are inspired by God and come straight from the heart of a man who deeply loves and honors God. In turn, they are directed straight toward the heart of God. Some of the Psalms are autobiographical in nature and simply reflect David's uncut version of him "keeping it real" with God. A good example of this is found in Psalm 51, wherein David repents and laments in sorrow over his sin with Bathsheba. Unlike many of us today, David here is not simply sorry that he got caught, but he is genuinely repentant for the part he played in wounding the heart of God. Although David wrote many of the Psalms, not all of them were penned by him, and most study Bibles include the specific authorship notation at the heading of the passage.

Throughout the history of the church, Psalms have been utilized for a wide variety of purposes. From hymns to prayers to responsive readings, the book of Psalms has represented the important scriptural link between ancient Judaism and contemporary Christianity. Although customs from the historical past are reflected throughout the verses, the timeless passions and expressions of the present are also clearly seen. While one verse may speak of building up Zion, the next verse will express a universal principle such as the assurance of God hearing the prayer of those who are truly in need (cf., Psalm 102:16-17). Although humanity may be "dwarfed by the immensity of the universe, (it is) yet taken up by the Lord, given glory and made its master—a principle perfectly realized in Jesus Christ and still to be realized in redeemed mankind" *(New Bible Commentary)*. Whatever one's need, mood, or concern, chances are that there is a verse in this largest book in the Bible that will coincide with those feelings or that subject matter.

II. EXPOSITION AND APPLICATION OF THE SCRIPTURE
A. The Excellence of God *(Psalm 8:1-3)*

The psalmist begins by acknowledging and establishing the exalted nature of the very name of God. In ancient times, the very name of God was treated with reverence and utter respect. Many versions of the Bible still maintain the all-uppercase spelling of the word LORD. In contemporary times, it seems that people name their children based on the phonetic sound rather than the meaning of the name. During the time that the book of Psalms was written, the meaning of a name carried the utmost importance. It was so important that when the nature, personality, or mission of a person's life was radically changed, then the person's name had to also be altered. (Saul's name was changed to Paul.) The Hebrew name used for LORD here is Jehovah, which means "the Self-existent or Eternal One" *(Strong's Exhaustive Concordance).* In order to see the glory of God, one need only to open one's eyes and observe *the moon and the stars* which God has ordered or ordained. The vast veil of darkness that nightly descends may hide some things but cannot cover the majesty of God. The heavenly bodies are a testimony to the glory of God.

B. The Potential of Humanity
(Psalm 8:4-9)

The psalmist raises a poignant question: "What is man that you are mindful of him?" As if trying to rationalize the reasoning behind a God who is so big—caring so passionately about a people so small—David juxtaposes two seemingly polar opposites. The answer is revealed in verse five. Through the divine process of creation, God has made us in His own image (Genesis 1:26) and a little less than God (angels, KJV). The very obvious implication here is that although we are not God, we are a lot like God. We are constructed from the same substance that is found in God. What an awesome revelation for anyone struggling with the curse of low self-esteem.

At first glance, verse five may seem as if it is attributing an extreme amount of power, authority and responsibility to created humanity. Verse six acknowledges that God has made humanity to be rulers over the works of God's hands. Not only are we to exercise rule over the works of God's hands, but God has also put "everything" under our feet. The *King James Bible* uses the term "dominion." This word refers to "the power or right of governing and controlling; sovereign authority, rule, control and domination" *(Webster's Encyclopedic Unabridged Dictionary,* p. 582). Many Christians seem somewhat uncomfortable with the notion of having such a great amount of authority from a spiritual or natural perspective. The term "ruler" somehow seems ill-fitting for the typical churchgoing individual. We usually reserve such terms for elected officials or for the Father, Son and Holy Ghost. But as children of the most high God, as heirs of the Kingdom, we *do* have the great privilege of ruling some things on the earth, including areas of parenthood, business, politics, and use of our own spiritual gifts. Who would be better equipped to serve in a governmental office, corporate position, or educational post than one whose intellect, emotion and will are controlled by the Spirit of God?

David delineates specific aspects of human dominion in verses 7 and 8. It seems that he names everything that came to his mind: "All flocks and herds, and the beasts of the field, the birds of the air, and the fish of the sea, all that swim the paths of the seas." He covers the sky above, the level earth and the liquid depths below. This passage has a scriptural link with Genesis 1:28-30, which verifies David's perspective as matching the perspective of God: "God blessed them and said to them, 'Be fruitful and increase in number; fill the earth and subdue it. Rule over the fish of the sea and the birds of the air and over every living creature that moves on the ground.' Then God said, 'I give you every seed-bearing plant on the face of the whole earth and every tree that has fruit with seed in it. They will be yours for food. And to all the beasts of the earth and all the birds of the air and all the creatures that move on the ground—everything that has the breath of life in it—I give every green plant for food.' And it was so."

A sense of completion is established as Psalm 8 concludes in the identical manner that it began—by establishing and extolling the excellence and majesty of the name of God.

III. SPECIAL FEATURES
A. Preserving Our Heritage

David realized his personal potential through remembering and recounting his spiritual origin. He realized that since he was a child of the King, he had king-sized potential. African Americans who are Christians have a rich spiritual heritage (which is of primary importance), but we also have a rich cultural heritage. Understanding this rich cultural heritage may require doing a little research to discover a grandfather or grandmother who lived a life worth investigating. In every family, there is usually an uncle, aunt, cousin, nephew, or niece who has made a big or small contribution to the community, city, state, country, or world. Family reunions or other gatherings are great times to break out the note pad, tape recorder, or video camera to preserve some priceless family history. Corral your family matriarch or patriarch and "milk them" for all the knowledge they can stand to divulge. When you finish with your extended family, check out the wealth locked inside the minds of your friends, neighbors and church members. You might be surprised at what you might learn from someone who lives next door or down the street. But don't stop there; discover the wealth, wisdom and regal heritage that you share by having an ancestry linked to Africa. Use all the resources at your disposal—from the library to the Internet—to search your history for its many traces of greatness. Greatness is all around you, but you must first open your eyes, admit it, accept it, believe it, and embrace it. Be proud of who you are…it was God's idea, after all.

B. Concluding Reflections

We were not created to live in mediocrity; neither were we designed to infringe on the rights of others by dominating them in a negative or harmful manner. Somewhere between those two extremes, we will discover the beautiful balance of assuming responsibility for doing the very best and the most with whatever assignment we have been given in life. We were created in the very image of God, and we dare not waste such a privilege by living less of a life than we are capable of living.

Potential is the inborn capacity and ability which we all possess. It is estimated that most people only utilize ten percent of their total human potential. At some point in life, you may have stumbled upon a "surprise" ability that was realized in the presence of challenging or difficult circumstances. Although we may be comfortable with the known resources currently within our reach, there are even greater discoveries to be found in the territory just beyond our reach. Of course, this will require a stretch. But just as those who came before us had to stretch in order to grow, the same is true today. Accept the challenge to re-discover your great legacy, and you will re-discover your great destiny.

Notice that our destiny is not self-designed, but rather is designed by the One who created us with a purpose. As Christians, we must remain focused so that the changing circumstances of life will not disorient us. Worship of the Creator does two things: it acknowledges God as the ground of our existence, and it conditions us to be acceptable to His will.

HOME DAILY BIBLE 📖 READINGS

for the week of March 5, 2006
God Made Us Special

Feb. 27, Monday
—Genesis 1:26-31
—God Creates Humankind
Feb. 28, Tuesday
—Genesis 2:7, 15-25
—God Creates Man and Woman
Mar. 1, Wednesday
—Genesis 9:8-17
—God Establishes a Covenant with Noah
Mar. 2, Thursday
—Psalm 63:1-8
—God Is Our Help and Strength
Mar. 3, Friday
—Psalm 73:21-28
—God Is Our Guide and Refuge
Mar. 4, Saturday
—Hebrews 2:5-10
—God Leaves Nothing Outside Our Jurisdiction
Mar. 5, Sunday
—Psalm 8
—Created a Little Lower than God

PRAYER

O God, our Father, give us insight into the various dimensions of how being special increases our sense of responsibility. Amen.

Lesson 2

God Created Wonderful Things

ADULT TOPIC: God Created Wonderful Things
YOUTH TOPIC: This Wonderful World!
CHILDREN'S TOPIC: God Is an Awesome Creator

KEY VERSE
Bless the LORD, O my soul.
O LORD my God, thou art
very great; thou art clothed
with honour and majesty.
—Psalm 104:1

DEVOTIONAL READING: Psalm 104:31-35
BACKGROUND SCRIPTURE: Psalm 104
PRINT PASSAGE: Psalm 104:1-13

OBJECTIVES
Upon the completion of this lesson, students should understand that:
1. Songs of praise are appropriate responses to God's love and care.
2. God's creative activity can be recognized on a daily basis.
3. Faith enables us to recognize that all of nature is the work of God.

Psalm 104:1-13—KJV
BLESS THE LORD, O my soul. O LORD my God, thou art very great; thou art clothed with honour and majesty.

2 Who coverest thyself with light as with a garment: who stretchest out the heavens like a curtain:

3 Who layeth the beams of his chambers in the waters: who maketh the clouds his chariot: who walketh upon the wings of the wind:

4 Who maketh his angels spirits; his ministers a flaming fire:

5 Who laid the foundations of the earth, that it should not be removed for ever.

6 Thou coveredst it with the deep as with a garment: the waters stood above the mountains.

7 At thy rebuke they fled; at the voice of thy thunder they hasted away.

8 They go up by the mountains; they go down by the valleys unto the place which thou hast founded for them.

9 Thou hast set a bound that they may not pass over; that they turn not again to cover the earth.

10 He sendeth the springs into the valleys, which run among the hills.

11 They give drink to every beast of the field: the wild asses quench their thirst.

12 By them shall the fowls of the heaven have their habitation, which sing among the branches.

13 He watereth the hills from his chambers: the earth is satisfied with the fruit of thy works.

Psalm 104:1-13—NRSV

BLESS THE LORD, O my soul. O LORD my God, you are very great. You are clothed with honor and majesty,

2 wrapped in light as with a garment. You stretch out the heavens like a tent,

3 you set the beams of your chambers on the waters, you make the clouds your chariot, you ride on the wings of the wind,

4 you make the winds your messengers, fire and flame your ministers.

5 You set the earth on its foundations, so that it shall never be shaken.

6 You cover it with the deep as with a garment; the waters stood above the mountains.

7 At your rebuke they flee; at the sound of your thunder they take to flight.

8 They rose up to the mountains, ran down to the valleys to the place that you appointed for them.

9 You set a boundary that they may not pass, so that they might not again cover the earth.

10 You make springs gush forth in the valleys; they flow between the hills,

11 giving drink to every wild animal; the wild asses quench their thirst.

12 By the streams the birds of the air have their habitation; they sing among the branches.

13 From your lofty abode you water the mountains; the earth is satisfied with the fruit of your work.

POINTS TO BE EMPHASIZED
ADULTS
Key Verse: Psalm 104:1
Print: Psalm 104:1-13
—God reveals Himself through the created order.
—The psalmist praises God for the act of creation.
—God has made the parts of creation so that they work together and support each other.
—God continues to watch over creation and cares for it.

YOUTH
Key Verse: Psalm 104:13
Print: Psalm 104:1-13
—God is Creator and Sustainer of the universe and continues to work in the natural order.
—The order, beauty and mystery of the universe are evidence of God's creative and sustaining power.
—God has given us the ability to find ways of using natural resources for the good of all.

—The natural order is dynamic, ever-changing, but kept in balance by God the Creator and Sustainer.

CHILDREN
Key Verse: Psalm 104:24
Print: Psalm 104:1-2, 14, 19-20, 25-28
—God is the Creator of the entire universe.
—God faithfully provides for the needs of all creation.
—The wonders and vastness of God's creation should motivate us to bless God.
—All of creation is dependent upon God for provisions.

TOPICAL OUTLINE OF THE LESSON

I. INTRODUCTION
   A. The Divine Capability of God
   B. Biblical Background

II. EXPOSITION AND APPLICATION OF THE SCRIPTURE
   A. Opening Salutation *(Psalm 104:1)*
   B. Personification of God *(Psalm 104:2-5)*
   C. Commander of the Sea *(Psalm 104:6-9)*
   D. Purposeful Creation *(Psalm 104:10-13)*

III. SPECIAL FEATURES
   A. Preserving Our Heritage
   B. Concluding Reflections

I. INTRODUCTION
A. The Divine Capability of God
If you were asked to describe God's personality, how would you describe it?

Do you find similarities between God's personality and your own? In this psalm, we learn intimate details about the personality and character of God. This is accomplished through understanding God's connection with nature. This hymn to the Creator extols the virtues of almighty God in a succession of poetic stanzas and triplets. The unnamed writer uses a stylized format matched with spiritual content to "turn creation truth into song, [and] environmental theory into wonder and praise" *(New Bible Commentary,* p 553).

One cannot help but to think, imagine and wonder if perhaps this psalm was inspired while the writer was alone with God in a beautiful, natural setting. Perhaps, it was an open field observing the growing vegetation, or at the edge of a body of water looking at the wildlife present, or in a field observing land animals as they grazed. These facts are not known because the physical presence of the writer is consistently sublimated throughout the psalm, while the full focus of this literary piece is riveted on God. This psalm makes the important social point that "Nothing is made for itself alone, but each is made for another, so that the needs of all are fully met" *(The Interpreter's Bible Commentary,* p. 550). The land is dependent on the sky for sun and rain. The sky is dependent on the water and land for the moisture it needs to drop rain back down on the earth. Animals are dependent on plants for food, and humans are dependent on animals for food. But in the final analysis, everything and everybody is utterly dependent upon

God for sustenance and ultimate survival. Without God holding life together, everything would fall apart. Life is only truly meaningful when viewed from the perspective of God being in full control. This has always been the standard with God and is even reflected in the first of the Ten Commandments found in Exodus 20:3: "You shall have no other gods before me."

B. Biblical Background

Unlike some of the other psalms, Psalm 104 has no given title in either the Hebrew or the Chaldee. Some have considered this a sort of "epitome of the history of creation as given in the book of Genesis" *(Adam Clarke's Commentary,* p. 516). These two pieces of literature bear many natural similarities, since both of them focus on the wonder of God's creation. One passage from Genesis that is a relevant example of this literary pairing is Genesis 1:1—2:4. Genesis reflects God's creation from the beginning perspective. Psalm 104 views God's creation from a developed perspective. This psalm "does not reason from creation to the existence of God, but vice versa. It proceeds from faith in the covenant God of kindness and fidelity (Exodus 34:6-7) to a new appreciation of creation. God's people Israel are at the center." *(Harper Collins Bible Commentary,* p. 433). Since God is such a gracious and faithful God, it is natural and normal that this great God would produce such a great and marvelous creation. Jesus reflects a similar sentiment when He states in Matthew 15:11: "What goes into a man's mouth does not make him 'unclean,' but what comes out of his mouth, that is what makes him 'unclean.'"

"Can both fresh water and salt water flow from the same spring? My brothers, can a fig tree bear olives, or a grapevine bear figs? Neither can a salt spring produce fresh water. Who is wise and understanding among you? Let him show it by his good life, by deeds done in the humility that comes from wisdom."

The concept is clear: since God is the ultimate possessor and dispenser of virtue, only virtuous creations can emerge from this source. God's creations are great and glorious simply because God is great and glorious. The human dilemma and question for the Christian becomes: How can a fallen being yield divine products? Even Romans 7:18 records the fact that "nothing good lives in me, that is, in my sinful nature." Our only recourse is also recorded in Romans 7:24-25: "Who will rescue me from this body of death? Thanks be to God—through Jesus Christ our Lord!" The challenge for humanity becomes striving to make sure this same source of glory lives inside so that our works and products can be reflective of God. As God is praised in the words of this psalm, the implication and subtle invitation is for the reader or singer to join in and participate in the process. The expression of the psalmist is from the depths of the heart; thus, this is the only way for the psalm to be properly read, recited, sung or understood. Each appearance of the word "O" in this chapter should be a reminder to read and understand this psalm from a perspective of personal passion and deep, meaningful feeling.

II. EXPOSITION AND APPLICATION OF THE SCRIPTURE
A. Opening Salutation *(Psalm 104:1)*

Psalms 103 and 104 both open with the words "Praise the Lord, O my soul." Some other versions of the Bible render this phrase as "Bless the Lord," but the meaning is still the same. This personal statement of faith and trust in God has come to be a mantra for many who have trusted God through good times and bad times. Job adopted a similar statement even in the face of his many troubles when he said: "Naked I came from my mother's womb and naked I will depart. The Lord gave and the Lord has taken away; may the name of the Lord be praised" (Job 1:21). The writer adds substance to the notion that biblical Scripture is empty without being accompanied by personal faith and belief. Therefore, in order to truly appreciate the psalms, one must have a relationship with the subject and direct object of the psalms.

B. Personification of God *(Psalm 104:2-5)*

The writer utilizes the literary devices of personification and simile to illustrate and emphasize the nature of God. A vivid picture of God is created when the psalmist suggests that God wraps himself in light as with a garment. This powerful image exceeds the bounds of human understanding, since we (human beings) are unable to even physically grasp light, much less wrap it around ourselves like clothing. Humans can relate to God enough to receive and respond to God's love. But we are also unlike God enough to constantly stand in awe of His power. The image of light is appropriate to the nature of God. Like God, light is pure, originates from above and illuminates dark places. Likewise, just as a tent is stretched wide to set up for inhabitation, so God stretches wide the heavens. Tents were once a common mode of housing because they were inexpensive and easily transportable.

Whereas humans are limited to more conventional means of transportation, God is portrayed as using simple, everyday things—like clouds and wind—and utilizing them in extraordinary, unconventional ways. Isn't that just like God—to take what is simple and to make it simply sensational? Strange things happen when touched and/or employed by God. The wind becomes a messenger, and the flames become a servant. Here, again, the psalmist's technique is to use common objects to illustrate uncommon concepts.

A similar comparison/contrast theme is reflected in the New Testament: "Where is the wise? where is the scribe? where is the disputer of this world? hath not God made foolish the wisdom of this world? For after that in the wisdom of God the world by wisdom knew not God, it pleased God by the foolishness of preaching to save them that believe" (1 Corinthians 1:20-21). Throughout Scripture, God seems to prove powerful points through simple means. Consider Jesus' statement regarding children and the kingdom of God in Mark 10:13-15: "People were bringing little children to Jesus to have him touch them, but the disciples rebuked them. When Jesus saw this, he was indignant. He said to them, 'Let the little children come to me, and do not hinder them, for the kingdom of God belongs to such as these. I tell you the truth, anyone who will not receive the kingdom of God like a little child will never enter it.'"

In other instances, Jesus made statements such as "The last shall be first" and "Bless those who curse you." Such perspectives undergird the unconventional, upside-down motif of the Kingdom.

Verse 5 acknowledges the fact that the foundations of the earth were set in place by God. When God puts something in place, it stays… forever. When God removes something, it goes… forever. God's works are not temporary, but permanent. A great deal of faith and confidence can be drawn from the fact that God's Word and work can be trusted and depended upon to be the same "yesterday, today and forevermore" (Hebrews 13:8). When we begin to view God in this manner, personal problems that seem insurmountable are put into perspective when we begin to see God for who God is. The absolute sovereign power of God is reflected in the words of Revelation: "What he opens no one can shut, and what he shuts no one can open" (Revelations 3:8).

C. Commander of the Sea
(Psalm 104:6-9)

The image of a garment that was introduced in verse 2 is continued in verse 6. God uses the water like a wide coat or shawl to cover the earth in a liquid blanket. Just as God can cover the earth with water, God can also cover our sins with His love. Throughout Scripture, water is often used to signify some type of physical or spiritual cleansing. We are told that God will cast our sins into the sea of forgetfulness and remember them no more. Then, in Hebrews 10:22, we are encouraged to "draw near to God with a sincere heart in full assurance of faith, having our hearts sprinkled to cleanse us from a guilty conscience and having our bodies washed with pure water."

In verses 7-8, we see a picture of the actual water itself being obedient and totally subservient to the will and direction of God. The literary device of personification is employed again to create the picture of the water being rebuked and the water responding by running away or "fleeing" from its coverage of the mountains. This account recalls what occurred on the third day of creation in Genesis 1:9-10: "And God said, 'Let the water under the sky be gathered to one place, and let dry ground appear.' And it was so. God called the dry ground 'land,' and the gathered waters he called 'seas.' And God saw that it was good." Many instances of the water being obedient to God are cited throughout the Bible. In Exodus, the water of the Red Sea divided for the Israelites to safely pass. In the Gospels, Jesus walks on the water, turns water into wine, and commands a sea storm to be still. God has obviously never had difficulty getting water to be obedient…it is just the people who present the greatest challenge.

In verse 9, the language changes from addressing God in the first person to addressing God in the third person again, as is done in verses 2-5. The promise given by God is that the waters—once they were commanded to subside—will never cover the earth again. This notion parallels with the command given by God in Genesis after the earth was covered by water for 150 days. When God gave the command, the waters receded, and God gave the rainbow—along with a promise: "Never again will all life be cut off by the waters of a flood; never again will there be a flood to destroy the earth" (Genesis 9:11).

D. Purposeful Creation
(Psalm 104:10-13)

Switching back to the third person in verse 10, the psalmist continues the narrative of God's interaction, commandments, and authority over the elements. It is God who provides for the springs to pour between the mountains. A ravine is "a narrow steep-sided valley commonly eroded by running water" *(Webster's Encyclopedic Unabridged Dictionary,* p. 1604). When heavy rain or a mountain spring pours into one of these ravines, the result is often a rapidly rushing waterfall that usually crashes at the bottom of the ravine in a rousing burst of spray and moisture. This is just another demonstration of God being able to take something simple and make it into something spectacular.

Verses 11-12 demonstrate that everything God does has an ultimate purpose. While water falling in a mountain ravine and birds nesting by the water may seem like isolated occurrences that are unrelated to anything else, they do serve a purpose in providing sustenance for the wild animals in the area. When things do not go as we might have imagined, humans have a tendency to wonder whether we have a purpose or if we truly matter to God in the grand scheme of life. Just as God has a purpose for mountain springs, then surely God has a purpose for everyone that has been divinely created. Not only do we matter to God, but there is also a practical link between all individuals. Since this link is not always apparent on the surface, we must exert some effort to discover our true reason for existence. But the answer to this question is well worth the effort it takes to discover.

The final verse to be examined in this passage (verse 13) provides a succinct summary of the great works of God as demonstrated in nature: "the earth is satisfied by the fruit of his work." Due to the fact that God is at work in nature, the whole earth receives positive benefits. This passage echoes Psalm 19:1—"The heavens declare the glory of God; the skies proclaim the work of his hands." A cursory observation of nature provides sufficient evidence that there is a God. The signature of God can be seen in a sunset, a seashell or in a baby's birth. We need look no further than our own, unique fingerprints in order to understand that there is a higher being beyond ourselves at work in the universe and holding it all together.

III. SPECIAL FEATURES
A. Preserving Our Heritage

Psalm 104 is a call for all to begin recognizing God's creative activity on a daily basis. When God has blessed people, it is easy to begin taking our blessings for granted. One blessing that has been earned by people of African American descent is the privilege of voting. Although it has been relatively recent that this right has been lawfully extended to people of color, there are masses of Black people who are still not even registered to vote. Even those who are registered sometimes fail to exercise their right to vote. Some may rationalize that their vote does not count anyway or that they do not want to get involved in the corruption of politics. But the position of Jesus on matters of the state is: "Give to Caesar (government) what is Caesar's and to God what is God's" (Matthew 22:21). Even beyond voting, we have a responsibility to make a difference within our community. One need not possess a great deal of money in order to make a positive, practical difference in the lives of others. Since we serve such a creative God, we should depend upon that power to help us to help ourselves and to help others.

B. Concluding Reflections

The very first action of God recorded in the Bible is related to the act of creation: "In the beginning God created the heavens and the earth." Psalm 104 is filled with examples of God's mastery over all of creation. Since we were created in the image of God, there is no way we could not contain some aspects of that divine creativity. Our creativity was given to us to explore and to multiply every gift and talent that has been entrusted to our care. We all must give an account of what we did with our creativity. We all should want to hear a positive assessment from God as is recorded in the parable of the talents found in Matthew 25:21—"Well done, good and faithful servant! You have been faithful with a few things; I will put you in charge of many things. Come and share your master's happiness!"

It must be taken into consideration that such participation in the divine glory in predicated upon deeds accomplished within the human arena—"Inasmuch as you did it to the least of these" should constantly remain the focus of piety. Notice that the prophets "found it necessary constantly to remind men that God requires more than sacrifices, more even than equity; he requires the humble spirit and the contrite heart. These things are repeated by Jesus Christ, who never ceased to warn men against hypocrisy and to plead for a piety that shrinks from ostentation" (*The Interpreter's Bible*). The point is that the nobility with which God created us and the dignity with which man is endowed does not exempt him from the requirement to obey the law of God. Without it, "religion becomes vague and preaching becomes indefinite. We cannot give it unless we return to the Bible and train ourselves in meditation on its commandments as well as its promises" (*The Interpreter's Bible*).

HOME DAILY BIBLE READINGS

for the week of March 12, 2006
God Created Wonderful Things

Mar. 6, Monday
—Psalm 19:1-6
—The Firmament Proclaims God's Handiwork

Mar. 7, Tuesday
—Psalm 66:1-9
—Make a Joyful Noise to God

Mar. 8, Wednesday
—Psalm 136:1-9
—God's Steadfast Love Endures Forever

Mar. 9, Thursday
—Psalm 104:1-13
—God, the Great Creator

Mar. 10, Friday
—Psalm 104:14-23
—God's Creation Is Balanced and Orderly

Mar. 11, Saturday
—Psalm 104:24-30
—Manifold Are God's Works

Mar. 12, Sunday
—Psalm 104:31-35
—Rejoice in the Lord

PRAYER
Eternal God, may we not seek to hide from Thee, but come to Thee with repentance and contrition as we depend upon Your abundant mercy. Amen.

God Created and Knows Us

UNIT I
The Glory of God's Creation

CHILDREN'S UNIT
Our Creator God

ADULT TOPIC: Searched and Known by God
YOUTH TOPIC: God Knows Us Like a Book
CHILDREN'S TOPIC: God Takes Care of Us

KEY VERSE
I will praise thee; for I am fearfully and wonderfully made: marvellous are thy works; and that my soul knoweth right well.
—Psalm 139:14

DEVOTIONAL READING: Psalm 100
BACKGROUND SCRIPTURE: Psalm 139
PRINT PASSAGE: Psalm 139:1-3, 7-14, 23-24

Psalm 139:1-3, 7-14, 23-24—KJV

O LORD, thou hast searched me, and known me.

2 Thou knowest my downsitting and mine uprising, thou understandest my thought afar off.

3 Thou compassest my path and my lying down, and art acquainted with all my ways.

.....

7 Whither shall I go from thy spirit? or whither shall I flee from thy presence?

8 If I ascend up into heaven, thou art there: if I make my bed in hell, behold, thou art there.

9 If I take the wings of the morning, and dwell in the uttermost parts of the sea;

10 Even there shall thy hand lead me, and thy right hand shall hold me.

11 If I say, Surely the darkness shall cover me; even the night shall be light about me.

12 Yea, the darkness hideth not from thee; but the night shineth as the day: the darkness and the light are both alike to thee.

OBJECTIVES
Upon the completion of this lesson, students should embrace the realization that:

1. God is intimately aware of our thoughts and actions.

2. It is futile to attempt to hide from God.

3. Confession of sins and surrender to God grant inner peace.

13 For thou hast possessed my reins: thou hast covered me in my mother's womb.

14 I will praise thee; for I am fearfully and wonderfully made: marvellous are thy works; and that my soul knoweth right well.

…..

23 Search me, O God, and know my heart: try me, and know my thoughts:

24 And see if there be any wicked way in me, and lead me in the way everlasting.

Psalm 139:1-3, 7-14, 23-24—NRSV

O LORD, you have searched me and known me.

2 You know when I sit down and when I rise up; you discern my thoughts from far away.

3 You search out my path and my lying down, and are acquainted with all my ways.

…..

7 Where can I go from your spirit? Or where can I flee from your presence?

8 If I ascend to heaven, you are there; if I make my bed in Sheol, you are there.

9 If I take the wings of the morning and settle at the farthest limits of the sea,

10 even there your hand shall lead me, and your right hand shall hold me fast.

11 If I say, "Surely the darkness shall cover me, and the light around me become night,"

12 even the darkness is not dark to you; the night is as bright as the day, for darkness is as light to you.

13 For it was you who formed my inward parts; you knit me together in my mother's womb.

14 I praise you, for I am fearfully and wonderfully made. Wonderful are your works; that I know very well.

…..

23 Search me, O God, and know my heart; test me and know my thoughts.

24 See if there is any wicked way in me, and lead me in the way everlasting.

POINTS TO BE EMPHASIZED

ADULTS

Key Verse: Psalm 139:14

Print: Psalm 139:1-3, 7-14, 23-24

—The human tendency to flee from God is circumvented by His ever-present nature.

—God is an ever-present and all-knowing God.

—God has an intimate knowledge of humanity.

—God's help is available when we as humans surrender to Him.

YOUTH

Key Verse: Psalm 139:13-14

Print: Psalm 139:1-3, 7-14, 23-24

—We are led and held by the right hand of God.

—God fearfully and wonderfully makes us.

—If we ask, God will assume the lead in the fulfillment of our destiny.

CHILDREN

Key Verse: Psalm 139:14

Print: Psalm 139:1-3, 7-14, 23-24

—God is in control of all things.

—God is present everywhere.

—God cares for us even before conception.

—God created our wonderful bodies.

—God knows everything about us.

TOPICAL OUTLINE OF THE LESSON

I. INTRODUCTION

   A. God Specializes in Searching Us and Knowing Us

   B. Biblical Background

II. EXPOSITION AND APPLICATION OF THE SCRIPTURE

   A. You Have Searched Me
      (Psalm 139:1-3)

   B. Where Can I Go?
      (Psalm 139:7-12)

   C. You Have Created Me
      (Psalm 139:13-14)

   D. Know My Heart
      (Psalm 139:23-24)

III. SPECIAL FEATURES

   A. Preserving Our Heritage

   B. Concluding Reflections

I. INTRODUCTION

A. God Specializes in Searching Us and Knowing Us

Do you have a friend or relative who knows you completely and with whom you withhold absolutely no secrets? Psalm 139 is one of the most beautiful, personal and delicate of the recorded psalms, and it explores the subject of intimate, personal knowledge. It has been adapted to various musical motifs and has been used to uplift the heart, mind and spirit of those who may be struggling with low self-esteem or feelings that God does not love them. The psalmist David allows the reader to have a glimpse into the inner workings of his very soul as he speaks to God in a very intimate way. Why is it important that God search us and know us? Everybody needs to be completely known by somebody. Part of what contributes to our genuine humanity is our ability to share our innermost thoughts, feelings and secrets. Those who choose to keep everything bottled up inside eventually pay the penalty for their insistence through a decline in their mental and/or emotional health. We are created to be in fellowship with God, in fellowship with ourselves and in fellowship with each other. When one or more of those factors are missing, we suffer. But when we share ourselves, we thrive.

Psalm 139 is a reflection of God's omniscience (verses 1-6), God's creation (verses 13-18) and God's holiness (verses 19-24). In reading this psalm, it is easy to see and to understand why David was considered to be a man after God's own heart. David's concept of God does not stem from a few surface experiences, but is based on a multifaceted, richly seasoned personal relationship that has stood the test of time and love. This psalm is not written "by one who would escape this God if he

"You have searched me" insinuates that the psalmist has been falsely accused and appeals to God for vindication. "It is high" means that God's presence is inaccessible or extraordinarily high. The psalmist asserts that he is fully known, in actions and thoughts, as he is in lifestyle and speech. God's Spirit represents God's presence that is inescapable. Hell (Sheol) is the realm of the dead and was ordinarily thought of as being without God's presence, but not in the opinion of the psalmist. God's light dispels even utter darkness, making the psalmist secure everywhere. "Curiously wrought" suggests the metaphor of God as creative weaver. "Inward parts" has to do with the seat of emotions. While God's thoughts cannot be comprehended, the psalmist is assured of being with God. The petition in verses 19-20 does not seek personal vengeance, as much as it does divine justice. Love and openness to God include opposing those who oppose God. "Any wicked way," or a way of pain, presumably means a manner of life that brings pain (the way of idolatry). "The way everlasting" describes the way of life that is ordained by God and which is right for all time.

could, or fly from [God] as a sinner, but one who knows he cannot escape and finds nothing to regret in such a truth" *(The Interpreter's Bible Commentary,* p. 712). David's perspective can serve as a template or an example of how intimately we can and need to know and understand God. The apostle Paul reflects his desire for us to fathom the magnitude of God's love: "And I pray that you and all God's holy people will have the power to understand the greatness of Christ's love—how wide and how long and how high and how deep that love is. Christ's love is greater than anyone can ever know, but I pray that you will be able to know that love. Then you can be filled with the fullness of God" (Ephesians 3:17-19, NCV). Everything that God is and everything that God does is ultimately based upon the matchless love of God. God can only fill us to the degree that we know and activate God's divine love.

B. Biblical Background

Strict literary classification of Psalm 139 is somewhat difficult to achieve. In some ways it resembles a hymn, in some ways it resembles a psalm of trust and in still other ways it resembles a highly personal prayer. *(The Interpreter's Bible Commentary,* p. 712). The structure of this psalm is comprised of four poetic paragraphs containing six verses each (1-6, 7-12, 13-18, 19-24). The tone and sense of personal experience reflected in the psalm is reminiscent of the sentiments espoused in the book of Job. While both Job and David seem to be on very personal speaking terms with God ("you have searched me and you know me"), at the same time, they both acknowledge that they are not aware of all there is to know about God and could never exhaust God's resources ("such knowledge is too wonderful for me, too lofty for me to attain"). This particular theological posture represents a very healthy and very necessary balance between familiarity and awe. Although we need to intimately know God, we also need to personally fear God in a positive way. Other than in the book of Job, nowhere else in Scripture do we find such a profound expression of what it means to request divine examination of one's life and soul. This is the psalmist's God, "Who knows every thought, word and deed, from whom there is no hiding, who has been privy even to one's formation in the dark concealment of the womb" *(The NIV Study Bible,* Psalm 139). The psalm both begins and ends with references to the searching and knowing nature of almighty God. God sees all and knows all, even when such scrutiny is uninvited and undesired. It is a process that is never-ending and can only be accomplished by God.

II. Exposition and Application of the Scripture

A. You Have Searched Me
(Psalm 139:1-3)

Since God is the creator and originator of our lives, it is not surprising that God knows what lies inside of our lives and what it takes for us to operate at optimum capacity. God is like the manufacturer of a wristwatch. In case of malfunction, it would not make sense to attempt impromptu repair by a novice. It would be a much wiser move to return it to the manufacturer to ensure expert repair. The manufacturer has access to the specs and knowledge of the intricate, original designs, and is able to provide the exact repair that is necessary for proper function.

David acknowledges the searching nature of the Lord. The Hebrew word for "search" used here is *chaqar* (khaw-kar), which means to penetrate, examine intimately, to find out, search, sound, seek or try *(Strong's Exhaustive Concordance).* Since we as people are so close to ourselves, it is easy for us to overlook the obvious. We then require the intensive eyes of the Lord to mount an investigation and locate areas that are in need of alteration. The term "known" is a primary Hebrew root word *yada* (yaw-dah). It is used in a wide variety of instances and basically means "to know." Other inferences could include a sense of observation, care and recognition *(Strong's Exhaustive Concordance).* Essentially, God knows us in whatever way we need to be known. That is why when Moses was told by God to tell Pharaoh to let God's people go, Moses asked God who he should say sent him. God replied, "I AM who I AM. This is what you are to say to the Israelites: I AM has sent me to you." (Exodus 3:14). Although this title for God may have seemed too general and vague, it was quite appropriate in that the needs of the Israelites would be so wide-ranging before they made it to Canaan, the Promised Land. Through giving them this name, God was saying, "Whatever you need, I AM." That God of the Old Testament is the same God we serve today. The promise given to the Israelites of the Old Testament is still in effect today and is concerned about even our mundane activities, such as sitting down, rising up, going out, lying down—and even our thought life.

B. Where Can I Go? *(Psalm 139:7-12)*

Introspectively, David contemplates the vastness of the universe and the fact that it is surpassed by the vastness of God. Hypothetically, he wonders aloud about his options in case he should someday decide to run from the presence of God's Spirit. Such an action would be ludicrous, simply due to the lack of options. He does a quick spot-check of the possibilities: "Let's see, what if I run to the heavens? No, of course You live there. What about the depths? No, I forgot You're a deep God. Let's try settling on the far side of the sea—real estate? There too? Last try: Surely if I turn the lights out, You can't see me then, right? Don't tell me You've got high tech night vision?" The apostle Paul arrived at a similar conclusion:

"Who shall separate us from the love of Christ? Shall trouble or hardship or persecution or famine or nakedness or danger or sword? ...No in all these things we are more than conquerors through him who loves us. For I am convinced that neither death nor life, neither angels nor demons, neither the present nor the future, nor any powers, neither height nor depth, nor anything else in all creation, will be able to separate us from the love of God that is in Christ Jesus our Lord" (Romans 8:35-39).

As twenty-first-century Christians, we are called to "update" this confession of David and of Paul. We must personally claim it and adapt it to our own situation. We embrace it by acknowledging that nowhere can we run from God's Spirit and by declaring that nothing can separate us from God's love.

C. You Have Created Me *(Psalm 139:13-14)*

David declares that God assembled all his parts together, even before he was ever born. The reference to the "inmost being" refers to the kidneys. This is a Hebrew idiomatic expression signifying "the innermost center of emotions and of moral sensitivity—that which God tests and examines when He 'searches' a person" *(The NIV Study Bible)*. Such an advanced level of knowledge and intentional planning by God even prior to human birth implies volumes with regard to reproductive ethics and the rights of the unborn. If God goes to such great lengths prior to one being born, what happens when that process is artificially interrupted? Even after birth, some people struggle with accepting their own particular physical package. Evidence of this fact is the proliferation and popularity of cosmetic surgery and real-life makeovers. It seems that few people are actually satisfied and content with who they are and how they are made. Light-skinned people want to be darker, and darker people want to be lighter. Those with thin lips want theirs to be broader, and those with broad lips want theirs to be thinner. Many heavier people want to lose weight, and some lighter-weight people want to gain. Some of our physical alterations are quite necessary for the sake of positive health benefits and a productive lifestyle. However, other alterations are desired simply to conform to a socially contrived, media-driven self-conception. The quest for so-called perfection can consume much time, money and emotional energy. It would be better to accept that we were "fearfully and wonderfully made."

D. Know My Heart *(Psalm 139:23-24)*

David concludes his communication with a bold and sweeping invitation for divine examination. With heart wide open, David declares: "Search me!" What a daring and dangerous statement to make to God. Such statements should only be made by those who truly desire to be delivered. A clean heart always precedes a delivered heart, and a searched heart always precedes a clean heart. So those who claim to want deliverance should immediately prepare for a divine strip search. Question: What will God strip? Answer: Anything that hinders a heart like God's. That could include pride, selfishness, jealousy, anger, fear and untruth. The Hebrew word for "heart" used here is *lebab,* which is a word widely used for the feelings, the will, the intellect and the center of anything *(Strong's Exhaustive Concordance).* When it comes to God's list of priorities, the heart comes first. While people usually place high value on the outward appearance, God always looks on the heart (1 Samuel 16:7). When God performs divine "open-heart surgery" on us, many of our offensive ways will be removed. This process is not painless, but the long-term result will be tremendously beneficial. Some of our offensive ways are quite obvious and are primarily offensive to others. Still others are very secret and mostly offensive to God. Whatever the case, when God's surgery is complete, the path will be cleared for us to be led in a manner that is not superficial or temporary, but in a way that is permanent and everlasting.

III. SPECIAL FEATURES
A. Preserving Our Heritage

A great resource within African American culture and history is the vast collection of Negro Spirituals. These songs reveal the struggles and victories of our ancestors and forebearers. It is important to sing these songs periodically so that we will not forget their sacrifice, their lessons and their legacy. One song they used to sing was entitled: "No Hiding Place Down Here." It highlighted the fact that at Judgment Day, the earth provides no space for a safe hiding place. This truth resonates with the truth of Psalm 139. The reality of God's omnipresence could be potentially good news as well as bad news. For those who reject obedience to God, there is certain judgment. But for the one who seeks first the kingdom of God, it is a guarantee of God's presence and not abandonment. It is a reminder that "Earth has no sorrow that heaven cannot heal." This was the kind of assurance that the captured Africans needed to make it through the Middle Passage to strange lands far away from home. This was the faith that brokenhearted mothers needed when their family was divided and sold on an auction block to a plantation in another state. This was the assurance that Black people clung to as they faced Jim Crow, unequal rights, and discrimination in the workplace. Even today, with all the advancements and accomplishments made by people of color, we still need God. This is true today, true tomorrow, and will be true forevermore.

B. Concluding Reflections

The value of a thing is determined by the relative rarity of the thing. You need not look any further than your own fingerprints in order to know that there is no one else who has ever lived or will ever live who is exactly like you. Your value, worth and importance are not based upon how physically attractive you are, how much money you have, or even your natural talent. Your ultimate worth is directly related to your relationship with God. It would be a great mistake to base your sufficiency and sense of significance upon your family, your race, your job or your education. You would be better to follow the life prescription of Jesus and "seek first the kingdom of God and his righteousness and all these things will be added unto you" (Matthew 6:33). Within our transitory world, only what we do for Christ will last.

HOME DAILY BIBLE READINGS

for the week of March 19, 2006
God Created and Knows Us

Mar. 13, Monday
—Psalm 100
—We Belong to God
Mar. 14, Tuesday
—Psalm 121
—Our Help Comes from the Lord
Mar. 15, Wednesday
—Psalm 146
—Our God Watches Over All
Mar. 16, Thursday
—Psalm 139:1-6
—God Is Acquainted with My Ways
Mar. 17, Friday
—Psalm 139:7-12
—God, You Are Always with Me
Mar. 18, Saturday
—Psalm 139:13-18
—Fearfully and Wonderfully Made
Mar. 19, Sunday
—Psalm 139:19-24
—Search Me, O God

CLOSING PRAYER

Eternal God, as we live in a world of conflicting loyalties and allegiances, grant unto us that perspective that comes from placing Your kingdom's priorities first in our lives. Anchor our soul in Your Word that we may live for Him who died for us. Amen.

Lesson 4

A Hymn of Praise to the Creator

UNIT I
The Glory of God's Creation

CHILDREN'S UNIT
Our Creator God

ADULT TOPIC: Worthy of Praise
YOUTH TOPIC: Praise God!
CHILDREN'S TOPIC: Praise God for His Creations

KEY VERSE
The LORD is gracious, and full of compassion; slow to anger, and of great mercy.
—Psalm 145:8

DEVOTIONAL READING: Psalm 150
BACKGROUND SCRIPTURE: Psalm 145
PRINT PASSAGE: Psalm 145:1-13

Psalm 145:1-13—KJV

I WILL extol thee, my God, O king; and I will bless thy name for ever and ever.

2 Every day will I bless thee; and I will praise thy name for ever and ever.

3 Great is the LORD, and greatly to be praised; and his greatness is unsearchable.

4 One generation shall praise thy works to another, and shall declare thy mighty acts.

5 I will speak of the glorious honour of thy majesty, and of thy wondrous works.

6 And men shall speak of the might of thy terrible acts: and I will declare thy greatness.

7 They shall abundantly utter the memory of thy great goodness, and shall sing of thy righteousness.

8 The LORD is gracious, and full of compassion; slow to anger, and of great mercy.

9 The LORD is good to all: and his tender mercies are over all his works.

OBJECTIVES
After study of this lesson, students should realize that:
1. Praising God should be continuous and shared within the community of faith.
2. Praise is the Christian's natural response to God's goodness and mercy.
3. Praise is a way to witness to others of God's greatness.

10 All thy works shall praise thee, O Lord; and thy saints shall bless thee.

11 They shall speak of the glory of thy kingdom, and talk of thy power;

12 To make known to the sons of men his mighty acts, and the glorious majesty of his kingdom.

13 Thy kingdom is an everlasting kingdom, and thy dominion endureth throughout all generations.

Psalm 145:1-13—NRSV

I WILL extol you, my God and King, and bless your name forever and ever.

2 Every day I will bless you, and praise your name forever and ever.

3 Great is the Lord, and greatly to be praised; his greatness is unsearchable.

4 One generation shall laud your works to another, and shall declare your mighty acts.

5 On the glorious splendor of your majesty, and on your wondrous works, I will meditate.

6 The might of your awesome deeds shall be proclaimed, and I will declare your greatness.

7 They shall celebrate the fame of your abundant goodness, and shall sing aloud of your righteousness.

8 The Lord is gracious and merciful, slow to anger and abounding in steadfast love.

9 The Lord is good to all, and his compassion is over all that he has made.

10 All your works shall give thanks to you, O Lord, and all your faithful shall bless you.

11 They shall speak of the glory of your kingdom, and tell of your power,

12 to make known to all people your mighty deeds, and the glorious splendor of your kingdom.

13 Your kingdom is an everlasting kingdom, and your dominion endures throughout all generations.

POINTS TO BE EMPHASIZED

ADULTS

Key Verse: Psalm 145:8

Print: Psalm 145:1-13

—Praising God is to be a continuous experience.

—Praise is to be shared with others within the community of faith.

—God's actions are praiseworthy.

—We will always have reasons to praise God.

YOUTH

Key Verse: Psalm 145:3

Print: Psalm 145:1-13

—God is worthy to be praised above all else.

—Our praise of God should include our thankfulness for His benefits.

—God is worthy of our praise because God is great, good, loving, all-powerful and eternal.

—The praise of God should be passed from one generation to another.

CHILDREN

Key Verse: Psalm 145:2

Print: Psalm 145:1-3, 8-18

—Daily worship is prescribed in the Scripture.

—Humans cannot comprehend the greatness of God.

—The good of God is seen in all of His creations.

—The kingdom of God is everlasting.

TOPICAL OUTLINE OF THE LESSON

I. **INTRODUCTION**
   A. Nothing but Praise
   B. Biblical Background

II. **EXPOSITION AND APPLICATION OF THE SCRIPTURE**
   A. Exalted Is the Lord
      (Psalm 145:1-2)
   B. Great Is the Lord
      (Psalm 145:3-7)
   C. Gracious Is the Lord
      (Psalm 145:8-13)

III. **SPECIAL FEATURES**
   A. Preserving Our Heritage
   B. Concluding Reflections

I. INTRODUCTION
A. Nothing but Praise

What are some of the ways that you express praise to God? Is your praise affected or impacted in any way by your circumstances? In Psalm 145, David delivers a glorious song of praise that is meticulously constructed to capture and convey the glorious greatness, powerful praise, wonderful worthiness and marvelous majesty of the King of kings and the Lord of lords. Using appropriately extreme language and larger-than-life metaphors, David superbly showcases the awesome attributes of *El Shaddai*. From beginning to end, the descriptive pen of this former shepherd profusely drips with a detailed description of a dynamic deliverer who is "gracious, compassionate, slow to anger and rich in love." This is a perfect example of the type of psalm to sing when one's praise to God and one's appreciation of God has simply exceeded the capacity for expression. Spiritually and emotionally speaking, one cannot always operate from a mountaintop perspective. However, if our love for God truly exceeds our love for ourselves and any other human beings, there ought to be some point in our lives where we are able to freely express what we say we possess. For David, Psalm 145 apparently captures the occasion and "exploits to the full the traditional language of praise and, as an alphabetic acrostic, reflects the care of studied composition" *(The NIV Study Bible)*. The psalm begins with a simple and very straightforward two-line introduction. The psalm also ends with a relatively simple statement of personal and group praise to "his holy name for ever and ever." But the four poetic paragraphs that come between the introduction and the conclusion descriptively develop four separate themes. Each theme is introduced with a thematic line (see verses 3, 8, 13b, 17, *The NIV Study Bible*).

B. Biblical Background

Tehillah, the traditional Hebrew name of the Psalter, occurs here in the psalm

Psalm 145 is a celebration of God's sovereignty and anticipates the final outpouring of praises contained in Psalms 146-150. Not only will the psalmist bless God's name, but so will all flesh. "Bless" connotes the submission appropriate to one who is king. Kingship carries a strong sense of the worldwide reign of God and is given special prominence. God's greatness is revealed by what He does, which provides the reason for blessing Him. The greatness of God is proclaimed by His works, His mighty acts, His miraculous deeds, His terrible acts—His terror-inspiring theophanies—and His splendor and majesty. God Himself reveals His essential character, as in His self-revelation to Moses. "Merciful and compassionate" come from the same Hebrew root and describe God's motherly love (see Psalm 131). The word "kingdom" is repeated to reinforce the opening focus on God's sovereignty. As the passage returns to focus on God's activity, it describes the result of God's faithful love. The destruction of the wicked is the result, not of God's intent, but, of the failure of persons to respond. God is faithful, just and kind to all who call upon Him in truth—but all the wicked He will destroy.

title. The word is defined as "laudation," with specific reference to a hymn. The root word is *halal*, which means "to be clear, to shine; hence to make a show, to boast; and thus to be (clamorously) foolish; to rave; to celebrate" *(Strong's Exhaustive Concordance).* Although the psalm begins as the psalm of an individual ("I will extol thee, my God"), it eventually segues and broadens its perspective to include all God's people ("All you have made will praise you, O Lord; your saints will extol you").

This psalm is not completely unique, but it borrows from several other styles and techniques utilized throughout the generous collection. Since it was originally written in Hebrew and later transcribed into English, on the surface one is unable to detect the fact that this psalm is constructed in an acrostic format. The verses begin with successive letters of the Hebrew alphabet. Often when such stylistic and "artificial" means are used to express subject matter that is highly personal and highly spiritual, there is an initial tendency to dismiss an acrostic format as somewhat detached at best and somewhat juvenile at worst. But this potential obstacle is obliterated by the psalmist through "introducing into the psalm such a degree of vigor and logical development that the signs of the mechanical method of its construction are not unduly prominent. His efforts combine to produce a hymn of impressive power and rich spiritual content" *(Interpreter's Bible Commentary).*

II. EXPOSITION AND APPLICATION OF THE SCRIPTURE
A. Exalted Is the Lord *(Psalm 145:1-2)*

As previously noted, David commences this psalm with a very individual tone. God is not regarded as some impersonal force that is sequestered behind the curtains of the heavenlies who seldom, if ever, intervene into the personal lives of mere mortals. No, this God is up close and personal. This God is the God of the here-and-now who is intimately acquainted and genuinely concerned about the everyday events of human life. David uses the word translated "extol" in the KJV and translated "exalt" in the NIV. The Hebrew word is *ruwm* (room), and it literally means "to be high, to rise, to bring up, lift up or promote" *(Strong's Exhaustive Concordance)*. Although God is portrayed in the perspective of a King, this exalted position is balanced and personalized by the phrase "my God the King." God is seen as high enough to rule, but low enough to know David by his first name. Such a relationship does not only merit occasional praise, but a willingness to "praise your name for ever and ever." While other people cannot always detect our rendering of "occasional praise," such praise is well-known by God, who is the object of such praise. The kind of praise that God desires, deserves and inhabits is praise that is pure and perpetual. In other words, it occurs every day, forever and ever. Praise is not just for when the battle is over and the victory has been won. We need some pre-problem praise, some praise in the middle of the problem—and then, when it's all over, there is nothing left to do but celebrate. In Psalm 34, David expressed it this way: "I will extol the Lord at all times; his praise will continually be on my lips."

B. Great Is the Lord *(Psalm 145:3-7)*

God's greatness and our praise go together like thunder and lightning, or like inhaling and exhaling. One seems strangely out of place without the other. We do not praise God in a vacuum or out of habit and tradition. Our praise of God should be rooted in a consistent consciousness of God's greatness and God's worthiness to be praised. The word "worthy" simply means "having worth, merit, or value; deserving acclaim" *(The American Heritage Dictionary)*. In the KJV, the term "worthy" only appears once in the Psalm (18:3). In this psalm, the KJV renders the same word "greatly." Regardless of which option is used, the central idea is that our regard for God and our expression of that regard should not be small, inconspicuous, or reserved; the greatness of God is so overwhelming that "no one can fathom" it. A more contemporary hymn writer expressed the same thought in this way: "Oh for a thousand tongues to sing my Great Redeemer's praise!"

When God demonstrates faithfulness and performs marvelous works in the lives of God's people, those people should not be content to internalize their appreciation. Every generation has the privilege and the responsibility to communicate God's works to the next generation. In Jewish culture, the religious education of the children was, and still is, a strictly followed ritual. Not only were parents mandated to teach their children about the things of God, but the wider spiritual community also played a significant part in the process of nurturing young minds and lives. In biblical history, it was an ingrained tradition to teach the children as is reflected in Deuteronomy 11:18-21:

"Fix these words of mine in your hearts and minds; tie them as symbols on your hands and bind them on your foreheads. Teach them to your children, talking about them when you sit at home and when you walk along the road, when you lie down and when you get up. Write them on the doorframes of your houses and on your gates, so that your days and the days of your children may be many in the land that the LORD swore to give your forefathers, as many as the days that the heavens are above the earth."

In contemporary times, we could learn much from the example set in Scripture regarding the teaching of our children. Not only was the instruction verbal (teaching), it was also visual (writing on the doorposts and symbols on the hands and foreheads). In the course of everyday life, it would be virtually impossible for them to overlook God's law.

Verses 5-7 are all extensions of verse four. These verses take the subject of "one generation" and report the actions of this subject. The first action is to "speak of the glorious splendor of your majesty." Beyond the verbal and visual applications of God's law, there is also the mental application of God's law: "I will *meditate* on your wonderful works." Meditation is somewhat of a lost art for many people in this fast-paced society. To meditate on some aspect of God's work or God's law requires time and a focused mindset. However, the spiritual dividends of meditation have a potentially tremendous effect upon our personal, spiritual growth.

The second action in this trilogy is to tell of God's awesome works and great deeds. For the typical Jewish family, these great deeds would have included seminal events in the history of God's people, such as the opening of the Red Sea and the fall of the Jericho walls. Verse seven highlights the concept of God's righteousness. The initial mention of God's righteousness in the Psalms appears in 4:1, but with a slightly different tone: "Answer me when I call to you, O my righteous God." David's references to God's righteousness refer to the faithfulness with which God acts: "This faithfulness is in full accordance with [God's] commitments (both expressed and implied) to His people and with His status as the divine King—to whom the powerless may look for protection, the oppressed for redress and the needy for help" *(The NIV Study Bible)*.

C. Gracious Is the Lord
(Psalm 145:8-13)

Verses 8-9 highlight six additional characteristics of God's character. Although it is God who reflects these characteristics, these same traits are capable of also being possessed and of being displayed by God's people. The character traits include the following:

Graciousness: A gracious person is generous, tactful, courteous, graceful and merciful.

Compassion: A compassionate person feels deeply and is sincerely sympathetic to the needs of others.

Slow to Anger: A slow-to-anger person exercises a great deal of self-control and harnesses his or her emotions in a mature manner.

Rich Love: A rich-in-love person possesses a deep and abundant supply of unconditional personal regard for others that is not contingent upon how the other person responds.

Goodness to All: A "good" person is one who reflects positive and desirable moral qualities above average.

Indiscriminate Compassion: A person with indiscriminate compassion is one who does not base love on merit, response, performance, or personal preference. Love is freely given to whoever is in need.

This treasure chest of characteristics as described by David are all found in the nature of God and are also available to those who submit to the authority of God.

Verses 10-12 contain another summons by David for everybody and everything to praise the Lord. This proclamation of praise does not go out only to the saints; everything that God has made should extol its maker and speak of God's glory and power (verse 11). Many elements of nature give praise to God instinctively through the serenade of the bird or through the raised "arms" of a tree. It is the human element that often lags behind nature in learning and remembering to give praise to God. This praise is not given just to produce noise or to participate in empty ritual. The purpose of the praise is found in verses 12-13a: So that everybody may know of the great things God *has* done, *is* doing and *will* do. The latter part of verse

12 mentions that important word *kingdom:* This notion of the kingdom of God holds a central place in the psalmist's view of God and the world. Like others of his fellows in late Judaism, he sees the realization of God's worldwide dominion as the goal of history. The kingdom of God is simply the rule of God. Jesus echoes this longing in the prayer He taught to His disciples: "Thy kingdom come, thy will be done." This Kingdom is not just a faraway goal or target for the distant future, but the longing is also for God's will to be done "on earth" and inside the life of each person.

The reason that David is so confident, dependent and complimentary toward the Lord is found in the simple truth of verse 13: "The LORD is faithful to all his promises and loving toward all he has made." These two characteristics of love and faithfulness are the basic building blocks of any worthwhile intimate relationships. If love is absent, there is no trust, patience, or hope. If faithfulness is absent, there is no perseverance, commitment, or longevity.

III. SPECIAL FEATURES
A. Preserving Our Heritage

Our greatest heritage that is truly worth preserving is that of our children. We must periodically ask ourselves: "What legacy am I leaving behind to those who will come after me?" Whether or not we have biological children, we are all responsible for touching the lives of those around us and for leaving them richer after having passed our way. One of the best ways to impact the present and future of our children is to model a good marriage in front of them. The current generation of young people sometimes tends to resent the institution of marriage because of what they have observed in their own families and in the general community. According to Linda Malone-Colon, Ph.D., "Too many of us have lost sight of certain values. African culture is based in collectivism, doing what benefits the community. But over the years we have become more individualistic. It's difficult to maintain a healthy relationship when you aren't thinking about what's good for the family, but rather about what's good for yourself" (*Essence* magazine, September 2004, p. 215). Unfortunately, the pandemic of divorce is even present within the church. Positive, practical and effective teaching about marriage and relationships must be modeled by the church. From the pastor to the pew, we have a responsibility to model biblical marriage—this means working to make our marriages go beyond just staying together.

B. Concluding Reflections

The goodness of the Lord is evident in the created world all around us. Sometimes, we allow the darkness of life's circumstances to block our view of God's love and grace. When this happens, we sometimes ask questions such as: "Where are You, God? Don't You even care about me?" If we would take the time to "light a candle" rather than "curse the darkness,"

we would find that night eventually turns to light; but it happens a lot sooner if we have the right attitude.

HOME DAILY BIBLE READINGS
for the week of March 26, 2006
A Hymn of Praise to the Creator

Mar. 20, Monday
—Psalm 105:1-11
—Glory in God's Holy Name
Mar. 21, Tuesday
—Psalm 138
—I Sing Your Praise
Mar. 22, Wednesday
—Psalm 149
—Sing to God a New Song
Mar. 23, Thursday
—Psalm 150
—Praise the Lord!
Mar. 24, Friday
—Psalm 145:1-7
—I Will Extol You, O God
Mar. 25, Saturday
—Psalm 145:8-13a
—Your Kingdom Is an Everlasting Kingdom
Mar. 26, Sunday
—Psalm 145:13b-21
—God Is Faithful

PRAYER
O Thou in whose image we were created, may we never cease to praise Your name in greatness and goodness in a world that is estranged from Thee. May others come to affirm and live by that higher dignity to which we have been called. Amen.

Lesson 5

When Tragedy Occurs

ADULT TOPIC: Living with Tragedy
YOUTH TOPIC: Overcoming Tragedy
CHILDREN'S TOPIC: Job Trusted God

DEVOTIONAL READING: Psalm 22:1-11
BACKGROUND SCRIPTURE: Job 1—3
PRINT PASSAGE: Job 1:14-15, 18-19, 22; 3:1-3, 11

Job 1:14-15, 18-19, 22; 3:1-3, 11—KJV

14 And there came a messenger unto Job, and said, The oxen were plowing, and the asses feeding beside them:

15 And the Sabeans fell upon them, and took them away; yea, they have slain the servants with the edge of the sword; and I only am escaped alone to tell thee.

.....

18 While he was yet speaking, there came also another, and said, Thy sons and thy daughters were eating and drinking wine in their eldest brother's house:

19 And, behold, there came a great wind from the wilderness, and smote the four corners of the house, and it fell upon the young men, and they are dead; and I only am escaped alone to tell thee.

.....

22 In all this Job sinned not, nor charged God foolishly.

.....

AFTER THIS opened Job his mouth, and cursed his day.

2 And Job spake, and said,

3 Let the day perish wherein I was born, and the night in which it was said, There is a man child conceived.

UNIT II
Living with Creation's Uncertainty

CHILDREN'S UNIT
Learning to Be Wise

KEY VERSE

He said unto her, Thou speakest as one of the foolish women speaketh. What? shall we receive good at the hand of God, and shall we not receive evil? In all this did not Job sin with his lips.—Job 2:10

OBJECTIVES
Upon completion of this lesson, students should realize that:

1. Difficulties in life are designed to test our faith.

2. We cannot equate our personal circumstances with the love of God for us.

3. Tragedy and bad things may happen to good people.

.....

11 Why died I not from the womb? why did I not give up the ghost when I came out of the belly?

Job 1:14-15, 18-19, 22; 3:1-3, 11 —NRSV

14 A messenger came to Job and said, "The oxen were plowing and the donkeys were feeding beside them,

15 and the Sabeans fell on them and carried them off, and killed the servants with the edge of the sword; I alone have escaped to tell you."

.....

18 While he was still speaking, another came and said, "Your sons and daughters were eating and drinking wine in their eldest brother's house,

19 and suddenly a great wind came across the desert, struck the four corners of the house, and it fell on the young people, and they are dead; I alone have escaped to tell you."

.....

22 In all this Job did not sin or charge God with wrongdoing.

.....

AFTER THIS Job opened his mouth and cursed the day of his birth.

2 Job said:

3 "Let the day perish in which I was born, and the night that said, 'A man-child is conceived.'"

.....

11 "Why did I not die at birth, come forth from the womb and expire?"

POINTS TO BE EMPHASIZED
ADULTS
Key Verse: Job 2:10
Print: Job 1:14-15, 18-19, 22; 3:1-3, 11
—Job lost his family and all of his possessions.
—Job neither sinned nor blamed God for his losses.
—God allowed Satan to test Job's faith.
—The prologue of the book of Job (chapters 1-2) narrates his losses—which is followed by poetic reflections.

YOUTH
Key Verse: Job 1:21
Print: Job 1:14-15, 18-19, 22; 3:1-3, 11
—God speaks to us in the vast range of experiences as creatures in the world of suffering and joy.
—The various changes in life can make us fearful, uneasy and frustrated.
—When multiple tragedies happened to blameless Job, he continued to praise God in spite of his circumstances.
—Extreme mental and physical suffering can lead us to question the meaning of life.

CHILDREN
Key Verse: Job 1:1
Print: Job 1:1-4, 8-11; 2:3-6; 3:1-3
—Good behavior does not ensure the absence of suffering and the presence of abundant joy.
—Job was a man of faith who possessed great integrity.

—God did not abandon Job in the midst of his suffering.

—Job made a wise decision to trust God, in spite of the circumstances in his life.

TOPICAL OUTLINE OF THE LESSON

I. INTRODUCTION
   A. Personal Perils of Job
   B. Biblical Background

II. EXPOSITION AND APPLICATION OF THE SCRIPTURE
   A. The Bad News Begins *(Job 1:14-15)*
   B. The Bad News Multiplies *(Job 1:18-19)*
   C. Refusing to Blame *(Job 1:22)*
   D. Writhing in Pain *(Job 3:1-3, 11)*

III. SPECIAL FEATURES
   A. Preserving Our Heritage
   B. Concluding Reflections

I. INTRODUCTION
A. Personal Perils of Job

Have you ever had a bad day? Have you ever had the kind of day when nothing seemed to go right and everything that *could* go wrong, *did* go wrong? Maybe your day was somewhat unpleasant, but it dare not compare with Job's perilous and precarious predicament. It would be an understatement to say that Job's situation was extreme. Most people can handle one problem at a time. Some can even juggle two or three simultaneous difficulties. But very few people have the inner capacity to psychologically comprehend what Job experienced. Few could emotionally persevere under the pressure of six simultaneous tragedies. First of all, the loss of livestock was unfortunate for Job because his herds were extensive and he lived in a society that was heavily dependent upon animals as a primary source of income. Moreover, during each of the separate attacks, several of Job's servants perished at the hands of marauding tribesmen. While the loss of human life is seriously regrettable, none of the previous losses prepared him for what came next: All of his children die in one single accident. The image presented in this story is one of multiple misery and layered losses. The subtle inference being suggested here is: If Job can go through all of *this*, surely you can deal with your own personal problem. Job's extreme situation serves as an example for all others who undergo suffering.

B. Biblical Background

There is a great deal of speculation surrounding the authorship and date of writing for the book of Job. The list of possible authors includes Job himself, Elihu, Moses and Solomon. Evidence that Job was not the author is that the writer (not Job or his friends) frequently uses the Israelite covenant name for God (Yahweh; the Lord). The unknown author most likely had access to oral and/or written sources from which, under divine inspiration, he composed the book that we now have. Of course, the subject matter of the prologue had to be divinely revealed since it contains information only God could know *(The NIV Study Bible, Introduction to Job)*.

The book struggles with the classic question of righteousness and suffering. If God is such a good, powerful, and almighty God, why would God allow a righteous person to suffer? Some scholars do not view the story of Job as an actual historical occurrence. This is primarily due to the nature and sequence of the writing. Legitimate questions are raised, such as: Would the God we know actually participate in a game with Satan? Would the God of Scripture and history use a righteous man as a pawn just to prove a point in response to a demonic dare? One of the ways to test the validity of a passage is simply to compare it to the rest of the Bible. Some scholars believe that at least the prologue of Job is the storyline from a dramatic play that was utilized in that time. In reading the prologue, one can clearly visualize the stage entrances made by the various characters and the messengers who come to report the news of each disaster. Regardless of its origin, the story raises important life questions that help us to understand the nature of God better as well as to understand ourselves better.

II. EXPOSITION AND APPLICATION OF THE SCRIPTURE

A. The Bad News Begins *(Job 1:14-15)*

Job was a resident of Uz (1:1) which is a sizable area east of the Jordan River (3). He is described as a blameless, upright, God-fearing, evil-shunning man. This fact only increases the anguish, pathos and dramatic flair of the story. (If Job had been a reprobate man or even an average man, the story would not have had quite as much of an edge.) Another obvious contrast is the great wealth with which the story begins, juxtaposed with the lightning-quick plunge of all Job's material assets.

The initial bearer of bad news for Job reported the loss of Job's oxen and donkeys. Job's prominence was obvious in

Job is a hero who was well-known beyond the confines of Israel. His homeland is in Uz, not in the Holy Land. Job as blameless and upright indicates that he feared God and turned away from evil. His children are mentioned to illustrate Job's piety and to prepare for the loss of their lives. The scene is a heavenly court modeled after an earthly one, wherein courtiers present themselves before the king and officially report to the Lord. Satan (as represented herein, not an adversary as in other books) is a member of the court whose particular task is to watch the actions of human beings and report back to the Lord. God is pleased by the utterly just action of Job, but Satan cynically intimates that Job is doing it only for the abundant blessings he receives in return. With divine permission, Satan instigates four attacks to wipe out Job's animals, servants and children. Contrary to Satan's prediction, Job does not curse God—but worships and blesses Him, acknowledging His power as almighty. Job curses the day of his birth, wishing that he had never been born. He demands from God the explanation of an unfair situation. Satan accused God of fencing Job in to protect him, but Job sees it as a hostile act.

that he possessed 500 of each of these animals. The fact that Job's oxen were plowing might indicate that Job also had great farmland. Sabeans were probably traveling Arab merchants from Sheba (Job 6:19). Traveling merchants would have needed a way to transport their belongings and their inventory of spices, gold and precious stones. Oxen and donkeys were perfectly suited as forerunners to the modern-moving truck. It was bad enough that the Sabeans stole 1000 animals. What made it worse was that they also killed the keepers of these animals. Perhaps they desired to destroy every witness to their crime. However, one servant escaped to relay the bad news to Job.

B. The Bad News Multiplies
(Job 1:18-19)

Following the initial report to Job in verse 14, two other messengers come bearing bad news of loss, making this the fourth messenger in verse 18. Job is not afforded the opportunity to mourn one tragedy when three additional ones are presented. Although the first three were bad, to the ancient Hebrew mindset, the news of all one's children perishing simultaneously would be an absolutely unthinkable atrocity. In Job 1:4-5, we get a glimpse of the character of Job and his children. The siblings periodically spent time with each other in extended periods of feasting. A typical celebration could last for several days, and this trend of extended feasting is still practiced in many African and middle-eastern countries today. The activities that typically occurred during the feasts with Job's children seem to be questionable at best. Not wanting to take a chance—and in an effort to absolve the children of possible sinful acts—Job offered a substitutionary burnt offering as a sacrifice for the sins of his children. Perhaps this intercessory gesture was made due to the typical presence of large amounts of wine at the feasts that would have easily altered the judgment of the children after so many days in succession.

While the first and third of Job's misfortunes were accomplished by human hands, the second and fourth mishaps reported to Job were initiated through natural causes. In verse 16, the seven thousand sheep (see verse 3) are burned up through fire that falls from heaven. In verses 18-19, the death of the children happens when a mighty wind causes the house of feasting to collapse. It is significant that there were a variety of causes for the negative occurrences in Job's life.

C. Refusing to Blame *(Job 1:22)*

Job's character is on prime time display as he refuses to draw a negative conclusion for his untoward circumstances. When bad things happen to people, it is a natural reaction to begin searching for causes and reasons. It is frustrating to be unable to locate a cause for our discomfort. Consequently, when a logical reason seems elusive, we create our own causes in order to medicate our pain. It just seems to feel better when we can identify a concrete culprit for our calamities. The truth is that there is not always a neatly packaged logical reason for the things that happen in our lives. (This is true for the good things as well as the negative things.) As we begin to see God as ultimately in control of ALL things, then it begins to matter less when the negative things do occur. God is a big target, and many conveniently resort to blaming God or the Devil whenever things go wrong. Job refuses to follow this typical pattern of casting blame to ease the pain.

D. Writhing in Pain *(Job 3:1-3, 11)*

Sometimes in the midst of pain, it helps to tell it like it is. Sometimes, the agony of life becomes overwhelming and the gray clouds of anguish block out the memory of better days gone by. It is then easy to be lured into the cave of doubt and negativity where we fall prey to the carnivorous, fire-breathing dragon called self-pity. When things are going well for us, we are tempted to look at the person in pain and lecture him or her not to complain; but, when the difficulty of life finds *our* address and knocks on the front door of *our* house, the tables are quickly turned and our wail sounds louder than the person whom we told not to moan.

After losing almost all his earthly possessions (including all of his children), Job, like any normal human being, was devastated. At that point, just about the only things he had left were his health and his wife. In chapter two of Job, Satan practically duplicates the exchange between him and God that occurred in chapter one. He reports to the throne room of God and presents himself to God right along with the other angels in what appears to be a daily, divine roll call. Astoundingly, the omniscient, omnipresent God again asks Satan where he has come from (2:2).

After a round of dialogue between the two, diametrically opposed forces, Satan prevails in his bargaining with God and "wins permission" to afflict Job's physical body. Again, it is difficult to picture God in the position of bargaining with Satan and using Job as a human pawn in this unlikely spiritual chess match. When Satan departs, 3:7 records that *God* afflicted Job with excruciating sores that covered his entire body. A gruesome portrait is painted of Job using broken pottery to scrape his oozing sores. This is pain at its pinnacle. As if things could not possibly get any worse, domestic strife is added to the mix. Job's wife starts talking crazy and gives him the horrible advice to just get it all over with by cursing God and dying. Job's response to his wife is indispensable to the central truth of the entire story. Job says, "Shall we accept good from God, and not trouble?" This statement to his wife in 2:10 served as an indication of Job's integrity. But Job's statement to his friends in 3:3-26 served as an indication of his humanity. His words are raw pain personified. Although he refused to curse God, he does curse the day of his birth. Job's sorrowful soliloquy is filled with regret and introspection as it mournfully winds through a convoluted and meandering maze of reflective misery. The questions raised—such as, "Why did I not perish at birth, and die as I came from the womb?" (3:11)—are merely rhetorical and are not intended to be actually answered by Job's friends. Job is venting, and the best thing that the friends can do at this point is to listen, to care, and to just be there.

III. SPECIAL FEATURES
A. Preserving Our Heritage

Of all the characters of the Old Testament, Black people ought to surely be able to identify with Job. Historically, the African race was rich in gold, diamonds, knowledge and natural resources. When America was founded and the international slave trade began, Africa was a primary target for slave labor. Those who were strong enough to endure the brutalities of the Middle Passage were subjected to a litany of losses not unlike those endured by Job. They lost property, friends, family members and health. In many cases, even their lives were lost. But like Job, they clung doggedly to a belief in a God who does not ultimately deny and desert the objects of God's love.

The hardships that the masses of African Americans suffer today are nowhere near the inhumane treatment endured by our fore-parents throughout the years. Consequently, we can take solace in knowing that if our fore-parents could make it under such harsh conditions, surely we can make it as well. We must adopt a "Job spirit" to help us persevere through economic challenges, educational obstacles and social difficulties. If God be for us, who can be against us?

B. Concluding Reflections

Life is sometimes like a country road in a hilly land: it is filled with steep drops, high climbs and a series of sudden twists and turns. The lack of predictability on our journey can throw us off course, make us feel lost and even tempt us to turn around. But if we give up, we will never make it to our ultimate destination. Sometimes, it is only our faith in God that keeps us going—especially when all our other external support systems break down. The anguish, faith and persistence of Job serve as a reminder that it is okay to be human and to lament our humanity. It is acceptable to raise real questions and to express genuine doubts about our past, present, or future circumstances. But, in the midst of our doubtful deliberations, it is also important to maintain our trust in the ability of God to deliver at God's divine discretion. God always has a way of turning our human question marks into divine exclamation points.

Notice that the tragedy that occurred in the life of Job was totally unexpected—he was a man who feared God and stayed away from evil. Job was *perfect*, an attribute that God Himself used to describe

Job. It is the fear of God that motivates man with the power to avoid evil, but Job learned to his dismay that being righteous and being insulated from the tragedies of life are two difference realities. Although Job had labored long in acquiring his wealth, he refused to blame God for taking his wealth (inclusive of his children), but for granting his wealth to him in the first place. Job's response to the devastating question is made clear through his action: do we serve God for our own self-gratification? The obvious answer is "no." Job's love and service to God was not self-seeking and self-calculation. Job realized that all that we possess is contingent upon the order or disorder of the nature of circumstances, and whereas our self-identity in intertwined with that which we have, tragedy seems to come with debilitating blows. But, when we change the perspective from which we view reality, the concept of God becomes our coping center and no weapon formed against us shall prevail. When tragedy comes into our lives, we must affirm that God does not save us from trouble, but that God saves us in the midst of trouble itself.

HOME DAILY BIBLE READINGS
for the week of April 2, 2006
When Tragedy Occurs

Mar. 27, Monday
—Job 1:1-5
—Job, a Blameless and Upright Man
Mar. 28, Tuesday
—Job 1:6-12
—Satan Determines to Strike Job
Mar. 29, Wednesday
—Job 1:13-22
—Job Loses All, but Remains Faithful
Mar. 30, Thursday
—Job 2:1-10
—Job Falls Ill, but Praises God
Mar. 31, Friday
—Job 3:1-10
—Job Curses His Day of Birth
Apr. 1, Saturday
—Job 3:11-19
—Job Wishes for Death
Apr. 2, Sunday
—Job 3:20-26
—Job Questions God's Benevolence

PRAYER
Eternal God, our Father, as we live in the world, but not of the world, we know that we are impacted by the circumstances that are common to the human race. Regardless of that which we have or may not have, grant us the grace to trust Your guidance and personal concern as expressed in Your love for us in the person of Jesus Christ, our Lord and Savior. Amen.

Lesson 6

When All Seems Hopeless

ADULT TOPIC: When All Seems Hopeless
YOUTH TOPIC: Keep Hope Alive!
CHILDREN'S TOPIC: Job's Young, Wise Friend

DEVOTIONAL READING: Job 36:24-33
BACKGROUND SCRIPTURE: Job 14; 32:1-8; 34:10-15; 37:14-24
PRINT PASSAGE: Job 14:1-2, 11-17; 32:6, 8; 34:12; 37:14, 22

UNIT II
Living with Creation's
Uncertainty

CHILDREN'S UNIT
Learning to Be Wise

KEY VERSE
If a man die, shall he live again? all the days of my appointed time will I wait, till my change come.
—Job 14:14

Job 14:1-2, 11-17; 32:6, 8; 34:12; 37:14, 22—KJV

MAN THAT is born of a woman is of few days, and full of trouble.

2 He cometh forth like a flower, and is cut down: he fleeth also as a shadow, and continueth not.

.....

11 As the waters fail from the sea, and the flood decayeth and drieth up:

12 So man lieth down, and riseth not: till the heavens be no more, they shall not awake, nor be raised out of their sleep.

13 O that thou wouldest hide me in the grave, that thou wouldest keep me secret, until thy wrath be past, that thou wouldest appoint me a set time, and remember me!

14 If a man die, shall he live again? all the days of my appointed time will I wait, till my change come.

15 Thou shalt call, and I will answer thee: thou wilt have a desire to the work of thine hands.

OBJECTIVES
Upon completion of this lesson, students should know that:

1. Persons should turn to God for strength rather than blaming God for their troubles.

2. Faith in God means trusting Him although His ways may not be understood.

3. Christians are obliged to offer each other comfort and hope in difficult times.

16 For now thou numberest my steps: dost thou not watch over my sin?

17 My transgression is sealed up in a bag, and thou sewest up mine iniquity.

…..

6 And Elihu the son of Barachel the Buzite answered and said, I am young, and ye are very old; wherefore I was afraid, and durst not show you mine opinion.

…..

8 But there is a spirit in man: and the inspiration of the Almighty giveth them understanding.

…..

12 Yea, surely God will not do wickedly, neither will the Almighty pervert judgment.

…..

14 Hearken unto this, O Job: stand still, and consider the wondrous works of God.

…..

22 Fair weather cometh out of the north: with God is terrible majesty.

Job 14:1-2, 11-17; 32:6, 8; 34:12; 37:14, 22—NRSV

"A MORTAL, born of woman, few of days and full of trouble,

2 comes up like a flower and withers, flees like a shadow and does not last.

…..

11 As waters fail from a lake, and a river wastes away and dries up,

12 so mortals lie down and do not rise again; until the heavens are no more, they will not awake or be roused out of their sleep.

13 Oh that you would hide me in Sheol, that you would conceal me until your wrath is past, that you would appoint me a set time, and remember me!

14 If mortals die, will they live again? All the days of my service I would wait until my release should come.

15 You would call, and I would answer you; you would long for the work of your hands.

16 For then you would not number my steps, you would not keep watch over my sin;

17 my transgression would be sealed up in a bag, and you would cover over my iniquity.

…..

6 Elihu son of Barachel the Buzite answered: "I am young in years, and you are aged; therefore I was timid and afraid to declare my opinion to you."

…..

8 But truly it is the spirit in a mortal, the breath of the Almighty, that makes for understanding.

…..

12 Of a truth, God will not do wickedly, and the Almighty will not pervert justice.

…..

14 "Hear this, O Job; stop and consider the wondrous works of God."

…..

22 Out of the north comes golden splendor; around God is awesome majesty.

POINTS TO BE EMPHASIZED
ADULTS
Key Verse: Job 14:14
Print: Job 14:1-2, 11-17; 32:6, 8; 34:12; 37:14, 22
—Job lamented the human condition.
—Elihu proclaimed that the breath of God vitalizes the human spirit.
—Elihu pleaded that God's intention for humankind is good and not wicked.
—Elihu encourages Job to look on the majesty of God.

YOUTH
Key Verse: Job 26:2-3
Print: Job 14:1-2, 11-17; 32:6, 8; 34:12; 37:14, 22
—God is willing to give wisdom, but in God's timing—not ours.
—Learning to pause for a moment and reflect on God's greatness and goodness is sometimes the best way to experience His glory.
—Job learned that human beings will not always understand life's tragedies, but despite this, they must trust God to be good and just.
—In the face of Elihu's affirmation that God is just, Job struggles with undeserved suffering.

CHILDREN
Key Verse: Job 33:12
Print: Job 2:11; 32:1-8; 33:12; 34:12; 37:14, 22
—In trying to explain suffering, humans must acknowledge that God is all-knowing.

—Elihu used God's wondrous acts in nature to help Job and his friends get a better understanding of the power of God.
—Job's friend, Elihu, explained that God is sovereign and in control of the universe.
—Job's friends (Eliphaz, Bildad and Zophar) attempted to explain Job's suffering to comfort him.

TOPICAL OUTLINE OF THE LESSON

I. INTRODUCTION
  A. The Futility of Life
  B. Biblical Background

II. EXPOSITION AND APPLICATION OF THE SCRIPTURE
  A. Man Born of a Woman *(Job 14:1-2)*
  B. A Case of Comparisons *(Job 14:11-12)*
  C. A Case of the "What Ifs?" *(Job 14:13-14)*
  D. Bargaining with God *(Job 14:15-17)*
  E. Appealing to a Higher Power *(Job 32:6, 8; 34:12; 37:14, 22)*

III. SPECIAL FEATURES
  A. Preserving Our Heritage
  B. Concluding Reflections

I. INTRODUCTION
A. The Futility of Life

There is something about being close to death that makes one contemplate the futility of life. This is exactly what Job does as he gives his extended reflections on his situation following Zophar's speech. Job aims most of his pessimistic critique not at himself or at God, but at the emptiness of life itself. Ultimate life questions are asked such as: Who can bring what is pure from the impure? If a man dies, will he live again? The reader is given an intimate look at the inner struggle inside the heart of a righteous man who trusts in God wholeheartedly but finds it difficult to reconcile God's love with his present circumstances. In so many words, Job wrestles with the grand "why" of his current situation. Why does God care in the first place? Why are we born? Job wonders out loud whether or not death would be preferable above life in some circumstances. Interlaced between the serious and delirious rants and ramblings of Job are very obvious traces of faith that are manifested to give balance to the doubt. The entire tone is quite familiar to the honest reader. Although Job was undeniably holy, he was also identifiably human.

B. Biblical Background

This section of Job presents a personal commentary on the mortality of man. Chapter 14 concludes the first round of the ongoing debate between Job and his friends. The three friends were Eliphaz from Teman, Bildad from Shuah, and Zophar from Naamah. When they heard about his troubles, they made their way to his side to lend moral support. After arriving at Job's place, they hardly recognized him because his illness had produced considerable physical disfigurement. Some people have a tendency to discredit Job's friends as insincere, but they did display a significant amount of concern and genuine sympathy. This was demonstrated in several ways. First, they tore their clothes, put dust on their heads and cried bitterly in solidarity with Job's plight. Then, putting aside their own concerns, they sat silently on the ground near Job for seven days and nights because they were identifying with the intense pain of their friend. Obviously, this is much more than the typical friend would do today.

When the friends finally open their mouths, they reveal their need for training on how to minister to sick people. They essentially give their personal insight into the reason they think that Job was suffering. Of course, the reasons they give are skewed toward their personal bias and reflect a lack of time deeply contemplating the issue. These friends' comments are not unlike contemporary situations in which a family member dies and people visit the house and say things such as: "I know how you feel." Such a comment is particularly disconcerting when the person who utters it has never had a close family member to die. And even if they have experienced something similar, no one knows how a person truly feels except that person. Consequently, as a result of all these different points of view, the conversation between

Job and his friends takes on a somewhat adversarial tone at times. No doubt, all parties believe very strongly in their own point of view.

II. EXPOSITION AND APPLICATION OF THE SCRIPTURE
A. Man Born of a Woman *(Job 14:1-2)*

The phrase "man born of a woman" is used by Job to indicate his sense of man's temporal frame and morally fallen nature. This phrase is also used in 15:14—"What is man, that he could be pure, or one born of woman, that he could be righteous?" It is a decidedly pessimistic commentary on the state of humanity that is regarded by Job as being, for one thing, totally troublesome, but most of all, very temporary. As Job speaks in such highly polished, well-developed language, one cannot help but wonder how he could muster such monumental elocutionary skills while simultaneously being in such great physical pain. Nevertheless, he uses sparkling similes and compares a man's life to a quickly growing flower that withers just as fast as it blossoms. Another well-crafted image is of a fleeting shadow that momentarily appears and then suddenly vanishes away.

B. A Case of Comparisons *(Job 14:11-12)*

Job continues his usage of memorable images drawn from nature and everyday life. When there is a drought and the water evaporates from the lakes and streams, all that is left is a parched, cracked, dry riverbed. The life-giving water is gone and so are all the other possibilities that are associated with it. Likewise, when a person perishes, only a similitude of the former physical glory remains. All of the possibilities that could have been have been arrested, and nothing is left but memories. A commonly held belief among the people of ancient Israel was that death was the absolute end of life. The concept of "eternal life" was not considered to be achievable by the individual. Their hope of life beyond death was based upon their descendents. Consequently,

Job questions the brevity of human life and asks how God can bring miserable persons to judgment. Job does not claim to be clean in an absolute sense, only innocent of the kind of wrongdoing that has caused his suffering. Job draws a comparison between the brief human life span and trees ever renewed by water, and mountains worn slowly away by water. Job entertains the impossible hope that he might escape the constraints of mortality and be enabled to speak with God beyond the grave. Elihu defends God's justice by attacking Job's character and upholding God's character and mode of governance. He calls on Job to repent (34:31-33) and gives his own verdict (34-37). Elihu assesses Job's claim that one gains no advantage from being just—God is too far away to be affected by human behavior. Most people's cries for help are insincere. In chapters 36-37, three speeches begin with an address to Job (36:2-4; 37:14-22) and then depict God as just and wise. The depiction of God is accomplished by describing God's masterpiece, the storm that vividly illustrates divine wisdom and power. Job soon finds the Almighty: God is in the storm that Elihu described, but differently than Elihu imagines.

it became very important for families to have a son and thus to perpetuate the family lineage *(The Learning Bible, 1976)*.

C. A Case of the "What Ifs?"
(Job 14:13-14)

As a result of his spiritual groping in prayer, Job rises from the level of meditation to one of personal, intimate dialogue with God. Although one might think that Job's previous tone of skepticism would preclude any possible, positive conclusion, the contrary is true: "Job's doubt…spurred by a prayer that will not let God go, undermines a negative certainty to prepare for an affirmative faith. The question of verse 14a is not asked by a thinker observing the human situation, but by a lover pre-imagining his partner's attitude: You would hide, …conceal me, appoint me a set time [make a date with me] …remember me …call, …long for [literally 'become pale with passion and desire,' or faint from delayed or thwarted expectation" *(The Interpreter's Bible, p. 1012)*. Job poses his famous question: "If a man die, will he live again?" Job demonstrates the fact that it is acceptable to inquire of God and to ask God the most pressing questions that impact our personal lives. If it is important enough for us to ask, God will answer.

D. Bargaining with God *(Job 14:15-17)*

Passionately, Job implores God, pursues God and imaginatively creates the environment and relationship that he desires. Job appeals to the divine "Daddy nature" of God as he assumes the position of the beloved child. Job speaks as if to say: "Daddy, you are the one who created me. You are responsible for my existence, and anytime you call for me, I will not linger with my own pursuits, but I will immediately respond to see what you need from me." (This idea is repeated in Job 23:12.)

The term "count my steps" suggests a very watchful posture. It can be used as a negative phrase describing how one might look upon a spy, a thief, or a traitor. (Due to a severe lack of trust, one would watch their steps very closely.) Even though Job invites this close attention from God, he adds a caveat. In essence, he says: "Even though You put all my moves under a microscope, please don't hold my (inevitable) sins against me." Job goes one step further by suggesting a solution for the collection of sins that might be accumulated: Put them in a bag and tie them tightly! The KJV renders verse 17a: "Thou sewest up my iniquity." This imagery conveys the concept that when God covers our sins, they cannot be uncovered.

E. Appealing to a Higher Power
(Job 32:6, 8; 34:12; 37:14, 22)

Elihu, while having respect for Job's age, speaks with timidity as well as boldness. He acknowledges that the Spirit gives humans wisdom, with which he overcomes the obstacle of his youth and voices his opinion. Since life, wisdom, and understanding are gifts from God and not the natural endowment of humans, the question is, does Elihu speak on the grounds that he possesses these God-given gifts? While Job's conception of his plight calls into question the nature of divine justice, there is the assurance in the faith that the Almighty will not pervert justice. God is faithful, and the very existence of humans is contingent upon the gift of God's breath (Job 34:14-15; cf., Psalm 104:29-30). God is the faithful One of whom Paul spoke (1 Corinthians 1:9), who calls us into "the fellowship of His son," and suffers none to be tempted above that which he is able to bear.

III. SPECIAL FEATURES
A. Preserving Our Heritage

The strategic importance of the father in the fabric of the family cannot be over-emphasized. This is particularly true among African American families. The destruction of the Black family during slavery may have some influence on the dysfunction of some Black families today. However, that does not excuse Black men from living up to their God-given responsibilities as fathers. Author Jawanza Kunjufu expresses this perspective regarding the issue: "I don't believe our major problem is racism," said Kunjufu. "The greatest demon in Black America is fatherlessness. The common variable for the (African American) dropout rate, the incarceration rate, and drug use, is that the daddy didn't stay."

It has been said that "hurt people, hurt people." What this simply means is that when people have been wounded by certain circumstances in life, they sometimes become perpetuators of the same pain in the lives of other people. Consequently, the unfortunate phenomenon of fatherlessness sometimes produces a ripple effect, and a generational curse is created. Abandonment by fathers has several different offshoots. One of them is the scourge of divorce within the community. The divorce rate among Black married couples is alarmingly high. To add to this, even when couples stay together, there is a strained or drained atmosphere within the marriage or the home. Sometimes, the father is not emotionally available because he has been consciously or subconsciously trained that a real man is to be "hard" and aloof. One last trend is the rising rate of couples that simply choose to live together rather than to get married. Some reasons that are given for this lifestyle choice range from the economic convenience that it provides, to simply not wanting to make a long-term commitment. Even with all the negative examples of fatherhood, thankfully there are still some positive examples within the Black community of successful fatherhood.

Since there are few courses available for teaching about successful fatherhood, individual families must model this behavior and churches must reinforce this behavior. God has already provided for us the example of what it means to be a loving, supportive and dependable father. We will succeed if we follow God's lead.

B. Concluding Reflections

Sometimes, the circumstances of life present to us deep questions that are very difficult to answer. We may even have well-meaning friends around us who try to console us and arrive at their own conclusions regarding our situation. If God is in control of everything, why doesn't God intervene? Is God listening to me? The book of Job is an invitation to join in the struggle to make some sense of these questions. There are some things that we will be able to discover in this life, and there are others that we may never fully know on this side. First Corinthians records: "For we know in part, and we prophesy in part. But when that which is perfect is come, then that which is in part shall be done away.... For now we see through a glass, darkly; but then face to face: now I know in part; but then shall I know even as also I am known" (13:9-10, 12). In our struggle, there is stretching—and in our stretching, there is growth, development and progress. We can resonate with Isaiah's experience of seeking to understand God. His conclusion is recorded in Isaiah 40:28: "His understanding no one can fathom." When we trust in God even when we do not completely understand God, then our weakness will eventually give way to God's strength and we can say along with the prophet Isaiah: "But those who hope in the Lord will renew their strength. They will soar on wings like eagles; they will run and not grow weary, they will walk and not be faint" (40:31).

HOME DAILY BIBLE READINGS

for the week of April 9, 2006
(Palm Sunday)
When All Seems Hopeless

Apr. 3, Monday
   —Job 14:1-6
   —Job Pleads for Respite Before Death
Apr. 4, Tuesday
   —Job 14:7-17
   —Job Petitions the Grave as Refuge
Apr. 5, Wednesday
   —Job 14:18-22
   —Mortal Finally Overcomes Mortal Life
Apr. 6, Thursday
   —Job 32:1-10
   —God's Spirit Makes for Understanding
Apr. 7, Friday
   —Job 34:11-15
   —God Repays According to Our Deeds
Apr. 8, Saturday
   —Job 36:24-33
   —Elihu Proclaims God's Majesty
Apr. 9, Sunday
   —Job 37:14-24
   —Around God Is Awesome Majesty

PRAYER

Eternal God, our Father, whereas troubles and trials are part of the human situation, grant us the grace to view life from the divine perspective: that in all things God works for good for those who love the Lord. Sustain our faith in Thee and we shall serve You with gladness of heart. Amen.

April 16, 2006
(Easter)

Lesson 7

God Responds with Life

UNIT II
Living with Creation's
Uncertainty

ADULT TOPIC: From Death to Life
YOUTH TOPIC: New Life
CHILDREN'S TOPIC: God Gives New Life

CHILDREN'S UNIT
Learning to Be Wise

DEVOTIONAL READING: Luke 24:1-9
BACKGROUND SCRIPTURE: Job 38:1-4, 16-17; 42:1-6; Mark 16
PRINT PASSAGE: Job 38:1, 4, 16-17; 42:1-2, 5;
      Mark 16:1-7, 9-14, 20

Job 38:1, 4, 16-17; 42:1-2, 5; Mark 16:1-7, 9-14, 20—KJV

THEN THE LORD answered Job out of the whirlwind, and said,

.....

4 Where wast thou when I laid the foundations of the earth? declare, if thou hast understanding.

.....

16 Hast thou entered into the springs of the sea? or hast thou walked in the search of the depth?

17 Have the gates of death been opened unto thee? or hast thou seen the doors of the shadow of death?

.....

THEN JOB answered the LORD, and said,

2 I know that thou canst do every thing, and that no thought can be withholden from thee.

.....

5 I have heard of thee by the hearing of the ear: but now mine eye seeth thee.

.....

KEY VERSE
He saith unto them, Be not affrighted: Ye seek Jesus of Nazareth, which was crucified: he is risen; he is not here: behold the place where they laid him.
—Mark 16:6

OBJECTIVES
Upon the completion of this lesson, students should understand that:

1. We come to know God's power and goodness through experiencing trouble.

2. The tests of life precede the testimony.

3. We can become so preoccupied with the problems of life that we fail to see the apparent solutions.

AND WHEN the sabbath was past, Mary Magdalene, and Mary the mother of James, and Salome, had bought sweet spices, that they might come and anoint him.

2 And very early in the morning the first day of the week, they came unto the sepulchre at the rising of the sun.

3 And they said among themselves, Who shall roll us away the stone from the door of the sepulchre?

4 And when they looked, they saw that the stone was rolled away: for it was very great.

5 And entering into the sepulchre, they saw a young man sitting on the right side, clothed in a long white garment; and they were affrighted.

6 And he saith unto them, Be not affrighted: Ye seek Jesus of Nazareth, which was crucified: he is risen; he is not here: behold the place where they laid him.

7 But go your way, tell his disciples and Peter that he goeth before you into Galilee: there shall ye see him, as he said unto you.

. . . . .

9 Now when Jesus was risen early the first day of the week, he appeared first to Mary Magdalene, out of whom he had cast seven devils.

10 And she went and told them that had been with him, as they mourned and wept.

11 And they, when they had heard that he was alive, and had been seen of her, believed not.

12 After that he appeared in another form unto two of them, as they walked, and went into the country.

13 And they went and told it unto the residue: neither believed they them.

14 Afterward he appeared unto the eleven as they sat at meat, and upbraided them with their unbelief and hardness of heart, because they believed not them which had seen him after he was risen.

. . . . .

20 And they went forth, and preached every where, the Lord working with them, and confirming the word with signs following. Amen.

Job 38:1, 4, 16-17; 42:1-2, 5; Mark 16:1-7, 9-14, 20—NRSV
THEN THE Lord answered Job out of the whirlwind.

. . . . .

4 "Where were you when I laid the foundation of the earth? Tell me, if you have understanding."

. . . . .

16 "Have you entered into the springs of the sea, or walked in the recesses of the deep?

17 Have the gates of death been revealed to you, or have you seen the gates of deep darkness?"

. . . . .

THEN JOB answered the Lord:

2 "I know that you can do all things, and that no purpose of yours can be thwarted."

. . . . .

5 I had heard of you by the hearing of the ear, but now my eye sees you.

……

WHEN THE sabbath was over, Mary Magdalene, and Mary the mother of James, and Salome bought spices, so that they might go and anoint him.

2 And very early on the first day of the week, when the sun had risen, they went to the tomb.

3 They had been saying to one another, "Who will roll away the stone for us from the entrance to the tomb?"

4 When they looked up, they saw that the stone, which was very large, had already been rolled back.

5 As they entered the tomb, they saw a young man, dressed in a white robe, sitting on the right side; and they were alarmed.

6 But he said to them, "Do not be alarmed; you are looking for Jesus of Nazareth, who was crucified. He has been raised; he is not here. Look, there is the place they laid him.

7 But go, tell his disciples and Peter that he is going ahead of you to Galilee; there you will see him, just as he told you."

……

9 Now after he rose early on the first day of the week, he appeared first to Mary Magdalene, from whom he had cast out seven demons.

10 She went out and told those who had been with him, while they were mourning and weeping.

11 But when they heard that he was alive and had been seen by her, they would not believe it.

12 After this he appeared in another form to two of them, as they were walking into the country.

13 And they went back and told the rest, but they did not believe them.

14 Later he appeared to the eleven themselves as they were sitting at the table; and he upbraided them for their lack of faith and stubbornness, because they had not believed those who saw him after he had risen.

……

20 And they went out and proclaimed the good news everywhere, while the Lord worked with them and confirmed the message by the signs that accompanied it.

POINTS TO BE EMPHASIZED
ADULTS
Key Verse: Mark 16:6
Print: Job 38:1, 4, 16-17; 42:1-2, 5; Mark 16:1-7, 9-14, 20

—God questions Job's knowledge and wisdom by asking him if he had walked in God's steps.

—Job acknowledged God's power to restore life.

—God's final answer to Job's questions is in the resurrected Jesus.

—Jesus appeared alive again to many disciples.

—The disciples spread the Good News of Jesus' resurrection.

YOUTH

Key Verse: Mark 16:6
Print: Job 38:1, 4, 16-17; 42:1-2, 5;
Mark 16:1-7, 9-14, 20

—God brings new life, as demonstrated by the eventual restoration of Job and the resurrection of Jesus.
—God affirms our asking questions and has answers for us that He provides in His own time and not ours.
—God speaks to Job from the whirlwind and to the disciples from the empty tomb, declaring His life-giving power.

CHILDREN

Key Verse: Mark 16:6
Print: Job 38:1, 4, 16-17; 42:1-2, 5;
Mark 16:1-7, 9-14, 20

—God has power to do things that no human can do.
—God revealed Himself to Job in a whirlwind and communicated with him.
—When Job was confronted with God's awesome power, he was humbled.
—The resurrection of Jesus is an awesome display of the power of God.
—God can bring newness into the lives of humans today.

TOPICAL OUTLINE OF THE LESSON

I. INTRODUCTION
   A. From Death to Life
   B. Biblical Background

II. EXPOSITION AND APPLICATION OF THE SCRIPTURE
   A. When God Speaks

(Job 38:1, 4, 16-17)
   B. Job Responds *(Job 42:1-2, 5)*
   C. The Resurrection *(Mark 16:1-7)*
   D. The Appearances
      (Mark 16:9-14, 20)

III. SPECIAL FEATURES
   A. Preserving Our Heritage
   B. Concluding Reflections

I. INTRODUCTION
A. From Death to Life

An aura of drama and mystery abounds whenever humans question God and whenever God questions humans. Many may have been reared in a culture that frowned upon the very idea of daring to ask God a question even when the pressures of life are intense. However, we see in the life of Jesus—our example—that the opposite practice is true. When Jesus was on the cross facing His most extreme physical, spiritual and emotional test, He responded out of His immense, human anguish with a deep and heartfelt question directed toward God: "My God, my God, why have you forsaken me?" This instance in the life of Jesus demonstrates at least three things: (1) it is a natural and normal life process to ask God questions; (2) God does not chastise or penalize His children for asking questions; and (3) sometimes, God answers our questions and sometimes God does not answer them.

Even though God did not directly provide an immediate answer to the impassioned query of Jesus while on the cross, there are times when an answer does come. In Job's case, after thirty-seven chapters, God finally responds… and what a response! Not only does God answer Job with words, God also provides a bonus of human and material restoration that undoubtedly exceeded the expectation and imagination of Job as well as his friends. It is an example of God's ability to do "immeasurably more than all we ask or imagine, according to his power that is at work within us" (Ephesians 3:20). God is a God who hears prayers, answers prayers, makes provisions and keeps promises. When we give God our trust, God is able to take things that look dead and give them life. His greatest demonstration of this divine ability is seen in the resurrection of Jesus Christ.

B. Biblical Background

What is it like when God speaks? After a lengthy and rambling, yet well-worded, request for an audience with God, Job is finally given an opportunity to hear God's response to his mountain of words. Ironically, the words spoken by God sound eerily familiar. It is almost as if the writer who recorded the speeches made by Job is the same writer who recorded the speech made by God. The bold, pictorial images are similar. The rambling, picturesque sentences are parallel in structure. The deep-yet-simple questions posed when God speaks are also quite comparable to the speeches made by Job.

There are two separate discourses given by Yahweh. The first discourse showcases the wisdom of God and occurs in Job 38:1—40:5; the second discourse emphasizes the power of God over forces in the cosmos and is found in Job 40:6—42:6. The rapid-fire barrage of successive, earthshaking questions is enough to overwhelm the mind of Job. He is totally unprepared to handle and cope with the sheer depth and extreme gravity of God's perspective on the simple subject matter of life. Instead of specific, detailed answers in response to Job's questions, the Almighty asks rhetorical questions. God says nothing about Job's suffering, nor does He

The Lord's sudden appearance in the storm fails to astonish, even though the ground work has been laid for it in Job's oaths and demands. God answers Job out of the whirlwind, evoking a brief response from Job. The speeches are examples of the mysterious communication of Creator to creature, showing that the world has a design (God is wise, able to govern), and that the world is also just (God upholds the righteous and puts down the wicked). Job had demanded to see God—who is hidden, in his opinion. God's speech was the occasion for Job to "see" God. "I despise myself"—that is, Job retracts and gives up his lawsuit against God. Job interceded for his friends as he had interceded for his children. God gives Job twice as much as he had before.

The women came to the tomb to find it empty; they were too late to anoint the body of Jesus. The question is: had the Twelve not told the women about Jesus' prediction of resurrection?"Do not be amazed" is a usual note in biblical stories of an unusual or unexpected sight (apparition). The women "fled… astonishment had come upon them" in spite of the angel's reassurance.

The name "Jesus of Nazareth" was given to Christ as a way of reproach, and it was under this name that He was crucified.

address Job's problem about divine justice. Job gets neither a bill of indictment nor a verdict of innocence. But, more important, God does not humiliate or condemn him—which surely would have been the case if the counselors had been right. The divine discourses, then, succeed in bringing Job to complete faith in God's goodness without his receiving a direct answer to his questions *(The NIV Study Bible,* p. 38).

This lesson also includes the awesome moment when the women received the Good News that Jesus was raised from the dead. As the women approached the tomb in their dogged determination to anoint Jesus' body, they had resigned themselves to the fact that their beloved Teacher was gone. Their hopes of His earthly messiahship had died with Him on Calvary. But what a surprise was in store for them at the tomb!

II. EXPOSITION AND APPLICATION OF THE SCRIPTURE
A. When God Speaks
(Job 38:1, 4, 16-17)

In Job 31:35, Job states, "Let the Almighty answer me." Perhaps he did not fully know for what he was asking. When Yahweh finally speaks, Job is put in check. The Lord prefaces the commentary by pointing out that Job's words have been without a significant foundation of knowledge and understanding. This statement holds merit for us today and suggests that if we knew more about God, perhaps we

would question less, or at least we would ask better. The story is told of a pastor who had endured many hours of petty complaints and insignificant issues raised by the membership. One by one, they would come to his office, and talk for hours, taking up his entire day with pettiness. When it seemed that the pastor could endure no more, he came up with a brilliant idea. He posted a large sign outside his door that raised the question: "Have you prayed about it?" The pastor reported that once the sign was hung, his counseling load decreased by more than fifty percent! There is a popular saying that states: Prayer changes things. That is true, but prayer also changes people...starting with the one who is doing the praying.

As a platform for His questions to Job, Yahweh establishes some time perspectives and spatial parameters for their imminent conversation. Since Job was not present during God's laying of the earth's foundation, then God as creator would know infinitely more than Job, a mere human. The following exercise may help to clarify the point that is being made. Take a sheet of paper and draw a circle that represents all the knowledge of the world, both known and unknown. Now make a mark to represent the amount of that knowledge that you personally know. The rest of the space represents what God knows. (The only inadequacy of this exercise is that it would be hard to find a piece of paper large enough to reflect God's vastness.)

One cannot help but to notice and observe the blatant sarcasm in which this discourse is drenched. In verse 17, Job is asked if he has ever seen death. In verse 21, after posing additional questions that are impossible to discern, Yahweh says to Job, "Surely you know, for you were already born! You have lived so many years!" It is a rare occurrence to discover such a sarcastic tone attributed to the personhood of God elsewhere within the Scripture.

B. Job Responds *(Job 42:1-2, 5)*

After listening to a lengthy litany of personal statements and observations from the Almighty, Job reflectively offers his response. Initially, he states the obvious: God can do anything. Although this may seem like a very simple statement, it is an extremely important theological concept with the potential to significantly impact much of one's thoughts and actions. A concept closely linked with God's omnipotence is God's sovereignty. The word "sovereign" is defined as: "Having supreme rank or power; independent, unsurpassed, excellent" *(American Heritage Dictionary)*. We must realize that God does not have to get our permission before He exercises His prerogative to perform a given act. God is God! The sooner we realize this, the sooner we will be able to remove the limits from our lives and understand that God is too big for any human box.

This seems to slowly sink into Job's consciousness as he acknowledges that everything in the plan of God will eventually come to fruition. That is one reason why it is so important to live within the revealed will of God: God's will, *will* always come to pass.

In the extended divine discourse, God had offered answers to Job that were relatively general in nature. However, in Job's reply to God, Job responds to specific questions. In verse 3, Job responds to the question regarding the obscuring of God's counsel. He pleads a case of ignorance. Job reasons that although his mouth had been moving, the words he spoke were not words that he had properly understood.

In verse 5, Job describes the difference between hearing God and seeing God. Seeing God results in Job sinking to the bottom in the sea of humility. The "dust and ashes" he mentions in verse 6 signify a state of great humility. (The only other biblical instances of this phrase are found in Job 30:19 and Genesis 18:27.) *(Ryrie Study Bible)*.

Although Job made some mistakes in navigating through his harrowing experience, verses 7-9 reveal that Job is commended by God and his friends are rebuked. Below is an assessment of why this occurred:

Even in his rage, even when he challenged God, Job was determined to speak honestly before him. The counselors, on the other hand, mouthed many correct and often beautiful creedal statements, but without living knowledge of the God they claimed to honor. Job spoke to God; they only spoke about God. Even worse, their spiritual arrogance caused them to claim knowledge they did not possess *(The NIV Study Bible)*.

In the end, Job's life span was 140 years, and he was blessed to be able to see the fourth generation of his children.

C. The Resurrection *(Mark 16:1-7)*

In Mark 16, we see a picture of the aftermath of a great storm. Jesus has been arrested, tried, crucified and buried, all in an extremely short amount of time. The disciples are devastated and in seclusion. Although Mary is in mourning, like a typical mother she is also moving to ensure that the body of Jesus is properly anointed. As Mary, Mary Magdalene and Salome moved toward the tomb, these three godly women represented a living picture of what it means to walk by faith since they had no way of removing the huge boulder that blocked the grave. When they encountered an angel in the tomb rather than Jesus, they were in shock. The angel had the difficult duty of reassuring the women in the midst of their astonishment while also informing them of the Resurrection and Jesus' current location. Notice should be taken of the differences between Matthew, Mark, Luke and John's Resurrection accounts. The minor differences in the progression of events are evidence of the human aspect in the retelling of the story. However, the most important element remains intact. In all four accounts, Jesus was not present inside the tomb! This fact that He had risen is a central cornerstone in the case for Christianity.

D. The Appearances *(Mark 16:9-14, 20)*

Verse 9 records that the first person to see Jesus in the resurrected state was Mary Magdalene. She then had the privilege and the responsibility of telling the Good News to the disciples who were secluded. Only a *sovereign* God could choose a once demonically possessed female to be the very first communicator of His resurrection to the rest of world. It is interesting to note the response from the disciples when Mary gave them the message: they did not believe her. However, their lack of belief was not enough to stop the story. In fact, when Jesus finally appeared to the disciples, He rebuked them for their lack of faith. In the end, they got a glimpse of God's glory and began themselves to effectively spread the message everywhere. This was only possible because "the Lord worked with them and confirmed his word by the signs that accompanied it." Whenever one is in doubt as to whether something is of God or not, the proof is in the godly, spiritual evidence that surrounds the thing. When God is in it, the spiritual proof is apparent to those who care to see.

III. Special Features
A. Preserving Our Heritage

Most African Americans can relate to what it feels like to suffer and to experience loss. Many can also identify with being falsely accused and maybe even falsely arrested. The experiences of Job and of Jesus are alike in some ways, but also very different in other ways. Both experienced great physical pain and tremendous emotional anguish. Both also experienced some measure of derision and blame in the midst of their suffering. However, the difference that sets Jesus apart from Job and from every other human being is that after Jesus died, Jesus rose again and still lives today. That is the good news. Although we do not have the capacity for physical resurrection, we do have the ability to rebound from our falling down, to bounce back from our blunder, and to shake off our former shakeups. When we lose it in this life, if we search hard enough we can find it again. This is our hope and this is our example in the life of our Lord.

B. Concluding Reflections

The story of Job provides an example of an imperfect man who trusted in a perfect God to ultimately deliver him from a horrible "Pandora's box" life experience. His deliverance was not without doubt, death, or scars from the memories of both. However, he eventually emerged victoriously even though the chances looked quite bleak.

Job's latter state surpassed his former state even though he had to pass through a barrage of bitterness to get there.

HOME DAILY BIBLE READINGS

for the week of April 16, 2006 *(Easter)*
God Responds with Life

Apr. 10, Monday
—Job 38:1-7
—Where Were You During the Creation?

Apr. 11, Tuesday
—Job 38:8-18
—Do You Understand My Creation?

Apr. 12, Wednesday
—Job 42:1-6
—I Know You, and I Repent

Apr. 13, Thursday
—Job 42:10-17
—Job's Fortunes Are Restored Twofold

Apr. 14, Friday
—Mark 16:1-8
—He Is Not Here

Apr. 15, Saturday
—Mark 16:9-14
—Jesus Appears to His Followers

Apr. 16, Sunday
—Mark 16:15-20
—Go and Proclaim the Good News

PRAYER
Our Father, when we must go through situations that we do not understand, grant unto us the grace to trust in Thee. May our bold faith in Thee give courage and hope to others. Amen.

Lesson 8

UNIT II
Living with Creation's Uncertainty

CHILDREN'S UNIT
Learning to Be Wise

Finding Life's Meaning

ADULT TOPIC: Where Is Peace Found?
YOUTH TOPIC: Jesus' Answers to Life Questions
CHILDREN'S TOPIC: God Makes Us Wise

KEY VERSE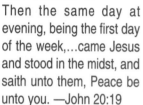

Then the same day at evening, being the first day of the week,...came Jesus and stood in the midst, and saith unto them, Peace be unto you. —John 20:19

OBJECTIVES

Upon completing this lesson, students should come to understand that:

1. As our faith matures, we find greater meaning, purpose and peace in life.
2. As faith is shared, Christians become more secure in their relationship with Christ.
3. Participation in the faith of others strengthens the Christian's personal faith.

DEVOTIONAL READING: Luke 24:36-48
BACKGROUND SCRIPTURE: Ecclesiastes 1:1-11; John 20:19-23
PRINT PASSAGE: Ecclesiastes 1:1-9; John 20:19-23

Ecclesiastes 1:1-9; John 20:19-23—KJV

THE WORDS of the Preacher, the son of David, king in Jerusalem.

2 Vanity of vanities, saith the Preacher, vanity of vanities; all is vanity.

3 What profit hath a man of all his labour which he taketh under the sun?

4 One generation passeth away, and another generation cometh: but the earth abideth for ever.

5 The sun also ariseth, and the sun goeth down, and hasteth to his place where he arose.

6 The wind goeth toward the south, and turneth about unto the north; it whirleth about continually, and the wind returneth again according to his circuits.

7 All the rivers run into the sea; yet the sea is not full; unto the place from whence the rivers come, thither they return again.

8 All things are full of labour; man cannot utter it: the eye is not satisfied with seeing, nor the ear filled with hearing.

9 The thing that hath been, it is that which shall be; and that which is done is that which shall be done: and there is no new thing under the sun.

.....

19 Then the same day at evening, being the first day of the week, when the doors were shut where the disciples were assembled for fear of the Jews, came Jesus and stood in the midst, and saith unto them, Peace be unto you.

20 And when he had so said, he showed unto them his hands and his side. Then were the disciples glad, when they saw the Lord.

21 Then said Jesus to them again, Peace be unto you: as my Father hath sent me, even so send I you.

22 And when he had said this, he breathed on them, and saith unto them, Receive ye the Holy Ghost:

23 Whose soever sins ye remit, they are remitted unto them; and whose soever sins ye retain, they are retained.

Ecclesiastes 1:1-9; John 20:19-23—NRSV

THE WORDS of the Teacher, the son of David, king in Jerusalem.

2 Vanity of vanities, says the Teacher, vanity of vanities! All is vanity.

3 What do people gain from all the toil at which they toil under the sun?

4 A generation goes, and a generation comes, but the earth remains forever.

5 The sun rises and the sun goes down, and hurries to the place where it rises.

6 The wind blows to the south, and goes around to the north; round and round goes the wind, and on its circuits the wind returns.

7 All streams run to the sea, but the sea is not full; to the place where the streams flow, there they continue to flow.

8 All things are wearisome; more than one can express; the eye is not satisfied with seeing, or the ear filled with hearing.

9 What has been is what will be, and what has been done is what will be done; there is nothing new under the sun.

.....

19 When it was evening on that day, the first day of the week, and the doors of the house where the disciples had met were locked for fear of the Jews, Jesus came and stood among them and said, "Peace be with you."

20 After he said this, he showed them his hands and his side. Then the disciples rejoiced when they saw the Lord.

21 Jesus said to them again, "Peace be with you. As the Father has sent me, so I send you."

22 When he had said this, he breathed on them and said to them, "Receive the Holy Spirit.

23 If you forgive the sins of any, they are forgiven them; if you retain the sins of any, they are retained."

POINTS TO BE EMPHASIZED
ADULTS
Key Verse: John 20:19
Print: Ecclesiastes 1:1-9; John 20:19-23
—The writer of Ecclesiastes was despondent over his failure to find purpose and meaning in life.

—The teacher declares that nothing new or redemptive is to be found in creation.

—The resurrection of Jesus gave peace to the disciples.

—The Holy Spirit enables the disciples to share their hope and peace with others.

YOUTH

Key Verse: John 20:21
Print: Ecclesiastes 1:1-9; John 20:19-23
—Real inner peace comes from God.

—People search for meaning in life and peace of mind that cannot be found apart from God.

—Some people have a perspective on life that is weary and pessimistic.

—The gospel of John presents a perspective on life that says that life has meaning and purpose.

CHILDREN

Key Verse: 1 Kings 3:9
Print: 1 Kings 4:29-34; Ecclesiastes 1:12; 2:2-6, 9-13

—God gave Solomon wisdom and the ability to make wise decisions.

—Solomon's wisdom was shared with others and preserved in the form of proverbs and songs.

—Solomon sought to obtain happiness and discovered that life had no meaning or fulfillment without God.

—Human efforts to find happiness without God are futile.

TOPICAL OUTLINE OF THE LESSON

I. INTRODUCTION
   A. The Quest for Purpose and Peace
   B. Biblical Background

II. EXPOSITION AND APPLICATION OF THE SCRIPTURE
   A. Everything Is Meaningless *(Ecclesiastes 1:1-3)*
   B. The Weariness of Repetition *(Ecclesiastes 1:4-9)*
   C. The Disciples' Struggle for Meaning *(John 20:19-20)*
   D. Tidings of Peace *(John 20:21-23)*

III. SPECIAL FEATURES
   A. Preserving Our Heritage
   B. Concluding Reflections

I. INTRODUCTION
A. The Quest for Purpose and Peace

The literal meaning of the word *Bible* is "little books." The Word of God is full of various little books and these books reflect a wide variety of different types of literature. It is essential to understand this in order to understand the book of Ecclesiastes. Just as a newspaper has different sections and the reader's mindset must change in order to process them, so the Bible student's perspective changes when reading Ecclesiastes. Otherwise, the pervasive use of cynicism in the book will prevent a proper understanding of the central message contained therein.

Ecclesiastes means "one who convenes and speaks at an assembly or an ecclesiastic or preacher." The author identifies himself as the son of David who was king in Jerusalem (1:1). Most agree that he is Solomon. What does one of the wealthiest men who ever lived have to say in retrospect? What advice could a man give who has been documented as having "seven hundred wives of royal birth and three hundred concubines"? In addition, Solomon is recognized as one of the wisest men who ever lived. With all of these superlative attributes and extreme accomplishments, the book of Ecclesiastes is certainly worthy of our attention. In the end, Solomon reaches the conclusion that wealth, women and wisdom are all meaningless without God.

The basic message of Ecclesiastes may be summarized in the form of three propositions: (1) when you look at life with its seemingly aimless cycles and inexplicable paradoxes, you might conclude that all is futile, since it is impossible to discern any purpose in the ordering of events; (2) nevertheless, life is to be enjoyed to the fullest, realizing that it is the gift of God; (3) the wise man will live his life in obedience to God, recognizing that God will eventually judge all men *(Ryrie Study Bible)*.

B. Biblical Background

Like the book of Job, Ecclesiastes raises a plethora of questions. Many of the questions raised by Solomon are left unanswered. Consequently, there is an even greater tendency for the general tone of meaninglessness to be heightened. Since Solomon has already had so many extreme experiences, he is able to probe the depths of human understanding and scale the heights of divinity with his persistent questioning. Sometimes, Solomon sounds as if he is "at odds with his own soul" *(The Interpreter's Bible Commentary)* as he grapples with the ultimate questions of life. In his expert examination of life, he figuratively sees the sea of mystery roll up and "wash the shores of time from the coasts of disillusionment" *(The Interpreter's Bible Commentary)*. The result is a book that seems to stretch from a reflective sense of melancholy, to a brooding devotion, to despair.

Historically, Ecclesiastes is not unique in its pursuit of life's meaning. Similar inquiries can be found in the literature of the Greeks, Egyptians and Chaldeans. The haunting question of "Why was I born?" is still as relevant a question now as it was when asked by Solomon. One must pay close attention to the clues that Solomon provides for this query. Some scholars believe that although there are some gleams of hope, there is generally no suggestion of redemption in Wisdom literature as a whole *(The Interpreter's Bible Commentary)*. Solomon does begin and almost ends his work with the refrain: "Meaningless, meaningless, all is meaningless." However, in the conclusion of Ecclesiastes, Solomon provides some sense of hope and direction: "Now all has been heard; here is the conclusion of the matter: Fear God and keep his commandments, for this is the whole duty of man." Herein is heard a ring of redemption and deliverance which is different from the previous air of agony and despair.

II. EXPOSITION AND APPLICATION OF THE SCRIPTURE
A. Everything Is Meaningless
(Ecclesiastes 1:1-3)

Ecclesiastes opens by identifying the words contained therein as coming from the Teacher. This term refers to a teacher of wisdom (12:9). The Greek translation of the word is *ekklesiastes*, from which we get the word "ecclesiastical." This teacher expresses total disgust for everything of earthly origin in verse 2. From his perspective, in the ultimate scheme of things, nothing really seems to matter. This is the basic theme that is consistently maintained throughout the writing. Everything is meaningless: "This key term occurs about 35 times in the book and only once elsewhere (Job 27:12). The Hebrew for it originally meant "breath." The basic thrust of Ecclesiastes is that all of life is meaningless, useless, hollow, futile and vain if it is not rightly related to God. Only when based on God and His Word is life worthwhile" *(The NIV Study Bible)*. The writer's reference to "everything" being useless refers to man-made pursuits and, of course, excludes God-initiated and God-ordained endeavors.

The first of many rhetorical questions contained in the book is raised in verse 3: "What does man gain from all his labor at which he toils under the sun?" This question is a result of Solomon's internal mental meanderings spilling over onto the pages of a book. Solomon writes from a gut-level perspective and provides the reader with a raw serving of his reality. One of the primary assignments of man is to work. In the book of Genesis, man was assigned to the task of earning a living: "By the sweat of your brow you will eat your food until you return to the ground, since from it you were taken; for dust you are and to dust you will return" (Genesis 3:19).

When men embrace their work with abandon and raise their career to the number one spot on their priority list, they begin to lose perspective on the true meaning of life. (While eight hours is currently a typical workday, the amount of time allotted for work in ancient times was much greater.) Although one's work is a very important factor in a healthy and balanced makeup of mankind, one's work should not supercede the importance of family relationships and obedience to God. The phrase "under the sun" is one that is later adopted by Jesus in Mark 8:36-38. It is another primary phrase used throughout Ecclesiastes (appears 29 times) and refers to this present world and all its many limitations (The NIV Study Bible).

B. The Weariness of Repetition
(Ecclesiastes 1:4-9)

After having so many possessions and after seeing so many wonders in the world, no doubt it was difficult for some things to make a significant impression on Solomon. The winds blow and the streams flow. People come and people go. The sun rises and the sun sets, but what is the ultimate meaning and significance for it all? In a poetic fashion, the writer examines the various elements of the created universe and highlights the repetitious, cyclical nature of each one. In verse 4, the generations are cyclical, but the earth remains the same. A possible ironic implication of this passage is that although most of humanity's attention and emphasis is placed upon each other, people are passing but the earth itself is lasting. The cycles of the sun are examined in verse 5. References to the phases of the sun usually relate directly to the passage of time. Genesis utilizes this concept. ("And there was evening, and there was morning—the first day.") Psalm 113:3 also embraces this phrase: "From the rising of the sun to the place where it sets, the name of the LORD is to be praised." For Solomon, even the mornings and nights are constant reminders of the futility of life. In verse 6, Solomon tackles the mystery of the wind. The wind has long been a source of intrigue for many people. In John 3:8, Jesus states: "The wind blows wherever it pleases. You hear its sound, but you cannot tell where it comes from or where it is going." In Jesus' case, He likens the mystery of the wind to the mystery of the Spirit.

People in ancient times believed and described the universe as being made up of four key elements: earth, fire, air and water. Having already dealt with the first three, Solomon now turns his attention toward the water in verse 7. He meditates on the fact that the sea is never full despite the constant emptying of the rivers' contents into the receptacle of the sea. Perhaps this was a very visual reminder of all the effort that is put into life with so little significant return at times. Solomon even includes the human body in his list of things that are labeled meaningless. For him, constant repetition without apparent results is meaningless and wearisome (verse 8).

The litany concludes in this section with a classic phrase that could be seen as one of the signature verses of the book: "There is nothing new under the sun." This saying is a time-tested proverb that has lasted throughout the centuries, possibly because of its ability to turn a complicated concept into a simple reality. Perhaps the reason why people think that something is new is because they have forgotten that which was old. This passage is written in poetic style and the author uses literary devices such as exaggeration in order to get his point across. Obviously, there have been new things introduced into the world such as the gasoline-powered car, space travel and the Internet. The book of Ecclesiastes is not designed or intended to convey fact, but to convey feeling.

C. The Disciples' Struggle for Meaning (John 20:19-20)

One of the things that the book of Ecclesiastes and this passage in John have in common is that both Solomon and the disciples struggled with faith and belief. When Mary Magdalene and the other women initially went to the disciples to tell them of the Good News of Jesus' resurrection, the reaction was one of disbelief: "But they did not believe the women, because their words seemed to them like nonsense" (Luke 24:11). It is clear throughout the entire book of John that Jesus is attempting to get His disciples to simply *believe* in Him. Thomas had not been present in the initial appearance of Jesus, and when the disciples themselves told him, he did not believe. But in John 20:29 when Jesus finally appeared to Thomas, it was only then that he believed. It is easy to be hard on Thomas because of his disbelief, but in all honesty there are areas in our own lives when we should trust God, but we fail to do so basically because of our unbelief. We are visual creatures and will often only believe something after we have seen it. However, Jesus issues the challenge to Thomas that is also a challenge to us today: "Because you have seen me, you have believed; blessed are those who have not seen and yet have believed." The central theme of the book of John is about belief. Another word for spiritual belief is faith. This relentless emphasis on belief and faith is observable throughout the New Testament. In 2 Corinthians 5:7, Paul declares: "We live by faith, not by sight." Although Paul realizes that faith is essential for success, he also understands that the walk of faith can also involve times of struggle. As you read the following excerpt from Romans 7:21-25, look and listen closely for a very similar spirit of inner struggle as was reflected in the life of Solomon as well as Job:

"So I find this law at work: When I want to do good, evil is right there with me. For in my inner being I delight in God's law; but I see another law at work in the members of my body, waging war against the law of my mind and making me a prisoner of the law of sin at work within my members. What a wretched man I am! Who will rescue me from this body of death? Thanks be to God—through Jesus Christ our Lord!"

The lives of Job, Solomon, Paul and Jesus are testimonies to the fact that a walk with God is not always an easy walk and will necessarily involve struggle and doubt at times. However, that is all a part of the road to growth and spiritual maturity. Hard times help us to personally stretch and to assist others in their time of need.

D. Tidings of Peace
(John 20:21-23)

After displaying his wounds from the Crucifixion, Jesus proceeded to give the disciples the standard Jewish greeting: "Shalom!" These disciples may have expected rebuke from the Lord, but He proceeded to give them a commission to go into all the world and preach the Gospel. He compared their calling to the calling He himself had received from God. Realizing that such a commission would involve opposition and would require great power to be effectively accomplished, He imparted unto them the power of the Holy Spirit through breathing on them. The Greek work for Spirit, *pneuma*, comes from the root word *pneo*, which means "to breathe hard or to blow" *(Strong's Exhaustive Concordance)*.

Some may be surprised by Jesus' statement in verse 23 when He ostensibly grants to the disciples the power to forgive sins or to withhold forgiveness of sins. However, the literal translation of this passage is rendered: "Those whose sins you forgive have already been forgiven; those whose sins you do not forgive have not been forgiven." God does not give or withhold forgiveness based upon human whim. But for those whom God has commissioned to proclaim the Gospel, God has extended the authority to forgive or not forgive sins based upon whether the hearers accept or reject the message of Jesus Christ *(NIV Study Bible)*.

III. Special Features
A. Preserving Our Heritage

When you read the book of Ecclesiastes, what genre of music do you most closely associate with the sentiments of this book? What about the Blues? Like Ecclesiastes, the Blues draws from the depths of personal struggle and painful experiences. Consider a line paraphrased from legendary Blues man B. B. King: "Nobody loves me but my mother, and she could be jivin' too!" Lyrics from the Blues are saturated with a sense of doubt and disbelief. It comes from the life lessons of a people who have been disappointed and disenfranchised in so many ways that skepticism has become almost second nature in some cases. However, it is gratifying that the Blues is not the only kind of song that African American people learned how to sing. From the roots of slavery many other positive musical branches sprouted, such as Ragtime, Jazz, and most assuredly, the Spirituals and gospel music. The gospel song is delivered with feeling and contains words of hope and a sure expectation of divine deliverance. So the next time you may be feeling a little low, you may moan and groan for a while, but don't forget to sing a gospel song full of faith.

B. Concluding Reflections

The resurrection of our Lord and Savior Jesus Christ is the crowning event of His life and of history. Because of Jesus' birth, we have Christmas and a great gift given to humankind. Because of Jesus' life, we have a powerful example of how to live our own lives in a way that will give great glory and honor to God. Because of Jesus' death, we have the forgiveness of sins and an extreme example of just how much God really loves us. Because of Jesus' resurrection, we have the power to conquer any obstacle that may attempt to block us from reaching our God-given destiny. Finally, because of Jesus' return, we have hope of joining God and enjoying the gift of eternal life. Truly there is a great deal of value and many levels of benefits that are contained in a personal relationship with God through our Lord and Savior Jesus Christ.

When viewed through the perspective of Ecclesiastes, there is a litany of contrasts that follows one another in a meaningless succession. The fact that God created humans in His own image presupposes a purpose that cannot be ascertained from a casual observation of the natural order of things. We find meaning in life to the exact extent that we embrace that which God has done in Jesus Christ and conform to that style of life that He has ordained.

HOME DAILY BIBLE READINGS

for the week of April 23, 2006
Finding Life's Meaning

Apr. 17, Monday
—Ecclesiastes 1:1-11
—Nothing New Under the Sun
Apr. 18, Tuesday
—Ecclesiastes 1:12-18
—The Futility of Seeking Wisdom
Apr. 19, Wednesday
—Ecclesiastes 2:1-11
—The Futility of Self-indulgence
Apr. 20, Thursday
—Ecclesiastes 2:12-17
—All Is Vanity
Apr. 21, Friday
—Ecclesiastes 2:18-26
—Of What Good Is Our Toil?
Apr. 22, Saturday
—Luke 24:36-48
—Jesus Gives the Disciples a Mission
Apr. 23, Sunday
—John 20:19-23
—Receive the Holy Spirit

PRAYER

O Thou, in whom we live and move and have our being, You have revealed the meaning of our existence in Your holy Word. May we conceal Your Word within our hearts so that we will live by Your design for our lives. Amen.

Lesson 9

In God's Time

ADULT TOPIC: Everything Has a Season
YOUTH TOPIC: Perfect Timing
CHILDREN'S TOPIC: A Time for Everything

DEVOTIONAL READING: Psalm 34:1-8
BACKGROUND SCRIPTURE: Ecclesiastes 3
PRINT PASSAGE: Ecclesiastes 3:1-8, 14-15

Ecclesiastes 3:1-8, 14-15—KJV

TO EVERY thing there is a season, and a time to every purpose under the heaven:

2 A time to be born, and a time to die; a time to plant, and a time to pluck up that which is planted;

3 A time to kill, and a time to heal; a time to break down, and a time to build up;

4 A time to weep, and a time to laugh; a time to mourn, and a time to dance;

5 A time to cast away stones, and a time to gather stones together; a time to embrace, and a time to refrain from embracing;

6 A time to get, and a time to lose; a time to keep, and a time to cast away;

7 A time to rend, and a time to sew; a time to keep silence, and a time to speak;

8 A time to love, and a time to hate; a time of war, and a time of peace.

.....

14 I know that, whatsoever God doeth, it shall be for ever: nothing can be put to it, nor any thing taken from it: and God doeth it, that men should fear before him.

UNIT II
Living with Creation's Uncertainty

CHILDREN'S UNIT
Learning to Be Wise

KEY VERSE
To every thing there is a season, and a time to every purpose under the heaven.
—Ecclesiastes 3:1

OBJECTIVES
Upon the completion of this lesson, students should understand that:

1. The futility of human existence implicates the necessity for belief in the faithfulness of God.

2. While there is a time for everything, our actions should be determined by God's timing.

3. It is incumbent upon Christians to discover God's purpose for their lives.

15 That which hath been is now; and that which is to be hath already been; and God requireth that which is past.

Ecclesiastes 3:1-8, 14-15—NRSV

FOR EVERYTHING there is a season, and a time for every matter under heaven:

2 a time to be born, and a time to die; a time to plant, and a time to pluck up what is planted;

3 a time to kill, and a time to heal; a time to break down, and a time to build up;

4 a time to weep, and a time to laugh; a time to mourn, and a time to dance;

5 a time to throw away stones, and a time to gather stones together; a time to embrace, and a time to refrain from embracing;

6 a time to seek, and a time to lose; a time to keep, and a time to throw away;

7 a time to tear, and a time to sew; a time to keep silence, and a time to speak;

8 a time to love, and a time to hate; a time for war, and a time for peace.

. . . . .

14 I know that whatever God does endures forever; nothing can be added to it, nor anything taken from it; God has done this, so that all should stand in awe before him.

15 That which is, already has been; that which is to be, already is; and God seeks out what has gone by.

POINTS TO BE EMPHASIZED
ADULTS
Key Verse: Ecclesiastes 3:1

Print: Ecclesiastes 3:1-8, 14-15

—There is an appropriate time for every human endeavor and experience.

—In contrast with human endeavors and experiences, the works of God endure forever.

—Time cannot change the eternal purpose of God.

—Ecclesiastes represents a pagan worldview that the author ultimately rejects.

YOUTH
Key Verse: Ecclesiastes 3:1
Print: Ecclesiastes 3:1-8, 14-15

—God sets up for us the balance that we need in our lives.

—God made time to be filled with activities that balance one another.

—God has approved a time for every purpose under heaven: for beginning and ending, for building up and tearing down, for happiness and sadness, for keeping and throwing away, for loving and hating, for war and peace.

—God's work endures forever and is perfect in its timing and completion.

CHILDREN
Key Verse: Ecclesiastes 3:1
Print: Ecclesiastes 3:1-8

—Solomon believed that everything had a designated, proper time.

—God has a divine plan in place that impacts the rhythm of the universe.

—God's timetable provides a balance for living.

—Humans are encouraged not to rebel against God's timetable but to find their place in the scheme of things.

TOPICAL OUTLINE OF THE LESSON

I. INTRODUCTION
   A. The Revolving Circle of Time
   B. Biblical Background

II. EXPOSITION AND APPLICATION OF THE SCRIPTURE
   A. Comparison and Contrast (Ecclesiastes 3:1)
   B. Life Is Full of Opposites (Ecclesiastes 3:2-8)
   C. The Conclusion of the Matter (Ecclesiastes 3:14-15)

III. SPECIAL FEATURES
   A. Preserving Our Heritage
   B. Concluding Reflections

I. INTRODUCTION

A. The Revolving Circle of Time

Do you use your time wisely, or are you in need of some help in the area of time management? Today's lesson explores the wide gamut of possibilities that inevitably occur in the ebb and flow of life. Solomon's pattern of poetic styling, phrasing and parallelism is continued here in the third chapter of Ecclesiastes. This beautiful and haunting piece of literature has been used in settings of poetry, drama—and has even been set to music. The passage presents a grand view of life and offers seven sets of various kinds of life circumstances for consideration by the reader. It is a highly reflective piece of writing and is therefore not intended to be understood in a very literal way. In order to be understood, the context must constantly be considered. The context is still an inside look into the mental musing of a man who has seen and had it all in life. At the end of his search for meaning and significance, he has traveled down the roads of wealth, possessions, relationships and power. At the end of these roads has been eventual emptiness and disappointment. Humanity will always be busy with endless comings and goings. It is easy to become wrapped up in the vicissitudes of life and lose sight of what really matters. We must move beyond existence and embrace real life—for without God, nothing truly satisfies.

B. Biblical Background

Solomon sees time as a divinely appointed entity that is predetermined and serves as a framework to control, order and direct the affairs of humanity. From his perspective, although people may think they have a broad-based free will, they can only act and operate within the parameters of a God-ordered existence. The concept of divine appointment can be seen in other places in Scripture. Psalm 31:14-15 records, "But I trust in you, O LORD; I say, 'You are my God.' My times are in your hands; deliver me from my enemies and from those who pursue me." Here David relies upon divine appointment to deliver him from his enemies. He reasons that since God is in control of his future, there is no need to fear. This sense of divine appointment is also echoed throughout the book of Proverbs, which was also primarily written by Solomon. Consider the following two verses from Proverbs 16:3-4: "Commit to the LORD whatever you do, and your plans will succeed. The Lord works out everything for his own ends—even the wicked for a day of disaster." Our personal goals will be reached and our personal plans will succeed only as we commit them to the sovereign will of the Lord. Whenever we choose to operate outside the will of God, we remove ourselves from the umbrella-like protection of God and expose ourselves to the dangers of the unknown, unprotected realm. For Solomon, everything that occurs is for the ultimate end of pleasing God and accomplishing God's will. This even includes God's control over, and cooperation with, those who act in a wicked way. Although God is not the source of wickedness, God does occasionally use it to ultimately accomplish a greater good. In the larger scheme of things, all evil will eventually be judged (Ezekiel 38:22-23; Romans 2:5-11).

II. EXPOSITION AND APPLICATION OF THE SCRIPTURE
A. Comparison and Contrast
(Ecclesiastes 3:1)

In verse 1, Solomon introduces the upcoming series of life's opposites. Emphasis is placed on the belief that all of the activities of humanity are under the direct influence of God. Although God has not revealed the reason for all of life's inconsistencies, God has given us life to enjoy while living in obedience to Him. This is vastly different from the solution of the Epicurean sensualists, "Let us eat, drink, and be merry, for tomorrow we die." Solomon advises that one's life must be regulated by an awareness of future divine judgment (12:14) *(Ryrie Study Bible)*. For Solomon, everything happens whenever it needs to happen…not a second sooner and not a second later. A sense of free will, personal freedom and self-determination are all absent in this perspective. Humanity's day-to-day activities (such as planting), as well as one's intimate feeling and emotions (such as hatred), are all products of God's divine will. The list of activities is representative of things that typically occur within the realm of human existence. In order to illustrate the wide range of life's possibilities, for each life item listed, its antithesis is also provided to emphasize the contrast.

B. Life Is Full of Opposites
(Ecclesiastes 3:2-8)

From the moment that life begins at birth, every human being is steadily marching toward an inevitable date with death. No one has control over when he or she is born. But we are responsible for what occurs while we are living. The birth of an individual is like the planting of a seed into the ground. This is an analogy that is frequently used throughout the Scripture. It was easily understood and easily transferable into action due to the people who lived in a largely agrarian society. Jesus used many parables and references related to sowing and reaping. Just as the plants need air, water, sunshine and fertilizer in order to grow, so people need the light of God's love and the water of God's Word in order to spiritually thrive. We must also stay connected to our source, as was stated by Jesus in John 15:5-6 (NASB):

"I am the vine, you are the branches; he who abides in Me and I in him, he bears much fruit, for apart from Me you can do nothing. If anyone does not abide in Me, he is thrown away as a branch and dries up; and they gather them, and cast them into the fire and they are burned."

In verse 3, the phrase "a time to kill" may sound a bit harsh for the average reader to accept coming from a spiritual guidebook like the Bible. Even the sixth commandment states: "Thou shalt not kill" (Exodus 20:13, KJV). The NIV updates this translation as "You shall not murder," which would be somewhat different from the general category of outright killing. The concept of there being "a time to kill" was written during the time when the prevailing philosophy was "an eye for an eye and a tooth for a tooth" (Exodus 21:23-35). There were, and still are, various instances in which killing is legally acceptable (the moral question is quite another issue altogether). The will of God was often demonstrated in the Old Testament through brutal wars against pagan nations. This same climate is not nearly as pronounced in the New Testament. In the New Testament, we are encouraged by Paul not to kill others but to "die daily" on our own accord, and, in Galatians 5:24, to put to death or "crucify" our own flesh and "sinful nature with its passions and desires." Another difference is that the Old Testament demanded the killing of a sacrificial animal, but the New Testament focuses upon a living sacrifice that dies to the old ways. There are some things in our lives that we need to "tear down" (kill), and there are others that we need to build up (heal).

Verse 4 focuses on the seasons of bitterness and their opposites. Life is filled with a wide range of actions that seem to be polar opposites at times. A life filled with only constant laughter and dance would seem almost as extreme as a life filled with constant weeping and mourning. The periodic presence of pain and sadness makes possible the proper appreciation for joy and happiness when it does occur.

Among scholars, there is no uniformity in agreement about the meaning of gathering stones and casting away stones that is mentioned in verse 5. The practice of gathering stones is usually related to the building process, and the casting away of stones is usually related to the deconstruction process. There are some things in life that should be built up and others that should be dismantled. Although everything in life is ultimately under the control and direction of God, the fulfillment of God's will also involves interaction and participation by God's people. God is gratified when we serve as contributors to the fulfillment of God's perfect will.

The *Midrash Qoheleth Rabbah* explains this verse in an altogether different manner and holds that the act of "casting away stones" is an obscure metaphor used in that period to imply the act of marital intercourse *(Interpreter's Bible Commentary)*. Gathering stones would then represent refraining from intercourse. Paul mentions the idea of periodic marriage abstinence in 1 Corinthians 7:5: "Do not deprive each other except by mutual consent and for a time, so that you may devote yourselves to prayer." If this idea of a metaphor being used here is accurate, then the rest of the verse which mentions an embrace would continue the parallel pattern already established and would thus fit well with such a unique interpretation. An embrace is a physical picture and expression of love, openness and personal acceptance.

Verse 6 refers to an activity with which people of all time should be able to identify. Whenever people misplace an item, the natural tendency is to begin to diligently search for that item. In the parable of the lost coin mentioned in Luke 15:8, Jesus states: "Suppose a woman has ten silver coins and loses one. Does she not light a lamp, sweep the house and search carefully until she finds it?" This parable was included in a series of stories about lost things. The other two lost items mentioned by Jesus were the lost sheep and the lost son. With the coin and the sheep, a search to retrieve them was made by their owners. But with the lost son, commonly called the Prodigal Son, no attempt was made by his father to go looking for him and bring him back home. The father simply waited for the son to return on his own volition. Perhaps these parables can serve as examples of a time to search and a time to give up searching.

When the concept of tearing or rending (verse 7) occurs in biblical literature, it usually refers to the practice of tearing one's garment as a sign of great sorrow and grief. In the Old Testament, the Israelites acted unfaithfully and were defeated by the men of Ai (Joshua 7:1-6). When Joshua heard the news, he "tore his clothes and fell facedown to the ground before the ark of the Lord, remaining there till evening." David had a similar reaction when told of the sickness of his son by Bathsheba. He refused food, did not bathe, and wept while lying prostrate on the ground for seven days. But when the boy finally died, he got up from the ground, bathed himself, applied lotions, put on fresh clothes and partook of a meal (2 Samuel 12). David's servants could not understand why David had fasted while the child was alive but when he died, David got up and ate. His explanation for his behavior is similar to the passage in Ecclesiastes and could be summarized by saying that there is a time for mourning and a time to stop mourning.

Perhaps the most difficult statement in this series is Solomon's observation in verse 8 that there is a time to love and a time to hate. This is especially difficult because of the scriptural assertions that "God is love" and that "love never fails." If love is so strong and if love conquers all, is hate ever appropriate? The term "hate" here is used hyperbolically. It is an extreme expression used for effect and does not signify evil maliciousness, but preference in relationship to something greater. In Luke 14:26, Jesus states, "If anyone comes to me and does not hate his father and mother, his wife and children, his brothers and sisters—yes, even his own life—he cannot be my disciple."

This simply means that devotion to one's family or even to oneself must take a back seat to devotion to God *(Ryrie Study Bible)*.

C. The Conclusion of the Matter
(Ecclesiastes 3:14-15)

Solomon observes that everything God does will endure forever. This fact stands in stark contrast to all that has been said regarding the strivings of humankind that will soon pass away. With God's work, nothing can be added or subtracted. Jesus echoes this notion in Matthew 5:18—"I tell you the truth, until heaven and earth disappear, not the smallest letter, not the least stroke of a pen, will by any means disappear from the Law until everything is accomplished." On the other hand, changes, revisions and improvements occur within the works of men quite frequently without consequence. This comparison and contrast is used to heighten the sense of awe and reverence due to almighty God. God was in control of what has happened in the past, what is happening in the present, and even what will happen in the future (verse 15).

III. SPECIAL FEATURES
A. Preserving Our Heritage

The knowledge and belief that God is in control of the past, present and future is one of the things that has helped in maintaining the sanity, focus and perseverance of African Americans throughout history. Blacks have been able to endure hardship, abuse, racism, poverty and psychological warfare because deep down in our hearts there has been the assurance that no matter what people may do to us, God is ultimately in control. Like the Israelites who were led from the captivity of the Egyptians, God provided a way out through the opening of the Red Sea. Many of our forefathers and foremothers have experienced miraculous provision and deliverance through the power of God. Even in contemporary times, anyone who has truly walked with God can testify that God is a great provider who supplies our needs according to God's riches in glory in Christ Jesus. Much of our gospel music lyrics acknowledge God's provision of the everyday necessities of life, such as food to eat, a place to sleep, eyes to see, ears to hear, and "the activity of my limbs." Other cultures that do not place such great emphasis on the simple essentials have not had to go without those essentials and consequently it is not something significant enough to sing about. But every test can lead to a testimony, and every testimony can lead to ultimate triumph in which we are edified and God gets the glory.

B. Concluding Reflections

Our lives and our relationship with God are not solely dependent upon circumstantial occurrences. Rather, our existence is impacted by the sovereign will of God who intervenes into circumstances and influences outcomes. As Christians, we must live above mere philosophies and embrace the belief that all things really do work together for God's good when we love God and when we are obedient to God's will (Romans 8:28).

HOME DAILY BIBLE READINGS

for the week of April 30, 2006
In God's Time

Apr. 24, Monday
—Psalm 34:1-8
—The Lord Is Good
Apr. 25, Tuesday
—Ecclesiastes 7:15-22
—Use Moderation and Respect God's Authority
Apr. 26, Wednesday
—Ecclesiastes 8:2-8a
—Every Matter Has Its Time
Apr. 27, Thursday
—Ecclesiastes 9:1-12
—Life Is in God's Hands
Apr. 28, Friday
—Ecclesiastes 3:1-8
—For Everything There Is a Season
Apr. 29, Saturday
—Ecclesiastes 3:9-15
—Whatever God Does Endures Forever
Apr. 30, Sunday
—Ecclesiastes 3:16-22
—Judgment and Future Belong to God

PRAYER

Eternal God, our Father, as we live in a world that is confused over the meaning of life and some who find life a composite of meaninglessness, may we stay focused on Your Son Jesus Christ in whom there is both purpose and meaning to our earthly sojourn. Amen.

A Treasure Worth Seeking

ADULT TOPIC: A Treasure Worth Seeking
YOUTH TOPIC: Wise Up!
CHILDREN'S TOPIC: Obey God

DEVOTIONAL READING: Proverbs 2:6-15
BACKGROUND SCRIPTURE: Proverbs 2—3
PRINT PASSAGE: Proverbs 2:1-5; 3:1-6, 13-18

KEY VERSE

Happy is the man that findeth wisdom, and the man that getteth understanding.—Proverbs 3:13

OBJECTIVES

Upon the completion of this lesson, students should understand that:

Proverbs 2:1-5; 3:1-6, 13-18—KJV

MY SON, if thou wilt receive my words, and hide my commandments with thee;

2 So that thou incline thine ear unto wisdom, and apply thine heart to understanding;

3 Yea, if thou criest after knowledge, and liftest up thy voice for understanding;

4 If thou seekest her as silver, and searchest for her as for hid treasures;

5 Then shalt thou understand the fear of the LORD, and find the knowledge of God.

.....

MY SON, forget not my law; but let thine heart keep my commandments:

2 For length of days, and long life, and peace, shall they add to thee.

3 Let not mercy and truth forsake thee: bind them about thy neck; write them upon the table of thine heart:

1. God is the source of true wisdom and understanding.

2. The spiritually wise are challenged to teach those new in the faith.

3. Trust in God should always take priority over personal preferences.

4 So shalt thou find favour and good understanding in the sight of God and man.

5 Trust in the LORD with all thine heart; and lean not unto thine own understanding.

6 In all thy ways acknowledge him, and he shall direct thy paths.

.....

13 Happy is the man that findeth wisdom, and the man that getteth understanding.

14 For the merchandise of it is better than the merchandise of silver, and the gain thereof than fine gold.

15 She is more precious than rubies: and all the things thou canst desire are not to be compared unto her.

16 Length of days is in her right hand; and in her left hand riches and honour.

17 Her ways are ways of pleasantness, and all her paths are peace.

18 She is a tree of life to them that lay hold upon her: and happy is every one that retaineth her.

Proverbs 2:1-5; 3:1-6, 13-18—NRSV
MY CHILD, if you accept my words and treasure up my commandments within you,

2 making your ear attentive to wisdom and inclining your heart to understanding;

3 if you indeed cry out for insight, and raise your voice for understanding;

4 if you seek it like silver, and search for it as for hidden treasures—

5 then you will understand the fear of the LORD and find the knowledge of God.

.....

MY CHILD, do not forget my teaching, but let your heart keep my commandments;

2 for length of days and years of life and abundant welfare they will give you.

3 Do not let loyalty and faithfulness forsake you; bind them around your neck, write them on the tablet of your heart.

4 So you will find favor and good repute in the sight of God and of people.

5 Trust in the LORD with all your heart, and do not rely on your own insight.

6 In all your ways acknowledge him, and he will make straight your paths.

.....

13 Happy are those who find wisdom, and those who get understanding,

14 for her income is better than silver, and her revenue better than gold.

15 She is more precious than jewels, and nothing you desire can compare with her.

16 Long life is in her right hand; in her left hand are riches and honor.

17 Her ways are ways of pleasantness, and all her paths are peace.

18 She is a tree of life to those who lay hold of her; those who hold her fast are called happy.

POINTS TO BE EMPHASIZED
ADULTS
Key Verse: Proverbs 3:13
Print: Proverbs 2:1-5; 3:1-6,13-18

—God promises wisdom to those who seek it.

—Faithfulness and obedience are the way to please God and people.

—Trust in God adds clarity and assurance in decision making.

—Wisdom is more valuable than any of the riches of earth.

YOUTH

Key Verse: Proverbs 3:5

Print: Proverbs 2:1-5; 3:1-6, 13-18

—God's wisdom is more valuable than material possessions.

—God offers the wisdom we need to find happiness.

—The fear of the Lord is the beginning of wisdom.

—Acquiring wisdom and understanding of God is our top priority.

—A successful life comes from trusting in the Lord's wisdom with all of one's heart.

CHILDREN

Key Verse: Proverbs 3:5

Print: Proverbs 2:1-5; 3:1-6, 13-18

—There is value in hearing, accepting and keeping God's commandments.

—True wisdom begins with respect for and faith in God.

—Commitment to God brings long-term guidance for living.

—Dependence upon God provides a sense of security and peace.

■ TOPICAL OUTLINE OF THE LESSON

I. INTRODUCTION
A. Proverbs as a Literary Style
B. Biblical Background

II. EXPOSITION AND APPLICATION OF THE SCRIPTURE
A. The Benefits of Wisdom
(Proverbs 2:1-5)
B. Formula for Favor
(Proverbs 3:1-6)
C. The Search for Wisdom
(Proverbs 3:13-18)

III. SPECIAL FEATURES
A. Preserving Our Heritage
B. Concluding Reflections

I. INTRODUCTION
A. Proverbs as a Literary Style

The book of Proverbs is a part of the category of Wisdom Literature in the Bible. Two other books in this quarter's study that fall into this category include Job and Ecclesiastes. In reading and studying all three books, it is easy to observe the similarities between them. All three are very practical in content and presentation. All three books speak directly to many of the real needs, concerns, desires, hurts, losses, gains, and experiences frequently encountered in everyday life. Central to the subject matter of Proverbs is the celebration of wisdom as essential for effective living. Other topics include general instruction and specific teaching on family, friends, death, lust, laziness, love, gluttony, revenge, justice, humility, pride, the tongue, poverty, wealth, goodness, sin, folly and success.

Solomon is considered to be the author of the majority of the book of Proverbs. First Kings 4 records the following insightful information regarding Solomon's wisdom:

- God gave to Solomon great wisdom and insight that was more extensive than the sand on the seashore.
- Solomon was considered to be wiser than any other man.
- He was able to speak three thousand proverbs.
- He knew over a thousand songs.
- He taught others about plants, animals, birds, reptiles and fish.
- People came from far and near just to listen to the wisdom of Solomon.

Proverbs was probably written sometime in the tenth century BC, when Israel's monarchy was united and prosperity prevailed throughout the land. Times of peace naturally made possible the luxuries of reading for pleasure and writing for the pure joy of personal expression. The advice offered in Proverbs sounds like a father speaking to a child, a teacher to a student, or an elder to a young person. Proverbs provides a picture of the kind of practical teaching and instruction done in families, schools and the royal palace. Generally, the proverbs in this collection give an uncomplicated picture of life. Certain actions are shown as always producing certain results. A wise person is able to recognize the right decision ahead of time and choose the path that leads to blessing, happiness and even wealth.

Since the wisdom of Proverbs is timeless, it is still very useful for teaching even in these current times. Proverbs uses short, simple sentences that are often parallel in structure. But each of those short sentences is packed with powerful truth and wisdom.

B. Biblical Background

The meaning the Hebrew word for "proverb" is generally wider in scope than the English understanding of the word. In Hebrew, this same word could be translated as "taunt" (Isaiah 14:4), "parable" (Ezekiel 17:2), or "oracle" (Numbers 23:7, 18). Consequently, the passages are not limited to concise truisms, but also include longer, more developed discourses in chapters 1-9 *(NIV Study Bible)*. The structural organization and division of the book of Proverbs is easily identified by the textual headings located above each section. The sections include the Prologue (1:1-7), the Superiority of Wisdom (1:8-9:18), the Central Collection of Solomon's Proverbs (10:1-22:16), the Thirty Sayings of the Wise (22:17-24:22), Additional Wise Sayings (24:23-34), Hezekiah's Collection of Solomon's Proverbs (chapters 25-29), Agur's Words (chapter 30), King Lemuel's Words (31:1-9), and the Epilogue highlighting the Ideal Wife (31:10-31) *(NIV Study Bible)*.

Important insight into interpreting the underlying purpose behind the writing of Proverbs is found in its own verses.

Proverbs 1:2-4 identifies the following concepts that are central to understanding why the book was written:

Wisdom—Wisdom is the proper understanding of that which is true, right and lasting.

Discipline—Disciplined training which is designed to produce a particular character trait within an individual.

Understanding Words of Insight—Deep and insightful words mean nothing unless they are properly understood by one with the ability to read beneath the surface.

Acquiring a Disciplined, Prudent Life — Prudence is concerned with a sense of discretion, modesty and economy (it is the opposite of extravagance, which incidentally is one of the characteristics for which Solomon was well-known).

Doing What Is Right, Just and Fair — Proverbs serves as a guideline for living a life of goodness, godliness and personal purity in every area of existence.

Giving Prudence to the Simple—Those who are simpleminded would tend to strive after immediate gratification rather than undergo the discipline of deferred gratification.

Give Knowledge and Discretion to the Young—Knowledge is usually a byproduct of age and maturity. Proverbs seeks to provide the young with a cumulative collection of insights from the elders so that they won't have to make the same mistakes and can get a head start on a wise life.

II. EXPOSITION AND APPLICATION OF THE SCRIPTURE

A. The Benefits of Wisdom
(Proverbs 2:1-5)

The speaker of these proverbs is not one who insistently forces wisdom upon the lives of the hearers. Instead, wisdom is firmly but courteously offered to the hearers for their acceptance or rejection. Young people are encouraged to "store up" the commands within them. Usage of this phrase is reminiscent of the psalmist who urged young men to avoid sin by hiding the Word of God in their hearts (Psalm 119:11). Scripture memorization was a significant aspect of the spiritual training for young people. One never outgrows the

"Seek wisdom and the Lord will keep you": the main point of the poem is that if you seek wisdom with all your strength, the Lord will give it to you, and wisdom will safeguard you from wicked men and seductive women with the result that you can walk on the blessed path. While wisdom will be given to anyone who earnestly seeks it, one cannot directly take it—it must be given as a gift. "The loose woman...the adulteress": loose is literally "foreign"—a foreign woman can be a woman outside the community who is forbidden as a marriage partner, a prostitute, or a woman otherwise dangerous to a man. Proverbs focuses not only on her sexuality, but also on her seductive and deceitful speech. The teacher invites the disciple to memorize the teaching and to be loyal, which leads to trust in God, the great Teacher. Such trust means not relying upon oneself, but honoring God with due worship and allowing God to become one's Teacher and Father. While trust in God is necessary, considering the reality that God reproves when educating disciples, there may be suffering. Note: "heart" is the seat of various emotions; "hide" is to treasure up, as something to be valued.

need to regularly internalize the Word of God through meditation and memorization.

Although meditation and memorization is commendable, it is not sufficient or adequate standing alone by itself to empower one for a lifestyle of wisdom. There must also be application in which the things that have been learned are applied to the situations of everyday life. The heart was considered the center or seat of the emotions. Everything that truly matters in our lives originates from the heart. When one is passionate enough to "call out" for insight and to "cry loud" for understanding, then these things will be achieved (verse 3). One must truly want it bad enough in order for it to be attained. Most of the things in life that we attain materialize because we desire them on a feeling level, rather than merely on a cognitive or mental level. Jesus captured the essence of this concept when He said in His teaching on the mountain: "Blessed are those who hunger and thirst for righteousness, for they will be filled" (Matthew 5:6).

This passionate personal search for God will take us beyond the convenience of a regularly scheduled Sunday-morning worship experience complete with air-conditioning and padded pews. A truly hungry search for God and godly wisdom will make us look for it like we lost some money (verse 4). We will look for God like a lucrative nest egg hidden in the ground. This will quite possibly involve physical discomfort, time infringement, social ostracism, and all-around inconvenience. But the final result of knowledge and fear (reverence) for God is worth the trouble required to accomplish the goal (verse 5).

B. Formula for Favor *(Proverbs 3:1-6)*

The commandments of God are not capricious. God did not give us guidelines because of nothing else to do that day or because they simply sounded good. Every command of God is rooted in a significant reason and motive. For example, we are told to "Remember the Sabbath day and keep it holy." The reason for this is that God knows there would be workaholics among us, and in an attempt to prevent undue stress, God sat aside a day of rest. Man was not made for the Sabbath, but the Sabbath was made for man (Mark 2:27). If we follow God's plan for longevity and prosperity, we will succeed in our endeavors just as a child succeeds when a parent extends time-tested advice from personal experience (3:1-2). Love and faithfulness are two concepts that are objectified by the writer, and they take on the imagery of jewelry pieces. The writer is speaking metaphorically in order to emphasize the importance of never forgetting what one has learned about God's wisdom (verse 3). Jewish custom called for phylacteries or portions of the Law to literally be worn on one's person as a form of memory-enhancing adornment.

Desirable results are promised for those who embrace the power of love and faithfulness. The reward is both social and spiritual in nature. The spiritual benefit is favor and a good name in the sight of God. The same is true from the social perspective. A person who is obedient to God need not necessarily be offensive to people. Unfortunately, some people believe that to be holy is to always be unpopular, sad, unattractive and generally as miserable as possible. But Jesus said in John 10:10b— "I have come that they may have life, and have it to the full." God's plan for our abundant life is not just in heaven, but begins on earth. The Spirit of God is a compelling force within the lives of Christians that draws non-believers to the light and power of God.

Our ultimate trust should not be in self, money, material goods, or human relationships. Our trust or ultimate dependence should be placed in a source that does not change from day to day depending upon the circumstances of life. As the foundation of a well-built building should rest on an immovable surface, so should our lives rest on a solid source. Our trust should not be given half-heartedly, because then we could only expect half-hearted results. Placing our entire trust in God means becoming vulnerable in many areas. As we grow to trust God with everything, there will be times when our specific future is unpredictable and some things will be out of our direct control. But as we resist the temptation to depend on our own understanding or on the ungrounded speculation of others, we will then see that God will guide our decision-making process in a way that may not reach perfection, but will safely put us at our God-ordained destination (3:5-6).

C. The Search for Wisdom
(Proverbs 3:13-18)

In 3:13-18, wisdom moves from being cast as personal adornment and is now projected as a woman. Perhaps the writer is appealing to the preferences of his predominately male audience as he writes that "she" is more profitable than silver and produces better returns on the investment than gold and rubies (3:13-15). Surely this would be an irresistible combination for a solid investment. Understanding humans have the capacity to want and desire a great deal of things. The writer seals all the possibilities and submits that just in case he has neglected to mention some particular desire, he is sure that nothing one could ever desire can compare to this wisdom (verse 17). One last image change for wisdom in this passage is the comparison of wisdom to a tree. Just like a tree, wisdom must be planted, watered, and attended to. When this happens on a regular basis, wisdom will provide the owner with shade during scorching summer days and with fruit in times of need.

III. SPECIAL FEATURES
A. Preserving Our Heritage

Proverbs is a collection of wisdom that was designed to be passed down from generation to generation. Each generation has the privilege and the responsibility to leave a material and an instructional legacy for the next generation so that each group does not have to start from the "bare bones" beginning. The one who starts the race with the benefit of collective knowledge from the past is more likely to finish the race as a winner. One of the great places to showcase and exercise this practice is at family reunions. At your next family reunion, make it a point to gather all the relatives together and allow the senior members of the tribe to speak their words of wisdom to the whole group. You need not wait for a family reunion; you can start within your own family and have a weekly family meeting. As a part of this event, make it a point to share three things you have learned in life. Even the younger ones may be able to get in on the action and share about life from their perspective.

B. Concluding Reflections

The book of Proverbs helps us to understand that wisdom is the divine revelation of God's plan in this world for the lives of all humanity. Wisdom is not just the mere accumulation of earthly knowledge or the matriculation through schools of higher education. While education is highly desirable and should be pursued by all people, information alone is useless without the wisdom that comes from God alone. This book of Proverbs elevates the belief that the people who embrace wisdom are prosperous and happy. Those who reject the gift of wisdom are frequently subjected to a painful existence. A belief that the one true and living God "rewards the righteous and punishes the wicked" is a primary principle that thoroughly permeates the book of Proverbs *(The Interpreter's Bible Commentary,* Proverbs).

HOME DAILY BIBLE READINGS
for the week of May 7, 2006
A Treasure Worth Seeking

May 1, Monday
—Proverbs 2:1-5
—Seek Wisdom
May 2, Tuesday
—Proverbs 2:6-15
—Wisdom Brings Knowledge, Prudence and Understanding
May 3, Wednesday
—Proverbs 2:16-22
—Follow the Way of the Good
May 4, Thursday
—Proverbs 3:1-12
—Trust and Honor God
May 5, Friday
—Proverbs 3:13-20
—Wisdom Is Precious
May 6, Saturday
—Proverbs 3:21-30
—Wisdom Brings Security
May 7, Sunday
—Proverbs 3:31-35
—Do What Is Right

PRAYER
O God, as we lift our voices to You for guidance, mercy and grace, grant that we may resolve by Your Spirit to live lives with integrity that reflect the quality that is resident in Thee. Amen.

Wisdom's Invitation

ADULT TOPIC: Wisdom's Invitation
YOUTH TOPIC: RSVP to Wisdom
CHILDREN'S TOPIC: Obey Wise Teachings

KEY VERSE
Doth not wisdom cry? and understanding put forth her voice? —Proverbs 8:1

DEVOTIONAL READING: Proverbs 8:10-21
BACKGROUND SCRIPTURE: Proverbs 8—9
PRINT PASSAGE: Proverbs 8:1-5, 22-31

Proverbs 8:1-5, 22-31—KJV

DOTH NOT wisdom cry? and understanding put forth her voice?

2 She standeth in the top of high places, by the way in the places of the paths.

3 She crieth at the gates, at the entry of the city, at the coming in at the doors.

4 Unto you, O men, I call; and my voice is to the sons of man.

5 O ye simple, understand wisdom: and, ye fools, be ye of an understanding heart.

.....

22 The LORD possessed me in the beginning of his way, before his works of old.

23 I was set up from everlasting, from the beginning, or ever the earth was.

24 When there were no depths, I was brought forth; when there were no fountains abounding with water.

25 Before the mountains were settled, before the hills was I brought forth:

OBJECTIVES
Upon the completion of this lesson, students should realize that:
1. God's Word is the source for knowing that which is right and just.

2. Wisdom is a gift from God.

3. There is a difference between wisdom, understanding and intelligence.

26 While as yet he had not made the earth, nor the fields, nor the highest part of the dust of the world.

27 When he prepared the heavens, I was there: when he set a compass upon the face of the depth:

28 When he established the clouds above: when he strengthened the fountains of the deep:

29 When he gave to the sea his decree, that the waters should not pass his commandment: when he appointed the foundations of the earth:

30 Then I was by him, as one brought up with him: and I was daily his delight, rejoicing always before him;

31 Rejoicing in the habitable part of his earth; and my delights were with the sons of men.

Proverbs 8:1-5, 22-31—NRSV

DOES NOT wisdom call, and does not understanding raise her voice?

2 On the heights, beside the way, at the crossroads she takes her stand;

3 beside the gates in front of the town, at the entrance of the portals she cries out:

4 "To you, O people, I call, and my cry is to all that live.

5 O simple ones, learn prudence; acquire intelligence, you who lack it."

.....

22 The LORD created me at the beginning of his work, the first of his acts of long ago.

23 Ages ago I was set up, at the first, before the beginning of the earth.

24 When there were no depths I was brought forth, when there were no springs abounding with water.

25 Before the mountains had been shaped, before the hills, I was brought forth—

26 when he had not yet made earth and fields, or the world's first bits of soil.

27 When he established the heavens, I was there, when he drew a circle on the face of the deep,

28 when he made firm the skies above, when he established the fountains of the deep,

29 when he assigned to the sea its limit, so that the waters might not transgress his command, when he marked out the foundations of the earth,

30 then I was beside him, like a master worker; and I was daily his delight, rejoicing before him always,

31 rejoicing in his inhabited world and delighting in the human race.

POINTS TO BE EMPHASIZED
ADULTS

Key Verse: Proverbs 8:1

Print: Proverbs 8:1-5, 22-31

—Wisdom desires to be found and wants people to exercise intelligence and prudence.

—God created wisdom before creating the earth.

—Wisdom was with God as God created the world.

—Wisdom rejoiced in front of God and took delight in humanity.

YOUTH

Key Verse: Proverbs 8:1

Print: Proverbs 8:1-5, 22-31

—Wise choices and the good life come from living in God's wisdom.

—Wisdom was with God before the beginning of time.

—God's wisdom is available to all persons.

—Proverbs affirms that wisdom is about making good choices.

CHILDREN

Key Verse: Proverbs 8:33

Print: Proverbs 8:1-5, 10-11, 32-35

—Knowledge of God's expectations is one of life's most important possessions.

—It is important to understand true intelligence and prudence.

—True happiness is found in following God's instruction.

—To be faithful to God's instruction is to find the fullness of life.

TOPICAL OUTLINE OF THE LESSON

I. INTRODUCTION
   A. The Clarion Call of Wisdom
   B. Biblical Background
II. EXPOSITION AND APPLICATION OF THE SCRIPTURE
   A. The Voice of Wisdom
      (Proverbs 8:1-5)
   B. Wisdom Exalted
      (Proverbs 8:22-31)
III. SPECIAL FEATURES
   A. Preserving Our Heritage
   B. Concluding Reflections

I. INTRODUCTION

A. The Clarion Call of Wisdom

With a distinctive voice that is compelling and clear, wisdom calls out for everyone to hear. In chapter 7, the spotlight is on the adulteress who boldly solicits the companionship of the passerby. She uses her kisses (13), flattery (15), sensuality (19-20) and reassurance (19-20) to convince the passerby to embrace her. When she finally is successful in attracting a willing victim, she leads him down the highway to hell (27). In stark contrast to chapter 7, chapter 8 is astounding. The transition is like moving from an underground dungeon—full of rotting bones— to a bright, airy palace filled with satin and sunshine. In spite of the contrast, there are also several similarities between the adulteress and the personification of wisdom. Both the adulteress and wisdom are characterized in the female gender. The target for both the adulteress (7:7) as well as wisdom (8:5) is those who are simple or unwise. Both the adulteress and wisdom use attention-getting actions such as calling out in order to attract those passing by. Each persuasion makes promises of glorious benefits—if she is the one that is chosen.

The primary difference between choosing the sly, seductive adulteress and choosing the prudent, time-tested wisdom is the results. To choose the adulteress is to choose death, and to choose wisdom is to choose life. The comparison is reminiscent of Jesus' assertion in Matthew 7:13-14: "Enter through the narrow gate. For wide is the gate and broad is the road that leads to destruction, and many enter through it. But small is the gate and narrow the road that leads to life, and only a few find it." Life is full of choices: some of them are good, and some of them are bad. Some choices are big, and others may seem small. But our ultimate destiny is significantly impacted by the small and larger choices that we make every day. Therefore, the wise one will practice making wise choices in the small things so that when the big decisions come, there won't be much of a real choice at all.

B. Biblical Background

Chapter 8 of Proverbs is organized into three primary sections: the first section includes verses 1-21, and it is an exhortation to follow the ways of wisdom along with the personal benefits of embracing the personified woman of wisdom; the second general section of this chapter covers verses 22-31 and highlights the exalted position of wisdom when placed on the same level with the Creator; finally, the chapter concludes with verses 32-36 that contain a variety of final exhortations. Two types of poetic content are offered in this chapter. Most of the verses are presented in "synonymous" or parallel form. This simply means that after the first line is stated, a second line repeats essentially the same idea, but with a slightly different twist or emphasis. An example of this is verse 5: "You who are simple, gain prudence; you who are foolish, gain understanding." The synonymous format is present in verses 1-12, 14-28, 31-33 and 35-36. The remaining verses utilize a triplet format (13, 29-30, 34).

Proverbs is written from a very practical perspective, but it does pay special attention to the work of God as Creator. Other forms of non-spiritual literature share the exalted view of wisdom that is found in the book of Proverbs. However, the sayings in Proverbs differ from the wisdom of other nations on the key point of where wisdom comes from. In Proverbs, wisdom comes from the Lord God and is said to have been with the Lord at the beginning of time (8:22-31) *(The Learning Bible)*. Proverbs extends an open invitation for all people to come to the house of wisdom and dine freely at her banquet table.

II. EXPOSITION AND APPLICATION OF THE SCRIPTURE

A. The Voice of Wisdom
(Proverbs 8:1-5)

In the first three verses of chapter 8, wisdom is personified and is presented in the third person as she pleads with humanity to take heed to the knowledgeable perspective and valuable advice she has to offer. The chapter begins with a question: "Does not wisdom call out?" Lady wisdom and understanding must raise her voice in order to capture the attention of the people who are busily passing by and living their lives oblivious to the need to take heed and make the necessary changes (8:1-2). This is a crucial time in the life of the young person who must listen to voices that are competing for attention and obedience. The challenge of the youth is to learn discretion by listening to the voice of wisdom: "She speaks neither out of heaven (by special revelation, as do the prophets) nor out of the earth (through voices from the dead—necromancy), but out of the center of the life of the city, where man's communal experience of the creation order (established by God's

wisdom) is concentrated. And it is there also that the godly, the truly wise, test human experience in the crucible of faith and afterward give divine wisdom a human voice in their wise instructions—as in Proverbs" *(NIV Study Bible)*.

The gates leading into the city (8:3) represented a point at which there was a great deal of busy activities and a high volume of human traffic. No doubt, there were buyers, sellers and beggars who would have frequented such a site.

In verse 4, wisdom stops being addressed in the third person and now calls out and raises her voice in the first-person singular. The transaction she offers is simple and straightforward. Those who are simple and foolish can come to her and exchange their shallow mentality for something much more enduring. Wisdom offers them a generous helping of prudence and understanding. Although she strongly desires for them to experience these virtues, she is not at liberty to force herself upon them. As Jesus asserts in Revelation 3:20: "Here I am! I stand at the door and knock. If anyone hears my voice and opens the door, I will come in and eat with him, and he with me."

B. Wisdom Exalted *(Proverbs 8:22-31)*

Proverbs 8:22 introduces a section of the writing that is essentially a hymn describing the role of wisdom at the beginning of creation. Some scholars interpret these verses as providing part of the background for the New Testament portrayal of Christ. The connection is seen in John 1:1-2, which records: "In the beginning was the Word, and the Word was with God, and the Word was God. He was with God in the beginning." This unusual portion of Scripture exalts wisdom as the first thing that God created and as the companion of God in the creation of the earth: "This is the highest conception of wisdom found in the canonical books. Wisdom therefore should be obeyed not only because of the advantages she brings, but also because of her essential nature and the high place she holds in the universe" *(The Interpreter's Bible Commentary).* The creation was made possible out of actions that flowed directly from the creative wisdom of God. The only thing that existed "before the world began" (8:23) was God. Therefore, in this case, the writer seems to be equating wisdom with one of the attributes contained in the divine nature of God. God is omnipresent (everywhere all the time), omnipotent (all-powerful) and omniscient (all-knowing). However, God is also all-wise, and God incorporates this trait into everything else about God.

Wisdom claims that her birth was prior to the creation of oceans and springs (8:24). The waters were created on the second day according to Genesis 1:6. Wisdom also predates the mountains, hills, fields, and even the dust of the ground. The word "dust" is mentioned only once in the book of Proverbs. It is the same word used in Genesis 2:7 when "the LORD God formed the man from the dust of the ground and breathed into his nostrils the breath of life, and man became a living being." Since the man was made from the dust, and wisdom came before the dust, wisdom is then presented as predating humanity. Wisdom is presented as being a witness to essentially all of creation from the marking of the horizon to the establishment of the clouds, seas and wells.

She identifies herself as the servant or craftsman present and assisting at the side of the Lord as God labored diligently in the creation of the cosmos. Craftsmen were sometimes referred to as wise men (see Bezalel who designed and constructed the tabernacle in Exodus 31:3). The term used here accentuates the considerable level of skill, talent and ability demonstrated in creation. There are some who unfortunately believe that skill has no place among spiritual things. However, Psalm 33:3 records: "Sing to him a new song; play skillfully, and shout for joy." Here, we see an intertwining of the emotive aspects of worship and the studied, educational aspects of practice. To concentrate on the practice part only would leave worship with a technically pure but spiritually cold atmosphere. To concentrate on the emotive aspects of worship without the presence of the technical, practiced expertise would create an imbalance. God expects the "true worshipers" to worship in spirit and in truth.

Wisdom's reaction to the creation of the universe is one of sheer delight. The words used to describe this experience are "rejoicing" and "delighting." The very first action recorded by God was to create. In Genesis 1:2, God created the heavens and the earth. God's reaction to this experience of creating something is recorded several times in the first chapter of Genesis. Three times following the creation of the earth, feelings are expressed through the use of the phrase: "And God saw that it was good" (8:10, 12, 26). Then, after humans are created in verse 31, "God saw all that he had made, and it was very good." Since the first recorded action of God was to create, and since we were created in the image of God and have the mind of Christ, it would just stand to reason that we should be creative people. This idea often stands in contrast to some churches and some Christians who seem to insist on eradicating all creativity and innovation in the name of preserving tradition. In the book of Proverbs, creativity is accompanied by delight and rejoicing (31). Whenever God uses us as a vessel to participate in the divine creative process, it is a blessing that should not be taken lightly, but thankfully embraced, cherished and nurtured.

III. SPECIAL FEATURES
A. Preserving Our Heritage

As wisdom lifts her voice through the book of Proverbs, it is evident that she is not a lady who believes in discrimination. On the contrary, Lady Wisdom is very much an "equal opportunity" employer. Regardless of race, class, gender, or denominational background, wisdom is available for the price of sacrifice, discipline and obedience. Although an employer may be able to deny someone a job based upon some discriminatory reason, no one but God has a monopoly on the wisdom market. A wise idea can be even more valuable than a job. Booker T. Washington encouraged his people by urging them to lift themselves up by their own bootstraps. Most people were born with the inbred ability to accomplish and achieve much more than they think or demonstrate over the entire course of their lives. Your specific type of creativity may not involve art, music, writing, or dance. You may, however, be able to creatively listen to someone, physically help someone, or creatively help in some other way. Don't waste your gifts. Keep your eyes open for every opportunity to tap into your inner source of divine creativity. Your creativity is anxiously waiting for your permission to let it come outside and play!

B. Concluding Reflections

Wisdom affords tremendous rewards and fringe benefits to those who are willing to take her advice and apply it to their lives. If you have wisdom, you have something better than riches, because wealth can be taken, but wisdom forever remains and most of the time increases with age. Fenelon wrote, "All that exists, exists only by the communication of God's infinite being. All that has intelligence, has it only by derivation from [God's] sovereign wisdom, and all that acts, acts only for the impulse of [God's] supreme activity" *(Interpreter's Bible Commentary).*

As we reflect upon this lesson, it will be to our advantage to remember that wisdom is not only personified, but also represents a twofold point of view: "1) Wisdom, the power of judging rightly, implying the knowledge of divine and human things; and 2) As an attribute of God, particularly displayed in the various and astonishing works of creation *(Clarke's Commentary).*

Wisdom does not take a passive role in the lives of humans, she cries out to draw attention to herself to the end that sinners may be persuaded to turn from their evil ways and accept the advice of wisdom that ensues in life.

Notice that wisdom is learned by slow and progressive degrees, but in God it is as eternally inherent as any of the other essential attributes of His nature. If there is a lack of wisdom, one must ask of God who gives to all men freely, but the wisdom God gives must be deployed for His purpose and not as a self-distinguishing quality of any human. Keep in mind then that wisdom is not accumulated philosophies, or scientific learning, but an attribute of God by which He created the world. God displays especially His wisdom in ordering and directing human beings, and in providing for their wants. "Hence, wisdom is represented ads offering its lessons of instruction continually, and using every means and opportunity to call me from folly and vice to sound knowledge, holiness and happiness *(Clarke's Commentary).*

HOME DAILY BIBLE READINGS

for the week of May 14, 2006
Wisdom's Invitation

May 8, Monday
—Proverbs 8:1-9
—Learn Prudence and Acquire Intelligence
May 9, Tuesday
—Proverbs 8:10-21
—Receive Advice, Wisdom, Insight and Strength
May 10, Wednesday
—Proverbs 8:22-31
—Wisdom Participated in Creation
May 11, Thursday
—Proverbs 8:32-36
—Listen to Wisdom's Instruction
May 12, Friday
—Proverbs 9:1-6
—Wisdom Extends an Invitation
May 13, Saturday
—Proverbs 9:7-12
—Wisdom Multiplies Our Days
May 14, Sunday
—Proverbs 9:13-18
—Folly Extends an Invitation

PRAYER

Eternal God, in our technological world, we have come to know how, but not why. Give us the grace to see Your divine purpose in our lives. Amen.

The Path of Integrity

ADULT TOPIC: Choosing the Path of Integrity
YOUTH TOPIC: The Path of Integrity
CHILDREN'S TOPIC: Do Good to Others

DEVOTIONAL READING: Proverbs 10:27-32
BACKGROUND SCRIPTURE: Proverbs 11
PRINT PASSAGE: Proverbs 11:1-14

KEY VERSE

The integrity of the upright shall guide them: but the perverseness of transgressors shall destroy them.
—Proverbs 11:3

Proverbs 11:1-14—KJV

A FALSE balance is abomination to the LORD: but a just weight is his delight.

2 When pride cometh, then cometh shame: but with the lowly is wisdom.

3 The integrity of the upright shall guide them: but the perverseness of transgressors shall destroy them.

4 Riches profit not in the day of wrath: but righteousness delivereth from death.

5 The righteousness of the perfect shall direct his way: but the wicked shall fall by his own wickedness.

6 The righteousness of the upright shall deliver them: but transgressors shall be taken in their own naughtiness.

7 When a wicked man dieth, his expectation shall perish: and the hope of unjust men perisheth.

8 The righteous is delivered out of trouble, and the wicked cometh in his stead.

9 An hypocrite with his mouth destroyeth his neighbour: but through knowledge shall the just be delivered.

10 When it goeth well with the righteous, the city rejoiceth: and when the wicked perish, there is shouting.

OBJECTIVES

Upon the completion of this lesson, students should realize that:

1. There is a difference between the letter of the law and the spirit of the law.

2. In order for faith to be valid, our behavior must match our belief.

3. Honest people sometimes suffer, while dishonest persons sometimes prosper as a fact of human experiences.

11 By the blessing of the upright the city is exalted: but it is overthrown by the mouth of the wicked.

12 He that is void of wisdom despiseth his neighbour: but a man of understanding holdeth his peace.

13 A talebearer revealeth secrets: but he that is of a faithful spirit concealeth the matter.

14 Where no counsel is, the people fall: but in the multitude of counsellors there is safety.

Proverbs 11:1-14—NRSV

A FALSE balance is an abomination to the LORD, but an accurate weight is his delight.

2 When pride comes, then comes disgrace; but wisdom is with the humble.

3 The integrity of the upright guides them, but the crookedness of the treacherous destroys them.

4 Riches do not profit in the day of wrath, but righteousness delivers from death.

5 The righteousness of the blameless keeps their ways straight, but the wicked fall by their own wickedness.

6 The righteousness of the upright saves them, but the treacherous are taken captive by their schemes.

7 When the wicked die, their hope perishes, and the expectation of the godless comes to nothing.

8 The righteous are delivered from trouble, and the wicked get into it instead.

9 With their mouths the godless would destroy their neighbors, but by knowledge the righteous are delivered.

10 When it goes well with the righteous, the city rejoices; and when the wicked perish, there is jubilation.

11 By the blessing of the upright a city is exalted, but it is overthrown by the mouth of the wicked.

12 Whoever belittles another lacks sense, but an intelligent person remains silent.

13 A gossip goes about telling secrets, but one who is trustworthy in spirit keeps a confidence.

14 Where there is no guidance, a nation falls, but in an abundance of counselors there is safety.

POINTS TO BE EMPHASIZED
ADULTS
Key Verse: Proverbs 11:3

Print: Proverbs 11:1-14

—The Lord considers deception as an abomination.

—Some adults discover that the workplace encourages them to do things that lack integrity.

—Integrity gives people a way to live, while pride and dishonesty will destroy a life.

—Providing wise guidance to people is an important duty for all Christians.

YOUTH
Key Verse: Proverbs 11:3

Print: Proverbs 11:1-14

—The Lord respects and is happy with people who are honest.

—A life of integrity is a transparent life that reflects what is factual, genuine and illuminating.

—Wisdom leads to humility and integrity.

—A leader's integrity, or the lack of it, can make a tremendous impact on those whom he leads.

CHILDREN
Key Verse: Proverbs 3:27
Print: Proverbs 3:27-31; 11:13, 25; 14:29; 19:22; 20:11

—The Scriptures instruct us on how to treat others with respect.

—Pride and dishonesty are negative traits that we must overcome.

—Dishonesty and pride can destroy personal integrity.

—Goals for conduct include doing good things and helping others.

TOPICAL OUTLINE OF THE LESSON

I. INTRODUCTION
   A. The Value of Righteousness
   B. Biblical Background

II. EXPOSITION AND APPLICATION OF THE SCRIPTURE
   A. An Inner Inventory *(Proverbs 11:1-3)*
   B. The Wide Reach of Righteousness *(Proverbs 11:4-14)*

III. SPECIAL FEATURES
   A. Preserving Our Heritage
   B. Concluding Reflections

I. INTRODUCTION
A. The Value of Righteousness

Would you consider yourself to be a righteous person? The central concept showcased in Proverbs 11 is righteousness. This is a term that is not frequently used in contemporary times even within the church. In fact, the average Christian would probably not consider himself or herself to be righteous. Most people would reserve that description for someone deemed to be a "Super Saint." Even though many may see it this way today, the Scriptures do not make such a distinction. Biblically speaking, righteousness is a spiritual and moral characteristic that is expected from and achievable by all who have the Spirit of God living on the inside. The book of Proverbs refers to the word "righteousness" some twenty-one times. Indeed, the rest of the Old and New Testaments are sprinkled with references to righteousness.

The first occurrence is in Genesis 15:6, where we see that Abraham believed God and it was credited to him as righteousness. This establishes the fact that sheer belief in God is a very necessary prerequisite for righteousness. In the New Testament, the book of Romans offers an extended exposition on righteousness in chapter 3. In what almost appears to be contradictory points of view, Paul affirms that there is no one righteous, not even one (Romans 3:10). Later in 4:5, Paul states, "To the man who does not work but trusts God who justifies the wicked, his faith is credited as righteousness." The key element here is the presence of two different kinds, or sources, of righteousness. One source of righteousness comes from the Law and is essentially self-made righteousness. This is the kind of self-righteousness so piously displayed by the Pharisees and Sadducees. Jesus roundly and bluntly condemned this self-centered style of righteousness: "For I tell you that unless your righteousness surpasses that of the Pharisees and the teachers of the law, you will certainly not enter the kingdom of heaven" (Matthew 5:20). Although works are an expected part of righteousness, works cannot be the source of one's righteousness. When righteousness starts from God and continues to flow from God, works will be a natural by-product of the process.

B. Biblical Background

In the context of Proverbs 11, the word "righteous" or "righteousness" comes from the Hebrew root word *tsaw-dak,* which means to be right (in a moral or forensic sense), to cleanse, clear self and to be or do justly *(Strong's Exhaustive Concordance).* To be righteous is to meet or exceed the standards of that which is just and right from God's perspective. Another word used in Scripture to describe the character of righteous individuals is the word "just." Let us consider two biblical examples of men who were considered to be just men. Genesis 6:9 records that Noah was a just man—perfect or blameless among his contemporaries. The passage also adds that he walked with God. David was a righteous man who was considered to be a man after God's own heart. Finally in the New Testament, Joseph, the husband of Mary, did not publicly expose Mary's pregnancy because he was a "just" man. It is possible that Joseph died before Jesus reached maturity because we do not hear anymore from him in Scripture. But in the lives of the Old Testament's "just men," there are plenty of moral errors to be observed. After the flood, Noah got drunk and naked, and his sons were forced to cover him in that condition. David, of course, committed adultery and became an accessory to murder. Yet, these men were still considered righteous in the sight of God. Although this may seem like a contradictory standard, the truth is that man looks on the outward appearance, but God looks on the heart.

As is reflected in Proverbs 11, righteousness is a characteristic that is valuable in all walks of life— from spirituality, to business, to family life, and beyond. Jesus said that the person who hungers and thirsts after righteousness is blessed and will be filled with this valuable commodity. The Scripture allows very little toleration for those who choose to appear righteous in one arena of life, but are unrighteous in the other areas of life. The key concept here is consistency and integrity. In the book of Revelation, the characteristic of integrity is highlighted in the message to the church at Laodicea: "I know your deeds, that you are neither cold nor hot. I wish you were either one or the other! So, because you are lukewarm—neither hot nor cold—I am about to spit you out of my mouth." The message is simple: Wherever you are, be who you are. We must move away from segmenting our spiritual experience and reserving it for Sunday mornings only. The Spirit of God desires to permeate all our life's experiences and to make an impact wherever we may go.

II. EXPOSITION AND APPLICATION OF THE SCRIPTURE
A. An Inner Inventory
(Proverbs 11:1-3)

Chapter 11 delves deeply into the psyche of a human being and deftly explores the mindset and motives of the inner self. A central concept in this chapter is that God cannot be excluded from the everyday affairs of life. In verse 1, God's position is made clear regarding dishonest weights. In the business and trade arena of that day, stone weights were used in conjunction with a scale to determine the weight and the cost of silver or other items being sold. Unscrupulous sellers sometimes "fixed" the weights and scale to make it register incorrectly in their favor. Proverbs singles out this unfair practice and acknowledges God's displeasure with it.

A righteous person reflects an attitude of personal humility (11:2). One who persists in practicing a pattern of pride is putting himself or herself on a pathway to personal peril. Our job is to humble ourselves, but it is God's job to exalt us. If we perform God's job, God is then forced to perform our job. But if we perform our job, God will always perform God's job. Pride points toward a disgraceful conclusion, but humility engenders wisdom. There is no spiritual ability without personal humility.

The word *integrity* is defined as adherence to moral and ethical principles (11:3). A person with integrity reflects soundness of morality, honesty and character that is wholly unimpaired *(Webster's Encyclopedic Unabridged Dictionary)*. The value of this important inner quality goes far beyond a person simply being considered to be nice. Like the compass

The day of wrath is any life-threatening disaster. In such danger, riches are of no use; value attaches itself only to that which assures ultimate protection—righteousness. "An hypocrite with his mouth": the difference between impiety and righteousness is so great that what is expressed by the godless harms others, whereas what is not expressed (knowledge) by the righteous benefits them. The statement that wisdom is more important than beauty is evaluating woman. Ear and nose rings were common adornments of women. The comparison to a pig seems to have been made on the basis of sound as well as humorous incongruity—"a ring of god in the snout of a pig." The persistent quest for what is good is ultimately a search that ends in gaining divine favor—hence: to seek happiness, seek excellence. To seek evil means that trouble will seek you out. Note that pride in condemnation and humility is praised; to be *humble* means "walking humbly before God." *Perverse* means "to turn aside." Godless man implies turning away from the right, and so profane or impure. Righteousness is the basis for salvation and a long life, whereas wickedness leads to death and destruction.

on a ship, personal integrity becomes an inner trustworthy guide that assists in helping us to make crucial decisions and in pointing us in the right direction. This trait is contrasted with duplicity that ends up in a state of moral shipwreck.

B. The Wide Reach of Righteousness
(Proverbs 11:4-14)

There is much written in the Scripture concerning the subject of money and wealth. Perhaps the most well-known biblical passage concerning wealth is found in 1 Timothy 6:10: "The love of money is the root of all evil." The main premise of this often misunderstood and misinterpreted passage is not that money is evil in itself, but that when money becomes one's main motive and central focus exalted above God and others, many problems tend to occur (11:4). Prosperity for the righteous is a welcome reality because they know how to keep it in the proper perspective, as will be seen in verse 10.

Verses 5, 6 and 8 are very similar to verse 3 in intent and direction. Everyone operates from some source of inner motivation and propulsion in order to give his or her life direction. Righteousness points up in a straight direction leading to life and peace. Wickedness points down in a crooked direction leading to danger and death. Verse 6 presents a picture of a trap that was commonly set to capture a bird or other animals. Evil desires serve as a trap that ensnares; but the upright are delivered from danger and escape the trap by exercising righteousness. The trouble that was intended for the righteous one is redirected toward the wicked one. The steps of the righteous person are ordered by God. Therefore, what the enemy of the righteous meant for evil actually turns out for their good.

Verses 7 and 10 share a common theme and subject matter. Both verses are concerned with the death of the wicked. For those without hope, death is the end—and all the material gain that has been so painstakingly acquired simply evaporates. In Jewish culture, death universally signaled a time for great mourning. Not only did mourning occur, but it was typically accompanied with the wearing of sackcloth and the application of ashes to the head. To express joy or happiness at the death of someone would have been the height of dishonor and disrespect. Yet, the writer of the text asserts that when the wicked die, there are shouts of joy.

The importance of one's words is highlighted in verses 9, 11-13. Unrighteous words are depicted as a weapon of the godless. This concept is also echoed in several other places throughout the Scripture. Regarding the tongue, James 3:6 records: "The tongue also is a fire, a world of evil among the parts of the body. It corrupts the whole person, sets the whole course of his life on fire, and is itself set on fire by hell." Although small, the tongue can contribute to anyone's fall. The mouth is capable of issuing blessings as well as curses. Blessings build people up and exalt cities. Negative talk destroys minds and poisons people. One of the most practically useful characteristics of a worthwhile friend is the ability to keep secrets and to maintain confidences (11:13). Gossip is the communication tool of the weak-minded person. But the righteous exercise discipline and forgo the urge to spread rumors.

This section closes with encouragement to include trusted friends and advisors in one's social circle of fellowship. Many people fall and make mistakes because they attempt to do it all alone. This advice is not just for nations, but also for individuals.

III. Special Features
A. Preserving Our Heritage

The writer of Proverbs recognized the special and significant connection between divinity and creativity. God is the source of creativity, and God gets pleasure from enabling and observing the creative process. The book of Genesis records that God took the animals to Adam in order to see what he would name them. Just as a human father receives great gratification from observing the creative process of his children, so our heavenly Father thoroughly enjoys when we flow in the gifts and abilities that we have been given. At the risk of sounding prejudiced, it seems that African Americans have somehow been given an extra measure of grace in order to excel in practically every phase of the arts, sports and academics. Having special ability is great, but it is not enough. Like a wild, untrained stallion, raw talent may be beautiful to the eyes, but it is not truly useful unless it is harnessed and trained. We must train our minds to view problems and obstacles like a bodybuilder views weights: although there is definite discomfort present, the results of the training far outweigh the pain and inconvenience of doing the exercise.

B. Concluding Reflections

Those who choose to live a life of righteousness are rewarded with an abundance of wisdom and a life of stability. Proverbs 10:28 records that one of the by-products of a righteous life is the characteristic of joy. Joy is not mere happiness, because happiness is dependent upon favorable circumstances. Joy requires a much greater element of depth because joy remains in effect regardless of the outer circumstances. Joy is the God-driven inner resolve to smile even when there seems to be little or no reason to do so. Once the tree of righteousness has been planted in our lives, we must then begin to water it daily through our thoughts, our words and our walk. When a sufficient amount of time has transpired to allow the sunshine of perseverance to test our resolve, an abundance of fruit will come forth. Righteousness is not just about the one who is righteous. It is also for those around us who will be impacted by our faithfulness and it is also for the benefit of the kingdom of God.

Righteousness is more than inward piety or in acting a way that is superior to the standards of the community in which ones lives. In fact, righteousness is acting in accord with divine or moral law whereby one is free from sin and guilt. In a commercial culture wherein honest in business transaction is essential for the buyer, Proverbs stresses "Just weights" as that in which the Lord delights. This is righteousness in practice as contrasted with wickedness and treachery, and it is rightfully embellished by the conception of "being humble." The humble man looks for nothing but justice; has the meanest opinion of himself; expect nothing in the way of commendation or praise; and can never be disappointed but in receiving praise, which he neither expects not desires." (*Clarke's Commentary*). The implication here is that should one seek personal recognition and gain, then there may be occasion to compromise one's integrity to attain that which is desired. While righteousness is the divine requisite by which one should relate to others, integrity prevents that relationship from being appropriated for one's own advantage.

HOME DAILY BIBLE 📖 READINGS
for the week of May 21, 2006

The Path of Integrity

May 15, Monday
—Proverbs 10:27-32
—God's Way Is a Stronghold
May 16, Tuesday
—Proverbs 11:1-5
—Wisdom, Not Pride
May 17, Wednesday
—Proverbs 11:6-10
—Righteousness, Not Treachery
May 18, Thursday
—Proverbs 11:11-15
—The Importance of Guidance and Counsel
May 19, Friday
—Proverbs 11:16-21
—Blameless Ways, Not Wickedness
May 20, Saturday
—Proverbs 11:22-26
—Generosity, Not Stinginess
May 21, Sunday
—Proverbs 11:27-31
—Goodness, Not Evil

PRAYER
Eternal God, You have created us to live in community wherein we share each other's woes and burdens as well as participate in the achievement of our highest communal aspirations. In and through it all, may our actions be governed by Your will that we may become what You would have us be. Amen.

Lesson 13

Living Out Wisdom

ADULT TOPIC: Living Out Wisdom
YOUTH TOPIC: Wise Women
CHILDREN'S TOPIC: Obey Your Parents

DEVOTIONAL READING: Proverbs 4:10-15
BACKGROUND SCRIPTURE: Proverbs 31
PRINT PASSAGE: Proverbs 31:8-14, 25-30

Proverbs 31:8-14, 25-30—KJV

8 Open thy mouth for the dumb in the cause of all such as are appointed to destruction.

9 Open thy mouth, judge righteously, and plead the cause of the poor and needy.

10 Who can find a virtuous woman? for her price is far above rubies.

11 The heart of her husband doth safely trust in her, so that he shall have no need of spoil.

12 She will do him good and not evil all the days of her life.

13 She seeketh wool, and flax, and worketh willingly with her hands.

14 She is like the merchants' ships; she bringeth her food from afar.

.....

25 Strength and honour are her clothing; and she shall rejoice in time to come.

26 She openeth her mouth with wisdom; and in her tongue is the law of kindness.

27 She looketh well to the ways of her household, and eateth not the bread of idleness.

UNIT III
Lessons in Living

CHILDREN'S UNIT
Wise Sayings to Guide Us

KEY VERSE

Favour is deceitful, and beauty is vain: but a woman that feareth the LORD, she shall be praised.
—Proverbs 31:30

OBJECTIVES

Upon completion of this lesson, students will understand that:

1. Parents are responsible to train and teach their children both by word and example.
2. Showing gratitude to others can become a manifestation of faith.
3. People who demonstrate their faith in a public manner may lead others to embrace faith in God.

28 Her children arise up, and call her blessed; her husband also, and he praiseth her.

29 Many daughters have done virtuously, but thou excellest them all.

30 Favour is deceitful, and beauty is vain: but a woman that feareth the LORD, she shall be praised.

Proverbs 31:8-14, 25-30—NRSV

8 Speak out for those who cannot speak, for the rights of all the destitute.

9 Speak out, judge righteously, defend the rights of the poor and needy.

10 A capable wife who can find? She is far more precious than jewels.

11 The heart of her husband trusts in her, and he will have no lack of gain.

12 She does him good, and not harm, all the days of her life.

13 She seeks wool and flax, and works with willing hands.

14 She is like the ships of the merchant, she brings her food from far away.

.....

25 Strength and dignity are her clothing, and she laughs at the time to come.

26 She opens her mouth with wisdom, and the teaching of kindness is on her tongue.

27 She looks well to the ways of her household, and does not eat the bread of idleness.

28 Her children rise up and call her happy; her husband too, and he praises her:

29 "Many women have done excellently, but you surpass them all."

30 Charm is deceitful, and beauty is vain, but a woman who fears the LORD is to be praised.

POINTS TO BE EMPHASIZED
ADULTS
Key Verse: Proverbs 31:30
Print: Proverbs 31:8-14, 25-30
—A wise woman is trusted and works hard.
—A wise woman is not afraid of the future and takes time to teach kindness.
—The fear of the Lord can be the basis for praising others.
—Persons may live our wisdom by defending the rights of those less fortunate than we are.

YOUTH
Key Verse: Proverbs 31:30
Print: Proverbs 31:8-14, 25-30
—A person who lives a life of honor should be praised.
—Social action is a necessity to assure the welfare of the needy and powerless in one's community.
—A virtuous person fits the description as recorded in Proverbs 31.
—Persons who are loyal to God and others should be respected.

CHILDREN
Key: Proverbs 6:20
Print: Proverbs 4:1-5; 6:20; 31:10, 26-28
—It is important to listen to and to follow the advice of wise parents.
—The qualities of a God-fearing mother can be found in Proverbs 31.

—Parents have a responsibility for wisely guiding and teaching their children.

—Godly parents can provide a loving home environment in which children feel secure.

TOPICAL OUTLINE OF THE LESSON

I. Introduction
   A. Women in the Bible
   B. Biblical Background

II. Exposition and Application of the Scripture
   A. Protecting the Needy *(Proverbs 31:8-9)*
   B. A Wife of Noble Character *(Proverbs 31:10-14)*
   C. Strong and Dignified *(Proverbs 31:25-30)*

III. Special Features
   A. Preserving Our Heritage
   B. Concluding Reflections

I. Introduction

A. Women in the Bible

Can you identify a woman in your past or present who has made a positive impact on you or has played a part in helping to shape your life? Ancient Israel was a patriarchal society wherein families and public culture were male-dominated. Women had few legal rights and were excluded from participation in many of the affairs within the religious hierarchy. Women were highly susceptible to abuse and misuse due to the very limited amount of social and legal rights and recourses afforded to them. Although they lived in an atmosphere of gender discrimination, the Scripture reveals that they still made a considerable impact upon their family life and upon society in general. Women are prominently featured throughout the Bible as involved in various roles and responsibilities including the positions of matriarch, prophetess, queen, judge, intercessor, entrepreneur, wife and mother. Below are some names to go with some of these categories *(The Complete Bible Handbook).*

Matriarchs: Sarah, Rebekah, Rachael and Leah
Prophetess: Miriam, Deborah, Huldah, Anna, and the four daughters of Phillip the evangelist as recorded in Acts 21:8-9.
Queen: Vashti, Esther, unnamed Queen of Sheba, and Candace
Judge: Deborah
Entrepreneur: Lydia

The prominent roles occupied by these and other women of the Scripture demonstrate the capacity of women to accomplish whatever God desircs and designs for them to become. In this study, we will examine some specific characteristics of an ideal woman from the perspective of Proverbs.

B. Biblical Background

Proverbs 31 is attributed to King Lemuel. This brief passage does not originate from an Israelite source. Consequently, other than this reference, particulars about King Lemuel are unknown. The book of Proverbs sometimes portrays women from a negative perspective as well as from a positive perspective. A contentious woman is described as an undesirable wife in Proverbs 19:13, 21:9, 25:24 and 27:15. Another negative prototype is presented in Proverbs 1-9 as well as 3, 22:14, 23:27, 27:13 and 29:3. In Proverbs 6:20—7:27, the longest section of the book deals frankly with the dilemma of illicit sexual experimentation (fornication or adultery). This issue is addressed so openly and so descriptively simply because it was, and still is, a real issue even within the church. The voice of wisdom speaks so candidly "not to titillate the passions of the reader, as so much modern literature does, but to portray the disillusionment of illicit love and its certain end in unquenchable remorse and bitter death" *(The Interpreter's Bible Commentary).* However, Proverbs' positive presentations of the woman outshine the negative. The ideal of the wise men was monogamy, which is definitely encouraged in 5:15-19." *(The Interpreter's Commentary,* Proverbs 31:10-31). The student is exhorted to "Drink waters from your own cistern, flowing water from your own well. (Ancient imagery compared marital sexual pleasure to drinking from a spring or well.) Should your springs be scattered abroad, streams of water in the streets? Let them be for yourself alone, and not for strangers with you. Let your fountain be blessed, and rejoice in the wife of your youth, a lovely hind, a graceful doe."

Much of the writing style and imagery used to convey King Lemuel's perspective on a proper marital relationship is quite reminiscent of writings found in the Song of Solomon or Song of Songs. There, Solomon writes, "How beautiful you are, my darling! Oh how beautiful! Your eyes behind your veil are doves. Your hair is like a flock of goats descending from Mt. Gilead. Your teeth are (white) like a flock of sheep just shorn, coming up for washing…Your lips are like scarlet ribbon; your mouth is lovely." Of course, Solomon goes into much more detail in this graphic description of his bride/wife. First Kings 11:1 records that Solomon "loved many foreign women besides Pharaoh's daughter—Moabites,

Ammonites, Edo-mites, Sidonians and Hittites." His life in this area gives new meaning to the term "trophy wife." It is interesting to note that even with all his wives and concubines, Solomon eventually recognized the value of a godly, faithful, marital relationship with one man and one woman.

II. Exposition and Application of the Scripture

A. Protecting the Needy
(Proverbs 31:8-9)

Even though he is a king and probably has access to an overabundance of possessions to satisfy his every need, it is obvious that King Lemuel also has a tender and compassionate heart for those within society who are less fortunate than others. In verse 8, he spotlights the importance to speak up or take up for those who for some reason are not able to speak up or take up for themselves. This category does not literally refer to those who are physically unable to talk. King Lemuel seeks to activate the social action conscience and consciousness of the student/reader. The literal translation for the phrase "left desolate" used in verse 8b is "sons of passing away." On many occasions throughout the Scripture, references are made to God's concern for those who have experienced considerable pain and loss in life. James 1:27 records: "Religion that God our Father accepts as pure and faultless is this: to look after orphans and widows in their distress and to keep one-self from being polluted by the world." Verse 9 repeats and concludes the references to the need for sensitivity to defending the rights of the poor and needy.

When it comes to assisting the needy, many people tend to adopt an attitude that is passive at best and distant/repulsive at worst. Most of us wait for those in need to come to us...then, we may just give a contribution as long as we don't have to get sweaty or get our hands soiled. Jesus assumed quite a different posture. He did not wait for someone in need to ask Him for service. In His first public reading of the Scripture, He displayed His heart for the disadvantaged by reading from Isaiah 61:1-2: "The Spirit of the Sovereign LORD is on me, because the LORD has anointed me to preach good news to the poor. He has sent me to bind up the brokenhearted, to proclaim freedom for the captives and release from darkness for the prisoners, to proclaim the year of the LORD's favor." At the Last Supper, when Jesus unexpectedly washed the disciples' feet, He said to them: "Now that I, your Lord and Teacher, have washed your feet, you also should wash one another's feet. I have set you an example that you should do as I have done for you" (John 13:14-15).

B. A Wife of Noble Character
(Proverbs 31:10-14)

The Epilogue for the book of Proverbs is an acrostic poem that extols the virtues of a noble wife who is the epitome of wisdom and the personification of godly womanhood. The primary emphasis is not placed upon this woman's exterior appearance. Unlike the adulteress described in chapter 7, any physical beauty or outer adornments are secondary to the primary attribute of her godly character. Physical beauty fades. Garments and jewelry can be lost, go out of style or wear out. But a woman with good character and wisdom has the power of God within her to take her beyond her personal limitations. Therefore, she need not worry about wearing rubies to impress others because her value exceeds any piece of jewelry.

In verse 11, the focus shifts from the noble wife, to the perspective of her husband. Any man worth his salt recognizes the great value of a good woman. Husbands and wives who are called by God to be purposefully joined together should never view the other as a threat. The purpose of marriage is not to compete with each other, but to help complete each other. Marriage is the institution designed by God to blend two distinct individuals into one. Therefore, when one spouse excels, both of them are blessed. Only an insecure man would be threatened by the accomplishments of his wife. Since this Proverbs woman walks in wisdom, she understands that part of her purpose regarding her husband is to always "do him good" rather than harm (verse 12).

The character of this woman is not just passive character. She is not just a holy woman who lounges around the house all day. Sister girl is busy! She exquisitely demonstrates her capacity to match her holiness with hard work. This woman uses her gifts to accomplish her destiny. Not every woman may be able to work with her hands like this woman. Perhaps another godly woman may work with her mind, but still achieve the equivalent of selecting wool, flax and food from afar (13-14, 27). She cheerfully takes responsibility for the duties within the household that she is uniquely designed to fulfill.

C. Strong and Dignified
(Proverbs 31:25-30)

Verse 25 gives a description of this wise woman's wardrobe. Her "fashions" of choice are strength and dignity. These two character traits present the very balanced approach to life that is adopted by this woman. Some women may be strong, but lack dignity. Others may be dignified, but lack strength. The Scriptures reflect a pattern of avoiding extremes in everything except in our extreme love and overboard obedience to God. The reason that this woman can "laugh" at the days to come is because she places her trust in God and therefore has no reason to fear the future.

One of the biggest challenges for some women may be to exercise discipline and control over the tongue. Most females are (from childhood) more verbally skilled than males, and just like anything that has power, it can be used positively or negatively. This particular woman has chosen to harness her tongue to build people up rather than to tear people down (26). Her words are well-seasoned and she does not give in to the urge to say whatever she feels. A wise woman realizes that some things, even though true, are better left unsaid. This ability to weigh her words is a skill that enables her to offer faithful instruction rather than verbal destruction.

In verse 28, the focus shifts to yet another aspect of the family—the children. Parents are considered by God to be the stewards of their children, and this role and responsibility should be taken very seriously. In 1 Timothy 3:4-5, Paul writes to Timothy regarding the necessary characteristics for spiritual leaders within the church; he provides these guidelines: "He must manage his own family well and see that his children obey him with proper respect. (If anyone does not know how to manage his own family, how can he take care of God's church?)" The Proverbs woman obviously manages her household in an admirable manner. Consequently, her children, as well as her husband, verbally express their appreciation. Sometimes, a simple "thank you" goes a long way. Women, wives and mothers should never be taken for granted for all the many things that they do for others. Just because something may be the role of a woman does not mean that they never need acknowledgement or appreciation for a cooked meal or a cleaned house. Even more, it would not hurt to do their usual task in their stead from time to time.

One cardinal rule in relating to women is that they usually prefer not to be compared to someone else. However, in this case, King Lemuel gets away with it by elevating this woman above many other women who may do noble things (29). Here, the *being* is elevated above the mere doing. A woman with charm can achieve that trait by attending classes and practicing what she sees others performing. Consequently, just because a person seems charming does not mean that she possesses godly character. The litmus test provided by King Lemuel is the fear of the Lord. This kind of fear does not involve fright, but deep reverence, respect and obedience toward the God who is the Giver of all wisdom.

III. SPECIAL FEATURES
A. Preserving Our Heritage

In his book *Race Matters*, Cornel West cites three ways in which Black women have been negatively stereotyped: "There is Jezebel (the seductive temptress), Sapphira (the evil manipulator), and Aunt Jemima (the sexless, long-suffering nurturer)." The problem with all stereotypes is that they fall short of capturing the true, holistic essence and variety of that which they attempt to represent. Historically, Blacks have been characterized not in a framework of humanity, but in a framework of caricature. (Chris Jackson, *Dating and Sexuality*). Historically, Black women have been the backbone of the Black community and have been present to lend support, love and endless encouragement. They have been the superglue of the family unit, and without their cooperation and perseverance, it is difficult to imagine the current state of the Black family. Black women should be celebrated and appreciated for all that they have done in the past and are doing in the present to contribute to the functionality of the Black family and community. From grandmothers to godmothers, from mothers to aunts, from teachers to church ladies and many other categories, we credit Black women today for birthing us, raising us, praising us, believing in us and helping us to reach the potential they knew we had inside.

B. Concluding Reflections

The world is a better place because of conscientious women who have walked in wisdom and obeyed the voice of God. In an essay on the Proverbs 31 woman, Sheila Graham writes: "The Proverbs 31 woman is spiritually strong and her life exhibits the Word of God. She begins with faith, seeks His wisdom, and everything else falls into place as she builds upon that solid foundation. She is trustworthy, generous, competent and shrewd, and it is by those traits that the world knows her faith." (Sheila Graham, 2003 Worldwide Church of God).

The truth is that the characteristics outlined in Proverbs 31 are also advisable for men. The world could use a few Proverbs 31 men! Holiness has no gender barriers. Colossians 3:23-24 reminds us, "Whatever you do, work at it with all your heart, as working for the Lord, not for men, since you know that you will receive an inheritance from the Lord as a reward. It is the Lord Christ you are serving."

HOME DAILY BIBLE 📖 READINGS

for the week of May 28, 2006
Living Out Wisdom

May 22, Monday
—Proverbs 4:1-9
—Advice for Children
May 23, Tuesday
—Proverbs 4:10-15
—Keep on the Right Path
May 24, Wednesday
—Proverbs 10:18-23
—Wise People Value Wise Conduct
May 25, Thursday
—Proverbs 31:1-9
—Advice from a Mother
May 26, Friday
—Proverbs 31:10-15
—Portrait of a Capable Wife
May 27, Saturday
—Proverbs 31:16-23
—What an Ideal Wife Is Like
May 28, Sunday
—Proverbs 31:24-31
—A Good Wife and Mother

PRAYER

Eternal God, You have granted us wisdom through Your Word, which was made flesh in Jesus Christ, our Savior. Grant that we may not demean Your love, but demonstrate Your will in every facet of our daily living. In Jesus' name, we pray. Amen.

Called to Be a Christian Community

GENERAL INTRODUCTION

The three units in this quarter will focus on Paul's letters to the Corinthians. They are highly practical letters designed to address various concerns and problems that plagued a church that was struggling to be the people of God in a lost world. The insights are not limited to the first century, but are applicable to Christians attempting to live as God's people today.

Unit I, *Servants of God,* contains four lessons that focus on selected passages from First Corinthians. These lessons explore how the Christian community becomes God's servant people through demonstrating unity, wisdom, togetherness and ministry. These lessons will occasion discussion on the continuous problems of commitment to human leaders rather than commitment to Christ. The parallels between the divisions within the Corinthian church and our present disunity become apparent as the faith community seeks to promote unity and reconciliation. While the Holy Spirit assists Christians in dealing with these problems, our plight is made more simple when we have "the mind of Christ" as the inspiration for our undertaking. During this unit, we shall come to understand the nature of the church, whose foundation is Christ, and the role and function of those who participate within it as fellow workers with God and servants to one another. As a matter of fact, any human leader that God uses to edify the church is a servant of God's larger purpose. We shall come face-to-face with the reality that being a Christian does not guarantee a trouble-free life—we invite trouble into our lives when we commit to Christ as Lord and Savior.

Unit II, *Called to Obedience,* has five lessons based on passages from First Corinthians. The lessons examine how members of the Christian community are called to be in relationship, to help the weak, to "win the race," to work for the common good, and to love one another. This unit provides opportunity to honestly discuss the issue of divorce, how one's relationship to a spouse may affect one's relationship to God, how respect for the other person's wishes should be affirmed without compromising one's own integrity, and God's design for marriage that is being challenged by contemporary culture. The unit provides opportunity to discuss acceptable accommodation with culture and unacceptable compromises that arise for the church when the Gospel encounters a new cultural context in which it is obliged to function. The question is when to give up personal rights and privileges for the sake of the greater good that becomes a ministry to others since the church as the body of Christ is composed of many members with various gifts and dispositions. While Christians are free, those who make poor choices will suffer the consequences thereof. The final lesson in this unit focuses on faith, hope and love as the enduring character marks of the Christ life.

Unit III, *The Spirit of Giving,* has four lessons based on selected passages from Second Corinthians, dealing with the spirit of giving as an essential part of life within the Christian community. The lessons explore the nature of giving by focusing on the themes of forgiveness, generosity, witness, and the grace of God. Herein, emphasis is upon one's attitudes and behavior toward others as an important step in expressing and accepting forgiveness. In the final analysis, the presence of Christ within the Christian community is necessary in inspiring and enabling forgiveness and reconciliation. The question may be raised, when Christians give expecting to be blessed, is this really giving? The final lesson in this unit places emphasis on the fact that Christians are not self-sufficient, but must constantly rely upon the grace of God to rectify or help us endure human frailties and weaknesses.

Because of the complex language Paul uses in these letters, the lessons for children are adapted to cover related themes. The general theme of what it means to live a Christian life within the church is reflected in these ways: Unit I focuses on growing spiritually; Unit II emphasizes obedience to God; and Unit III highlights joyful service.

Lesson 1

Servants of Unity

ADULT TOPIC: Living in Unity
YOUTH TOPIC: Let's Get Together!
CHILDREN'S TOPIC: Be Peaceful

UNIT I
Servants of God

CHILDREN'S UNIT
We Grow Spiritually

DEVOTIONAL READING: 1 Corinthians 1:2-9
BACKGROUND SCRIPTURE: 1 Corinthians 1:10-17
PRINT PASSAGE: 1 Corinthians 1:10-17

1 Corinthians 1:10-17—KJV

10 Now I beseech you, brethren, by the name of our Lord Jesus Christ, that ye all speak the same thing, and that there be no divisions among you; but that ye be perfectly joined together in the same mind and in the same judgment.

11 For it hath been declared unto me of you, my brethren, by them which are of the house of Chloe, that there are contentions among you.

12 Now this I say, that every one of you saith, I am of Paul; and I of Apollos; and I of Cephas; and I of Christ.

13 Is Christ divided? was Paul crucified for you? or were ye baptized in the name of Paul?

14 I thank God that I baptized none of you, but Crispus and Gaius;

15 Lest any should say that I had baptized in mine own name.

16 And I baptized also the household of Stephanas: besides, I know not whether I baptized any other.

17 For Christ sent me not to baptize, but to preach the gospel: not with wisdom of words, lest the cross of Christ should be made of none effect.

KEY VERSE

Now I beseech you, brethren, by the name of our Lord Jesus Christ, that ye all speak the same thing, and that there be no divisions among you; but that ye be perfectly joined together in the same mind and in the same judgment.—1 Corinthians 1:10

OBJECTIVES
Upon completion of this lesson, students are expected to:

1. Know more about the book of First Corinthians;

2. Understand the major problem of division that existed in the church;

3. Identify who informed the apostle about this and other problems; and,

4. Explain how Paul called for unity in the church.

1 Corinthians 1:10-17—NRSV

10 Now I appeal to you, brothers and sisters, by the name of our Lord Jesus Christ, that all of you be in agreement and that there be no divisions among you, but that you be united in the same mind and the same purpose.

11 For it has been reported to me by Chloe's people that there are quarrels among you, my brothers and sisters.

12 What I mean is that each of you says, "I belong to Paul," or "I belong to Apollos," or "I belong to Cephas," or "I belong to Christ."

13 Has Christ been divided? Was Paul crucified for you? Or were you baptized in the name of Paul?

14 I thank God that I baptized none of you except Crispus and Gaius,

15 so that no one can say that you were baptized in my name.

16 (I did baptize also the household of Stephanas; beyond that, I do not know whether I baptized anyone else.)

17 For Christ did not send me to baptize but to proclaim the gospel, and not with eloquent wisdom, so that the cross of Christ might not be emptied of its power.

POINTS TO BE EMPHASIZED
ADULTS
Key Verse: 1 Corinthians 1:10
Print: 1 Corinthians 1:10-17
—Paul called on the members of the church at Corinth to resolve their differences.
—Discuss the founding of the church at Corinth and Paul's return visit.
—Paul's proclamation of the Gospel is focused on Christ.
—The faith community should promote unity and reconciliation.

YOUTH
Key Verse: 1 Corinthians 1:10
Print: 1 Corinthians 1:10-17
—God's message of unity is much more important than any human messenger.
—Dissension within the group prevents the achievement of common goals.
—We follow Christ, rather than the person who brought us to Christ.
—Jesus will give us the right words to proclaim the cross of Christ.

CHILDREN
Key Verse: Mark 9:50
Print: Genesis 33:1-11; 1 Corinthians 1:10
—It was difficult for Esau and Jacob to interact after Jacob stole Esau's birthright.
—Jacob did not know what to expect when Esau returned from the fields.
—Once Jacob and Esau met again, they were reconciled and at peace with one another.
—The story of Jacob and Esau teaches us the difficulty that arises when one takes advantage of another.
—Paul appealed to the Corinthians to put away any divisions among church members and to become united in mind and purpose.

TOPICAL OUTLINE OF THE LESSON

I. INTRODUCTION
   A. Unity
   B. Biblical Background

II. EXPOSITION AND APPLICATION OF THE SCRIPTURE
   A. The Call to Unity
      (1 Corinthians 1:10)
   B. The Challenge to Unity
      (1 Corinthians 1:11-12)
   C. The Commitment to Unity
      (1 Corinthians 1:13-17)

III. SPECIAL FEATURES
   A. Preserving Our Heritage
   B. Concluding Reflections

I. INTRODUCTION
A. Unity

The one word that characterizes the church at Corinth is "division." All of their difficulties were rooted in the fact that they were divided doctrinally, spiritually, ecclesiastically, morally and socially. This division had eroded their Christian identity.

Understanding this problem and seeking to eradicate it from this congregation was one of the major challenges the apostle Paul faced. He knew that if they could amend their ways, their growth and development as a church would be unhindered. He charged this congregation *that there be no divisions among you.* Unity was what they needed.

Paul had received information concerning their dissensions. These dissensions had originated because they had aligned themselves with four major persons that had influences upon them. With four leaders recognized as heads in this church, the church was evolving into a "four-headed" monster, and not the organism united in bringing the kingdom of God into the lives of people. This division showed that they misunderstood their relationship with Christ, with their teachers (leaders), and with each other.

B. Biblical Background

The church at Corinth was established by the apostle Paul on his second missionary journey (see Acts 18). The city was known for the famous temple to Aphrodite, the Greek goddess of love. The temple normally housed some one thousand priestesses, who were religious prostitutes. The city was so notorious that to live like a Corinthian became synonymous with these and other ungodly practices. In 1 Corinthians 6:9-11, Paul lists the sins that were evident in the city and reminded the Corinthian Christians, "such were some of you."

In Corinth, Paul met tentmakers Aquila and Priscilla, a Jewish couple that had been exiled from Rome. He preached regularly in the synagogue there and soon a number of Gentiles and Jews believed Jesus Christ as Lord and Savior. Even the leader of the synagogue, Crispus, was converted, along with his household (Acts 18:8). Paul's ministry continued in Corinth for one-and-a-half years, as he taught "the word of God among them" (Acts 18:11).

Also mentioned in Paul's letter is Apollos (see Acts 18:24—19:1). He was "mighty in the Scriptures," but he knew "only the baptism of John" until he was mentored by Aquila and Priscilla who expounded "the way of God more perfectly." As a result, he received a letter of support from the church at Ephesus to the churches in Achaia, who wanted him to minister in that area.

The problems Paul addresses in this epistle are: division over leadership, immorality, lawsuits against a Christian brother, misunderstandings of marriage and celibacy, discredit of his apostleship, undervaluation of the Lord's Supper, misuse of spiritual gifts, and erroneous beliefs concerning the doctrine of the Resurrection.

II. EXPOSITION AND APPLICATION OF THE SCRIPTURE
A. The Call to Unity (1 Corinthians 1:10)

Now I beseech you, brethren, by the name of our Lord Jesus Christ, that ye all speak the same thing, and that there be no divisions among you; but that ye be perfectly joined together in the same mind and in the same judgment. The word "beseech" is better translated "exhort." It is from the same Greek word used of the Holy Spirit (see John 14:16, 26; 15:26; 16:7) and for "advocate" (see 1 John 2:1). The Greek word means "to come alongside to help." The apostle was coming alongside the Corinthians so that the sin of division and factions would not destroy them.

To help them to become amenable to his exhortation for unity, Paul stressed three important points. First, he called them *brethren.* This was to show that the Corinthians were members of the body of Christ—the church. It was also to show that both he and they shared the same relationship, as part of the family of God (see Ephesians 3:13-14).

Secondly, he used the possessive pronoun *our* in reference to the name of the Lord Jesus Christ. Here, he was emphasizing the ownership they all had—they both shared a common ownership that further bound them to each other.

Thirdly, to give credence and substance to his exhortation, Paul used *the name of our Lord Jesus Christ.* The authority of that name and the reverence they were to have for it would cause them to heed his exhortation. He would show that both he and the Corinthians fell under the authority of that name and were responsible for rendering obedience to it at all times. This is further evidenced by Paul's use of the title or name *Lord.* By calling Jesus Christ "Lord," he was establishing the fundamental truth about Him and His role in the church. "Jesus Christ is Lord" is the proclamation of all believers (see 1 Corinthians 12:3). In verses 1-9 of this first chapter, Paul calls Jesus Christ *Lord* in every verse except 1, 4, 5 and 6. And even in verses 4-6, the subject is still focused on Jesus' lordship. This emphasis on Jesus Christ as Lord was to appeal to their Christian loyalty (see Romans 15:30; 2 Thessalonians 4:12; 2 Timothy 2:3-4).

Paul invoked the name that would cause them to behave in a way that would bring glory and honor to all that it denoted.

Paul was exhorting them to *speak the same thing.* The Greek phrase is "that you all agree." Speaking the same thing means having agreement about what is preached, taught, sung and even written. It emphasizes an agreement in biblical doctrines. If there is to be unity in the church, it must start with sound, healthy doctrine.

This agreement would be evident when there were no longer any divisions among them. The Greek word translated "divisions" is better translated "schisms"—used to express a difference of opinion, a rent or tear (as in one's clothing), or an alienation of feeling. The congregation was literally torn apart as a piece of cloth.

Paul then said, *but be ye perfectly joined together.* The Greek word translated "perfectly joined together" can be translated "made complete." This word speaks of repairing, mending, or restoring broken nets, broken bones and dislocated joints (see Matthew 4:21; Galatians 6:1). The idea here is that of putting back together something that has been torn or broken. Paul would have the Corinthians "made complete," that is, put back together from the schisms or divisions that existed. He would have them united *in the same mind* (*mind,* here, probably means intellect or feelings) and *in the same judgment* (*judgment,* here, probably means opinion). Paul wanted them united in intellect, feelings and opinions. Our unity must be in like motives and principles, attitudes and opinions, beliefs and perspectives.

B. The Challenge to Unity
(1 Corinthians 1:11-12)

For it hath been declared unto me of you, my brethren, by them which are of the house of Chloe, that there are contentions among you. Paul exhorted them to unity because he had received reports of their division from *the house of Chloe.* Those of Chloe's household must have been reliable sources whom Paul believed to be trustworthy. Chloe was a Christian who seemed to be well-known and respected. Since Paul spent eighteen months in this city and in this church, he must have developed some very special relationships. Chloe's relationship with Paul appears to be on this order.

The Greek word translated "contentions" can also be translated "strifes" or "wranglings," which speaks of disputes, arguments and squabbles, even implying brawls and/or altercations. Verse 12 explains the basis for these contentions (verse 11) and divisions (verse 10).

Now this I say, that every one of you saith, I am of Paul; and I of Apollos; and I of Cephas; and I of Christ. The contentions reported by Chloe were based on church members aligning themselves under certain leaders or teachers. The church was divided into four basic groups: (1) those who followed Paul; (2) those who followed Apollos; (3) those who followed Cephas (Peter—cf., John 1:42); and (4) those who followed Christ. It seems that those who followed Christ were not seeking to give genuine allegiance to Him; rather, by using Christ's name, they were seeking to show their superiority over the other groups. If they were truly of Christ, they would have aligned themselves with the love that seeks reconciliation.

The list reveals the division of Jews and Gentiles. It appears that the Gentile converts claimed Paul as their leader and apostle; however, the Jewish converts gave allegiance to the authority of the apostle Peter. Since Apollos was a Jew

from Alexandria, and had distinguished himself with his eloquence, oratory and literary culture, it is likely that he appealed to the more educated and the philosophical among them. Both the Judaizers and the followers of Apollos rejected Paul. The Judaizers rejected him as an apostle; the followers of Apollos did not think much of Paul as a preacher. Meanwhile, those aligned with Christ considered themselves superior to all of them.

The divisions seemed to be based on the following: one faction followed Paul because of his edification; some followed Peter because of his ethnicity; some followed Apollos because of his education; and others followed Christ because they wanted exaltation.

C. The Commitment to Unity
(1 Corinthians 1:13-17)

These verses show Paul's commitment to the unity he advocated. *Is Christ divided? was Paul crucified for you? or were ye baptized in the name of Paul?* Paul fired a series of rhetorical questions. The answer to all of them is an obvious "No!" But their rhetorical nature does not diminish their importance. In fact, Paul set forth three fundamental truths concerning Christ's exclusive claim as Savior. *Is Christ divided?* In other words, "Is He unsure about who He is and what He came to do?" The answer, of course, is "No!" He is one (see John 17:21-22). *Was Paul crucified for you?* In other words, "Was it

Paul's blood that purchased your redemption?" The answer is "No!" Only Christ was crucified for us (Acts 2:22-23; 1 Corinthians 2:2; Romans 5:6-10). *Were ye baptized in the name of Paul?* No one had been baptized on the authority of Paul.

There are three truths Paul affirms in this verse that are exclusive to Christ: 1) Jesus is the Christ; 2) He redeemed us by His sacrificial death on the cross; and 3) we are consecrated to and identified with Him in water baptism. We cannot attribute these truths to anyone but Christ. And as Christ is undivided and incapable of division, so His church must reflect its founder and sustainer. In 1 Corinthians 12:12, Paul parallels the human body, which is made up of many parts, with the body of Christ.

This verse shows the significance of Christ's ministry to the believer's faith. The first part of the verse, *Is Christ divided?*, emphasizes Christ as the originator of our faith—He has the authority to do so. The second part of the verse, *Was Paul crucified for you?*, emphasizes Christ as the obtainer of our faith—He has secured our atonement. The third part of the verse, *Were ye baptized in the name of Paul?*, emphasizes Christ as the object of our faith—He is our administrator.

I thank God that I baptized none of you, but Crispus and Gaius; lest any should say that I had baptized in mine own name. And I baptized also the household of Stephanas: besides, I know not whether I baptized any other. Paul rejoiced that he baptized only a few converts in Corinth.

In so doing, he removed all pretenses that he was making disciples for himself. Therefore, the Corinthians could not put him in Christ's place. Although it was commanded by the Lord that His apostles baptize (see Matthew 28:19), Paul rejoiced that his ministry to the Corinthians resulted in him only baptizing a few of them. His writing indicates his interpretation that this was not accidental, but providential.

We know from Acts 18:8 that Crispus was the ruler of the Jewish synagogue in Corinth. He was among the first persons to be converted under Paul's preaching. His conversion resulted in many other persons being saved. According to Romans 16:23, Gaius was among those believers who hosted the apostle and showed him kindness. Since it is believed that Paul wrote this letter (Romans) from Corinth, it would be safe to assert that he was referring to this Gaius.

For Christ sent me not to baptize, but to preach the gospel: not with wisdom of words, lest the cross of Christ should be made of none effect. Here, Paul showed his commitment to the ministry to which he was called. He was not confused about his identity and role in the body of Christ. His ministry was to preach the Gospel. He was not diminishing the ordinance of baptism; rather, he was emphasizing the important role of preaching in his ministry. He shows that preaching was his *priority*. And, in 1 Corinthians 2:2, he showed his *passion* for preaching; Acts 20:18-20 showed his *perpetual practice* of preaching;

and in 2 Timothy 4:1-2, he showed his *purpose* in preaching.

He would let no one sway him from his ministry to proclaim the Word of God. Further, he would never be associated with anything that would destroy the unity and fellowship of the body of Christ.

III. SPECIAL FEATURES
A. Preserving Our Heritage

One of the sad commentaries of our history as Baptists is the many times we have multiplied by division. Our local churches, districts, state conventions, and even our beloved national convention have all fallen victim to this recurrence. Our challenge as Christian Black people is to hear and heed the message of Jesus and the appeal of the apostle Paul to "be of one mind and one spirit."

Our denomination is rich in tradition, steeped in adherence to sound doctrine, deeply committed to the relevance and power of the Scriptures, and possessing genuine love for the Lord. Let us harness our traditions and not allow the shadows of division to cover the great truth of our identity.

B. Concluding Reflections

Paul was determined to eradicate a major problem in the Corinthian church—division. But he would not just point out the problem; he would give ways and instructions as to how that problem should be dealt with. One of the purposes of this epistle was to bring a confused congregation into unity manifested by speaking the same thing and possessing the same mind and the same judgment. A divided church will always malfunction; a unified church will always bring production.

HOME DAILY BIBLE READINGS
for the week of June 4, 2006
Servants of Unity

May 29, Monday
—Romans 10:9–13
—God Is Lord of All
May 30, Tuesday
—Colossians 1:15–20
—We Are Reconciled in Christ
May 31, Wednesday
—Ephesians 4:1–6
—One Body and One Spirit
June 1, Thursday
—1 Corinthians 1:1–9
—Called Together in Christ
June 2, Friday
—1 Corinthians 1:10–17
—Be United in Christ
June 3, Saturday
—1 Corinthians 1:18–25
—We Proclaim Christ Crucified to All
June 4, Sunday
—1 Corinthians 1:26–31
—God Brings Us to Christ

PRAYER
Heavenly Father, thank You for all the things You have provided to ensure our unity with each other, and with You. We bless You for all You have done. In Jesus' name, we pray. Amen.

Lesson 2

Servants of Wisdom

ADULT TOPIC: Finding Wisdom
YOUTH TOPIC: The Gift of True Wisdom
CHILDREN'S TOPIC: Trust God

DEVOTIONAL READING: Ephesians 1:15-21
BACKGROUND SCRIPTURE: 1 Corinthians 2
PRINT PASSAGE: 1 Corinthians 2:1, 6-16

1 Corinthians 2:1, 6-16—KJV

AND I, brethren, when I came to you, came not with excellency of speech or of wisdom, declaring unto you the testimony of God.

.....

6 Howbeit we speak wisdom among them that are perfect: yet not the wisdom of this world, nor of the princes of this world, that come to nought:

7 But we speak the wisdom of God in a mystery, even the hidden wisdom, which God ordained before the world unto our glory:

8 Which none of the princes of this world knew: for had they known it, they would not have crucified the Lord of glory.

9 But as it is written, Eye hath not seen, nor ear heard, neither have entered into the heart of man, the things which God hath prepared for them that love him.

10 But God hath revealed them unto us by his Spirit: for the Spirit searcheth all things, yea, the deep things of God.

11 For what man knoweth the things of a man, save the spirit of man which is in him? even so the things of God knoweth no man, but the Spirit of God.

UNIT I
Servants of God

CHILDREN'S UNIT
We Grow Spiritually

KEY VERSE

Which things also we speak, not in the words which man's wisdom teacheth, but which the Holy Ghost teacheth; comparing spiritual things with spiritual.—1 Corinthians 2:13

OBJECTIVES

Upon completion of this lesson, students are expected to:

1. Understand Paul's commitment to preaching the Gospel;
2. Know the difference between the wisdom of God and the wisdom of the world;
3. Know the important role of the Holy Spirit in revealing the things of God to those who are saved.

12 Now we have received, not the spirit of the world, but the spirit which is of God; that we might know the things that are freely given to us of God.

13 Which things also we speak, not in the words which man's wisdom teacheth, but which the Holy Ghost teacheth; comparing spiritual things with spiritual.

14 But the natural man receiveth not the things of the Spirit of God: for they are foolishness unto him: neither can he know them, because they are spiritually discerned.

15 But he that is spiritual judgeth all things, yet he himself is judged of no man.

16 For who hath known the mind of the Lord, that he may instruct him? But we have the mind of Christ.

1 Corinthians 2:1, 6-16—NRSV

WHEN I came to you, brothers and sisters, I did not come proclaiming the mystery of God to you in lofty words or wisdom.

.....

6 Yet among the mature we do speak wisdom, though it is not a wisdom of this age or of the rulers of this age, who are doomed to perish.

7 But we speak God's wisdom, secret and hidden, which God decreed before the ages for our glory.

8 None of the rulers of this age understood this; for if they had, they would not have crucified the Lord of glory.

9 But, as it is written, "What no eye has seen, nor ear heard, nor the human heart conceived, what God has prepared for those who love him"—

10 these things God has revealed to us through the Spirit; for the Spirit searches everything, even the depths of God.

11 For what human being knows what is truly human except the human spirit that is within? So also no one comprehends what is truly God's except the Spirit of God.

12 Now we have received not the spirit of the world, but the Spirit that is from God, so that we may understand the gifts bestowed on us by God.

13 And we speak of these things in words not taught by human wisdom but taught by the Spirit, interpreting spiritual things to those who are spiritual.

14 Those who are unspiritual do not receive the gifts of God's Spirit, for they are foolishness to them, and they are unable to understand them because they are spiritually discerned.

15 Those who are spiritual discern all things, and they are themselves subject to no one else's scrutiny.

16 "For who has known the mind of the Lord so as to instruct him?" But we have the mind of Christ.

POINTS TO BE EMPHASIZED
ADULTS
Key Verse: 1 Corinthians 2:13
Print: 1 Corinthians 2:1, 6-16
—Paul wrote to the Corinthians at a time in which people were exploring many religions.
—Paul used theological argument to

convince his readers that the wisdom of which he was speaking was rooted in the ancient past and came from God, not humans.

—Paul summarizes the content of the Gospel as "Christ crucified." He reminds the Corinthians that he did not preach with dazzling rhetoric or intricate wisdom.

—The Holy Spirit assists humans in their search for wisdom.

YOUTH
Key Verse: 1 Corinthians 2:13

Print: 1 Corinthians 2:1, 6-16

—Human beings cannot discover wisdom, which comes only through divine revelation.

—God's wisdom is given to us in Scripture and is understood through the Spirit.

—God's wisdom is given to those who have the mind of Christ.

—God sent the Spirit to offer us the gifts of God's grace and blessing.

CHILDREN
Key Verse: Proverbs 3:5

Print: Luke 15:1-10; 1 Corinthians 1:9

—The story of the lost sheep illustrates how God seeks a lasting relationship with followers.

—Jesus taught this parable because of grumbling about the nature of His ministry.

—God never stops loving us and is always faithful.

—Each person is precious to God, just as the one lost sheep was important to the shepherd and the one lost coin was important to the woman who lost it.

—When a person repents and is committed to Christ, it is a cause for rejoicing.

TOPICAL OUTLINE OF THE LESSON

I. INTRODUCTION
   A. Wisdom
   B. Biblical Background

II. EXPOSITION AND APPLICATION OF THE SCRIPTURE
   A. The Preeminence of God's Wisdom *(1 Corinthians 2:1, 6-8)*
   B. The Provision of God's Wisdom *(1 Corinthians 2:9-13)*
   C. The Purpose of God's Wisdom *(1 Corinthians 2:14-16)*

III. SPECIAL FEATURES
   A. Preserving Our Heritage
   B. Concluding Reflections

I. INTRODUCTION
A. Wisdom

The divisions in the Corinthian church were the result of human wisdom, orchestrated and operated by men who majored in philosophy and oratory. Some of the Corinthians accused Paul of using human wisdom to present the Gospel. He wrote to refute this accusation, and to make clear his perspective on preaching. He did so by explaining the distinction between the wisdom of the world (human wisdom) and the wisdom of God (the Holy Bible).

By *the wisdom of this world*, Paul meant that wisdom that has its origin from human beings. He called this wisdom foolish, because it is unable to secure salvation for lost humankind. The wisdom of God comes from God. It is that wisdom that is mysterious or hidden, and it contains truths and principles that human nature and reason could never grasp or discover. This wisdom is beyond human ability to comprehend; we do not possess the tools or capacity to obtain it.

Paul rejected and repudiated human wisdom, but approved and applied God's wisdom. This is the wisdom that will secure humanity's salvation. This is the wisdom that he used when he came preaching to the Corinthians. He declared that he did not come as a philosopher but as a witness and proclaimer of the Gospel. He spends this chapter explaining the significance and supremacy of God's wisdom over human wisdom. If a person is to be saved, that person can only be saved by the preaching of the wisdom of God; that wisdom is best seen in God's revelation and provision for humanity's salvation through the cross.

B. Biblical Background

In the first section of chapter 1 (verses 1-17), Paul discussed the critical issue of division and contention among the Corinthians. He explained the reason why the issue existed and uttered a plea for them to be united. This call to unity was further explained in his discussion on wisdom. He asserted that human wisdom had become the priority of the church, and they had abandoned the wisdom of God.

It was his purpose in the remaining verses of chapter one to show the destructive nature of human wisdom and the dynamic nature of the Gospel. He showed that human wisdom is folly—insufficient to lead people to Christ. God decreed that the Gospel would be the only means of salvation. Paul explained that neither human wisdom nor any other human distinctions can secure one's salvation.

Paul set forth how God revealed His Word to the apostles, and then to us. He did so by His Holy Spirit, which is responsible for inspiration and illumination. But only those who are spiritual—saved by God's wisdom and the preaching of the Cross, and filled with His Spirit—have access to these truths, for they are spiritually discerned.

II. EXPOSITION AND APPLICATION OF THE SCRIPTURE

A. The Preeminence of God's Wisdom (1 Corinthians 2:1, 6-8)

And I, brethren, when I came to you, came not with excellency of speech or of wisdom, declaring unto you the testimony of God. Since the Corinthians lived in a Greek culture that was dominated by philosophical thought and ideologies, rhetoric and oratory, they developed a passion for this way of life. They saw it as the ultimate expression of their identity.

This was true of both Jews and Greeks—for even though the Jews maintained their Jewish synagogue's exclusivity, their assimilation into this culture caused them to embrace Hellenism. Anything that was outside of this cultural identity became a challenge for them, to the point that they were ready to reject it outright.

When the apostle Paul came to this city, he was challenged to make the Gospel of Christ known and accepted, and not to become entrapped by seeking to please a people who were enticed by wisdom. Instead, Paul presented the Gospel in the appropriate way. He did not tickle their fancy, but proclaimed to them "the testimony of God." He knew that they suffered from the "itching ear" syndrome (2 Timothy 4:3), but he also knew that they were suffering from depravity and were children stamped with the Adamic (sin) nature (see Romans 3:10-18; 5:12). He would not give them what they expected, but what they needed—the Good News of Jesus Christ.

This is why he wrote emphatically, "For I determined not to know any thing among you, save Jesus Christ, and him crucified" (1 Corinthians 2:2). "Jesus Christ crucified" is his way of expressing the "whole" plan of salvation, and not just Jesus' crucifixion. The major reason for this focus on the Cross was that to the Jews it was "a stumbling block," and to the Greeks "foolishness" (1 Corinthians 1:23). Both groups had rejected God's revelation of redemption through the Cross.

Understanding the power of the Gospel was essential for the Corinthians. They were mixed up about many things. Paul would make sure that they were not mixed up concerning the truth of the Gospel or the wisdom of God. He presented the Gospel clearly, distinctly and perfectly, under the influence and power of the Holy Spirit.

Howbeit we speak wisdom among them that are perfect: yet not the wisdom of this world, or of the princes of this world, that come to nought. Those who sit in the pew should not be inundated with the preacher's opinions or theories; they should hear the wisdom and Word of God. Paul was determined that this would always be his course of action.

Paul's preaching illustrates God's power. "Mystery of God" is something hidden that God can reveal. "Testimony of God" suggests that God bears witness through Paul's preaching. "Jesus Christ, and him crucified" includes both Paul's preaching and the manner of life. "Demonstration of the Spirit and of Power" intimates that Paul saw himself as a channel for the Holy Spirit exerting power. "Wisdom for the mature": Paul speaks positively of wisdom. God's Spirit imparts a deeper wisdom than any human speculation can achieve, a wisdom which only the mature (those who have been taught by the Spirit) can understand. "This age and the rulers of this age" refer to political leaders (Acts 4:25-28), or cosmic, demonic powers (Ephesians 1:20-21), or both. "As it is written" has reference to several Old Testament passages (see Isaiah 64:4; 52:15; 65:16). The unspiritual or natural person is a two-dimensional figure living in a three-dimensional world. The spiritual (*pneumatikos*) person is guided by God's Spirit. The mind of Christ, guided by the Spirit of God, seeks what is truly God's. Those with the Spirit have the mind of Christ, and no one is in the position to instruct Christ.

In this verse, he begins to explain why God's wisdom was most important. He says *we* speak wisdom. The "we" refers specifically to the apostles. They had received this wisdom. But in a real sense, it refers to all those who were/are saved. He spoke it *among them that are perfect*. The Greek word for "perfect" means "mature, full grown, those that are complete." Is Paul referring here to mature Christians? The answer is found by referring to the context. No. He has addressed both the saved and unsaved. First Corinthians 1:18ff summarizes this whole section: "For the preaching of the cross is to them that perish foolishness; but unto us which are saved it is the power of God." Then he says in 1 Corinthians 2:5, "That your faith should not stand in the wisdom of men, but in the power of God." The context reveals that he is speaking about the saved and unsaved. Therefore, the reference to those "who are perfect" has to do with those who are saved.

But we speak the wisdom of God in a mystery, even the hidden wisdom, which God ordained before the world unto our glory (verse 7). The wisdom that Paul spoke was the wisdom that originated from God. But this wisdom was spoken in a *mystery*, hidden from those who were of the world. Those who adhered to the world's wisdom rejected the wisdom of God because they could not receive it or comprehend it (see 2 Corinthians 4:4). Jesus said emphatically, "I thank thee, O Father, Lord of heaven and earth, because thou hast hid these things from the wise and prudent, and hast revealed them unto babes."

God's wisdom was *ordained before the world unto our glory*. Before time and in eternity, God predetermined this saving wisdom, and this wisdom was for our glorification—the ultimate aspect of our salvation (see Romans 8:18, 29-30). This means *the princes of this world* will be among those who will not be saved (1 Corinthians 1:26-29).

Which none of the princes of this world knew: for had they known it, they would not have crucified the Lord of glory (verse 8). Paul's conclusion here is astounding. None of the princes of this world knew the wisdom of God. The persons of authority and those in leadership did not know God's wisdom. Though he is speaking of all people in this capacity, he specifically was making reference to the Jewish rulers and Gentile leaders (see Mark 9:31; 10:33-34). Then he explained what they did to prove that they did not know God's wisdom as *they . . . crucified the Lord of glory*. They rejected God's Son, thus rejecting God's Word, will and wisdom.

B. The Provision of God's Wisdom
(1 Corinthians 2:9-13)

But as it is written, Eye hath not seen, nor ear heard, neither have entered into the heart of man, the things which God hath prepared for them that love him (verse 9). Paul refers to Isaiah 64:4 and

65:17. Though he does not quote it exactly, the meaning of the verse is maintained or explained. Since the New Testament clarifies and fulfills the Old Testament, Paul brings the Isaiah passage into the revelation of the New Testament. Remember that the Old Testament is a shadow of what is to come; the New Testament is the real thing. For example: the Old Testament speaks of a lamb for the sacrifice (see Genesis 3:21; 22:7-8, 13-14; Exodus 12:3-13; Leviticus 16:5-15, 20-22). It is an actual lamb. But when we come to the revelation in the New Testament, the lamb is not an animal, but a real person—and that person is none other than the Lord Jesus Christ (see John 1:29; Revelation 5:5-9, 12).

This is one of the most succinct verses in Scripture that describes the human inability to know anything that is of God. Left alone, human beings will never have the eyes to see, neither the ears to hear, nor the heart or mind to comprehend the things or revelations of God. Without God, human beings are truly lost, having no means—to understand the things of God.

But God hath revealed them unto us by his Spirit: for the Spirit searcheth all things, yea, the deep things of God. For what man knoweth the things of a man, save the spirit of man which is in him? even so the things of God knoweth no man, but the Spirit of God (verses 10-11). God has revealed His wisdom, His revelation and His truth to us by way of His Spirit. This refers to the Holy Spirit. It is the ministry of the Holy Spirit to make known the revelation of God to believers. Jesus told His disciples that when the Comforter (the Holy Spirit) comes: *"He shall teach you all things"* (John 14:26); *"He will guide you into all truth"* (John 16:13).

In the Trinitarian assignment, the Holy Spirit is responsible for communicating and translating God's truth into human understanding. Paul explains how the Holy Spirit is able to communicate God's revelation. The Holy Spirit knows the depths of God and the thoughts of God. He knows God, because He is God. Then Paul illustrates this point. As no one knows what is in a person's mind, but that person—so no one but God can know what is in the mind of God. Only God's Spirit can know God's mind.

The great blessing of these verses is that God takes the initiative to make Himself known to humanity. This is very important because we cannot come to God; we cannot find God. God must come to humanity. This is the only way that we can possess the revelation of God, and be in relationship with God.

Now we have received, not the spirit of the world, but the spirit which is of God; that we might know the things that are freely given to us of God (verse 12). Paul explained further that not only has God revealed "the things he has prepared for those who love Him," but God has also given to us His Spirit. Paul says that we have *received...the spirit which is of God.* It is debatable whether the "we" in verse

12 refers to all believers or only to the apostles who were inspired to speak and write the revelation they received from the Holy Spirit. Verse 13 supports that here Paul had himself and the other apostles chiefly in mind; however, all believers have received the Spirit of God. The Spirit is the medium whereby humans obtain all the things of God. To receive God's Spirit is another way of speaking about salvation. This means that only those who are saved can receive the things God has prepared and revealed (see 1 Corinthians 2:14-16).

When Paul said, *That we might know the things that are freely given to us of God,* he was not addressing the spiritual blessings from God that we receive and enjoy as believers. Instead, his reference was about God's revelation. What the apostles *received* was given to them in order that they would *know*.

Which things also we speak, not in the words which man's wisdom teacheth, but which the Holy Ghost teacheth; comparing spiritual things with spiritual. The *things . . . we speak* refers back to the things revealed. What they were speaking was the revelation of God. Paul set forth a significant process: what they received, they received in order to know; and what they received and knew, they did so in order to speak it. The whole purpose of God giving His revelation was for its communication. This is what inspiration is and this is what it does—it makes the revelation known. We have access to knowing God's revelation because of inspiration.

Paul again emphasized that what they spoke was not taught by *man's wisdom.* Human beings do not have access to this kind of revelation. They were able to speak the revelation because it was taught by the Holy Spirit. The reference to teaching here is different than the reference to teaching in John 14:26. In John, the teaching ministry of the Holy Spirit is for all believers. The teaching referred to here is exclusively for the apostles. This teaching allows them to compare *spiritual things with spiritual.* The phrase literally means "joining spiritual thoughts to spiritual words."

C. The Purpose of God's Wisdom
(1 Corinthians 2:14-16)

But the natural man receiveth not the things of the Spirit of God: for they are foolishness unto him: neither can he know them, because they are spiritually discerned. One aspect of divine wisdom is that it reveals and exposes those who cannot possess that wisdom. Here, Paul calls this person *the natural man,* meaning the person who is unsaved. The person who has not received the Holy Spirit cannot receive *the things of the Spirit of God.* As God has revealed the things He has prepared for those who love Him (verse 10), those who are operating in the natural cannot love God, for such persons are in no position to receive the things of God.

Notice the position of persons in the natural state. They do not have the Spirit of God or access to the things of God that He has freely given. They do not possess the knowledge of the things of God nor can they discern those things. In Romans 8:5-8, Paul explains, "For they that are after the flesh do mind the things of the flesh...."

But he that is spiritual judgeth all things, yet he himself is judged of no man. Another aspect of the wisdom of God is that it gives the believer the ability to judge (a better translation is discern) all things— that is, all spiritual things. The indwelling of the Holy Spirit makes this possible. Though believers can discern all spiritual things, we are not discerned or appreciated by those living in the natural. Unbelievers (natural man) have animosity and contempt for believers (spiritual man) because unbelievers cannot understand spiritual things.

For who hath known the mind of the Lord, that he may instruct him? But we have the mind of Christ (verse 16). Another aspect of the wisdom of God is to show the great privilege all believers have. We are highly privileged because we *have the mind of Christ*. This explains how we can be spiritual, and judge, discern and understand all spiritual things or truths, and how we are not like those living in the natural state of being.

Paul explains how the spiritual beings can know and understand all spiritual truths by raising a very important question: *Who knows the mind of the Lord that he may instruct or teach Him?* The person in the natural state of being is in no position to know the mind of the Lord. Isaiah said, "For my thoughts are not your thoughts, neither are your ways my ways, saith the Lord" (Isaiah 55:8). Isaiah is stating that the unsaved (see Isaiah 55:7) cannot know God's thoughts or His ways. Isaiah's statement can apply to all people, for there are thoughts and ways of God that we will never possess or practice (see Isaiah 55:9). However, Isaiah's context is directed toward the unbeliever (the wicked or the unrighteous—Isaiah 55:7). As long as persons are devoid of God's Spirit (unsaved), they will never be able to think God's thoughts or have God's ways. But once a person is saved, that person can think on the thoughts of God and have the ways of God.

The second part of the question is: *Who can instruct the Lord?* The idea here is that when the unspiritual confront the spiritual, they are seeking to teach and instruct the spiritual. The unspiritual are calling the spiritual into question and trying to correct them, because the unspiritual have no concept of spiritual things. In so doing, they are unknowingly calling the Lord into question and seeking to instruct the Lord. This, of course, is absurd, yet it demonstrates the folly of the unspiritual.

Paul concludes, *But we have the mind of Christ.* This means we have access to the Lord's mind, to His thoughts. But the Greek word for "mind" is better translated "understanding." We have the Lord's understanding or are able to understand the truths of the Lord. Though we have this access, that understanding will not always come without effort. This is why Paul admonished Timothy: "Study to show thyself approved unto God, a workman that needeth not to be ashamed, rightly dividing the word of truth" (2 Timothy 2:15).

III. SPECIAL FEATURES

A. Preserving Our Heritage

Having historically been a people with little or no political, social or economic power, African American Christians have long relied on the Holy Spirit to give them the godly wisdom needed to make it through difficult times. Having the mind of Christ has helped our people survive injustices and hardships that would have caused many others to buckle under.

Although we have garnered significantly more economic, social and political power, the Black Christian community cannot afford to put more value on these human resources. Indeed, there will always be times when economic or political resources will not be enough. Godly wisdom is a great jewel of the Black Christian community—one we can ill afford to cast aside as we move up among the ranks of the rich and powerful.

B. Concluding Reflections

The difference between the wisdom of God and the wisdom of the world is the difference between life and death, between light and darkness, between knowledge and ignorance. This difference should cause many to seek after God's wisdom rather than the wisdom of the world. But, many still reject God's wisdom.

Let us be diligent declarers and demonstrators of that wisdom.

HOME DAILY BIBLE READINGS

for the week of June 11, 2006
Servants of Wisdom

June 5, Monday
—James 1:2–8
—Faith and Wisdom
June 6, Tuesday
—James 3:13–18
—Two Kinds of Wisdom
June 7, Wednesday
—Ephesians 1:15–21
—A Spirit of Wisdom
June 8, Thursday
—Colossians 1:24–29
—Warn and Teach Everyone in Wisdom
June 9, Friday
—1 Corinthians 2:1–5
—Faith Not Based on Human Wisdom
June 10, Saturday
—1 Corinthians 2:6–10
—We Speak God's Wisdom
June 11, Sunday
—1 Corinthians 2:11–16
—Words Not Taught by Human Wisdom

PRAYER

Heavenly Father, we thank You for Your revelation, inspiration and illumination of Your Word by Your Holy Spirit. Continue to teach us and develop us so we can truly manifest "the mind of Christ." Amen.

Lesson 3

Servants Together

ADULT TOPIC: Building Together
YOUTH TOPIC: Faithful Teamwork
CHILDREN'S TOPIC: Obey God's Word

DEVOTIONAL READING: Matthew 13:3-9
BACKGROUND SCRIPTURE: 1 Corinthians 3:1-15
PRINT PASSAGE: 1 Corinthians 3:1-15

KEY VERSE

For we are labourers together with God: ye are God's husbandry, ye are God's building.
—1 Corinthians 3:9

OBJECTIVES

Upon completion of this lesson, students are expected to:

1. Access the maturity level of the Corinthians;
2. Understand the interconnected relationship each apostle has to one another;
3. Know what constitutes the foundation and formation of the church; and,
4. Learn about the test that will prove the validity of every believer's work.

1 Corinthians 3:1-15—KJV

AND I, brethren, could not speak unto you as unto spiritual, but as unto carnal, even as unto babes in Christ.

2 I have fed you with milk, and not with meat: for hitherto ye were not able to bear it, neither yet now are ye able.

3 For ye are yet carnal: for whereas there is among you envying, and strife, and divisions, are ye not carnal, and walk as men?

4 For while one saith, I am of Paul; and another, I am of Apollos; are ye not carnal?

5 Who then is Paul, and who is Apollos, but ministers by whom ye believed, even as the Lord gave to every man?

6 I have planted, Apollos watered; but God gave the increase.

7 So then neither is he that planteth any thing, neither he that watereth; but God that giveth the increase.

8 Now he that planteth and he that watereth are one: and every man shall receive his own reward according to his own labour.

9 For we are labourers together with God: ye are God's husbandry, ye are God's building.

10 According to the grace of God which is given unto me,

as a wise masterbuilder, I have laid the foundation, and another buildeth thereon. But let every man take heed how he buildeth thereupon.

11 For other foundation can no man lay than that is laid, which is Jesus Christ.

12 Now if any man build upon this foundation gold, silver, precious stones, wood, hay, stubble;

13 Every man's work shall be made manifest: for the day shall declare it, because it shall be revealed by fire; and the fire shall try every man's work of what sort it is.

14 If any man's work abide which he hath built thereupon, he shall receive a reward.

15 If any man's work shall be burned, he shall suffer loss: but he himself shall be saved; yet so as by fire.

1 Corinthians 3:1-15—NRSV

AND SO, brothers and sisters, I could not speak to you as spiritual people, but rather as people of the flesh, as infants in Christ.

2 I fed you with milk, not solid food, for you were not ready for solid food. Even now you are still not ready,

3 for you are still of the flesh. For as long as there is jealousy and quarreling among you, are you not of the flesh, and behaving according to human inclinations?

4 For when one says, "I belong to Paul," and another, "I belong to Apollos," are you not merely human?

5 What then is Apollos? What is Paul? Servants through whom you came to believe, as the Lord assigned to each.

6 I planted, Apollos watered, but God gave the growth.

7 So neither the one who plants nor the one who waters is anything, but only God who gives the growth.

8 The one who plants and the one who waters have a common purpose, and each will receive wages according to the labor of each.

9 For we are God's servants, working together; you are God's field, God's building.

10 According to the grace of God given to me, like a skilled master builder I laid a foundation, and someone else is building on it. Each builder must choose with care how to build on it.

11 For no one can lay any foundation other than the one that has been laid; that foundation is Jesus Christ.

12 Now if anyone builds on the foundation with gold, silver, precious stones, wood, hay, straw—

13 the work of each builder will become visible, for the Day will disclose it, because it will be revealed with fire, and the fire will test what sort of work each has done.

14 If what has been built on the foundation survives, the builder will receive a reward.

15 If the work is burned up, the builder will suffer loss; the builder will be saved, but only as through fire.

POINTS TO BE EMPHASIZED
ADULTS

Key Verse: 1 Corinthians 3:9
Print: 1 Corinthians 3:1-15

—Understanding and maturing in the Christian faith requires beginning with the basics.
—The Corinthians considered themselves mature and spiritual, but Paul replies that they are people of the flesh and infants in Christ.
—Jealousy and quarreling within the church is a symptom of spiritual immaturity.
—God makes the words of the Gospel take root and spring up into a living community of faith.
—Paul uses the metaphor of building the church to illustrate the cooperative ministry of the church and our accountability to God's judgment.

YOUTH

Key Verse: 1 Corinthians 3:7
Print: 1 Corinthians 3:1-15

—Spiritual people have learned that jealousy and quarreling are not growth-producing.
—God's servants know how to work together.
—Each Christian has a part to play in building on the foundation of Jesus Christ.

CHILDREN

Key Verse: James 1:22
Print: Matthew 7:24-27; 1 Corinthians 3:10-11

—Jesus used a parable to illustrate the need to build lives on the strong foundation of God's Word.
—Jesus used the analogy of rock and sand to illustrate a proper foundation for living.
—A good foundation gives stability in difficult times.
—Each person must build (with care) on that foundation.
—Following Christ is like building a house on a solid, rock foundation.

TOPICAL OUTLINE OF THE LESSON

I. INTRODUCTION
  A. Maturity
  B. Biblical Background

II. EXPOSITION AND APPLICATION OF THE SCRIPTURE
  A. The Carnality of the Corinthians *(1 Corinthians 3:1-4)*
  B. The Correlation of Christian Leaders *(1 Corinthians 3:5-10)*
  C. The Confirmation of Christian Labor *(1 Corinthians 3:11-15)*

III. SPECIAL FEATURES
  A. Preserving Our Heritage
  B. Concluding Reflections

I. INTRODUCTION
A. Maturity

Paul chastised the Corinthian church because of their immaturity. The nature of their immaturity was that they had ample time and opportunity to grow and develop spiritually; however, they were still *babes in Christ*. The manifestation of this immaturity was evident by their division. They had fragmented into cliques and factions that were hindering the church from growing and understanding the essential doctrines of the faith.

Paul was disappointed with their struggle with the flesh. They had showed no signs of moving away from this destructive lifestyle. As long as they remained in this condition, they would not be spiritual. That is, they would not be yielding to the influence and authority of the Holy Spirit, by not allowing themselves to follow His commands and to grow in the ways that only He could provide. This also meant that they would be prey to false teaching and false teachers. Paul explained this very clearly in Ephesians when he addressed all believers coming into "the unity of the faith, and of the knowledge of the Son of God, unto a perfect man, unto the measure of the stature of the fulness of Christ" (Ephesians 4:13). He instructed the Ephesians on how they could be matured and unified. Then he added, "That we henceforth be no more children, tossed to and fro, and carried about with every wind of doctrine, by the sleight of men, and cunning craftiness, whereby they lie in wait to deceive." He was explaining to them how vulnerable believers are when they are "children," immature believers. He shared that as long as they remained in that state, they would never be able to obtain sound doctrine.

They would always be drifting and tossed from one doctrinal position to another. The danger of this was that they were worldly—influenced and dominated by the thinking and practices of the world. As a result, their lives would never experience the power, purpose and productivity of the ministry of the Holy Spirit.

B. Biblical Background

From 1 Corinthians 1:18 through 2:16, Paul points out that the Corinthians were divided because of human wisdom. They had allowed that which was not of God to become ingrained in their Christian teaching and practices. Now, in 3:1-15, Paul shows them that their human wisdom had hindered their spiritual growth. This lack of growth manifested itself in their inappropriate understanding of Christian leaders and teachers. They had divided themselves into "mini-churches" within the one church. Paul writes to correct this deadly doctrinal position, and to show the true place of Christian leaders and teachers, and the perception the Corinthians should have of them.

II. EXPOSITION AND APPLICATION OF THE SCRIPTURE

A. The Carnality of the Corinthians
(1 Corinthians 3:1-4)

And I, brethren, could not speak unto you as unto spiritual, but as unto carnal, even as unto babes in Christ. Paul sets forth the spiritual condition of the Corinthians. It is this condition that explains why they were divided, not doctrinal, and not developing. Instead of repudiating them at first, he softens his rebuke by properly identifying them. He identifies them in light of their relationship with Christ, and then the level of their conformity to Christ.

In their relationship with Christ, they were *brethren*. This was to show both Paul's and their relationship with Christ. Paul wanted them to know that they were all in the family of God. He was establishing the fact that the Corinthians were saved; they were believers. He did not want them to have any doubts about their position in Christ. However, their progress in Christ was a different story.

Paul was displeased with their lack of spiritual growth and development. He was disgusted because they were immature and infantile in Christ. He had expected them to be on a much higher spiritual level. He wanted to teach them the deeper truths of the faith; he wanted to expose them to the broader and more profound Christian principles. But they were still on the earliest level of faith maturity.

The term *spiritual* does not mean that they did not possess the Holy Spirit, and as a result were not saved. It means that they were not on the level of maturity that distinguished the unbeliever from the believer. They were still "babes in Christ." They were not spiritually sensitive and capable of handling the deeper doctrinal truths. From the letter, we learn that they had trouble in a number of areas: they had trouble with disciplining unruly members; they were suing each other; they were unsure about marriage and singleness; they were eating food offered to idols; they misunderstood the Lord's Supper; and they abused the spiritual gifts, were disorderly in worship, and did not understand the doctrine of the Resurrection. They were a long way from where they should have been in the faith. When Paul says that he could not speak unto them *as unto spiritual*, he could have had these very issues in mind.

Paul referred to them as *carnal*. Again, he did not mean that they were unbelievers or unsaved. The word "carnal" literally means "fleshy ones," or controlled by the flesh. This

Like infants, people of the flesh think only of their own needs and self-interests. Paul reacts to a criticism that he has been too simple in his gospel. He explains that though he has wisdom to impart, he could impart it only to spiritual people—the mature—but the Christians are infants and do not qualify. Jealousy and quarreling are listed among the desires of the flesh (see Galatians 5:20). The emphasis in this lesson is placed on God's initiative. Paul experienced the grace of God when God called him. Starting churches was like laying the foundation of a building (see Romans 15:20). The Day of Judgment is often envisioned as destruction of the world by fire. Paul uses the building metaphor to make his point: God's temple, the individual body is a temple. Since the community is a temple where God is present, those who divide and destroy it will suffer condemnation. "Becoming truly wise": Rather than following human leaders who claim to be wise, belonging to Christ gives one all he needs. Most divisive and harmful is the "wisdom" that finds its center in this age, and not in God's wisdom—Christ and the Cross.

refers to their fallen nature, their bodily desires. These desires caused them to rebel against God, opposing what He commands. This helps us understand that carnality is a dangerous and dreadful condition. It dulls one's spiritual senses; it makes one deaf to truth; it makes one indifferent to teaching and preaching; and it makes one quench the Holy Spirit.

I have fed you with milk, and not with meat: for hitherto ye were not able to bear it, neither yet now are ye able (verse 2). Paul noted the work that he did among them. *He fed* [them] *with milk*. He was pointing out the foundational work that he had done. He gave them the Gospel in its simplest form, and they *ate* and *digested* it. As unbelievers, they grasped the basic principles of the Gospel and embraced salvation. Paul calls the simple and elementary truths of salvation *milk*.

He did not feed them *with meat*. He did not teach them the more detailed truths of the faith. They did not have the spiritual maturity to grasp the deeper truths. "Milk" and "meat" do not refer to different doctrines. The difference between milk and meat is that meat is the more expansive development of the doctrine; milk is the lesser development. For example, Jesus Christ as Savior and Lord is the basic truth of the faith. To be saved, one must believe and grasp this truth. This is milk. But one can take that truth and go deeper into its development. For example, one can say that Jesus Christ our Savior and Lord is the Son of God, the Second Person of the Trinity. This means that He is a distinct Person from God the Father and God the Holy Spirit. The ministry of God the Son is exclusive to the Son. He does not do what the Father does or what the Holy Spirit does. He makes possible our propitiation, expiation, regeneration, justification, sanctification, glorification, etc. He is our substitute, God's perfect sacrifice, and our good, great and chief Shepherd. He is the virgin-born Son of Mary. He is both human and divine. But His humanity is not mixed with His divinity. As the early church said, "He is one person with two natures." The doctrine is the same—the doctrine of the Son of God; but there are deeper truths related to it.

For ye are yet carnal: for whereas there is among you envying, and strife, and divisions, are ye not carnal, and walk as men? (verse 3). Paul's indictment of the Corinthians is unavoidable. He wanted to speak of them in better terms, but he needed to give a true assessment. If they were to correct themselves, they needed the truth to accomplish that goal. He confronted them by condemning them for their lack of spiritual development. They were *carnal*. Then he described the behavior that characterizes carnality. It is demonstrated through *envying, and strife, and divisions*. The presence and practice of these sins indicates what was in their hearts and heads. The destructive nature of these sins was being manifested through a deficiency in doctrines, deeds and duty. They should have been behaving as spiritual adults, but they were behaving as spiritual babies.

Since Paul's indictment and confrontation of the Corinthians was a true assessment, and that carnality is revealed by the manifestation of *envying, strife and divisions*, there are many persons in our churches who need to be confronted. Like the Corinthians, they should be on meat; but tragically, they are still on milk. We need to challenge our brothers and sisters in Christ to become mature in Christ Jesus.

For while one saith, I am of Paul; and another, I am of Apollos; are ye not carnal? (verse 4). The manifestation of their divisions revealed their carnality. Some were giving allegiance to Paul, others to Apollos. This is childish behavior; adults in Christ do not behave this way.

B. The Correlation of Christian Leaders *(1 Corinthians 3:5-10)*

Who then is Paul, and who is Apollos, but ministers by whom ye believed, even as the Lord gave to every man? The question in this verse is rhetorical, but also revelatory. It was designed to reveal the true place Paul and Apollos occupied. They were *ministers* or subordinates. The Greek word for "ministers" refers to any type of menial worker of any status. They were ministers *by whom ye believed*. The Lord used them to preach the Gospel to the Corinthians, resulting in the Corinthians' salvation. Paul and Apollos were not the source of salvation, but rather the servants.

The phrase rendered *even as the Lord gave to every man* is better translated,

"even as the Lord gave opportunity to each one." The salvation of the Corinthians could not be credited to Paul or Apollos, but to the Lord. He gave each of them the opportunity to preach the Gospel. The Lord used them to serve the Corinthians; as a result, they believed and were saved. This means that Paul and Apollos were not to be elevated to the position of the Lord.

I have planted, Apollos watered; but God gave the increase (verse 6). In this verse, Paul explains the distinction between his work and that of Apollos'. He also set forth the distinction between his and Apollos' work and God's work. His ministry was one of "planting"; Apollos' ministry was one of "watering." That means, his ministry was foundational; and Apollos' ministry was constructional—building upon the foundation Paul had laid. Planting and watering show the relationship of the two ministers. One was as important as the other. But it was the Lord who assigned them to these ministerial roles (verse 5).

Planting and watering also show the sequential order of the ministerial roles—planting always precedes watering. But although Paul planted, he was not preeminent over Apollos. Paul was Apollos' partner. One ministry needed the other ministry.

Paul explained further *but God gave the increase*. Here, he distinguished his and Apollos' work from God's work. God was responsible for the productive work. It was

He who effected salvation in the hearts of the Corinthians.

So then neither is he that planteth any thing, neither he that watereth; but God that giveth the increase (verse 7). Paul emphasized how much more significant God is in the ministry. God must be pre-eminent. By showing the significant work of God, Paul was establishing who should receive the recognition and glory. What he and Apollos did was nothing compared to what God had done. They had planted and watered the seed, but making it grow and produce was beyond human ability.

The repetition of the ministry of God, by the phrase *God that giveth the increase*, is intentional. It was to give emphasis to the appropriate place He occupied and the exclusive power that He alone possessed. In Acts (see Acts 2:42-43, 46-47), the apostles did many signs and wonders; but it was the Lord who added to the church. This is what Paul established in these verses. The Corinthians would give God His proper due and recognition.

Now he that planteth and he that watereth are one: and every man shall receive his own reward according to his own labour (verse 8). In verse 6, Paul cited his and Apollos' dependance on each other. In verse 7, he showed their dispensability. In verse 8, he showed their unity. In pointing out their individuality—in terms of ministry (verse 6)—and their inferiority (verse 7), Paul also was setting forth God's superiority and sovereignty to establish the church's integrity.

In addition to their individuality, their dependability, their dispensability, and their unity, Paul also stressed their exclusivity—that is, in terms of receiving rewards. *Every man shall receive his own reward according to his own labour.* This is the principle of Matthew 10:10. The worker performs the ministry, and the recipients of that ministry provide the meat (provision).

The point Paul was making is that God will give each person what he or she has earned. By elevating Paul and Apollos to the place reserved for the Lord, the Corinthians gave them unearned and undeserved recognition. But they had no need to be discouraged; the Lord is a great accountant. He appropriately rewards His leaders and workers. What the Corinthians were doing was inappropriate; what God will do will be just and appropriate.

For we are labourers together with God: ye are God's husbandry, ye are God's building (verse 9). Paul speaks of the ministers (and the church) in glowing terms. On the one hand, we are partners with God (*labourers together*), and on the other hand, we are products of God (*God's husbandry . . . God's building*). This is a profound truth. God had included Paul and Apollos in His ministry to the world and the church. But what He does for all those who believe is make them recipients of His grace. He saves us and then places us into the body of Christ.

The meaning of *God's husbandry* and *God's building* are important here. God's husbandry means that Paul and Apollos (and we) are laborers in God's field. God's building means that they (we) are God's temple. God produced us and He possesses us. Paul was helping the Corinthians understand that God owns everything, including the church (see 1 Timothy 3:15).

According to the grace of God which is given unto me, as a wise masterbuilder, I have laid the foundation, and another buildeth thereon. But let every man take heed how he buildeth thereupon (verse 10). Paul goes further to explain his and Apollos' privileges, which are the privileges of all believers. That which has come to him was by God's "grace" (see 1 Corinthians 15:10). His life was an expression and manifestation of God's grace.

He was a *wise masterbuilder,* meaning he was a skillful architect. From the verse, apparently "architect" involved both designing and building, which is a different understanding from our day. The present-day architect only designs; the general contractor builds. Paul did both. God revealed the plans to him for the design of the building. And God gave him the skill to construct the building. He received from God how to organize and build the church, especially the Corinthian church. He became God's architect by God's grace. Divine grace gifted him and enabled him to function in the calling on his life.

As God's architect, he *laid the foundation,* the first and most basic part of the building. Paul laid the foundational truths of the Gospel and of the doctrine in Corinth, during those eighteen months he spent in the city (see Acts 18). Then *another buildeth thereon*. He laid the foundation, and Apollos built on that foundation.

The warning, *but let every man take heed how he buildeth thereon*, was directed to the *false teachers* who had caused divisions in the church. Paul was warning them about how they build or do ministry. Ministers must be careful. If the structure of the church is to be in line with its foundation, those who build must use the right material. This was not being done in Corinth. Paul would demonstrate in the succeeding verses why the foundation is so important to the building.

C. The Confirmation of Christian Labor *(1 Corinthians 3:11-15)*

For other foundation can no man lay than that is laid, which is Jesus Christ (verse 11). The preeminence of the Lord Jesus Christ had to be understood by the Corinthians. There is only one foundation—the Lord Jesus Christ. He is the focal point of Scripture (see Luke 24:27; John 5:39) and the foundation of the church. If the church is to be authentic, it must be built on God's exclusive and essential foundation, Jesus Christ.

The Corinthians needed to know the true foundation of the church. It was not Paul; it was not Apollos; it was not Cephas. It was and is the Lord Jesus Christ. A foundation built on anyone else is flawed and false and will fail. Paul did not want this fledgling body to fail.

Now if any man build upon this foundation gold, silver, precious stones, wood, hay, stubble (verse 12). Paul's warning continued to include the type of works that are done. He listed those works under six descriptions: *gold, silver, precious stones, wood, hay, stubble*. These works were given in order of importance.

To *build upon this foundation* speaks of the work of those who follow the apostles and prophets. The apostles and prophets were responsible for laying the foundation (2:20; 4:11). Now we need those who will build upon the foundation. Those who build must know that they will be held accountable for what they build.

Every man's work shall be made manifest: for the day shall declare it, because it shall be revealed by fire; and the fire shall try every man's work of what sort it is (verse 13). The work everyone does will be made known. The reference to *the day* refers to the "Day of Judgment," or the day of accountability that will disclose each person's work. The means of testing and evaluating will be done by *fire* that *shall try every man's work*. The Lord will use fire to determine the nature and substance of each believer's work. That is, the fire will determine if the work is *gold, silver, precious stones, wood, hay, or stubble*. Paul used the analogy of fire to give description and clarity to the evaluative process.

If any man's work abide which he hath built thereupon, he shall receive a reward (verse 14). The phrase, *If any man's* (believer's) *work abide which he hath built thereupon* addresses enduring the test or passing the test of the fire. If a believer's work passes the test, he *shall receive a reward.* The Lord will reward him or her for the work.

If any man's work shall be burned, he shall suffer loss: but he himself shall be saved; yet so as by fire (verse 15). If a person's work fails the fire test, the result will be the opposite of reward. Such persons *shall suffer loss.* There will be no reward coming for those whose work is burned. Verse 13 clarifies which materials will endure the fire and which will be burned. The gold, silver and precious stones will endure the fire; the wood, hay and stubble will be consumed. However, Paul adds a word of comfort and hope for those whose work will be burned. Though their work shall be burned, *he himself shall be saved.* These individuals will not lose their salvation.

It is also clear that the "gold, silver, and precious stones" refer to appropriate or righteous deeds that can withstand; the "wood, hay, stubble" refer to unrighteous deeds, or deeds that looked like Christian labor, but were not. It is important to remember that the Lord alone will make this determination, for He controls the fire—or the time of accountability (see 2 Corinthians 5:10).

III. Special Features
A. Preserving Our Heritage

Within the Black church, which has been a lighthouse for the people, far too many within the body have rallied around the personality of the leader rather than rooting themselves in the foundation of Jesus Christ. What hope do our churches have when they are more dependent on a charismatic pulpiteer than on Jesus?

As our people experience progress in new areas of society, we must keep our feet on a firm foundation. Knowing the possibility of this, James Weldon Johnson wrote about this in the song that would become known as the Negro National Anthem: "Lest our hearts, drunk with the wine of the world we forget Thee." The Black church, standing on the foundation of our Savior, must remain the place of strength on whom our people can depend.

B. Concluding Reflections

We have seen from this lesson the distinctions between workers, but yet they are unified. They have their own work, but that work is not separate or individualistic. We need and depend on each other in order to build and develop the church. Our work is in cooperation and in conjunction with God's work. The work they do is not theirs, but God's. He has privileged each believer with the opportunity to work *for Him* and to work *with Him*. Let our work therefore be substantive and valuable, so that we will glorify the Lord, bringing honor and distinction to His name.

HOME DAILY BIBLE READINGS

for the week of June 18, 2006
Servants Together

June 12, Monday
—Matthew 13:3–9
—Spreading God's Word
June 13, Tuesday
—Matthew 13:24–30
—Growing Together
June 14, Wednesday
—Hebrews 5:7–14
—The Need for Teachers
June 15, Thursday
—Ephesians 3:14–21
—Strengthened with Power Through the Spirit
June 16, Friday
—1 Corinthians 3:1–9
—Servants Through Whom You Believe
June 17, Saturday
—1 Corinthians 3:10–15
—Building on the Foundation of Christ
June 18, Sunday
—1 Corinthians 3:16–23
—Do Not Boast About Human Leaders

PRAYER

Eternal God, our Father, we praise You for the responsibilities You grant us in the body of Christ, and the accurate accounting of our labor You will do on the day of accounting. We thank You for all You do. In Jesus' name, we pray. Amen.

Lesson 4

Servants in Ministry

CHILDREN'S UNIT
We Grow Spiritually

ADULT TOPIC: Serving Responsibly
YOUTH TOPIC: Leaders: Servants and Stewards
CHILDREN'S TOPIC: Be Responsible

KEY VERSE

Let a man so account of us, as of the ministers of Christ, and stewards of the mysteries of God.

—1 Corinthians 4:1

DEVOTIONAL READING: Matthew 23:8-12
BACKGROUND SCRIPTURE: 1 Corinthians 4:1-13
PRINT PASSAGE: 1 Corinthians 4:1-13

OBJECTIVES
Upon completion of this lesson, students should understand that:
1. Christian leaders/ministers are stewards of God's truths;
2. Christian ministers must be faithful;
3. Sufferings and trials prove the credibility of Christian ministers;
4. God will hold each Christian minister accountable.

1 Corinthians 4:1-13—KJV

LET A man so account of us, as of the ministers of Christ, and stewards of the mysteries of God.

2 Moreover it is required in stewards, that a man be found faithful.

3 But with me it is a very small thing that I should be judged of you, or of man's judgment: yea, I judge not mine own self.

4 For I know nothing by myself; yet am I not hereby justified: but he that judgeth me is the Lord.

5 Therefore judge nothing before the time, until the Lord come, who both will bring to light the hidden things of darkness, and will make manifest the counsels of the hearts: and then shall every man have praise of God.

6 And these things, brethren, I have in a figure transferred to myself and to Apollos for your sakes; that ye might learn in us not to think of men above that which is written, that no one of you be puffed up for one against another.

7 For who maketh thee to differ from another? and what hast thou that thou didst not receive? now if thou didst receive it, why dost thou glory, as if thou hadst not received it?

8 Now ye are full, now ye are rich, ye have reigned as kings without us: and I would to God ye did reign, that we also might reign with you.

9 For I think that God hath set forth us the apostles last, as it were appointed to death: for we are made a spectacle unto the world, and to angels, and to men.

10 We are fools for Christ's sake, but ye are wise in Christ; we are weak, but ye are strong; ye are honourable, but we are despised.

11 Even unto this present hour we both hunger, and thirst, and are naked, and are buffeted, and have no certain dwelling-place;

12 And labour, working with our own hands: being reviled, we bless; being persecuted, we suffer it:

13 Being defamed, we entreat: we are made as the filth of the world, and are the off scouring of all things unto this day.

1 Corinthians 4:1-13—NRSV

THINK OF us in this way, as servants of Christ and stewards of God's mysteries.

2 Moreover, it is required of stewards that they be found trustworthy.

3 But with me it is a very small thing that I should be judged by you or by any human court. I do not even judge myself.

4 I am not aware of anything against myself, but I am not thereby acquitted. It is the Lord who judges me.

5 Therefore do not pronounce judgment before the time, before the Lord comes, who will bring to light the things now hidden in darkness and will disclose the purposes of the heart. Then each one will receive commendation from God.

6 I have applied all this to Apollos and myself for your benefit, brothers and sisters, so that you may learn through us the meaning of the saying, "Nothing beyond what is written," so that none of you will be puffed up in favor of one against another.

7 For who sees anything different in you? What do you have that you did not receive? And if you received it, why do you boast as if it were not a gift?

8 Already you have all you want! Already you have become rich! Quite apart from us you have become kings! Indeed, I wish that you had become kings, so that we might be kings with you!

9 For I think that God has exhibited us apostles as last of all, as though sentenced to death, because we have become a spectacle to the world, to angels and to mortals.

10 We are fools for the sake of Christ, but you are wise in Christ. We are weak, but you are strong. You are held in honor, but we in disrepute.

11 To the present hour we are hungry and thirsty, we are poorly clothed and beaten and homeless,

12 and we grow weary from the work of our own hands. When reviled, we bless; when persecuted, we endure;

13 when slandered, we speak kindly. We have become like the rubbish of the world, the dregs of all things, to this very day.

POINTS TO BE EMPHASIZED
ADULTS
Key Verse: 1 Corinthians 4:1
Print: 1 Corinthians 4:1-13

—Paul regards his suffering not merely as misfortunes or trials, but as identifying marks of the authenticity of his apostleship.

—Paul's concern is not whether he is winning popularity contests among Corinthians, but whether he is trustworthy.

—God holds us responsible for our attitudes and actions as disciples.

—Paul views Christian leadership as servanthood and stewardship of responsibility.

YOUTH
Key Verse: 1 Corinthians 4:2
Print: 1 Corinthians 4:1-13

—As Christians, we are servants of God and responsible to God for the way we treat others.

—The ability to lead is a gift from God and there is no need to boast.

—God's leaders must be trustworthy stewards.

CHILDREN
Key Verse: 1 Corinthians 4:2
Print: Matthew 25:14-23, 28-29; 1 Corinthians 4:1-2

—Much is expected of those who are blessed with much.

—The parable illustrates that equal opportunities do not come to everyone.

—The result of our actions and responses is not necessarily just and fair.

—We sometimes make decisions out of fear rather than out of responsibility or principle.

—The parable emphasizes that we must take good care of what we have been given.

—When we do a good job of caring for a few things, God trusts us to care for many things.

TOPICAL OUTLINE OF THE LESSON

I. INTRODUCTION
   A. Faithful
   B. Biblical Background

II. EXPOSITION AND APPLICATION OF THE SCRIPTURE
   A. Critical Requirement
      (1 Corinthians 4:1-5)
   B. Conceit Repudiated
      (1 Corinthians 4:6-9)
   C. Credibility Reaffirmed
      (1 Corinthians 4:10-13)

III. SPECIAL FEATURES
   A. Preserving Our Heritage
   B. Concluding Reflections

I. INTRODUCTION
A. Faithful

The challenge facing each child of God is to be faithful to the Lord's calling on his or her life. Often the flesh is a personal challenge that causes us to follow and yield to the pull and pleasures of the world. Success is not our calling; success is the calling and goal of those who live after the flesh and the world's system. We are called to faithfulness. The Lord requires that we be dutiful stewards of His assignment for our lives. God's desire is that we obey Him (see Exodus 19:1-6; 1 Samuel 15:22; 1 Peter 1:14-16) and that obedience is visibly manifested through our faithfulness. The message given to the church at Smyrna (Revelation 2:8-11) was: "Be thou faithful unto death" (verse 10). The Lord expects all followers to adhere to this command.

B. Biblical Background

In chapter 4, Paul continues his discussion on the true role and proper understanding of Christian ministers. He rejected the folly and fallacy of the Corinthians and was repulsed by their lack of spiritual maturity. They were misguided and therefore had misjudged their Christian ministers. Paul wanted the Corinthians to regard their ministerial leaders as servants of the Lord Jesus Christ. They were to view them as stewards of the oracles (teachings of truth) of God, who were charged to faithfully impart these truths to others. Paul gave them instructions on the appropriate way that the Corinthians should relate to these ministers. They were not in position to judge them; rather, they needed to yield that judgment to the Lord. Only Christ can occupy this judicial position. He alone possesses the appropriate authority and can make adequate assessment of those who serve in His church.

Since the Corinthians were following the teachings and authority of false ministers (who misused the office) who sought to satisfy their own greed and need for glory, Paul wanted this congregation to know the difference between him and his colleagues and these false ministers. Sadly, many of today's churchgoers do not know the difference either. Paul did not want the Corinthians to be confused. His intent was to admonish them, not abash them. After all, he was their spiritual father, the one who shared the Gospel with them— won them to Christ. He had taught them the basic truths of the faith.

More important than a minister's personal characteristics is how that minister relates to the Lord. The teachers themselves, as servants of Christ, are answerable only to the Lord. Servants and stewards are roles defined by superiors. Sit in judgment: the Lord establishes the true perspective for judging behavior. Judgment is a time for unveiling secrets. "Puffed up" suggests an inflated self-image that leads to boasting (see Romans 3:21), and carries with it the illusion that one has already arrived. Since only the Lord knows the heart, boasting and blaming are ruled out. Apostles are like prisoners of war, last in the victory parade, a spectacle to everyone— thrown to beasts in the arena or to triumphal processions where military conquerors displayed their captives. The missionary lives a vagabond's existence. Starting churches was like having children: as their father, Paul expected the church to imitate his behavior. "My ways in Jesus Christ" is what Paul taught and how he behaved; arrogant behavior was a root problem in the church. Some in Corinth felt that they were already in God's final kingdom, rich and full (verse 8).

II. EXPOSITION AND APPLICATION OF THE SCRIPTURE

A. Critical Requirement
(1 Corinthians 4:1-5)

Let a man so account of us, as of the ministers of Christ, and stewards of the mysteries of God (verse 1). Paul was concerned that the Corinthians have a proper understanding of the role and function of ministers or servants of God. In verse 1, he was referring to himself, Apollos and Peter, but it can apply to all Christian ministers. The Greek word for *ministers* or "servants" literally means "under-rowers," and referred to the lowest level of slaves, those who rowed on the lowest level of the ships. Paul's assessment of himself and his colleagues is refreshing. Those of us who lead must first have an accurate assessment of ourselves, if we are to be the executioners of the Lord's precepts and principles, and examples of His people.

The word *account*, which means "to think of," or "to regard," picks up this idea. Proper regard and appropriate respect must be given to all ministers. How they are regarded will have much to do with the impact of a church's ministry.

Stewards refers to those slaves who were appointed as managers or overseers of their master's financial affairs or houses, and were to appropriately distribute their masters' provisions. Here, Paul is emphasizing the managerial duties entrusted to ministers. The Lord has entrusted His *mysteries* to them—that is, those things that were hidden that have now been made known. Every minister is called to be a good steward of the Word of God, accurately dispensing that Word (2 Timothy 2:15) and being aware of the Lord's accounting of that assignment.

Moreover it is required in stewards, that a man be found faithful (verse 2). This verse establishes the fundamental requirement of ministers of the Gospel. The Greek word *moreover* gives the requirement its emphasis. It means "as to the rest," or "what else remains is." What remains is the highest and greatest requirement for stewards: *that a man be found faithful*. Fidelity is the chief requirement for ministers.

There are three emphases of faithful ministry: (1) as it relates to the Lord of the work—*appointment*; (2) as it relates to rightly dividing God's Word—*assignment*; and (3) as it relates to edifying believers and being an example to them of God's Word—*deportment*. Ministers are to be faithful to: the Head of the church (being under Him not over Him); the household of the faith (being among them but not above them); and the world, bringing it hope and healing (being in the world, but not of the world).

But with me it is a very small thing that I should be judged of you… (verse 3). Since ministers are to be faithful, who should judge that faithfulness? In Paul's estimation, their judgment, or that of any human being, mattered little or not at all in terms of his own commitment to faithfulness. It is important to clarify that Paul was not addressing judicial judgment, where condemnation and punishment are the issues. He was speaking about their opinion of him. His aim was to please his Master, not them. Although none of them could judge Paul, he would not put himself in the judge's seat and judge himself.

For I know nothing by myself; yet am I not hereby justified: but he that judgeth me is the Lord (verse 4). Paul did not intend to convey that he had no awareness of himself. He meant that he could find nothing in his conscience that would accuse him of any unfaithfulness. His conscience was clear and could not charge himself with being slack in his ministerial duties; however, he added, *yet am I not hereby justified.* He was not free from judgment or being judged. Neither was he acquitted, for his judgment was not up to him. He had no authority to determine his own faithfulness; that belonged to someone else. He explained, *But he that judgeth me is the Lord.* Only the Lord could make an accurate judgment of his faithfulness.

Therefore judge nothing before the time, until the Lord come, who both will bring to light the hidden things of darkness... (verse 5). If the Corinthians judged him, that judgment would be premature and presumptuous. The appropriate thing was to wait *until the Lord comes.* The coming of the Lord is the opportune time, for He can rightly judge only when all believers have completed their work.

We know that when the Lord Jesus Christ returns, He will come as Judge (see Matthew 25:31-46; 2 Timothy 4:1). Two things will occur when the Lord Jesus comes as Judge. He *will bring to light the hidden things of darkness....* That which is concealed from human knowledge will be revealed. In 1 Corinthians 13:9-10, Paul wrote, "For we know in part, and we prophesy in part. But when that which is perfect is come, then that which is in part shall be done away." Our knowledge is partial and imperfect; but, when the Perfect One comes (see 2 Corinthians 5:21; Hebrews 4:15; 1 Peter 2:22; 1 John 3:5), it will be complete.

The *hidden things of darkness* refers to those things that are unknown to us. *Evil works* are those that are done in a way that avoids detection. It could also refer to dark and immoral deeds. *The counsels of the hearts* refer to the hidden and unknown motives, intentions and desires in the hearts of people. When Christ comes, He will reveal all deeds done in secret and will reveal all hidden motives, inclinations and moods.

Then shall every man have praise of God. All those who have been faithful will receive praise from God. He will commend His faithful workers. In the Parable of the Talents (Matthew 25:14-30), Jesus explained that the servants whose talents were increased received commendation from their lord (Matthew 25:21). This is what Paul says that the Lord will do on the Day of Judgment. He will judge righteously; and the righteous will be rewarded for their faithfulness.

B. Conceit Repudiated
(1 Corinthians 4:6-9)

And these things, brethren, I have in a figure transferred to myself and to Apollos for your sakes... (verse 6). Paul reminded the Corinthians of his teaching that ministers are servants. He used *a figure transferred* to explain his and Apollos' true identity. He used the figure or metaphor of agriculture, of architecture, and of servants to convey his teaching and explanation. He did it for their benefit to keep them from harming themselves. He would never do anything to destroy the work that he, Apollos and the Lord had done.

The purpose of his instruction was *that ye might learn in us not to think of men above that which is written.* Paul taught them to follow the Scriptures and never to place a minister above the teaching found therein. If they had followed his teaching, they would not be full of pride and conceit. Their elevation, distinction and separation of their ministers into factions were evidence of their own sin—the dreaded sin of pride—which was the driving force behind their divisions. Paul wanted them to learn and to obey the Scriptures that they might avoid the sin Satan committed (see Isaiah 14:12-16) and heed the warning of Proverbs 16:18.

For who maketh thee to differ from another? and what hast thou that thou didst not receive? now if thou didst receive it, why dost thou glory, as if thou hadst not received it? (verse 7). The Corinthians' sin of pride was manifesting itself in boasting and conceit. They were claiming superiority over their fellow believers. Paul wanted them to question their attitude of superiority, beginning with who would make them greater than their fellow believers. If they were superior, it came from God and not from another human being. Therefore, they had no grounds for their superiority complex or their boasting.

Now ye are full, now ye are rich, ye have reigned as kings without us: and I would to God ye did reign, that we also might reign with you (verse 8). Paul resorted to sarcasm to illustrate their high opinion of themselves. The Corinthians felt that they had "arrived" and had already reached perfection. They had done it, however—without Paul and Apollos—which meant that what they said they possessed was far from the truth. The accolades they gave themselves were false assessments.

Paul also stated that he *would to God* that the time to reign with Christ had come, that he and Apollos *might reign* with them. The reign of Christ and believers was in the distant future. Therefore, what the Corinthians had done could only be branded folly. Paul revealed what was at the heart of their cliquish and divisive practices. They felt they were in position of royalty; in reality, they were rebels.

For I think that God hath set forth us the apostles last... (verse 9). The Corinthians felt that they should be treated as royalty, but the apostles were far from being treated as kings. In the world's estimation, they were last, the least, the lowest, and the most afflicted and persecuted of all men. The apostles' experience was not one of privilege, but of pain and persecution. Death was their allotment. To be *appointed to death* meant to be always under the threat of death; but it also meant to be treated as those who are condemned to death—convicts, prisoners, or persons who had lost all the privileges and comforts of life. Paul was thankful to be treated this way, for this was proof that he and Apollos were not of the world, but of God.

The Greek word for *spectacle* can also be translated "theater." It means that they were gazed upon as one watches a show in the theater. They were on exhibit to the world, and people were amazed at how they endured the suffering they experienced. Paul was saying that the lot of a believer is not pomp and circumstance, but pain and suffering. It was the proof that they were true believers (see 2 Timothy 3:12; Philippians 1:27-28).

C. Credibility Reaffirmed
(1 Corinthians 4:10-13)

We are fools for Christ's sake, but ye are wise in Christ; we are weak, but ye are strong; ye are honourable, but we are despised (verse 10). Paul contrasted the apostles (himself and Apollos and others) and the Corinthians in three ways. First, the apostles were fools for Christ; the Corinthians were wise. Second, the apostles were weak; the Corinthians were strong. Third, the apostles were despised; the Corinthians were honorable. These contrasts are interesting because they show the different perspectives of each group. To be foolish, weak and despised was the apostles' view of themselves. To be wise, strong and honorable was how the false teachers viewed themselves and the Corinthians.

All that Paul says in this verse is to be seen as irony. The whole design of his irony was to show the foolishness of the Corinthians. For the Corinthians to regard themselves as wise, strong and honorable, and the apostles as the opposite, was ludicrous. Paul desired to show the Corinthians how foolish, weak and despised they really were, with their self-confident attitude and their self-exaltation. Paul was also emphasizing that he would rather be a fool, weak and despised for Christ, than to be wise, strong and honorable, and be Christ-less.

Even unto this present hour we both hunger, and thirst,... (verse 11). Paul gave further proof that he and the apostles were truly of Christ. They had suffered hunger, thirst, and rough living conditions. These things happened to Christ also. Paul submitted to these afflictions and was overjoyed to suffer for Christ's sake.

The apostles (verses 12-13) labored with their hands, toiling to the point of exhaustion. The Greeks considered this type of labor to be beneath them. Paul and the others were assaulted with abusive and injurious words, but responded with words of blessing (see Matthew 5:44). They were persecuted but they endured. They were slandered but they exhorted. They met their slander with kindness and did not retaliate, nor were they resentful. Instead, they sought reconciliation. Whatever mistreatment they received, they met it with love, endurance, patience, kindness and humility.

III. SPECIAL FEATURES
A. Preserving Our Heritage

Rewards for faithful service are promised to all believers, but many African Americans can and should be recognized for the service they have given—not for glory or fame, but to help uplift the condition of our people. One such person is Dr. Dorothy Height, who has received the Congressional Gold Medal, the highest honor of appreciation bestowed upon a civilian for distinguished services, achievements and special contributions to the nation. As President of the National Council of Negro Women for more than forty years, she has distinguished herself as one who fights to level the field for those who consigned to the sidelines. She is rightfully honored for her longevity and her fidelity to her people.

B. Concluding Reflections

How important it is for us to have the right assessment of our ministers. We must recognize them not as "super-saints," but as the stewards, the caretakers of the revelations of God. We must see them as the ones responsible for protecting, preserving, preaching, teaching and practicing God's truth. Our estimation of them must be based on their handling of the Word of God rather than external variables.

HOME DAILY BIBLE READINGS
for the week of June 25, 2006
Servants in Ministry

June 19, Monday
—1 Peter 4:1–11
—Good Stewards of God's Grace
June 20, Tuesday
—John 13:2b–9
—Jesus Washes Peter's Feet
June 21, Wednesday
—John 13:12–17
—Serve One Another
June 22, Thursday
—Mark 10:41–45
—Become a Servant
June 23, Friday
—1 Corinthians 4:1–7
—Stewards of God's Mysteries
June 24, Saturday
—1 Corinthians 4:8–13
—We Are Fools for Christ
June 25, Sunday
—1 Corinthians 4:14–21
—A Fatherly Admonition on Responsibility

PRAYER
Eternal God, our Father, we praise You for the many faithful examples of Christian men and women You have given us. We seek to follow in their footsteps so that we may bring You glory in all things. In the name of Jesus, we pray. Amen.

Lesson 5

Called to Relationships

ADULT TOPIC: Living in Relationships
YOUTH TOPIC: One Special Person
CHILDREN'S TOPIC: God Teaches Us to Trust

DEVOTIONAL READING: 1 John 4:7-16
BACKGROUND SCRIPTURE: 1 Corinthians 7:1-20, 23-40
PRINT PASSAGE: 1 Corinthians 7:2-15

1 Corinthians 7:2-15—KJV

2 Nevertheless, to avoid fornication, let every man have his own wife, and let every woman have her own husband.

3 Let the husband render unto the wife due benevolence: and likewise also the wife unto the husband.

4 The wife hath not power of her own body, but the husband: and likewise also the husband hath not power of his own body, but the wife.

5 Defraud ye not one the other, except it be with consent for a time, that ye may give yourselves to fasting and prayer; and come together again, that Satan tempt you not for your incontinency.

6 But I speak this by permission, and not of commandment.

7 For I would that all men were even as I myself. But every man hath his proper gift of God, one after this manner, and another after that.

8 I say therefore to the unmarried and widows, It is good for them if they abide even as I.

9 But if they cannot contain, let them marry: for it is better to marry than to burn.

UNIT II
Called to Obedience

CHILDREN'S UNIT
We Obey God

KEY VERSE

For I would that all men were even as I myself. But every man hath his proper gift of God, one after this manner, and another after that.
—1 Corinthians 7:7

OBJECTIVES
Upon completion of this lesson, students are expected to:

1. Understand the proper use of the body in marriage;

2. Know the difference between sex within marriage and celibacy;

3. Have a proper understanding of the sexual relationship; and,

4. Understand the responsibility of a believer and an unbeliever in marriage.

10 And unto the married I command, yet not I, but the Lord, Let not the wife depart from her husband:

11 But and if she depart, let her remain unmarried, or be reconciled to her husband: and let not the husband put away his wife.

12 But to the rest speak I, not the Lord: If any brother hath a wife that believeth not, and she be pleased to dwell with him, let him not put her away.

13 And the woman which hath an husband that believeth not, and if he be pleased to dwell with her, let her not leave him.

14 For the unbelieving husband is sanctified by the wife, and the unbelieving wife is sanctified by the husband: else were your children unclean; but now are they holy.

15 But if the unbelieving depart, let him depart. A brother or a sister is not under bondage in such cases: but God hath called us to peace.

1 Corinthians 7:2-15—NRSV

2 But because of cases of sexual immorality, each man should have his own wife and each woman her own husband.

3 The husband should give to his wife her conjugal rights, and likewise the wife to her husband.

4 For the wife does not have authority over her own body, but the husband does; likewise the husband does not have authority over his own body, but the wife does.

5 Do not deprive one another except perhaps by agreement for a set time, to devote yourselves to prayer, and then come together again, so that Satan may not tempt you because of your lack of self-control.

6 This I say by way of concession, not of command.

7 I wish that all were as I myself am. But each has a particular gift from God, one having one kind and another a different kind.

8 To the unmarried and the widows I say that it is well for them to remain unmarried as I am.

9 But if they are not practicing self-control, they should marry. For it is better to marry than to be aflame with passion.

10 To the married I give this command—not I but the Lord—that the wife should not separate from her husband

11 (but if she does separate, let her remain unmarried or else be reconciled to her husband), and that the husband should not divorce his wife.

12 To the rest I say—I and not the Lord—that if any believer has a wife who is an unbeliever, and she consents to live with him, he should not divorce her.

13 And if any woman has a husband who is an unbeliever, and he consents to live with her, she should not divorce him.

14 For the unbelieving husband is made holy through his wife, and the unbelieving wife is made holy through her husband. Otherwise, your children would be unclean, but as it is, they are holy.

15 But if the unbelieving partner

separates, let it be so; in such a case the brother or sister is not bound. It is to peace that God has called you.

POINTS TO BE EMPHASIZED
ADULTS
Key Verse: 1 Corinthians 7:7
Print: 1 Corinthians 7:2-15

—Some Corinthians may have concluded that sexuality was part of a fleshly, unspiritual existence and that believers ought to renounce physical pleasures.

—Paul offers a single consistent position: celibacy is good, and sex within marriage is acceptable and expected.

—Paul believed that a Christian should remain married to an unbeliever and that the Christian might eventually convert the other person.

YOUTH
Key Verse: 1 Corinthians 7:17
Print: 1 Corinthians 7:2-15

—We must seek God's counsel when it comes to choosing a marriage partner.

—Developing lasting relationships involves careful consideration of feelings and obligations to the partner.

—Responsibility, obligation and respect are necessary to a healthy relationship.

CHILDREN
Key Verse: 1 Corinthians 7:32a
Print: Matthew 6:25-33; 1 Corinthians 7:32a

—God provides for our basic needs.

—God takes care of all of creation—plants, animals, and all of nature.

—If believers strive to please God first, God will provide what they need to live a good life.

—God wants us to be free from anxiety.

—Worrying brings only negative consequences.

TOPICAL OUTLINE OF THE LESSON

I. INTRODUCTION
  A. Marriage and Singleness
  B. Biblical Background

II. EXPOSITION AND APPLICATION OF THE SCRIPTURE
  A. The Difference Between Marriage and Celibacy
    (1 Corinthians 7:2-5)
  B. The Delight of Celibacy
    (1 Corinthians 7:6-7)
  C. The Directives for Marriage
    (1 Corinthians 7:8-15)

III. SPECIAL FEATURES
  A. Preserving Our Heritage
  B. Concluding Reflections

I. INTRODUCTION
A. Marriage and Singleness

With the divorce rate at 50 percent or higher among American Christians, it is expedient that Paul's biblical instruction become a major aspect of the church's ministry to the saints. Couples need to take more seriously the covenantal structure of marriage and not treat it as a personal convenience, but, rather, as a perpetual commitment made to God and to the spouse.

It is possible that some of the Jewish Christians in Corinth were pressuring single Gentile believers to get married. But some of the Gentiles, perhaps because of past experiences, were inclined to remain single. Those Gentiles, reacting to the sexual sin of their past, came to look at celibacy not only as the ideal state, but the only, truly godly state, which is how the Jews viewed marriage. Paul acknowledged that singleness is good, honorable and excellent, but he does not support the claim that it is a more spiritual state or that it is more acceptable to God than marriage.

B. Biblical Background

Paul's writings in 1 Corinthians 7 contain extensive teaching on marriage and singleness that is in a class by itself. The Corinthians, evidently, had many different opinions about marriage. They were uncertain about fornication, adultery and celibacy. Some frowned on the marital relationship, seeking to gratify themselves without submitting to this sacred institution. Paul addressed this issue to clarify these critical issues. If followed, his message to them would foster healing and wholeness in families and in the church.

While studying this passage, it should be kept in mind that Paul and the other believers expected the imminent return of Christ. Nevertheless, Paul's admonishments are just as valid for today's Christians as they were for the early Corinthians. Despite strong biblical directives, there is still a great deal of confusion about celibacy, and the role and structure of marital relationships.

II. EXPOSITION AND APPLICATION OF THE SCRIPTURE
A. The Difference Between Marriage and Celibacy
(1 Corinthians 7:2-5)

Paul had received a letter from the Corinthians that apparently contained a number of the church's concerns and problems. Among those concerns was the issue of marriage. In these verses, Paul addressed the conflict over singleness and celibacy. In the very first verse, he established that celibacy is good: *It is good for a man not to touch a woman.* This phrase was the Jewish way of speaking about the sexual relationship (see Genesis 20:6; Proverbs 6:29). Paul advised that it is a blessed state for Christians who are gifted or called to live as singles. There are those for whom sex is not a compelling desire or who are sufficiently disciplined to forgo sex outside of marriage.

Nevertheless, to avoid fornication,... (verse 2). Paul explained further the right way to live single. Many of the Corinthians had immoral lifestyles. Fornication was ingrained in their culture and was a part of their daily lives. They did not view it as sin. Paul cautioned that the way to protect themselves in the sight of God was to *let every man have his own wife, and let every woman have her own husband.* By placing emphasis on the adjective *own,* Paul was speaking of marriage and its true design—one man and one woman committed to a sacred and sanctified covenantal relationship.

Paul did not reduce marriage to a "legal" way to gratify one's sexual desires; Paul was establishing the sacredness of sex, which can only be manifested through the sanctity of marriage. Furthermore, Paul compared the marriage relationship to the relationship that Christ has with His church. Upheld in this light, marriage is greater than a haven for sexual fulfillment; it is a picture of the awesome relationship of Christ and His church.

Let the husband render unto the wife due benevolence: and likewise also the wife unto the husband (verse 3). Paul further explains the commitment the husband and wife should have as it relates to the sexual relationship. There are two important principles Paul sets forth regarding this special relationship: (1) it is due; and (2) it is an act of benevolence. It is merited by the nature of the relationship. It is also a benevolent act of giving in love that benefits both individuals.

Paul's instruction in this verse suggests that some of the married Corinthians were abstaining from sexual relations with their spouses. This meant that they were confused about both practices—marriage and celibacy. A life of celibacy is not designed to include marriage, and married individuals were not to be celibate.

The wife hath not power of her own body, but the husband: and likewise also the husband hath not power of his own body, but the wife (verse 4). Paul explained further this responsibility by clarifying the couple's understanding of their bodies. In marriage, ownership of each spouse's body is exchanged. Prior to marriage, the woman had authority over her body and the man had authority over his body. But when they married, those authorities were given to the other. This means that the husband cannot deny his wife his body because it belongs to her, and vice versa.

In this light, since the husband and wife exchange authority over their bodies, the husband is to satisfy his body—that is, the body of his wife; the wife is to satisfy her body—that is, the body of her husband. If this principle and truth is believed and practiced throughout the marital relationship, many more marriages will survive "until death do us part." If the husband views his wife as "his own flesh" (Ephesians 5:28-29) and the wife does the same for the husband, the divorce rate will greatly decrease. Interpreted this way, whether the couple's experiences are bad or good, or whether they face sickness or health, riches or poverty, they will never "hate" their own flesh.

Defraud ye not one the other, except it be with consent for a time... (verse 5). Paul's instruction further shows that the Corinthians did not hold marriage as a holy state as they did celibacy. Those who followed this belief and separated from their spouse and embraced celibacy soon became regarded as "super-saints," believing they had reached a higher level of spirituality. Such teaching threatened the marital relationship, and Paul had to give clear instructions to overrule this distorted and potentially damaging belief.

The Greek word for *defraud* means "deprive." Paul was not giving an opinion, but a command. Married couples were to stop depriving each other of sexual relations; it is unhealthy for the marriage.

Abstaining from the sexual relationship is only acceptable *with consent* or agreement. Both partners must agree to the abstinence. The couple must agree to abstain from the sexual relationship, but they were to do so only *for a time*. By instructing the married couple to consent to a set time,

Paul was showing the importance of unity and respect within the relationship. The only reason why couples were to abstain was *that ye may give yourselves to fasting and prayer.* The only occasion for abstinence is spiritual nourishment and development. Taking time for special personal prayer and fasting is essential in the life of the believer. Since married couples should pray together regularly, Paul may have been referring here to a special time of fasting and prayer. He also may be advocating that if either spouse is dealing with a personal issue or concern, he or she needs abstinence. Establishing the right environment for problem solving, decision making and receiving divine direction is critical to the marital relationship.

Once the time agreed upon has ended, the spouses should resume their physical intimacies, *that Satan tempt you not for your incontinency.* Satan is aware of a couple's period of abstinence and will do whatever he can to disrupt and destroy this relationship. He knows that adultery is one of the best means to accomplish this goal. The word *incontinency* means "lack of self-control." After abstaining from a pleasurable activity to which we are accustomed, we must take swift action to protect ourselves from the enemy's temptation.

B. The Delight of Celibacy
(1 Corinthians 7:6-7)

But I speak this by permission, and not of commandment (verse 6). Paul's discussion about celibacy and marriage was not given for them to conclude that he was commanding them to marry. He could only give them permission. In fact, our marital status does not determine our spirituality or Christian maturity.

For I would that all men were even as I myself... (verse 7). Paul here stated his desire and God's design. The freedom of the single life had allowed Paul to work and minister without having to concern himself with providing for a family. A family brings joys and pleasures to a minister; but it also brings many challenges as well (see 1 Corinthians 7:32-34). The responsibilities of caring for a family would limit much of the ministry Paul was called to accomplish. It was his desire that all believers had his freedom—then they could devote a greater amount of time and energy to the Lord's work.

Despite Paul's personal desire, he acknowledged that every believer has a *proper gift of God*. Not everyone is gifted to be celibate; not everyone has the gift of marriage. Each person has a gift and calling from God. It is important that each believer knows what that gift is, otherwise that believer may have difficulty in following God's call. Those who are called to celibacy should never marry; and those who cannot maintain a celibate lifestyle should marry.

C. The Directives for Marriage
(1 Corinthians 7:8-15)

I say therefore to the unmarried and widows, It is good for them if they abide even as I (verse 8). From verses 10, 11 and 34, we may conclude that the *unmarried* were those who were previously married—not widows (verse 8) nor virgins (verse 34)—but who are now single. The context of verse 8 suggests that the term "the unmarried" referred to women. The context suggests that they were divorced before being saved. Both the divorced and the widows were instructed by Paul to *abide even as I*, or to remain single. They were advised to maintain their current marital status.

But if they cannot contain, let them marry: for it is better to marry than to burn (verse 9). Though it was his instructions that the unmarried and widows remain unmarried, he understood that not all previously married individuals could handle the celibate life. Therefore *if they cannot contain* (control) their sexual desires, they should marry. This phrase, *let them marry,* is a command. They were to marry because celibacy was not for them.

Those persons who could handle the burning fires and desires for sex were advised to marry: *For it is better to marry than to burn.* They would not be able to bring glory to God or to serve Him appropriately if they had no control in this area.

And unto the married I command, yet not I, but the Lord, Let not the wife depart from her husband (verse 10). Verses 10 and 11 deal with Christians who are married to Christians; however, verses 12-14 address Christians married to unbelievers. Paul's instruction to *the married* was a command from the Lord: *Let not the wife depart from her husband.* The married should remain married, and should not seek divorce. According to Matthew 19:7-8, Moses had permitted divorce because of the "hardness" of their hearts. Jesus further stated that divorce was permitted only because of adultery (see Matthew 5:31-32).

The emphasis here is the prohibition against divorce. It emphasizes the permanence of marriage—*till death do us part.* This is a command from the Lord. The idea of command shows the importance of this relationship to the Lord. For Jesus Christ to be our Lord, we must be obedient to His commands. In the case of marriage, we show our obedience by being faithful to our spouses, and by keeping our vow of permanence (avoiding divorce).

The believer should never view a command as a burden; rather, believers should embrace it as a delight and an honor. If the command is seen only as obligatory, then the full benefit of the Lord's design through that command will not be actualized. We will do it grumbling and complaining, instead of doing it with gladness and rejoicing. Viewed as delight, marriage can be filled with celebration and excitement; even the times of challenge will be times of appreciation, rather than desperation or lamentation.

But and if she depart, let her remain unmarried, or be reconciled to her husband... (verse 11). Jesus had commanded that if the wife departs, she may do so but she cannot remarry (Mark 10:12). The sacredness of the relationship and union of marriage is of such that those who marry need to understand its full meaning. The word *depart* here means divorce. If she divorces her husband, she has to remain in that state or *be reconciled to her husband.* If a wife left her husband, she was not to attempt remarriage. Jesus taught that when a person who is not divorced on biblical grounds remarries, that person commits adultery (Matthew 19:9). A marriage cannot be voided simply because one spouse leaves the other.

The other option given to a wife who *departs* from her husband was to be reconciled to him. *Reconciliation* is the calling on the believer's life (see 2 Corinthians 5:18-20). Therefore, she must be willing to do what is necessary to reconcile the union. By remaining in the marriage, a Christian spouse has an opportunity to demonstrate proof of Christ love.

But to the rest speak I, not the Lord: If any brother hath a wife that believeth not, and she be pleased to dwell with him, let him not put her away. Verses 12-14 deal with Christians being married to non-Christians. Paul was careful to acknowledge here that his counsel was his own and not from the Lord. What did Paul mean? He meant that Scripture did not give a specific command regarding this issue. However, this does not mean that what is written here was not inspired by the Holy Spirit.

In the Old Testament, the Jews were obliged to put away their idolatrous wives (Ezra 10). But the marriages Paul addressed here were unions that occurred prior to conversion.

The instruction was that if a Christian brother was married to an unbelieving wife, and she is happy to live with him and remain married, the brother was not to *put her away*, meaning divorce her. The believer could not divorce an unbelieving wife if she wanted to remain married to him. This teaching is very clear.

And the woman which hath an husband that believeth not... (verse 13). What is true of the believing husband married to an unbelieving wife is also true of a believing wife married to an unbelieving husband.

In his second letter to the Corinthians, Paul wrote these words of warning: "Be ye not unequally yoked together with unbelievers: for what fellowship hath righteousness with unrighteousness? and what communion hath light with darkness? (2 Corinthians 6:14ff). It is important to understand that Paul was telling the Corinthian believers to remain with their unbelieving spouses because these believers and unbelievers were married before they were saved; therefore, these marriages were lawful. To ask them to abolish their marriages since they came to Christ would be against the purpose of marriage. They would commit a sin by divorcing because they had no biblical grounds for such an act. Furthermore, if there were children involved, severing this relationship would create much despair.

For the unbelieving husband is sanctified by the wife, and the unbelieving wife is sanctified by the husband... (verse 14). For believers who were contemplating leaving or divorcing their unbelieving spouses, Paul added further clarification and comfort. The unbelieving spouse is *sanctified* by the believer, and even the children are *holy*. The idea of being sanctified here does not mean that an unbeliever becomes saved because of his or her marriage to a believer. Rather, it means that God will protect and provide for the union. Furthermore, by remaining in the marriage, the believing spouse becomes a channel of sanctification to the unbelieving spouse. The idea of the children being *holy* does not mean that they are saved. Rather, it means that they are also "covered" or legitimized by the believer.

But if the unbelieving depart, let him depart... (verse 15). This verse is a great conclusion to this section. If the unbelieving spouse wants a divorce, the believer is free to let the departure occur. The divorce is acceptable to God based upon 2 Corinthians 6:14ff, since they are unequally yoked. The believer will not be *under bondage*; that is, he or she will be free to remarry. Paul then added, *God hath called us to peace*. The believer must do what he or she can to keep the marriage intact; however, if the unbeliever insists on the divorce, the believer must grant it to avoid turmoil, fighting and despair. We are to live in peace (see Romans 12:18).

III. SPECIAL FEATURES
A. Preserving Our Heritage

Four hundred years of chattel slavery in this country have left its legacy upon our people in the form of fractured family relationships, including marriage. Few slaves were allowed to marry, but those determined to make a public commitment of their union adopted the practice of "jumping the broom."

Just as external forces threatened the sanctity of marriage for our people during slavery, other forces are active today. Black Christians must resist the temptation to adopt worldly practices and commit to the godly relationship that God designed marriage to be.

B. Concluding Reflections

The Corinthians felt that celibacy was a higher spiritual plane than marriage. In fact, there were those who were married who were denying their spouses the physical intimacies that were due them; others were contemplating divorce to become celibate.

Paul's instruction was that all relationships should remain as they were, according to the believers' gifts, as God has given to each person his own gift. Some are to be married, others celibate.

As believers, we must know what our gift is. Let us take very seriously Paul's directives, so that we will not fall prey to the behavior of the Corinthians. We must pray for divine understanding in this so that we may bring honor and glory to Him.

HOME DAILY BIBLE READINGS

for the week of July 2, 2006
Called to Relationships

June 26, Monday
—1 John 4:7–16
—God Is Love
June 27, Tuesday
—1 Corinthians 7:1–5
—Instructions for Husbands and Wives
June 28, Wednesday
—1 Corinthians 7:6–11
—Advice to the Unmarried and Widows
June 29, Thursday
—1 Corinthians 7:12–16
—If You Have an Unbelieving Spouse
June 30, Friday
—1 Corinthians 7:17–24
—Live as God Called You
July 1, Saturday
—1 Corinthians 7:25–31
—Remain as You Are
July 2, Sunday
—1 Corinthians 7:32–40
—Unhindered Devotion to the Lord

PRAYER

Heavenly Father, You made us and know us. Help us to know and follow the path You have laid out for us, that we might know how to live our lives and bring honor to Your name. In the name of Jesus Christ, our Lord, we pray. Amen.

Lesson 6

Called to Help the Weak

ADULT TOPIC: To Eat or Not to Eat
YOUTH TOPIC: A Matter of Taste?
CHILDREN'S TOPIC: God Teaches Us to Love

DEVOTIONAL READING: Mark 9:42-48
BACKGROUND SCRIPTURE: 1 Corinthians 8:1-13
PRINT PASSAGE: 1 Corinthians 8:1-13

1 Corinthians 8:1-13—KJV

NOW AS touching things offered unto idols, we know that we all have knowledge. Knowledge puffeth up, but charity edifieth.

2 And if any man think that he knoweth any thing, he knoweth nothing yet as he ought to know.

3 But if any man love God, the same is known of him.

4 As concerning therefore the eating of those things that are offered in sacrifice unto idols, we know that an idol is nothing in the world, and that there is none other God but one.

5 For though there be that are called gods, whether in heaven or in earth, (as there be gods many, and lords many,)

6 But to us there is but one God, the Father, of whom are all things, and we in him; and one Lord Jesus Christ, by whom are all things, and we by him.

7 Howbeit there is not in every man that knowledge: for some with conscience of the idol unto this hour eat it as a thing offered unto an idol; and their conscience being weak is defiled.

8 But meat commendeth us not to God: for neither, if we eat, are we the better; neither, if we eat not, are we the worse.

9 But take heed lest by any means this liberty of yours

UNIT II
Called to Obedience

CHILDREN'S UNIT
We Obey God

KEY VERSE

But meat commendeth us not to God: for neither, if we eat, are we the better; neither, if we eat not, are we the worse. But take heed lest by any means this liberty of yours become a stumbling-block to them that are weak.—1 Corinthians 8:8-9

OBJECTIVES

Upon completion of this lesson, students should understand that:

1. Knowledge is measured by our Christian practices, not our pride;

2. Christians should avoid any practice that causes our weaker brother or sister to stumble;

3. There are boundaries that faith set for our lives; and,

4. We should renounce practices to protect the faith of other Christians.

become a stumblingblock to them that are weak.

10 For if any man see thee which hast knowledge sit at meat in the idol's temple, shall not the conscience of him which is weak be emboldened to eat those things which are offered to idols;

11 And through thy knowledge shall the weak brother perish, for whom Christ died?

12 But when ye sin so against the brethren, and wound their weak conscience, ye sin against Christ.

13 Wherefore, if meat make my brother to offend, I will eat no flesh while the world standeth, lest I make my brother to offend.

1 Corinthians 8:1-13—NRSV

NOW CONCERNING food sacrificed to idols: we know that "all of us possess knowledge." Knowledge puffs up, but love builds up.

2 Anyone who claims to know something does not yet have the necessary knowledge;

3 but anyone who loves God is known by him.

4 Hence, as to the eating of food offered to idols, we know that "no idol in the world really exists," and that "there is no God but one."

5 Indeed, even though there may be so-called gods in heaven or on earth—as in fact there are many gods and many lords—

6 yet for us there is one God, the Father, from whom are all things and for whom we exist, and one Lord, Jesus Christ, through whom are all things and through whom we exist.

7 It is not everyone, however, who has this knowledge. Since some have become so accustomed to idols until now, they still think of the food they eat as food offered to an idol; and their conscience, being weak, is defiled.

8 "Food will not bring us close to God." We are no worse off if we do not eat, and no better off if we do.

9 But take care that this liberty of yours does not somehow become a stumbling block to the weak.

10 For if others see you, who possess knowledge, eating in the temple of an idol, might they not, since their conscience is weak, be encouraged to the point of eating food sacrificed to idols?

11 So by your knowledge those weak believers for whom Christ died are destroyed.

12 But when you thus sin against members of your family, and wound their conscience when it is weak, you sin against Christ.

13 Therefore, if food is a cause of their falling, I will never eat meat, so that I may not cause one of them to fall.

POINTS TO BE EMPHASIZED
ADULTS
Key Verse: 1 Corinthians 8:8-9
Print: 1 Corinthians 8:1-13
—Paul's comments on eating food offered to an idol are linked to the practice of buying meat used in temple sacrifices.
—Christians are called to avoid eating

meat once dedicated to an idol, if doing so will be a stumbling block to another person.

—Eating meat dedicated to idols was a hot issue in Corinth because it raised problems of boundaries between the church and pagan culture.

—Paul's concern is not that the weak will be offended by the actions of eating meat dedicated to idols; his concern is that they will fall away from Christ.

—Paul's conclusion is that he is willing to give up eating meat if that is necessary to protect the weak from stumbling.

YOUTH

Key Verse: 1 Corinthians 8:9

Print: 1 Corinthians 8:1-13

—Christians should be guided in what they do by concern for another's good rather than the rightness of their position.

—Christians need to be concerned that we may intentionally or unintentionally lead others astray.

—Leading a person into a sin is against Christ.

CHILDREN

Key Verse: Mark 12:31b

Print: Mark 12:28-34; 1 Corinthians 8:1

—The great commandment directs us to love God with our heart, soul, mind and strength, and others as ourselves.

—Loving God and others is more important than tithes, offerings and other sacrifices.

—Living by the first commandment requires a compassionate heart, understanding what is expected of us, and acting accordingly.

—Some of the Jewish scribes understood Jesus' mission and accepted His teachings.

—Knowledge builds up the individual person, but love builds up others.

TOPICAL OUTLINE OF THE LESSON

I. INTRODUCTION
  A. Idolatry
  B. Biblical Background

II. EXPOSITION AND APPLICATION OF THE SCRIPTURE
  A. The Proper Understanding of Knowledge *(1 Corinthians 8:1-3)*
  B. The Proper Perspective of Idols *(1 Corinthians 8:4-7)*
  C. The Proper Practice of Liberty *(1 Corinthians 8:8-13)*

III. SPECIAL FEATURES
  A. Preserving Our Heritage
  B. Concluding Reflections

I. INTRODUCTION

A. Idolatry

Idolatry was so ingrained in the Greco-Roman world that it had pervaded every aspect of life. Feasts, social interaction, entertainment, shops, political positions and practices, execution and administration of justice, sports, and religious practices were inundated with this ungodly practice. Icons and statues were a common sight and part of the architecture and cultural norm. It was an accepted way of living. Their writings, their conversations and their thinking were saturated with vestiges of idolatry; they were unconsciously idolatrous.

The particular concern in this passage was meat offered to idols. The offering of meat was a highly spiritual practice. This practice was done to rid the meat of evil spirits that had attached themselves to it. They believed that sacrificing the meat to the gods rendered evil "spiritless." As a result, this meat was very valuable and very popular, especially at social events.

The problem for the Corinthian Christians was threefold: (1) this was a superstitious practice and to buy such meats would mean they were catering to such beliefs; 2) the meat was offered to idols, thus associating all those who ate it with idolatry; and, 3) if they were seen purchasing and eating this meat, others would conclude that these believers had abandoned their faith and returned to their former lifestyle. Some, therefore, refused to purchase this meat because of its pagan connotation; others felt there was nothing wrong in its consumption. But there was a larger issue: the impact this practice had on weaker or immature believers, and the attitude of stronger believers who felt no obligation to protect weaker believers.

B. Biblical Background

Among the many problems that the Corinthian church had, a critical problem was their worldliness. They were unable to be in the world but not of the world. They resisted breaking ties with their pagan surroundings. They knew Christ but were not ready to surrender all to Him. Therefore, false teachers easily persuaded them. They would change their doctrinal direction with every wind of change. This problem manifested itself in the eating of meats offered to idols, among other ways.

The Corinthians had enlisted the advice of the apostle to know the lawfulness of eating meat that was used as sacrifices offered to idols. At the council of Jerusalem, The Holy Spirit directed their decision that the Gentile converts should abstain "from meats offered to idols, and from blood, and from things strangled, and from fornication" (Acts 15:28-29). So, the church was well aware of the seriousness and magnitude of this problem. Having been present at the Jerusalem Council (see Acts 15:1-2), Paul was knowledgeable of the church's teaching on the matter.

The basis of the problem had to do with stronger believers acting in a way that was detrimental to weaker believers. Paul established the importance of the relationship between the strong and weaker believers. He explains how the strong believers can have communion with and be helpful to weaker believers. He instructed the strong to be mindful of the weak. They were to be an aid to the spiritually immature rather than a hindrance. Though they were free in Christ, they were not to use that freedom in a way that would be detrimental to weaker believers.

II. Exposition and Application of the Scripture

A. The Proper Understanding of Knowledge

(1 Corinthians 8:1-3)

In verse 1, Paul identified one of the major attitudes that the Corinthian believers were manifesting. The more mature believers were saying *all have knowledge,* and Paul agreed with them. Their *knowledge* dictated that there was nothing sinful in eating meat that had been offered to idols. The Corinthians were using this claim to defend their actions and they stated their position in such a way that they would not be contested. But the apostle would not allow them to get away with such flawed reasoning. He did not dispute that they had such knowledge, but he did condemn them by declaring that *knowledge puffeth up.* The Greek word for *puffeth up* literally means "to blow, to fill with wind, to inflate"; then, "to render vain and conceited." Puffed-up knowledge makes one haughty and egotistical. It calls attention to oneself. Their truth was rooted in an attitude of superiority.

He added, *but charity edifieth.* The word *charity* is better translated "love." The Greek word used here for love means "that which seeks the best for another no matter the cost." This love edifies. *Edification* means "to build up, to strengthen, to undergird, to nourish and nurture." True love blesses and benefits others. Unlike knowledge that is self-centered, love is others-centered.

The more knowledgeable believers were full of knowledge but void of love. They were concerned about themselves but not about others. If the problem of the strong helping the weak is to be corrected, it must begin with the strong possessing and manifesting love. Pride will always destroy; love will always build. The Corinthians needed to join love to their knowledge.

In verse 2, Paul further condemned believers there by stating that they were not as knowledgeable or as mature as they thought: *If any man think that he knoweth anything, he knoweth nothing yet as he ought to know.* That is, if a person is proud or arrogant as a result of what he thinks he knows,

Many Christians ate food consecrated to idols. Much meat sold in the marketplaces had come from animals sacrificed in pagan temples. Some Christians (weak believers) had scruples about eating such meat. Others felt superior to such scruples and contemptuous toward those troubled by them. Paul rebuked the superior with their "knowledge." Paul's principles are love for others that build up community, and renunciation of one's rights for the sake of others. True blessedness consists not in knowing, but in being known by God, and it is in love that one is thus known. Note: social clubs and guilds held banquets in pagan temples; since no real acknowledgment or worship of the idol was involved for Christians, many felt that there was no objection to attending. Paul warns of the influence by example upon a brother or sister for whom such indulgence would be a violation of conscience and therefore destructive. Note: liberty is the freedom that strong believers have, based on their enlightened attitude. It is better to limit one's liberty than to cause a weak Christian harm. Knowledge without love has destructive power. "You sin against Christ" because the church is the body of Christ.

that person is really devoid of knowledge. What a severe condemnation the apostle hurled at the Corinthians! But the only antidote for their arrogance and pride was the truth.

Verse 3 is similar to what the apostle John said in 1 John 4:7-8: "Every one that loveth is born of God, and knoweth God; He that loveth not knoweth not God; for God is love." Both Paul and John understood the relationship between love and knowledge. Love is essential to knowledge. One cannot claim to know God and not love God; and one cannot love God and not know God. And love for God is manifested in love for others (see 1 John 4:21). The Corinthians were boasting of knowledge but not of their love; they were missing the main ingredient. Devoid of love, they also were devoid of true knowledge. Love is the highest expression of knowledge. The apostle was pointing out their lack of spiritual maturity.

B. The Proper Perspective of Idols
(1 Corinthians 8:4-7)

Having refuted their knowledge defense, in verse 4, Paul turned to attacking the problem of eating meat offered or sacrificed to idols. First, they all knew that *an idol is nothing in the world.* That is, there is no such thing as an idol. Since idols are made of wood, stone and precious jewels—all inanimate objects—they have no life; they are useless. They exist only in the minds of those that created them. Idols are nothing (see Isaiah 41:23-24; 44:8-10; 45:19; Jeremiah 10:14). *There is none other God but one.* This is the message throughout Scripture (see Deuteronomy 4:35; 6:4; cf.; Isaiah 43:10; 45:20-22; 46:9; Ephesians 4:6). God, the one and only God, is everything!

In verses 5 and 6, Paul reiterates the point made in verse 4—idols are only *called gods.* He reinforced these facts to give emphasis to the powerful truth of the monotheistic nature and essence of God. In verse 6, he gives the revelation of God as Father, the undisputed message of the New Testament (Matthew 28:19; John 1:14, 18; Romans 8:14-17; 1 Corinthians 1:3). As Father *of whom are all things,* He is Creator, the source of all things. And *we,* all believers, *are in him.* All believers exist for Him (see Ephesians 4:6). Then Paul affirmed that just as there is only one God, *there is one Lord Jesus Christ* (see also Ephesians 4:4). Paul would write in his second letter that there were those who preached "another Jesus" (2 Corinthians 11:4). But only Lord Jesus Christ is the only one begotten of the Father (see John 3:16, 18; 1 John 4:9). Paul offered the "full" name of Jesus to show that he was speaking of none other. He speaks not just of Jesus, or of Jesus Christ—but "the Lord Jesus Christ." This distinguishes Him as having no equal. The Christ *by whom are all things* acknowledges Him as the Maker and Sustainer of all things (see John 1:1-2; Colossians 1:16-17; Ephesians 3:9). All things are through Jesus Christ (see Romans 6:23; Ephesians 2:18; Colossians 1:18-20) *and we by him.* That is, we have become children of God and Christians because of Him (see Colossians 1:13-14).

However, Paul stated, *not all men have this knowledge*. Does this knowledge refer to the knowledge of who God is or does it refer to the truth concerning idols? It seems that both ideas are referenced here. Not all people have knowledge of God as Father and of Jesus Christ as Lord and Savior. And not all persons in the Corinthian church had the knowledge that idols are not real. It would seem that the two ideas go together. If a person truly knows who God is, that person would also know that idols are nonexistent. There were believers among the Corinthians who did not have a full understanding of God and, as a result, regarded idols as having meaning or purpose. They were not mature in their understanding of God as Father and Jesus Christ as Lord.

For some with conscience of the idol unto this hour eat it as a thing offered unto an idol. Some of the weaker believers had become so accustomed to idols that they thought of meat they ate as if the idol was something real. Therefore, being weak-minded, they were defiled. Though the act of eating these meats was not wrong, in their minds it was wrong because it pricked against their conscience—for, *their conscience being weak is defiled.* A *weak* conscience judges something wrong which in itself is not wrong. This leads to confusion and guilt. To be freed from this confusion, the believer needs more knowledge, which will enable him to understand that the act itself is not sinful. Such believers should, therefore, refrain from the practice until they come to this level of understanding (cf., Romans 14:23).

C. The Proper Practice of Liberty
(1 Corinthians 8:8-13)

In these verses, Paul established the truth concerning these foods. Regardless of whether or not one ate them, there was no spiritual value to be gained. *But meat commendeth us not to God....* The Greek word translated *commendeth* literally means "to stand near." The idea is that eating does not bring us closer to God. The Greek word for *better* can be translated "to excel"; the Greek word for *worse* can be translated "to come behind." Eating does not cause believers to excel or to come behind their relationship to God. Since God has given no commandment to refrain or to practice in a certain way regarding eating or not eating, the practice has no spiritual significance.

Despite a clear divine directive, *But take heed lest by any means this liberty of yours become a stumblingblock to them that are weak.* Though eating or not eating has no spiritual value, the issue is a much deeper one. How one uses his or her liberty is the issue. A believer should not and must not use Christian liberty (lawful power and right) in a way that it becomes a *stumblingblock* to his weaker believers. The Greek word for *stumblingblock* can also be translated "offenses." It refers to that which causes an occasion to sin or persons to fail. Paul says that if a weaker believer observes a stronger believer doing something he believes to be sinful, it will be spiritually detrimental for him.

A believer has the right to his liberty but does not have the right to use that liberty in a way that will harm the spiritual life of Christian brothers and sisters. Every believer must always remember that we are to "each esteem other better than" ourselves (Philippians 2:3), and we are to "be of the same mind one toward another" (Romans 12:16).

Verses 10 and 11 take us a step further. If a weaker believer sees a strong believer sitting and eating this meat in the idol's temple, his conscience will be *emboldened* to eat those things that are offered to idols, and through his knowledge *shall the weak brother perish, for whom Christ died?* Paul explained how a weaker brother can be encouraged to do something that he believes is sinful. The matured believer is at liberty to eat this meat in the idol's temple because he has the knowledge that idols are nothing. But he must live and act responsibly. He must consider the welfare of his fellow believer. His act can cause the weaker believer to *perish*. The Greek word for *perish* can also mean "ruin." The idea of ruin is not that he will lose his salvation, but it will cause him to sin. He is not strong enough to resist the temptation to participate in this act because he saw another and more mature believer doing it.

Paul's rhetorical question ending, *for whom Christ died*, puts the matter in perspective. The death of Christ was to save us from sin (see Matthew 1:21; Luke 19:10; Romans 5:8; 1 John 3:5; 4:9-10). Therefore, to cause a brother or sister to sin disrespects the great sacrifice that He made—He paid a great price (see 1 Peter 1:18-19). As believers, our goal and purpose is to always honor and glorify the Christ who died for us. We dishonor Him when we cause others to participate in the very thing for which He died.

Verse 13 is Paul's instruction as to how the stronger believer can aid the weak believer. Paul states that if eating meat causes a believer to sin (offend), then the stronger believer should refrain from doing so. The statement, *while the world standeth*, refers to the duration of the world, as long as time lasts, or simply, forever. Believers should never do anything that will offend a fellow believer. This is the principle that all believers should practice, and they must do it *forever*.

III. SPECIAL FEATURES
A. Preserving Our Heritage

The Black preacher has historically been the person looked up to by the Black community. In times past, the Black preacher has been a counselor, advisor, lawyer and confidant for those inside the body and out. For that reason, the personal behavior of a minister is always under scrutiny. Many "weaker" members of the household of faith will believe that if the pastor/minister does something, then that behavior is acceptable. While Paul's caution regarding stronger members and weaker ones applies to all believers, those who are postured in the limelight of the faithful must be careful to guard the way their actions will be interpreted by those with lesser knowledge of the faith.

B. Concluding Reflections

The presence of mature and strong believers is critical to the church of Jesus Christ. It is the design of the apostle Paul to commend those believers who were no longer babes, or no longer carnal. He called these believers "spiritual." They were being guided and groomed by the Holy Spirit. They were growing and glowing (strong) in the Word of God and were overcoming the Wicked One—having the strength of character and being controlled by the Holy Spirit to walk away from temptation, taking the "way of escape" provided by the Lord. They were unwavering in their doctrinal understanding, not swayed by false teachings.

The warning of this lesson is clearly expressed: we must be careful not to use our liberty in a way that will cause another believer to sin. Every believer is responsible for the welfare and well-being of brothers and sisters in Christ. We must have rooted in our minds and spirits that we will aid and assist in the maturity and spiritual development of all believers. Nothing in this life should cause us to be a detriment to our fellow believers. Using our liberty to cause another to sin is wrong. Let us be committed to "bearing one another's burdens."

HOME DAILY BIBLE READINGS

for the week of July 9, 2006
Called to Help the Weak

July 3, Monday
    —John 1:1–5
    —Called to Life and Light
July 4, Tuesday
    —Mark 9:42–48
    —Do Not Tempt Others
July 5, Wednesday
    —Mark 12:28–34
    —Love Your Neighbor as Yourself
July 6, Thursday
    —Romans 14:13–19
    —Do Not Make Another Stumble
July 7, Friday
    —1 Corinthians 8:1–6
    —We Have One God, One Lord
July 8, Saturday
    —1 Corinthians 8:7–13
    —Do Not Create a Stumbling Block
July 9, Sunday
    —1 Corinthians 10:23—11:1
    —Do All to God's Glory

PRAYER

Gracious God, our heavenly Father, continue to teach us the value of the strong bearing the burden of the weak. Help us to know that we are responsible for each other as members of Your family. Amen.

Lesson 7

Called to Win the Race

CHILDREN'S UNIT
We Obey God

ADULT TOPIC: Called to Win
YOUTH TOPIC: Called to Be a Winner
CHILDREN'S TOPIC: God Teaches Us Courage

KEY VERSE
Know ye not that they which run in a race run all, but one receiveth the prize? So run, that ye may obtain.
—1 Corinthians 9:24

DEVOTIONAL READING: Hebrews 12:1-12
BACKGROUND SCRIPTURE: 1 Corinthians 9:24—10:13
PRINT PASSAGE: 1 Corinthians 9:24—10:13

OBJECTIVES
Upon completion of this lesson, students are expected to:
1. Know the importance of self-control in running the Christian race;
2. Take the example of the Israelites as a warning to the Corinthians; and,
3. Understand the gravity of temptation and how to deal with it.

1 Corinthians 9:24—10:13—KJV

24 Know ye not that they which run in a race run all, but one receiveth the prize? So run, that ye may obtain.

25 And every man that striveth for the mastery is temperate in all things. Now they do it to obtain a corruptible crown; but we an incorruptible.

26 I therefore so run, not as uncertainly; so fight I, not as one that beateth the air:

27 But I keep under my body, and bring it into subjection: lest that by any means, when I have preached to others, I myself should be a castaway.

.....

MOREOVER, BRETHREN, I would not that ye should be ignorant, how that all our fathers were under the cloud, and all passed through the sea;

2 And were all baptized unto Moses in the cloud and in the sea;

3 And did all eat the same spiritual meat;

4 And did all drink the same spiritual drink: for they drank of that spiritual Rock that followed them: and that Rock was Christ.

5 But with many of them God was not well pleased: for they were overthrown in the wilderness.

6 Now these things were our examples, to the intent we should not lust after evil things, as they also lusted.

7 Neither be ye idolaters, as were some of them; as it is written, The people sat down to eat and drink, and rose up to play.

8 Neither let us commit fornication, as some of them committed, and fell in one day three and twenty thousand.

9 Neither let us tempt Christ, as some of them also tempted, and were destroyed of serpents.

10 Neither murmur ye, as some of them also murmured, and were destroyed of the destroyer.

11 Now all these things happened unto them for examples: and they are written for our admonition, upon whom the ends of the world are come.

12 Wherefore let him that thinketh he standeth take heed lest he fall.

13 There hath no temptation taken you but such as is common to man: but God is faithful, who will not suffer you to be tempted above that ye are able; but will with the temptation also make a way to escape, that ye may be able to bear it.

1 Corinthians 9:24—10:13—NRSV

24 Do you not know that in a race the runners all compete, but only one receives the prize? Run in such a way that you may win it.

25 Athletes exercise self-control in all things; they do it to receive a perishable wreath, but we an imperishable one.

26 So I do not run aimlessly, nor do I box as though beating the air;

27 but I punish my body and enslave it, so that after proclaiming to others I myself should not be disqualified.

.....

I DO not want you to be unaware, brothers and sisters, that our ancestors were all under the cloud, and all passed through the sea,

2 and all were baptized into Moses in the cloud and in the sea,

3 and all ate the same spiritual food,

4 and all drank the same spiritual drink. For they drank from the spiritual rock that followed them, and the rock was Christ.

5 Nevertheless, God was not pleased with most of them, and they were struck down in the wilderness.

6 Now these things occurred as examples for us, so that we might not desire evil as they did.

7 Do not become idolaters as some of them did; as it is written, "The people sat down to eat and drink, and they rose up to play."

8 We must not indulge in sexual immorality as some of them did, and twenty-three thousand fell in a single day.

9 We must not put Christ to the test, as some of them did, and were destroyed by serpents.

10 And do not complain as some of them did, and were destroyed by the destroyer.

11 These things happened to them to serve as an example, and they were written down to instruct us, on whom the ends of the ages have come.

12 So if you think you are standing, watch out that you do not fall.

13 No testing has overtaken you that is not common to everyone. God is faithful, and he will not let you be tested beyond your strength, but with the testing he will also provide the way out so that you may be able to endure it.

POINTS TO BE EMPHASIZED
ADULTS
Key Verse: 1 Corinthians 9:24
Print: 1 Corinthians 9:24—10:13
—Like athletes, believers must exercise self-control if they are to win a race.

—We are not to follow the examples of idolaters, those who indulge in sexual immorality, those who put Christ to the test, or those who complain.

—We must be alert, for we could fall when we think we are standing.

—We all face testing, but God will not let us be tested beyond our strength.

—The self-control to which Paul is calling believers is the discipline of giving up privileges for the sake of others.

YOUTH
Key Verse: 1 Corinthians 9:24
Print: 1 Corinthians 9:24—10:13
—Growing Christians are like runners in a race determined to win.
—Knowledge of the law by itself does not offer salvation.
—God is faithful and will provide a way for us to endure any testing our faith may encounter.

CHILDREN
Key Verse: 1 Timothy 1:7
Print: Daniel 1:8-15;
1 Corinthians 10:11-13

—During Babylonian captivity, things were done to attempt to eradicate the heritage of the Jews.

—Daniel and three other trainees were pious Jews who did not want to defile themselves with anything considered unclean by Jewish dietary laws.

—Like Daniel, if believers trust in God and obey God's laws, God will be with them in every situation.

—Both Daniel and Paul are examples of what happens when God's people follow a spiritual path, rather than a secular one designed by other humans.

—God is faithful and just and will assist believers in overcoming all obstacles.

TOPICAL OUTLINE OF THE LESSON

I. **INTRODUCTION**
   A. Self-control
   B. Biblical Background

II. **EXPOSITION AND APPLICATION OF THE SCRIPTURE**
   A. Committed to Win
      (1 Corinthians 9:24-27)
   B. Failed to Win
      (1 Corinthians 10:1-5)
   C. Exhorted to Win
      (1 Corinthians 10:6-13)

III. Special Features
    A. Preserving Our Heritage
    B. Concluding Reflections

I. Introduction
A. Self-control

In this section of his first letter, Paul exhorts the Corinthians to self-control and self-denial. The Corinthians were cautioned not to fall into the lifestyle of the Israelites, nor yield to the temptations which destroyed many of them (verse 6). But Paul reassured that God is merciful and faithful. He would not allow them to be tempted beyond their ability (verse 13).

For them to avoid the pitfalls, sins and punishments of the Israelites, their lives must be characterized by self-control. This fruit of the Spirit (*temperance*—Galatians 5:23) would enable them to persevere under any and all circumstances, and their lives will become examples, not of sinfulness, but of the presence and power of the Holy Spirit.

B. Biblical Background

Having urged the strong believers to waive their right of liberty for the sake of the weaker believers, the apostle moved to demonstrate how he had lived and ministered among the Corinthians, according to that same principle. He identified himself as an apostle and was entitled to all the rights of an apostle. In fact, the Corinthians were proof of his apostleship (verses 1-3; 2 Corinthians 3:1-3). As an apostle, he had the same right to be supported as any other apostle (verses 4-6). In verses 7-14, he sets forth why he was entitled to this right.

Paul chose not to exercise this right among the Corinthians. By doing so, they could not say that he was ministering for money or possessions. He knew that they would question his intentions so he would deny them that opportunity (verses 15-18). He also refused to exercise his rights by putting himself on the level of others, so that he might save some (verses 19-23). He did so to gain an incorruptible crown that would be made available only to those who deny themselves and who put forth a great effort (verses 24-27).

II. Exposition and Application of the Scripture
A. Committed to Win
(1 Corinthians 9:24-27)

Seeking to motivate the Corinthians to self-control, Paul shared his personal story (verse 24). He was not ashamed to tell his audience of his strengths and his weaknesses. Since the Corinthian church was predominantly Gentile, Paul used an illustration with which they were familiar—the games. Specifically, he wrote of those who run in a race (see Hebrews 12:1). Like the Olympic Games today, these games were very popular in Paul's day also. The winner would be highly honored. In fact, they would deify him, making him immortal. He would become famous and rich from the fortune he would accumulate.

Paul used the example of an athlete to establish his emphasis on self-control. The

Corinthians would easily understand his illustration and his emphasis. Athletes were a prime example of self-denial and self-control. In verse 24, Paul raised a rhetorical question. All who compete in the race run, but only one receives *the prize*. It was not enough to train and compete; it was all about winning. Paul then exhorts the Corinthians, *So run, that ye may obtain*. A better translation of the Greek word *obtain* is "win." If the Corinthians wanted to be winners in the body of Christ, they had to be committed to self-control and self-denial as the athletes were.

And every man that striveth for the mastery is temperate in all things. Now they do it to obtain a corruptible crown; but we an incorruptible (verse 25). The Greek word translated "striveth for the mastery" is also translated "agonizes," which describes the effort dispensed and the powers employed as the athlete engages in his particular event. *Temperate in all things* means abstinence from everything harmful and moderate, and judicious use of foods and drinks. The Greek word is also translated "self-controlled" (cf., Acts 24:25; 1 Corinthians 7:9; Galatians 5:23; 2 Peter 1:6). It does not refer to the actual competition or event, but to the strenuous time of preparation and training that is essential to compete and be competitive.

In a race, this training, agony, abstinence and preparation are all to win a *corruptible crown*. The word *corruptible* means "fading." The winner in the games would receive a garland, diadem, or wreath made of olive, pine, parsley, and similar plants or limbs. But these would soon fade. If the athletes would go through this agonizing process of self-discipline to receive a fading crown, the believer should put forth a much greater effort to receive *an incorruptible crown* which will last throughout eternity. This crown is an imperishable reward for service rendered (see 2 Timothy 4:8; 1 Peter 1:4).

In verse 26, Paul expressed his personal commitment: *I therefore so run…*, that is, he put forth the effort necessary because he realized the importance of his ministry to the world and to the church. But his running is *not as uncertainly*. This means he does not run inconspicuously or without aim. He runs in clear view of all; all eyes are fixed on him. He is totally aware of the reasons for his ministry.

He then changes metaphors: *So fight I, not as one that beateth the air,* using an image that refers to boxing. The idea of *beating the air* refers to shadow boxing. He was not throwing empty punches in the air; his fight was real and his opposition was real (see Ephesians 6:10-18).

Part of his fight was with his own body: *But I keep under my body, and bring it into subjection....* The phrase *I keep under my body* literally means "to smite under the eye," to bruise or to smite. It suggests that Paul would punch himself in the eye and beat on his body, if necessary, to keep his body under control. It was his desire *to bring it into subjection*—to make it his slave. He would not allow his body to interfere with his ministry. The body here refers not only to the physical body but to the inclinations, passions and desires of the heart—the sin nature.

Paul's reason for the subjection of his body: *lest that by any means, when I have preached to others, I myself should be a castaway.* The Greek word translated *cast away* is better translated "reprobate," "one rejected," or "disqualified." It seems to refer to an athlete who trains hard for the games but is disqualified for violating the rules of the sport. Another translation of this Greek word is to be "unworthy of the prize"—for the prize is eternal life (see James 1:12; 1 Timothy 6:12). Paul was showing the serious nature of his ministry. He wanted to be faithful and self-controlled in order to please his Lord (2 Timothy 2:4). He did not want to devote his life to the preaching ministry, sharing all its requirements with others, only to be disqualified for not meeting these requirements himself.

B. Failed to Win *(1 Corinthians 10:1-5)*

Paul turned from himself to using the Israelites as an example. He was a positive example, but Israel was a negative example. They could only be an example of what believers should avoid.

Moreover, brethren, I would not that ye should be ignorant... (verse 1). Paul uses the affectionate term *brethren* to give the Corinthians much-needed counsel concerning self-control. Stating the formula whenever he had something significant or special to say, *I would not that ye should be ignorant* (see Romans 1:13; 11:25; 1 Corinthians 12:1; 2 Corinthians 1:8), he recounted the history of the Israelites, *our fathers.* Since the majority of the Corinthian Christians were Gentiles and the *fathers* were Jewish, how are we to understand this reference? Abraham is the father of the faithful, which includes both Jews and Gentiles (see Romans 4:8-16; Galatians 3:6-9, 13-14). Since the Gentiles are also children of Abraham, all of the descendants of Abraham would be related to them through Christ.

The fact that they were *under the cloud* speaks of God's protective and providential presence in their lives: a pillar of cloud by day; a pillar of fire by night (Exodus

13:21). The Israelites were under the guidance and direction of the Lord as they journeyed from Egypt to the Promised Land (see Numbers 9:15-23; 14:13; Psalm 78:14). *And all passed through the sea.* God had parted the Red Sea and the children of Israel crossed over to freedom on dry land (see Exodus 14:21-22). This event sealed the deliverance of Israel from Egypt (see Exodus 14:23-31). This deliverance was the foundation of their faith and beliefs. Throughout the Old Testament, this event is repeated as a reminder of what God did for His people.

And were all baptized unto Moses in the cloud and in the sea (verse 2). God knew that for Moses to be effective as His leader among His people, they had to recognize his divine appointment and submit to his authority. Just as baptism unites us to Christ after we repent and confess Him as Lord, so this symbolic baptism did the same for Israel and their relationship with Moses. He was their leader and they were to be his followers.

And did all eat the same spiritual meat; And did all drink the same spiritual drink; for they drank of that spiritual Rock... (verses 3-4). The Israelites ate the *spiritual meat* and drank from the *spiritual rock*. The meat refers to the manna. By adding the word *spiritual* to these two experiences, Paul stressed the role of the Spirit, who transformed the meat and the water from a physical use to a spiritual reality. But *spiritual* also refers to what God produced for His people, and what He had provided for them.

The actual manna and water had more significance than just satisfying their appetites. They were also designed to satisfy their spiritual appetites. Just as they were nourished physically, they were also nourished spiritually in their understanding that the Lord would provide for them.

Paul offered two important points about the rock: (1) it followed them; and (2) it was Christ. The fact that the rock followed them indicates that this provision of water was not a one-time blessing. This was a continuous miracle. This rock was Christ. He was the source of the supply. It also means that Christ was present with the people. As they drank, they were refreshed by the water, and were assured by the presence of the Lord.

Verse 5 is very blunt, but its warning is beneficial: *But with many of them God was not well pleased: for they were overthrown in the wilderness.* The Israelites had been highly favored; however, God was not pleased with the greater number of them. The displeasure of God was manifested through His wrath: *They were overthrown in the wilderness.* Numbers 14:29-34 details the results of their disobedience.

Paul gave the Corinthians a carefully crafted explanation of how punishment and judgment can come upon people who ignore the commands of God.

C. Exhorted to Win
(1 Corinthians 10:6-13)

Now these things were our examples, to the intent we should not lust after evil things, as they also lusted (verse 6). The

Israelites' experiences are the example for the Corinthians and all other believers. The Greek word for *examples* literally means "types." They were types and models of caution and warning for believers to avoid doing what they did.

Numbers 11:4-5ff reveals how the Israelites, in their lust, longed for the food and their lifestyle in Egypt. In fact, throughout their wandering in the wilderness, this was their constant desire (see Exodus 16:3; 17:3; Numbers 11:18, 20; 14:2-4; 20:3-5; 21:5).

Neither be ye idolaters, as [were] *some of them; as it is written, The people sat down to eat and drink, and rose up to play* (verse 7). Paul listed the lustful sins of Israel and admonished the Corinthians not to follow their example. The first sin they were to avoid was idolatry, which was the very first sin that was committed when the Israelites were camped at Mt. Sinai (see Exodus 32). But even in making the golden calf, the people did not believe they had sinned. In fact, they were proclaiming this a worship celebration to the Lord (see Exodus 32:5).

Neither let us commit fornication, as some of them committed, and fell in one day three and twenty thousand (verse 8). In Paul's warning to avoid *fornication*, he recounted the events that took place in Numbers 25:1-9. From this passage in Numbers, it can be gleaned how idolatry and fornication are intimately connected. The first leads to the last. In fact, they seem to be inseparable (see Exodus 32:1-6). This was also true in Corinth; the temple

of Venus was a testimony to these sins. Because these sins were so prevalent in their culture, the Corinthian Christians were under constant threat.

The large number of Israelites slain as a result of these sins—well over 20,000—emphasized the seriousness of Paul's warning. They also show how serious the Lord is about sin.

Neither let us tempt Christ, as some of them also tempted, and were destroyed of serpents (verse 9). To tempt someone is to try or test with either a good or evil intent. The Israelites tempted God by putting His patience to the test. They *spoke against God and against Moses*. They expressed their discontent and complained about their conditions. The punishment of Israel would befall the Corinthians if they committed the same sin.

Neither murmur ye, as some of them also murmured, and were destroyed of the destroyer (verse 10). The idea of murmuring is to speak and complain about God's goodness and to do so with a rebellious spirit. Paul explained that the Israelites were *destroyed of the destroyer*. According to Numbers 14:29, Israel was condemned to die in the wilderness. This devastation was to be done by the destroyer. The "destroyer" here is understood by many to mean the "death angel" or the "angel of death." Many believe that this refers to the angel in Exodus 12:23; 2 Samuel 24:15-16; and 2 Chronicles 32:21.

Numbers 14:22 states that on ten separate occasions, the Israelites had murmured against the Lord. There is a subtle difference between tempting Christ and murmuring against God. Both are expressed verbally and can be used as synonyms. But tempting God refers to questioning and complaining about His goodness and testing His patience. Murmuring refers to expressing one's dissatisfaction with God's sovereign will.

Now all these things happened unto them for examples... (verse 11). The diabolical sins and the devastating punishments of Israel were intended by God to be used for examples to succeeding generations of believers. They were also written *for our admonition.* The phrase, *upon whom the ends of the world are come,* refers to the last age or dispensation.

Wherefore let him that thinketh he standeth, take heed lest he fall (verse 12). We must never overestimate our strengths. We should never believe that we can conquer any and everything, and do not need assistance. We must never think that certain sins and punishments might never befall us. If we think we are secure, we had better be careful; we may be in greater danger than we realize.

Instead of self-control and self-denial, the Corinthians had self-confidence. They were depending on themselves and their own strength rather than on God. Paul warned them to be careful, for they were more vulnerable for the *fall.* The reference to *fall* is falling into temptation that leads to sin, and being a recipient of its poison.

With the list of sins and their consequences still fresh on their minds, the Corinthians probably contemplated how they could avoid these sins and their dreaded consequences (verses 7-10). They knew that their culture was saturated with enticements and temptations abounded. Paul shared that help was available to them to be overcomers and live victoriously. Though they could not avoid temptation, they could avoid yielding to it. God had made special provision to enable them to be victors and not victims of temptation.

There hath no temptation taken you but such as is common to man; but God [is] *faithful....* The Greek word for *temptation* simply means "to prove" or "to test or try." It is a neutral word whose meaning is based on the context. That is, it can refer to testing or proving one's righteousness or it can be a testing or trying to induce one to do evil. We can understand this definition when we explain further that God does not tempt any man to do evil (cf., James 1:13)—but Satan does (cf., Matthew 6:13).

Paul affirmed that temptation *is common to man.* This means that it is typical of all humans. Those who were thinking that temptation only comes to nonbelievers need to readjust their thinking. *But will with the temptation also make a way to escape.* Paul was not teaching that we can escape being tempted. However, we can rejoice in knowing that in being tempted we have a way of escape. Since we have a way of escape, when we yield to temptation, we do so on our own volition. We choose to sin; no one forces or controls us. Sin is the choice we make. But for those who are willing, God will bring us through our temptation by giving us a way of escape, *so that ye may be able to bear [endure] it.*

III. Special Features
A. Preserving Our Heritage

It is a sad commentary that many of our people have fallen prey to the temptations of the world. They are selling their souls for clothes, shoes, cars, houses, money and drugs. Having been historically deprived of many of life's rewards, pleasures, or enticements, there is a craving in their spirits to acquire a certain lifestyle, and to do so by any means necessary.

We must be both sensitive and aggressive, working to reclaim the values and virtues that made us a resilient and overcoming people. The fire of survival and of self-respect must burn again in our communities, lest cold indifference send a chill throughout our community that can never be overcome.

B. Concluding Reflections

The Corinthians were admonished to run the Christian race with diligence and self-control. They knew that in the athletic games, all contestants ran, but only one received the prize. But in the Christian race, the crown of life, a reward from the Lord, is available to all who serve the Lord with fidelity and trust. Paul warned the Corinthians to avoid the sins of the Israelites, and to trust God, who will aid them in their times of temptation. They needed to cease their self-confidence and be aided by the Spirit to be self-controlled. If they have this fruit of the Spirit, they will live victorious lives.

HOME DAILY BIBLE READINGS
for the week of July 16, 2006
Called to Win the Race

July 10, Monday
—Hebrews 12:1–12
—Run the Race with Perseverance
July 11, Tuesday
—Ephesians 6:10–20
—Keep Alert and Always Persevere
July 12, Wednesday
—James 1:19–27
—Be Doers, Not Just Hearers
July 13, Thursday
—Philippians 3:12–16
—Press on Toward the Goal
July 14, Friday
—1 Corinthians 9:22*b*–27
—Run for the Gospel's Sake
July 15, Saturday
—1 Corinthians 10:1–7
—Do Not Follow Our Ancestors
July 16, Sunday
—1 Corinthians 10:8–13
—God Will Help You Endure Testing

PRAYER
Almighty Father, grant to us Your discerning power to be able to tell what is right and wrong, and the courage to stand up and fight for that which is right. Amen.

Lesson 8

Called to the Common Good

ADULT TOPIC: All for One
YOUTH TOPIC: Called to Share Your Gifts
CHILDREN'S TOPIC: God Teaches Us How to Use Gifts

KEY VERSE 💡
But the manifestation of the Spirit is given to every man to profit withal.
—1 Corinthians 12:7

DEVOTIONAL READING: 1 Corinthians 12:27-31
BACKGROUND SCRIPTURE: 1 Corinthians 12:1-13
PRINT PASSAGE: 1 Corinthians 12:1-13

OBJECTIVES
Upon completion of this lesson, students should understand:
1. The role of the Trinity in spiritual gifts;
2. The main purpose for spiritual gifts;
3. The description of some of the spiritual gifts; and,
4. How the church is like a body.

1 Corinthians 12:1-13—KJV

NOW CONCERNING spiritual gifts, brethren, I would not have you ignorant.

2 Ye know that ye were Gentiles, carried away unto these dumb idols, even as ye were led.

3 Wherefore I give you to understand, that no man speaking by the Spirit of God calleth Jesus accursed: and that no man can say that Jesus is the Lord, but by the Holy Ghost.

4 Now there are diversities of gifts, but the same Spirit.

5 And there are differences of administrations, but the same Lord.

6 And there are diversities of operations, but it is the same God which worketh all in all.

7 But the manifestation of the Spirit is given to every man to profit withal.

8 For to one is given by the Spirit the word of wisdom; to another the word of knowledge by the same Spirit;

9 To another faith by the same Spirit; to another the gifts of healing by the same Spirit;

10 To another the working of miracles; to another prophecy; to another discerning of spirits; to another divers kinds of tongues; to another the interpretation of tongues:

11 But all these worketh that one and the selfsame Spirit, dividing to every man severally as he will.

12 For as the body is one, and hath many members, and all the members of that one body, being many, are one body: so also is Christ.

13 For by one Spirit are we all baptized into one body, whether we be Jews or Gentiles, whether we be bond or free; and have been all made to drink into one Spirit.

1 Corinthians 12:1-13—NRSV

NOW CONCERNING spiritual gifts, brothers and sisters, I do not want you to be uninformed.

2 You know that when you were pagans, you were enticed and led astray to idols that could not speak.

3 Therefore I want you to understand that no one speaking by the Spirit of God ever says "Let Jesus be cursed!" and no one can say "Jesus is Lord" except by the Holy Spirit.

4 Now there are varieties of gifts, but the same Spirit;

5 and there are varieties of services, but the same Lord;

6 and there are varieties of activities, but it is the same God who activates all of them in everyone.

7 To each is given the manifestation of the Spirit for the common good.

8 To one is given through the Spirit the utterance of wisdom, and to another the utterance of knowledge according to the same Spirit,

9 to another faith by the same Spirit, to another gifts of healing by the one Spirit,

10 to another the working of miracles, to another prophecy, to another the discernment of spirits, to another various kinds of tongues, to another the interpretation of tongues.

11 All these are activated by one and the same Spirit, who allots to each one individually just as the Spirit chooses.

12 For just as the body is one and has many members, and all the members of the body, though many, are one body, so it is with Christ.

13 For in the one Spirit we were all baptized into one body—Jews or Greeks, slaves or free—and we were all made to drink of one Spirit.

POINTS TO BE EMPHASIZED
ADULTS
Key Verse: 1 Corinthians 12:7
Print: 1 Corinthians 12:1-13
—Our confession of faith in Christ is itself a work of the Holy Spirit.
—The spiritual gifts in the church are, first of all, gifts of God's free grace.
—All members of the community receive gifts of the Spirit, the purpose of which is for the benefit of the faith community as a whole.

—The diverse gifts are all "activated by one and the same Spirit."

—The church, the body of Christ, is composed of many members.

YOUTH

Key Verse: 1 Corinthians 12:4-5
Print: 1 Corinthians 12:1-13

—Spiritual gifts differ, but all are useful in building the body of Christ.

—We are all members of one body that has many gifts of one Spirit.

—There are a variety of gifts, but the same Lord.

CHILDREN

Key Verse: 1 Corinthians 7:7b
Print: 1 Corinthians 12:4-20, 26

—Gifts of the Holy Spirit are manifested in different ways in different people.

—Believers are empowered by the Holy Spirit in order to strengthen the body of Christ.

—All believers have unity in Christ though their spiritual gifts may differ.

—All gifts are needed to bolster the church's spiritual growth.

TOPICAL OUTLINE OF THE LESSON

I. INTRODUCTION
   A. Unity
   B. Biblical Background

II. EXPOSITION AND APPLICATION OF THE SCRIPTURE
   A. The Importance of the Gifts
      (1 Corinthians 12:1-6)

   B. The Importance of the Holy Spirit
      (1 Corinthians 12:7-11)
   C. The Importance of Unity
      (1 Corinthians 12:12-13)

III. SPECIAL FEATURES
   A. Preserving Our Heritage
   B. Concluding Reflections

I. INTRODUCTION
A. Unity

Unity is at the heart of this lesson. Though the apostle is dealing with the counterfeiting of gifts by the Corinthian church, he assumed responsibility for correcting this false teaching and bringing unity in the church.

This lesson is one of the most important in this study, in that the gifts of the Holy Spirit are essential with respect to regeneration and sanctification. In fact, regeneration makes these gifts possible— for they are received at that point (see Romans 11:29). Sanctification enables the believer to discover and develop these gifts. As the believer matures, the reality, responsibility and accountability of the gifts become evident. The Holy Spirit helps in the development and demonstration of these gifts.

Because these gifts are important, the enemy has done a good job of bringing confusion, division, misunderstanding and, consequently, weakness into the church. In fact, he has so counterfeited the gifts that there are those who cannot tell the real from the counterfeit. The enemy has kept us bickering and arguing so much that we do not and cannot fulfill God's design in and for our lives.

Unlocking the true teaching and meaning of these gifts will go a long way in helping us with our *true* role as individual believers, and our *triumphant* role as a corporate body.

Though there are many gifts, there is one Spirit; and though there are many members, there is only one body. Throughout this lesson, Paul is emphasizing the relationship between diversity and unity. It is his position that diversity is intended to express itself in unity.

B. Biblical Background

Among the many problems the Corinthian church had was the misuse of spiritual gifts. A number of the members felt like they were superior because they claimed to possess the spiritual gift of tongues. In reality, what they had was an imitation of the gift. In their attempt to be different and special, they brought into the church the babbling of the pagans where they worked themselves into a frenzy resulting in an utterance that they believed allowed them to communicate with the gods. Unfortunately, they called this utterance the "gift of tongues."

There are certain truths that can be applied to genuine gifts from the Spirit:
1. God's purpose and plan are connected to them—*my function in the body of Christ;*
2. They represent God's desire to use the believer to his or her full potential;
3. God wants the believer to be involved in the development and assistance of other believers (1 Corinthians 12:7);
4. God's power is manifested when believers know and use their gift(s);
5. God's confidence and the believer's commitment and conformity to Christ are the result;
6. God's evangelization of the world is manifested through the gifts; and,
7. God is glorified when the gifts enable the saints to be edified.

II. Exposition and Application of the Scripture

A. The Importance of the Gifts
   (1 Corinthians 12:1-6)

Now concerning spiritual gifts, *brethren, I would not have you ignorant* (verse 1). Paul begins discussing the problem the church had with spiritual gifts. The word "gifts" is in italics in the *King James Version* of the Bible, which means the word is not in the original language. It was added to give clarity and context. Paul was writing about spiritual things, and the context indicates that those things are gifts.

Paul believed that proper knowledge would lead to proper behavior and ministry. The Corinthians were suffering from a lack of knowledge; he would clarify that issue once and for all.

Ye know that ye were Gentiles, carried away unto these dumb idols, even as ye were led (verse 2). Paul now reviewed their former condition and life-style. When they were unsaved, they *were Gentiles*, or a better translation is, "pagans." In Ephesians 2:11-12, he describes what it meant to be Gentiles, or "under the power of the flesh," enslaved by carnal desires and passions. They were of the uncircumcision, which is a term of reproach and insult. They were without knowledge of the Messiah or the Savior. They were not citizens, like the Jews, which gave them access to true worship, the Law, the Temple, and the ordinances. They did not have "the covenants of promise," and as a result, had no hope.

The one characteristic of these Gentiles was their religion. It was a religion built on idolatry. These Gentiles were *carried away unto these dumb idols*. The Greek word translated *carried away* is better translated "led astray." The word describes a prisoner being escorted by an armed guard to prison. This means that these Gentiles were enslaved to the worship of idols. The fact that Paul calls these idols *dumb* speaks of their worthlessness. They were worshiping a dead, worthless piece of wood or stone, and could not break away from it.

Wherefore I give you to understand, that no man speaking by the Spirit of God calleth Jesus accursed: and that no man can say that Jesus is the Lord, but by the Holy Ghost (verse 3). It seems from this verse that there were some church members in Corinth who were publicly calling Jesus accursed in the gathered worship assembly. Paul made swift work of this ungodly practice by condemning it with all of the apostolic authority he could muster. The word *accursed* refers to a person or thing that is set aside for destruction and is targeted for divine displeasure. Paul says that it is not possible for the Spirit to say this. No one can curse Jesus Christ and be under the influence or control of the Holy Spirit.

The Holy Spirit will never speak ill of the Lord Jesus Christ; He would never blaspheme His name. But He will always proclaim *that Jesus is the Lord*. To simply say that Jesus is the Lord is not what Paul was advocating, for anyone can say that. In Matthew 7:21, Jesus emphatically admonished, "Not every one that saith unto me, Lord, Lord,

---

Paul gives a perspective of spiritual gifts to the Corinthians. Gifts (*charistmata*), services (*diakoniai*) and activities (*energemata*) are different ways of describing the manifestations of the Spirit. Paul emphasizes their variety, their common source, and their intended purpose: to serve the common good. Utterances of wisdom and knowledge describe speech that informs and enlightens. Faith, gifts of healing and working of miracles belong together. Prophecy is paired with discernment of spirits, or the ability to evaluate prophetic speech. Various kinds of tongues require their interpretation. All are spiritual activities because their source is the same Spirit. The weaker, less honorable, less respectable inferior members are sexual organs; all are indispensable and require honor and respect. They are compared to the more respectable members, the parts of the body not covered with clothing. The body suffers and rejoices as a single organism. The church as the body of Christ does not appear to be self-evident to the Corinthians. Paul had the universal church in view. The apostles (literally those sent) may refer to missionaries rather than to the twelve apostles.

shall enter into the kingdom of heaven; but he that doeth the will of my Father which is in heaven." Paul means that believers will proclaim the lordship of Jesus Christ not only in words but also in living. They will revere Him as the absolute authority and sovereign God. First John 4:2-3 can be applied here, for it speaks of a believer who confesses, with the aid of the Holy Spirit, that Jesus Christ has come in the flesh. The person testifying to the truth of Jesus Christ will agree with what God the Father has spoken. Likewise, what God the Father says will agree with the Holy Spirit.

In 1 Corinthians 12:4-6, reference is made to the Spirit, the Lord, and God, which is Paul's way of referring to the Trinity. Paul would have us know that each Person in the Godhead has an important role to play as it relates to spiritual gifts. *Now there are diversities of gifts, but the same Spirit* (verse 4). Each person of the Godhead has an important role to play relative to spiritual gifts. He did so to show which person of the Trinity the believer initially encounters—the Holy Spirit. He is the one who must first convict of sin (John 16:8).

The Holy Spirit gives *diversities of gifts*. The Greek word for *diversities* is also translated "varieties," meaning many different types. This seems to suggest that whatever is needed and should be done in the body of Christ, the Lord has bestowed a gift just for it.

The Greek word Paul uses for gifts is *"charismata"* (cha-ris-ma-ta). The Greek word used for gifts is related to *charis—* this is the Greek word for "grace." *Charismata* literally means "grace gifts." They are produced by grace, given by grace and utilized by grace. This means that these gifts are unearned and undeserved, for grace means God granting to us that which we do not deserve.

Though there are a variety of spiritual gifts, *the same Spirit* is the one responsible for these various gifts. This gift(s) enables believers to function and serve in the church (the body of Christ) to edify the saints, thus causing the church to glorify God, grow in grace and knowledge of the Lord Jesus Christ and to share the Gospel with the world.

The same Lord refers to the Lord Jesus Christ (see Romans 10:9). Since He is Head of the church (see Ephesians 1:22; 4:15; 5:23) and chief Administrator, He determines to whom these gifts will be granted. Since spiritual gifts are given for the benefit of all the saints (the whole church, see verse 7), then each gift is used to edify the body of Christ. As each gift does its ministry, the whole church and the members therein are ministered unto.

Even with all of these gifts in operation, God is in control of it all: *And there are diversities of operations, but it is the same God which worketh all in all*. The Greek word translated *operations* literally means "energies," or "the results of the energy," and is also translated "workings," or "effects." *God* here refers to God the Father (see Ephesians 4:6). Since God the

Father is preeminent in the Godhead, He determines the effects or results of the energy that He provides for each gift. This also means that the same person dispensing his gift will not always have the same effect, even if he is using his gift for the same person, at the same time or at a different time. ...*which worketh all in all.* All of these "effects" can be traced back to God the Father. No one will be confused about who is working in the life of a believer who is faithfully using his or her spiritual gift. God will always or should always get the glory for what occurs.

Paul's point to the Corinthians was that no one can boast when it comes to any aspect of spiritual gift(s). Everything that has to do with spiritual gifts must be credited to the Godhead. Those who claim that they can do anything in this area are misguided or full of pride. The ministry of spiritual gifts is a total work of God!

B. The Importance of the Holy Spirit
(1 Corinthians 12:7-11)

After explaining the origin of the gifts, Paul moved to articulate their purpose: *But the manifestation of the Spirit is given to each one for the profit of all.* God, by His Spirit, bestows the gifts on the church. They are the manifestations of the Spirit, who is representative of the Triune God. We know from verses 4-6 that the Trinity is involved in the total ministry of the gifts from bestowal to manifestation.

The Greek word translated *manifestation* means "to make known" or "to give evidence." From this word we can begin to develop the purpose of spiritual gifts. They are given to give evidence to the Holy Spirit's presence and power. Spiritual gifts put the Holy Spirit on display: they reveal Him. If sinners are to be saved, saints edified, and the Lord Jesus Christ exalted, then the Holy Spirit must be active and operative in each of these areas.

Paul also says that gifts are *for the profit of all.* The Greek word translated *profit* literally means "to bring together," but also means "to benefit," or "to be advantageous." Spiritual gifts are to bring together and benefit or edify believers. When edification takes place, maturation, evangelization and exaltation occur.

Verses 8-10 offer a listing of some of these gifts. Paul here verified that every believer receives at least one gift: *For to one is given... to another... to another....* The Greek word translated *another* means "another of a different kind." In this case it refers to different persons. The gifts he lists are:

The Word of Wisdom (Acts 15:19-21), which involves the application of a comprehensive and balanced understanding of the Scriptures to practical issues.

The Word of Knowledge (Acts 5:3; 20:25; 27:22-26)—The believer who possesses this gift is able, by the Holy Spirit, to discover truths and principles from the Scriptures, and to interpret and explain these truths. This gift is essential for preachers and teachers. The gift of wisdom and the gift of knowledge go together, for knowledge comes before wisdom. One can possess the knowledge without wisdom but one cannot possess wisdom without knowledge.

The Gift of Faith—This gift of faith is certainly much more than saving faith (see Romans 10:9; Ephesians 2:8), and the ordinary faith to trust God for everyday needs (see Matthew 6:11, 25-33). This gift is extraordinary faith in God's ability to do impossible things. There is a close relationship among this gift and the gifts of healings and miracles.

The Gift of Healing refers to the supernatural ability to heal people of physical diseases in response to the laying on of hands, praying, commanding to be healed, or some combination of them by the person having the gift. The gifts of healings (double plural in the Greek text) suggest that the healing extends to the body, the mind and the emotions.

The Working of Miracles refers to the supernatural ability to supersede the natural law. It is a gift in which the person invokes the miraculous intervention of God and performs powerful acts in a given situation with God receiving recognition for the supernatural intervention.

The Gift of Prophecy is primarily concerned with forth-telling (preaching, proclamation), not foretelling (prediction), though some aspects of foretelling (prediction) may occur. The Greek word for *prophecy* means "to speak" or "to proclaim." A believer with this gift proclaims the Word of God, which has already been revealed, in an effective manner.

Discerning of Spirits: "Discern" is from the Greek word meaning "to separate, discriminate." Discernment is the Spirit-endowed ability to discriminate between truth and error in teaching or between good and evil in behavior. The qualifying phrase *"of spirits"* limits the field of operation of this gift. It is the ability to know by which spirit a person is motivated, since Satan is the great counterfeiter of God's message and work (see 2 Corinthians 11:4, 12-15).

Divers Kinds of Tongues (Acts 2:4, 11) is the supernatural ability given spontaneously by the Holy Spirit to an individual to speak in a language or languages unknown to the speaker.

Interpretation of Tongues (1 Corinthians 14:26-27) is the gift whereby a believer is given a supernatural ability spontaneously by the Holy Spirit to translate the languages of one using the gift of tongues.

But all these worketh that one and the selfsame Spirit, dividing to every man severally as he will (verse 11). The Holy Spirit is sovereign in the ministry and distribution of spiritual gifts. We do not determine which gift or gifts we receive. We do not lay hands on individuals and confer gifts upon them. The Holy Spirit does this. Those who claim to have the power to dispense gifts to others are attempting to act in the role and place of the Holy Spirit, which is the definition of blasphemy.

C. The Importance of Unity
(1 Corinthians 12:12-13)

For as the body is one, and hath many members, and all the members of that one body, being many, are one body: so also is Christ (verse 12). Paul's point is to emphasize that though the human body is made up of many parts, those parts make up one body. Within the body of Christ, though there are individual members, they do not and cannot function apart from themselves; they are combined to allow the body to function as one entity, according to its design. Christ is the Head of the body (the church). Without the head, the body cannot exist. And as Christ is one (see Ephesians 4:5), so the church is one.

For by one Spirit are we all baptized into one body, whether we be Jews or Gentiles, whether we be bond or free; and have been all made to drink into one Spirit. Verse 13 answers the question: How do the many members become one body? Paul answered by reiterating that there is one Spirit. This is his emphasis throughout this chapter: There is "one" and only one Spirit—the Holy Spirit.

We all refers to all that are in the body of Christ, whether *Jews or Gentiles… bond or free*, all believers are *baptized into one body*. The Greek word *baptizo* means "to immerse or submerge." In Scripture, it was used to describe a person taking a bath, dyeing garments, or drawing water by dipping in a cup. The grammar used here indicates that this baptism is a one time act or experience. When believers are saved, they are Spirit-baptized and they share the same indwelling that the disciples had on the Day of Pentecost (see Acts 2:3-4; 8:14-17; 10:44-48; 19:2-6). It must be added that speaking in tongues was the confirmation that identified all other people with the Jews. What was true of the Jews was to be true of all other believers. By the baptism of the Spirit all believers are incorporated into the body of Christ. This is how the church was formed and united as *one body*. Therefore, the body of Christ is comprised of believers who are immersed with the Holy Spirit by the Lord Jesus Christ. This means that every believer must be Spirit-baptized. This baptism unites all believers, for in the context of this verse, the unity of the body of Christ is under discussion.

Paul added, *and have been all made to drink into one Spirit*. This drinking refers to the Spirit going "in," just as water goes inside of us. The drink makes reference to the "indwelling" of the Holy Spirit. According to theologian Albert Barnes, the *drink* probably refers to their partaking together the Lord's Supper. Essentially, by drinking the same cup which commemorates the death of Christ, they had partaken of the same influences of the Holy Spirit.

Paul puts together two important experiences that occur when a sinner is saved. One is Spirit baptism, immersed in the Spirit, therefore being placed into the body of Christ and to be used for its edification. The other is the indwelling of the Spirit, ensuring that the believer has eternal life, or new life in Christ.

III. SPECIAL FEATURES

A. Preserving Our Heritage

The Civil Rights Movement is a prime example of the unity within a body. Those who believed the time had come for America to treat all of her citizens as equals banded together—Black and White, rich and poor, young and old. They did not have perfection, but unity. They used a diversity of means and resources to achieve a common goal. Those who had economic means gave money. Those who had political power used pressure. Those who had time and opportunity, like the many students involved, gave themselves to be used as visible agents of protest across the South. Tragically, some gave the most by giving their lives, like Medgar Evers, James Chaney, Michael Schwerner, and Andrew Goodman.

B. Concluding Reflections

God gives us gifts *(charismata)* and calls us (Romans 8:30) and these are *irrevocable*. The Greek word for irrevocable means "not to be taken back." God's gifts and calling are *"without repentance"* (KJV). God will not "change His mind."

With this tremendous promise, let us be faithful to God's calling on our lives, and live to bring honor and glory to the Lord. However, just because our gifts are secured does not mean we can just do anything with them or nothing at all. To the contrary, we must do the work of Him that sent us while it is day, for the night comes when no man can work (John 9:4).

HOME DAILY BIBLE READINGS

for the week of July 23, 2006
Called to the Common Good

July 17, Monday
—1 Corinthians 14:6–12
—Strive to Excel in Spiritual Gifts

July 18, Tuesday
—1 Timothy 6:13–19
—Be Rich in Good Works

July 19, Wednesday
—1 Corinthians 12:1–6
—Varieties of Gifts

July 20, Thursday
—1 Corinthians 12:7–11
—All Gifts Activated by the Spirit

July 21, Friday
—1 Corinthians 12:12–20
—The Body Consists of Many Members

July 22, Saturday
—1 Corinthians 12:21–26
—If One Member Suffers, All Suffer

July 23, Sunday
—1 Corinthians 12:27–31
—Strive for the Greater Gifts

PRAYER

God our Father, help us to be committed to using the gifts You have given us to enhance the quality of life for all people. Let us be ever mindful that these gifts are not given to us for or own purpose or glory. You have entrusted these gifts to us to edify Your people and Your Kingdom. Amen.

Lesson 9

Called to Love

ADULT TOPIC: Love Comes First
YOUTH TOPIC: Called to Love
CHILDREN'S TOPIC: God Teaches Us How to Love

KEY VERSE

Now abideth faith, hope, charity, these three; but the greatest of these is charity.
—1 Corinthians 13:13

DEVOTIONAL READING: John 3:16-21
BACKGROUND SCRIPTURE: 1 Corinthians 13:1-13
PRINT PASSAGE: 1 Corinthians 13:1-13

OBJECTIVES

Upon completion of this lesson, students will understand that:

1. Without love, spiritual gifts and religious practices are void;
2. Love should have priority in the lives of Christians;
3. Only as love presides over our common life in the church will spiritual gifts find their rightful place.

1 Corinthians 13:1-13—KJV

THOUGH I speak with the tongues of men and of angels, and have not charity, I am become as sounding brass, or a tinkling cymbal.

2 And though I have the gift of prophecy, and understand all mysteries, and all knowledge; and though I have all faith, so that I could remove mountains, and have not charity, I am nothing.

3 And though I bestow all my goods to feed the poor, and though I give my body to be burned, and have not charity, it profiteth me nothing.

4 Charity suffereth long, and is kind; charity envieth not; charity vaunteth not itself, is not puffed up,

5 Doth not behave itself unseemly, seeketh not her own, is not easily provoked, thinketh no evil;

6 Rejoiceth not in iniquity, but rejoiceth in the truth;

7 Beareth all things, believeth all things, hopeth all things, endureth all things.

8 Charity never faileth: but whether there be prophecies, they shall fail; whether there be tongues, they shall cease; whether there be knowledge, it shall vanish away.

9 For we know in part, and we prophesy in part.

10 But when that which is perfect is come, then that which is in part shall be done away.

11 When I was a child, I spake as a child, I understood as a child, I thought as a child: but when I became a man, I put away childish things.

12 For now we see through a glass, darkly; but then face to face: now I know in part; but then shall I know even as also I am known.

13 And now abideth faith, hope, charity, these three; but the greatest of these is charity.

1 Corinthians 13:1-13—NRSV

IF I speak in the tongues of mortals and of angels, but do not have love, I am a noisy gong or a clanging cymbal.

2 And if I have prophetic powers, and understand all mysteries and all knowledge, and if I have all faith, so as to remove mountains, but do not have love, I am nothing.

3 If I give away all my possessions, and if I hand over my body so that I may boast, but do not have love, I gain nothing.

4 Love is patient; love is kind; love is not envious or boastful or arrogant

5 or rude. It does not insist on its own way; it is not irritable or resentful;

6 it does not rejoice in wrongdoing, but rejoices in the truth.

7 It bears all things, believes all things, hopes all things, endures all things.

8 Love never ends. But as for prophecies, they will come to an end; as for tongues, they will cease; as for knowledge, it will come to an end.

9 For we know only in part, and we prophesy only in part;

10 but when the complete comes, the partial will come to an end.

11 When I was a child, I spoke like a child, I thought like a child, I reasoned like a child; when I became an adult, I put an end to childish ways.

12 For now we see in a mirror, dimly, but then we will see face to face. Now I know only in part; then I will know fully, even as I have been fully known.

13 And now faith, hope, and love abide, these three; and the greatest of these is love.

POINTS TO BE EMPHASIZED
ADULTS
Key Verse: 1 Corinthians 13:13
Print: 1 Corinthians 13:1-13
—Religion minus love is futile and meaningless.
—Love's permanence contrasted with tongues, prophecy and knowledge.
—Faith, hope and love are the enduring character marks of the Christian life.
—Love will endure eternally.

YOUTH
Key Verse: 1 Corinthians 13:3
Print: 1 Corinthians 13:1-13
—Love is the greatest and most distinctive characteristic of our relationship with God and others.

—Love is an active, dynamic and healing response to life's situations.
—Love should be the one quality that separates believers from unbelievers.
—Unlike earthly things, love never ends.

CHILDREN

Key Verse: 1 Corinthians 13:8a
Print: 1 Corinthians 13:4-13; John 3:16
—Love is the most important aspect of Christian character because it is inspired by God's love.
—The most powerful gift is worthless unless it is powered and tempered by love.
—It is impossible to love unconditionally without the indwelling of the Holy Spirit.
—Love is an active, dynamic, healing response to life's situations.
—Love should be the one quality that separates believers from nonbelievers.

TOPICAL OUTLINE OF THE LESSON

I. INTRODUCTION
  A. Love
  B. Biblical Background

II. EXPOSITION AND APPLICATION
    OF THE SCRIPTURE
  A. The Priority of Love
     (1 Corinthians 13:1-3)
  B. The Perception of Love
     (1 Corinthians 13:4-7)
  C. The Preeminence of Love
     (1 Corinthians 13:8-13)

III. SPECIAL FEATURES
  A. Preserving Our Heritage
  B. Concluding Reflections

I. INTRODUCTION
A. Love

The thirteenth chapter of 1 Corinthians is believed to be the best and most comprehensive treatise on love. Though love is discussed throughout Scripture, it is generally in fragment. Here, Paul knits superb explanation of love into a beautiful and meaningful tapestry. Paul then seemed to dip deeply into the recesses of the consciousness and character of God, pulling out nuggets of truth and precious pearls of eternity.

At the close of Paul's explanation on the Holy Spirit's ministry of giving gifts to all believers (chapter 12), Paul appealed to the Corinthians (verse 31) to stop seeking greater gifts because that is futile. Each believer has received from God the gift(s) he or she will possess; there is no need to seek greater gifts. What the Corinthians needed was to seek a more excellent way—the way of love. This would give them satisfaction and contentment, and allow them to experience the unity that identifies them as the body of Christ.

Since Paul admonished the Corinthians to seek the more excellent way of love. Apparently, the attribute of God that had inspired their salvation was missing in those who were of God.

B. Biblical Background

Paul was not content to simply set forth the doctrine of spiritual gifts in a clear and comprehensive way. They needed to know more. The Corinthians' problem was not just the misuse and misunderstanding of the gifts. Theirs was a deeper problem: they did not manifest love.

The *King James Version* uses the word *charity* to translate the Greek word for unconditional love—agape. However, charity does not capture the contemporary understanding of this awesome word for God's love. Therefore, throughout this lesson, love will be used in the place of charity, even in quoting the KJV translation.

II. Exposition and Application of the Scripture

A. The Priority of Love
(1 Corinthians 13:1-3)

Though I speak with the tongues of men and of angels, and have not charity, I am become as sounding brass, or a tinkling cymbal (verse 1). Paul began his discussion of the "more excellent way" (1 Corinthians 12:31) by addressing the issue of tongues. This apparently was a major issue because it is mentioned frequently in this writing, especially in chapter 14. The Corinthians seem to have valued this gift above others. Paul wrote that even if a person possesses all the human languages, and the language of angels, and did not have love, that person's speaking is no more significant than *a sounding brass or a tinkling cymbal,* two instruments used in pagan worship.

This means that the gift of tongues, without love, is merely a noisy sound that makes no sense. Instruments that are designed to make music, but make only noise, are useless. So is the one who speaks the best of human and divine languages without love. The *sounding brass* refers to the instrument that was worn on the thumb and middle finger. This was a small and undignified instrument. The word *tinkling* of the cymbal refers to the clanging sound of a cymbal. Paul may have adopted this illustration because of the Corinthians who were speaking in ecstatic utterances claiming it was the gift of languages. But even if they did practice the genuine gift, without love the end result would be the same.

And though I have the gift of prophecy, and understand all mysteries, and all knowledge; and though I have all faith, so that I could remove mountains, and have not charity, I am nothing (verse 2). The gift of prophecy was another important gift in the Corinthian church. The gift of prophecy is the supernatural ability to effectively utter or proclaim the Word. According to Paul, even one who possesses the gift of prophecy, knows all mysteries (the secret revelations of God that are now revealed) and has *all knowledge* (omniscience), but does not have love, that person is *nothing*.

The gift of faith is certainly much more than saving faith (see Romans 10:9; Ephesians 2:8) or the faith to trust God for everyday needs (see Matthew 6:11, 25-33). In this verse, we see an example of the kind of faith that can *remove mountains* (see Mark 11:22-24). But one who possesses the gift of such faith, but has no love, is *nothing*.

And though I bestow all my goods to feed the poor, and though I give my body to be burned, and have not charity, it profiteth me nothing (verse 3). The gift of benevolence, where a believer gives all his *goods to feed the poor*; and (2) the gift of martyrdom, the sacrificing of one's life or well-being for the cause of Christ *profiteth...nothing* if done in the absence of love.

Eloquent language, prolific prophecy encompassing all knowledge, mountain-moving faith, elaborate, benevolence, and martyrdom without love profits nothing for the kingdom of God. They do not bring edification to the body of Christ, which is the primary reason for the spiritual gifts (see 1 Corinthians 12:7; 14:3-4, 12-17, 26).

The Corinthians, who boasted about their spirituality (see 1 Corinthians 1:4-7; 2 Corinthians 8:7), were likely alarmed by Paul's words. They believed that their gifts, elevated them above others. But Paul cautioned them take their focus off of themselves and manifest God's love as they were gifted to do; otherwise, they would be doing nothing of worth. This is the condemnation of any believer who feels that he or she can exercise spiritual gifts without love.

B. The Perception of Love
(1 Corinthians 13:4-7)

Charity suffereth long, and is kind; charity envieth not; charity vaunteth not itself, is not puffed up (verse 4). Having discussed what happens when love is not manifested, Paul shifts his emphasis to explain why love is so valuable to the exercise of spiritual gifts. The term *suffereth long* is better understood as longsuffering or patient. The Greek word used refers to being patient with people (see Ephesians 4:2), rather than with circumstances or events.

Paul speaks of love out of his personal experiences, and, by implication, extends it to everyone. Tongues (14:18), prophetic powers (14:37), mysteries and knowledge (2:6-13; 4:1; 15:51), faith or the power to heal (Romans 15:18-19), giving away possessions (4:11; 9:18), and handing over his body (2:4:10-12) relate to Paul's personal experiences. "Boast" is used in a positive sense. This profile of love are terms used in Paul's own ministry: patient and kind (2 Corinthians 6:6), not envious or boastful (3:7, 21), not arrogant or rude (2 Corinthians 2:17; 4:1-2), does not insist on its own way (10:24, 33), not irritable or resentful (4:14), does not rejoice in wrongdoing but rejoices in the truth (2 Corinthians 6:10; 11:29), bears, believes, hopes, endures (9:27; 2 Corinthians 6:3-10). As valuable as they are, both knowledge and prophetic speech give an incomplete picture. The "complete" probably refers to the end time, when God is fully revealed. The phrase "In a mirror, dimly" compares life to looking in a mirror that yields an unclear image. Paul thinks of conversion as being fully known by God. These three—faith, hope and love—are difficult to separate (see Colossians 1:4-5; 1 Thessalonians 1:3).

Love enables one to be long-tempered, so it is never inconvenienced, never taken advantage. Love does not seek revenge. The word *kind* means to be useful, to serve, or to be gracious. Love seeks the well-being of others and seeks to benefit and bless them.

Love envieth not.... This statement is the beginning of eight observations that Paul made about the feelings and behaviors that love does *not* manifest. Envy is an ungodly desire for what someone else owns or has accomplished meshed with a desire to diminish or destroy that accomplishment.

Love vaunteth not itself. Love does not brag or boast. Bragging or boasting involve showing off, attempting to elevate ourselves in order to draw attention to ourselves from others.

Love is not puffed up. In other words, love is not arrogant. Arrogance, which can also be regarded as pride, means being conceited, haughty, or snobbish.

Doth not behave itself unseemly, seeketh not her own, is not easily provoked, thinketh no evil. Persons motivated by love do not act in ways that are unbecoming. Love does not have poor manners or rude behavior (see 1 Corinthians 11:20-22, 27, 29-30). *Unseemly* behavior has offended many persons, especially those who enter the doors of the church.

Love seeketh not her own. It is never consumed with its own needs and desires. Love is not prejudiced or racist, sexist, classist or snobbish. It is genuinely concerned for others, not itself.

Love is not easily provoked. The Greek word translated *provoked* means to incite to anger, and deals with a sudden outburst of anger or an uncontrollable angry reaction. Love is self-control in action.

Love thinketh no evil. This means that love never keeps a record of wrongs done to it. This is how forgiveness is related to love. Forgiveness is the act of canceling all debts (acts of offense) made against the offended. Those who fail to exercise love by keeping records of wrongs done to them only put themselves in bondage.

Paul then shifted the context of his letter to show what love does: *rejoiceth not in iniquity, but rejoiceth in the truth* (verse 6). Love will never justify sin; it will never parade sin as something to be prized. When a sin is committed, love is wounded. Love will always side with truth; it will always affirm truth; it will always honor truth (see 1 John 3:16-19; 4:20).

Beareth all things, believeth all things, hopeth all things, endureth all things (verse 7). The Greek word translated *beareth* means to cover, to hide and to support or protect. *All things* refers to all the things of God; *all things* that are righteous and true (see Philippians 4:8). Love, therefore, does not seek to make the faults of others known by trying to call undue attention to them. Love does not deny or dismiss faults; but it chooses not to amplify them either. Love also supports and protects all that is righteous and truthful concerning them.

Love believeth all things. Love has faith in others and is not unnecessarily suspicious of them. Love believes that a person's motives and intentions are right and earnest. It is always ready to believe the best about others. Love will warmly receive those who have been mistreated.

*Love hopeth all things....*never gives up hope, no matter how hopeless a situation may be (see Luke 15:11-24). It desires the best for others and will hold out until that occurs. When all signs of hope for a person are gone, love continues hoping for the best, especially in regards to the repentance of a sinner.

Love endureth all things. The Greek word for endure is a military term meaning "to endure or sustain the assaults of an enemy." Love can sustain or endure any assaults made upon it. Whether that is suffering or persecution from others, love will survive under any and all of these (see 2 Timothy 2:1; Hebrews 12:2).

C. The Preeminence of Love
(1 Corinthians 13:8-13)

Charity never faileth: but whether there be prophecies, they shall fail; whether there be tongues, they shall cease; whether there be knowledge, it shall vanish away (verse 8). Having explained the nature of love, Paul concluded his great discourse by encouraging the Corinthians that love never fails. From this point on (in verses 8-13), Paul would defend the unfailing nature of love.

The Greek word that Paul uses for *fail* (in relation to love) literally means falling, withering or decaying. It refers to a flower that falls to the ground and—being detached from the tree, it withers and decays. Love will never fall, wither, or decay! In defending the unfailing quality of love, Paul contrasts it in relation to the gifts of prophecy, tongues (languages) and knowledge.

Love will never fail, whereas *prophecies...shall fail.* Love will never fail, but *tongues...shall cease* and *knowledge...shall vanish away.* There will come a time when the gifts of prophecy, tongues and knowledge will fail. He explains that by using two Greek words.

The first Greek word he uses regarding the gifts of prophecy and knowledge, (translated *fail* and *vanish away*) means "to reduce to inactivity" or "to abolish." One day the gifts of prophecy and knowledge will be reduced to inactivity or be abolished. The second Greek word used for the gift of tongues—translated *cease,* literally means to stop or "to come to an end." One day, the gift of tongues will also come to an end. When these events will occur is uncertain, although many believe that the gift of tongues ceased after the first century.

Verses 9 and 10 should be studied together to maintain the complete thought: *For we know in part, and we prophesy in part. But when that which is perfect is come, then that which is in part shall be done away.* Paul showed them the relationship between the gifts of knowledge and prophecy and the coming of *that which is perfect*. Compared to the *perfect*, our knowledge is limited or partial and so is our prophecy. So when the *perfect* comes, these gifts will be done away.

Paul then turned their attention to his own spiritual development. *When I was a child, I spake as a child, I understood as a child, I thought as a child: but when I became a man, I put away childish things* (verse 11). When he was immature, as a *child*, he acted accordingly. But after maturing into an adult, he was transformed and no longer needed his childish ways. Barnes has determined, "There will be, doubtless, as much difference between our present knowledge, and plans, and views, and those which we shall have in heaven, as there is between the plans and views of a child and those of a man."

In verse 12 Paul continued his discourse about knowing *in part*, and the coming of the full knowledge—*Now I know only in part; then I will know fully, even as I have been fully known* (NRSV).

Though we have the full revelation of God in the Bible, we still do not know or understand everything there is to know about God's mysteries. We *now see through a glass, darkly*. There are many things that we will not know as long as we are on this side of life; we see through a glass (mirror) darkly. The mirrors of ancient times were made of polished metal or brass, and the images were marred and obscure. Paul uses this illustration to show that we do not yet have a clear understanding. Just as the images in the mirror are obscure, so our knowledge and prophecy is obscure or imperfect.

But what is unclear or obscure will be clarified: *but then face to face*. The words *but then* refer to the coming of the perfect. The phrase *face to face* means seeing clearly, without anything to obscure one's view. *But then shall I know even as also I am known*. Paul would one day know fully just as he also has been fully known. Nothing would be hidden then.

And now abideth faith, hope, charity, these three... (verse 13). The word *abideth* also means to remain or continue. It refers to a person remaining in a certain place or being in a certain state or condition. A better translation here is the word "permanent." Although prophecy and knowledge will fail and tongues will cease, faith, hope and love are permanent.

The greatest of these is [love]. Faith will one day give way to sight; hope will give way to fruition; but love will not give way to anything. Love will always be love.

Love is more important than faith or hope, not simply because it will endure longer, but also because it exerts a wider influence than hope or faith. Love overcomes more evils and is the key to harmony among all humankind. Love is an essential ingredient to society and to the Kingdom. Faith and hope generally have individual application; love has a corporate application. The kingdom of God stands upon the foundation of love.

Believers are saved by faith but the kingdom of God depends on Love.

Love supersedes the power of tongues, the power of knowledge, the power of understanding all mysteries and even above all faith. Love is the more excellent way.

III. Special Features
A. Preserving Our Heritage

The vestiges of years of racism, hatred and discrimination have infected African Americans with a particular brand of self hatred. We have learned to hate our complexion, our culture, our hair, our history, and each other. Our people would do well to take Paul's admonishment to heart. No matter how great our accomplishments as a people, if we are lacking love for ourselves and for each other, these achievements ring a hollow sound.

B. Concluding Reflections

Paul's exposition on love is a departure from most of his writings, much of which focuses on faith. His writing here gives us insight into how much the apostle truly loved the church.

The Greek word translated "love" or "charity" in this chapter is *agape*, generally understood as "unconditional love." It is the height and depth of love which God possesses and to which His people should aspire. Unlike the Greek, our English language has only one word for love. But like the Greek-speaking Corinthians, there is today a great deal of confusion about the role and significance of love. Today, many people are confused because they cannot understand love beyond the realm of feeling. But agape is far more than feeling, it is action which is demonstrated whether the feeling exists or not.

HOME DAILY BIBLE READINGS
for the week of July 30, 2006
Called to Love

July 24, Monday
—John 3:16–21
—God So Loved the World
July 25, Tuesday
—Romans 8:31–39
—God's Love in Christ Jesus
July 26, Wednesday
—John 13:31–35
—Love One Another
July 27, Thursday
—Romans 13:8–14
—Loving One Another Fulfills the Law
July 28, Friday
—1 John 3:11–18
—Let Us Love
July 29, Saturday
—1 Corinthians 13:1–7
—Love Defined
July 30, Sunday
—1 Corinthians 13:8–13
—The Greatest Gift Is Love

PRAYER
Kind and generous Father, we thank You for providing us with Your greatest characteristic—love. Help us not to just say it, but to manifest it—not only to our neighbors, but also to our enemies. Amen.

Lesson 10

Giving Forgiveness

ADULT TOPIC: Forgiving and Reconciling
YOUTH TOPIC: Restoring Relationships Through Forgiveness
CHILDREN'S TOPIC: God Answers Prayers

DEVOTIONAL READING: Matthew 18:21-35
BACKGROUND SCRIPTURE: 2 Corinthians 2:5-11; 7:2-15
PRINT PASSAGE: 2 Corinthians 2:5-11; 7:2-15

2 Corinthians 2:5-11; 7:2-15—KJV

5 But if any have caused grief, he hath not grieved me, but in part: that I may not overcharge you all.

6 Sufficient to such a man is this punishment, which was inflicted of many.

7 So that contrariwise ye ought rather to forgive him, and comfort him, lest perhaps such a one should be swallowed up with overmuch sorrow.

8 Wherefore I beseech you that ye would confirm your love toward him.

9 For to this end also did I write, that I might know the proof of you, whether ye be obedient in all things.

10 To whom ye forgive any thing, I forgive also: for if I forgave any thing, to whom I forgave it, for your sakes forgave I it in the person of Christ;

11 Lest Satan should get an advantage of us: for we are not ignorant of his devices.

.....

2 Receive us; we have wronged no man, we have corrupted no man, we have defrauded no man.

UNIT III
The Spirit of Giving

CHILDREN'S UNIT
We Serve with Joy

KEY VERSE
For godly sorrow worketh repentance to salvation not to be repented of: but the sorrow of the world worketh death.—2 Corinthians 7:10

OBJECTIVES
Upon completion of this lesson, students should affirm:
1. That God is a God of forgiveness;
2. The importance of attitude in forgiveness;
3. That godly sorrow is essential to forgiveness; and,
4. That forgiveness must be modeled for others to imitate.

3 I speak not this to condemn you: for I have said before, that ye are in our hearts to die and live with you.

4 Great is my boldness of speech toward you, great is my glorying of you: I am filled with comfort, I am exceeding joyful in all our tribulation.

5 For, when we were come into Macedonia, our flesh had no rest, but we were troubled on every side; without were fightings, within were fears.

6 Nevertheless God, that comforteth those that are cast down, comforted us by the coming of Titus;

7 And not by his coming only, but by the consolation wherewith he was comforted in you, when he told us your earnest desire, your mourning, your fervent mind toward me; so that I rejoiced the more.

8 For though I made you sorry with a letter, I do not repent, though I did repent: for I perceive that the same epistle hath made you sorry, though it were but for a season.

9 Now I rejoice, not that ye were made sorry, but that ye sorrowed to repentance: for ye were made sorry after a godly manner, that ye might receive damage by us in nothing.

10 For godly sorrow worketh repentance to salvation not to be repented of: but the sorrow of the world worketh death.

11 For behold this selfsame thing, that ye sorrowed after a godly sort, what carefulness it wrought in you, yea, what clearing of yourselves, yea, what indignation, yea, what fear, yea, what vehement desire, yea, what zeal, yea, what revenge! In all things ye have approved yourselves to be clear in this matter.

12 Wherefore, though I wrote unto you, I did it not for his cause that had done the wrong, nor for his cause that suffered wrong, but that our care for you in the sight of God might appear unto you.

13 Therefore we were comforted in your comfort: yea, and exceedingly the more joyed we for the joy of Titus, because his spirit was refreshed by you all.

14 For if I have boasted any thing to him of you, I am not ashamed; but as we spake all things to you in truth, even so our boasting, which I made before Titus, is found a truth.

15 And his inward affection is more abundant toward you, whilst he remembereth the obedience of you all, how with fear and trembling ye received him.

2 Corinthians 2:5-11; 7:2-15—NRSV

5 But if anyone has caused pain, he has caused it not to me, but to some extent—not to exaggerate it—to all of you.

6 This punishment by the majority is enough for such a person;

7 so now instead you should forgive and console him, so that he may not be overwhelmed by excessive sorrow.

8 So I urge you to reaffirm your love for him.

9 I wrote for this reason: to test you and to know whether you are obedient in everything.

10 Anyone whom you forgive, I also

forgive. What I have forgiven, if I have forgiven anything, has been for your sake in the presence of Christ.

11 And we do this so that we may not be outwitted by Satan; for we are not ignorant of his designs.

.....

2 Make room in your hearts for us; we have wronged no one, we have corrupted no one, we have taken advantage of no one.

3 I do not say this to condemn you, for I said before that you are in our hearts, to die together and to live together.

4 I often boast about you; I have great pride in you; I am filled with consolation; I am overjoyed in all our affliction.

5 For even when we came into Macedonia, our bodies had no rest, but we were afflicted in every way—disputes without and fears within.

6 But God, who consoles the downcast, consoled us by the arrival of Titus,

7 and not only by his coming, but also by the consolation with which he was consoled about you, as he told us of your longing, your mourning, your zeal for me, so that I rejoiced still more.

8 For even if I made you sorry with my letter, I do not regret it (though I did regret it, for I see that I grieved you with that letter, though only briefly).

9 Now I rejoice, not because you were grieved, but because your grief led to repentance; for you felt a godly grief, so that you were not harmed in any way by us.

10 For godly grief produces a repentance that leads to salvation and brings no regret, but worldly grief produces death.

11 For see what earnestness this godly grief has produced in you, what eagerness to clear yourselves, what indignation, what alarm, what longing, what zeal, what punishment! At every point you have proved yourselves guiltless in the matter.

12 So although I wrote to you, it was not on account of the one who did the wrong, nor on account of the one who was wronged, but in order that your zeal for us might be made known to you before God.

13 In this we find comfort. In addition to our own consolation, we rejoiced still more at the joy of Titus, because his mind has been set at rest by all of you.

14 For if I have been somewhat boastful about you to him, I was not disgraced; but just as everything we said to you was true, so our boasting to Titus has proved true as well.

15 And his heart goes out all the more to you, as he remembers the obedience of all of you, and how you welcomed him with fear and trembling.

POINTS TO BE EMPHASIZED
ADULTS
Key Verse: 2 Corinthians 7:10
Print: 2 Corinthians 2:5-11; 7:2-15
—Scripture reveals that God is a merciful and forgiving God.
—Experiencing God's forgiveness depends on the attitude of the person.
—Godly grief leads to repentance. The

church should offer forgiveness as an act of reconciliation.

—The experience of Paul and the Corinthian church models possibilities of healing and reconciliation within the Christian community.

YOUTH

Key Verse: 2 Corinthians 7:10

Print: 2 Corinthians 2:5-11; 7:2-15

—Once a person has repented and been forgiven, it is our responsibility to accept that person joyfully into the fellowship.

—Satan gains an advantage when we fail to accept or offer forgiveness.

—Joy accompanies true repentance.

CHILDREN

Key Verse: Matthew 7:8

Print: Matthew 7:7-12; 2 Corinthians 1:10-11

—God's answers to prayers are good.

—Prayer is a privilege that comes with great benefits.

—God can be trusted to answer our prayers.

—Intercessory prayer can reap unexpected blessings for both the initiator and the person for whom we pray.

TOPICAL OUTLINE OF THE LESSON

I. INTRODUCTION
   A. Forgiveness
   B. Biblical Background

II. EXPOSITION AND APPLICATION OF THE SCRIPTURE
   A. The Request for Forgiveness *(2 Corinthians 2:5-11)*
   B. The Reasons for Forgiveness *(2 Corinthians 7:2-11)*
   C. The Responsibility of Forgiveness *(2 Corinthians 7:12-15)*

III. SPECIAL FEATURES
   A. Preserving Our Heritage
   B. Concluding Reflections

I. INTRODUCTION
A. Forgiveness

Our culture is so contaminated with unforgiveness that anyone at anytime can explode with violent, vindictive reactions that result in bodily harm. "Getting even" is the order of the day. And what is so unfortunate and disheartening is that this cultural trend and propensity is escalating and has gained momentum that will only lead to more unnecessary violence.

If the church is to bring a cure to this Christ-less, cultural malady, she must be spreading and practicing this godly virtue, for where forgiveness is, love is, joy is, peace is, hope is, and, above all, God is.

B. Biblical Background

One of the problems Paul dealt with was forgiveness. One of the members of the church was involved in an incestuous relationship; he had an affair with his father's wife. This was a shameful, disgraceful and embarrassing act, so much so that even the pagans would not tolerate such behavior. Added to this ghastly act was the Corinthian church's failure to discipline this unruly member; as a result, they were worse than the pagans. In 2 Corinthians 7:12, we learn that the person who had suffered the wrong and the one who did it were still alive. Paul scolded the church for allowing this sin to exist in the church. Added to their shame was the existence of pride. Instead of mourning and exhibiting humility, they were filled with pride because of it. They were elated over the occurrence of this ungodly act. They had allowed this guilty member to remain in their fellowship, and they were not disturbed or troubled by their decision. This further infuriated and incensed the apostle. Therefore, he had decided what ought to be done. He instructed them to "deliver such an one unto Satan for the destruction of the flesh" (1 Corinthians 5:5). "Delivering him to Satan" meant excommunication; but it also meant some sort of punishment or affliction that Satan would bring upon him. It was Paul's desire that once excommunicated and afflicted, the condemn man's "spirit may be saved." That is, that he might repent and be corrected by these afflictions, and be in position to return to the fellowship of the church. The church is to "restore" a fallen member. This is the protocol for disciplining an unruly member (see Galatians 6:1).

In 2 Corinthians 2, Paul returns to this important issue. The sorrow and grief caused by the incestuous member was not only felt by the apostle, but was the lot of the Corinthian congregation. He was satisfied with the way they handled the situation, and was pleased with the action taken. He was willing that the offender be restored to the fellowship, if they would permit it. The offender had suffered sufficiently.

This lesson focuses on Paul's response to this unforgettable event, and his call for forgiveness by the whole church. He knew that if healing was to occur, forgiveness had to be manifested. He admonished the church to follow his example, since he was the one offended. He had forgiven this brother; they must do the same.

Out of this experience come some of the most important instructions on forgiveness. Because Paul experienced this offense firsthand, he helps us by showing us what we should do when we find ourselves in similar situations. Forgiveness should never be an afterthought; it must be in the foreground of our fellowship.

II. EXPOSITION AND APPLICATION OF THE SCRIPTURE

A. The Request for Forgiveness
(2 Corinthians 2:5-11)

But if any have caused grief, he hath not grieved me, but in part: that I may not overcharge you all (verse 5). The "grief" referred to here was caused by that notorious, incestuous man who had his father's wife (1 Corinthians 5:1). Paul writes to explain his position. He states that if this offender had grieved or brought sorrow to any one, "he hath not grieved me." Though Paul was initially disturbed and sorrowed by this act, he was only grieved "in part." To a small degree, the offense saddened him, but now it was no longer a problem for him. His pain and grief had subsided. This was his position now that the offender had confessed and asked for forgiveness. Paul was ready to see to it that he received what was appropriate.

Since it was not an issue for him, Paul prayed that it was not going to be an issue for anyone else. He did not want this sinful act to cause undue grief and sorrow among the members of the church. He had dealt with it personally—now it was time for them to do the same. His concern was that he "not overcharge [them] all." He wanted to guard against the impression that he was bearing down hard upon them, charging them with indifference or laying the blame on them. He was free; he wanted the church to be free as well.

Sufficient to such a man is this punishment, which was inflicted of many (verse 6). This was the reason why Paul's sorrow no longer existed. The accused had received sufficient punishment. He had already been "inflicted" by the church and he had received the appropriate amount of punishment. The Greek word for "punishment" refers to an official disciplinary action. This action was enacted "of many," or by the majority of the members. No doubt, this was the act of excommunicating the accused. Paul was pleading with the church not to do anything that would harm this member.

So that contrariwise ye ought rather to forgive him, and comfort him, lest perhaps such a one should be swallowed up with overmuch sorrow (verse 7). The phrase "so that contrariwise" suggests that there were still some members who felt that the accused should receive more punishment than he had already received. But Paul had a different or contrary position; he believed that the discipline was sufficient. Therefore, he insisted that they "ought rather to forgive him." The word for "forgive" means "to cancel a debt." The offender was indebted to the church because he had sinned against her. They were the ones who were in position to cancel his indebtedness. Therefore, when appropriate discipline is given and a person repents of his sins, it is then the responsibility of the church to "forgive him." Jesus said in Luke 17:3-4, "Take heed to yourselves: If thy brother trespass against thee, rebuke him; and if he repent, forgive him. And if he trespass against thee seven times in a day, and seven times in a day turn again to thee, saying, I repent; thou shalt forgive him." If we rebuke a person who trespasses against us and he repents, he is to be forgiven. Paul knew what the Master taught, and he was following that teaching to the letter.

Paul makes an important point when he says, "comfort him, lest perhaps such a one should be swallowed up with overmuch sorrow." The Greek word for "comfort" means "to come alongside," "to encourage," "to strengthen." Paul wanted the church to come alongside this brother and strengthen him and encourage him. If they did not do so, he might be overwhelmed by much or excessive sorrow. Too much punishment can be detrimental; in fact, we call it abuse. Forgiveness was the order of the day; otherwise, they could lose this brother by too much punishment. Now that he has been disciplined, the Corinthians were to grant him comfort and not crush his spirit.

Wherefore I beseech you that ye would confirm your love toward him (verse 8). Paul presents the one virtue that is needed at all times and in all situations and circumstances: love. He appeals to love. He wanted them to "confirm" their "love toward him." Discipline without love leads to abuse; but discipline coupled with love leads to restoration. For them to manifest forgiveness, love had to be in their hearts, for love covers a "multitude of sins" (1 Peter 4:8). Those who love will always forgive; those who don't love will never forgive.

For to this end also did I write, that I might know the proof of you, whether ye be obedient in all things (verse 9). The purpose of his writing was that he "might know the proof" of them. That is, that he might put them to the test. He was testing them to see if they would "be obedient in all things." If they were willing to show their love and forgive this brother, then they would have passed the test of obedience.

To whom ye forgive any thing, I forgive also: for if I forgave any thing, to whom I forgave it, for your sakes forgave I it in the person of Christ (verse 10). Paul is saying that he forgave so that the Corinthians might forgive also. He wanted the brother restored, and once restored, the unity and fellowship in the church would also be restored. The phrase "in the person of Christ" is better translated "in the presence of Christ." This means that Christ is always present and because He is, the church should always do those things that honor and please Him (see Colossians 3:17). Because of that, the church must live knowing that she will have to give an account for all she has done (see 2 Corinthians 5:10).

"Lest Satan should get an advantage of us: for we are not ignorant of his devices" (verse 11). The church must always know that Satan is forever present to disrupt, disturb, disgust and destroy. He always wants to "get an advantage over us." The Corinthians had come to a critical point: they could either yield to love and show that they respect the "presence of Christ," or they could be unforgiving and give place to Satan. Paul's advice was clear to them. He wanted them to follow Christ. He encouraged them by reminding them that "we are not ignorant of his devices." The church knows the devices, the "schemes," the "thoughts" of the enemy. This knowledge will allow the church to always recognize his presence and avoid his pitfalls and traps.

B. The Reasons for Forgiveness
(2 Corinthians 7:2-11)

In 2 Corinthians 7:2-3, Paul entreats the Corinthians, in accordance with the wish which he had expressed in 2 Corinthians 6:13, to receive him as a teacher and a spiritual father; as a faithful apostle of the Lord Jesus. To get them to comply, he assures them of his integrity and honesty in ministry. In verse 2, he says, "Receive us; we have wronged no man, we have corrupted no man, we have defrauded no man." He admonishes the Corinthians to "receive" them—that is, to make room for them in their affections; to treat them as friends. They should know that they "have wronged no man." That is, done no injustices to anyone. The idea of not corrupting refers to morals; he was a good example. And, they did not "defraud" anyone. This refers to deception or trickery. They had done no such things.

In verse 3, Paul explains further, "I speak not *this* to condemn *you:* for I have said before, that ye are in our hearts to die and live with *you.*" Paul was not seeking to find fault with them or to reproach them, because they had a special place in his and his colleagues' hearts and if it was left up to them, they would spend the rest of their days living and dying among them. They were very special people in Paul's life.

"Great *is* my boldness of speech toward you, great *is* my glorying of you: I am filled with comfort, I am exceeding joyful in all our tribulation" (verse 4). He had the highest praise and love for this congregation. Here he speaks with "boldness of speech toward them." That is, he speaks openly and freely. He is not hindered by any ill will or malice. He praises them, especially since they had agreed to comply with his command to send an offering to the poor saints in Jerusalem (2 Corinthians 9:4). His relationship with them encouraged him and strengthened him to have joy in the midst of persecution.

"For, when we were come into Macedonia, our flesh had no rest, but we were troubled on every side; without *were* fightings, within *were* fears" (verse 5). When Paul and his co-laborers in the ministry came to Macedonia, their "flesh had no rest." Paul expressed his concern over the situation in Corinth. He had no rest or relief concerning the events that were occurring in Corinth. In fact, he was uncertain as to their affairs. He was very concerned that things may have gotten worse, especially since he had sent them a very severe letter (see 2 Corinthians 2:4). He was not sure how they had reacted to it. He had sent his troubleshooter Titus to investigate the situation (2 Corinthians 2:13). He was concerned about how they would treat him, and what kind of report Titus would bring from his assignment. He was also concerned about how they would respond to the incestuous brother, whether they had forgiven him or not.

Paul describes his condition as "without were fightings, within were fears." He had both external and internal concerns. The Greek word for "fightings" refers to "conflicts," "strife." These conflicts were without. That is external. This probably refers to the serious conflicts and fights he had with those who opposed his ministry. "Fears" refers to anxieties over the church's plight.

Nevertheless God, that comforteth those that are cast down, comforted us by the coming of Titus (verse 6). Paul was so anxious about the situation in Corinth that he became "cast down." The Greek word refers to someone that is down or depressed. But God lifted his depression, for He comforted him. God removed his depression by sending Titus back to him. The coming of Titus was so special, for Paul was not only glad to see him, but he brought great news from the Corinthian church. Titus' report dealt with the Corinthians' *earnest desire . . . mourning . . . fervent mind toward* Paul (verse 7). The Corinthians had responded favorably. They had an earnest desire to see him and to have fellowship with him. They mourned because they had disappointed and grieved him by their behavior or misbehavior. They had a fervent mind—that is, they were zealous to stand with him and to support him. This response led him to say, "I rejoiced the more."

For though I made you sorry with a letter, I do not repent, though I did repent: for I perceive that the same epistle hath made you sorry, though it were but for a season (verse 8). This verse expresses Paul's concern over the letter he had sent. Though the letter brought them "sorrow," he would not repent (he had no regrets), though he did repent. This statement, "I do not repent, though I did repent," reveals the mixed emotions the apostle was feeling concerning his letter. He did have some remorse, but he also had confidence, for though they had sorrow, their sorrow was only temporary. It was the sorrow that leads to repentance (verse 9). Repentance means, "a changing of the mind or of the heart," "a turning away from sin." The sorrow that the Corinthians had led them to turn away from sin. Paul calls it being made "sorry after a godly manner," or sorrow according to the will of God. The Corinthians repented of their pride, selfishness, unforgiveness, strife, disobedience and lack of love. Paul was pleased that his letter and ministry did not cause them any "damage" or loss; it caused them much gain.

For godly sorrow worketh repentance to salvation not to be repented of: but the sorrow of the world worketh death (verse 10). This verse sets forth the distinction between "godly sorrow" and "the sorrow of the world." Godly sorrow, a true mourning and remorse over sin, leads to repentance, which produces salvation (see 1 Thessalonians 1:9). This sorrow turns the soul toward God, to embrace and submit to Him. The sorrow of the world—disappointment, despair, self-pity, despondency, depression and discouragement—produces death. This sorrow turns away from God and embraces and glorifies the things of the world.

"For behold this selfsame thing, that ye sorrowed after a godly sort, what carefulness it wrought in you, yea, *what* clearing of yourselves, yea, *what* indignation, yea, *what* fear, yea, *what* vehement desire, yea, *what* zeal, yea, *what* revenge! In all things ye have approved yourselves to be clear in this matter" (verse 11). This verse explains what the godly sorrow of the Corinthians produced in them. It produced a "clearing of yourselves," that is, vindication—they vindicated themselves. It produced "indignation," that is, outrage—they were outraged over their sin. It produced "fear," that is, reverence for God. It produced "vehement desire," that is, yearning or longing; probably referring to their longing to please God and the great apostle. It produced "zeal," strong earnestness. It produced "revenge," that is, "an avenging of wrongs" or amends for the wrongs they did.

C. The Responsibility of Forgiveness
(2 Corinthians 7:12-15)

"Wherefore, though I wrote unto you, *I did it* not for his cause that had done the wrong, nor for his cause that suffered wrong, but that our care for you in the sight of God might appear unto you" (verse 12). Paul now states the main reason why he wrote that severe letter to the Corinthians. It was not because of him "that had done the wrong"—the man accused of incest (see 1 Corinthians 5:1). It was not because of him "that suffered wrong"—that the wrong which he suffered might be corrected, and he be restored to the fellowship of the saints. His purpose in writing was so that the Corinthians would recognize that he truly cared for them. He was their father in the ministry; he was their pastor and he would do anything to strengthen their faith, deepen their hope, and expound their love. He truly cared for them.

"Therefore we were comforted in your comfort: yea, and exceedingly the more joyed we for the joy of Titus, because his spirit was refreshed by you all" (verse 13). The Corinthians' comfort led to the comfort of Paul and his co-laborers. And they were especially comforted by the joy Titus experienced because they "refreshed" his spirit. He had boasted to Titus about them, and what he said of them, they had proved true. Therefore, he was "not ashamed," that is, not disappointed. In fact, all that he speaks, he speaks in truth (verse 14). And Titus had gained the same respect for them that Paul had, because "he remembereth the obedience of you all." They were obedient to the apostle; and Titus was a witness to it, for he observed that they obeyed with "fear and trembling" (verse 15).

III. SPECIAL FEATURES
A. Preserving Our Heritage

The tragedies in our community stem from a number of causes. One cause is the breakdown of the influence that the church has had. No longer is the church revered, as in the past. Though it still possesses some influence, the musical drums of the hip-hop culture are slowly silencing its commanding voice. It is rapidly gaining control of the minds of our youth, and dragging them down the road of despair and disappointment.

Those of us who are a part of the church need to wake up and be busy renewing the minds of our youth by the profound and powerful principles of God's holy Word. This is their "only" hope!

B. Concluding Reflections

For forgiveness to be genuine, it must be based on repentance. For a person to repent, he must manifest godly sorrow. This sorrow is the sorrow of the sinner who mourns with copious tears over his sins. This sorrow is based on an understanding of wrongs done, and a grasp of the principles and requirements of God's Word. This is how one comes to forgiveness.

HOME DAILY BIBLE 📖 READINGS
for the week of August 6, 2006
Giving Forgiveness

July 31, Monday
—Matthew 6:9–15
—Forgive Others Their Trespasses
Aug. 1, Tuesday
—Matthew 18:21–35
—Jesus Teaches About Forgiveness
Aug. 2, Wednesday
—Mark 11:20–25
—Forgive, So God May Forgive You
Aug. 3, Thursday
—Colossians 3:12–17
—You Also Must Forgive
Aug. 4, Friday
—2 Corinthians 2:5–11
—Forgive and Console Your Offender
Aug. 5, Saturday
—2 Corinthians 7:2–7
—Paul's Pride in the Corinthians
Aug. 6, Sunday
—2 Corinthians 7:8–16
—Paul's Joy at the Corinthians'
   Repentance

PRAYER
Gracious heavenly Father, thank You for showing us the power of forgiveness and demanding that we forgive others, lest You will not forgive us. Keep us faithful to what You require of us. Amen.

Lesson 11

Giving Generously

CHILDREN'S UNIT
We Serve with Joy

ADULT TOPIC: Giving Generously
YOUTH TOPIC: Giving Graciously
CHILDREN'S TOPIC: Jesus Christ Is Lord or Good News About Jesus

KEY VERSE

For ye know the grace of
our Lord Jesus Christ, that,
though he was rich, yet for
your sakes he became
poor, that ye through his
poverty might be rich.
—2 Corinthians 8:9

DEVOTIONAL READING: Luke 20:45—21:4
BACKGROUND SCRIPTURE: 2 Corinthians 8:1-15
PRINT PASSAGE: 2 Corinthians 8:1-15

2 Corinthians 8:1-15—KJV

MOREOVER, BRETHREN, we do you to wit of the grace of
God bestowed on the churches of Macedonia;

2 How that in a great trial of affliction the abundance of
their joy and their deep poverty abounded unto the riches of
their liberality.

3 For to their power, I bear record, yea, and beyond their
power they were willing of themselves;

4 Praying us with much entreaty that we would receive the
gift, and take upon us the fellowship of the ministering to the
saints.

5 And this they did, not as we hoped, but first gave their
own selves to the Lord, and unto us by the will of God.

6 Insomuch that we desired Titus, that as he had begun, so
he would also finish in you the same grace also.

7 Therefore, as ye abound in every thing, in faith, and utterance, and knowledge, and in all diligence, and in your love
to us, see that ye abound in this grace also.

8 I speak not by commandment, but by occasion of the
forwardness of others, and to prove the sincerity of your love.

9 For ye know the grace of our Lord Jesus Christ, that,

OBJECTIVES

Upon completion of this
lesson, students are ex-
pected to:
1. Know that God exempli-
fies generous giving;
2. Understand that giving
must be sacrificial;
3. Know that only grace
makes possible gener-
ous giving; and,
4. Accept the challenge to
give as God requires.

though he was rich, yet for your sakes he became poor, that ye through his poverty might be rich.

10 And herein I give my advice: for this is expedient for you, who have begun before, not only to do, but also to be forward a year ago.

11 Now therefore perform the doing of it; that as there was a readiness to will, so there may be a performance also out of that which ye have.

12 For if there be first a willing mind, it is accepted according to that a man hath, and not according to that he hath not.

13 For I mean not that other men be eased, and ye burdened:

14 But by an equality, that now at this time your abundance may be a supply for their want, that their abundance also may be a supply for your want: that there may be equality:

15 As it is written, He that had gathered much had nothing over; and he that had gathered little had no lack.

2 Corinthians 8:1-15—NRSV

WE WANT you to know, brothers and sisters, about the grace of God that has been granted to the churches of Macedonia;

2 for during a severe ordeal of affliction, their abundant joy and their extreme poverty have overflowed in a wealth of generosity on their part.

3 For, as I can testify, they voluntarily gave according to their means, and even beyond their means,

4 begging us earnestly for the privilege of sharing in this ministry to the saints—

5 and this, not merely as we expected; they gave themselves first to the Lord and, by the will of God, to us,

6 so that we might urge Titus that, as he had already made a beginning, so he should also complete this generous undertaking among you.

7 Now as you excel in everything—in faith, in speech, in knowledge, in utmost eagerness, and in our love for you—so we want you to excel also in this generous undertaking.

8 I do not say this as a command, but I am testing the genuineness of your love against the earnestness of others.

9 For you know the generous act of our Lord Jesus Christ, that though he was rich, yet for your sakes he became poor, so that by his poverty you might become rich.

10 And in this matter I am giving my advice: it is appropriate for you who began last year not only to do something but even to desire to do something—

11 now finish doing it, so that your eagerness may be matched by completing it according to your means.

12 For if the eagerness is there, the gift is acceptable according to what one has—not according to what one does not have.

13 I do not mean that there should be relief for others and pressure on you, but it is a question of a fair balance between

14 your present abundance and their need, so that their abundance may be for your need, in order that there may be a fair balance.

15 As it is written, "The one who had much did not have too much, and the one who had little did not have too little."

POINTS TO BE EMPHASIZED
ADULTS
Key Verse: 2 Corinthians 8:9
Print: 2 Corinthians 8:1-15
—The act of giving generously is a response to Jesus' example of total unselfishness.
—Believers are to give of themselves sacrificially to help others in both physical and spiritual need.
—Living sacrificially is a way of spreading the Gospel of Christ that is more effective than some verbal teaching.

YOUTH
Key Verse: 2 Corinthians 8:9
Print: 2 Corinthians 8:1-15
—Motivation for giving should be a response to God's grace, not dictated by human demands.
—Effective giving is done with love.
—Our giving should be influenced by Jesus' example of unselfishness.

CHILDREN
Key Verse: 2 Corinthians 4:5a
Print: Matthew 28:1-10, 16-20; 2 Corinthians 4:5
—The Good News of the Gospel is that Jesus lived, died, rose again, and lives forever.
—The Good News is for people from all nations.
—Just as Mary Magdalene told the disciples of Jesus' resurrection, children can tell others about Jesus.
—Jesus' resurrection proved His sovereignty over life and death and gives all believers hope for everlasting life.
—Jesus provided a mechanism for His earthly ministry to continue after His ascension.

TOPICAL OUTLINE OF THE LESSON

I. INTRODUCTION
  A. Generosity
  B. Biblical Background

II. EXPOSITION AND APPLICATION OF THE SCRIPTURE
  A. The Model of Giving
    (2 Corinthians 8:1-6)
  B. The Mandate for Giving
    (2 Corinthians 8:7-11)
  C. The Measurement of Giving
    (2 Corinthians 8:12-15)

III. SPECIAL FEATURES
  A. Preserving Our Heritage
  B. Concluding Reflections

I. INTRODUCTION
A. Generosity

Giving is a core manifestation of love. The old saying goes, "You can give without loving, but you can't love without giving." John 3:16 tells us "For God so loved the world, that he gave his only begotten Son, that whosoever believeth in him should not perish, but have everlasting life." Therefore, since God's love moved

Him to give so generously to humanity, it is essential that the people of God be a giving people. Appropriate use of our possessions is at the heart of the Master's message. His desire is that we avoid covetousness and selfishness (see Luke 12:15; 16:19-31) and manifest love.

Giving can be miserly or generous. One can give only according to what is required or one can be a generous giver, going beyond what is required. When examined by Scripture, this latter description is to define those within the family of God (Malachi 3:8-10; 2 Corinthians 9:6-7). This is demonstrated by the greatest example of all, God Himself (see John 3:16; Romans 8:32; Ephesians 2:4-5; 3:20; 2 Corinthians 8:15). We are admonished by the apostle Paul to "be ye therefore followers (imitators) of God, as dear children" (Ephesians 5:1).

There is no substitute for generosity—the generous giver is free from the hindrances that enslave the many who fail to give appropriately. The deep sense of awareness of and appreciation for the gifts and blessings we receive from God should yield a tremendous sense of freedom to share with others accordingly. God will dispense or withhold His gifts depending on His own purpose and His own design. Though He keeps His promises (Malachi 3:10-11), "[He] will have mercy on whom [He] will have mercy" (see Romans 9:15).

Furthermore, giving should not just be practiced from expectation, but from appreciation. We should not give just to receive from God; we should give to reverence God and please Him. Giving with the expectation of receiving something in return only robs the giver of the joy that can only come from pure giving. Giving motivated solely by expectation suffocates the joy and privilege of praising and thanking God for what He has already given. Appreciation, rather than expectation is at the heart of the generous giver.

B. Biblical Background

Paul made an appeal to render aid to the poor saints in Jerusalem. Many of them had fallen on hard times. They had lost their livelihood. Some had been imprisoned and their lands and possessions had been confiscated. They were struggling to survive. Persecution had raised its ugly head in their midst, and many of them had been forced to abandon their way of living. Being sensitive to their great need, the apostle wrote to the Corinthians to send financial aid to help bring some relief to their destitution.

The Corinthian church had many spiritual blessings (1 Corinthians 1:10; 2 Corinthians 8:7), but they were also in position to offer financial assistance to these ailing saints. The admonition of the apostle was *see that ye abound in this grace also* (verse 7), *prove the sincerity of your love* (verse 8) and *perform the doing of it.* (verse 11). He would awaken their sense of responsibility and give them an opportunity to respond favorably to this great need.

To help them fulfill their Christian obligation, Paul set before them two models of generous giving. The first was the churches of Macedonia (verses 1-5) and the second was the Lord Jesus Christ (verse 9). He gave them both a human and divine example: the visible and the supreme. The Macedonian churches were comprised of many impoverished members, yet they gave *riches* (verse 2), and Christ who was rich became poor, so that the poor might become rich. The Corinthian church was to follow these examples by having a *willing mind* (verse 12) and showing *the proof of* [their] *love, and of our boasting on your behalf* (verse 24).

The Corinthians had given Paul cause to be full of joy, and he had confidence that they could do all things. The Greek word translated "confidence" refers to being courageous, bold, or daring. The obedience and attitude of the Corinthians gave Paul the courage and the daring to believe that he could trust them and that they would not fail him. His faith in them was renewed and he was certain that they would remain faithful to the things he had taught them. He felt good about his relationship with them.

II. EXPOSITION AND APPLICATION OF THE SCRIPTURE
A. The Model of Giving *(2 Corinthians 8:1-6)*

Moreover, brethren, we do you to wit of the grace of God bestowed on the churches of Macedonia (verse 1). Paul had ended in the seventh chapter with, "I rejoice therefore that I have confidence in you in all things." It was this confidence that led Paul to write them concerning a special offering for the poor saints in Jerusalem. He was convinced that they would give it, so he began in verse 1 with *moreover* or better, "now," preparing to ask them to give this special gift.

Paul wanted the Corinthian church to understand what God did that enabled the Macedonian church to give in the way that they did. He lifted up to them the Macedonian church as his model of giving by *grace*. It was the enabling and empowering *grace of God* that gave them that ability to give. Though the great need in Jerusalem would most certainly motivate them to give, it was God's grace that caused them to give on the magnitude that they did. The churches of Macedonia (based on Acts 16 and 17) included Philippi, Thessalonica and Berea.

How that in a great trial of affliction the abundance of their joy and their deep poverty abounded unto the riches of their liberality (verse 2). Even though the Macedonian believers were undergoing great persecution and living in poverty, they gave liberally and generously because of *the abundance of their joy.*

How do poor people give riches? This seems to be oxymoronic; however, it is possible for poor people to give riches. Why? Because giving, according to God's standard, is not based on the amount, but on the percentage. Suppose, for example, that one person has a hundred dollars and another has five thousand dollars; both give an offering. The one with $100 gives $80 and the one with $5000 gives $1000. According to God's standard, the one who gave $80 gave more, even though it was a smaller monetary amount. Jesus, speaking of the woman who gave two mites, explained: "Verily I say unto you, That this poor widow hath cast more in, than all they which have cast into the treasury: For all they did cast in of their abundance; but she of her want did cast in all that she had, even all her living" (Mark 12:43-44).

For to their power, I bear record, yea, and beyond their power they were willing of themselves (verse 3). The word *power* here means "ability." Paul was testifying that the Macedonian churches gave *beyond* their natural ability. They exceeded what the apostle expected them to give. Furthermore, *they were willing of themselves*; they were not forced or coerced—they gave of their own accord. They had purposed in their hearts what they should give (see 2 Corinthians 9:7). They also prayed *with much entreaty* that Paul and his co-laborers would permit them to give. That is, the Macedonians insisted that Paul and the others allow them the privilege of participation in giving to the poor saints in Jerusalem, though they were beset with their own economic challenges. Still, they were determined to give (verse 4).

And this they did, not as we hoped, but first gave their own selves to the Lord, and unto us by the will of God (verse 5). The Macedonians gave beyond what Paul had expected. They could give on this level because they *first gave their own selves to the Lord.* When a person gives his or her whole self to the Lord, nothing will hinder that person from pleasing the Lord. Whatever is asked, that person will gladly and unreservedly do it. The person who has surrendered to God will also submit to leadership.

The Macedonians gave themselves *first...to the Lord, and unto us by the will of God.* They made the Lord their priority and they placed themselves under the authority of the Lord's leaders. In so doing, they submitted to the will of God.

Insomuch that we desired Titus, that as he had begun, so he would also finish in you the same grace also (verse 6). Paul assigned Titus to be responsible for collecting the donation from the Corinthians. Since Titus had already begun receiving the collection, it was Paul's desire that *he would also finish* collecting the offering. *The same grace* refers to the grace that the Macedonians had both received and manifested. It was Paul's desire that the Corinthians would follow the model given by the Macedonians. As they abounded in this grace, he prayed that the Corinthians would abound in grace as well. In 1 Corinthians 16:2, Paul admonished them to lay in store from that which God had prospered them so that there would be no need for gathering when He returned.

B. The Mandate for Giving
(2 Corinthians 8:7-11)

Therefore, as ye abound in every thing, in faith, and utterance, and knowledge, and in all diligence, and in your love to us, see that ye abound in this grace also (verse 7). After explaining the depth of the Macedonians' commitment, Paul then exhorted the Corinthians to follow their example. First, Paul complimented them about their abundance of virtues; he would then use that to exhort them to add an additional virtue to their corporate character. The Corinthians had abounded *in faith* (justifying, sanctifying and sustaining faith), *utterance* (words of truth—doctrine), *knowledge* (using knowledge in everyday life), *diligence* (eagerness) and *love*

(the unconditional, sacrificial love of God). As they had demonstrated an abundance of these virtues, Paul wanted them to *abound in this grace also*—the grace of giving. Paul may have been suggesting here that giving would complete their circle of virtues. In fact, their generous giving would be the visible sign of all these other virtues. Paul here seems to have suggested that they were incomplete without this grace. Therefore, to demonstrate their *faith, utterance, knowledge, diligence* and *love*, they needed to give. It would be the crowning manifestation of their Christian living.

I speak not by commandment, but by occasion of the forwardness of others, and to prove the sincerity of your love (verse 8). Paul was not using his apostolic authority to enlist an offering, though it was his prerogative to do so. He would not command them to give, for giving must be done voluntarily. He would emphasize this later (2 Corinthians 9:7). He would also give them the opportunity to *prove the sincerity of* [their] *love.* The authenticity and truthfulness of their love for God and His people would manifest itself if they abounded in the grace of giving.

For ye know the grace of our Lord Jesus Christ, that, though he was rich, yet for your sakes he became poor, that ye through his poverty might be rich (verse 9). After expounding on the Macedonians' generosity, Paul presented the preeminent model of giving—the Lord Jesus Christ.

He is the supreme example of every area of the Christian life. He models everything we are to do as believers.

Paul then explained how Christ gave. Jesus Christ, who is grace (John 1:14; 2 Corinthians 13:14), manifested God's grace fully by what He did. What did He do? Being rich (deity; King of kings and Lord of lords; owner and ruler of all), by choice He became poor (human—John 1:14; Galatians 4:4-5) so that through His poverty (laying aside His glory—John 17:1-5; suffering and death—Hebrews 12:2; cf., Romans 5:6-10), *we might be rich* (see John 3:16; Romans 8:1, 9-10, 14-17, 31-24; 1 Corinthians 1:4-8; 1 Peter 1:3-4; Ephesians 2:4-5).

And herein I give my advice: for this is expedient for you, who have begun before, not only to do, but also to be forward a year ago (verse 10). Since the Corinthian believers were the first to start giving to this important cause and since a year had already passed since they started, it was expedient for them to continue what they started. Therefore, Paul urged them to *perform the doing of it.*

C. The Measurement of Giving
(2 Corinthians 8:12-15)

For if there be first a willing mind, it is accepted according to that a man hath, and not according to that he hath not (verse 12). In order for the Corinthians to give, they *needed a willing mind*; they needed to have a spirit that was ready and eager to give. As they were preparing to give, Paul reminded them that a person can only give from what he or she has. Paul wanted them to have a *willing mind,* which would guide them in the right way to give.

Paul did not intend to burden them; therefore he would not require them to give beyond what they were able (verse 13). What he required of them, he required of all believers. He would treat everyone equally (verse 14). At this time, the Corinthians had *abundance* and the Jerusalem saints were in *want.* The time would come when their circumstances would be reversed. But what Paul required of the Corinthians in abundance or want, he would require of the Jerusalem saints in want or abundance, *so that there may be equality.* The responsibilities of the Christian life are the same for all believers (verse 14).

As it is written, He that had gathered much had nothing over; and he that had gathered little had no lack (verse 15). Paul related a powerful principle found in Exodus 16:2-18. The Lord had sent manna to the Israelites in the wilderness to provide sustenance. He fixed it so that those who received much had no surplus, and those who received little had no want. How this occurred, we are not told. This may also reflect what happened in Acts 4:32-35, where those who had plenty gave to those who had little or nothing at all. This is probably what Paul was teaching here; it seems to follow his words in verse 14. God's plan is that the "haves" render aid to the "have-nots."

III. Special Features

A. Preserving Our Heritage

As we seek to maintain identity, integrity and involvement in our nation, it is essential that we support our educational institutions, such as American Baptist College, that have distinguished themselves through the years by providing educational opportunities to those who otherwise may have had none.

Many of the founders of historically Black schools had little money—such as Mary McLeod Bethune—but they possessed great faith in God. As they joined their limited resources with their immeasurable faith, those who had economic means or political clout joined their cause.

If our forbears could, by faith, give of themselves and their meager resources so generously with so few resources, how much more can we do today? Our generous support of these historic institutions will go a long way in helping to educate those who had potential but little opportunity to actualize it.

B. Concluding Reflections

Paul drew upon two examples to encourage the Corinthians to give. One was from the Macedonian churches; the other was from the life of Christ. The Macedonians were practical models, and the Lord Jesus Christ is the perfect model. Both models were challenging. The Macedonians gave a generous gift, although they were much poorer than the Corinthians. The challenge of Jesus Christ, of course, is much greater. He gave what no one else could—He gave His life.

HOME DAILY BIBLE READINGS

for the week of August 13, 2006
Giving Generously

Aug. 7, Monday
—Luke 20:45—21:4
—The Widow's Offering

Aug. 8, Tuesday
—Acts 6:1–6
—Chosen to Serve the Poor

Aug. 9, Wednesday
—Romans 12:3–8
—Generosity, A Gift from God

August 10, Thursday
—1 Corinthians 15:58—16:4
—The Collection for the Saints

Aug. 11, Friday
—Galatians 5:16–26
—Generosity, A Fruit of the Spirit

Aug. 12, Saturday
—2 Corinthians 8:1–7
—Excel in Generosity

Aug. 13, Sunday
—2 Corinthians 8:8–15
—Rules for Giving

PRAYER

Our God and Father, we thank You for showing us how to give. Help us to be more generous with our possessions, and especially help us to truly honor You through our giving. Amen.

Giving Is a Witness

ADULT TOPIC: Reasons for Giving
YOUTH TOPIC: Giving: A Witness to God's Generosity
CHILDREN'S TOPIC: Giving with Joy

DEVOTIONAL READING: Psalm 37:16-24
BACKGROUND SCRIPTURE: 2 Corinthians 9:1-15
PRINT PASSAGE: 2 Corinthians 9:3-15

2 Corinthians 9:3-15—KJV

3 Yet have I sent the brethren, lest our boasting of you should be in vain in this behalf; that, as I said, ye may be ready:

4 Lest haply if they of Macedonia come with me, and find you unprepared, we (that we say not, ye) should be ashamed in this same confident boasting.

5 Therefore I thought it necessary to exhort the brethren, that they would go before unto you, and make up beforehand your bounty, whereof ye had notice before, that the same might be ready, as a matter of bounty, and not as of covetousness.

6 But this I say, He which soweth sparingly shall reap also sparingly; and he which soweth bountifully shall reap also bountifully.

7 Every man according as he purposeth in his heart, so let him give; not grudgingly, or of necessity: for God loveth a cheerful giver.

8 And God is able to make all grace abound toward you; that ye, always having all sufficiency in all things, may abound to every good work:

9 (As it is written, He hath dispersed abroad; he hath given

UNIT III
The Spirit of Giving

CHILDREN'S UNIT
We Serve with Joy

KEY VERSE

God is able to make all grace abound toward you; that ye, always having all sufficiency in all things, may abound to every good work.—2 Corinthians 9:8

OBJECTIVES

Upon completion of this lesson, students should know:

1. The reasons for Christian giving;

2. The practice of bountiful giving;

3. The responsibility of Christians to give to the needy; and,

4. The value of God's unspeakable gift—the Lord Jesus Christ.

to the poor: his righteousness remaineth for ever.

10 Now he that ministereth seed to the sower both minister bread for your food, and multiply your seed sown, and increase the fruits of your righteousness;)

11 Being enriched in every thing to all bountifulness, which causeth through us thanksgiving to God.

12 For the administration of this service not only supplieth the want of the saints, but is abundant also by many thanksgivings unto God;

13 Whiles by the experiment of this ministration they glorify God for your professed subjection into the gospel of Christ, and for your liberal distribution unto them, and unto all men;

14 And by their prayer for you, which long after you for the exceeding grace of God in you.

15 Thanks be unto God for his unspeakable gift.

2 Corinthians 9:3-15—NRSV

3 But I am sending the brothers in order that our boasting about you may not prove to have been empty in this case, so that you may be ready, as I said you would be;

4 otherwise, if some Macedonians come with me and find that you are not ready, we would be humiliated—to say nothing of you—in this undertaking.

5 So I thought it necessary to urge the brothers to go on ahead to you, and arrange in advance for this bountiful gift that you have promised, so that it may be ready as a voluntary gift and not as an extortion.

6 The point is this: the one who sows sparingly will also reap sparingly, and the one who sows bountifully will also reap bountifully.

7 Each of you must give as you have made up your mind, not reluctantly or under compulsion, for God loves a cheerful giver.

8 And God is able to provide you with every blessing in abundance, so that by always having enough of everything, you may share abundantly in every good work.

9 As it is written, "He scatters abroad, he gives to the poor; his righteousness endures forever."

10 He who supplies seed to the sower and bread for food will supply and multiply your seed for sowing and increase the harvest of your righteousness.

11 You will be enriched in every way for your great generosity, which will produce thanksgiving to God through us;

12 for the rendering of this ministry not only supplies the needs of the saints but also overflows with many thanksgivings to God.

13 Through the testing of this ministry you glorify God by your obedience to the confession of the gospel of Christ and by the generosity of your sharing with them and with all others,

14 while they long for you and pray for you because of the surpassing grace of God that he has given you.

15 Thanks be to God for his indescribable gift!

POINTS TO BE EMPHASIZED
ADULTS
Key Verse: 2 Corinthians 9:8
Print: 2 Corinthians 9:3-15
—Paul makes the case for giving as a dutiful response to God for what God has provided.
—Giving is divinely inspired by personal commitment and not compelled.
—Bountiful giving as a response to God's generosity is rewarded bountifully.
—Scripture urges giving to the poor.

YOUTH
Key Verse: 2 Corinthians 9:11
Print: 2 Corinthians 9:3-15
—We witness to our faith by giving of our money and time.
—Giving to the needs of Christians and others should be done cheerfully and not be coerced.
—Our giving to meet the needs of others should be in response to God's generous gifts to us.
—Enrichment and many thanksgivings come to those who learn the art of generosity.

CHILDREN
Key Verse: 2 Corinthians 9:7c
Print: Matthew 6:19-21;
2 Corinthians 9:1-8
—The treasury, during biblical times, was an offering box shaped like an inverted trumpet to prevent theft.
—During Jesus' time, a widow, who did not have a profession, was dependent on the generosity of others to survive.

—God is more concerned with our attitude toward giving than the monetary value of the gift.
—God will reward us to the same extent with which we are willing to share our possessions with others.
—Believers are required to live selfless lives—placing the needs of others before our own.

TOPICAL OUTLINE OF THE LESSON

I. INTRODUCTION
  A. Cheerful Giving
  B. Biblical Background

II. EXPOSITION AND APPLICATION OF THE SCRIPTURE
  A. Preparation for Giving
     (2 Corinthians 9:3-5)
  B. Purposeful Giving
     (2 Corinthians 9:6-7)
  C. The Promises for Giving
     (2 Corinthians 9:8-15)

III. SPECIAL FEATURES
  A. Preserving Our Heritage
  B. Concluding Reflections

I. INTRODUCTION
A. Cheerful Giving

One's attitude in giving is critical to its reception by God. God looks first and foremost at the heart (1 Samuel 16:7), it is most important that our hearts be involved in our giving, and that our hearts be in line with what God expects of us. James said, "Ye have not, because ye ask not. Ye ask, and receive not, because ye ask amiss" (James 4:2-3). The word "amiss" means "to be self-indulgent and seek the gratification of the flesh." It refers to having wrong motives and a wrong attitude. We are instructed that "the Lord loves a cheerful giver." He loves the giver that is joyous, praise-filled, spirited, lively and rejoicing. God desires givers who are happy to show His love by giving to others. He takes delight in givers who are happy to give back to Him. The bewildered spirit, the burdened spirit and the boastful spirit will hinder cheerful giving. One must have a blessed and bountiful spirit to qualify.

B. Biblical Background

In continuing his admonition to the Corinthians, here the apostle's interest shifted to instruct them on the need to help the poor saints in Jerusalem. He went a step further to set forth some important reasons why believers should give. He encouraged the Corinthians with instructions and principles to enable them to give in a way that pleased the Lord.

Paul had boasted about the Corinthians. He had told the other believers that they would not let him down. They would be ready to give as required. He cautioned them not to bring shame on him or on themselves. So, he made provision to send a delegation ahead of himself to collect their contribution. He wanted them to be properly notified, even though they already knew about the request and their responsibility. He wanted them to be generous in their giving, not covetous, self-seeking, greedy and stingy. He reminded them of the law of the harvest, a law they had knowledge of: those who sow little reap little; those who sow plentifully reap plentifully.

He instructed them that giving is an individual and personal act. It is an act of the heart, an act of purpose, and should never be demanded or exacted by coercion, compulsion, manipulation, or exploitation. Therefore, he encouraged them to give out of joy. For their joyful giving, Paul assured them that God would "make all grace abound toward" them. God knows how to bless those who give as He commands and requires and He does so liberally.

Paul explains the purpose of the delegation. "Ministry to the saints" is another name for the collection (8:4). "The brothers" are those mentioned in 8:18, 22. "Voluntary gift" means that it should be like Christ's gift. Paul uses a Proverb (9:6-15) to express the general experience of giving. The gift should be deliberate and voluntary. The quotation, "God loves a cheerful giver," is based on the Hebrew Scriptures (Septuagint); of Proverbs 22:9: "A generous man will himself be blessed." God's generosity toward human beings is a recurrent biblical theme. Willingness to give is seen as an expression or test of one's confession of faith. God's graciousness is the ultimate reason to give—the gift of God's love to humans is a blessing of unspeakable value. Note: "The gift which...through us" is to be delivered at Jerusalem will be the occasion of many thanksgivings to God on the part of those who receive it. There is "thanks to God" not only for the generosity inspired, but also for the gift of Christ. Note also: their charity was superabundant, and God had furnished the disposition, the occasion, and the means by which that disposition was to be made manifest.

II. Exposition and Application of the Scripture

A. Preparation for Giving
(2 Corinthians 9:3-5)

Yet have I sent the brethren, lest our boasting of you should be in vain in this behalf; that, as I said, ye may be ready (verse 3). In verses 1 and 2, Paul had indicated that it was superfluous or unnecessary for him to write to them about the ministry of giving to the poor saints at Jerusalem. This was for three reasons: (1) they were willing to give; (2) he had boasted of them to the Macedonians by informing them that the Corinthians were prepared to give a year ago; and (3) their zeal to give stirred up others to be involved in this honorable ministry.

Therefore he had *sent the brethren*. This delegation consisted of Titus and two other Christian brothers whose names were not given (see 2 Corinthians 8:16-22). Their presence was Paul's safety net to ensure that his *boasting of* [them] *should* [not] *be in vain in this behalf*. He wanted to ensure that his bragging was not empty or untrue. His bragging would be true if the offering was *ready*, or prepared.

Lest haply if they of Macedonia come with me, and find you unprepared, we (that we say not, ye) should be ashamed in this same confident boasting (verse 4). Paul was also concerned that if any of the Macedonians came with him and the offering was not ready, he would be embarrassed. He apparently had boasted to the Macedonians about the zeal and commitment of the Corinthians and there was no reason to disbelieve the great apostle. The Macedonians held Paul in high esteem as a man of integrity in ministry. The possibility of him coming to Corinth with them, only to discover that his boasting was unwarranted would damage his credibility. So, Paul was insistent and persistent in imploring the Corinthians to be faithful to their promise and have a generous offering ready.

Therefore I thought it necessary to exhort the brethren, that they would go before unto you, and make up beforehand your bounty, whereof ye had notice before, that the same might be ready, as a matter of bounty, and not as of covetousness (verse 5). Paul thought it necessary to give specific instruction to Titus and his colleagues with words of exhortation. His instructions were that they would go ahead of him, collect the offering (which he had already told them of) and ensure that it was ready for Paul's arrive. His desire was that the offering be given voluntarily and graciously rather than as something that he was extorting or demanding of them. He knew that giving was not to be compelled; but with a cheerful and benevolent spirit. This is why he added, *as a matter of bounty, and not as of covetousness*: he would appeal to their love, but he would not arouse their covetous spirit.

Two spirits tend to challenge the giver: the spirit of grace and love, and the spirit of covetousness and lust. The gracious and loving spirit is of God and is benevolent and seeks to look beyond self to others.

The covetous and lustful spirit is of the world, satanic and prideful, seeking to satisfy self while ignoring others. These two spirits seem to be in competition with each other. It is the ministry of the Holy Spirit to ensure that the Christian giver follows the gracious and loving spirit, and shuts the door to the spirit of covetousness and lust. Paul wanted the Corinthians to be under the control of the Holy Spirit.

Paul recognized that the covetous spirit rises when a person is provoked or irritated by those who seek to pressure him into giving. The greatest gifts come from the heart that is motivated by love and concern for others, not coercion or guilt.

B. Purposeful Giving
(2 Corinthians 9:6-7)

But this I say, He which soweth sparingly shall reap also sparingly; and he which soweth bountifully shall reap also bountifully (verse 6). Apparently reasonably assured that a generous gift would be ready, Paul turned his attention to divine revelation, utilizing a basic principle in nature. Paul did not ignore the importance of divine involvement in the giving process. This process is not directly quoted in the Old Testament, but is implied in Proverbs 11:24-25; 19:17; and Ecclesiastes 11:1. Jesus; teaching in Luke 6:38 also give confirmation to Paul's teaching here. This principle of giving is also affirmed in Galatians 6:7: "Be not deceived; God is not mocked: for whatsoever a man soweth, that shall he also reap."

Paul was instructing the Corinthians in the principle of the harvest—sowing and reaping. Employing imagery that was familiar to them, Paul used principles from, their agrarian life-style to encourage the Corinthians to follow the principles of Scripture. To inspire them to be generous in their giving, this great truth was put before them. One who sows sparingly (little) shall reap sparingly. Those who sow bountifully shall reap bountifully. "Bountifully" literally means "with blessing," either meaning, with blessings in mind or with a blessed spirit, intended to be a blessing to others; in either case, it seems to suggest "liberally," or "generously." No one can expect to reap (harvest) without sowing (planting), and even then only in proportion to how much is sewn.

Every man according as he purposeth in his heart, so let him give; not grudgingly, or of necessity: for God loveth a cheerful giver (verse 7). After explaining the biblical principle of sowing and reaping, Paul explained the true way to give. This verse is crucial to pleasing God. Giving is to be done by every believer. In Exodus 23:15, Moses said, "And none shall appear before me empty" (see also Exodus 34:20; Deuteronomy 16:16). There are no exemptions or exceptions.

There are several kinds of giving, but all giving, done in love, is purposeful. The widow who gave two mites as her offering exhibited sacrificial giving. She gave generously from what she had (Mark 12:41-44). Giving may be a spontaneous act of generosity and love, such as that which the woman demonstrated toward Jesus when she anointed His head with expensive perfume (Matthew 26:6-13). Systematic giving is both planned and organized (1 Corinthians 16:2). Tithing is God's plan for the faithful to engage in systematic giving. Each of these forms of giving are generated by and from the heart.

Giving is not to be done *grudgingly*. This word means "sorrow" or "grief," even "pain." No one should give an offering or gift with which he or she is grieved to part.

Paul indicated that giving is not to be done *of necessity*. This word means under pressure or compulsion. Unfortunately, far too many members of the body give under pressure or out of appeals designed to induce guilt. God desires that our giving be joyful and happy (see 2 Corinthians 8:2). It should always be a privilege and a pleasure to give. God loves this kind of giving because the giver expresses a spirit of thanksgiving and praise and seeks to please God.

C. The Promises for Giving
(2 Corinthians 9:8-15)

And God is able to make all grace abound toward you... (verse 8). God will bless the cheerful giver. *Grace* speaks of blessings; God will lavish His *grace* on cheerful givers. The cheerful giver's life will be impacted and blessed. God will give abundantly to them; their material needs will be substantially met. They will lack nothing (see Philippians 4:19).

Giving bountifully and cheerfully results in God's abundant return.

The cheerful giver will be a blessing to others and *abound to every good work*. A genuine heart for giving is a heart determined to please God. When God is pleased, He gives a great return; He will bless the individual to be positioned to have more, and therefore give more.

The cheerful giver will abound. He will *disperse abroad* (verse 9). As the farmer scatters the seed, cheerful givers will scatter or share their gifts. *Righteousness* refers to the act of almsgiving. They will always be in position to give in this way.

Quoting from Isaiah 55:10, Paul showed how God will bless the sower with seed (verse 10). He will also *minister bread for* [the cheerful giver's] *food, and multiply* [his] *seed sown, and increase the fruits of* [his] *righteousness*. God gives the seed; the sower plants the seed, resulting in bread. This bread will be food for the cheerful giver, and that giver's seed will be multiplied. He will *increase the fruits of righteousness*, receiving both material and spiritual blessings.

Being enriched in every thing to all bountifulness, which causeth through us thanksgiving to God. Paul assured the Corinthians that cheerful givers would be blessed and enriched in everything. This abundant blessing would enable them to give liberally and generously. Such giving would cause Paul and his co-laborers to give thanksgiving to God. The Lord would be glorified because the Corinthians would have given generously and the

Jerusalem saints would be cared for and sustained. God would be glorified because He initiates such giving and caring. He is the source behind such love and kindness. Praise is the natural response of those who realize God's worth and value in their lives. "If it had not been [for] the Lord who was on our side, where would we be?" (Psalm 124:1). Gratitude and praise for what God has done is an automatic, loving response for those who recognize that they are loved by Him.

For the administration of this service not only supplieth the want of the saints, but is abundant also by many thanksgivings unto God (verse 12). Their cheerful giving offered from caring hearts would have a twofold effect: (1) it would supply *the want of the saints*. The aid that the poor saints in Jerusalem were desperately in need of would be supplied. They would be ministered unto, lifting them from starvation and the other ravages of poverty; and (2) it would result in *many thanksgivings unto God*. Paul and his co-laborers would give thanks (verse 11), but many other thanksgivings also would take place. Essentially, the Corinthians would thank God for allowing them to give generously and to help their ailing fellow believers; the Jerusalem saints would thank God for supplying their needs. Thanksgiving would be expressed by all and everyone would give praise and recognition to God for all that He had done.

While by the experiment of this ministration they glorify God for your professed subjection unto the gospel of Christ, and for your liberal distribution unto them, and unto all men. The Corinthians' generosity, which would cause the Jerusalem saints to *glorify God*, would give testimony to their salvation. Good works do not result in salvation (see Ephesians 2:8-9), but they are evidence of our salvation (see Matthew 5:16; James 2:14-26; Titus 3:8; cf. Titus 1:16).

And by their prayer for you, which long after you for the exceeding grace of God in you (verse 14). What could the poor saints do for their generous fellow believers? They could offer *prayer*. The Jerusalem saints were praying that God's grace would be graciously and abundantly bestowed upon the Corinthians in their giving. Both the Jerusalem and the Corinthian believers would be offering what they had for the benefit of the other.

Thanks be unto God for his unspeakable gift (verse 15). No matter how much a person gives, God is the greatest Giver. What has He given that manifests the superlative nature of His giving? Paul described it as *his unspeakable gift*. This gift is so valuable and so generous that there are no words to describe it. While Paul does not identify the gift specifically, from Scripture we may know that gift is God's only begotten Son, our Lord Jesus Christ (see John 3:16-17; Romans 8:32; Galatians 4:4; 1 John 4:9-10, 14; see also Isaiah 9:6). God's most gracious gift is also the gift that shows us how to give (see John 10:11, 15, 17-18; 1 John 3:16).

The Corinthians were greatly impacted by Paul's appeal; they responded and gave their offering to support the poor saints in Jerusalem (see Romans 15:25-27).

III. SPECIAL FEATURES
A. Preserving Our Heritage

Today, many challenges threaten the survival of those dwelling in the Motherland. The threat of genocide of the western Sudanese people has caused thousands to lose their lives through starvation and sickness. Furthermore, because of HIV/AIDS, Africans are dying by the thousands and thousands more children have been orphaned. It behooves us to share our resources to help bring aid and relief to this troubled people—for they are our people.

Our Foreign Mission Board and Woman's Auxiliary have devoted themselves to rendering aid to alleviate their suffering. One agency or person cannot do it alone; however, together in faith we can accomplish much by the grace of God.

B. Concluding Reflections

The generosity of God is both our example and our motivation to give. He makes His grace abound toward us and enables us to give above and beyond our natural and normal ability. Our giving is to benefit others. The "good works" that we do are also the result of His grace.

When we give, God gives abundantly in return. The return is never the motivation for cheerful giving; yet we should rejoice in His generosity toward those who demonstrate their love for Him through their giving.

HOME DAILY BIBLE READINGS
for the week of August 20, 2006
Giving Is a Witness

Aug. 14, Monday
—James 1:12–17
—Every Giving Act Is from Above
Aug. 15, Tuesday
—Luke 6:32–38
—Give and You Shall Receive
Aug. 16, Wednesday
—Matthew 6:1–6
—Do Your Giving Quietly
Aug. 17, Thursday
—Romans 15:25–29
—Pleased to Share Their Resources
Aug. 18, Friday
—2 Corinthians 9:1–5
—Arrangements for the Jerusalem Collection
Aug. 19, Saturday
—2 Corinthians 9:6–10
—A Cheerful Giver
Aug. 20, Sunday
—2 Corinthians 9:11–15
—Generosity Glorifies God

PRAYER
Heavenly Father, help us to be cheerful givers. Grant us hearts that are free to give as You have commanded. May we rejoice in our ability to give more for Your sake. In the name of Jesus we pray. Amen.

Lesson 13

The Giving of Sufficient Grace

KEY VERSE

He said unto me, My grace is sufficient for thee: for my strength is made perfect in weakness.
—2 Corinthians 12:9

ADULT TOPIC: Leaning on Grace
YOUTH TOPIC: God's Strength in Tough Times
CHILDREN'S TOPIC: Work with a Cheerful Heart

DEVOTIONAL READING: James 4:1-10
BACKGROUND SCRIPTURE: 2 Corinthians 12:1-10
PRINT PASSAGE: 2 Corinthians 12:1-10

OBJECTIVES

Upon completion of this lesson, students should understand that:

1. Great privileges may result in pride;
2. Pride is dismantled by pain and suffering;
3. Grace allows us to live with difficulties; and,
4. God's strength is made perfect in our weaknesses.

2 Corinthians 12:1-10—KJV

IT IS not expedient for me doubtless to glory. I will come to visions and revelations of the Lord.

2 I knew a man in Christ above fourteen years ago, (whether in the body, I cannot tell; or whether out of the body, I cannot tell: God knoweth;) such an one caught up to the third heaven.

3 And I knew such a man, (whether in the body, or out of the body, I cannot tell: God knoweth;)

4 How that he was caught up into paradise, and heard unspeakable words, which it is not lawful for a man to utter.

5 Of such an one will I glory: yet of myself I will not glory, but in mine infirmities.

6 For though I would desire to glory, I shall not be a fool; for I will say the truth: but now I forbear, lest any man should think of me above that which he seeth me to be, or that he heareth of me.

7 And lest I should be exalted above measure through the abundance of the revelations, there was given to me a thorn in the flesh, the messenger of Satan to buffet me, lest I should be exalted above measure.

8 For this thing I besought the Lord thrice, that it might depart from me.

9 And he said unto me, My grace is sufficient for thee: for my strength is made perfect in weakness. Most gladly therefore will I rather glory in my infirmities, that the power of Christ may rest upon me.

10 Therefore I take pleasure in infirmities, in reproaches, in necessities, in persecutions, in distresses for Christ's sake: for when I am weak, then am I strong.

2 Corinthians 12:1-10—NRSV

IT IS necessary to boast; nothing is to be gained by it, but I will go on to visions and revelations of the Lord.

2 I know a person in Christ who fourteen years ago was caught up to the third heaven—whether in the body or out of the body I do not know; God knows.

3 And I know that such a person—whether in the body or out of the body I do not know; God knows—

4 was caught up into Paradise and heard things that are not to be told, that no mortal is permitted to repeat.

5 On behalf of such a one I will boast, but on my own behalf I will not boast, except of my weaknesses.

6 But if I wish to boast, I will not be a fool, for I will be speaking the truth. But I refrain from it, so that no one may think better of me than what is seen in me or heard from me,

7 even considering the exceptional character of the revelations. Therefore, to keep me from being too elated, a thorn was given me in the flesh, a messenger of Satan to torment me, to keep me from being too elated.

8 Three times I appealed to the Lord about this, that it would leave me,

9 but he said to me, "My grace is sufficient for you, for power is made perfect in weakness." So, I will boast all the more gladly of my weaknesses, so that the power of Christ may dwell in me.

10 Therefore I am content with weaknesses, insults, hardships, persecutions, and calamities for the sake of Christ; for whenever I am weak, then I am strong.

POINTS TO BE EMPHASIZED
ADULTS
Key Verse: 2 Corinthians 12:9
Print: 2 Corinthians 12:1-10
—Throughout the Scripture, we find numerous examples of people calling on God in their distress and affirming their trust in God even in times of struggle.
—God is glorified through human trust and dependence on God's grace.
—The expression of God's grace in the lives of believers often influences unbelievers to turn to Christ.
—Paul uses his own life as an example of how believers are to receive and respond to the grace of Christ.

YOUTH
Key Verse: 2 Corinthians 12:10
Print: 2 Corinthians 12:1-10
—God's grace is sufficient to empower us in our weakness.

—The power of the Gospel does not rely on human strength or ability.

—Paul experienced God's grace in his weakness.

CHILDREN

Key Verse: 2 Timothy 2:22b
Print: 2 Timothy 2:15-16, 19-21, 22; 2 Corinthians 12:19

—Christians can please God by striving for excellence.

—Every Christian should know the Scripture and live a disciplined life.

—Believers must prepare themselves to receive the fullness of God's grace by allowing God to purify, sanctify and anoint them as holy vessels if they are to become committed, useful Christian workers.

—The believer continuously seeks piety, faith, love and harmony with other believers.

—Believers should not engage in silly, idle chatter that may cause others to lose sight of God and what God requires of them.

TOPICAL OUTLINE OF THE LESSON

I. INTRODUCTION
  A. Sufficient Grace
  B. Biblical Background

II. EXPOSITION AND APPLICATION OF THE SCRIPTURE
  A. The Privileges Resulting from Pain *(2 Corinthians 12:1-5)*
  B. The Purpose of Pain *(2 Corinthians 12:6-8)*

C. The Prescription for Pain
   (2 Corinthians 12:9-10)

III. SPECIAL FEATURES
  A. Preserving Our Heritage
  B. Concluding Reflections

I. INTRODUCTION
A. Sufficient Grace

In this chapter, Paul enlightened the Corinthians about yet another aspect of giving. Previously, he had admonished them to give. Here he addressed divine giving. God has given His grace, which makes possible all the gifts He has given to us (Romans 8:32), including the gift of His Son (John 1:14, 17; Titus 2:11; 3:4).

Paul discovered what the Lord called "sufficient grace." It is grace that enables the believer to endure and persevere in spite of pain, problem, or discomfort. Hid grace is sufficient because it is complete; that is, it lacks nothing and supplies all of our spiritual needs. Paul discovered that God's all sufficient grace would cover him in his struggle with his "thorn in the flesh."

B. Biblical Background

In this section of Paul's second letter to the Corinthians, the issue of boasting continues as a theme. He had repeatedly cautioned the Corinthian believers about bragging on their spiritual gifts or their level of spirituality. However, here he found it necessary to expound on certain of his experiences with the Lord, which could be interpreted as boasting. Yet for the sake of their edification, Paul was willing to give the appearance of boasting or glorying in his own spiritual experiences. By sharing more about his own experiences, he could help the Corinthians understand that they had wronged him and had been misguided by false teachers. In his reluctant personal exposé, Paul, described a spiritual experience wherein he saw and heard things that human language could not express.

II. EXPOSITION AND APPLICATION OF THE SCRIPTURE
A. The Privileges Resulting from Pain *(2 Corinthians 12:1-5)*

It is not expedient for me doubtless to glory. I will come to visions and revelations of the Lord (verse 1). Paul described an unusual, supernatural experience.

Paul speaks of an experience that, while puzzling to the human mind, challenges our faith to enable us to grasp that which is in the world of the Spirit of God. Before sharing his experience, however, Paul expounded on the issue of boasting, reminding them that it is not expedient. He gives us this opening statement so that we would not think that he is stuck on himself and is unbearably egotistical. Talking about himself was not something he was eager to do; but rather, his purpose was to share information. Paul deemed boasting to be useless activity (see 2 Corinthians 10:8, 13; 11:10).

I will come to visions and revelations of the Lord. Paul would not boast to prove himself, but he would give confirmation of his apostolic authority. Therefore, his was not an attempt at self-praise, but to show how what he experienced was "of the Lord" (Jesus Christ).

Both *visions and revelations* are avenues God uses to communicate His truth. *Visions* occur in varying forms but generally refer to a visual or auditory experience where an individual receives a message from God (see Acts 10:9-23). *Revelations* here refers to an uncovering or unveiling of divine truth to humanity. God does this by removing the dark cloud of ignorance, lifting us from obscurity to grasp His truth.

Paul speaks of a different order of boasting: strength in weakness. In experiencing visions and revelations of the Lord, Paul speaks of himself in the third person: "I know a person" is an oblique reference. "Fourteen years ago" would place this experience shortly after Paul's conversion, probably around AD 30ff. The language suggests an ecstatic experience in which he was taken out of the body. The third heaven references the highest ecstasy. Paradise is where God dwells. "Hearing unrepeatable things" describes the revelations in greater details. "Things that are not to be told" is a reference to their sacred nature. The experience itself enables Paul to distinguish his ordinary self from the one caught up into heaven. No one knows the object of Paul's "thorn in the flesh." "Messenger of Satan" is literally an angel of Satan. Some have thought that the thorn in the flesh refers to an illness or a physical disability, while others have suggested that it was a specific opponent or opposition of fellow Jews. Power of Christ: Christ transmits the power He experienced in the Resurrection. "Weak...strong" expresses the paradox of the Cross.

I knew a man in Christ above fourteen years ago... (verses 2-3). In describing his vision, Paul spoke about himself in the third person, probably to stress that he was not boasting. He recounted a visionary event that occurred fourteen years prior to his letter. So unusual was this experience that twice Paul revealed that he could not tell whether he was *in the body...or...out of the body.* He was not sure whether or not his spirit left his body during the experience.

He was *caught up to the third heaven.* The Greek word for *caught up* means to "snatch away," "seize with eagerness" or "carry away" (cf., Acts 8:39; 1 Thessalonians 4:17). It is the same word from which the theological term "rapture" is derived. It describes the supernatural removal of the saints from one place to another (see 1 Thessalonians 4:13-17.

The *third heaven* was believed to be the dwelling place of God. The Jews believed in three heavens. The third was the highest and most majestic. Paul did not say how he got there. He only revealed that he was *caught up* and that he had nothing to do with it.

How that he was caught up into paradise, and heard unspeakable words, which it is not lawful for a man to utter (verse 4). Paul equated being *caught up to the third heaven* with being *caught up into paradise.* The word *paradise* is of Persian origin meaning "a royal garden." This same word is used in Genesis 2:8 to describe the Garden of Eden. The Jews used it to refer to heaven or as the place where

the righteous dead abode (see Luke 23:43; Revelation 2:7). In this place, he heard *unspeakable words,* great revelation that was not lawful or permitted for him or anyone to reveal.

Of such a one will I glory: yet of myself I will not glory, but in mine infirmities (verse 5). If the Corinthians wanted to boast, they could boast of a man who had known a supernatural experience. Since he was so highly privileged by his experience, such a man should be the subject of boasting. He had received special favor from God.

Even though he was speaking of himself, he would not let anyone know he had such an experience. If the false teachers had defamed his name, there is no telling what they would say had he told them of such an experience. Their criticisms would have increased. Therefore, Paul explained, *of myself I will not glory.* He would keep the event a secret and instead glory in his *infirmities.* He would highlight those things that the world despises.

There is no explanation as to why Paul had never shared this incredible vision before; however, some conjecture can be made. It lends insight into why he endured great persecution and suffering (see 2 Corinthians 11:23-28). It also helps to explain why he was so tenacious and faithful to preaching the Gospel (see Romans 1:16; 1 Corinthians 2:2; 2 Corinthians 4:5). He was immovable and determined to fulfill his ministerial assignment (see Philippians 3:12-14; cf. Acts 20:22-24).

B. The Purpose of Pain
(2 Corinthians 12:6-8)

For though I would desire to glory, I shall not be a fool... (verse 6). The false apostles were boasting extensively. But Paul would not join them in this ungodly act although he had much on which to boast. The Lord had used him in special and sundry ways. His boasting would not be meaningless and empty like these false apostles. And if he boasted, he would *not be a fool* or not be foolish. Unlike the false apostles, he would be telling *the truth*. But he refrained from such actions *lest any man should think of me above that which he seeth me to be, or that he heareth of me.* Paul had no need to be placed on a pedestal. He knew where he belonged.

And lest I should be exalted above measure through the abundance of the revelations... (verse 7). While Paul sought to keep himself in check, God also helped to preserve his humility. The phrase *lest I should be exalted above measure*, occurs twice in this verse, and reveals the seriousness of pride in the life of the believer and how easy it is to fall prey to its clutches. God had highly privileged him: he had received from the Lord abundance of revelations (see Acts 9:3-16; 16:9-10; 18:9-10; 22:17-21; 23:11; Ephesians 3:1-6). This privilege could have caused him to swell with pride. However, to prevent him from exalting himself and being lifted up in pride, he *was given...a thorn in the flesh.* The *thorn in the flesh* was a trial, which as painful to him as a thorn would be piercing through the flesh. The word *thorn* refers to something sharp, such as a stake which was used for impaling or spearing criminals or victims. This metaphor described the pain that the condition or circumstance had inflicted upon Paul. He used this analogy to demonstrate the intensity of his pain.

He likened this thorn to be *a messenger of Satan*. Though God permitted the thorn, Satan was the one who inflicted the pain and was sent to buffet or torment him. The Greek word that Paul uses for *buffet* refers to harsh or severe treatment from another (see Matthew 26:67).

The thorn was Paul's source of pain, but this pain was designed to keep him from exalting himself above measure. That is, it was designed to keep him from spiritual pride, which can yield destruction (see Genesis 3). Without this pain, Paul would have succumbed to pride, which "goeth before destruction" (Proverbs 16:18). For centuries, theologians have speculated as to the nature of Paul's infirmity; all are vain theories or conjecture. Whatever its manifestation, Paul clearly understood that the thorn inflicted upon him served to humble him, thus enabling him to give faithful and earnest service to the Lord.

For this thing I besought the Lord thrice, that it might depart from me (verse 8). Prayer is to be our constant action and something that we do always. The nature of pain, however, seems to drive us and make our prayer more intense, more intimate and sometimes more frequent.

We cry out to the Lord as never before when we are in severe pain. Therefore pain can be productive; it brought Paul to prayer just as it moves believers to pray today.

Like all human beings, Paul probably thought he would be better served by the removal of this condition. Paul petitioned the Lord three times to take away affliction. Paul ceased to pray on the matter after the Lord gave Him an answer. When God answers us in prayer, there is no need to continue beseeching the throne of grace. We must always be content with His answer, no matter what it is.

C. The Prescription for Pain
(2 Corinthians 12:9-10)

And he said unto me, My grace is sufficient for thee: for my strength is made perfect in weakness. Most gladly therefore will I rather glory in my infirmities, that the power of Christ may rest upon me (verse 9). The Lord answered Paul's prayer: his affliction would not be removed. Surely, this was a difficult answer to receive. No one wants to hear that answer. And yet, in faith we accept that any answer from God always has our best interest in view, even when it does not seem so in our understanding. God denied Paul's petition to remove his affliction, but granted His most potent treatment.

My grace is sufficient for thee: God said no to Paul, but He did grant His grace. God's grace would give him strength. God's grace would cover Paul to endure the pain of his affliction—his suffering. He will always have available to him the power of God's abundant grace.

Grace is God's unmerited favor; unearned and undeserved. There is nothing human beings can do or become to receive this grace. Even the most faithful, most dedicated servant of the Lord cannot earn grace. In granting us grace, God gives us what we do not deserve. God gave Paul the prescription that could handle any pain or affliction. Since grace is potent enough to cover our sins and grant us salvation (see Ephesians 2:8-9), which is our greatest affliction, and ensure our sanctification (see 2 Peter 3:18), it can cover our afflictions, sufferings and pain.

The word *sufficient* means that every need Paul had would be met. God's grace would always be available to him even during the most torturous moments. Therefore, no sin, sorrow, suffering, sickness, shortage or satanic attack are beyond the grace of God. Grace can handle any situation, circumstance and experience.

Why did God not remove the thorn? God wanted Paul to depend on Him in ways he would not have otherwise. Perhaps Paul would not have matured in certain areas of his life if he did not have this impaling condition. Finally, Paul's thorn required him to trust and obey God. He desires that every believer maintain a posture of dependence on Him. Paul stop praying because God gave him grace for the journey; Paul accepted that this was God's will for his life.

God explained that his *strength is made perfect in weakness*. In order for a believer to receive and experience God's strength, he or she must be in posture of weakness. This requires a believer to come to an experience that no human being can resolve. Our extremities are God's opportunities. When we cannot handle a situation, we are then postured to allow God to take over. This is a constant thread throughout Scripture. Through grace God helps those who cannot help themselves. Contrary to the phantom verse, "God helps those who help themselves," God's Word continuously demonstrates that the opposite is true. There is no need for God to help those who can help themselves.

Most gladly therefore will I rather glory in my infirmities, that the power of Christ may rest upon me. Instead of responding to God's answer with grumbling or complaint he responded with joy and gladness. He is glad yet still in pain—irony that can only make sense to people of faith. The Macedonian church knew what it meant to experience both affliction and joy (2 Corinthians 2:2). This is the way of the believer. Paul preferred to *glory in* [his] *infirmities* (weaknesses), so that the power of Christ could rest upon him. Paul understood that the power of God comes as believers give recognition to God and rejoice in our weaknesses. Paul was suggesting that a life of pain can be a life of power, but only through the grace of God.

It is easy to embrace hopelessness when facing insurmountable odds. But to live in joy, one needs a surrendered spirit to God's will, and an acceptance of God's grace. This is what Paul did.

Therefore I take pleasure in infirmities, in reproaches, in necessities, in persecutions, in distresses for Christ's sake: for when I am weak, then am I strong (verse 10). Once he understood God's will Paul was satisfied. Since God would not remove his painful condition, Paul made himself content. Reflecting on his experiences, Paul would later reveal "I have learned, in whatsoever state I am, therewith to be content" (Philippians 4:11).

He would suffer, but he would do so surrounded by God's sufficient grace; he resolved to surrender to God's will. It was this surrendered position that gave him joy because his weakness would amplify the power of Christ. Therefore, he took *pleasure in infirmities* (weaknesses), *in reproaches* (contempt and scorn from others), *in necessities* (destitution), *in persecutions* (bodily attacks), in *distresses* (needs and difficulties) *for Christ's sake*. Paul could rejoice because his suffering and infirmity was for a cause. His suffering was for Christ's sake, a cause to which the apostle had devoted his life.

III. SPECIAL FEATURES
A. Preserving Our Heritage

The painful yet proud history of African Americans gives credence to the fact that God's grace is sufficient to cover all afflictions. Indeed, it would appear that racism and prejudice have been the "thorn in the flesh" of our people. Despite the piercing pain of this 400-year affliction, our people have survived and even thrived. We have overcome circumstances that would have caused the extinction of others. We have borne the pain of hatred because of our color and condition. But God's grace has been sufficient and more in meeting the needs of our people.

God has not removed racism and prejudice from our experience as a people, but through His grace we have been empowered to "keep on keeping on" from generation to generation. Instead of bragging on who we have become, we would do well to concentrate on thanking God and giving Him glory for His sustaining grace.

B. Concluding Reflections

On this side of the journey, we will never understand the fullness of God and His mysterious ways. He gave Paul a thorn to humble him and as a reminder to depend on God's grace to endure. Through grace, Paul was able to meet the great challenge of living with pain.

His power to do this was not a result of his own power, strength, or stamina; it was the grace of God. He has provided what we need to face the challenges of life—His amazing grace.

Let us follow the example of the apostle Paul and turn to God for help in our thorny experiences, and pray that we discover what he discovered: when we are weak, in Him we will be strong!

◼ HOME DAILY BIBLE 📖 READINGS

for the week of August 27, 2006
The Giving of Sufficient Grace

Aug. 21, Monday
—Romans 5:12–21
—Grace Abounds All the More
Aug. 22, Tuesday
—James 4:1–10
—Grace for the Humble
Aug. 23, Wednesday
—1 Peter 5:5–10
—The God of Grace Will Restore
Aug. 24, Thursday
—1 Corinthians 15:3–10
—Paul Receives God's Grace
Aug. 25, Friday
—2 Corinthians 11:23–29
—Paul Experiences Many Difficulties
Aug. 26, Saturday
—2 Corinthians 12:1–7*a*
—Paul's Deep Spiritual Experience
Aug. 27, Sunday
—2 Corinthians 12:7*b*–13
—God's Grace Is Sufficient

PRAYER

Heavenly Father, teach us how to suffer for Thee, and to follow the example of the apostle Paul. Continue to help us learn the value of surrendering ourselves to Your will, even if that way is one of pain and suffering. Let us remember that our lives belong to You. In Jesus Christ's name, we pray. Amen.

GLOSSARY OF TERMS

Acrostic – writing (i.e., poetry) in which a row of letters (usually the first or final letter) is taken in order from a word or phrase.

Adjuration – a solemn oath or strong advisement.

Agrarian – an agricultural society.

Allegory – a kind of parable, containing a statement of a few simple facts followed by the explanation or interpretation. The object is to convey a moral truth.

Amalgamate – to unite, mix, combine, or consolidate.

Anathema – a strong curse.

Anomaly – a departure from the regular arrangement, general rule, or usual method.

Antithetical – exactly opposite or a direct opposite.

Apologist – someone who writes or speaks in defense or justification of a doctrine, faith, action, etc.

Apostasy – to rebel against or fall away from the tenets of one's faith.

Apostles – persons sent out with a special message. The official name given to the twelve disciples, chosen by our Lord to be with Him during His ministry and to whom He entrusted the organization of the church.

Beatitudes – (lit. "blessed") the opening words of Jesus in the Sermon on the Mount wherein He describes the blessed life of those residents of the kingdom of God.

Carnivorous – the behavior of a flesh-eating being.

Ceremonially Unclean/Clean – adherence to the laws God established for the Israelites to provide guidance for dietary and other circumstances. Cleanness was fundamental to maintaining holiness in the Israelite community. To be clean included being free from disease or defilement. In the New Testament, ceremonially unclean Jews were considered defiled and, therefore, could not worship or make offerings in the temple/synagogue.

Charlatan – a person who pretends to have knowledge or abilities that he does not have; an imposter.

Communitas – (or community) the people living in the same district, city, etc., under the same laws.

Coterie – a small, intimate—somewhat select—group of people associated for social or other reasons.

Debauchery – the extreme indulgence of a person's appetites, especially for sensual pleasure. It may also involve orgies and the act of morally leading people astray.

Derision – ridicule or scorn.

Deutero-Isaiah – chapters 40—55 of the book of Isaiah in the Old Testament. These chapters are often referred to as Second Isaiah and are of later authorship than the preceding chapters. This section of Isaiah also contains the very meaningful so-called Servant Songs (chapters 42:1-4; 49:1-6; 50:4-9; 52:13; and 53:12).

Diaspora – a dispersion of a people from their original homeland. Generally, the term refers to the Jewish Diaspora, when the majority of Jews were dispersed outside of Israel from the sixth century BC, when they were exiled to Babylon. The other common use for the diaspora is the African Diaspora, when tens of thousands of Africans were deported to the Western Hemisphere for slave trading.

Dichotomy – a situation or circumstance with seemingly contradictory qualities, conditions, or circumstances.

Ecclesiastical – (fr: Greek, an assembly of citizens) of or related to the church.

El Shaddai – (Hebrew) meaning "God Almighty"; "El" is a synonym for another Hebrew noun for God used more frequently: Elohim.

En masse – (French: "in mass") in group, as a whole, or altogether.

Epicurean – associated with the devotion to sensual pleasure; often associated with fine food or drink.

Epithet – a term used to characterize a person, thing, or name used; a descriptive substitute for the name or title of a person (ex., Lamb of God = Jesus).

Epitomize – serving as an ideal or general example of something.

Essenes – a Jewish religious community of men in Palestine and Syria, forming the first cells of organized monasticism in the Mediterranean world.

Evangelist – a person announcing good news. Anyone who proclaims the mercy and grace of God, especially as unfolded in the Gospel. It came to be employed in the early church as the designation of a special class (Ephesians 4:11).

Excommunicate – a formal church censure depriving a person of the rights of membership; being dis-fellowshiped from a group or community.

ff. – folios; following pages.

Gnostics – (Greek, "knowledge") a faction among the Christians who believed their superior knowledge distinguished them from other believers. Some Gnostics divided Christians into groups (the spiritual and the carnal). The "spiritual" Christians believed they were in a special or higher class than "ordinary" Christians because they had received special knowledge. Some of these "spiritual" Christians believed they were not responsible for what they did and could not really sin. They believed that knowledge was superior to faith.

Hermeneutics – the science of interpretation, especially the biblical text. It is the area of theology dealing with the principles of exegesis.

Hyperbolically – (fr: hyperbole) speaking or writing in words that represent an extreme exaggeration.

Ignominy – personal humiliation, dishonor, or disgrace.

Importunity – making an urgent demand; being excessively persistent in making a request; being "pushy."

Introspective – quality of self-examination or searching inside oneself.

Jim Crow – American laws that enforced racial segregation in the U.S. South between late 1877 and the early 1960s. The term was derived from a minstrel-show routine, and became a derogatory term for Black people.

Juxtapose – to place side by side, usually for comparison or contrast.

Magistrate – a civil officer with power to administer and enforce law, such as a judge or justice of the peace.

Meanderings – (fr. Meander) to follow a winding or turning course; wandering.

Metamorphosis – a marked or complete change of character, appearance, or condition.

Middle Passage – the journey made by slave traders on ships during the seventeenth and eighteenth centuries, traveling nearly 4000 miles from the west coast of Africa across the Atlantic to the Americas, where they were sold or, in some cases, traded for goods. The name came because it was the middle leg of a three-part voyage, one that began and ended in Europe.

Midrash Qoheleth Rabbah – rabbinical commentary on the book of Ecclesiastes. Midrash Rabbah most commonly refers to the famous compilation of rabbinical comments on each of the five volumes of the Torah.

Mortification – (1) related to feelings of shame or humiliation; (2) to discipline the body and its appetites through self-denial or self-inflicted deprivation.

Motif – a central or recurrent theme or dominant idea, usually related to an artistic or literary work.

Myrrh – a yellowish or reddish-brown fragrant gum resin—obtained from several trees and shrubs found in India, Arabia and eastern Africa—used in perfume and incense. Also called balm of Gilead.

New Covenant – the new agreement God has made with mankind, based on the death and resurrection of Jesus Christ. The concept originated with the prophet Jeremiah that God would accomplish for His people what the old covenant failed to do (Jeremiah 31:31).

Old Covenant – the covenant of law. The agreement God made with His people. God would make a promise to individuals or a group of people, and if they were obedient or followed the law, God would reward them.

Omnipotence – having sovereign or universal power; usually used in reference to the unlimited power of God.

Ostensibly – as it appears outwardly; the outward impression.

Ostentation – an excessive display or outward show meant to impress others; boastful.

Pandora's Box – term derived from Greek mythology, meaning the source of many unpredictable troubles; an unending source of evil.

Pedigree – a recorded or known line of descent, a list of ancestors, or a record of ancestry.

Pericope – a defined passage of Scripture; a full story within the Bible. In contemporary translations of the Bible, pericopes are headed by subtitles, such as "Jesus Heals a Paralytic" (John 5:17-26, NRSV). A pericope is defined by subject matter, rather than by chapter and verse. A pericope may include portions of two chapters or only a portion of a verse at its opening or close.

Plethora – possessing a great number; an excess or overabundance.

Prologue – the beginning (i.e., preface or introduction) of a literary work.

Putrid – someone who is morally corrupt, depraved, very disagreeable, or unpleasant.

Shema – the Jewish confession of faith which begins, "Hear, O Israel: The Lord our God, the Lord is one!" (Deuteronomy 6:4-9).

Sophomoric – a person who has the characteristics of a sophomore, often regarded as self-assured, opinionated, although immature and inexperienced.

Splendiferous – extraordinary or impressive in a showy manner.

Stanza – a division of a poem or lyrics consisting of a series of lines arranged together in a (often repeating) pattern of meter and rhyme.

Sublimate – to alter one's natural (instinctive) expression or action to a form that is considered more socially or culturally acceptable.

Temporal – related to earthly matters; finite.

Transfiguration – the sudden, glorying change in appearance that occurred with Jesus on the mountain (see Matthew 17:1-9).

Triplet – a group of three lines of verse in poetry or lyrics.

Truncate(d) – to cut off; appearing as cut short.

Vilify – to degrade; to use abusive or slanderous language.

BIBLIOGRAPHY OF RESOURCES

Achtemeir, Paul J. *Harper Collins Bible Commentary*. San Francisco: HarperSanFrancisco, 1996.

The American Heritage Dictionary of the English Language, Fourth Edition. Boston: Houghton Mifflin, 2000.

Barker, Kenneth, General Ed. *The NIV Study Bible*. Grand Rapids, Mich., 1995.

Barnes, Albert. *Barnes' Notes on the New Testament*. Public Domain.

Bowker, John. *The Complete Bible Handbook*. London: DK Publishing, 1998.

Clarke, Adam. *Adam Clarke's Commentary on the Holy Bible*. Nashville: World Publishing, 1997.

Cone, James H., and Wilmore, Gayraud S. eds. *Black Theology: A Documentary History*. Maryknoll, New York: Orbis Books, 1979.

Davies, Peter, ed. *The American Heritage Dictionary*. Boston: Houghton Mifflin Company, 1969.

Easton, M.G. *Easton's Bible Dictionary*. Public Domain.

Essence. September 2004, vol. 34, no. 9. New York: Essence Communications, Inc.

Graham, Sheila. "2003 Worldwide Church of God." Internet: http://www.wcg.org/lit/church/index/womens.htm.

Haley, Alex. *Roots: A Saga of an American Family*. New York: Doubleday, 1976.

The Interpreter's Bible Commentary, Volume III: Kings—Job. Nashville: Abingdon Press, 1955.

The Interpreter's Bible Commentary, Volume IV: Psalms—Proverbs. Nashville: Abingdon Press, 1955.

The Interpreter's Bible Commentary, Volume V: Ecclesiastes. Nashville: Abingdon Press, 1954.

Jackson, Chris. *The Black Christian Singles Guide to Dating and Sexuality.* Grand Rapids: Zondervan, 1999.

Jamieson, Robert, Fausset, A.R., and Brown, David. *Commentary Critical and Explanatory on the Whole Bible.* Public Domain.

Kee, Burke, Berneking, Rhodes, ed. "Introduction to Proverbs," *The Learning Bible: Contemporary English Version.* New York: American Bible Society, 1995.

Mitchell, Henry H. "The Holy Spirit: A Folk Perspective." Internet: www.pulpit.org.

Moore, Thomas (1779-1852). "Come Ye Disconsolate," *A Collection of Motetts or Antiphons.* London: 1792.

Orwell, George. *Animal Farm.* New York: Harcourt, Brace, and Company, 1946.

Ryrie, Charles ed. *Ryrie Study Bible: Introduction to Ecclesiastes.* Chicago: Moody Publishers, 1999.

Strong, James. *The New Strong's Exhaustive Concordance Hebrew and Chaldee Dictionary.* Nashville: Thomas Nelson Publishers, 1990.

Strong, James. *Strong's Exhaustive Concordance.* Public Domain.

Webster's Encyclopedic Unabridged Dictionary. New York: Gramercy Books, 1996.

Wenham, Motyer, Carson, France, editors. *New Bible Commentary.* Downers Grove, Ill: InterVarsity Press, 1994.

t, Cornel. *Race Matters.* Boston: Beacon Press, 1993.